ISBN 978-1-5278-8124-2
PIBN 10906716

Lancashire Parish Register Society.

---

# The Registers

OF THE

# Parish Church of Ormskirk.

# Lancashire Parish Register Society.

---

## Patrons.

The Right Rev. the LORD BISHOP OF MANCHESTER.
The Right Rev. the LORD BISHOP OF LIVERPOOL.

## Council.

Lt.-Col. FISHWICK, F.S.A., The Heights, Rochdale, *President.*
JAMES CLAYTON, Radcliffe.
HENRY BRIERLEY, B.A., Mab's Cross, Wigan, *Hon. Secretary.*
WILLIAM FARRER, Thornburgh House, Leyburn, R.S.O., Yorkshire.
J. HOLME NICHOLSON, M.A., Ellerhow, Wilmslow (*the late.*)
Major PARKER, Browsholme Hall, Clitheroe.
ARTHUR SMITH, B.A., LL.B., Wigan.
Rev. Canon STANNING, M.A., Leigh Vicarage, Lancashire.
CHARLES W. SUTTON, M.A., Manchester Free Library.
J. R. FAITHWAITE, Manchester and Salford Bank, *Hon. Treasurer.*

# The Registers

OF THE

# arish Church of Ormskirk

IN THE

# County of Lancaster.

## Christenings, Burials, and Weddings

1557—1626.

TRANSCRIBED AND EDITED BY

JOSIAH ARROWSMITH, WIGAN.

THE INDEXES BY

MRS. C. M. ROYDS AND MRS. H. BRIERLEY.

*Printed by permission of the Rev. J. E. Woodrow,*
*Vicar of Ormskirk.*



Rochdale:

PRINTED FOR THE LANCASHIRE PARISH REGISTER SOCIETY,
BY JAMES CLEGG, AT THE ALDINE PRESS.

1902

# Preface.

ORMSKIRK is a pleasant country town situate on the North Road from Liverpool through Preston, and is about midway between those two towns, and vies with its neighbour Wigan in the possession of a handsome church.

Ormskirk Church is known to have certainly existed in the reign of Richard I., and is dedicated to SS. Peter and Paul. Its ancient parish—a vicarage—comprised 31,000 acres and included the townships of Ormskirk, Bickerstaffe, Burscough, Lathom, Scarisbrick, and Skelmersdale.

The parishes surrounding Ormskirk are Rufford, Eccleston, Wigan, Prescot, North Meols, Halsall, and Aughton. At the time of the commencement of the present Registers there existed chapels at Scarisbrick and Skelmersdale, and a domestic chapel at the Manor House—as it was then called—of Lathom. 

The Register which is here transcribed is the earliest extant. It is contained in a volume of 225 parchment leaves, each leaf measuring 13½in. by 6½in., strongly bound in parchment, and is a monument of careful preservation on the part of its successive custodians. It appears to have been transcribed for the most part by one hand, and to judge from the entry in the Register (printed herein) the cost was not excessive.

Enquiry has been made at the Ancient Chapelries but no separate Chapel Registers are known to exist for the period covered by this volume.

Search for Episcopal Transcripts has been made at Chester and every important variation or addition found there has been embodied and noted in this volume. The most striking features of this volume are the enormous varieties of surnames, representing so many Lancashire and Westmorland townships, and the large number of Burials in the church itself. The latter have been counted and number 2,442 in 69 years.

The total number of entries in this volume is

| | |
|---|---|
| Christenings ... ... | 4,003 |
| Burials ... ... ... | 5,423 |
| Marriages ... ... ... | 1,456 |
| Total ... | 10,882 |

The whole of the present volume has been carefully collated with the Original, and it is believed that every unusual spelling not accounted for in the Table of Errata is a correct copy of the original.

The Society is under sincere obligation to the Rev. J. E. Woodrow, the Vicar of Ormskirk, who has most kindly facilitated the transcription of the original Register.

The compilers of the Index—which it will be noted, is unusually long and most careful in detail—desire to put on record their obligations to Miss Amy Wilson, of Wigan, and our member Miss Fanny Wrigley, for their enthusiastic help in its compilation.

# Table of Contents.

## 5th of Januarie 1600.

The names of the Churche wardens $w^{ch}$ cawesed this e to be writen and payde for the wrytinge thereof $XX^s$

ROGER WALWORTHE

THOMAS x ASCOUGH

RAFFE x BYRTCHWOOD

JOHN x ORMISHAW

WILLM x HOOLME

JOHN x LANCASTER

wryten in the p^9sents of

RIC̄ AMBROSE vicar

# The Registers of the Parish of Ormskirk.

[1] **The Regester Booke** of all suche as haue beene Christened Maried and Buried within the parishe of Ormis$^{h}$ Since the Beginninge of her ma$^{ties}$ moste happie Raigne which did begine to Englands Joye And Comforte the Seventithe daye of November Anno dni 1557

[1] The "T" of "The" is formed into a human face in original.

## CHRISTENINGS.

### 1557.

o. 1 George Martyndale baptized* ... ... ... ... ... 19 Nouember
Jane Cropper ... ... ... ... ... ... ... 10 December
Thomas Shawe ... ... ... ... ... ... 21 Januarie
Thomas Whytestones ... ... ... ... ... 25 „
Thomas Ormishawe ... ... ... ... ... ... 3 ffebruarie
Peeter Scarsbrecke ... ... ... ... ... ... 13 „
Catherin Langley ... ... ... ... ... ... 14 „
Elizabeth Gill ... ... ... ... ... ... ... 6 Martch
Ellis Gill ... ... ... ... ... ... ... ... 7 „

### 1558.

Margaret Windrowe ... ... ... ... ... ... 29 Martch
Elin Blunndell fi: John ... ... ... ... ... 30 „
Alis Kewquicke ... ... ... ... ... ... „ „
Jenet Cowper fi: Rich ... ... ... ... ... 31 „
Edward Halworth fi: Rich ... ... ... ... 19 Aprill
Rich Mellinge fi: John of Latham ... ... 3 „
Rich Johnson fi: Rich ... ... ... ... ... 10 „
o. 2 Margaret Parker ... ... ... ... ... ... 6 Maye
Harvie Asshorst ... ... ... ... ... ... 17 „

* The word "baptized" or "bap" is repeated after each entry in the original, but is omitted in the Transcript.

Elizabeth Parker ... ... ... ... ... ... 10 June
Ector Mawdisley ... ... ... ... ... ... „ „
Wittm Walcar ... ... ... ... ... ... ... 15 „
Henrie Lathwhat ... ... ... ... ... ... 16 „
Catherin Lathom ... ... ... ... ... ... 17 „
Margaret Price ... ... ... ... ... ... ... 25 „
Hugh Henryson ... ... ... ... ... ... 8 Julye
Elin Somner ... ... ... ... ... ... ... 13 „
John Aphrith basł ... ... ... ... ... ... 15 „
John Ormishawe ... ... ... ... ... ... 17 „
Thomas Mawdisley ... ... ... ... ... ... 24 Auguste
Jaine Whyte ... ... ... ... ... ... ... 27 „
Catherin Rainforth ... ... ... ... ... ... 6 September
Robert Hoolme base ... ... ... ... ... 8 „
Johne Shorlicars basł ... ... ... ... ... 21 „
Cislie Smalshaw ... ... ... ... ... ... 22 „
Margaret Skelton ... ... ... ... ... ... 25 „
Marierie Hardman ... ... ... ... ... ... „ „
John Jackeson ... ... ... ... ... ... ... 27 „
Cecelie Hunter ... ... ... ... ... ... ... 21 October
Elin Mawdisley ... ... ... ... ... ... 23 „
Marierie Smyth ... ... ... ... ... ... „ „
George Macon ... ... ... ... ... ... ... 10 Nouember
ffrances Watkinson ... ... ... ... ... ... „ „
Jamis Werall ... ... ... ... ... ... ... 30 „
. . . Haughton ... ... ... ... ... ... 9 December
Alis Asmall ... ... ... ... ... ... ... 26 „
Fo. 3 Mararet Rainforth ... ... ... ... ... ... 1 Januarie
Elizabeth Woodhowse ... ... ... ... ... 10 „
Janie Whytestones ... ... ... ... ... ... 12 „
Izabell Talior ... ... ... ... ... ... ... 30 „
Elizabeth Breykell ... ... ... ... ... ... „ „
Marierie Goulbron ... ... ... ... ... ... 1 ffebruarie
Gilbert Johneson ... ... ... ... ... ... 6 „
Marierie Waynewright ... ... ... ... ... 8 „
Barth Waynewright ... ... ... ... ... ... 14 „
Jamis Hunte ... ... ... ... ... ... ... 15 „
Edward Butler ... ... ... ... ... ... ... 20 „
Thomas Gorsutch ... ... ... ... ... ... 21 „
. . . Gill ... ... ... ... ... ... ... „ „
. . . Swyfte ... ... ... ... ... ... „ „
Elizabeth Whytestones ... ... ... ... ... 25 „
Thomas Hoolme ... ... ... ... ... ... 28 „
Izabell Hoolme ... ... ... ... ... ... ... „ „
Richard Ascough ... ... ... ... ... ... 12 Martch
Elin Molinex ... ... ... ... ... ... ... 20 „
A Chylde of Jhames Bankes ... ... ... ... „ „

## 1559.

| Fo. | Name | Day | Month |
|---|---|---|---|
| | Wiłłm Ambrose | 26 | Martch |
| | Jamis Ley | 27 | „ |
| | Wiłłm Gyles | 8 | Aprill |
| | Henrie Gyles | „ | „ |
| | Jane Mawdisley | 16 | „ |
| | Jane Haughton | 20 | „ |
| | Edward Johneson | 24 | „ |
| | Elizabeth Gobin | 11 | Maye |
| | Jane Whytestones | 27 | „ |
| | Jane Barton | 7 | June |
| | Elizabeth Hesketh | 13 | „ |
| | John Barton | 17 | „ |
| Fo. 4 | Elizabeth Alerton | 18 | „ |
| | George Smyth | 28 | „ |
| | Jamis Gill | 29 | „ |
| | George Hill | 4 | Julye |
| | Anne Hill | „ | „ |
| | Richard Coppo | „ | „ |
| | Margaret Westhead | 9 | „ |
| | Elizabeth Crofte | 18 | „ |
| | Elizabeth Ascrofte | 20 | „ |
| | Elizabeth Woodes | 23 | „ |
| | Wiłłm Cocket | 7 | Auguste |
| | Hugh Mawdisley | 12 | „ |
| | Elizabeth Alerton | 14 | „ |
| | Hugh Henrieson | 17 | „ |
| | Robert Sutch | 23 | „ |
| | Robert Acker | 24 | „ |
| | Izabeth Holland | „ | „ |
| | Hugh Lyuesley bast | 27 | „ |
| | Wiłłm Morecrofte | 31 | „ |
| | Marget Walles | 1 | September |
| | Thomas ffletcher | 3 | „ |
| | Jaine Martin | 8 | „ |
| | Wiłłm Seale | 12 | „ |
| | Mathew Atherton | 15 | „ |
| | Elin Thakarowe bast | „ | „ |
| | Richard Hyłł | „ | „ |
| | George Dunkon | 17 | „ |
| | Marie Abrā | 21 | „ |
| | Jaine fforshaw | „ | „ |
| | Nicolas Gill | „ | „ |
| | Elin Blundell | 8 | October |
| | John Jackeson | 17 | „ |
| | Anne Haughton | 1 | Nouember |
| Fo. 5 | John Cropp | 5 | December |

| | | | |
|---|---|---|---|
| | Jamis Gill | 7 | December |
| | David Chadocke | 9 | „ |
| | Elizabeth Hey | 17 | „ |
| | Ann Asco | 18 | „ |
| | Cuthbert Garard | „ | „ |
| | Peeter Chadocke | 20 | „ |
| | Rodger Webster | 25 | „ |
| | Johne She & Thomas She bast | 30 | „ |
| | Elizabeth Macon | 15 | Januarie |
| | Anne Hill | 26 | „ |
| | George Barton | 1 | ffebruarie |
| | Marierie Wilson | 15 | „ |
| | Wiłłm Prescot | 21 | „ |
| | Richard Barton | 22 | „ |
| | Wiłłm Alker | „ | „ |
| | Anne ffryth | 7 | Martch |
| | Tho: Blundell | 8 | „ |
| | Ewan Mawdisley | 10 | „ |
| | Ryč Towne | 17 | „ |
| | Margaret Westhead | 19 | „ |

## 1560.

| | | | |
|---|---|---|---|
| | Tho: Greves | 26 | Martch |
| | . . . Robertson | 1 | Aprill |
| | Wiłłm Shawe | 7 | „ |
| | Jamis Peycocke | 15 | „ |
| | Katherin Barton | 28 | „ |
| | Rič Garston | 3 | Maye |
| | Jaine Scarsbrecke | 4 | „ |
| | Alys Hatton bast | 9 | „ |
| | Rodger Scarsbrecke | 30 | „ |
| | Marierie Blundell | 10 | June |
| | Elin Sutch | „ | „ |
| | John Melling of Latham | 9 | „ |
| | John Wilson | 5 | „ |
| Fo. 6 | Elin Haughton | 2 | July |
| | Elin Hunte | 6 | „ |
| | John Lathwhat bast Heñ Lathw pat | „ | „ |
| | Elin Morecrofte | 8 | „ |
| | Robert She | 21 | „ |
| | Elizth She | „ | „ |
| | Elin Barton | 29 | „ |
| | Jaine ffarclough | 1 | Auguste |
| | Tho: Rylands | 2 | „ |
| | Wiłłm Harison | 7 | „ |
| | Elynor Home | 15 | „ |
| | Wiłłm Wolsey | 18 | „ |
| | Elynor Crofte | 19 | „ |

| |  |  |  |
|---|---|---|---|
| | ffrances Locker | 25 | Auguste |
| | Tho: Scarsbrecke | 26 | „ |
| | Jane Lee | 30 | „ |
| | George Cropp | 1 | September |
| | Ric̄ Goulbron | „ | „ |
| | Elin Barton | 7 | „ |
| | Tho: Seale | 8 | „ |
| | Wiłłm Gobin | „ | „ |
| | Jdeth Parker | 10 | „ |
| | Marie Longe | 21 | „ |
| | Elin Ambros | 7 | October |
| | Edwarde Wardman | 17 | „ |
| | Tho Munke | 18 | „ |
| | Wiłłm Hill | 19 | „ |
| | John Waynewright | 20 | „ |
| | Marierie Hunter | 30 | „ |
| | Hugh Asmall | 8 | Nouember |
| | Tho: Langley | 11 | „ |
| | George Whytestones | 15 | „ |
| | Anne Morecrofte | 21 | „ |
| | Marierie Barwicke | 29 | „ |
| | Anes Ormishaw | 30 | „ |
| . 7 | Jamis Molines | 15 | December |
| | Elnor Halsall | 28 | „ |
| | Alis Anderton | 30 | „ |
| | Tho: Cropp | 3 | Januarie |
| | Robert Gyll | „ | „ |
| | Elyz[th] Asmall | 4 | „ |
| | Edw: Hunter | 30 | „ |
| | Tho: Allerton | 16 | ffebruarie |
| | Wiłłm Robertson | 21 | „ |
| | Margaret Crane | 22 | „ |
| | Elizabeth Donkon̄ | 27 | „ |
| | Rodger Gredgeson | 5 | Martch |
| | Henry Killshaw | 7 | „ |
| | Ric̄ greene bast | „ | „ |
| | Jane Asmall | 16 | „ |
| | Emlin Killshaw | 19 | „ |

## 1561.

|  |  |  |
|---|---|---|
| Sislie Talior | 27 | Martch |
| John Swifte | 30 | „ |
| Sybell Waringe | 2 | Aprill |
| Wiłłm Shawe | 16 | „ |
| Wiłłm Alker | 23 | „ |
| Peeter Rigbie | 24 | „ |
| John Mawdisley | 21 | Maye |
| John Whytestones | „ | „ |

| | | | |
|---|---|---|---|
| | Richard Lee | 11 | June |
| | Elin Jackeson | „ | „ |
| | Riĉ Morecrofte | 14 | „ |
| | John ffysher bast Tho: fishêr pater | 17 | „ |
| Fo. 8 | John Mawdisley | 1 | July |
| | Jane Haughton | 4 | „ |
| | John Robinson | 7 | „ |
| | Marierie Smallshaw | 10 | „ |
| | John Alerton bast | 14 | „ |
| | Tho: Cobon | 23 | „ |
| | Tho: Ascoe | 24 | „ |
| | Riĉ Westhead | 27 | „ |
| | Tho: Huyton | 30 | „ |
| | Henrie farclough | 9 | Auguste |
| | Henrie Henrieson bast Jacobe Henrī pater | 12 | „ |
| | Henrye Blundell | 15 | „ |
| | Henrye Seale | 17 | „ |
| | George Swyfte | 18 | „ |
| | Jenet Blundell | 21 | „ |
| | Alis Breykell | 26 | „ |
| | Marget Shorlicars | 31 | „ |
| | Jane Morecrofte | 3 | September |
| | Edmond Hill | 7 | „ |
| | Margaret Asshorst | 12 | „ |
| | John Morecrofte | 13 | „ |
| | Elin Scarsbrecke | 14 | „ |
| | Christopher Wolsay | 16 | „ |
| | . . . Ascrofte | 28 | „ |
| | Edwarde ffarclofe | 29 | „ |
| | Margaret Barton | 22 | October |
| | Marget Alker | 23 | „ |
| | Marget Asmall | 24 | „ |
| | Elin Webster | 25 | „ |
| | Anne Thorneton | „ | „ |
| | Wiƚƚm Pecocke | 31 | „ |
| | Robert Cowp̄ | 7 | Nouember |
| | Tho: Molines | 10 | „ |
| | Elizabeth Gorsutch | 22 | „ |
| | Wiƚƚm Lathwhat | 23 | „ |
| | Richard Haughton | 25 | „ |
| | Xpofer Swyfte | 26 | „ |
| | Catherin Barton | 29 | „ |
| | Eliz[th] Chadocke | 30 | „ |
| Fo. 9 | Marierie Croston | 9 | December |
| | Anne Waynewright | 12 | „ |
| | Tho: Cocket | 17 | „ |
| | Anne Stanley | 21 | „ |
| | Peeter Coockeson | 22 | „ |
| | Eliz[th] Willson | 28 | „ |

| | | |
|---|---|---|
| Eliz[th] Westhead | 28 | December |
| Catherin Blundell | 31 | „ |
| Robert Arton | 4 | Januarie |
| Jane Prescot | 7 | „ |
| Jamis Blundell | 13 | „ |
| Robert Mawdisley | 14 | „ |
| Rodger Sutch | 15 | „ |
| Marierie Gorsutch | 18 | „ |
| Grace She | 25 | „ |
| Henrie Lufkin | 31 | „ |
| Tho: Browne bast | 6 | ffebruarie |
| Elin Holland | 8 | „ |
| Margaret Cropp | 13 | „ |
| Ector fforshaw | „ | „ |
| Windrowes iij children bap and bur | 18 | „ |
| Anne Mowdisle | 28 | „ |
| Johne Gilbertson | 1 | Martch |
| Alis Crofte | 14 | „ |
| John Ascrofte | 18 | „ |
| Margaret Mosse | 22 | „ |

## 1562.

| | | |
|---|---|---|
| Robert Hardman | 26 | Martch |
| Marierie Scarbrecke | 27 | „ |
| Marget Bocher | 1 | Aprill |
| John Loccar | 25 | „ |
| Alis Hey | 26 | „ |
| 10 Alis Jackeson | 2 | Maye |
| Alis Corbott | 3 | „ |
| Mode Blundell | 10 | „ |
| Eliz[th] Wrest de Aughton | 13 | „ |
| Eliz[th] Swyfte | 14 | „ |
| Lyonell Hoolme | 18 | „ |
| Henry Werall | 25 | „ |
| Tho: Morgan | 10 | June |
| Tho: Dauie | 24 | „ |
| Perret Waringe | 12 | July |
| John Blundell | 27 | „ |
| Henrie Ambrose | 29 | „ |
| Eliz[th] Shepte | 31 | „ |
| Ric̃ Greaves | 6 | Auguste |
| Hugh Marclough | 10 | „ |
| Hugh Westhead | 15 | „ |
| Catherin Yate | 18 | „ |
| Tho: Hattoñ | 20 | „ |
| Jdeth Barton | 22 | „ |
| Omfray Gill | 31 | „ |

Rodger Lea ... ... ... ... ... ... ... 5 September
Jamis Wolsy de Aughton ... ... ... ... 8 „
Eliz$^{th}$ Morecroft ... ... ... ... ... ... 18 „
John Coockeson bap: and bur̄ ... ... ... 23 „
Marierie Coockeson ... ... ... ... ... ... „ „
Robert Rutter ... ... ... ... ... ... ... 24 „
Tho: Hill ... ... ... ... ... ... ... 30 „
Tho: Waringe ... ... ... ... ... ... ... 3 October
Marierie Waringe ... ... ... ... ... ... „ „
Margaret Smallshaw ... ... ... ... ... ... „ „
Margaret Haughton ... ... ... ... ... ... „ „
Elino$^{r}$ Werall ... ... ... ... ... ... 8 „
Alis Seven Alies Blancherd ... ... ... ... 13 „
George Prescot ... ... ... ... ... ... ... 17 „
Alis Sutch ... ... ... ... ... ... ... „ „
Izabell Atherton ... ... ... ... ... ... 19 „
Elin ffarclof ... ... ... ... ... ... ... 23 „
John Clapam ... ... ... ... ... ... ... 24 „
Henry Smyth ... ... ... ... ... ... ... 30 „
Fo. 11 Kathine Asmalle ... ... ... ... ... ... 1 Nouember
Martine Morecrofte ... ... ... ... ... ... 10 „
Ector Kylshawe ... ... ... ... ... ... 22 „
Peter Or$^{9}$ell ... ... ... ... ... ... ... 26 „
An Barton ... ... ... ... ... ... ... „ „
John Jackson ... ... ... ... ... ... ... 2 December
Margreat Scaresb$^{9}$eke ... ... ... ... ... „ „
Robarte Modisley ... ... ... ... ... ... 4 „
Jenet Ambrose ... ... ... ... ... ... ... 14 „
Emlin Keckwicke ... ... ... ... ... ... 17 „
Thomas Hunte ... ... ... ... ... ... ... 19 „
An Cropp ... ... ... ... ... ... ... 21 „
Anne Jackson ... ... ... ... ... ... ... 26 „
Jenet & Marget Jackson bap: & bu: ... ... 28 „
An ffarcloughe ... ... ... ... ... ... ... 17 Januarie
Robarte Smyth ... ... ... ... ... ... 21 „
Yzabell Asmoll ... ... ... ... ... ... ... „ „
Elz: pker b: ... ... ... ... ... ... ... 22 „
Emlyn Jumpe ... ... ... ... ... ... ... 26 „
Rychard Mason ... ... ... ... ... ... 14 ffebruarie
Mawde Smyth ... ... ... ... ... ... ... 18 „
Wiłłm Travas ... ... ... ... ... ... ... 25 „
Henrie Morcrofte ... ... ... ... ... ... „ „
Elz: Coppowe ... ... ... ... ... ... ... „ „
Rycharde Taylior ... ... ... ... ... ... 26 „
Emlyn Haughton ... ... ... ... ... ... 1 Marche
Gabrill Barton ... ... ... ... ... ... ... 8 „
Wiłłm ffletcher ... ... ... ... ... ... 9 „
Richarde Hunter ... ... ... ... ... ... 10 „

## 1563.

| |  |  |  |
|---|---|---|---|
| | . . . Cropp | 25 | Marche |
| | Katherine Holme | 26 | ,, |
| | Tho: Wiswall | 27 | ,, |
| | Henrie Westehed | ,, | ,, |
| 12 | Ector & Katherin Modisley | 1 | Aprill |
| | Anne Aspinwall | 8 | ,, |
| | Elin Shaw | 9 | ,, |
| | Eloner Molinex | 12 | ,, |
| | Jahne Hoolme | ,, | ,, |
| | Katherin Willson Alis Pamer | 13 | ,, |
| | Anne Wakker | 23 | ,, |
| | Wiłłm Rylance | 25 | ,, |
| | George Waynewright | ,, | ,, |
| | Hugh Barker | ,, | ,, |
| | Elin Hesketh | 28 | ,, |
| | Eliz[th] Hadocke | 29 | ,, |
| | Elin Aerton | 2 | Maye |
| | John Tarleton | 3 | ,, |
| | Gouther Woulsey | 23 | ,, |
| | ffardinando Moscrop | ,, | ,, |
| | Henry Lathwhat | 30 | ,, |
| | Eliz[th] Aspinwall | 10 | June |
| | Claris ꝑker | 11 | ,, |
| | Jamis Lathwhat | 1 | July |
| | John Swyfte | 8 | ,, |
| | Elin Shawe | ,, | ,, |
| | Elin Prescot | 18 | ,, |
| | Marierie Ascrofte | 23 | ,, |
| | Marierie Hatton | 10 | August |
| | Eliz[th] Hoolme | 16 | ,, |
| | Jenet Hey | 15 | ,, |
| | Emlin Pecocke | 28 | ,, |
| | Marget Mawdisley | 31 | ,, |
| | Tho: Keckquicke | 14 | September |
| | Margaret Whytestones | ,, | ,, |
| | Wiłłm Lea | 20 | ,, |
| 13 | Mawde Blundell | 10 | October |
| | Wiłłm Wolsey | 16 | ,, |
| | Eliz[th] Seale | ,, | ,, |
| | Tho: Adamson alias Wiłłmson | 7 | Nouember |
| | Jenet Sumner | ,, | ,, |
| | Wiłłm Mason | 17 | ,, |
| | Tho: Coppoe | 5 | December |
| | . . . Traves | 16 | ,, |
| | . . . Shorlicars | 24 | ,, |
| | Catherin Aspinwall | 10 | Januarie |

Eliz^th Smyth ... ... ... ... ... ... ... 21 Januarie
Gilbert Blundell ... ... ... ... ... ... 25 „
Alis Wardmann ... ... ... ... ... ... 28 „
Jams Asshorste ... ... ... ... ... ... ... „ „
Tho: Ormishaw ... ... ... ... ... ... 31 „
Wiłłm Sutch ... ... ... ... ... ... ... „ „

[*No entries for ffebruarie*]

Wiłłm Barton ... ... ... ... ... ... ... 5 Martch
Margaret Mossocke ... ... ... ... ... ... 7 „
Ellin Ascroft ... ... ... ... ... ... ... 10 „
Eliz^th Bycarstaffe ... ... ... ... ... ... 15 „

## 1564.

Eliz^th Halle ... ... ... ... ... ... ... 5 Aprill
Anne Wlles [*sic*] ... ... ... ... ... ... 6 „
Ewan Dye ... ... ... ... ... ... ... ... 8 „
Marierie Yate ... ... ... ... ... ... ... 20 „
Fo. 14 Hugh Barton ... ... ... ... ... ... ... 3 Maye
Margaret Gobin ... ... ... ... ... ... „ „
Marierie Gill ... ... ... ... ... ... ... 11 „
Eliz^th Jackesoñ ... ... ... ... ... ... ... 29 „
Wiłłm Henrison ... ... ... ... ... ... 7 June
Tho: Ambrose ... ... ... ... ... ... ... 9 „
Ric̃ Gill ... ... ... ... ... ... ... ... 12 „
Grace Werall ... ... ... ... ... ... ... 13 „
Jamis windrow ... ... ... ... ... ... ... 3 Julye
Henry Alker ... ... ... ... ... ... ... 8 „
Anne Longlay ... ... ... ... ... ... ... 10 „
Marie Goulbron ... ... ... ... ... ... 11 „
Grace Barton ... ... ... ... ... ... ... 17 „
. . . Lea ... ... ... ... ... ... ... 19 „
Edward Killshaw ... ... ... ... ... ... 29 „
Henry Aspinwall ... ... ... ... ... ... 2 Auguste
Henry Morecrofte ... ... ... ... ... ... „ „
Eliz^th Waynewright ... ... ... ... ... ... 3 „
Jame Henrison ... ... ... ... ... ... ... „ „
Henrie Barker ... ... ... ... ... ... ... 10 „
Eliz^th Whytestones ... ... ... ... ... ... 20 „
Tho: Asley ... ... ... ... ... ... ... 23 „
Jamis Smalsha ... ... ... ... ... ... ... 24 „
. . . Haughton ... ... ... ... ... ... 29 „
Tho: Morecrofte ... ... ... ... ... ... 30 „
Katherin Hoolme ... ... ... ... ... ... 31 „
Tho: Henryson ... ... ... ... ... ... 1 September
Christopher Hunter ... ... ... ... ... ... 4 „

| |  |  |  |
|---|---|---|---|
| | Robert Hunter | 4 | September |
| | Marierie Prescot | 9 | „ |
| | Ellis Coockeson | 15 | „ |
| | John Gilbertson | 19 | „ |
| | Catherin Waynwrigh | 21 | „ |
| | Margaret Halsall | 23 | „ |
| | Tho: Shawe | 29 | „ |
| 5 | Jdeth Haughton | 1 | October |
| | John Wethingeton | 4 | „ |
| | Tho: Craine | 14 | „ |
| | Emlin Westhead | 15 | „ |
| | Emlin Morecroft | „ | „ |
| | Eliz$^{th}$ Lathwhat | 30 | „ |
| | Emlin Windrow | 6 | Nouember |
| | Adame Chadocke | 10 | „ |
| | Jayne Harison | 16 | „ |
| | Eliz$^{th}$ Morer | „ | „ |
| | Jamis Blundell | 18 | „ |
| | Homfrey Towne | 20 | „ |
| | Willm Kewquicke bast | 21 | „ |
| | Tho: Hodgeson | 22 | „ |
| | Tho: Hunter | 27 | „ |
| | Elin Sūmner | „ | „ |
| | Anne Barton | 28 | „ |
| | Jamis Bankes | 29 | „ |
| | Eliz$^{th}$ Rutter | „ | „ |
| | Emlin Lufkin | 2 | December |
| | Marierie Garrard | „ | „ |
| | Willm Webster | 17 | „ |
| | Jamis Blundel | 18 | „ |
| | John Craine bap: et bur̄ | 26 | „ |
| | Anne Barton | 30 | „ |
| | Enlin Loccar | 5 | Januarie |
| | Margaret Jumpe | „ | „ |
| | Emlin Hunte | 7 | „ |
| | Edward Morecrofte | 8 | „ |
| | Ector Sutch | 9 | „ |
| | Mawde Smyth | 12 | „ |
| | Margaret ffforshaw | „ | „ |
| | Peete Waynewright | 19 | „ |
| | Willm Breykell | 20 | „ |
| | Parsevall Cropp | 24 | „ |
| 16 | Margaret Masonn | 8 | ffebruarie |
| | Jaine Robertsoñ | 24 | „ |
| | Grace Aspinwall | „ | „ |
| | Willm Arton | 5 | Martch |
| | Henry Gill | 15 | „ |

## 1565.

| | | |
|---|---|---|
| Willm Hesketh | 25 | Martch |
| Tho: Whytstones | ” | ” |
| Elizth Jollie | 31 | ” |
| Margaret Gill | 3 | Aprill |
| Henry Mollinex | 8 | ” |
| Nicolas Barton | ” | ” |
| Jaine Atherton | 18 | ” |
| Tho: Hardman | 29 | ” |
| Ottuwell Barton | 30 | ” |
| Alis Aspinwall | 11 | Maye |
| Willm & Alis Stanley b | 28 | ” |
| Thurston ffarclough | ” | ” |
| Tho: Prescokot bast | 31 | ” |

[*No entries for June*]

| | | |
|---|---|---|
| Marie Haselgreave | 12 | Julie |
| Gilbert Blundel alias Coocke bast | 13 | ” |
| Tho: Woodes | 28 | ” |
| Alis Sumner | 5 | Auguste |
| Tho: ffirkin | 7 | ” |
| Ric̃ Holland | 9 | ” |
| Willm Talior | ” | ” |
| Tho: Lytham bast | 16 | ” |
| Marierie Whatton | 17 | ” |
| Jane wa: | 18 | ” |
| Elin Wolsay | 28 | ” |
| Fo. 17 Henry Wildinge | 9 | September |
| Margaret Lathom bast Hugh Lathom pater | 12 | ” |
| Jamis Mosse | 17 | ” |
| Tho: Busshell | 28 | ” |
| Jone Westhead | 29 | ” |
| Emlin Greaves | 30 | ” |
| Henry Mawdisley | 8 | October |
| Willm Whytestones bast | 14 | ” |
| Robert Shawe | 16 | ” |
| Jaine Tasker bast | 18 | ” |
| Claris Killshawe | 22 | ” |
| Elin Morecrofte | 25 | ” |
| Sara Garrarde | 28 | ” |
| Jane Shorlikers | 1 | Nouember |
| Elizth Cropp | 3 | ” |
| Henry Gorsutch | 8 | ” |
| Robert Blundell | 25 | ” |
| Tho: Rutter | 7 | December |
| Marie Letherbarow | 9 | ” |

| | | |
|---|---|---|
| Eliz[th] Artoun ... ... ... ... ... ... ... | 10 | December |
| Willm Lea ... ... ... ... ... ... ... | 16 | „ |
| Ric Brygehowse ... ... ... ... ... ... | 18 | „ |
| Eliz[th] Kewquicke ... ... ... ... ... ... | 20 | „ |
| John } John } Mawdisley dueeli ... ... ... ... | 22 | „ |
| Hector Morcrofte ... ... ... ... ... ... | 23 | „ |
| Gilbarton Barton ... ... ... ... ... ... | 29 | „ |
| John Lea bap: et bur ... ... ... ... ... | 1 | Januarie |
| Ric Ambrose ... ... ... ... ... ... ... | „ | „ |
| Hamlet . . . ... ... ... ... ... ... | 13 | „ |
| Grace Artherton ... ... ... ... ... ... | 19 | „ |
| Ric Bankes ... ... ... ... ... ... ... | 25 | „ |
| Elin Smyth ... ... ... ... ... ... ... | 31 | „ |
| Tho: Hill ... ... ... ... ... ... ... ... | 2 | ffebruarie |
| Elin Mawdisley ... ... ... ... ... ... | 3 | „ |
| . . . Mwdisley ... ... ... ... ... ... | 4 | „ |
| Margaret Ascrofte ... .. ... ... ... | 7 | „ |
| Peeter Martindaill de Aughton ... ... ... | „ | „ |
| Elin Alker ... ... ... ... ... ... ... ... | 12 | „ |
| Catherin Sutch ... ... ... ... ... ... ... | „ | „ |
| Tho: Yat ... ... ... ... ... ... ... ... | 17 | „ |
| Willm Blundell ... ... ... ... ... ... | 20 | „ |
| Marie Ascough ... ... ... ... ... ... ... | 26 | „ |
| Jo* . . . . . . } . . . Aspinwall } baptizati ... ... ... | 28 | „ |
| Jamis Swyfte ... ... ... ... ... ... ... | 5 | Martch |
| . . . Haughton ... ... ... ... ... ... | 6 | „ |
| Jamis She ... ... ... ... ... ... ... ... | 7 | „ |
| Anne Henrison de Aughton ... ... ... ... | „ | „ |
| Edwarde . . . ... ... ... ... ... ... | 8 | „ |
| George Traves ... ... ... ... ... ... ... | 10 | „ |
| Catherin Prescot ... ... ... ... ... ... | „ | „ |
| Margaret Toppinge ... ... ... ... ... ... | 12 | „ |
| Mawde Waringe ... ... ... ... ... ... | 18 | „ |
| John Waringe bap: et bur ... ... ... ... | 19 | „ |
| Sibell Barton ... ... ... ... ... ... ... | 21 | „ |
| Ann Crofte ... ... ... ... ... ... ... | 24 | „ |

## 1566.

| | | |
|---|---|---|
| Jenet Withingeton ... ... ... ... ... ... | 29 | Martch |
| Tho: Croston ... ... ... ... ... ... ... | 26 | Aprill |
| Catherin . . . ... ... ... ... ... ... | 28 | „ |
| Anne Crofte ... ... ... ... ... ... ... | 12 | Maye |
| Elin Sankey ... ... ... ... ... ... ... | „ | „ |
| Hughe Cropp ... ... ... ... ... ... ... | „ | „ |

* Other letters follow, but the entry is so blurred it is impossible to make it out, but the final letter is an "e."

Margaret Smyth ... ... ... ... ... ... 13 Maye
Edward Sumner ... ... ... ... ... ... „ „
Ric̃ Ormishawe ... ... ... ... ... ... 14 „
Gabrell Haughton ... ... ... ... ... ... 26 „
Fo. 19 Elizth Coockeson ... ... ... ... ... ... 3 June
. . . Stonton ... ... ... ... ... ... 4 „
Henry Webster ... ... ... ... ... ... ... 8 „
Wittm Sumner ... ... ... ... ... ... ... „ „
Margaret Swyfte ... ... ... ... ... ... „ „
Edward Garstange ... ... ... ... ... ... 14 „
Alis Goulbron ... ... ... ... ... ... ... 19 „
Allexander Orrell ... ... ... ... ... ... „ „
Elizth Hoolme ... ... ... ... ... ... ... 30 „
Anne ffarclough ... ... ... ... ... ... 5 Julie
Margaret Brookefild ... ... ... ... ... ... ... 13 „
Emannwell Morecrofte ... ... ... ... ... 3 August

[*No entries for September*]

Jenet Veale base Emlin Clarke mater ... ... 7 October

[*No entries for November*]

Tho: Gill ... ... ... ... ... ... ... ... ... 4 December
Elin Waynewright ... ... ... ... ... ... 9 „
John Toppinge ... ... ... ... ... ... ... 13 „
Adam Waynewright ... ... ... ... ... ... 17 Januarie
Anne Loccar ... ... ... ... ... ... ... 20 „
John Styam ... ... ... ... ... ... ... 21 „
Elizabeth Barton ... ... ... ... ... ... 23 „
Gilbart Waringe ... ... ... ... ... ... 24 „
Ric̃ Smyth ... ... ... ... ... ... ... ... 27 „
Ric̃ Cropp ... ... ... ... ... ... ... ... 28 „
Ric̃ Prescot ... ... ... ... ... ... ... 30 „
Fo. 20 Marierie Morecrofte ... ... ... ... ... ... 3 ffebruarie
John Woodhowse ... ... ... ... ... ... 17 „
Catherin Blackeledge ... ... ... ... ... ... „ „
Jamis Gill ... ... ... ... ... ... ... ... 18 „
John Morcrofte ... ... ... ... ... ... 20 „
Elizth Matthew ... ... ... ... ... ... ... 21 „
Izabell Coockeson ... ... ... ... ... ... 23 „
Elin Tasker ... ... ... ... ... ... ... 25 „
Elizth Gobbin ... ... ... ... ... ... ... 28 „
Marierie Leadbetter ... ... ... ... ... ... „ „
Elizth Macon ... ... ... ... ... ... ... 7 Martch
Ric̃ Tasker ... ... ... ... ... ... ... 8 „
Tho Jackeson ... ... ... ... ... ... ... „ „
Marierie Whytestones ... ... ... ... ... 17 „
Margaret Bowille ... ... ... ... ... ... 22 „

## 1567.

| | Name | Day | Month |
|---|---|---|---|
| | Ewañ Ascought | 28 | Martch |
| | Annes Towne | 1 | Aprell |
| | John Spencer | 7 | „ |
| | Margaret Lawrance doughter | 8 | „ |
| | John ffletcher | 9 | „ |
| | Hugh Hodgeson | 29 | „ |
| | Anne Waynewright | 6 | Maye |
| | John Hunte | „ | „ |
| | Edwarde Blundell | 9 | „ |
| | Willm Blundell | 18 | „ |
| | David Smvlte | 24 | „ |
| | Tho Asshorste | 31 | „ |
| | Willm Barton | 8 | June |
| | Elin Banister | 9 | „ |
| | Elin Windrowe | „ | „ |
| | Anne Jumpe | 11 | „ |
| | John Ambrose | 15 | „ |
| | Rodger Clapam | 22 | „ |
| | Jamis Smalshaw | 26 | „ |
| 1 | Rodge Westhead | 2 | Julye |
| | Henry Halsall | 4 | „ |
| | Bryham Swyfte | 5 | „ |
| | Marierie Holland | „ | „ |
| | Robert Ley | 6 | „ |
| | John Sutch | 10 | „ |
| | Rodger Sutch | „ | „ |
| | Emlin Sankey | 13 | „ |
| | Henry Hoolme | 20 | „ |
| | John Harison | 25 | „ |
| | Rodger Barton | 7 | Auguste |
| | Anne Parre | 10 | „ |
| | John Swyfte | „ | „ |
| | . . . Marcer | „ | „ |
| | Anne Allerton | 2 | September |
| | Ric̃ Swyfte | 3 | „ |
| | Anne Wane | „ | „ |
| | Hugh Leyland | 9 | „ |
| | Willm Hasellgreave | 16 | „ |
| | Rodger Hesketh | 17 | „ |
| | Gilbart Sefton | „ | „ |
| | Jane . . . base | „ | „ |
| | Henry Hoolme | 23 | „ |
| | Henry Hunter | 26 | „ |
| | Anne Woofall | 2 | October |
| | Elizth Litham | „ | „ |

| | | | |
|---|---|---|---|
| | Jamis Cadicke | 6 | October |
| | Gilbert Henryson | 9 | „ |
| | Jaine Lufkin | 10 | „ |
| | Gilbart Killshaw | 12 | „ |
| | Margaret Whytestones | 14 | „ |
| | Tho Harieson | 27 | „ |
| Fo. 22 | Tho: Hoolme | 2 | Nouember |
| | Anne Hoolme | „ | „ |
| | Catherin Ascrofte | 4 | „ |
| | Edwarde Abott | 6 | „ |
| | Elizabeth Craine | 7 | „ |
| | Bryhan Cocket | 10 | „ |
| | Ric̃ Batersbie | 18 | „ |
| | Edward Cowp | 1 | December |
| | Hamle Williamson | 7 | „ |
| | ffardinando ffloyde | 12 | „ |
| | ffardinando Garrard | 13 | „ |
| | Willm Barton | 21 | „ |
| | Willm Parker | „ | „ |
| | Ric̃ Waynwright | 29 | „ |
| | Hamlet Willmson | 30 | „ |
| | Margaret Barton | 9 | Januarie |
| | Robert Smolte | 14 | „ |
| | Tho: Codrey | 15 | „ |
| | Edward Aspinwall | 17 | „ |
| | Margaret Talior | 21 | „ |
| | Peeter Leye | 24 | „ |
| | Henry Watkinson | 1 | ffebruarie |
| | Peeter Barton | „ | „ |
| | John Walison | 4 | „ |
| | Margaret Howden | 5 | „ |
| | Omfrey Greaves | 10 | „ |
| | Margaret Shawe | 13 | „ |
| | Susanna Mossocke | 15 | „ |
| | Marierie Chadocke | 17 | „ |
| | Jamis Prescot | 20 | „ |
| | Anes Cosey | 23 | „ |
| | Jamis Blundell | „ | „ |
| | Henry Sumner | „ | „ |
| | Eliz$^{th}$ Wythingeton | 26 | „ |
| Fo. 23 | Elin Morcrofte | 2 | Martch |
| | Willm Hill | 4 | „ |
| | Ric̃ Cocket | 7 | „ |
| | Rodger Cropp | „ | „ |
| | Eles Aspinwall | 10 | „ |
| | Tho: Lawranson | 18 | „ |
| | Eliz$^{th}$ Mawdisley | 20 | „ |

## 1568.

| | | |
|---|---|---|
| Jaine Tasker | 26 | Martch |
| Margareett Hesketh bast | 30 | „ |
| Richard Gille | 5 | April |
| Tho Barton fill Wiłłm | 11 | „ |
| Eliz^th^ Morecrofte fił Jamis | 18 | „ |
| Thomas Sumner | 25 | „ |
| Margaret Masonn | 29 | „ |
| Roberte Laylloyd fiłł Ellis | 2 | Maye |
| Jamis . . . . | 6 | „ |
| Jamis Ormishaw fił Gilbart | 9 | „ |
| Wiłłm Leye fill: John | 10 | „ |
| Margaret Cropp fiłł George | 13 | „ |
| Robert Hadocke fill Tho: | 20 | „ |
| Izabell Mollinex | 31 | „ |
| Jaine Jackeson fiłł Hugh | 5 | June |
| Margaret Styhom fil John | „ | „ |
| Edwarde Yate fiłł John | 7 | „ |
| Sislie Lancaster | 14 | „ |
| John Lancaster | „ | „ |
| Eliz^th^ Wildinge | „ | „ |
| Anne Aspinwall fill Omfrey | 23 | „ |
| Jhamis Whatton fill Tho: | 7 | Julie |
| Anna Bongke fiłł Henry | 11 | „ |
| John Aspinwall | 14 | „ |
| Ric̃ Holland | „ | „ |
| Tho: Smyth fil Jamis | 15 | „ |
| Jaine Awker | 16 | „ |
| Eliz^th^ Ryāson fił Edm: | 18 | „ |
| Margaret Barton fił Mather | 23 | „ |
| Alis Yate fił Edw: | 26 | „ |
| Wiłłm Wryght fill Tho: | 29 | „ |
| Anna Mawdisley fill Jamis | 30 | „ |
| Wiłłm fforshaw fiłł George | 28 | Auguste |
| Elizabeth Jackeson fiłł Jamis | 31 | „ |
| Eliz^th^ Sefton fill Tho: | 1 | September |
| Margaret Smalshaw fiłł Tho: | 6 | „ |
| Edwarde Blundell fil John | 9 | „ |
| Jamis Stopforth fill Wiłłm | 10 | „ |
| Wiłłm Ley & Ellin Ley | 11 | „ |
| Elin Aspinwall fi Wiłłm | 18 | „ |
| Ric̃ Aiscrofte fi: Jo: | 20 | „ |
| Bodger [*sic*] Ley fil Hector | 22 | „ |
| Hugh Hodgeson | 27 | „ |
| Izabell Westhead fill Ric̃ | 29 | „ |
| Edw: Aspinwall fi Tho: | 6 | October |
| Robart Lathwat fi Robart | 9 | „ |

| | | | |
|---|---|---|---|
| | Silvester Jackeson fi Adam | 14 | October |
| | Ric̃ ffarclough fiłł Rodger | 16 | „ |
| | George Ambrose fill Tho: | 1 | Nvember |
| | Anne Whytestones fill Wiłłm | „ | „ |
| | John Smyth fill Symon | 8 | „ |
| | Wiłłm Saile fi Radall | „ | „ |
| | Henry Smyth fi: George | 14 | „ |
| | Edw: Scarsbreck fi: Mr Edw: | 24 | „ |
| | Marierie Barton fill Cristophe | 28 | „ |
| Fo. 25 | Elizth Croston fi: Edmunde | 8 | December |
| | Elin Stopforth | 12 | „ |
| | Ric̃ Winder fi: Henrie | 10 | Januarie |
| | Hector Whytestones fi: Tho: | „ | „ |
| | Izabell Windraw fi: Raffe | 16 | „ |
| | Gabrell Gorsutch fi: Jamis | 19 | „ |
| | Anne Prescott fi: Peeter | 21 | „ |
| | Marierie Gardn9 & Eideth Gardn9 fi Robert | 23 | „ |
| | Alis Mawdisley fi: Wiłłm | 2 | ffebruarie |
| | John Layland fi: Hugh | 4 | „ |
| | ffrances ffogge fi Rodger | 8 | „ |
| | Elizth Aspinwall fill Elis | 20 | „ |
| | Tho: Morecrofte fil Wiłłm | 24 | „ |
| | John Morecrofte fi Raffe | 25 | „ |
| | Elin Aiscrofte fil John | 27 | „ |
| | Anne Coockeson fi Henry | „ | „ |
| | Elin ffoa9clough fi Wiłłm | 28 | „ |
| | Margaret Waringe fi Wiłłm | 15 | Martch |
| | Sislie Waynewright fi Wiłłm | 16 | „ |
| | Robert Garrard fi: Henry | 17 | „ |

## 1569.

| | | | |
|---|---|---|---|
| | Elizth Blackeledge | 27 | Martch |
| | Marierie Webster fi: Henrye | 28 | „ |
| | Anne Cōillay fi Rob̃ de Prescot | 3 | Aprill |
| | Anne Cropp fi Peeter | 6 | „ |
| | Jaine Sutch fi Lucke | 13 | „ |
| | Catherin Cawdrey fił: Wiłł: | 15 | „ |
| | John Swifte fi: Lionell | 18 | „ |
| | Hugh Massie fi: Ric̃ | 21 | „ |
| | Elin Halworth fill: Wiłłm | 28 | „ |
| Fo. 26 | Elin Barton fi: Wiłłm | 12 | Maye |
| | Laurance Aspinwall fill Ranold | 31 | „ |
| | Henry Nelson fil Tho: | 3 | June |
| | Jaine Barton fi: Tho: | 7 | „ |
| | Elizth Standanought fiłł Ed: | 7 | Julie |
| | Tho: Jackeson fi: Robert | 10 | „ |
| | Izabell Morecrofte fi: Wiłłm | 18 | „ |

Alis Waynewright fi: Tho: ... ... ... ... 28 Julie
Wiłłm Butchert fi: Lyonell ... ... ... ... 4 Auguste
Eliz[th] Scarsbrecke fi: Johne ... .. ... ... 7 „
Abraham Hunte fi: Ja: ... ... ... ... ... ... 14 „
Wiłłm Butcherd fi: Lionel ... ... ... ... 27 „
Ric̃ Gleaste fil: Tho: ... ... ... ... ... 10 September
Hector Alcar fi: Tho: ... ... ... ... ... 14 „
Izabell Sumner fi: Christopher ... ... ... 23 „
Margerie Elliot fi: Ja: ... ... ... ... ... 24 „
Anthoney Cadicke fi: Wiłl: ... ... ... ... 28 „
Hugh & Raffe Sefton fi: George ... ... ... 2 October
Edmunde Hadocke ... ... ... ... ... ... 12 „
Jenet Morcrofte fi: Raffe ... ... ... ... 24 „
Christopher Waringe fi: Ric̃ ... ... ... ... 16 November
Margaret Withingeton fi: Tho: ... ... ... 22 „
Elin Hardmañ fill: Tho: ... ... ... ... 25 „
Wiłłm Johneson fi: Christ: Margerie Litham mat[9] bast ... ... ... ... ... ... ... 27 „
Margaret Worthington fi: Ric̃ ... ... ... 6 December
Eliz[th] Bycarstafe fi: Hug: ... ... ... ... ... 12 „
Jaine Brookefeelde fi: Jo: Margerie Litherland mater ... ... ... ... ... ... ... ... ... 27 „
Loare Ridinge fi: Rob: Emlin Marow mater... 26 „
Anne Gobbin fi: Tho: ... ... ... ... ... 9 Januarie
Ric̃ ffude fi: David ... ... ... ... ... ... 20 „
Margerie ffedgger fill Thirsten ... ... ... „ „
Jaine Barker fil: Alexander ... ... ... ... 3 ffebruarie
Nicolas Sumner fi: Jo: ... ... ... ... ... 24 „
Eliz[th] Cropp fil: Ric̃ ... ... ... ... ... ... 12 Martch
Eliz[th] Hoolme fi: Henrie ... ... ... ... ... 13 „
Alis Craine fi: Ranould ... ... ... ... ... „ „
Ellin Carter fi: Ja: ... ... ... ... ... ... „ „
Wiłłm ffarrer fi: Gilƀ ... ... ... ... ... 14 „

## 1570.

Catherin Cropp fi: Raph ... ... ... ... ... 7 Martch
Eliz[th] Smyth fi: Jo: ... ... ... ... ... ... 27 „
Margerie Leye fi: Henrie ... ... ... ... „ „
Ric̃ Swifte fil: Ja: ... ... ... ... ... ... 30 „
Emlyn Whitestones fi: Hecł ... ... ... ... 2 Apriłł
Ann Ambrose fi: Tho: ... ... ... ... ... 5 „
Letysse Asmoll fi: Hug: ... ... ... ... 6 „
Emlyn Ierland fi: Ric̃ ... ... ... ... ... 10 „
Gilbarte Asmoll fi: Ranold ... ... ... ... 12 „
Hùgh Keickwicke fi: Will: ... ... ... ... 14 „
Ann Mawdisley fi: Hector ... ... ... ... 16 „
Ann Madisley fi: Roƀt ... ... ... ... ... 18 „

Henrie Ascrofte fi: Jo: ... ... ... ... ... ... 27 Aprill
Ric̃ Allerton fi: Jo: ... ... ... ... ... 5 May
Silvester Keickwicke ... ... ... ... ... 9 "
Edward Soomner fi: Gilb̃ ... ... ... ... ... 11 "
Tho: Preskote fi: Will ... ... ... ... ... ... 13 "
ffrances Morcrofte fi: Ja: ... ... ... ... ... 23 "
Margerie Gobbin fi: Jo: ... ... ... ... ... ... 26 "
Marie Longlaye fi: Jo: ... ... ... ... ... ... 31 "
Fo. 28 Silvester Halworth fi: Will ... ... ... ... ... 7 June
Gabrill Laithom fi: Jo: ... ... ... ... ... ... 18 "
Jane Cockett fi: Hen: ... ... ... ... ... ... 22 "
Eliz$^{th}$ Aspinwall fi: Will: ... ... ... ... ... ... 24 "
Margerie Tasker fi: Tho: ... ... ... ... ... 25 "
Katherin Halworth filī lio: Ly [*sic*] ... ... 3 Julie
George Cropp fi: Jeor: [*sic*] ... ... ... ... ... 13 "
Edward Hunter fi: Rob̃t ... ... ... ... ... ... 17 "
John Holme filia Pet: ... ... ... ... ... ... 20 "
Katherin Bancke fi: Ric̃ ... ... ... ... ... ... 23 "
Margaret Scarisbreak fi: M$^{r}$ Ed: ... ... ... 24 "
Alis Yeatt fi: Jo: ... ... ... ... ... ... ... 31 "
Ann Letherbarow fi: Jo: ... ... ... ... ... 17 Auguste
Stephen Aspinwall fi: Hom: ... ... ... ... ... 21 "
Henrie Smith fi: Rob̃t ... ... ... ... ... ... 25 "
John Houghton fi: Ewan ... ... ... ... ... 6 September
Anne Barton fi: Peeter ... ... ... ... ... ... 8 "
Jamis Cowp fi ... ... ... ... ... ... ... ... 10 "
Mawde Westhead fi: Hector ... ... ... ... ... 11 "
Jamis Whytestones fi: Hugh ... ... ... ... ... 21 "
Edw: Batersbee fi: John ... ... ... ... ... 23 "
Edw: Waiworth fi: Ric̃ ... ... ... ... ... ... 30 "
Rodger Barton fi: George ... ... ... ... ... 1 October
Jaine Gill fi: Tho: ... ... ... ... ... ... ... 10 "
Jaine Clarke fi: Jo: ... ... ... ... ... ... 19 "
Elon Asscrofte fi: Raffe ... ... ... ... ... ... 23 "
Fo. 29 Marie Haughton fi: Jamis ... ... ... ... ... 2 November
Wiłłm Haughton fi: Tho: ... ... ... ... ... 8 "
Margaret fforshaw fi Jo: ... ... ... ... ... ... 10 "
Claris Lathom fi: Henrie ... ... ... ... ... 11 "
Silvester Shawe fi: Rodger ... ... ... ... ... " "
Edwarde Mosse fi: Hugh ... ... ... ... ... 16 "
Jaine Masoñ fi: Ranolde ... ... ... ... ... 24 "
ffrances Rylans fi: Robert ... ... ... ... ... 1 December
John Blackeledge fi: Ewan ... ... ... ... ... 2 "
George Mollinex fi: Henrie ... ... ... ... ... 8 "
Syslye Prescot fill Henrie ... ... ... ... ... 9 "
Catherin Rim̃er fi: Jo: de Halsall ... ... ... 23 "
Anne Whytestones fi: Tho: ... ... ... ... ... 25 "
Margaret Ascrofte fi: Jo: ... ... ... ... ... 2 Januarie
Jamis Leay fi: Hector ... ... ... ... ... ... 11 "

Hector Mawdisley fi: Witt Juvenor [?] ... ... 14 Januarie
Anne Windrowe fi: Tho: ... ... ... ... ... 16 „
Emlin Barton fi: Tho: ... ... ... ... ... ... 23 „
Tho: Allerton fi: Witm ... ... ... ... ... 25 „
Eliz[th] Bongke fi: Henrie ... ... ... ... ... ... 26 „
Rodger Winder fi: Henrie ... ... ... ... ... 30 „
Jamis Saille fi: Randall ... ... ... ... ... ... 1 ffebruarij
Izabell Chadocke fi: Ric ... ... ... ... ... ... 5 „
Margerie Prescot fi: Robert ... ... ... ... ... 9 „
Anne Smyth fi: John ... ... ... ... ... ... 18 „
Gabrell Kilshaw fi Witm ... ... ... ... ... „ „
John Morcrofte fi: Henrie ... ... ... ... ... 19 „
Johan Asmall filia Ric ... ... ... ... ... ... 23 „
John Styam fi: Jo: ... ... ... ... ... ... ... 27 „
Tho: Mawdisley fi: Ric ... ... ... ... ... ... 1 March
Ric Sakey fi: Rodger ... ... ... ... ... ... 4 „
Jaine Whytestones fi: Henrie ... ... ... ... 8 „
Jaine Waynewright fi: Tho: ... ... ... ... ... 9 „
Witm Gill fi: Cristopher ... ... ... ... ... 11 „
Elin Longeton fi: Ric ... ... ... ... ... ... „ „
Elin Aspinwall fi: Ellis ... ... ... ... ... ... 13 „
Emlin Smolte fi: Edmund ... ... ... ... ... 16 „
Catherin Haile fi: Ellis ... ... ... ... ... ... 17 „
Tho: Aspinwall fi: Witm ... ... ... ... ... 24 „

## 1571.

Jamis Robinson fi: Lowrance ... ... ... ... ... 29 Martch
Edw: Aspinwall fi: Jamis ... ... ... ... ... 18 Aprill
John Mawdisle fi: Hector senior ... ... ... ... 30 „
Anne Leye fi: John ... ... ... ... ... ... ... 9 Maye
Eliz[th] Edmundson fi: Lawrance ... ... ... ... 17 „
Eliz[th] fi: Robert ... ... ... ... ... ... ... ... ... 18 „
Robert Shawe fi: Jamis ... ... ... ... ... ... 31 „
Cislie Cowp fitt Hugh ... ... ... ... ... ... 1 June
Eliz[th] Barton fi: Alexsander ... ... ... ... ... 2 „
Emlin Jackeson fi: Robr ... ... ... ... ... 5 „
Eliz[th] Banke fi: Henrie ... ... ... ... ... ... 8 „
Alis Sutch fi: George ... ... ... ... ... ... 24 „
Anne Hunter fi: Tho: ... ... ... ... ... ... 25 „
Jaine Morecrofte fi: Bryhan ... ... ... ... 29 „
Peeter & Witm Ormishaw fi: Gilbert ... ... 30 „
John Hodgeson fi: Robert ... ... ... ... ... „ „
Edward Garrard fi: Henrie ... ... ... ... ... 4 July
Tho: Aspinwall fi: Jamis ... ... ... ... ... 5 „
Catherin Robinson fi: Robert ... ... ... ... 14 „
Richard Whytestones fi: Hector ... ... ... 21 „
Catherin Lunte fi: Trymor ... ... ... ... ... 26 „
George Prescot fi: George ... ... ... ... ... 29 „

| | | | |
|---|---|---|---|
| Fo. 31 | William Swifte fi : Jo : ... ... ... ... ... ... | 8 | Auguste |
| | Alis Swifte fi : Ric̃ ... ... ... ... ... ... ... | 12 | „ |
| | Roger Keickwicke fi : Jo : ... ... ... ... ... | 18 | „ |
| | Alis Standanought fi : Ed : ... ... ... ... ... | 19 | „ |
| | Marget Swifte fi : Ric̃ mat : Jenet bounde ... | 21 | „ |
| | Tho : Topping fi : Jo : mat Sislye weauer ... | 26 | „ |
| | Margaret Suche fi : Lucke ... ... ... ... ... | 3 | September |
| | John Elliott fi : Tho : ... ... ... ... ... ... | „ | „ |
| | Tho : Blundell fi : Christ ... ... ... ... ... | 5 | „ |
| | James Lithom fi : Witt ... ... ... ... ... ... | 7 | „ |
| | Margaret Blundell fi : Jo : ... ... ... ... ... | 8 | „ |
| | Eline Morcrofte fi : Raw : ... ... ... ... ... | 12 | „ |
| | Tho : Cropp fi : Ric : ... ... ... ... ... ... ... | 23 | „ |
| | Anne Suche fi : Christ ... ... ... ... ... ... | 24 | „ |
| | Margerie ffaircloughe fi : ... ... ... ... ... ... | 6 | October |
| | Jane Smalshawe fi : Tho : ... ... ... ... ... | 14 | „ |
| | Eline Rydynge fi : Robt ... ... ... ... ... ... | 16 | „ |
| | Tho : Tuner fi : Ja : ... ... ... ... ... ... | 18 | „ |
| | William Ric̃son fi : Edmund ... ... ... ... ... | 28 | „ |
| | John Alerton fi : Hen : ... ... ... ... ... ... | 30 | „ |
| | Jenet Alerton fi : Hen : ... ... ... ... ... ... | „ | „ |
| | John Cawsey fi : Hu : ... ... ... ... ... ... | 2 | November |
| | Grace Wainwright fi : Will : ... ... ... ... ... | 18 | „ |
| | John Holme fi : Pet : ... ... ... ... ... ... | „ | „ |
| | Elizth Aspinwall fi : Hom : ... ... ... ... ... ... | 19 | „ |
| | Elizth Suche fi : Ja : ... ... ... ... ... ... ... | 20 | „ |
| | Emlin Ambrose fi : Tho : ... ... ... ... ... | 24 | „ |
| | Ellis Gleaste fi : Tho : ... ... ... ... ... ... | 29 | „ |
| Fo. 32 | Ranould Gill fill Hugh ... ... ... ... ... ... | 1 | December |
| | Edw : Brighowse fi : Ric̃ ... ... ... ... ... ... | 6 | „ |
| | Anne Ambose [*sic*] fi : Tho : ... ... ... ... ... | 8 | „ |
| | Anne Worthingeton fi : Ric̃ ... ... ... ... ... | 18 | „ |
| | Richard Morecrofte fi : Witt ... ... ... ... ... | 23 | „ |
| | Rodger Mawdisley fi : Hector minor ... ... | 24 | „ |
| | Elizth Beconsay fi : Jamis ... ... ... ... ... ... | „ | „ |
| | Hugh ffletcher fill Ric̃ ... ... ... ... ... ... | 30 | „ |
| | Edw : Kewquicke fill Ric̃ ... ... ... ... ... | 3 | Januarie |
| | Tho : Swifte fil John & mater Mrgerie Haughton bast ... ... ... ... ... ... ... ... ... ... ... | 4 | „ |
| | Elizth Barton fit Tho : ... ... ... ... ... ... | „ | „ |
| | Elizth Mowdisley fi Jo : et mater Alis Killshaw | 7 | „ |
| | Ric̃ Hesketh fi : Tho : ... ... ... ... ... ... | 9 | „ |
| | Anne Killshaw fi : Ric̃ ... ... ... ... ... ... | „ | „ |
| | Anne Whytestones fi : Henri ... ... ... ... ... | 13 | „ |
| | Wittm Brigehowse fi : Hamlet ... ... ... ... | 14 | „ |
| | Gabrell Hunter fi : Jamis ... ... ... ... ... | 18 | „ |
| | Charles Iarland fil : Ric̃ ... ... ... ... ... ... | „ | „ |
| | Ric̃ Swyfte fill Ewan ... ... ... ... ... ... | 19 | „ |
| | Silvester Tunstual fi : Gowther ... ... ... | 20 | „ |

| | | | |
|---|---|---|---|
| | Annes Shawe fi: Henrie | 25 | Januarie |
| | Ellin Waynewright fil G: | 4 | ffebruarie |
| | Wilm Sefton fi: George | 13 | „ |
| | Marie Cropp fil Ric̃ | 22 | „ |
| | Peeter Aspinwall fi: Wiłł | 23 | „ |
| | Peeter Barton fi Will: | 26 | „ |
| | Hugh Wosey fi: Peeter | 28 | „ |
| | Elizth Farrer fi: Gilƀ | 1 | March |
| | Catherin Yate fi: Edw: | „ | „ |
| | Tho: Whyte fi: Jamis | 7 | „ |
| | Henrie Anderton fi: Edmond | 8 | „ |
| | Emlin Bycarstaf fi: Hugh | 9 | „ |
| | Tho: Blundell fi: Hen: | 13 | „ |
| | Peeter Talior fi: Wiłł | „ | „ |
| | Godfray Cropp fi Peeȓ | „ | „ |
| 33 | Anne Mowdsley fi: ffillip | 14 | „ |
| | Elizth Gobbin fi: Jo: | 16 | „ |
| | Edw: Asshirst fi: Jo: | 22 | „ |
| | John Stopforth fi: Raffe et Maget Herlickers | 23 | „ |

## 1572.

| | | | |
|---|---|---|---|
| | Silvester Ascrofte fi: John | 26 | March |
| | Jaine Gill fi: Wiłłm | 2 | Aprill |
| | Annes Aspinwall fi: Tho: | 17 | „ |
| | Izabell Barton fi Ric | 18 | „ |
| | Gilbart Sumner fi: | „ | „ |
| | Catherin Traves fil Henrie | 19 | Maye |
| | Margaret Gill fi: ꝑsevall | 21 | „ |
| | Anne Whytestones fi Roƀt | „ | „ |
| | Margaret Orton fi: John | 28 | „ |
| | Edward Banke fi Henrie | 29 | „ |
| | Gilbert Garrard fi Wiłł | „ | „ |
| | Hugh Ascrofte fi Jamis | 30 | „ |
| | Anne Blundell fi: Peeter | 2 | June |
| | John Marow fi: Tho: | 9 | „ |
| | Elin Wariner fi: Tho: | 14 | „ |
| | Elizth Lathom fi: Jo: | 20 | „ |
| | Edw: Parke fi: Ric̃ | „ | „ |
| | Robert Ley fi: Jo: | 29 | „ |
| | Alis Vrmiston fi: Lyonell | 8 | Julye |
| | Alexsander Scarsbrecke fi Mr Edw: armigeri | 30 | „ |
| 34 | Anne Willson fi: Cristopher | 3 | Auguste |
| | Marget Woodes fi: Robert | 12 | „ |
| | Jaine Atkinson fi: Jo: | 15 | „ |
| | Marie Chisnall fi: Tho: | 19 | „ |
| | Ro: Hollande fi: Tho: | 21 | „ |
| | Ma°get Raskem fi: Jo: et mater Ellin Ranforth de Eccleston | 23 | „ |

| | | | |
|---|---|---|---|
| | Marie Mawdisley fi : Ric̃ | 3 | September |
| | Eliz[th] Mawdisley fi : Ric̃ | 4 | „ |
| | Adrian Haidocke fi Charles | 7 | „ |
| | Catherin Crofte fi Tho : | 14 | „ |
| | Omfrey Hill fi Jo : | 15 | „ |
| | Peeter Barton fi Gilb̃ | 16 | „ |
| | Hugh Aiscrofte fi Raffe | 18 | „ |
| | Eliz[th] Sankey fi Rodger | 28 | „ |
| | Marget Scarsbrecke fi Tho : | 2 | October |
| | Henrie Matthew fi George | „ | „ |
| | Jamis Mollinex | 22 | „ |
| | Hugh Craine f | 30 | „ |
| | Elin Tyrer | 4 | November |
| | Marie Mowdisley | 6 | „ |
| | Jamis Prescot | 13 | „ |
| | Jenet Ormishaw f | 14 | „ |
| | Wiłłm Westhead | „ | „ |
| | Eliz[th] Coket | 22 | „ |
| | Jamis Smyth fi : Tho : | 2 | December |
| | Elin Browne fi : Will : | 6 | „ |
| | Marie Gill fi Ric̃ et mater Margett Kekewquick | 10 | „ |
| | Rodge Stonton fi Ja : Marget Welshe | 30 | „ |
| Fo. 35 | Ric̃ Mollinex | 1 | Januarie |
| | Wiłłm Bobinso [*sic*] | „ | „ |
| | Marie Claton | 2 | „ |
| | Edw : Killshaw | 3 | „ |
| | Alis Yat fi Wiłł et mater Ann Wayshe | 4 | „ |
| | Johane Martindaill fillia John | 10 | „ |
| | Ric̃ Cowp fi : Hugh | „ | „ |
| | Edw : Cosey fi : Hugh | 11 | „ |
| | Anne Sailes fi Randall | 12 | „ |
| | Wiłłm Waynewright | 24 | „ |
| | Henrie fformebie | 1 | ffebruarie |
| | Sara Morecroft | 2 | „ |
| | Catherin Gowbron fi Jo : de Halsall | 10 | „ |
| | Jaine Morecrofte fi Raffe | 13 | „ |
| | Tho : Byckstaff fi Ja : de Aught | 14 | „ |
| | Margerie Masoñ fi : Ri : | „ | „ |
| | Wiłłm Carr fi : Wiłł | 19 | „ |
| | Henry Swyfte fi : Ja : | „ | „ |
| | Peeter ffloyde fi : David | 26 | „ |
| | Agnes Smyth fi : Jo : | 6 | March |
| | Rob̃ Shawe fi : Edm | 12 | „ |
| | Elin Lunte fi : Trymovr | 14 | „ |
| | Edw : Barton fi : George | „ | „ |
| | Peter Cropp fi : Tho : | 16 | „ |
| | Emlin Harkar fil Tho : | „ | „ |
| | Wiłłm Barton fi : Lewes | 23 | „ |

## 1573.

| | | |
|---|---|---|
| Marget Sanforth fi ... ... ... ... ... ... ... | 27 | Marche |
| Ric̃ Brockefild ... ... ... ... ... ... ... ... | 29 | „ |
| Catherin Stanton et mater Marget Rimmer ... | 31 | „ |
| Peeter Houkeshey fi ... ... ... ... ... ... ... | 4 | Aprill |
| Will̃m Mawdisley fi Rob̃ ... ... ... ... ... ... | „ | „ |
| Will̃u Ascrofte ... ... ... ... ... ... ... ... | 16 | „ |
| Ellyn Haughton fi: Rob̃ ... ... ... ... ... ... | 20 | „ |
| Gilbart Morcrofte fi: Will̃u ... ... ... ... ... | „ | „ |
| Alis Spencer fi Peeter ... ... ... ... ... ... | 24 | „ |
| Ma'gerie Sutton ... ... ... ... ... ... ... | 3 | Maye |
| Isake Prescott fill Pet' ... ... ... ... ... ... | 16 | „ |
| Elizbeth Asmall ... ... ... ... ... ... ... | 21 | „ |
| John Webster ... ... ... ... ... ... ... ... | 23 | „ |
| Catherin Awerton fi: Henrie ... ... ... ... ... | 25 | „ |
| Eideth Halliwall ... ... ... ... ... ... ... | 29 | „ |
| Anne Lea fi Hector ... ... ... ... ... ... ... | 31 | „ |
| Henrie Cropp ... ... ... ... ... ... ... ... | 3 | June |
| Jenet Spencer ... ... ... ... ... ... ... ... | 4 | „ |
| Anne Sumner ... ... ... ... ... ... ... ... | „ | „ |
| Ja: Cropp ... ... ... ... ... ... ... ... ... | 14 | „ |
| Edward M'Crofte fi Will̃ ... ... ... ... ... | 17 | „ |
| Ric̃ Brigehowse fi Ric̃ ... ... ... ... ... ... | 22 | „ |
| Catherin Wrthingeton fi Ric ... ... ... ... ... | 24 | „ |
| Will̃m Gowbron ... ... ... ... ... ... ... | 14 | Julye |
| Ric̃ Halle fi Ellis ... ... ... ... ... ... ... | „ | „ |
| Ri: Jumpe fi Edw: ... ... ... ... ... ... ... | 18 | „ |
| Tho: Catrell fi George mater Eliz: Beconsō... | 21 | „ |
| Anne Macristie fi Jo: ... ... ... ... ... ... | 22 | „ |
| Will̃m Sefton fi George ... ... ... ... ... ... | 25 | „ |
| Vrsola Aspinwall fi Will̃m ... ... ... ... ... | 28 | „ |
| Arthor Styham fi Jo: ... ... ... ... ... ... | 8 | Auguste |
| Ric̃ Aspnall fi Tho: ... ... ... ... ... ... ... | 16 | „ |
| Ric̃ ffintch fi Tho: ... ... ... ... ... ... ... | 17 | „ |
| Henrie Rimmer fi Jo: ... ... ... ... ... ... | 21 | „ |
| Ja: Kewquicke fi John ... ... ... ... ... ... | 26 | „ |
| Margerie Walener ... ... ... ... ... ... ... | „ | „ |
| Elizth Banke ... ... ... ... ... ... ... ... | „ | „ |
| 7 Nicolas Prescot fi Peter ... ... ... ... ... ... | 3 | September |
| John Lathom fi Hugh ... ... ... ... ... ... | 4 | „ |
| Emlin Prescot ... ... ... ... ... ... ... ... | 20 | „ |
| Marget Jackeson fi: Ro: ... ... ... ... ... | „ | „ |
| Will̃m Goodes fi Jo: et mater Ellin Lathwhat | 30 | „ |
| Omfrey Mowdisley fi: ... ... ... ... ... ... | 7 | October |
| Will̃m Laythom fi ... ... ... ... ... ... ... | 8 | „ |
| Jamis ffletcher ... ... ... ... ... ... ... ... | 9 | „ |
| Rodger Tasker fi Tho: ... ... ... ... ... ... | 12 | „ |

| Name | Day | Month |
|---|---|---|
| Hugh ffarclough | 15 | October |
| Raffe Cadicke | 16 | " |
| Henrie Freskoth | 17 | " |
| Henrie Hunter fi Tho: | 21 | " |
| Wiłłm Holton fi: Gilbert | 23 | " |
| Jo: Cowp fi Ro: | 27 | " |
| Annes Jackeson fi Hugh | 29 | " |
| Alis Smolte fi Edmund | 1 | November |
| Ranoold Gill fi Cristopher | " | " |
| Raffe Gleaste fi Tho: | 15 | " |
| Tho: Wilkinson fi Henrie de Aug: | 19 | " |
| Wiłłm Turner fi Ja: | 21 | " |
| Catherin Hesketh fi Ro: | " | " |
| Jaine Windrow fi: Tho: | 22 | " |
| Jo: Lithon fi Wiłłu | " | " |
| Catharin Garrard fi Wiłłu | 26 | " |
| Ed: Morecrofte fi Raph | " | " |
| Ric̃ Beconsay fi Ja: | 4 | December |
| Rodger Kekuike fi Ather et matr Catherin Gill de Aughton | 5 | " |
| Elin Leye fi Jo: | 6 | " |
| Marget Sutch fi Cristopher | 12 | " |
| Marie Whatton fi Tho: | 13 | " |
| Fo. 38 Anne Hodgeson fi Ewan | 15 | " |
| Wiłłm Pemberton fi Rodge | 22 | " |
| Anne Asmall fill Elise | 29 | " |
| Margaret Shawe fi Jo: | 1 | Januarie |
| Elizth Sutch fi Wiłłm | 2 | " |
| Jaine Morecrofte fi Ro: | 8 | " |
| John Jackeson fi Jon: | 17 | " |
| Alis Asmall fi Wiłłm | 18 | " |
| Elin Sutch fi Jamis | 20 | " |
| Elizth Awerton fi Jo: | 24 | " |
| Catherin Minshaw fi Ri: | 14 | ffebruarie |
| Tho: Hill fi Jo: | 18 | " |
| Allexander Hesketh fi Tho: | 22 | " |
| Peeter Barton fi Gabrell et mater Anne Asmali | 23 | " |
| Tho: Morcrofte fi | 24 | " |
| Ric̃ Jackeson fi Tho: et mater Izabell | 26 | " |
| Elin Sutch | 23 | Maꝰch |
| Tho: Waynewright fi Will: | 25 | " |

## 1574.

| Name | Day | Month |
|---|---|---|
| John Westhead fi Gilbart | 28 | March |
| Marie Scarsbrecke fi Edw: Esqꝰ | 29 | " |
| John Barton fi Lewas | 3 | Aprill |
| Tho: Brigehowse fi Hamlet | 4 | " |
| Cuthbart fformbey fi Tho: | " | " |

| | Name | Day | Month |
|---|---|---|---|
| | Gabrell Crofte fi Tho: | 4 | Aprill |
| | Loyd Gill fi Hugh | 6 | „ |
| | Jaine Withingeton fi Tho: | „ | „ |
| | Willm Carr fi Cristopher | 9 | „ |
| | Willm Cropp fi Jo: | 10 | „ |
| | Ellin Killshaw fi Willm: | 12 | „ |
| | Cislie Ascrofte fi Jo: | „ | „ |
| 39 | Tho: Sutton fi Ja: | 14 | „ |
| | Eliz$^{th}$ Prescot fi Ric̃ | 15 | „ |
| | Jamis Waynewright fi Ewan | 17 | „ |
| | Margaret Sutch fi Georg | 22 | „ |
| | Jamis Robinson fi Rob̃ | 30 | „ |
| | Sislie Hunter fi Rob̃ | 4 | Maye |
| | Anne Waynewright | 17 | „ |
| | Peeter Burie | 19 | „ |
| | Jane Atherton fi Jamis | 2 | June |
| | Marget Yate fi Edw: | 6 | „ |
| | Annes Shawe fi Will | 11 | „ |
| | Claris Worthingeton fi Ric̃ | 16 | „ |
| | Jain ffasicarlay | 22 | „ |
| | Robert Barton fi Tho: | 7 | Julye |
| | Homffray Woodfall fi Ja: | 24 | „ |
| | Ed: Gorsutch fi Ja: | 30 | „ |
| | Bryhan Morecrofte | 9 | August |
| | Henrie Hadocke | 10 | „ |
| | Dorethie Mellinge | 19 | „ |
| | Tho: Sumner | 24 | „ |
| | Tho: Marcer | „ | „ |
| | Marget Hesketh fi maꝰ Robert | 30 | „ |
| | John Hunte fi Ja: | 7 | September |
| | Alis Jumpe fi Tho: | 9 | „ |
| | Jamis Irlande fi Ric̃ | 17 | „ |
| | Hugh Noris fi Edw: | 22 | „ |
| | Jaine Ambrose fi Tho: | 25 | „ |
| 40 | Jenet Lathon fi Henrie | 3 | October |
| | Richard Kekuicke fi Willu | 4 | „ |
| | Anne Rydinge fi Rob̃ | 7 | „ |
| | Ric̃ Woodes fi Rob̃ | 10 | „ |
| | Hector Whytestones fi | 12 | „ |
| | Eliz$^{th}$ Saile fi Randle | 16 | „ |
| | Elin Whytestones fi Rob̃ | „ | „ |
| | Eliz$^{th}$ Billinge fi Jo: | 18 | „ |
| | Thomas Hatclife fi Edw: | „ | „ |
| | Gilbart Gill fi Parsivall | 1 | November |
| | Rodger Lea fi Hugh | „ | „ |
| | Gilbart Ballshaw de Halsall | 5 | „ |
| | Anne Sutch fi Hugh et mater Jenet Weltch | 7 | „ |
| | Edw: Letherbarow fi Tho: | 17 | „ |
| | Eliz$^{th}$ Pye de Aughton | 19 | „ |

| | | |
|---|---|---|
| Peeter Scarsbrecke fi Gilb̃ | 26 | November |
| Wiĩĩm Assherst fi Tho: | 27 | " |
| Henrie Mawdisley fi Hector | 1 | December |
| Eliz[th] Ambrose fi Tho: | 5 | " |
| Tho: Letherbarow fi Peter de Aught: | 9 | " |
| Jamis Alker fi Rodge | 25 | " |
| Abraham Prescot | 2 | Januarie |
| John Gill fi Ric̃ | 5 | " |
| Ric̃ Howden fi Henrie | 13 | " |
| Marget Waliner fi Tho: | 26 | " |
| Alis Scarbrecke fi Tho: | 29 | " |
| Anne Smyth fi Tho: | 1 | ffebruarie |
| Elin Barton fi Myles | 4 | " |
| Wiĩĩm Cosey fi Jamis | 6 | " |
| Homfrey Barton fi Gilb̃ | 9 | " |
| Tho: Gowbron fi John | 12 | " |
| Elin Butler fi Gilb̃ | 15 | " |
| Tho: Westhead fi Ric̃ | 16 | " |
| John Acar fi Tho: | 19 | " |
| Tho: Aspmall fi' Elis | " | " |
| Fo. 41 Robert Sutton fi Tho: | 21 | " |
| Ewan Lea fi | 23 | " |
| Jame Banester | " | " |
| Anne Woodes fi Henrie | 3 | March |
| Henrie Birche fi: Jo: | 5 | " |
| Wiĩĩm Shawe fi: Henrie | 8 | " |
| Jaine Bykarstaff fi Hugh | 15 | " |
| Ewan Mawdisley fi Wiĩĩu | 16 | " |
| Jamis ffarclough fi Henrie | 18 | " |
| Edw: Stopforth fi George | 21 | " |
| Henrie Barton fi Lewes | 23 | " |

## 1575.

| | | |
|---|---|---|
| John Graine fi Rañ | 3 | Aprill |
| Henrie Walworth fi Ric̃ | " | " |
| John Gill fi: Wiĩĩu | 5 | " |
| Ellin Aspinwall fi Wilĩ | 8 | " |
| Jaine Mawdisley fi Rob̃ | 18 | " |
| Elis Waynwright fi Ewan | 19 | " |
| John Whytestones fi Tho: | 20 | " |
| Henrie Becconsa fi Jam: | 21 | " |
| Alis Haide fi Ric̃ | 23 | " |
| Marget Killshaw fi Tho: | 25 | " |
| Clares Leyes fi Henrie | " | " |
| Eliz[th] Yate fi Lawrance | 28 | " |
| Allexander Sumner fi Jo: | 9 | Maye |
| Ellin Bylame fi: Jo: | " | " |
| Tho: Wardeman fi: Rob̃t | 13 | " |

| | | |
|---|---|---|
| John Blackeledge fi Ewan | 13 | Maye |
| Izabell Smalshaw fi Wittm | 17 | " |
| Wittm Prescott fi: Witt | 18 | " |
| Jaine Hesketh fi Edmund | 20 | " |
| Jaine Pemberton fi Rodger | 22 | " |
| Jamis Rigbie fi ... | 23 | " |
| Wittm Lea fi: Pawle | 2 | June |
| Ric̃ Blundell fi: Ja: | 5 | " |
| Eliz[th] Jackeson fi. Alexander | " | " |
| Anne Wittmson fi Cristopher | " | " |
| Marie ffarrer fi: Rob̃ | 17 | " |
| Henrie Whytestones fi: Tho: | 30 | " |
| Eliz[th] Worthingeton fi: Ric̃ | 2 | Julye |
| Tho: Gobbin fi: John | 3 | " |
| Ellin Hesketh fi: Rob̃ | 18 | " |
| Eliz[th] Cruick [?] fi Jamis | 28 | " |
| Ric̃ Holland fi Tho: | 8 | Auguste |
| John Jarrard fi Henrie | 12 | " |
| Wittm Cowp fi Hugh | 13 | " |
| John Cowsey fi Hugh | 14 | " |
| Izabell Lathom̃ fi Jo: | " | " |
| George Whytestones fi: Hugh | 17 | " |
| Eliz[th] Goodes fi John | 19 | " |
| Tho: Mawdisley fi Henrie | 27 | " |
| John Sutch fi George | 7 | September |
| James Spencer fi Jo: | 10 | " |
| Tho: Barker fi: John | 15 | October |
| Anne Morecrofte fi Witt | 16 | " |
| Tho: Cropp fi: Tho: | 25 | November |
| Omfrey Morecrofte fi: Henrie | 3 | December |
| John Shawe fi: Hugh | 9 | " |
| Wittm Cropp fi: Ric̃ | 12 | " |
| Catherin Lea fi John | 18 | " |
| Wittm Blundell | 20 | Januarie |
| Jaine Scarsbreck | 27 | " |
| Ric̃ Gill | 22 | ffebruarie |
| Emlin Gleast | 25 | " |
| Catherin Haiton | 15 | March |
| Jamis Gorsutch | 22 | " |

## 1576.

| | | |
|---|---|---|
| Edward Hunt | 10 | Aprill |
| Agnes Gleaste | 11 | " |
| Henrie Gill | 20 | " |
| Tho: ffloide | " | " |
| Tho: Ormishaw | 22 | " |
| Marie Mollinex | " | " |
| Thomas & Jaine Haile | 7 | Maye |

| | | | |
|---|---|---|---|
| | Ric̃ Shawe | 12 | Maye |
| | Tho: Mellinge | 13 | „ |
| | Catherin Hainde | 15 | „ |
| | Gilbert Andertoñ | 26 | „ |
| | Wiłłm Marclew | 5 | June |
| | Ewan Cropp | 7 | „ |
| | Alis Talior | 11 | „ |
| | ffrances Gowbron | 13 | „ |
| | . . . Morecrofte | „ | „ |
| | Wiłłm Manne | 15 | „ |
| | Ellin Hill | 17 | „ |
| | Godfrey Ormishaw | 2 | Julye |
| | Ellin Cropp | 8 | „ |
| | ffrances Gorsutch | 24 | „ |
| | Henrie Hall | 27 | „ |
| | Jenet Waynewright | 28 | „ |
| | Marget Mawdisley | 31 | „ |
| Fo. 44 | Wiłłm Sailles | 6 | Auguste |
| | Jaine Halsall | 9 | „ |
| | Marget Jumpe | „ | „ |
| | Hugh Worthingeton | 14 | „ |
| | Marie Lathom | 16 | „ |
| | Jamis Lithom | 20 | „ |
| | Gilb̃ Jackeson | 24 | „ |
| | Maꝰgerie Barkar | „ | „ |
| | Alis Voce | 30 | „ |
| | Tho: fforshaw | „ | „ |
| | Peeter Blundell | „ | „ |
| | John Mollinex | 22 | September |
| | Margaret Sutch | 25 | „ |
| | Ric̃ Lea | 1 | October |
| | Henrie Pearte | 7 | „ |
| | Jaine Sutch | 8 | „ |
| | Tho: Burie | „ | „ |
| | Hamlet Gill | 9 | „ |
| | Ric̃ Mowdisley | 15 | „ |
| | Edward Norris | 17 | „ |
| | Henrie Woodes | 19 | „ |
| | Henrie Robertson | 26 | „ |
| | Sislie Allerton | 2 | November |
| | Wiłłu Hankin | 10 | „ |
| | Tho: Ashton | 11 | „ |
| | Marget Sutton | 18 | „ |
| | Gowther Mason | 25 | „ |
| | Margerie Spencer | „ | „ |
| | Marget Aspinwap | 26 | „ |
| | Ellin Burie | 27 | „ |
| | Jamis Blackeledge | „ | „ |
| Fo. 45 | George Longeton | 1 | December |

| Name | Day | Month |
|---|---|---|
| Eliz[th] Shawe | 2 | December |
| Rob̃ Mollinex | 6 | " |
| Willm Whatton | " | " |
| George Brigehowse | 7 | " |
| Jaine Modisley | " | " |
| Jenet ffrance | 9 | " |
| Henrie Atherton | 10 | " |
| Parnell Cropp | 12 | " |
| Edward Stanley fi : Henrie Armi : | 14 | " |
| Edw : Scarsbrecke | 17 | " |
| Eliz[th] Prescott | 22 | " |
| Elin Lathom fi : Heñ | 2 | Januarie |
| Edw : Gill | 12 | " |
| Marget Spencer fi : Ric̃ | 17 | " |
| Elin Ormishaw fi : Rodge | 21 | " |
| Rachell Sanforth | 2 | ffebruarie |
| Jaine Scarsbrecke fi : Ed : Armig : | 4 | " |
| Hamlet Tusoñ | 15 | " |
| Tho : Shawe | 20 | Marche |
| Eliz[th] Shawe | " | " |
| Hamlet Prescot | 23 | " |
| Anne Goulbron | " | " |

## 1577.

| Name | Day | Month |
|---|---|---|
| Ric̃ Cowp fi Ro : | 25 | Marche |
| Jamis Masoñ fi : Gabrell | 6 | Aprill |
| Tho : Aspinwall fi : Willm | 10 | " |
| Edw : Scarsbrecke | 11 | " |
| Jaine Cowp | 12 | " |
| John Aspinwall fi : Nicolas | " | " |
| George Sutton | 20 | " |
| John Wallworth | 24 | " |
| 5 Jenet Jumpe fi : Parsevall | 1 | Maye |
| Peeter Scarsbrecke | 11 | " |
| Elline Millingeton | 12 | " |
| Randle Cowp | 23 | " |
| Ric̃ Smyth | 28 | " |
| Elline Dalton fi : Willm | 3 | June |
| Agnes Mawdisley | " | " |
| Eliz[th] Anderton | " | " |
| Peeter Brigehowse fi : Ric̃ | 5 | " |
| Catherin Blundell fi : Jackeob | 6 | " |
| Eliz[th] Irland | 18 | " |
| John Hesketh fi : Bartholomew | 25 | " |
| Marget Blanchet fi : Steven bast | " | " |
| Ric̃ Aspinwall | 27 | " |
| Anne Eccleston | 14 | Julie |
| Joanie Styam | 15 | " |

| | Name | Day | Month |
|---|---|---|---|
| | John Ascrofte fi: Raffe | 20 | Julie |
| | John Shorlicars fi: Rob̄ | 29 | „ |
| | Eliz$^{th}$ Barton | 3 | Auguste |
| | Emlin ffinch | „ | „ |
| | Edw: Barton | 4 | „ |
| | Omfrey Carr | 13 | „ |
| | Omfrey Lytham | 15 | „ |
| | John Swifte fi: Ellis | 22 | „ |
| | Wil̄lu Briges bast | „ | „ |
| | Peeter Sutch fi: Cris̄ | 29 | „ |
| | Gabrell Westhead | 2 | September |
| | Thurston ffarclough fi Henr̄ | 9 | „ |
| | Ric̃ Prescot fi Tho: | 10 | „ |
| | Edwarde Gilbartson fi Hugh | 14 | „ |
| | Eliz$^{th}$ Hughson | 19 | „ |
| | Edw: Hesketh fi Tho: | 20 | „ |
| | Alis Hill fi Jo: | 21 | „ |
| | Jaine Wetherbie bap: et bur̄ bast | 25 | „ |
| | Marget Barton fi: Jamis bast | 27 | „ |
| Fo. 47 | Marget Blanch bap: et bur̄ bast | 5 | October |
| | Anne Billinge | 12 | „ |
| | Marget Mellinge | „ | „ |
| | Eliz$^{th}$ Jackeson | „ | „ |
| | Jamis Lunte | 17 | „ |
| | Wil̄lm Croston de Halsall | 21 | „ |
| | George Abbot fi John | 29 | „ |
| | Wil̄lm p̄ker fi Edward | 5 | November |
| | Jaine Chadocke | 6 | „ |
| | Jaine Sutch | 10 | „ |
| | Jaine Sailes fi Rān: | 21 | „ |
| | John Lea fi Ector | 26 | „ |
| | Eliz$^{th}$ Burscough de Aughton | 29 | „ |
| | Joanie Morcrofte fi Hom: bap: et bur̄ | 5 | December |
| | Jamis Beconso | 8 | „ |
| | Eideth Woodhowse | „ | „ |
| | Allexander Blundel | 18 | „ |
| | Wil̄lm Cowson | 23 | „ |
| | Catherin Voce | 29 | „ |
| | John Ambrose | „ | „ |
| | Eliz$^{th}$ fferrer | 31 | „ |
| | Jaine Waringe fi Paule | 6 | Januarie |
| | Alis Gill fi Wil̄l | 13 | „ |
| | Eliz$^{th}$ Yat fi: Edw: | 18 | „ |
| | Anne Ambrose fi Henrie | 21 | „ |
| | John Sefton fi George | 30 | „ |
| | Humfrey Waynewright fi Jo: | „ | „ |
| | Ric̃ Whytstones fi: Raffe | „ | „ |
| | Tho: Robertson fi Rob̄t Hen̄son | 1 | ffebruarie |
| | Marget Balshaw fi Jo: | 3 | „ |

Jamis Prescot fi Wiłł ... ... ... ... ... 5 ffebruarie
Anne Haughton fi Tho: bast ... ... ... ... 6 „
Eliz[th] Cristophers doughter ... ... ... ... „ „
Marget Prescot fi Peeter ... ... ... ... ... 13 „
Anne Jackeson fi Ja: ... ... ... ... ... 17 „
Margerie Whytestones fi: Hugh ... ... ... „ „
Edw: Hesketh ... ... ... ... ... ... ... ... 18 „
Jaine Prescot fi Tho: bast ... ... ... ... 22 „
Anthony Crooke fi Ja: ... ... ... ... ... 23 „
Alis Blundell fi Adam ... ... ... ... ... 24 „
Omfrey Talior fi Tho: bast ... ... ... ... 26 „
Elin Morecrofte fi Tho: ... ... ... ... ... 1 March
Emlin Morecrofte fi Rob̃ ... ... ... ... ... 2 „
Margaret ffletcher fi Ric̃ ... ... ... ... ... 6 „
Eliz[th] Lufkin ... ... ... ... ... ... ... ... 9 „
Alis Spencer fi Ja: ... ... ... ... ... ... 10 „
Alis Waringe fi Ja: ... ... ... ... ... ... 15 „
Catherin Davie fi Bryhan ... ... ... ... 24 „

## 1578.

Lawrance Goulbron fi Anthoney bast ... ... 25 March
John Mawdisley ... ... ... ... ... ... ... 1 Aprill
Tho: Lathom fi: Gilb̃ ... ... ... ... ... ... 5 „
Wiłłm Masoñ fi Edward bast ... ... ... ... 7 „
Ric̃ Barton fi George ... ... ... ... ... ... „ „
Henrie Lathwhat fi: Tho: ... ... ... ... ... 18 „
ffrances Scarsbrecke fi: Ja: ... ... ... ... „ „
John Spencer fi Wiłł ... ... ... ... ... ... 19 „
Catherin Blund fi Rob̃t ... ... ... ... ... 20 „
Ellin Killshaw fi Tho: ... ... ... ... ... ... 23 „
Ric̃ Spencer fi Jo: ... ... ... ... ... ... ... 24 „
Jamis Henrison ... ... ... ... ... ... ... „ „
Anne fferar fi Rob̃t bast ... ... ... ... ... 2 Maie
Alis Wythingeton fi George bast ... ... ... 5 „
George Scarsbrecke fi Ed: Armig: ... ... 11 „
John Sumner ... ... ... ... ... ... ... ... 12 „
Katherin Brookefeeld ... ... ... ... ... ... 19 „
Jamis Sumner fi Hugh ... ... ... ... ... „ „
Elin Blundell fi: Ottuwell ... ... ... ... 23 „
Jamis Swifte fi Rob̃t ... ... ... ... ... ... 3 June
Marget Lathom ... ... ... ... ... ... ... 6 „
Tho: Alker fi Roger ... ... ... ... ... ... 15 „
Douse Byrtch fi Jo: bast ... ... ... ... ... 28 „
Richard Mason fi Gabrell ... ... ... ... ... 1 July
Jamis Killshaw fi Wiłłm ... ... ... ... ... 3 „
Jaine Kocket ... ... ... ... ... ... ... ... 21 „
Marie Garrard fi Wil ... ... ... ... ... ... 23 „
Jamis ffo̅rbie fi Tho: ... ... ... ... ... ... 10 August

| | | | |
|---|---|---|---|
| | Jamis Bankes fi Heñ | 15 | August |
| | Ric̃ Mawdisley fi Rob̄t | 20 | „ |
| | Henrie Gyles fi Ric̃ bast | 27 | „ |
| | Hugh Morecrofte fi Ja: bast | 2 | September |
| | Gabrell Hesketh fi Barth: Arg: | 3 | „ |
| | Williame Lathwhat fi Pe: | 7 | „ |
| | Mary Morcrofte fi Wil̄l | 10 | „ |
| | Wil̄lim Bradley fi Jo: bap: bur̄ | 19 | „ |
| | Eliz$^{th}$ Suche fi Lucie | 20 | „ |
| | Edwarde Jumpe fi Tho: | 18 | October |
| | Marie Ormishawe fi: Rog: bast | 19 | „ |
| | Lore Aspinwall fi: Eliz: | 26 | „ |
| | Thomas Lathom fi Hugh | 17 | November |
| | Alis Moudiseley | 23 | „ |
| | Elline Mason fi Ra: | 29 | „ |
| | Eliz$^{th}$ Barker fi Jo: | 21 | December |
| | Thomas Towson | 29 | „ |
| | Jaine Hankin fi Rob̄t bap: et bur̄ | „ | „ |
| Fo. 50 | John Rydinge | 16 | Januarie |
| | Rodger Morcrofte fi Wil̄l | 24 | „ |
| | Marie Hall fi Ellis | 28 | „ |
| | Gabrell Morcrofte fi Hom: | 10 | ffebruarie |
| | Anne Heie fi Jo: | 15 | „ |
| | Eliz$^{th}$ Aspinwall fi Pet$^{r}$ | 27 | „ |
| | Doretie Scarsbreke fi Tho: | 28 | „ |
| | Izabell Maudesley fi Hen: | 29 | „ |
| | Katheren Cadicke fi: Wil̄l | 1 | Marche |
| | Jahn Bereye fi Jo: | 11 | „ |
| | Richard Mellinge fi Rodg | 15 | „ |
| | Thomas Mulinexe | 23 | „ |
| | Margret ffarre | 30 | „ [*sic*] |

## 1579.

| | | | |
|---|---|---|---|
| | James Blundell fi Jo: | 25 | Marche |
| | Richard Chadoke | 29 | „ |
| | Jahne Whytstones | 30 | „ |
| | Elline Holme | 2 | Aprill |
| | Katheran Somner fi Gilb̄ | 11 | „ |
| | Eliz$^{th}$ Rylandes fi Rob̄t | 29 | „ |
| | Robart ffarclough | 30 | „ |
| | Elline Parker | 3 | Maie |
| | William Kilshawe fi Jo: | 6 | „ |
| | Elline & Evan Gille fi Wil̄l | „ | „ |
| | Margrete Morcrofte fi Rob̄t | „ | „ |
| | Tho: Mason fi Ric̃ | 9 | „ |
| | John Sutton fi Tho: | 13 | „ |
| | Margerie Cropp fi Pit$^{9}$ | 27 | „ |
| Fo. 51 | Ellin Hancocke fill ffrances | 8 | June |

| Name | Day | Month |
|---|---|---|
| Homfrey Lea fi: Jo: ... ... ... ... ... ... | 30 | June |
| Homfrey Aspinwall fi Henrie ... ... ... ... ... | 6 | Julie |
| Margerie Gille fi Cristopher ... ... ... ... ... | 13 | „ |
| George Mawdisley fi Jo: ... ... ... ... ... ... | „ | „ |
| Henrie Lea fi Henrie ... ... ... ... ... ... | 22 | „ |
| Anne Mylner fi Tho: ... ... ... ... ... ... | 28 | „ |
| Robt Butler fi Tho: bast ... ... ... ... ... | 30 | „ |
| Elizth Orrell fill Willm ... ... ... ... ... ... | 16 | Auguste |
| Alis Carre fi Cristopher ... ... ... ... ... ... | 22 | „ |
| Henrie Prescot fi: Hugh ... ... ... ... ... ... | 30 | „ |
| Elizth Sallet fi Johne bast ... ... ... ... ... | 3 | September |
| Lyonell Swyfte fi Jo: ... ... ... ... ... ... | 22 | „ |
| Marget Barton fi Gabr ... ... ... ... ... ... | 30 | „ |
| Elizth Mellinge fi Ric ... ... ... ... ... ... | 2 | October |
| Ranovld Mason ... ... ... ... ... ... | 4 | „ |
| Rodge Goulbron fi John ... ... ... ... ... ... | „ | „ |
| Elizth Barton fi: Will ... ... ... ... ... ... | 9 | „ |
| Catherin Scarsbrecke ... ... ... ... ... ... | „ | „ |
| Nicolas Shawgh fi Will ... ... ... ... ... ... | „ | „ |
| Willm Barton fi Myles ... ... ... ... ... ... | 21 | „ |
| Henrie Goulbron fi: Ric ... ... ... ... ... ... | 22 | „ |
| Willu Farclough fi: Henrie ... ... ... ... ... | 23 | „ |
| Henrie Bridges fi Jo: ... ... ... ... ... ... | 24 | „ |
| Elizth ffforshaw ... ... ... ... ... ... ... | 9 | November |
| Richard Kekewqick fi: Hugh ... ... ... ... ... | 10 | „ |
| Adam Barton fi Raffe ... ... ... ... ... ... | 16 | „ |
| Ric Masson fi Gabr ... ... ... ... ... ... ... | 20 | „ |
| Jaine Brigehowse fi Hamlet ... ... ... ... ... | „ | „ |
| Ellin Smyth fi Tho: ... ... ... ... ... ... | 22 | „ |
| Ric Blackeledge fi Ewan ... ... ... ... ... ... | 27 | „ |
| Catherin Cowsey ... ... ... ... ... ... ... | 7 | December |
| Rowland Barton fi Crist ... ... ... ... ... ... | 10 | „ |
| Emlin Voce fi Gilb ... ... ... ... ... ... ... | 18 | „ |
| Jaine Wainewright ... ... ... ... ... ... ... | 22 | „ |
| Jaine Mawdisley fi Will ... ... ... ... ... ... | 23 | „ |
| Marie Martindaille fi ... ... ... ... ... ... | 24 | „ |
| Marget Owarde fi Will ... ... ... ... ... ... | 3 | Januarie |
| John Walker fi Jo: ... ... ... ... ... ... ... | „ | „ |
| Marget Gilbson fi Hugh ... ... ... ... ... ... | 6 | „ |
| John and Richard Allerton fi Tho: ... ... | 9 | „ |
| Catherin Lailond fi Tho: ... ... ... ... ... | 10 | „ |
| Will Gyles ... ... ... ... ... ... ... ... | 14 | „ |
| Margerie Sailes fi Ann Ball ... ... ... ... ... | 18 | „ |
| Emlin Lathom fi: Gilb ... ... ... ... ... ... | 19 | „ |
| Ellin Shorlikares ... ... ... ... ... ... ... | „ | „ |
| Henrie Henrieson ... ... ... ... ... ... ... | 22 | „ |
| Jenet Blundell ... ... ... ... ... ... ... ... | 30 | „ |
| Tho: Eccleston fi Jo: ... ... ... ... ... ... | 1 | ffebruarie |
| John Balshaw ... ... ... ... ... ... ... | 3 | March |

Marie ffletcher fi Ric ... ... ... ... ... 5 March
Ellin Morecroft fi Rob ... ... ... ... ... 6 „
Hugh Wright fi Will ... ... ... ... ... 12 „
Marget Westhead fi Jo: ... ... ... ... ... 18 „
John Mawdisley fi fflip [*sic*] ... ... ... ... 19 „
Marget Livesley fi: Tho: ... ... ... ... „ „
Mari ffarrer fi Robt ... ... ... ... ... ... „ „

## 1580.

. . . Walworke ... ... ... ... ... ... 29 Marche
Catherin Kewquicke de Augh ... ... ... ... 30 „
Izabell Barton f: Lewes * ... ... ... ... 31 „
Fo. 53 Marie Aspinwal fi Will ... ... ... ... ... 5 Aprill
Eliz^th^ Whytestones fi: Hugh ... ... ... ... 10 „
Anne Sutch fi Ja: ... ... ... ... ... ... 24 „
Ewan Allerton fi Jo: ... ... ... ... ... 9 Maye
Tho: Blundell fi: Jo: bast ... ... ... ... 14 „
Richard Anderton fi Raffe ... ... ... ... 16 „
Ric Chadocke fi Hugh ... ... ... ... ... 18 „
Edward Worthington fi Tho: ... ... ... ... 23 „
Ellin Hesketh fi Tho: ... ... ... ... ... 27 „
Henri Willmsonn fi Will Oliverson ... ... 6 June
Peeter Lunte fi: Henrie ... ... ... ... ... 10 „
Tho: Ierland fi: Ric ... ... ... ... ... „ „
Willm Traves fi Ric ... ... ... ... ... ... 16 „
Raphe Orrell fi Jo: ... ... ... ... ... ... 17 „
Emllin Lathwhat fi Peter ... ... ... ... ... 19 „
Tho: Woodhouse fi Hugh ... ... ... ... 10 Julye
Anne Warener fi Tho: ... ... ... ... ... „ „
Margerie Hodgeson fi Jo: ... ... ... ... ... 17 „
Eliz^th^ Morecrofte fi Tho: ... ... ... ... ... 23 „
Jenet Edwardes doughter ... ... ... ... ... 25 „
Ric Burie fi John ... ... ... ... ... ... 31 „
Edw: Smyth fi Johne ... ... ... ... ... 3 Auguste
Richard Morecrofte fi Ric ... ... ... ... ... 17 „
Eliz^th^ Blundell bast ... ... ... ... ... ... 20 „
Gilb Barton fi Jo: bast ... ... ... ... ... 21 „
Silvester Hunt fi John ... ... ... ... ... 24 „
Ric Barton fi Adam ... ... ... ... ... ... 5 September
Tho: Sanderson fi Ja: ... ... ... ... ... 16 „
Henrie Bykarstaffe de Aught bast ... ... ... 18 „
John Tarleton de Rannford ... ... ... ... ... „ „
Willm Barton fi Ja: bast ... ... ... ... ... 24 „
John Macristie fi Jo: bast ... ... ... ... 25 „
John Preskot fi Tho: ... ... ... ... ... 27 „
Fo. 54 Margery Hill fi Ric ... ... ... ... ... ... 4 October
Margery Barker fi Raph bast ... ... ... ... 7 „
Margaret Alaxanders doughter ... ... ... 10 „

* This entry in a different hand.

Ric̃ Hill fi Jo: ... ... ... ... ... ... ... ... 10 October
Margaret Allarton fi Witt ... ... ... ... ,, ,,
Margart Talylior fi Robt ... ... ... ... ... ... 16 ,,
Jane Moodye fi: Tho: ... ... ... ... ... 18 ,,
Roberte Withington fi Raph ... ... ... ... ... 26 ,,
Jane Jackson fi Robt ... ... ... ... ... ... 28 ,,
Ideth Preskott fi Ja: ... ... ... ... ... ... 1 November
Anne Hawghton fi Hugh ... ... ... ... ... ... 2 ,,
Witt͂m Aspinwall fi Ran̄ ... ... ... ... ... ... 3 ,,
Witt͂m Morcrofte fi Hom̄ ... ... ... ... ... ... 4 ,,
Margret Holline fi Ric̃ ... ... ... ... ... ... 5 ,,
Anne Lathom fi Ric̃ ... ... ... ... ... ... ... 8 ,,
Anne Hankin fi Robt ... ... ... ... ... ... ,, ,,
Margreat Parker fi Ed: ... ... ... ... ... ... 19 ,,
Witt͂m Lathwat fi Tho: ... ... ... ... ... ... 25 ,,
Anne Whitstons fi: Raph ... ... ... ... ... ,, ,,
Jane Scarsbrick fi: Gilb ... ... ... ... ... ... 28 ,,
Witt͂m Kilshawe fi Alan ... ... ... ... ... ... 4 December
James Blundell fi Jo: ... ... ... ... ... ... 9 ,,
Katherin Waynwright fi Tho: ... ... ... ... ,, ,,
Alis Gill fi: David ... ... ... ... ... ... ,, ,,
Tho: Asley de Aughton ... ... ... ... ... ... 20 ,,
Rowland Ryding fi: Robt ... ... ... ... ... 23 ,,
James Waynwright fi Geor ... ... ... ... ... 24 ,,
Rauph Cocket alis Ledbetr̃ bast ... ... ... ... 29 ,,
John Golbourne fi Ant: bast ... ... ... ... ... 3 Januarie
Tho: Stopford fi Witt͂m bast ... ... ... ... ... 16 ,,
Roberte Gill fi: Ric̃ ... ... ... ... ... ... ... 20 ,,
Marie Latham fi Jo: ... ... ... ... ... ... ... 26 ,,
Ellin Sefton fi Geor: ... ... ... ... ... ... ,, ,,
Oliver Lune A stranger ... ... ... ... ... ... 2 ffebruarie
Witt͂m Ryc͛son ... ... ... ... ... ... ... 6 ,,
Ric̃ Lithom fi Witt͂m ... ... ... ... ... ... 13 ,,
Marie Haughton fi Ric̃ ... ... ... ... ... ... 15 ,,
Izabell Modisley fi: Tho: ... ... ... ... ... 18 ,,
Edward Smolt fi: Edm̄ ... ... ... ... ... ... 19 ,,
Jenet Alerton fi: Tho: ... ... ... ... ... ... ,, ,,
Jane Lowe fi: Tho: ... ... ... ... ... ... 22 ,,
Robt Cosey fi: Hugh bast ... ... ... ... ... 24 ,,
Jane Lowe fi: Ja: ... ... ... ... ... ... ... ,, ,,
John Tasker fi: Hen: bast ... ... ... ... ... 26 ,,
John Kilshawe fi: Tho: ... ... ... ... ... 28 ,,
Jane Scersbreke fi: Witt͂m ... ... ... ... ... ,, ,,
Thomas Preket fi: Ric̃ ... ... ... ... ... ... 1 Marche
Margerie Smolt fi: Robt ... ... ... ... ... ... 5 ,,
Thomas Ambrose fi: Tho ... ... ... ... ... 6 ,,
George Barton fi: Ric̃ ... ... ... ... ... ... 9 ,,
Thomas Modisley fi: Jo: ... ... ... ... ... 17 ,,
Katherin Spenser ... ... ... ... ... ... ... 21 ,,

## 1581.

| | Name | Day | Month |
|---|---|---|---|
| | Marie Eccleston fi Raph ... ... ... ... ... ... | 13 | Aprill |
| | Izabell Harker ... ... ... ... ... ... ... ... | „ | „ |
| | John Harison fi Rob̄t ... ... ... ... ... ... | 20 | „ |
| | Elizth Barton fi Gill ... ... ... ... ... ... | „ | „ |
| | Willm Spenser fi Hugh ... ... ... ... ... ... | 22 | „ |
| | James Moudsley fi Rob̄t ... ... ... ... ... ... | 3 | Maye |
| | Ellis Anderton fi Rob̄t ... ... ... ... ... ... | 12 | „ |
| | James Ormishawe fi Gilb... ... ... ... ... ... | 14 | „ |
| | Henrie Scersbreke fi Willm ... ... ... ... ... | 16 | „ |
| | John Smithe fi Willm ... ... ... ... ... ... | 23 | „ |
| | Jane Sefton fi Willm bast ... ... ... ... ... | 1 | June |
| | Ric̄ & Ellin Babott bast ... ... ... ... ... ... | „ | „ |
| | Richard Modsley fi Ric̄ ... ... ... ... ... ... | 5 | „ |
| | Emblin Ashurts fi Tho: ... ... ... ... ... ... | 12 | „ |
| | John Preskott fi Willm ... ... ... ... ... ... | 12 | Julye |
| | John Barker fi Willm ... ... ... ... ... ... | 13 | „ |
| | James Kilshawe fi Ector bast ... ... ... ... ... | 17 | „ |
| | Tho: Watkinson fi Ric̄ ... ... ... ... ... ... | 24 | „ |
| | Elizth Morcrofte fi Willm... ... ... ... ... ... | 26 | „ |
| | Elner Hesketh fi: Rob̄t ... ... ... ... ... ... | 27 | „ |
| Fo. 56 | James Modisley fi Simiō ... ... ... ... ... ... | 9 | August |
| | Elizh Morcrofte fi Ric̄ ... ... ... ... ... ... | 10 | „ |
| | Cristopher Hūter fi Tho: bast ... ... ... ... | „ | „ |
| | Ellin fformbey fi Tho: ... ... ... ... ... ... | 12 | „ |
| | Marie Cimsters [*probably Simister*] doughter... | 13 | „ |
| | Hugh ffletcher fi: Myles ... ... ... ... ... ... | 14 | „ |
| | John Mardondaile fi Henrie ... ... ... ... ... | 16 | „ |
| | Emline Sumner fi: Jo: ... ... ... ... ... ... | 3 | September |
| | Marie Brigehowse fi: Hamlet ... ... ... ... ... | 14 | „ |
| | Godfrey Atherton fi: Oliver ... ... ... ... ... | 17 | „ |
| | Marget Bispam fi: Edm: ... ... ... ... ... ... | 19 | „ |
| | John Mollinex fi Will bast ... ... ... ... ... | 26 | „ |
| | Rob̄t Bradshaw fi: Jo: ... ... ... ... ... ... | 28 | „ |
| | Brichet Blundell fi: Jo: ... ... ... ... ... ... | 30 | „ |
| | Alis Masoñ fi: Ric̄ ... ... ... ... ... ... | 2 | October |
| | Tho: Smolte fi: Ja: ... ... ... ... ... ... | 4 | „ |
| | Jaine ffidler fi: Tho: ... ... ... ... ... ... | 6 | „ |
| | Ellin Whytestones fi: Ric̄ ... ... ... ... ... | 8 | „ |
| | Izabell Lathwhat fi: Peeter ... ... ... ... ... | 9 | „ |
| | Jaine Lawransoñ fi: Anthoney ... ... ... ... | 25 | „ |
| | Jaine Spenser ... ... ... ... ... ... ... ... | „ | „ |
| | Gabrell Walker fi Ric̄ ... ... ... ... ... ... | 9 | November |
| | John Cropp fi Raffe... ... ... ... ... ... ... | 18 | „ |
| | Katherin Balshaw fi: Jo: ... ... ... ... ... ... | „ | „ |
| | Tho: Killshaw fi Jo: ... ... ... ... ... ... | 20 | „ |
| | Marget Grffie [*sic*] ... ... ... ... ... ... ... | 3 | December |
| | John Irland fi Ri: ... ... ... ... ... ... ... | 13 | „ |

| | | |
|---|---|---|
| Ric̃ Huton fi: Jo: ... ... ... ... ... ... ... | 8 | Januarie |
| Jaine ffarclough fi: Henrie ... ... ... ... | 11 | „ |
| Marget Butler fi Tho: ... ... ... ... ... ... | „ | „ |
| Anne ffarrer fi: Rob̃ ... ... ... ... ... ... | 12 | „ |
| Marget Waynwright fi Tho: ... ... ... ... ... | 16 | „ |
| Eliz[th] Mawdisley fi Robt ... ... ... ... ... ... | 17 | „ |
| Tho: Voce fi Gilb̃ ... ... ... ... ... ... ... | 19 | „ |
| Ric̃ Shawe fi: Jo: ... ... ... ... ... ... ... | 22 | „ |
| Dorethi Dicket [*or Ditket*] fi: Will ... ... | 24 | „ |
| ffrances Lathom fi: Gilb̃ bast ... ... ... ... | 26 | „ |
| Jaine Ballshaw fi: Gilb̃ ... ... ... ... ... ... | 27 | „ |
| Raffe Parson fi Jo: ... ... ... ... ... ... ... | 29 | „ |
| John Mason fi: Cuth ... ... ... ... ... ... | 30 | „ |
| Peeter Marclough ... ... ... ... ... ... ... | 3 | ffebruarie |
| Emllin Barton fi: Gabrell ... ... ... ... | 7 | „ |
| Marie Wright fi: Will ... ... ... ... ... ... | „ | „ |
| Gilb̃ Blundell fi: Ja: ... ... ... ... ... ... | 12 | „ |
| Ellin Rithrop fi: Hamlet... ... ... ... ... ... | 17 | „ |
| John Blundell fi: Ro: ... ... ... ... ... ... | „ | „ |
| Catherin Ascough fi: Tho: ... ... ... ... ... | 19 | „ |
| Catherin Traves fi: Henrie ... ... ... ... ... | 20 | „ |
| Izabbell Gleaste fi: Tho: ... ... ... ... ... | 23 | „ |
| Marie Haughton fi: Hugh ... ... ... ... ... | 1 | March |
| Silvester Goulbron fi: Jo: ... ... ... ... ... | „ | „ |
| Jaine Lea fi: Hecton [*sic*] ... ... ... ... ... | 5 | „ |
| Margerie Rainfforth fi: Jo: ... ... ... ... ... | 7 | „ |
| John Shorlikers fi Rob̃ ... ... ... ... ... ... | 9 | „ |
| Izabell Kequicke fi: Will ... ... ... ... ... | 10 | „ |
| Jaine ffletcher fi Ric̃ ... ... ... ... ... ... | 12 | „ |
| Anne Scarsbrecke fi: Gabrell ... ... ... ... ... | 15 | „ |
| Marget Smyth fi: Tho: ... ... ... ... ... ... | 20 | „ |
| Ric̃ Oliverson ... ... ... ... ... ... ... ... | 23 | „ |
| Willm Morecrofte fi Ric̃ ... ... ... ... ... ... | 24 | „ |

## 1582.

| | | |
|---|---|---|
| Willm Kilshaw fi: Ja: ... ... ... ... ... ... | 29 | Marche |
| Edw: Barton fi: . . . ... ... ... ... ... | 30 | „ |
| Marget Gill: fi Willm ... ... ... ... ... ... | 1 | Aprill |
| Margerie Mellinge fi: Anthoney ... ... ... | „ | „ |
| Marie Koket fi: Jo ... ... ... ... ... ... ... | 3 | „ |
| John Kilshaw fi Tho: ... ... ... ... ... ... | „ | „ |
| Tho: Davie fi: Bryhan ... ... ... ... ... ... | 9 | Maie |
| John Rutter fi: Jo: ... ... ... ... ... ... | 10 | „ |
| Eideth Lea fi Ewañ ... ... ... ... ... ... ... | 14 | „ |
| Mawde Hunter fi Rob̃ ... ... ... ... ... ... | 15 | „ |
| Rauph Hoolme fi Will ... ... ... ... ... ... | 16 | „ |
| Tho: Lunte fi Trymor ... ... ... ... ... ... | 27 | „ |
| Marie Jackeson fi: Ja: ... ... ... ... ... ... | 30 | „ |

Jamis Hey fi: John ... ... ... ... ... ... ... 31 Maie
Henrie Mollinex fi: Tho: ... ... ... ... 3 June
Marie Worthingeton fi: Ric̃ ... ... ... ... 4 „
Alis Whytestones fi Tho: ... ... ... ... 10 „
Gilbert & Peeter Wackefeeld fi Hugh ... ... 13 „
Katherin Bycarstaffe fi Hugh ... ... ... ... 17 „
Gabrell Masoñ fi Gab̃ ... ... ... ... ... 20 „
John Walthew fi: Ric̃ ... ... ... ... ... „ „
Jaine Worthingetoñ fi Hugh ... ... ... ... 4 Julye
George Gill fi: Gilb̃ ... ... ... ... ... 16 „
Margerie Lappinge fi: Ja: bast ... ... ... „ „
Margerie Allerton fi: Will bast ... ... ... „ „
Tho: Mawdisley fi Hector ... ... ... ... 19 „
Jaine Aspinwall fi Tho: ... ... ... ... ... 24 „
Edmunde Cropp fi Peeter ... ... ... ... 26 „
Anne Tum̃soñ fi Ja: ... ... ... ... ... 27 „
Jane and Joanie Orrell fi: John bast ... ... 1 August
Eliz[th] Cockeson fi: Ja: ... ... ... ... ... „ „
Eliz[th] Swyfte ... ... ... ... ... ... ... 2 „
Eliz[th] Colson fi: Jo:... ... ... ... ... ... 4 „
Ric̃ Smalshaw fi: Rob̃ ... ... ... ... ... 14 „
Willm Kadicke fi: Will ... ... ... ... ... 20 „
Rob̃t Cruke fi: Ja: ... ... ... ... ... ... 25 „
Fo. 59 Ric̃ Preskot fi Rob̃ bast ... ... ... ... ... 4 September
Elenor Morecrofte fi Rob̃t ... ... ... ... 5 „
Willm Allerton fi: Jo: ... ... ... ... ... 6 „
Anne Waringe fi: Ja: ... ... ... ... ... 7 „
Henrie Stopforth fi Tho: ... ... ... ... 8 „
Willm Jackeson fi Jamis ... ... ... ... ... 11 „
Jane Martindaile fi: Hugh ... ... ... ... 12 „
Margerie Gilb̃soñ fi Hugh ... ... ... ... 16 „
Margerie Sutton fi Tho: ... ... ... ... ... 21 „
Jamis Halsall fi Rob̃ ... ... ... ... ... 22 „
Edward Wadingeton fi Will ... ... ... ... 23 „
Willm Hoolme fi Ric̃ ... ... ... ... ... 25 „
Marget Harrisoñ fi Hugh ... ... ... ... „ „
Anne Waringe fi: Harie ... ... ... ... ... 5 October
Jamis Barton fi Adam ... ... ... ... ... 9 „
Willm Hill fi Jo: ... ... ... ... ... ... 13 „
John Mowdisley fi Will ... ... ... ... ... 17 „
Jane Mollinex fi Henrie ... ... ... ... ... 8 November
Jaine Blackeledge fi Ewan ... ... ... ... 9 „
Willm Haiton fi Tho: ... ... ... ... ... „ „
Brtholomew [*sic*] Kar fi John ... ... ... ... 10 „
John Sumner ... ... ... ... ... ... ... 11 „
Joanie Butl[r] fi: Jo: ... ... ... ... ... ... 15 „
Grace Asley fi Ja: de Aug ... ... ... ... 24 „
Henrie Plombe fi Ja: ... ... ... ... ... 1 December
Anne Masoñ fi Hugh ... ... ... ... ... 8 „

Henrie Whaley fi: Niccolas ... ... ... ... ... 22 December
Henrie Milnor fi Tho: ... ... ... ... ... ... " "
John Lowe fi Tho: ... ... ... ... ... ... ... 29 "
John Preskot fi: Hugh bast ... ... ... ... ... 5 Januarie
Katherin Swifte fi Hug: ... ... ... ... ... ... 8 "
Alis Preskot fi: Tho: bast ... ... ... ... ... 10 "
Raffe Lea a stranger bast ... ... ... ... ... 13 "
o Tho: Lunte fi: Rob̃ ... ... ... ... ... ... 14 "
Katherin ffarclough fi Rodĝ: ... ... ... ... ... 15 "
Omfrey Gill fi Davie ... ... ... ... ... ... 17 "
Alis Lathom fi Hugh ... ... ... ... ... ... 20 "
Silvester Sutch fi: Tho: ... ... ... ... ... ... 26 "
John Preskot fi: Jo: bast ... ... ... ... ... 28 "
Wiłłm Preskot fi: Ric̃ ... ... ... ... ... ... 7 ffe̊bruarie
John Chadocke fi: Hugh ... ... ... ... ... 8 "
Eliz[th] Boer fi: Tho: ... ... ... ... ... ... 9 "
Alis Morecrofte fi Tho: ... ... ... ... ... ... 10 "
Wiłłm Harison fi Rob̃t ... ... ... ... ... ... " "
Jamis Balshaw fi: Jo: ... ... ... ... ... ... 12 "
Alis Swifte fi Rob̃ ... ... ... ... ... ... ... 16 "
Anne Cowsey fi Hugh ... ... ... ... ... ... " "
Henrie Anderton fi Rob̃t ... ... ... ... ... 17 "
Izabell Scarsbrecke fi Tho: ... ... ... ... ... 26 "
George Haughton fi Hugh ... ... ... ... ... " "
Ric̃ Whytestones fi Hugh ... ... ... ... ... 8 Marche
Cuthbart Morecrofte fi: Hom: ... ... ... ... 14 "
Hector Walles fi Tho: ... ... ... ... ... ... 23 "
Margerie Cropp fi: Ric̃ ... ... ... ... ... ... 24 "

## 1583.

Eliz[th] Allerton fi Tho: ... ... ... ... ... ... 30 Marche
Marget Mawdisley fi Tho: ... ... ... ... ... 4 Aprill
John ffisher fi: Ric̃ bast ... ... ... ... ... ... 5 "
. . . Ascroft ... ... ... ... ... ... ... ... 14 "
Rodger Preskot fi: Tho: ... ... ... ... ... 23 "
Marget Layland fi . . . ... ... ... ... ... 2 Maie
Marie Page fi: Cristopher ... ... ... ... ... 19 "
Elloner fformby fi Tho: ... ... ... ... ... ... 30 "
Johne Mason fi: Tho: ... ... ... ... ... ... 11 June
Joanie Whytestones ... ... ... ... ... ... ... 12 "
Henrie Mawdisley fi Jo: ... ... ... ... ... ... 23 "
51 Rodger Barton fi Myles ... ... ... ... ... ... 24 "
Marget Westhead fi: Ric̃ ... ... ... ... ... " "
Henrie Preskot fi Wiłł ... ... ... ... ... ... 29 "
Tho: Barton fi: Ja: ... ... ... ... ... ... 5 Julye
Rodger ffidler fi Tho: ... ... ... ... ... ... 8 "
Jamis Smalshaw fi: Tho: ... ... ... ... ... 12 "
Marget Barton fi: Gilb̃ ... ... ... ... ... ... 14 "

Rob̄t Kilshaw fi ... ... ... ... ... ... 15 Julye
Edward Rithrope fi Hamlet ... ... ... ... 29 „
John Diket fi Wiłłm ... ... ... ... ... 31 „
Dorethie Parker fi Edw: ... ... ... ... ... „ „
Jamis Waringe ... ... ... ... ... ... ... 2 August
Ellin Babot fi Tho: ... ... ... ... ... ... 3 „
John Killshaw fi: Jo: ... ... ... ... ... 16 „
Ellin Hill fi: Ric̃ ... ... ... ... ... ... 24 „
Tho: Haughton fi: Ric̃ ... ... ... ... ... 29 „
Tho: Yeate fi Ewan ... ... ... ... ... 5 September
Edwarde Scarsbricke ... ... ... ... ... 9 „
John Jacsone fi Ja: ... ... ... ... ... ... 15 „
Henrie Barton fi Ric̃ ... ... ... ... ... 18 „
Hughe Askough fi Tho: ... ... ... ... ... 21 „
Tho: Hyton fi Tho: ... ... ... ... ... 23 „
Anne Martindall fi Ja: ... ... ... ... ... 28 „
Ric̃ Jonsone fi: Wiłłm ... ... ... ... ... „ „
Katheren Aspinwall fi Hugh ... ... ... ... 29 „
John Ric̃son fi Ric̃ ... ... ... ... ... ... 1 October
Gilbrte Jackson fi: Ja: ... ... ... ... ... 2 „
Hugh Scarsbricke fi Jo: bast ... ... ... ... „ „
Mary Mason fi Gilb: ... ... ... ... ... „ „
Wiłłm Butelor fi: Tho: ... ... ... ... ... 4 „
Margery fforshawe ... ... ... ... ... ... 6 „
Gabrell Gill fi Gilb̄ ... ... ... ... ... ... 9 „
Henerie Burges fi Wiłłm ... ... ... ... ... „ „
. . . . Marrall fi Tho: ... ... ... ... ... 10 „
Anne Marson fi Wiłłm ... ... ... ... ... 13 „
Fo. 62 Wiłłm Woofall fi Cris̃ bast ... ... ... ... ... 22 „
Jane & Eliz[th] Hunter fi Tho:... ... ... ... „ „
Ric̃ Preskote fi Wiłłm ... ... ... ... ... 23 „
Tho: Kilshaw fi Alane ... ... ... ... ... 24 „
Tho: Jackson fi John bast ... ... ... ... 25 „
Wiłłm Cadicke fi Ric̃ ... ... ... ... ... 30 „
Symonde Tayrare fi Gill ... ... ... ... ... 6 November
Jahn Haughton fi Ric̃ ... ... ... ... ... 11 „
Eliz[th] Morcrofte fi Wiłłm ... ... ... ... 15 „
Hughe Whytstons fi: Raph ... ... ... ... 16 „
Emline Willimson fi Christe ... ... ... ... 23 „
Myles Abote fi Jo: ... ... ... ... ... ... 25 „
Jenet fflecher fi miles ... ... ... ... ... 28 „
Rolonde Holiwell fi Alex ... ... ... ... 29 „
Eliz[th] Preskot fi Tho ... ... ... ... ... 15 December
Richard Barton fi: Jo: ... ... ... ... ... 17 „
Jamis Morecrofte fi Ric̃ ... ... ... ... ... 23 „
Ric̃ Blundell fi: Rob̄ ... ... ... ... ... 24 „
Janie Morecrofte fi Ja: ... ... ... ... ... 5 Januarie
Eliz[th] Talior fi Rob̄ ... ... ... ... ... ... 24 „
Edward Eccleston fi: Raph ... ... ... ... 25 „

Jaine Traves fi Ric̃ ... ... ... ... ... ... ... 29 Januarie
Omfrey Lathwhat fi Peetr ... ... ... ... 1 ffebruarie
Henrie Hesketh fi: Bartholomew Esqr ... ... 3 „
Myles Boothe fi: Wilł ... ... ... ... ... ... 26 „
Tho: Cowdocke fi Wilm ... ... ... ... ... 27 „
Anne Balle fi Ric̃ ... ... ... ... ... ... ... „ „
Jamis Talior fi: Jo: ... ... ... ... ... ... 5 March
Alis Henrieson fi: Ric̃ ... ... ... ... ... ... 18 „
Henrie Mawdisley fi Symon ... ... ... ... „ „
Dennis the Irishemans child bast ... ... ... 21 „

63 **1584.**

Marie Worthingeton fi: Hugh ... ... ... 28 March
Emlin Ireland fi Ric̃ ... ... ... ... ... ... „ „
Anne Suche fi Rodgr bast ... ... ... ... „ „
Jane Mason fi Ryc̃ ... ... ... ... ... ... ... 4 Aprill
Elizth Sumner fi: Jo: ... ... ... ... ... ... 14 „
Wiłłm ffletcher fi: Ric̃ ... ... ... ... ... ... 17 „
Johne Mellinge fi Ric̃ ... ... ... ... ... ... 22 „
John Waynewright fi: Tho: ... ... ... ... ... 25 „
Edw: Scarsbrecke fi Wiłłi ... ... ... ... „ „
Anne Mawdisley fi Rob̃ ... ... ... ... ... ... 27 „
Anne Ambrose fi Tho: ... ... ... ... ... ... „ „
Anne Coolso fi: Jo: ... ... ... ... ... ... 30 „
Henrie Masoñ fi: Cuthbert ... ... ... ... „ „
Marget Cowp fi Hugh ... ... ... ... ... ... 2 Maye
Ellene Molinex fi Tho: ... ... ... ... ... ... 4 „
Marget ffoge fi Jo: ... ... ... ... ... ... ... 8 „
Genet Balshaw fi . . . ... ... ... ... ... 10 „
Ric̃ Cocket fi Jo: ... ... ... ... ... ... ... 12 „
Marget Barker fi Jo: ... ... ... ... ... ... „ „
Hugh Penket fi Henrie bast ... ... ... ... 13 „
Rob̃t Keckewicke fi Hugh bast ... ... ... 15 „
Tho: Shawe fi Jamis ... ... ... ... ... ... 18 „
Marget Holland fi Hugh ... ... ... ... ... „ „
Jamis Taylior fi Jo: ... ... ... ... ... ... 19 „
Elin Asmall fi Tho: ... ... ... ... ... ... 26 „
Wiłłm Hulme fi Tho: ... ... ... ... ... ... 31 „
Jaine Bower fi Tho: ... ... ... ... ... ... „ „
Hugh Rainforth fi John de Aug: ... ... ... „ „
Jamis Wadingeton fi Wiłł ... ... ... ... ... 5 June
Margreat Asshurst fi Tho: ... ... ... ... ... 13 „
Gabrill Mowdisley fi Ric̃ ... ... ... ... ... 29 „
Richard Shawe fi Rodger ... ... ... ... ... 30 „
Fo. 64 Alis Blundell fi: Jo: bast ... ... ... ... ... 3 July
Thomas Martindall fi Henrie ... ... ... ... 5 „
Elene Carre fi Jo: ... ... ... ... ... ... ... „ „
Wiłłm Spakem̃ fi: Ric̃ ... ... ... ... ... ... 7 „

Tho: Stopforth fi Witt ... ... ... ... ... 10 July
Ryc̃ Modisley fi: Phĩ ... ... ... ... ... 12 „
Eliz[th] Bradley fi Jo: ... ... ... ... ... ... 22 „
Ric̃ Morecrofte fi: Rob̃ ... ... ... ... ... 2 Auguste
Ellin Butchard fi Ed: ... ... ... ... ... 13 „
Rodg̃ Barton fi: Gabriell... ... ... ... ... „ „
Hugh Askowe fi Ric̃ ... ... ... ... ... 15 „
Witm Rim̃er fi Ja: bast ... ... ... ... ... 31 „
Witlm Swifte fi *Homfrey ... ... ... ... 12 September
Hugh Wallen fi Jo: ... ... ... ... ... ... „ „
Crister Parkinson fi Rodg̃ a strañ ... ... ... 14 „
Alis Smallshaw fi Rob̃ ... ... ... ... ... 18 „
Anne Asley fi Ja: de Aug ... ... ... ... 28 „
Marget Smyth fi Henri bast ... ... ... ... 1 October
Ellin Blundell fi Jo: ... ... ... ... ... 2 „
Marie Waringe fi Tho: bast ... ... ... ... 7 „
Rauph Cowp̃ fi Ja: ... ... ... ... ... ... 8 „
Rodger Aspinwall fi Hugh ... ... ... ... 10 „
Jamis Blundell fi Jo: ... ... ... ... ... 12 „
Cristopher Darwen fi John bast ... ... ... 14 „
Tho: Henrieson ... ... ... ... ... ... 17 „
Hugh Badger fi Tho: bast ... ... ... ... 18 „
Witm Kilshaw fi Tho: ... ... ... ... ... 26 „
Jaine Morecrofte fi: Ric̃ ... ... ... ... ... „ „
Marget ffarclough fi Hen: ... ... ... ... 3 November
Hugh Mason fi Gabrell ... ... ... ... ... „ „
Ellin Hill fi John ... ... ... ... ... 5 „
Jaine Mellinge fi Rap̃ ... ... ... ... ... 9 „
Ellin Smulte fi Rob̃ ... ... ... ... ... ... 14 „
Fo. 65. Marget Lea fi Ewan ... ... ... ... ... ... 15 „
Eliz[th] Lawranson fi Doughter ... ... ... ... 17 „
Raffe Killshaw fi Hector ... ... ... ... ... 22 „
Henrie Bradshaw fi P̃ter ... ... ... ... ... „ „
Anne Lathom fi Hugh ... ... ... ... ... 26 „
Eliz[th] Harwood fi Witt ... ... ... ... ... 30 „
Katherin Gilbertson fi Hugh ... ... ... ... 1 December
Marget Haughton fi Hugh ... ... ... ... 6 „
Marget Hunte fi: Jo: ... ... ... ... ... 8 „
Elin Adamson fi Witt ... ... ... ... ... 9 „
Eliz[th] Waringe fi Jamis ... ... ... ... ... 13 „
Richard Corker fi Witt bast ... ... ... ... 16 „
Marie Kequicke fi Geor̃ ... ... ... ... ... „ „
Alis Vace fi Gilb̃ ... ... ... ... ... ... 18 „
Henrie Sutch fi Jamis ... ... ... ... ... 21 „
Marget Tumson fi John ... ... ... ... ... 24 „
Margerie Goulbron fi John ... ... ... ... 26 „
Ric̃ Waringe fi Jo: ... ... ... ... ... ... „ „
Marget Marclough fi Tho: ... ... ... ... „ „

* Written over "Rob" struck through.

| | | |
|---|---|---|
| Wiłłm Shawe fi Tho: | 1 | Januarie |
| Alis Smyth fi Tho: | 3 | „ |
| Catherin Penketh fi Henr̄ | 8 | „ |
| Ellin Hoolme | 9 | „ |
| Rodger Scarsbrecke fi Gabrell | 11 | „ |
| Henrie Allerton fi Jo: | 12 | „ |
| Marie Scarsbrecke fi Tho: | 13 | „ |
| Henrie Morecrofte fi Tho: | 14 | „ |
| John Cowson fi Jo: | 20 | „ |
| Ellin Sumner fi Hugh | „ | „ |
| Rob̄t Sanforth fi Jo: | 22 | „ |
| Gilb̄ Asshort fi Ja: | 27 | „ |
| Edwarde Cadicke fi Wiłł | „ | „ |
| John Wright fi Tho: | 28 | „ |
| Marget Stopforth fi Henrie | „ | „ |
| John Jackeson fi Ja: | 29 | „ |
| Elin Swifte fi: Ewan | 30 | „ |
| Katherin Autie fi Wiłl | 1 | ffebruarie |
| Tho: Lunte fi Hen̄ | 2 | „ |
| Robert and Henrie Diket fi Wiłł | 4 | „ |
| Rodger Barton̄ fi Ja: | 6 | „ |
| Jamis Milner fi Tho: | 8 | „ |
| Katherin Wilson fi Wiłł | 9 | „ |
| Tho: Balshaw fi John | „ | „ |
| Alis Morecrofte fi Ri: | 7 | March |
| Katherin Aiscrofte fi | „ | „ |
| Marie Wainewright fi Hugh | 8 | „ |
| Hugh Mason fi Tho: | 11 | „ |
| . . . Henrieson fi Rob̄ | „ | „ |
| Richard Woodhowse fi Hugh | 12 | „ |
| John Preskot fi Tho | 13 | „ |
| ffrances ffarrer fi Rob̄ | 18 | „ |
| Wiłłm Grason fi Tho: de Prekot | „ | „ |
| Jamis Huton fi Hugh bast | 21 | „ |
| Izabell Jackeson fi Jamis | 22 | „ |

## 1585.

| | | |
|---|---|---|
| Jaine Halliwell | 25 | March |
| Alis Blackeledge fi: Ewan | 30 | „ |
| Jaine fformbie fi: Tho: | 31 | „ |
| Wiłłm Preskot fi Tho: | 3 | Apriłł |
| Wiłłm Jackeson fi: Ric̄ | 5 | „ |
| Ewan Modisley fi Henrie | 11 | „ |
| Gefferey Page fi: Crist[r] | 15 | „ |
| Alis Haughton fi Hugh | 8 | Maye |
| Eliz[th] Scarsbrecke fi Wiłł | 14 | „ |
| Wiłłm Hoolme | 15 | „ |
| ffrançes Scarsbrecke fi Edw: Arm̄ | „ | „ |

Ric̃ Mowdisley fi Wiłłm ... 18 Maye
Henrie Anderton fi Raffe ... 20 „
Fo. 67 Richard Ascough fi Tho: ... 5 June
Jamis Modisley fi Tho: ... 6 „
Tho: Whytestones fi Ri: ... 8 „
Elin Morecrofte fi Gilb̄ ... 18 „
Anne Stanley fi: Henri Esq$^{r}$ ... 19 „
Marget Chadocke fi Hugh ... 20 „
Rob̄t Martindaile fi Henrie ... 21 „
Marie Hesketh fi Barthlū Esq$^{r}$ ... 22 „
Katherin Whyte fi Edw: ... 26 „
Marget Sutch fi Henrie ... 29 „
Margerie Ritherop ... 3 July
Jamis Ascough fi Jo: ... 13 „
Rodger ffarclough fi Rodg: ... 28 „
Tho Johnsson fi Edwardson ... 29 „
Anne Mowdisley fi Jo: ... 4 August
Elin Preskot fi Ric̃ ... 6 „
Jaine ffoge fi Jo: ... 10 „
Rob̄t Glaisbarow fi: Ri: bast ... 12 „
Rob̄t Read fi Ja: ... „ „
Anne Lailand fi Ric̃ ... 25 „
Wiłłm Wainewright fi Tho ... 27 „
Ellin Butler fi Tho: ... 30 „
Gabrell Ashton fi Raffe ... „ „
Wiłłm Sanke fi Rodger ... 1 September
Rob̄t Gobbin ... 5 „
Gilb̄ Babot fi Tho: ... 9 „
Wiłłm Wainewright fi Symon bast ... „ „
Ellin Glaisbarow fi Tho: ... 12 „
Alis Brighowse fi Ric̃ ... 13 „
Eliz$^{th}$ Abraham fi Tho: ... 22 „
Fo. 68 Katherin Charles fi Nicolas ... 4 October
Anne Barton fi Wiłłm ... 5 „
ffrances Haille fi Jamis ... 7 „
Jaine Hesketh fi Rob̄ ... 20 „
Jaine Gilbertson fi Tho: ... 30 „
Anne Suthe fi Tho: ... 4 November
Jamis ffidler fi Tho: ... 12 „
Rodger Haughton fi Ric̃ ... 13 „
Marget Morcrofte fi Ric̃ ... 16 „
Eliz$^{th}$ Killshaw fi Ja: ... 19 „
Wiłłm Whytestones fi Raffe ... „ „
Alis Kocket fi Henrie ... 20 „
Eideth Gill fi Gilb̄ ... 26 „
Jamis Oliverson fi Cristopher ... 27 „
Wiłłm Hill fi Ric̃ ... „ „
Eliz$^{th}$ Killshaw fi Tho ... 28 „
John Bower fi Jo: ... 2 December

| | | |
|---|---|---|
| Anne Harlinge fi Tho: ... | 2 | December |
| Jaine Wainewright fi Peeter ... | 4 | ,, |
| Tho: Lyon fi John strange ... | 9 | ,, |
| Henrie Barker fi: Ric̃ ... | 15 | ,, |
| Anne Masoñ fi Gabrell ... | 20 | ,, |
| Jamis Morcrofte fi Tho: ... | 27 | ,, |
| John Killshaw fi: Allen ... | 31 | ,, |
| Wiłłm Wainewright fi Ja: ... | 2 | Januarie |
| Tho: Blundell ... | 7 | ,, |
| Richard Gill fi: Henrie ... | 8 | ,, |
| Ric̃ Allerton fi Tho: ... | 9 | ,, |
| Katherin Butchert fi Edw: ... | 11 | ,, |
| Wiłłm Morecrofte fi Tho: ... | 28 | ,, |
| Richard Preskot fi Jo: bast ... | 5 | ffebruarie |
| Jamis Wiłłmson fi: Ri: ... | ,, | ,, |
| Anne Talior fi Rob̃ ... | 6 | ,, |
| Tho: Butler fi Jo: A stranger ... | 10 | ,, |
| Edward Marson fi Wiłłu ... | 12 | ,, |
| Marget Ambrose fi Henrie ... | 20 | ,, |
| Marget Shaw fi Wiłł ... | 25 | ,, |
| Alis Becconsawe fi: Gilb̃ ... | 3 | March |
| Anne Strange fi Myles ... | 8 | ,, |
| Brichet Gilb̃son fi Hugh ... | 9 | ,, |
| Ellis Longe fi: Piter ... | 10 | ,, |
| Jamis Bispam fi. Edmund ... | 11 | ,, |
| Eliz[th] Killshaw fi Jo: ... | 18 | ,, |
| Eliz[th] Aspinwall fi Hugh ... | 23 | ,, |
| Jaine Jackeson fi Ric̃ ... | 24 | ,, |

## 1586.

| | | |
|---|---|---|
| Marie Allerton fi Tho: ... | 28 | Marche |
| Marget Wholey fi Nicõ ... | ,, | ,, |
| Johnnie Martindaille fi Hugh ... | 29 | ,, |
| Eliz[th] Hesketh fi Myles ... | 1 | Aprill |
| Eliz[th] Aspinwall fi Nicol ... | ,, | ,, |
| Wiłłm Gill fi Davie ... | 7 | ,, |
| George Swifte fi Rob̃ ... | ,, | ,, |
| Anne Jameson fi Jo: bast p coniugat̃ ... | 10 | ,, |
| Ric̃ Barton fi Lewes ... | ,, | ,, |
| Wiłłm Swyfte ... | 20 | ,, |
| Tho: Hill fi Ric̃ ... | 1 | Maye |
| Margret Salfe fi Ran: ... | 6 | ,, |
| Jane Mason fi Tho: ... | 20 | ,, |
| Henrie Morcrofte fi Wiłł ... | 6 | June |
| Anne Walker fi Ric̃ ... | 20 | ,, |
| Mageret Moody fi Tho ... | 3 | Julie |
| John Voce fi Ric bast ... | 4 | ,, |
| Jane Morcrofte fi Hen: bast ... | 6 | ,, |
| Robte Bower fi Tho: ... | 17 | ,, |

| | | |
|---|---|---|
| Willm Tomson fi: Jo: ... ... ... ... ... | 30 | Julie |
| Alis ffletcher fi Ric ... ... ... ... ... ... | 1 | Auguste |
| Tho: Smolte fi Evan ... ... ... ... ... | 5 | " |
| Jane Waynwright fi Tho: ... ... ... ... | 6 | " |
| Hugh Barton fi Gabr bast ... ... ... ... | 17 | " |
| Tho: Wadington fi Willm ... ... ... ... | 18 | " |
| Alis Barton fi Gabr ... ... ... ... ... ... | 29 | " |
| Elene Balshawe fi Gilb ... ... ... ... ... | 30 | " |
| Marie Barton fi James ... ... ... ... ... | 4 | September |
| Grace Preskot fi John ... ... ... ... ... | " | " |
| Raffe Mellinge fi: Anthoney ... ... ... ... | " | " |
| Anne Tasker fi Henrie bast ... ... ... ... | " | " |
| Anne Henrison fi Edw: ... ... ... ... ... | 5 | " |
| Anne fforshaw fi . . . ... ... ... ... | 10 | " |
| Marget Coockeson ... ... ... ... ... ... | 15 | " |
| Eliz[th] Westhead fi Ric ... ... ... ... ... | 28 | " |
| Andrew Atherton fi Oliver ... ... ... ... | 1 | October |
| Marget Sanke fi Rodger ... ... ... ... ... | 5 | " |
| Katherin Bartonn fi Jamis ... ... ... ... | 9 | " |
| Ric Lathwhat fi Ja: bast ... ... ... ... | 11 | " |
| Henrie Gill fi Tho: ... ... ... ... ... ... | 18 | " |
| Ellinor Robinson fi Will ... ... ... ... ... | 27 | " |
| Eliz[th] Haile fi Henrie ... ... ... ... ... | 28 | " |
| Marget Barton fi: Jo: ... ... ... ... ... | 3 | November |
| Peeter Hunter fi: Tho: ... ... ... ... ... | 18 | " |
| Eliz[th] Darwen fi Willm ... ... ... ... ... | 20 | " |
| Tho: Badger fi Hugh ... ... ... ... ... | " | " |
| Fo. 71 Jamis Gill fi Gilb ... ... ... ... ... ... | 8 | December |
| Jamis Preskot fi Jo: ... ... ... ... ... | 15 | " |
| Tho: Marclough fi Ewan ... ... ... ... | 16 | " |
| George Sutch fi Jamis ... ... ... ... ... | 18 | " |
| Robert Butler fi Tho: ... ... ... ... ... | 21 | " |
| Ellin Butler fi Tho: ... ... ... ... ... | " | " |
| Emllin Scarsbrecke fi Tho: ... ... ... ... | " | " |
| John Shurlikars fi: . . . ... ... ... ... | 23 | " |
| Dorethie Blundell fi Cristo ... ... ... ... | 25 | " |
| Omfrey Gill ... ... ... ... ... ... ... | 29 | " |
| Ellin Blundell fi Rob ... ... ... ... ... | 6 | Januarie |
| Anne Worrall fi Ri: ... ... ... ... ... | 8 | " |
| Tho: Eccleston fi Ric bast ... ... ... ... | 10 | " |
| Tho: Blundell fi Rob ... ... ... ... ... | 11 | " |
| Willm Modisley ... ... ... ... ... ... | 16 | " |
| John Balshaw fi Jo: ... ... ... ... ... | 18 | " |
| Jenet Voce fi: Gilb ... ... ... ... ... ... | 20 | " |
| George Gill fi Par ... ... ... ... ... ... | 3 | ffebruarie |
| John Shawe fi Will ... ... ... ... ... ... | 23 | " |
| Marget Killshaw fi Alex ... ... ... ... ... | 26 | " |
| Katherin Croocke fi Jo: bast ... ... ... ... | 27 | " |

[*No entries for March—space left blank*]

# 1587.

72

[*No entries for Aprill—space left blank*]

|  |  |  |
|---|---|---|
| Houmphere Morecroft fi Wiłłm ... ... ... | 1 | Maye 1687* |
| John Kilshaw fi Ja: ... ... ... ... ... ... | 8 | „ |
| Tho Whytestones fi Raffe ... ... ... ... | 9 | „ |
| Anne Burscough fi Tho: ... ... ... ... | 12 | „ |
| Ellin Crosley fi Homfrey ... ... ... ... ... | 17 | „ |
| Ellin ffarclough fi Henr̄ ... ... ... ... ... | 28 | „ |
| George Rethrop fi Wiłł ... ... ... ... ... | „ | „ |
| John Cubon fi Tho: ... ... ... ... ... | 2 | June |
| Hector Lea fi Ewañ... ... ... ... ... ... | 8 | „ |
| Wiłłm Woodes fi Lawrance ... ... ... ... | 15 | „ |
| Anne Barker ... ... ... ... ... ... ... | 19 | „ |
| Rodger Wholey fi Nicol bap et bur̄ ... ... | 22 | „ |
| Anne Hesketh fi barth esqr ... ... ... ... | 5 | Julie |
| Anne Kocket fi Jo: ... ... ... ... ... ... | 15 | „ |
| Wiłłm Jackeson fi Ri: ... ... ... ... ... | 19 | „ |
| Richard Adamson fi Wiłł ... ... ... ... | 20 | „ |
| Doretha Stanley fi Henri esqr ... ... ... ... | 21 | „ |
| George Hesketh fi Rob̄ ... ... ... ... ... | 22 | „ |
| Marie Sefton fi George ... ... ... ... ... | 27 | „ |
| Jamis Waltheu fi Ri: ... ... ... ... ... | „ | „ |
| Elizth Lea fi Jamis ... ... ... ... ... ... | 30 | „ |
| Anne Ambrose fi Ri: vic ... ... ... ... | 2 | August |
| Elizth Cowsey fi Jam: ... ... ... ... ... | 4 | „ |
| Katherin Holland fi Hugh ... ... ... ... | 13 | „ |
| Wiłł Aiscroft fi Ja: ... ... ... ... ... ... | 22 | „ |
| Henrie Killshaw fi Tho: ... ... ... ... ... | 11 | September |
| Edmund Killshaw fi Wiłł ... ... ... ... | 12 | „ |
| Gabrihell Haughton fi Om̄ ... ... ... ... | 19 | „ |
| Myles Swyfte fi Oł m̄sr ... ... ... ... ... | 30 | „ |
| 73 Eline Cowp fi Ja: ... ... ... ... ... ... | 20 | October |
| Eline Haughton fi Rowland ... ... ... ... | 20 | „ |
| Margaret fi Hen bast ... ... ... ... ... | 14 | „ [*sic*] |
| Wiłłm Moudisley fi Jo: ... ... ... ... ... | 5 | November |
| Ric̄ Forshewe fi Rob̄t ... ... ... ... ... | 7 | „ |
| Henrie Golbron fi Jo: ... ... ... ... ... | 23 | „ |
| Jane Jacson fi Ja: ... ... ... ... ... ... | „ | „ |
| Eline Ascrofte fi Jo: ... ... ... ... ... | „ | „ |
| Elizth ffletcher fi Milse ... ... ... ... ... | 1 | December |
| Elizth Hill fi: Ric̄ ... ... ... ... ... ... | 8 | „ |
| Elizth Cadicke fi Rob̄t ... ... ... ... ... | 10 | Januarie |
| Margret Swifte fi: Wiłłm ... ... ... ... | 11 | „ |
| John Harison fi Hugh ... ... ... ... ... | 10 | „ |

* The whole of this entry (year, &c.) is in a different hand and ink, and is inserted in the blank space left for April, 1587.

George Tireyer fi Wittm ... ... ... ... ... ... 18 Januarie
Tho: Becall fi Gilb: ... ... ... ... ... ... 24 „
Paynters doughters Child ... ... ... ... 26 ffebruarie
Katherin Morcrofte fi Ric ... ... ... ... 5 Marche
Eamie Oliverson ... ... ... ... ... ... 17 „

## 1588.

Anne fforbie fi: Jo: ... ... ... ... ... ... 26 Marche
Hughe Marson fi: Wittm ... ... ... ... 4 Aprill
Eline Milere fi: Tho: ... ... ... ... ... ... „ „
Tho: Westehed fi Pet ... ... ... ... ... 11 „
James Chadoke fi: Hugh ... ... ... ... 13 „
Margret Hardman fi Jo: ... ... ... ... ... 14 „
Ric Golibrannd fi: Hugh gent ... ... ... „ „
Henrie Mason fi Gab ... ... ... ... ... 17 „
Hector Whitstons fi Ric ... ... ... ... ... 26 „
Peter Billinge fi Jo: ... ... ... ... ... 30 „
Anne Hesketh fi: Jo: ... ... ... ... ... 2 Maye
Jane Preskot fi: Jo: ... ... ... ... ... 27 „
Fo. 74 John Hesketh fi: Tho: bap et bur bastard ... 1 June
Margeret ffogge fi: Jo: ... ... ... ... ... 6 „
Robte Knowles fi: Hen: ... ... ... ... 14 „
Margreat Morcrofte fi: Tho: ... ... ... ... 23 „
Eliz[th] Parker fi Tho: de Aught bast ... ... 3 July
Tho: Swifte fi: Micell bast ... ... ... ... „ „
Henrie Kilshawe fi Jo: ... ... ... ... ... 20 „
Jane Sankie fi Rodger ... ... ... ... ... 31 „
John Eagles fi Jo: ... ... ... ... ... ... 8 Auguste
Elline Waringe fi: Jo: bast ... ... ... ... 9 „
Tho: Prescott fi Tho: ... ... ... ... ... 10 „
Margreat Robinson fi: Wittm ... ... ... ... 12 „
Eliz[th] Prescott fi: Ric ... ... ... ... ... „ „
Cuthbart Hallsall fi: Ric ... ... ... ... 22 „
Robt fidler fi: Tho: ... ... ... ... ... 31 „
Alis Kequicke fi: George ... ... ... ... „ „
Eliz[th] Haughton... ... ... ... ... ... ... 1 September
Gabrell Cropp fi: George bast ... ... ... 15 „
John Hulme fi: Ric ... ... ... ... ... 16 „
Jaine Houlme fi: Witt ... ... ... ... ... „ „
Ellin Mawdisley fi Symon ... ... ... ... 25 „
Anne Waringe fi Ja: ... ... ... ... ... 9 October
Raffe Hesketh fi Ric bast ... ... ... ... 21 „
Jamis Dalton fi John ... ... ... ... ... 24 „
Omfrey Lunte fi Hen: ... ... ... ... ... 27 „
Katherin Garrard fi Rob ... ... ... ... ... „ „
Anne Ambrose fi Ric bap et bur ... ... ... 30 „
Katherin Hayton fi Tho: ... ... ... ... 1 November
Emllin Kewquicke fi: Witt ... ... ... ... „ „

Ellin Killshaw fi: Hector ... ... ... ... 18 November
Richard Barton fi Ja: ... ... ... ... ... 19 „
Riĉ Morecrofte fi Tho: ... ... ... ... ... 22 „
Edmund Walker fi Riĉ ... ... ... ... ... 24 „
Riĉ Clapam̃ fi Rodg: ... ... ... ... ... 1 December
John Wadingeton fi Wiłł ... ... ... ... 5 „
Katherin Garrard ... ... ... ... ... ... „ „
Alis Lei fi Ewañ ... ... ... ... ... ... 6 „
Wiłłm Arnoulde fi: Riĉ ... ... ... ... ... 9 „
Omfrey Aspinwall fi Riĉ ... ... ... ... ... 12 „
Henrie Lathwhat fi Wiłł ... ... ... ... ... 22 „
Marie Preskot fi Tho: ... ... ... ... ... 25 „
Marie Ambrose fi Riĉ vic ... ... ... ... 26 „
Anne Oliverson fi Xpr̃ ... ... ... ... ... 30 „
Wiłłm Barton fi Jac ... ... ... ... ... ... 5 Januarie
Marget Sutch fi John ... ... ... ... ... 9 „
Jamis Lathwhat fi Ja: ... ... ... ... ... 10 „
Katherin Nallier fi Wiłł ... ... ... ... ... 16 „
John Peeter fi Jo: bap et bur̃ ... ... ... ... 19 „ bur̃ 20
Richard Swyfte fi Jo: ... ... ... ... ... 21 „
Rob̃rt Abbott fi Jo: ... ... ... ... ... 22 „
Ellenn Haughton fi Ri: ... ... ... ... ... 26 „
Edward Allerton fi Jo: ... ... ... ... ... 2 ffebruarie
Emlyine M^9rofte [*sic*] fi Edw: bast ... ... 10 „
Rauffe Holland fi George ... ... ... ... 20 „
Rob̃t Woods fi Wiłłm bast ... ... ... ... 6 Marche
Edward Wiswall fi Tho: bast ... ... ... 7 „
Johne Burscough fi Tho: ... ... ... ... 18 „
Edward Brigehowse fi: Tho: bast ... ... „ „

## 1589.

Izabell Strange fi Myles ... ... ... ... ... 26 March
Eliz^th Bartoñ fi . . . . ... ... ... ... ... 27 „
Riĉ Martindaile ... ... ... ... ... ... „ „
Marget ffasikerley fi Hugh ... ... ... ... 1 Aprill
Henrie Todd fi Wiłł bast ... ... ... ... ... 2 „
Elleñ Westhead fi Riĉ ... ... ... ... ... 11 „
Alis ffarrer fi Rob̃ ... ... ... ... ... ... „ „
Rodger Kewquicke fi Hugh ... ... ... ... 12 „
Wiłłm Rithrope fi Hamlet ... ... ... ... „ „
Gabriell Haskeine fi Hen: ... ... ... ... 14 „
Marget Coockeson fi Ja: ... ... ... ... „ „
Omfrey Hill fi Riĉ ... ... ... ... ... ... 16 „
Eliz^th Butchard fi Edward ... ... ... ... 23 „
Jaine Hunter fi Tho: ... ... ... ... ... 6 Maye
Elline Hoolme fi Will: Ju: ... ... ... ... 8 „
Johne Au'toñ fi Wiłł ... ... ... ... ... „ „
Marie Masonn fi Gabrell ... ... ... ... ... 11 „

Gilƀ Scarsbrecke fi Tho: ... ... ... ... 18 Maye
Ellin Sutch fi Raffe ... ... ... ... ... ... ... „ „
Katherin Lathom̄ fi Henrie ... ... ... ... „ „
Alis Lathwhat fi Peter ... ... ... ... ... ... 24 „
Marie Hill fi Jo: ... ... ... ... ... ... ... 25 „
Edw: Ambrose fi Ellis ... ... ... ... ... ... 29 „
Hugh Mason fi Tho: ... ... ... ... ... ... 4 June
Jam̄ Rydinge fi: Rodger ... ... ... ... ... 5 „
Tho: Ballshaw fi Gilƀ: ... ... ... ... ... ... 15 „
Alis Westhead fi Tho: bast ... ... ... ... „ „
Marget Assheton fi Raffe ... ... ... ... ... 27 „
Cuthbart Asley fi Jamis de Aug: ... ... ... 2 Julye
Roƀt Cosey fi Hugh ... ... ... ... ... ... „ „
Anne Barton fi Ja: ... ... ... ... ... ... ... 6 „
Gowther & Cuthbart Hodgekinson̄ fi Ric̃ ... 9 „
Jamis Sharrocke fi Jo: ... ... ... ... ... ... 10 „
Jane Pousy fi Ri: ... . ... ... ... ... ... 15 „
Eideth Haughton fi Hugh ... ... ... ... ... 18 „
Grace Morecrofte fi Tho: ... ... ... ... „ „
Marget Cubon̄ fi Tho: ... ... ... ... ... ... 30 „
Edward Aspinwall fi Peeter ... ... ... ... ... 7 August
Henrey Mowdisley fi Jam: ... ... ... ... ... 12 „
Eliz[th] Jackeson fi Ja: ... ... ... ... ... ... 24 „
Fo. 77 Henrie Robinson̄ fi Tho: ... ... ... ... 26 „
Emlin Gill fi Roƀ ... ... ... ... ... ... ... 27 „
Ric̃ Penketh fi Henrie ... ... ... ... ... ... „ „
Roƀt Gill fi Parsivall ... ... ... ... ... ... 31 „
Raffe Gill fi Gilƀ ... ... ... ... ... ... ... „ „
Henrie ffletcher fi Myles ... ... ... ... ... ... 3 September
Marie Dikit alias Bathe fi ... ... ... ... ... „ „
Gilƀ Roƀtson fi Roƀ ... ... ... ... ... ... 5 „
Henrie Hoolme fi Ric̃ ... ... ... ... ... ... 12 „
Anne Barton fi Jo: ... .. ... ... ... ... ... 13 „
Jamis & Johne Haile fi Henrie ... ... ... ... 15 „
Marie Barton fi Myles ... ... ... ... ... ... 17 „
Eliz[th] Gobbin fi John ... ... ... ... ... ... 18 „
Anne Woosey fi Ja: de Aughton bast ... ... 20 „
Ric̃ Goulƀron fi Omfrey supposed ... ... ... 26 „
Tho: Hey fi: Nicolas ... ... ... ... ... ... 3 October
Wiłłm More fi Tho: ... ... ... ... ... ... 9 „
Anne Blundell fi Edw: ... ... ... ... ... ... 10 „
Marie Sankey fi Rog[r] ... ... ... ... ... 24 „
Eliz[th] Gill fi Hen: ... ... ... ... ... ... ... „ „
Edward Charles fi Peeter ... ... ... ... ... 25 „
Henrie Balshaw fi: Jo: ... ... ... ... ... ... 16 November
John Hill fi Ric̃ ... ... ... ... ... ... ... 22 „
Tho: Killshaw fi Hector ... ... ... ... ... ... 26 „
Roƀt Crosley fi Omfrey ... ... ... ... ... 6 December
Marie Kequicke fi Wiłł de Aug: ... ... ... 8 „

| | | |
|---|---|---|
| Willm Garrard fi Cuthebart | 11 | December |
| Brychet Cowdocke fi Will | 12 | ,, |
| Johnnie Aiscrofte fi Jo: | 17 | ,, |
| Robart Barton fi Nic bast | ,, | ,, |
| Loare Talior fi Rob | 24 | ,, |
| Marget Ambrose fi Ric | 27 | ,, |
| Henrie Sutch fi George | 30 | ,, |
| 8 Emie Preskot bast | 9 | Januarie |
| Tho: Koket fi Bryhan | 11 | ,, |
| Marie Baron fi Gilb | 28 | ,, |
| Izabell Aspinwall fi Tho: | 2 | ffebruarie |
| Edw: Blundell fi Jo: | 3 | ,, |
| Anne Croston fi Jo: de Hal | 6 | ,, |
| Tho: Arnoold fi Ri | ,, | ,, |
| Philip Atherton fi Oli: | ,, | ,, |
| Marie Wadingeton fi Willi | 10 | ,, |
| John Modisley fi Jo: | 12 | ,, |
| John Aiscrofte fi Hug: | 21 | ,, |
| Ric Mosse fi Ri: | ,, | ,, |
| John Jackeson fi Ri: | 24 | ,, |
| Richard Killshaw fi Allen | ,, | ,, |
| Richard Robinson fi Will | 27 | ,, |
| . . . Killshaw fi Ja: | 28 | ,, |
| Ric Parpointe fi Raffe | 1 | Marche |
| Allex[r] Shorliker fi Rob | ,, | ,, |
| Eliz[th] Cartwright fi | 10 | ,, |
| Jane Preskot fi George | 15 | ,, |

## 1590.

| | | |
|---|---|---|
| Henrie Swifte fi Will | 26 | Marche |
| Marget Holland fil Jo: | 2 | Aprill |
| Anne Mellinge fi Anthoney | 3 | ,, |
| Jane Hesketh fi Tho: bast | 9 | ,, |
| Marget Spencer fi Tho: de Rufford | ,, | ,, |
| Elyne Whythington fi Raffe | 22 | ,, |
| Anne Oliverson fi Xpor | 25 | ,, |
| Parcevall Edwdson fi Peeter | 29 | ,, |
| Margerie Cowson fi John | 30 | ,, |
| 79 Tho: Woodes fi Will | 4 | Maye |
| Jamis Butle fi Will de Halsall bast | 11 | ,, |
| Hugh Lea fi Willm | 12 | ,, |
| Ewan Westhead fi Peeter* | 6 | June |
| Anne Peeters fi Jo* | ,, | ,, |
| Willm Griffie fi David* | 10 | ,, |
| Tho: Spencer fi Will | 13 | ,, |
| Eliz[th] Standanought fi Tristrom | 14 | ,, |

* These 3 names entered by mistake at bottom of Fo. 78 and struck through.

| | | |
|---|---|---|
| Henrie Prekot fi Witt de Halsall ... ... ... | 30 | June |
| Anne ffogg fi Jo: ... ... ... ... ... ... | 2 | Julye |
| Henrie Voce fi Pe ... ... ... ... ... ... | ” | ” |
| Richard Babbot fi Tho: ... ... ... ... ... | 12 | ” |
| Edward & Jamis Aspinwall fi Hugh ... ... | 23 | ” |
| Katherin Killshaw fi Jo: ... ... ... ... ... | 25 | ” |
| Jamis Killshaw fi Jo: ... ... ... ... ... | 26 | ” |
| Margerie Holland fi Rap ... ... ... ... ... | 27 | ” |
| Ellin Werall fi Ri: ... ... ... ... ... ... | 28 | ” |
| Ric̃ Lathom fi Henrie ... ... ... ... ... | 10 | August |
| Tho: Hesekth fi John ... ... ... ... ... | 12 | ” |
| Tho: Crooke fi John ... ... ... ... ... | 13 | ” |
| Marget Jackesoñ fi Jam ... ... ... ... ... | 17 | ” |
| Dorethie Miller fi Tho: ... ... ... ... ... | 18 | ” |
| Martha Ambrose fi: Ric̃ vic ... ... ... ... | 21 | ” |
| Margerie Haughton fi Homfrey ... ... ... | 28 | ” |
| Ellin Shawe fi Wittm ... ... ... ... ... | 31 | ” |
| Margerie Hunt fi John ... ... ... ... ... | 1 | September |
| Henrie Spencer fi Jo: ... ... ... ... ... | 8 | ” |
| Marget ffarrer fi Rob̃ ... ... ... ... ... | 19 | ” |
| Jaine Voce fi Ric̃ ... ... ... ... ... ... | 23 | ” |
| Eliz$^{th}$ Sutton fi Wittm ... ... ... ... ... | 24 | ” |
| Richard Rigmaiden fi Witt bast ... ... ... | 29 | ” |
| Fo. 80 Marget Kewquicke fi Ja: ... ... ... ... | 1 | October |
| Richard Morecrofte fi Witt bast ... ... ... | 11 | ” |
| Tho: Lathwhat fi Witt ... ... ... ... ... | 12 | ” |
| Richard Huton fi Tho: ... ... ... ... ... | 13 | ” |
| Cuthbart Mason fi Gabrell ... ... ... ... | ” | ” |
| Katherin Kewquicke fi Hugh ... ... ... ... | 30 | ” |
| Anne Whytestones fi Ric̃ ... ... ... ... | 3 | November |
| Marget Werden fi Mi: de Raiñ ... ... ... | 4 | ” |
| Ellis Ambrose fi Henrie ... ... ... ... ... | 5 | ” |
| Marget Lathwhat fi Ja: ... ... ... ... ... | ” | ” |
| Anne Swifte fi Jamis bast ... ... ... ... | 9 | ” |
| Wittm Chadocke fi Hugh ... ... ... ... | ” | ” |
| Jaine Skinner fi Tho: ... ... ... ... ... | 11 | ” |
| Peeter Bore fi John ... ... ... ... ... ... | 17 | ” |
| Katherin Soknell [?] fi ffrancis bast a Stranger | 22 | ” |
| Alis Ince fi Hamlet bast ... ... ... ... ... | 8 | December |
| Alex$^{r}$ Gowbron fi Homfrey ... ... ... ... | 14 | ” |
| Izabell Smyth fi Hen: ... ... ... ... ... | 21 | ” |
| Alis Hardmañ fi John ... ... ... ... ... | 30 | ” |
| Eliz$^{th}$ Preskot fi Tho: ... ... ... ... ... | 5 | Januarie |
| George Croocke fi Jon: ... ... ... ... ... | 7 | ” |
| Ewan Lea fi Wittm bast ... ... ... ... ... | 11 | ” |
| Marie Gill fi Davie ... ... ... ... ... ... | 18 | ” |
| Wittm Baron fi Gilb̃ ... ... ... ... ... | 24 | ” |
| Eliz$^{th}$ Gleaste fi Jo: de P$^{9}$skot ... ... ... | 4 | ffebruarie |
| Henrie Allerton fi Tho: ... ... ... ... ... | 11 | ” |

| | | |
|---|---|---|
| Wiłłm Shurlikar fi Ja: | 18 | ffebruarie |
| Claris Haughton fi Ri: | 21 | " |
| Anne Rithrope fi Hamlet | 25 | " |
| Alis Sumner fi Hugh | 26 | " |
| John Barton fi Ja: | 1 | March |
| Marie Blundell fi Edw: | 5 | " |
| Marget Hill fi Jo: | 6 | " |
| Jamis ffidler fi Tho: | " | " |
| Marie Mowdisley fi Symon | 7 | " |
| Phillip Martindaille fi Hugh bast | 16 | " |
| Edw: Martindaille fi Hen | " | " |
| Jamis Morecroft fi Tho: | 21 | " |
| Anne Wiłłson fi Jo: de Meales | 22 | " |

## 1591.

| | | |
|---|---|---|
| Margerie Golb̄ron fi Wiłł bast | 28 | March |
| Alis the doughter of Kath: Holland bast | " | " |
| Tho: Morecrofte fi Wiłł | 3 | Aprill |
| Alis Barton fi Gow: | 6 | " |
| Jamis Morecrofte fi Ri: | 8 | " |
| Gilb̄ Tyrer fi Wiłł | 10 | " |
| Izabell Aiscrofte fi Jon: | 11 | " |
| Wiłłm Alker fi Ja: | " | " |
| Anne Standishe fi Hugh | 12 | " |
| Marget Kocket fi Bry: | 2 | Maie |
| Henrie Woodes fi Wiłł | 13 | " |
| Katherin Rydinge fi Rog: | 14 | " |
| Jaine Preskot fi Tho: | 16 | " |
| Ellin ffletcher fi Rob̄ | 26 | " |

[*No entries for June*]

| | | |
|---|---|---|
| Tho: Lawrance fi Ant | 11 | July |
| Rob̄rt Mosse fi Ric̄ | 13 | " |
| Eliz^th^ Talior fi Edm̄: | 16 | " |
| Joaine Orum Alis Jonghi bast | 21 | " |
| Tho: Barton fi Ja: | 25 | " |
| Homfrey Scarsbrecke fi Gab: | 29 | " |
| Peter Asmall fi Ric̄ | 5 | August |
| Anne Lea fi Ewan | 7 | " |
| John Halsall fi Ric̄ | " | " |
| Eliz^th^ Keckwicke fi Rob̄t | 12 | " |
| Margratt Swifte fi Jo: | " | " |
| Christopher Wignall fi Wiłłm | 16 | " |
| Katherin ffletcher fi Mil: | 9 | September |
| Anne Gill fi: Rob̄t | 11 | " |
| Ric̄ Morcrofte fi Hen: | 12 | " |
| Gabriell Shawe fi: Tho: | 13 | " |
| Grace Waringe fi: Hen: | 14 | " |

Henrie Spenser fi: Pit ... ... ... ... ... 21 September
Rauph Kilshawe fi Hector ... ... ... ... 24 „
John Pinĩgton fi: Hom: ... ... ... ... ... 8 October
Anne Sutche fi: Ja: talior ... ... ... ... 15 „
George Aspes fi: Rodg: bast ... ... ... 19 „
Margreat Barton fi: Ric̃ ... ... ... ... ... 24 „
Margery Jackson fi: Ja: ... ... ... ... 30 „
Wiłłm Webster fi: Hen: ... ... ... ... „ „
Hughe Hoolme fi: Ric̃ ... ... ... ... ... 1 December
Tho: Cockett fi: Jo: ... ... ... ... ... 15 „
Hughe Grifith fi: David ... ... ... ... ... 19 „
Margrat Paulsey fi: Ric̃ ... ... ... ... ... 31 „
Tho: Lathom fi: Hen: ... ... ... ... ... 1 January
George Smalshaye fi: Tho: ... ... ... ... 4 „
Jane Hill fi: Ric̃ ... ... ... ... ... ... 18 „
Christofer Blundell fi: Jo: ... ... ... ... 19 „
John Alerton fi: Tho: ... ... ... ... ... 27 „
Gauther Atherton fi: May: bast ... ... ... 28 „
Myles Gerard fi: Cuth: ... ... ... ... ... 30 „
Eliz$^{th}$ Brighouse fi: Ric̃ ... ... ... ... ... 31 „
Fo. 83 George Charles fi: Pił ... ... ... ... ... 2 ffebruarie
Tho: Lea fi: Tho: ... ... ... ... ... 6 „
Elen Clapem fi: Ric̃ ... ... ... ... ... 10 „
Henry Worthington fi: Hugh ... ... ... ... 14 „
Henrie Atherton fi: Gotf: ... ... ... ... 15 „
Katherin Peter fi: Jo: ... ... ... ... ... 28 „
Margrat Cropp fi: George ... ... ... ... 1 Marche
Symond Turner fi: Hom: ... ... ... ... 5 „
Wiłłm Clapham fi: Rodg: ... ... ... ... 13 „
Ric̃ & Jo: Butler fi: Tho: ... ... ... ... 14 „

## 1592.

Wiłłm Kilshaw fi: Hom: ... ... ... ... 25 Marche
Genett Barton fi: Rodg: ... ... ... ... „ „
Ric̃ Ashurts fi: Tho: ... ... ... ... ... „ „
Anne Ambrose fi: Ellis ... ... ... ... 2 Aprill
John Hulme fi: Tho: ... ... ... ... ... „ „
Jane Gill fi: Rodg$^{9}$: de Halsall ... ... ... 5 „
Elin Lea fi: Wiłłm bast ... ... ... ... 9 „
James Brighouse fi: Ric̃ bast ... ... ... ... 11 „
Margreat Hill fi: Ric̃ de Scer: ... ... ... 13 „
Margreat Waynwright fi: Sy: ... ... ... 26 „
Eliz$^{th}$ Barton fi: Miles ... ... ... ... ... 30 „
Ric̃ Singleton fi Wiłł bast ... ... ... ... 7 Maye
Jenet Aiscrofte fi Hugh ... ... ... ... ... 9 „
Jamis Preskot fi: Tho: ... ... ... ... ... 12 „
Izabell Cubbon fi: Tho: ... ... ... ... „ „
Anne Robinsoñ fi Wiłł ... ... ... ... ... 17 „

| | | |
|---|---|---|
| Alis Stopforth fi Hen: ... ... ... ... ... | 21 | Maye |
| Edward Haughton fi Rog⁹: ... ... ... ... ... | 30 | „ |
| Sara Marsoñ fi Wiłł ... ... ... ... ... ... | 19 | June |
| Elizth Rutter fi: Jo:... ... ... ... ... ... | 26 | „ |
| Anne Kokket fi Ri: bast ... ... ... ... | 2 | Julye |
| Richard Lawe fi: Jo: ... ... ... ... ... ... | 6 | „ |
| Ewan Rycrofte fi: Wiłł ... ... ... ... ... ... | 9 | „ |
| Edw: & Jaine Hoolme fi Phil ... ... ... | 18 | „ |
| Ellizth Hollond fi John ... ... ... ... ... | 21 | „ |
| Katherin Mason fi Tho: ... ... ... ... ... ... | 24 | „ |
| Anne Harison fi: Rob̄ ... ... ... ... ... | 5 | Auguste |
| Edward Asmall fi Tho: ... ... ... ... ... ... | 7 | „ |
| Amye Allerton fi: Tho: ... ... ... ... ... ... | 18 | „ |
| Wiłłm Masoñ fi: Gab̄ ... ... ... ... ... | 19 | „ |
| Anne & Emlin Gill fi: Gilb̄ ... ... ... ... | 2 | September |
| Elizth Hunte fi John... ... ... ... ... ... | 8 | „ |
| Marget Blundell fi Edw: ... ... ... ... ... ... | 12 | „ |
| Ma'get Glaisbarow fi: Ric̄ bast ... ... ... | 25 | „ |
| John Knowles fi: Tristrom ... ... ... ... | 29 | „ |
| Marget Balshaw fi: John ... ... ... ... | 8 | October |
| Anne Barton fi: Arthor ... ... ... ... ... ... | 9 | „ |
| Margerie Dowber fi: Will bast ... ... ... | 11 | „ |
| Henrie Hoolme fi: Wiłł ... ... ... ... ... ... | 12 | „ |
| Wiłłm Gyles fi: Rob̄ ... ... ... ... ... ... | 15 | „ |
| Jaine Butler fi: Gilb̄ de Aughton ... ... ... | 25 | „ |
| Jaine Whytestones fi: Ra: ... ... ... ... ... | 26 | „ |
| Anne Holland fi: Jo: ... ... ... ... ... ... | 30 | „ |
| Jamis Jackeson fi Ri: ... ... ... ... ... | 4 | November |
| Henrie Sankey fi: Rodg⁹: ... ... ... ... ... | 17 | „ |
| Raffe Mellinge fi: Wiłł ... ... ... ... ... ... | 21 | „ |
| Anne Withingeton fi: Raffe ... ... ... ... ... | 22 | „ |
| Gowther Barton fi: Ja: ... ... ... ... ... ... | 24 | „ |
| Jaine Cockesoñ fi Silvester ... ... ... ... ... | „ | „ |
| Elizth Westhead fi: Peeter ... ... ... ... ... | 26 | „ |
| Jaine Sutch fi: Jo: ... ... ... ... ... ... | „ | „ |
| Richard Lathwhat fi: Wiłł ... ... ... ... ... | 28 | „ |
| Wiłłm Modisley fi: Phillip ... ... ... ... ... | 2 | December |
| Robert Gobbin fi Jo: ... ... ... ... ... ... | 5 | „ |
| Anne Hadley fi John ... ... ... ... ... | 9 | „ |
| Trustrom Haughtō fi Homfrey ... ... ... | 14 | „ |
| Margerie Boothe fi: Wiłł ... ... ... ... ... | 15 | „ |
| Henrie Ambrose fi Ri: vic̄ ... ... ... ... ... | 24 | „ |
| Peeter Barton fi John ... ... ... ... ... ... | 25 | „ |
| Edw: ffleetewood fi: Peeter bast ... ... ... | 26 | „ |
| Richard Chadocke fi Adam̄ ... ... ... ... | 2 | Januarie |
| John Robinson fi Tho: ... ... ... ... ... ... | 10 | „ |
| Peeter Stanley fi Wiłł gent ... ... ... ... ... | 12 | „ |
| Ewan Mowdisley fi: Hector ... ... ... ... | 14 | „ |
| Anne Morcrofte fi: Tho: ... ... ... ... ... | 20 | „ |

John Longley fi Witt ... ... ... ... ... 21 Januarie
Tho: Wittm fi Ja: ... ... ... ... ... ... 29 „
Robt Lathome fi: Hen: ... ... ... ... ... 9 ffebruarie
Wittm Sutch fi: George ... ... ... ... ... 12 „
Katherin Asmall fi: Witl ... ... ... ... 15 „
Jaine Atherton fi: John bast ... ... ... ... „ „
Gabrell Roase fi Raffe ... ... ... ... ... 21 „
Tho: Chadocke fi Hugh ... ... ... ... ... 24 „
Gilb Gill fi Tho: ... ... ... ... ... ... 25 „
Eliz[th] Swifte fi: Jo: ... ... ... ... ... „ „
John Croston fi Henrie ... ... ... ... ... 28 „
Eideth Standishe fi Hugh ... ... ... ... 2 Marche
Richard Spencer fi Witl ... ... ... ... ... 4 „
Jams Webster fi John ... ... ... ... ... 11 „
Tho Barton fi Gilb ... ... ... ... ... ... „ „
Omfrey Martindaile fi Henrie ... ... ... ... „ „
Silvester Weltch fi Gilb ... ... ... ... ... 16 „
Hugh Aughton fi Ric ... ... ... ... ... 19 „
Hugh Skinner fi Tho: ... ... ... ... ... 22 „

## 1593.

Fo. 86 Richard Sutton fi Witt ... ... ... ... ... 11 Aprill
Anne Barker fi Henrie bast ... ... ... ... 14 „
Anne Karter fi Tho: ... ... ... ... ... 22 „
Jenet Wadingeton fi Witl ... ... ... ... 29 „
Emlin Bonnde fi Lawrance ... ... ... ... 1 Maye
Anne Hill fi Jo: ... ... ... ... ... ... 4 „
Edw: Ambrose fi Ellis ... ... ... ... ... 6 „
Jaine Barton fi Gowther ... ... ... ... ... 12 „
Jaine Preskot fi Hugh ... ... ... ... ... 16 June
Marget Mawdisley fi Tho: ... ... ... ... 19 „
Marget Scarsbrecke fi Ja: ... ... ... ... 21 „
Jenet Waynewright fi Ri: ... ... ... ... 22 „
Hugh Rithrope fi Hamlet ... ... ... ... 28 „
Alis Swyfte fi Nic: ... ... ... ... ... ... 22 July
Tho: Mawdisley fi Symon ... ... ... ... 4 Auguste
Ellin Holland fi Robt ... ... ... ... ... 15 „
Jaine Aspinwall fi Ric ... ... ... ... ... „ „
Elnor Mason fi Tho: ... ... ... ... ... 17 „
Eliz[th] Medowes fi: Tho: ... ... ... ... ... 23 „
A Chylde of Rodg[9]: Rydinges ... ... ... 28 „
Tho: Webster fi Rodg[9]: ... ... ... ... 31 „
Anne Cowson fi Jo: ... ... ... ... ... 9 September
Richard Stryker fi Myhell ... ... ... ... 13 „
Hugh Voce fi Ric ... ... ... ... ... ... 19 „
Marget Barton fi Jam: ... ... ... ... ... 27 „
John Greaves fi Omfrey ... ... ... ... ... 30 „
Marget Balshaw fi Edw: ... ... ... ... ... 4 October

|  |  |  |
|---|---|---|
| Willm Morecroft fi Tho: | 15 | October |
| Jaine Garrard fi Cutb | 19 | „ |
| Marget Kellet fi: Ric̃ | 24 | „ |
| Robrt Buler fi John | 25 | „ |
| Henrie Alker fi Jam: | 27 | „ |
| Ellin ffarrer fi Rob̃ | „ | „ |
| Edw: Gill fi: Rob̃t | 1 | November |
| Henrie Hesketh fi Tho: | 9 | „ |
| Silvester Lathwhat fi Jam: | 10 | „ |
| Henrie Bankes fi: Edward | 14 | „ |
| Edw: ffogge fi John | 15 | „ |
| Willm Cadicke fi: Rob̃ | 28 | „ |
| Anne Halsall fi Ri: | 29 | „ |
| Jaine Killshaw fi: John | 30 | „ |
| A childe of one Dawber | „ | „ |
| Marget Gollie fi Tho: | 10 | December |
| Tho: Woodes fi Will | 14 | „ |
| Ellin Killshaw fi Allen | 15 | „ |
| Richard Mowdisley fi John | 16 | „ |
| Margerie Westhead fi Tho: bast | „ | „ |
| Jenet ffletcher fi Ri: | 19 | „ |
| Jamis Hey fi Ric̃ | 24 | „ |
| Alis Whytesaid fi Rob̃ | 13 | Januarie |
| Joanie Morecrofte fi Ric̃ | 15 | „ |
| Anne Oliverson fi Tho: | 18 | „ |
| Hector Morecrofte fi Tho: | „ | „ |
| Hugh Shawe fi Willm | 20 | „ |
| Gabrell Gill fi Ric̃ | 22 | „ |
| Hugh Mowdisley fi Hen: bast | 23 | „ |
| Jaine Gore fi Adam | 26 | „ |
| Henrie Blundell fi John | 28 | „ |
| John Sutch fi Jamis | 3 | ffebruarie |
| Jaine Mason̄ fi Gabrell | 6 | „ |
| Eliz^th^ Woosey fi Gowther | 7 | „ |
| Hugh Turner fi Omfrey | 18 | „ |
| John Sutch fi George | 19 | „ |
| Eliz^th^ Hatley fi John | 20 | „ |
| John Hey fi Tho: | 24 | „ |
| Henrie Hill fi Ric̃ | 28 | „ |
| Jamis Charles fi Peeter | 3 | Marche |
| Jenet Aiscroft fi Jo: | 7 | „ |
| Jaine Clapam fi Ric̃ | „ | „ |
| Agnes Cocket fi Bryhan | 9 | „ |
| ffardinandow Cropp fi Hugh | 10 | „ |
| Richard Preskot fi Rob̃ | 17 | „ |
| Eliz^th^ A stranger | 19 | „ |
| Ric̃ Kewquicke fi Ro: | 21 | „ |
| Jonie & Izabell Robinson fi Will | 22 | „ |

## 1594.

Catherin Mellinge fi Anthoney ... ... ... 26 Marche
Gilbart Sharrocke fi John ... ... ... ... 1 Aprill
Alis Oliverson fi Crist ... ... ... ... ... 7 „
Marget Powsey fi Ric̃ ... ... ... ... ... „ „
Jaine Marche fi Witt ... ... ... ... ... 9 „
Marget Harison fi Tho: ... ... ... ... ... 11 „
Eliz^th Blackeledg fi Ewañ ... ... ... ... 16 „
Rodger ffletcher fi Rob̃ ... ... ... ... ... 21 „
Peeter Voce fi Ric̃ ... ... ... ... ... ... 25 „
Margerie Sutch fi Jo: ... ... ... ... ... 28 „
Raffe Longley fi Ewan ... ... ... ... ... „ „
Peeter Hoolme fi Tho: ... ... ... ... ... 5 Maye
Marget Kewquicke fi Hugh ... ... ... ... 8 „
Jaine Robertes doughter fi Rob̃ ... ... ... 16 „
Anne Killshaw fi Tho: ... ... ... ... ... 17 „
Peeter Ambrose fi Ellis ... ... ... ... ... 20 „
Henrie Kare fi Tho: ... ... ... ... ... 21 „
Tho: Webster fi Hen: ... ... ... ... ... 28 „
Ellin Ormishaw fi John ... ... ... ... ... 2 June
Henrie Longeworth fi Will ... ... ... ... 15 „
Jaine Woosey fi Hen: ... ... ... ... ... 17 „
Richard Barton fi Gilb̃ ... ... ... ... ... 22 „
Fo. 89 John Greaves fi Tho: ... ... ... ... ... 9 Julye
Jaine Mawdisley fi Tho: ... ... ... ... „ „
ffardinando & Margerie } Cropp fi George ... ... ... „ „
Thomas Talior fi Ric̃ bast ... ... ... ... 16 „
Joanie Peeter fi John ... ... ... ... ... 28 „
Anne Barton fi Myles ... ... ... ... ... 30 „
Anne Stanley fi Edw: de Morehall ... ... 5 Auguste
Eliz^th Holland fi George de Halsall ... ... 8 „
Wittm Lea fi Ewañ ... ... ... ... ... ... 14 „
John Waringe fi Hen: ... ... ... ... ... 31 „
Jane Prekot fi John ... ... ... ... ... ... 6 September
Tho: Yate fi Edward ... ... ... ... ... 15 „
Gabriell Ambrosse fi Ri: Vic̃ ... ... ... ... 16 „
Margerie Cropp fi Tho: bast ... ... ... ... 22 „
Eliz^th Clapam fi Rodger ... ... ... ... ... „ „
Mawde Tyrer fi Witt ... ... ... ... ... 26 „
Rob̃t Carre fi Edmund ... ... ... ... ... 30 „
Margerie Yates Chyld bast ... ... ... ... 4 October
Eliz^th Rycroft fi Witt ... ... ... ... ... 22 „
Henrie Smyth fi Tho: ... ... ... ... ... 24 „
Marie Hey fi Tho: de Halsall ... ... ... 7 November
Anne Tarbocke fi Jo: de Halsall ... ... ... 12 „
Marget Lunte fi Henr: ... ... ... ... ... 15 „

| | | |
|---|---|---|
| Jaine Cowdocke fi Witt ... ... ... ... ... ... | 15 | November |
| Hugh Wildinge fi Henrie ... ... ... ... ... | 17 | " |
| Gabrell Butler fi Tho: ... ... ... ... ... ... | 20 | " |
| Symond Westhead fi Ric ... ... ... ... ... ... | 22 | " |
| Marget Morecrofte fi Ric bast ... ... ... ... | " | " |
| Jaine Holland fi Rob ... ... ... ... ... ... | 23 | " |
| Hugh Lathom fi Henrie ... ... ... ... ... | 3 | December |
| Alis Barton fi Gowther ... ... ... ... ... ... | 6 | " |
| John Prekot fi Tho: ... ... ... ... ... ... | " | " |
| Emlin Barton fi John ... ... ... ... ... ... | 8 | " |
| Edward Lathwhat fi Henrie ... ... ... ... ... | 10 | " |
| Katherin Haughton fi Omfrey ... ... ... ... ... | 11 | " |
| Katherin Barker fi: Hen: ... ... ... ... ... | 17 | " |
| Eliz[th] Spencer fi Tho: ... ... ... ... ... ... | 18 | " |
| Allexander Lee fi Ri: ... ... ... ... ... ... | 24 | " |
| Wittm Preskot fi Tho: ... ... ... ... ... ... | " | " |
| Anne Cropp fi Raffe ... ... ... ... ... ... | 25 | " |
| Ellin Ellam fi Raffe ... ... ... ... ... ... | 2 | Januarie |
| Eliz[th] Coockeson fi Silvester ... ... ... ... ... | 3 | " |
| Marget Hey fi Tho: ... ... ... ... ... ... | 5 | " |
| Alis Wignall fi Wittm ... ... ... ... ... ... | 8 | " |
| Anne Killshaw fi John ... ... ... ... ... ... | 25 | " |
| Tho: ffletcher fi Ric ... ... ... ... ... ... | 5 | ffebruarie |
| Tho: Weardon fi Tho: ... ... ... ... ... ... | 6 | " |
| John Plumbe fi Edw: ... ... ... ... ... ... | 19 | " |
| Cuthbart Chadocke fi Adam ... ... ... ... ... | " | " |
| Marie Longley fi Wittm ... ... ... ... ... ... | 20 | " |
| Jaine Barnes fi Ric ... ... ... ... ... ... | 5 | Marche |
| Jane Swifte fi Witt ... ... ... ... ... ... | 9 | " |
| Ellene Blackeledge fi Rob ... ... ... ... ... | 10 | " |
| Jamis Roase fi Raffe ... ... ... ... ... ... | 11 | " |
| Ann Aspinwall fi: Tho: ... ... ... ... ... ... | 15 | " |
| Tho: Hoolme fi Edw: ... ... ... ... ... ... | 16 | " |
| Tho: Hunt fi John ... ... ... ... ... ... | 22 | " |

## 1595.

| | | |
|---|---|---|
| John Skinner fi Tho: ... ... ... ... ... ... | 28 | Marche |
| Eliz[th] Cubon fi Rob ... ... ... ... ... ... | 31 | " |
| Margret Withington fi Raphe ... ... ... ... ... | 4 | Aprill |
| Margret Leae fi Wittm bast ... ... ... ... ... | 6 | " |
| Anne Hill fi Wittm ... ... ... ... ... ... | 7 | " |
| Genett Cropp fi: Peet ... ... ... ... ... ... | " | " |
| Eline Croston fi: Hen: ... ... ... ... ... ... | 12 | " |
| Edw: Parker fi: Tho: ... ... ... ... ... ... | 13 | " |
| Alis Barton fi Wittm ... ... ... ... ... ... | " | " |
| Edw: Smithe fi: Tho: ... ... ... ... ... ... | 28 | " |
| Jane Modisley fi: George bast ... ... ... ... | 30 | " |
| Robt Taylor fi: Hen: ... ... ... ... ... ... | 12 | Maye |

Anne Balshawe fi: Jo: ... ... ... ... ... ... 23 Maye
Margret Stanley fi: Edw: Junior gent ... ... 29 „
Anthony Chadoke fi: Hugh ... ... ... ... ... „ „
Hughe Barton fi: Adam ... ... ... ... ... ... 30 „
Robt Sutche fi Jo: ... ... ... ... ... ... ... 11 June
Jayne Aspinwall fi: Edw: ... ... ... ... ... 14 „
Symond Ince fi Hamlet bast ... ... ... ... ... 16 „
Henrie A Stranger ... ... ... ... ... ... ... 20 „
Tho: Haughton fi Georg ... ... ... ... ... 24 „
Alis Butler fi: Jo: ... ... ... ... ... ... ... 27 „
ffrances Spencer fi Willm ... ... ... ... ... 2 Julye
Margret Lawranson fi: Anth: ... ... ... ... 15 „
Eline Hyton fi Tho: ... ... ... ... ... ... 24 „
Henrie Hulme fi: Willm ... ... ... ... ... 25 „
Rodger Barton fi Gawth: ... ... ... ... ... 29 „
Dorite Garrard fi Cuth: ... ... ... ... ... ... 1 Auguste
Katherin Alerton fi: Tho: ... ... ... ... ... 4 „
Fo. 92 ffardinando Wadington fi Willm ... ... ... 2 September
James Aspinwall fi Willm ... ... ... ... ... 5 „
James Molinxe fi Willm bast ... ... ... ... ... 15 „
Edw: Halsall fi Tho: gent ... ... ... ... ... 16 „
Marye Barton fi Ja: ... ... ... ... ... ... ... 17 „
Ric̃ Cropp fi Jo: ... ... ... ... ... ... ... 25 „
Katherin Wignall fi: Edw: ... ... ... ... ... „ „
George Webster fi: Brin: ... ... ... ... ... 1 October
Eline fforshwe fi Willm ... ... ... ... ... ... 4 „
A Childe of Rodger Suche ... ... ... ... ... 5 „
John Gobine fi: Hen: ... ... ... ... ... ... „ „
Silvester Lathwhat fi: Willm ... ... ... ... ... 6 „
Willm Dunkon als Sheal fi: Jo: ... ... ... ... „ „
Henrie Vace fi: Ric̃ ... ... ... ... ... ... 7 „
Jane Standishe fi: Hugh ... ... ... ... ... ... 11 „
Elizth Page fi: Cristo ... ... ... ... ... ... 12 „
Anne Yeate fi: ... ... ... ... ... ... ... 15 „
Margerie Kenian fi: Hen: ... ... ... ... ... 16 „
Willm Heskethe fi Ric̃ ... ... ... ... ... ... 31 „
Robte Leae fi Willm ... ... ... ... ... ... 5 November
Tho: Rithrope fi Hamlet ... ... ... ... ... 16 „
Mary Modisley fi Tho: ... ... ... ... ... ... 23 „
Henrie Simkin fi Ric̃ ... ... ... ... ... ... „ „
Elinior ffairclough fi Ric̃ ... ... ... ... ... 25 „
Alis Orton fi: Tho: ... ... ... ... ... ... 26 „
Peeter Morcrofte fi: Tho: ... ... ... ... ... 3 December
Doritie Streyker fi Mich: ... ... ... ... ... 13 „
Eline Morcrofte fi Ric̃ ... ... ... ... ... ... 16 „
John Draninge fi: Char: ... ... ... ... ... 20 „
Alis Lancestere fi Jo: ... ... ... ... ... ... 25 „
Fo. 93 Rodger Sutche fi Georg: ... ... ... ... 3 Januarie
Margerie Barton fi: Hen: ... ... ... ... ... „ „

| | | |
|---|---|---|
| Eline Dobere fi : Wittm ... ... ... ... ... ... | 4 | Januarie |
| Mawde Blundell fi Gilb ... ... ... ... ... ... | 8 | " |
| Robte ffogge fi : Jo: ... ... ... ... ... ... | 10 | " |
| John Rydinge fi : Rodg: ... ... ... ... ... | 18 | " |
| Tho : Blundell fi : Jo: ... ... ... ... ... ... | 25 | " |
| John Hesketh fi : Tho: ... ... ... ... ... ... | 28 | " |
| Elizth Turnere fi : Hnm : ... .. ... ... ... ... | " | " |
| Ewane Swifte fi : Jo: ... ... ... ... ... ... | 29 | " |
| John Harden fi Wittm ... ... ... ... ... ... | 31 | " |
| Rodger Leae fi Ja : ... ... ... ... ... ... ... | 4 | ffebruarie |
| Katherin Lathom fi : Ri : gent de Ecclestone | 14 | " |
| Jenet Hill fi : Ric ... ... ... ... ... ... ... | 16 | " |
| Katherin Alkare fi : Ja : ... ... ... ... ... ... | " | " |
| Cislie Mulinxe fi : Tho : ... ... ... ... ... ... | 9 | Marche |
| Richard Werall fi : Ric ... ... ... ... ... ... | 13 | " |
| Margret Lathom fi : Ric ... ... ... ... ... ... | 16 | " |
| Elizth Barton fi : Ja :... ... ... ... ... ... ... | " | " |
| Tho : Bounde fi : Lawr: ... ... ... ... ... | 21 | " |

## 1596.

| | | |
|---|---|---|
| Cuthberte Gathe fi : Jo: ... ... ... ... ... ... | 25 | Marche |
| Gabriell Holden fi : Jo: ... ... ... ... ... ... | 27 | " |
| Alis Vace fi : Hughe bast ... ... ... ... | 29 | " |
| Anne Walche fi : Gilb ... ... ... ... ... ... | 7 | Aprill |
| Margrete Golbrone fi : Hom : ... ... ... ... | 15 | " |
| Anne Hill fi : Richard ... ... ... ... ... ... | 28 | " |
| Ric Westhed fi : Tho : ... ... ... ... ... ... | 1 | Maye |
| Sislie Waringe fi : Ja: ... ... ... ... ... ... | 5 | " |
| Ric ffletcher fi : Hughe ... ... ... ... ... ... | 8 | " |
| Wittm Swifte fi : Nicolas ... ... ... ... ... ... | 11 | " |
| Anne Craine fi : Edw: ... ... ... ... ... ... | 13 | " |
| Tho : ffarington fi : Tho : gnt ... ... ... | 16 | " |
| Claris Blundell fi : Ja : ... ... ... ... ... ... | 21 | " |
| Eline Blundell fi : Ja: ... ... ... ... ... ... | 28 | " |
| Wittm Lowe fi : Jo: ... ... ... ... ... ... | 29 | " |
| Milis Mudisley fi : Robt ... ... ... ... ... ... | " | " |
| Jane Woosey fi : Crstr : ... ... ... ... ... ... | 30 | " |
| Margery Robinson fi : Wittm ... ... ... ... | 7 | June |
| Marey Heye fi : Tho: ... ... ... ... ... ... | 8 | " |
| Christophere Cropp fi : Raph ... ... .. ... | 10 | " |
| Jane Wollen fi : Edw: ... ... ... ... ... ... | 12 | " |
| Margreat Hoolme fi : Philip ... ... ... ... | 14 | " |
| Margery ffrithe fi : Gilb ... ... ... ... ... ... | 15 | " |
| Wittm Brechell fi : Wittm ... ... ... ... ... | 22 | " |
| John Shepard fi : Hen : bast ... ... ... ... | 28 | " |
| Ric Ascrofte fi : Hugh ... ... ... ... ... | 1 | Julye |
| Anne Marson fi : Robt ... ... ... ... ... ... | 6 | " |
| Claris Kewquicke fi : Robt ... ... ... ... ... | 22 | " |

Cristopher Greaves fi: Hom: ... ... ... 22 Julye
Edw: Mason fi: James bast ... ... ... ... 27 „
Robt Woodes fi: Willm ... ... ... ... ... 1 Auguste
Jane Westhed fi: David ... ... ... ... ... 6 „
Alixander Barker fi: Hen: ... ... ... ... 7 „
Tho: Sutche fi: Jo: ... ... ... ... ... 10 „
Margerie Wainwright fi: Sy: ... ... ... ... „ „
George Cadicke fi: Rob ... ... ... ... ... 11 „
Symon Martindaill fi: Hen: ... ... ... ... 24 „
Marget Halsall fi: Ri ... ... ... ... ... ... 27 „
Fo. 95 Anne Ince fi Hamlet bast ... ... ... ... 3 September
Eliz[th] Ormishaw fi: Ric bast ... ... ... ... 4 „
Ellin Rutter fi John ... ... ... ... ... ... 7 „
Anne Hoolme fi Will ... ... ... ... ... ... 9 „
Marget Butler fi: Tho: ... ... ... ... ... 18 „
Katherin Waterworth fi Will bast ... ... ... „ „
Marget Aiscough fi: John ... ... ... ... ... 27 „
Robert Charles fi Peeter ... ... ... ... ... „ „
Tho: Sharrocke fi John ... ... ... ... ... 30 „
John Coockeson fi Jamis ... ... ... ... ... 1 October
Anne Irland fi Jo: ... ... ... ... ... ... ... 2 „
Tho: Sutch fi Rodger ... ... ... ... ... 4 „
Richard Gleaste fi: Ellise ... ... ... ... ... 5 „
Edw: Blackeledge fi Ewan ... ... ... ... ... 7 „
John Clapam fi: Ric ... ... ... ... ... ... 9 „
Hugh Cropp fi: George ... ... ... ... ... 10 „
Catherin Kocket fi: Bryhan bast ... ... ... 12 „
Anne Powsey fi: Ric ... ... ... ... ... ... 13 „
Alis Wildinge fi Will ... ... ... ... ... ... 18 „
Izabell Swifte fi Ric ... ... ... ... ... ... 21 „
Tho: Hoolme fi Tho: ... ... ... ... ... ... „ „
Anne Martindaile fi Hugh ... ... ... ... ... 24 „
Gabrell Gill fi Gilb ... ... ... ... ... ... 30 „
Jamis Hunte fi: Abraham ... ... ... ... ... 5 November
Willm Sutch fi Jam: ... ... ... ... ... ... 8 „
Eideth Cropp fi: Peeter ... ... ... ... ... 14 „
Alis Coockesonn fi: Ric ... ... ... ... ... 17 „
Silvester Shaw fi: Will ... ... ... ... ... 19 „
Richard Thomson fi Will ... ... ... ... ... „ „
Gabirell Ormishaw fi: John ... ... ... ... 23 „
Jaine Harison fi: Tho: ... ... ... ... ... 2 December
Tho: Gill fi: Ric ... ... ... ... ... ... 6 „
Henrie Waynewright fi Hugh ... ... ... ... „ „
Claris Westhead fi Rod ... ... ... ... ... 10 „
Richard Mason fi: Tho: ... ... ... ... ... 16 „
Eliz[th] Bycarstaffe fi Jo: ... ... ... ... ... 21 „
Fo. 96 Peeter Barton fi Rob ... ... ... ... ... ... 26 „
Willm Morecrofte fi Ric ... ... ... ... ... „ „
Ellin Beykell fi: Henrie ... ... ... ... ... 28 „

| | | |
|---|---|---|
| Marget Killshaw fi Gilb̄ ... ... ... ... ... ... | 9 | Januarie |
| Dorethie Lathom fi Hen: ... ... ... ... ... | 12 | " |
| Tho: Peeter fi: John ... ... ... ... ... ... | 16 | " |
| Jamis Spencer fi: Edw: ... ... ... ... ... ... | 17 | " |
| Gilbert Sefton fi Thomas ... ... ... ... ... | 18 | " |
| George Lathwhat fi: Hen ... ... ... ... ... | 21 | " |
| Henrie Barton fi: Gilb̄ ... ... ... ... ... ... | 22 | " |
| Catherin Irland fi: Ric̃ ... ... ... ... ... ... | 23 | " |
| Ric̃ et Ric̃ Carr fi: Edm: ... ... ... ... ... | 24 | " |
| Marget Hesketh fi Gabriell gẽt ... ... ... | 27 | " |
| Symond Smyth fi: Tho: ... ... ... ... ... ... | 8 | ffebruarie |
| Henrie Harison fi: Omfrey ... ... ... ... ... | 16 | " |
| Trymor Haighton fi: Omfrey ... ... ... ... ... | 18 | " |
| Henrie Aiscrofte fi: Silvester ... ... ... ... ... | 22 | " |
| Ric̃ Lytham fi: Edw: ... ... ... ... ... ... | 24 | " |
| Eliz^th Ambrose fi: Ric̃: ... ... ... ... ... ... | 2 | March |
| Tho: Webster fi: Hen: ... ... ... ... ... ... | 6 | " |
| Margerie Woosey fi: Gaw: ... ... ... ... ... | 8 | " |
| Marie Lathom fi: Ric̃ ... ... ... ... ... ... | " | " |
| Dorethie Lathwhat fi: Ja: ... ... ... ... ... | 10 | " |
| Eliz^th Cowdocke fi: Wiłł... ... ... ... ... ... | 13 | " |
| Tho: Cropp fi: Hugh ... ... ... ... ... ... | " | " |
| Jamis Chadocke fi Adame ... ... ... ... ... | 22 | " |
| Henrie Barton fi: Jo: ... ... ... ... ... ... | 24 | " |
| Marie Haughton fi: Ric̃ ... ... ... ... ... ... | " | " |
| Sislie Cropp fi . . . bast... ... ... ... ... | " | " |

[*In the Original the entries for the month of May follow on here but in the Transcript they are inserted in the proper place.*]

## 1597.

| | | |
|---|---|---|
| Margaret Preskot fi Jo: ... ... ... ... ... | 3 | Apriłł |
| Henrie Bebot fi: Tho: ... ... ... ... ... ... | 5 | " |
| Anne Aiscroft fi Jo: ... ... ... ... ... ... | 8 | " |
| Katherin Killshaw fi: Hector ... ... ... ... ... | 9 | " |
| Richard Keckwicke fi: Wiłł ... ... ... ... ... | 13 | " |
| Tho: Holland fi John ... ... ... ... ... ... | 15 | " |
| Jaine Lathwhat fi Rob̄ bast ... ... ... ... ... | 25 | " |
| Jaine Ascough fi: Tho: ... ... ... ... ... | 5 | Maie * |
| Ann Mowdisley fi Symon ... ... ... ... ... | 6 | " |
| Lettis Clarke fi: Edw: ... ... ... ... ... ... | 19 | " |
| Jamis Stopforth fi Hen: ... ... ... ... ... | 25 | " |
| Ric̃ ffidler fi: Tho: ... ... ... ... ... ... ... | 12 | June |
| Marie Ryylanes fi Tho: ... ... ... ... ... ... | 26 | " |
| James Banester fi: Nico ... ... ... ... ... ... | 7 | July |

* The entries for this month will be found at the bottom of page 96 of the Original.

| | | | |
|---|---|---|---|
| | Edw: Simkin fi: Ric̃ | 9 | July |
| | James Smithe fi: Gilb̃t | 10 | „ |
| | George ffrithe fi: Hugh | 16 | „ |
| | Margerie Easthead fi Jo: | 21 | „ |
| | Doretie Lea fi: Euan | 23 | „ |
| | Anne Stanley fi: Edw: Esquire | „ | „ |
| | Jane Haskeyne fi: Rodger | 28 | „ |
| | Jonye Skinner fi: Tho: | 23 | Auguste |
| | Jaine Rosse fi Rauph | 27 | „ |
| | Margreat Lathwhat fi: Rob̃t | 4 | September |
| | Margreat Balshawe fi: Tho: | 6 | „ |
| | John Kilshawe fi Edw: | 8 | „ |
| | Peeter Blundell fi Ja: | 16 | „ |
| | Marie Morecrofte fi ... | 21 | „ |
| | John Ambrose fi: Tho: | 28 | „ |
| | Rob̃t Hunter fi Tho: | 29 | „ |
| | Katherin Hunte fi Jo: | 2 | October |
| | Jaine Croston fi: Tho: | 9 | „ |
| | Ric̃ Lighe fi: Ric̃ | „ | „ |
| | Elline Sankie fi: Ric̃ | 22 | „ |
| | Henrie Windrowe fi Ric̃ | 24 | „ |
| | Edw: Morcrofte fi Tho: | 25 | „ |
| Fo. 98 | Anne Traves fi: Tho: | 13 | November |
| | Alis Whytehead fi Hen: | 3 | December |
| | Jaine Killshaw fi Allen | 9 | „ |
| | Marie Sumner fi Willm | 10 | „ |
| | Sislie Smyth fi Tho: | 13 | „ |
| | Ric̃ Sumner fi: Edw: | 15 | „ |
| | Marget Leadbetter fi: Peeter | „ | „ |
| | Marie Sheparde fi: Henrie bast | 3 | Januarie |
| | Marget Coockeson fi: Silvester | 9 | „ |
| | Jenet Westhead fi: Tho: | 15 | „ |
| | Jenet Halsall fi: Rob̃ | 16 | „ |
| | Hugh Gleaste fi: Elice | 8 | ffebruarie |
| | John Hill fi Will | 11 | „ |
| | Eliz[th] Westhead fi David | 15 | „ |
| | Emllin Woodes fi Ric: | 19 | „ |
| | George fforshaw fi Will | 4 | Marche |
| | Hugh Irland fi: John bast | 17 | „ |
| | Jamis ffogge fi John | 23 | „ |

## 1598.

| | | |
|---|---|---|
| George Preskot fi Tho: | 28 | Marche |
| Jamis Gleaste fi Ric̃ | 31 | „ |
| Willm Barton fi Gilb̃ | 11 | Aprill |
| Henrie Clapam fi Rodger | 18 | „ |
| Thurstan Barton fi: Gowther | 11 | Maye |
| Jaine Ambrose fi John | 18 | „ |

| | | |
|---|---|---|
| John Barton fi: Tho: ... ... ... ... ... | 27 | Maye |
| Alis Cropp fi George ... ... ... ... ... | 7 | June |
| Richard Rithrope fi Hamlet ... ... ... ... | 10 | " |
| Willm Mowdisley fi Ector ... ... ... ... | 3 | Julye |
| Richard Aiscrofte fi: Silvester ... ... ... | 8 | " |
| Jamis Wildinge fi Henrie ... ... ... ... ... | 16 | " |
| Robert Lathwhat fi Will ... ... ... ... ... | 1 | Auguste |
| Edward Barton fi Arthor ... ... ... ... ... | 2 | " |
| Susanna Cumbarbatch fi Ric ... ... ... ... | 6 | " |
| Alis Spencer fi Peeter ... ... ... ... ... | 13 | " |
| Edmund Aspinwall fi Will ... ... ... ... | 15 | " |
| Ellin Keckwicke fi Hugh ... ... ... ... | 17 | " |
| Margaret Sutch fi George ... ... ... ... | 20 | " |
| Robart Allerton fi Tho: ... ... ... ... ... | " | " |
| Ric Walne fi Hen: ... ... ... ... ... ... | 13 | September |
| Tho: Seale fi Jo: ... ... ... ... ... ... | " | " |
| Anne Keckwicke fi Willm ... ... ... ... | 14 | " |
| Moude Molnexe fi Tho ... ... ... ... ... | 18 | " |
| Edw: Worthington fi Hugh ... ... ... ... | 20 | " |
| Anne Barton fi Hen: ... ... ... ... ... | 27 | " |
| George Smith fi Hen: ... ... ... ... ... | 26 | October |
| Raphe Windrowe fi Ric ... ... ... ... ... | 30 | " |
| Peeter Barton fi Hugh ... ... ... ... ... | " | " |
| James Halsall fi Ric ... ... ... ... ... | 2 | November |
| Nicolas ffarmbie fi John ... ... ... ... ... | " | " |
| Thomas Barkere fi Hen ... ... ... ... ... | 4 | " |
| Anne ffletcher fi Tho: ... ... ... ... ... | 7 | " |
| Eliz[th] Morcrofte fi Tho Junior ... ... ... | 12 | " |
| Elline Eashhead fi: Jo: ... ... ... ... ... | " | " |
| Tho: Cowbann fi Robt ... ... ... ... ... | 13 | " |
| Alis Darbie fi John ... ... ... ... ... ... | 19 | " |
| Katherin Blundell fi Ja: ... ... ... ... ... | " | " |
| Izabell Walworthe fi Rodger ... ... ... ... | " | " |
| Anne Waringe fi Cristopher bast ... ... ... | 25 | " |
| Doretye Breckhell fi: Hen: ... ... ... ... | 3 | December |
| . . . Woods fi Willm ... ... ... ... ... | 8 | " |
| John Blundell fi: Hen: ... ... ... ... ... | 9 | " |
| Ric Cropp fi: Hen: baste ... ... ... ... | 11 | " |
| Robt Kenion fi Hen: ... ... ... ... ... | 14 | " |
| ffardinandow Tomson fi Jo ... ... ... ... | 15 | " |
| Tho: Barton fi Willm ... ... ... ... ... | " | " |
| Katherin Blacklidge fi John ... ... ... ... | 16 | " |
| Willm Sefton fi Gilbt ... ... ... ... ... | 9 | Januarie |
| Marie Ascrofte fi: John ... ... ... ... ... | 12 | " |
| Hugh Barton fi James ... ... ... ... ... | 25 | " |
| John Lea fi Rodger ... ... ... ... ... ... | 18 | ffebruarie |
| Gilberte Hoolme fi Edw: ... ... ... ... | 1 | Marche |
| Willm & Tho: Ambrose fi Ellis ... ... ... | 5 | " |
| Roberte Hey fi Tho: ... ... ... ... ... | 6 | " |

Elline Lathwhat fi Jamis ... ... ... ... ... ... 12 Marche
Ric̃ & Anne Ormishawe fi Tho: ... ... ... 13 „
James Greaues fi Tho: ... ... ... ... ... 15 „
John Ascrofte fi Willm ... ... ... ... ... 16 „
Ric̃ Swifte fi Jo: ... ... ... ... ... ... 20 „

## 1599.

Elline Kilshawe fi Gilbt ... ... ... ... ... ... 25 Marche
John Vace fi: Ric̃ ... ... ... ... ... ... 26 „
Margreat Blundell fi Jo: ... ... ... ... ... 3 Aprill
Philipe Ascrofte fi Hugh ... ... ... ... ... 9 „
Jaine Sankie fi Ric̃ ... ... ... ... ... ... 28 „
Fo. 101 Marget Cropp fi Peeter ... ... ... ... ... 1 Maye
Edward Gibson fi Peeter ... ... ... ... ... 6 „
Elline Brecell fi Willm ... ... ... ... ... 9 „
Anne Alker fi: Ja: ... ... ... ... ... „ „
Henrie Prescott fi: Tho: ... ... ... ... 13 „
Tho: Ambrose fi: Ric̃ ... ... ... ... ... 24 „
Marie Ambrose fi: Tho: ... ... ... ... 27 „
Jenet Spencer fi Ja: ... ... ... ... ... 29 „
Margrat Mowdisley fi: Tho: ... ... ... ... 1 June
Jane Sutch fi Rodger ... ... ... ... ... „ „
Peeter Chadoke fi Adam ... ... ... ... ... 14 „
Margreat Gleaste fi Ellis ... ... ... ... ... 15 „
Hugh Cropp fi Ric̃ ... ... ... ... ... ... 18 „
Marie Mason fi: Ja: bast ... ... ... ... 22 „
Anne Clarke fi Edw: ... ... ... ... ... 25 „
Tho: Charles fi: Peeter ... ... ... ... ... 27 „
Elline Atherton fi: Alexander ... ... ... 1 July
Robert Rutter fi Jo: ... ... ... ... ... 11 „
Tho Gerrard fi Cuthbert ... ... ... ... ... 12 „
Tho: Gobin fi Jo: ... ... ... ... ... ... 14 „
Henrie Keuqick fi Robt ... ... ... ... ... 19 „
James Hoolond fi Jo: ... ... ... ... ... 26 „
Margreat Blundell fi Gilbt ... ... ... ... 3 Auguste
Margreat Voce fi Hugh ... ... ... ... ... 4 „
Anne Woosey fi Goouther ... ... ... ... 6 „
Raph Carre fi: Edmund ... ... ... ... ... 8 „
Alis Butler fi Tho: ... ... ... ... ... ... 12 „
Marie ffrithe fi Gilbt ... ... ... ... ... 15 „
Homfray Taylor fi Ric̃ bast ... ... ... ... 16 „
Rodger Walshe fi Gilbt ... ... ... ... ... 17 „
Fo. 102 Tho: Cadicke fi Robt ... ... ... ... ... 19 „
Anne Sutche fi Jo: ... ... ... ... ... ... 22 „
Ric̃ Brighouse fi Willm ... ... ... ... ... 24 „
Rodger Barnet fi Ric̃ bast ... ... ... ... 26 „
. . . Standishe fi Hugh ... ... ... ... 31 „

| | | |
|---|---|---|
| Eliz$^{th}$ Harison fi Tho: | 6 | September |
| Henrie Lathwhat fi Hen: | " | " |
| John Spenser fi Edw: | 16 | " |
| Marie Woodes fi Ric̃ | 21 | " |
| Tho: Butlere fi John | 23 | " |
| Eliz$^{th}$ Lathwhat fi Rodgꝰ | 25 | " |
| Tho: Smyth fi John | 27 | " |
| Ric̃ Woodes fi James | " | " |
| Eline Lea fi Ric̃ | 2 | October |
| John Cropp fi Raph... | 6 | " |
| Doretie Ambrose fi Jo: | " | " |
| Cristopher Bleswicke fi Raph | 8 | " |
| Margerat Chadoke fi Ja: | 12 | " |
| Jane Barton fi John | 21 | " |
| Eliz$^{th}$ Stanley fi Edw Esquire | 25 | " |
| Jaine Barton fi: Tho: | 4 | November |
| Henrie Jolie fi: Tho: | 11 | " |
| John Morcrofte fi Tho: | 17 | " |
| Tho: Haughton fi: Hom: | 20 | " |
| Alis Pinington fi Hom | " | " |
| Jamis Parker fi Tho: | 28 | " |
| John Easthead fi Jo: | 29 | " |
| Henrie Barton fi: Ja: | 30 | " |
| Alis Hoolme fi Wiłłm | 6 | December |
| Henrie Morcrofte fi Ric̃ | 9 | " |
| Margreat Halsall fi Edw: | 10 | " |
| ffrances Waringe fi Cristo: | 20 | " |
| Ric̃ ffletcher fi Hugonis | 7 | Januarie |
| Marie Lynaker fi Tho: | 8 | " |
| Katherin ffletcher fi Tho: | 10 | " |
| Omfrey Morecrofte fi Edw: | 22 | " |
| Richard Skinner fi Tho: | 23 | " |
| Marie Shawe fi Gabriełł | 26 | " |
| Henrie Ormishaw fi Jo: | 1 | ffebruarie |
| Wiłłm Greaves fi Omfrey | 2 | " |
| Geffrey Clapam fi Ric̃ | 3 | " |
| Jaine Blackeledge fi John | 4 | " |
| Margerie Blundell fi Hen: | " | " |
| Alis Cropp fi George | 6 | " |
| Anne Aspinwall fi Peeter | 7 | " |
| Mowde Waringe fi Henrie | 10 | " |
| Richard Ireland fi Jo: bast | 2 | March |
| John Holliwell fi Tho: bast | 4 | " |
| Robart Lowe fi John | 9 | " |
| Jaine Stryker fi Myhell | 18 | " |
| Ric Westhead fi Tho: | 22 | " |
| Robart Killshaw fi: Allen | 23 | " |
| Hugh Barton fi: Gowther | 24 | " |

## 1600.

Andrew Barton fi Witl bast ... ... ... ... 26 March
Henry Woodes fi Ric ... ... ... ... ... 3 Aprill
Marget Anglesdaile fi: John ... ... ... ... 13 „
Hugh Spencer fi Peeter ... ... ... ... ... „ „
Marget Gill fi: Ric ... ... ... ... ... 25 „
. . . Coockeson fi Silvester ... ... ... 29 „
Jamis Yate fi: Tho: ... ... ... ... ... 3 Maye
Gilb Westhead fi Rodg: ... ... ... ... ... 9 „
Richard Poole fi Raffe ... ... ... ... ... 14 „
Tho Westhead fi Davie ... ... ... ... ... 18 „
ffardinandow Haughton fi: Ric ... ... ... 24 „
Fo. 104 Witlm Ascough fi: Tho: ... ... ... ... 3 June
Ellin Swifte fi Phillip ... ... ... ... ... 8 „
Marget Traves fi: John bast ... ... ... ... 12 „
Hugh Lathwhat fi Witl ... ... ... ... ... 18 „
Tho: Sutton fi: Rob ... ... ... ... ... 25 „
Witlm Cropp fi Hugh ... ... ... ... ... 1 July
Emlin Dunkon fi: John ... ... ... ... ... 2 „
Edmund Dalton fi Tho: ... ... ... ... 4 „
Katherin Stopforth fi Hen: ... ... ... ... 6 „
Tho: ffrith ... ... ... ... ... ... ... 7 „
Marget Darbie fi: John ... ... ... ... ... 11 „
Tho: Rigbie fi John ... ... ... ... ... 2 Auguste
Marie Hoolme fi Ric ... ... ... ... ... 8 „
Gilbart Asshurste fi Edward bast ... ... ... 10 „
Tho: Ormishaw fi Tho: bast ... ... ... ... 24 „
Ric Houlte fi Hugh bast ... ... ... ... ... 27 „
Henrie Smyth fi: Tho: ... ... ... ... ... 14 September
Tho: Gleaste fi Elis ... ... ... ... ... 21 „
John Sumner fi Edward ... ... ... ... ... 22 „
Witlm Wildinge fi: Hen: ... ... ... ... 30 „
Marget Ince fi Hamlet ... ... ... ... ... „ „
Jaine Voce fi Hugh ... ... ... ... ... 4 October
Edw: Windrow fi Ric ... ... ... ... ... 10 „
Katherin Ascough fi: John ... ... ... ... 19 „
Henrye Withingeton fi Witl ... ... ... ... 27 „
Katherin Tomson fi John ... ... ... ... 1 November
John Clapam fi Rodg: ... ... ... ... ... 13 „
Izabell Gill fi: Ric ... ... ... ... ... 27 „
Julian Hesketh fi: Gabriell gēt ... ... ... 28 „
Margerie Coockeson fi Tho: ... ... ... ... „ „
Marie Lidya fi: Tho: bast ... ... ... ... 29 „
Marget Webster fi: Henrie ... ... ... ... 30 „
Jaine Lea fi: Rodger ... ... ... ... ... 10 December
Katherin Blagden fi: John ... ... ... ... 12 „
Ellin Houghton fi: Richard ... ... ... ... 15 „

| | | | |
|---|---|---|---|
| | Anne Huton fi: Ric̃ | 17 | December |
| 105 | Anne Whytestones fi: Ric̃ bast | 24 | " |
| | Anne Shawe fill George | 3 | Januarie |
| | Margaret Morecrofte fi: Tho: | 6 | " |
| | Willm Atherton fi Tho: de Aughton | 10 | " |
| | Ric̃ Waringe fi Robert | 16 | " |
| | Katherin Lea fi: Ewan | 22 | " |
| | Marie Brigehowse fi Tho: | 26 | " |
| | Tho: Aspinwall fi: Willm | 29 | " |
| | Gilbert Sumner fi Will | 8 | ffebruarie |
| | Katherin Hulme fi: Tho: | 9 | " |
| | Anne Blackeledge fi Ewan | 13 | " |
| sp: | Katherin Whytestones fi: George bast | " | " |
| | Elin Sutch fi George | 15 | " |
| | Izabell Harber fi: John | 16 | " |
| sp: | Anne Hey fi: John bast | 22 | " |
| | Elizabeth Halsall fi: Ric̃ | 25 | " |
| | Anne Chadocke fi: Jamis | 4 | Martch |
| | Ric̃ Mercer fi: Robert | 8 | " |
| | Margaret Leee [*sic*] fi Richard | " | " |
| | Edw: Cowbron fi: Robert | 10 | " |
| | Henrie Cropp fi Raffe | 13 | " |
| | Gilbert Ambrosse fi: Tho: | 22 | " |

## 1601.

| | | | |
|---|---|---|---|
| | Myles and Robert Lathwhat fi: Henrie | 1 | Aprill |
| | Izabell Barton fi Henrie | " | " |
| | Elizabeth fforshaw fi Will | 7 | " |
| | Hugh Smyth fi: John | 10 | " |
| | Elnor Walworth fi: Rodger | 14 | " |
| | ffrances Stanley fi: Edw: Stanley of Bycarstaffe Esq[r] | " | " |
| | Willm Morecrofte fi: Edw: | " | " |
| | Edw: Stanley fi: M[r] Henrie | 19 | " |
| | Anne Molinex fi: Tho: | 25 | " |
| 106 | John Barton fi: Henrie | 11 | Maye |
| | Willm Waringe fi Gilbert | 16 | " |
| | Elizabeth ffletcher fi: Tho: | " | " |
| | Katherin Sutch fi Jamis | 17 | " |
| | Jamis Blundell fi: Edw: | 3 | June |
| | John Haughton fi: George | 8 | " |
| | Rodger Sankey fi: Ric̃ | 21 | " |
| | Margaret ffletcher fi: Hughe | " | " |
| | Dorethie Mawdisley fi: Tho: | 23 | " |
| | Marie Cropp fi George | 26 | " |
| | Jayne Morecrofte fi: Gabrell | 29 | " |
| | Alis Killshawe fi: Edw: : | 2 | July |
| | Peeter Barton fi: Hugh | " | " |

Edward Briscow fi: Willm ... ... ... ... 4 July
Ellin Toppinge fi: Omfrey ... ... ... ... 8 „
Ellin Robinson fi Willm ... ... ... ... ... „ „
Margaret Rimer fi Hugh bast ... ... ... ... 28 „
Tho: Killshaw fi: Gilbert ... ... ... ... 7 Auguste
Margaret Mason fi: Arthor ... ... ... ... 8 „
Anne Smyth fi Henrie ... ... ... ... ... 11 „
Margaret Haughton fi: Jamis ... ... ... ... 13 „
Jaine Mawdisley fi: Ector ... ... ... ... 21 „
Elin Davie fi Johnie ... ... ... ... ... 25 „
. . . Cocket fi: Robert ... ... ... ... 2 September
Susanna Dutton fi: Tho: ... ... ... ... 4 „
Willm Parre fi: Edw: de Rainforth ... ... 24 „
Tho: Windrow fi: Richard ... ... ... ... 29 „
Henrie Clarke fi: Edw: ... ... ... ... ... 3 October
Ellin Barker fi: Henrie ... ... ... ... ... 4 „
Cuatherin Morecroft fi: Ric̃ ... ... ... ... 4 „
Marie Ambrose fi George ... ... ... ... 13 „
John Poole fi: Raffe ... ... ... ... ... 14 „
Willm Hankin fi Jamis ... ... ... ... ... 22 „
Jaine Cropp fi: ffardinand ... ... ... ... 25 „
Fo. 107 John Longley fi: Tho: ... ... ... ... ... 28 „
Edw: Hoolme fi: Tho: ... ... ... ... ... 29 „
Gilbert Blundell fi: Jamis ... ... ... ... 31 „
Margaret Hunter fi: Tho: ... ... ... ... 1 Nouember
Ric̃ Hunter fi: Cristopher ... ... ... ... 2 „
sp: Jamis Bowker fi: Will ... ... ... ... ... 4 „
Marie and Margaret Lawranson fi: Tho: ... 6 „
Marie Brigehowse fi Will ... ... ... ... 11 „
Tho: Sutch fi: Silvester ... ... ... ... 13 „
Jamis Mawdisley fi: Robert ... ... ... ... 19 „
George Scasbrec̃ fi Jamis ... ... ... ... 23 „
Ric̃ Alker fi: Jamis ... ... ... ... ... 24 „
Jamis Hesketh fi: Edw: ... ... ... ... 25 „
sp: Gilbert Leae fi: Willm ... ... ... ... ... 28 „
Pawle fferris fi: Rowland ... ... ... ... 6 December
Richard Waringe fi: Cristopher ... ... ... 8 „
Dorethie Stanley fi: Willm ... ... ... ... 10 „
Lewes Holland fi: Robert ... ... ... ... „ „
Jamis Aiscroft fi: Jamis ... ... ... ... ... 14 „
Hugh Swifte fi: John ... ... ... ... ... 16 „
John ffornbey fi: John ... ... ... ... ... 19 „
Margaret Blundell fi Jamis ... ... ... ... 20 „
Richard Wood fi: Ric̃ ... ... ... ... ... 21 „
Jamis Towne fi: Robert ... ... ... ... ... 27 „
Catherin Scarsbrecke fi: ffardinand ... ... 17 Januarie
Ewann Swifte fi: Jamis ... ... ... ... ... „ „
sp: John Speakeman fi: Ric̃ ... ... ... ... 18 „
Eliz[th] Morcrofte fi: Edw: ... ... ... ... 21 „

Loare Hey fi: Tho: ... ... ... ... ... 24 Januarie
Margreat Withingeton fi: Robert ... ... ... 4 ffebruarie
Emlin Hodgekinson fi: Rodger ... ... ... 7 "
Willm Gollie fi: Tho: ... ... ... ... ... ... 13 "
Silvester Cadicke fi: Robert ... ... ... ... " "
Robert Gill fi: Ric ... ... ... ... ... ... 14 "
Tho: Ambrose fi: John ... ... ... ... ... 3 Martch
Elizabeth Lathwhat fi: Jamis ... ... ... 6 "
Elizabeth Killshawe fi: Willm ... ... ... 7 "
Alis Hesketh fi: Mr Gabriell ... ... ... ... 8 "
. . . Barton fi: John ... ... ... ... 9 "
Grace Sowthwork fi: Willm ... ... ... ... 19 "

## 1602.

Ellin Woosey fi: Gowther ... ... ... ... 2 Aprill
Anne Simkin fi: Ric ... ... ... ... ... 3 "
Homfrey Greaves fi: Tho: ... ... ... ... " "
Margaret Gerrerd fi: Robert ... ... ... ... 9 "
Marierie Hayton fi: Ric ... ... ... ... ... 15 "
Anne Gleast fi: Elice ... ... ... ... ... 20 "
John Hoolme fi: Willm ... ... ... ... ... 22 "
Jayne Awtie fi: Tho: de Croston ... ... ... 25 "
Gabrell Thornow fi: Tho: ... ... ... ... 2 Maye
John Barton fi: Henrie ... ... ... ... ... " "
Ellin Yate fi: Tho: ... ... ... ... ... 3 "
Richard & Thomas Barton fi: Tho: ... ... 5 "
Ellin Sefton fi: Edmunde ... ... ... ... 9 "
Tho: Bankes fi: Edw: ... ... ... ... ... 16 "
Richard Jackeson fi: Ric ... ... ... ... 24 "
Ellin Lathwhat fi: Henrie ... ... ... ... " "
Elizabeth Halsall fi: Edw: ... ... ... ... 6 June
Hamlet Dayle fi: Willm ... ... ... ... 16 "
Henrie Kennion fi: George ... ... ... ... " "
Marie Bankes fi: Edw: ... ... ... ... ... 28 "
Margaret Charles fi: Peeter ... ... ... ... 29 "
Marie Sefton fi: . . . ... ... ... ... 4 July
Ellin Haughton fi: Omfrey ... ... ... ... 11 "
Tho: ffogge fi: John ... ... ... ... ... 24 "
Ellin Turner fi: Omfrey ... ... ... ... 25 "
John Carre fi Edmund ... ... ... ... ... 6 August
Jamis Cowp fi: Ric: ... ... ... ... ... 8 "
Jayne Sutton fi: Robert ... ... ... ... 10 "
Anne Henrieson fi: Tho: ... ... ... ... 12 "
Willm Lathwhat fi: Willm ... ... ... ... " "
Cuthbert Weltch fi: Gilbert ... ... ... ... 15 "
Gabrell Lunt fi: Robert ... ... ... ... 28 "
Thomas Swifte fi: Phillipe ... ... ... ... 12 September
Margaret Heye fi: Nicolas ... ... ... ... 14 "

| | | | |
|---|---|---|---|
| sp: | Emie Shawe fi: Tho: | 14 | September |
| | Hugh Medowes fi: Tho: | 21 | „ |
| | Jenet Blessinge fi: Raffe | 23 | „ |
| | Omfrey Alerton fi Tho: | 2 | October |
| | Alis Windrowe fi: Richard | 10 | „ |
| | Catherin Westhead fi: Rodger | 21 | „ |
| | Gilbert & Elizabeth Gill fi: Ric̃ | 29 | „ |
| sp | Alis Mollinex fi: John | 7 | November |
| | Hugh Rainforth fi Jamis | 11 | „ |
| | Willm Aspinwall fi: Peeter | „ | „ |
| | Edw: Mawdisley fi: Robert | 14 | „ |
| | Anne Mawdisley fi: John | 18 | „ |
| | Anne Lyon fi: George | „ | „ |
| | Ric̃ Killshawe fi: Gilbert | 19 | „ |
| | Elizth Marcer fi: Robert | 9 | December |
| | Elizabeth Blackeledge | 11 | „ |
| sp: | Catherin Sankey fi: Nicolas | 14 | „ |
| | John ffletcher fi: Tho: | 21 | „ |
| sp | Anne Windrow fi Rodger | „ | „ |
| sp | Homfrey Traves fi: Willm | „ | „ |
| | Tho: Garrerd fi: Tho: | 24 | „ |
| | Elizth Mawdisley fi: Ric̃ | „ | „ |
| | Henrie & Catherin Duncon fi: John | 25 | „ |
| | Willm Prescotte fi: Tho: | „ | „ |
| | Ric̃ Lathom fi: Gultheric | 31 | „ |
| | . . . Mason fi: Gowther | 7 | Januarie |
| | Anne Johnson fi: Ric̃ | 8 | „ |
| | Jamis Greaves fi: Homfrey | 26 | „ |
| | Jamis Anglesdaile fi: John | 31 | „ |
| sp | Jaine Higham fi: John | 2 | ffebruarie |
| | Nicolas Morecrofte fi Tho: | „ | „ |
| | Ric̃ Sutch fi: John | 7 | „ |
| | Margaret Coockeson fi: Silvester | 8 | „ |
| | Ric̃ Peeter fi: John | 11 | „ |
| | Robert Spencer fi: Ric̃ | 13 | „ |
| | Tho: Hooton fi: Ric̃ | 15 | „ |
| | Elizth Crayne fi: Robert | 20 | „ |
| | Elizth Woodes fi: Willm | „ | „ |
| Fo. 110 | Martha Smyth fi: Tho | 22 | „ |
| | Tho: Toppinge fi: John | 25 | „ |
| | Margaret Skinner fi: Tho: | 28 | „ |
| | Ric̃ Mawdisley fi: John | 2 | Martch |
| sp: | Griffie Whytestones fi: Ric̃ | 3 | „ |
| | Ellin Scarsbrecke fi: Fardinandow | 5 | „ |
| | Robert Webster fi: Henry | 10 | „ |
| | John Wildinge fi: Henry | 18 | „ |
| | Willm Swifte fi: Jamis | „ | „ |
| | Marie Derbie fi: John | 19 | „ |

## 1603.

Jaine Ollerton fi: Ric̃ ... ... ... ... ... 27 Martch
Ellin Kenion fi: Henry ... ... ... ... ... 30 „
Dorethie Wholey fi: Robert ... ... ... ... 1 Aprill
Claris Stopforth fi: Henry ... ... ... ... „ „
Margaret Morecroft fi: Ric̃ ... ... ... ... 3 „
Jaine Tomson fi: John ... ... ... ... ... „ „
Henrie Haiton fi: John ... ... ... ... ... 5 „
Dorethie Wolworke fi: Rodger ... ... ... 6 „
John Ince fi: Hamlet ... ... ... ... ... 8 „
Margaret Morecroft fi: Gabriell ... ... ... „ „
Jamis Lathom fi: Henry ... ... ... ... ... „ „
Ellin Shawe fi: George ... ... ... ... ... „ „
Edw: Gorsutch fi: Nicolas .. ... ... ... „ „
Sislie Holland [? Hellam] fi: John ... ... 12 „
Ellizth Ambrose fi: Tho:... ... ... ... ... 15 „
Izabel Gleaste fi: Ellis ... ... ... ... ... 20 „
George Blundell fi: Edmund ... ... ... 1 Maye
Margreat Knowles fi: Willm ... ... ... ... 5 „
Ellin Blundell fi: Henry ... ... ... ... ... 8 „
Tho: Ambrose fi: George ... ... ... ... 13 „
Jo: Blundell fi: John ... ... ... ... ... 17 „
Edw: Sumner fi: Edw: ... ... ... ... 19 „
Tho: Nelson fi: Fard: ... ... ... ... ... 24 „
Susan Morecrofte fi: Henry ... ... ... ... 6 June
Omfrey Tomson fi Willm ... ... ... ... 9 „
Nicolas Wilkinson fi: John ... ... ... ... 16 „
Tho: Hankin fi: Willm ... ... ... ... 20 „
Henry Mawdisley fi: Tho: ... ... ... ... 2 July
Alis Sutch fi: Willm ... ... ... ... ... 10 „
Jamis Asley fi: Tho: ... ... ... ... ... 13 „
Henry Heddringeton fi: Jhne ... ... ... ... 19 „
III Tho: fforshawe fi: Willm ... ... ... ... 7 Auguste
sp: Alis Sumner fi: Gilbert ... ... ... ... „ „
Marie Sutch fi: George ... ... ... ... ... 12 „
Marie Toppinge fi: Omfrey ... ... ... ... 16 „
Howcroft Doughtie fi: Micall ... ... ... 4 September
Ellin Asmall fi: Peeter ... ... ... ... ... 8 „
Raffe Woodcocke fi: Jhon ... ... ... ... 11 „
Marie Layland fi: Tho: ... ... ... ... ... 13 „
Ellin Cropp fi: ffardinand ... ... ... ... 17 „
Hugh Morecrofte fi: Edw: ... ... ... ... 21 „
Elizabeth Sutch fi: Rodger ... ... ... ... 23 „
sp: Johne Lea fi: Ewan ... ... ... ... ... 1 October
Elizabeth Rigbie fi: Tho: ... ... ... ... 5 „
sp: Thomas Mawdisley fi: Tho: ... ... ... ... 8 „
sp: Elizabeth Tyrer fi: Jamis ... ... ... ... 14 „

Thomas Brighowse fi: Wilt ... ... ... ... 16 October
Elizabeth Woosey fi: Hugh ... ... ... ... 20 „
Tho: Morecrofte fi: Richard ... ... ... 21 „
Anne Sutch fi: Silvester ... ... ... ... ... „ „
Ellin Hill fi: Willm ... ... ... ... ... 24 „
Hugh Gerrerd fi: Robert ... ... ... ... „ „
Anne Lea fi: Rodger ... ... ... ... ... 25 „
Catherin Chadocke fi: Adam ... ... ... 27 „
Hugh Irelande fi: Ric ... ... ... ... ... 3 Nouember
sp: Willm Sharrocke fi: Willm ... ... ... ... 4 „
Richard Mellinge fi: Tho: ... ... ... ... 9 „
Jaine ffletcher fi: Hugh ... ... ... ... ... 10 „
Jenet Lathwhat fi: Henry ... ... ... ... 23 „
Anne Hoolme fi: Tho: ... ... ... ... ... „ „
John Waringe fi: Cristopher ... ... ... ... 25 „
Richard Hodgekinson fi: Ric ... ... ... 27 „
Anne Sumner fi: Willm ... ... ... ... ... „ „
Anne Kewquicke fi: Willm ... ... ... ... 29 „
Marie Cropp fi: Rodger ... ... ... ... ... 15 December
Thomas Lee fi: Ric ... ... ... ... ... 21 „
Ellin Atherton fi: Tho: ... ... ... ... 24 „
Willm Withingeton fi: Robert ... ... ... 26 „
Cristopher Smyth fi: John ... ... ... ... 28 „
Gilbert Swifte fi: Jamis ... ... ... ... ... „ „
Fo. 112 Katherin Gill fi: Henry ... ... ... ... ... 2 Januarie
Willm Garlecke fi: Myles ... ... ... ... 4 „
Willm Ambrose fi: John ... ... ... ... 13 „
sp: Jaine Penketh fi: Henry ... ... ... ... 17 „
Henry Sefton fi: Edmund ... ... ... ... 19 „
sp: Anne Gerrerd fi: Tho: ... ... ... ... ... 22 „
Robert Smyth fi: Tho: ... ... ... ... ... 29 „
Jaine Haughton fi: Jamis ... ... ... ... „ „
Willm Poole fi: Raffe ... ... ... ... ... „ „
Henry Gobbin fi: John ... ... ... ... ... 7 ffebruarie
Jenet Hunter fi: Cristopher ... ... ... ... 12 „
sp: Jenet Blundell fi: Edw: ... ... ... ... 13 „
Ellen Blackestons fi: Ric of Croston ... ... 16 „
Betrige Whytestones fi: George ... ... ... 19 „
. . . . Blundell fi: Robert ... ... ... ... 21 „
Ellin Morecrofte fi: Cuthbert ... ... ... 24 „
Elizbeth Breykell fi: Wilt ... ... ... ... 25 „
Willm Mason fi: Arthor ... ... ... ... ... 26 „
Anne Ambrose fi: Ric ... ... ... ... ... 29 „
Jamis Ashton fi: John ... ... ... ... ... 1 Martch
Jamis & Rodger Barton fi: Willm ... ... ... 4 „
Anne Willson fi: John ... ... ... ... ... 6 „
Tho: Blackeledge fi: Ewan ... ... ... ... 9 „
Thomas Smulte fi: Robert ... ... ... ... 13 „
Margaret Lathwhat fi: Willm ... ... ... 14 „

George Clapam fi: Rodger ... ... ... ... 21 Martch
Gabriell Derbie fi: John ... ... ... ... 24 „
Wiftm Spencer fi: John ... ... ... ... ... „ „

## 1604.

Marie Ascough fi: Tho: ... ... ... ... 25 Martch
Alis Crayne fi: Wiftm ... ... ... ... ... 5 Aprill
Henry Sefton fi: Ric ... ... ... ... ... 8 „
Katherin Davie fi: John ... ... ... ... ... 15 „
Anne Brigehowse fi: Tho: ... ... ... ... 21 „
Samuwell Kenion fi: Henrie ... ... ... ... 2 Maye
Wiftm Swifte fi: Phillip ... ... ... ... ... 4 „
Ellin Anderton fi: Henry ... ... ... ... 8 „
Edward Cropp fi: Raphe ... ... ... ... 11 „
John Swifte fi: John ... ... ... ... ... „ „
Thomas Kewquicke fi: Edward ... ... ... 12 „
Jamis Aiscrofte fi: John ... ... ... ... ... 20 „
John Waringe fi: Robert ... ... ... ... 21 „
Jaine Worthingeton fi: Hugh ... ... ... 24 „
Jaine Millner fi: Wiftm ... ... ... ... ... 25 „
Homfrey Morecrofte fi: Gabriell ... ... ... „ „
Marie Ambrose fi: Elice ... ... ... ... 26 „
Margaret Whytestones fi: Ric ... ... ... 27 „
Isacke Ambrose fi: Richard ... ... ... ... 29 „
Jamis Lancaster fi: John ... ... ... ... 3 June
Anne Whittle fi: Raphe ... ... ... ... ... „ „
George Wright fi: Rangle ... ... ... ... 10 „
Rodge Barton fi: Richard ... ... ... ... 11 „
Margaret Tomson fi: John ... ... ... ... 12 „
Marie Diconson fi: Edwarde ... ... ... ... „ „
Anne Aspinwall fi: Wiftm ... ... ... ... 18 „
Jamis Stanley fi: Wiftm ... ... ... ... ... 21 „
Emlin Clarke fi: Edw: ... ... ... ... ... „ „
Richard Yate fi: Tho: ... ... ... ... ... 3 July
Margaret Stanley fi: Wiftm ... ... ... ... 4 „
Martha Woosey fi: Gowther ... ... ... ... 5 „
Gabriell Brigehowse fi: Peeter ... ... ... 12 „
Ellin Whylewright fi: Tho: ... ... ... ... 13 „
Wiftm Lunte fi: Robert ... ... ... ... ... 15 „
Izabell Woodes fi: Wiftm ... ... ... ... 16 „
George Woodes fi: Wiftm ... ... ... ... 29 „
Ellin Sunforth fi: Henry ... ... ... ... 3 Auguste
Margery Haso* fi: Tho: ... ... ... ... „ „
Katherin Howton fi: Richard ... ... ... 4 „
Emanuell Morecrofte fi: Henrie ... ... ... 13 „
Margaret Westhead fi: Ric ... ... ... ... 19 „
Rodger Lathwhat fi: Jamis ... ... ... ... 20 „

* Appears to be Hastin in Chester Transcript.

Wiƚƚm Talior fi: Ric̃ ... ... ... ... ... ... 26 Auguste
Gabriell Singleton fi: ffrancis ... ... ... 29 „
Marie Barton fi: John ... ... ... ... ... ... „ „
Margaret Cowp̃ fi: Hugh ... ... ... ... 30 „
Tho: Butler fi: Tho: ... ... ... ... ... 6 September
Henrie Cockeson fi: Wiƚƚm ... ... ... ... 16 „
Peeter Rimmer fi: Hugh ... ... ... ... 23 „
Sislie Brigehowse fi: Wiƚƚm ... ... ... ... 24 „
Fo. 114 Marie Smyth fi: Tho: ... ... ... ... ... 1 October
Hector Mawdisley fi: Rodger ... ... ... 6 „
Wiƚƚm Sheppord fi: Henry of Aughton ... 10 „
Ellin Whittle fi: Ric̃ ... ... ... ... ... ... 13 „
Margaret Asley fi: Tho: ... ... ... ... 16 „
A base Chyld of Henry Penketh ... ... ... 24 „
Edward Croston fi: Edw: ... ... ... ... ... 25 „
Richard Hualsall fi: Edw: ... ... ... ... 30 „
Jaine Stopforth fi: Wiƚƚm ... ... ... ... 4 November
spū Johne Lea fi: Ewan ... ... ... ... ... 5 „
Izabell Waynewright fi: Symond ... ... ... 8 „
Joanie Eccleston fi: John ... ... ... ... ... 17 „
spū Anne Lea fi: Ewan ... ... ... ... ... ... 20 „
Margaret ffletcher fi: Tho: ... ... ... ... 25 „
Elizabeth Barton fi: Tho: ... ... ... ... „ „
Marie Sefton fi: Wiƚƚm ... ... ... ... ... 7 December
Elizabeth Barton fi: Jamis ... ... ... ... 9 „
Ellin Kadicke fi: Robert ... ... ... ... 13 „
Edward Henrieson fi: Tho: ... ... ... ... „ „
Brian & Thomas Traves fi: John ... ... ... 15 „
Robert Woode fi: Richard ... ... ... ... „ „
Marie Johnson fi: Gilbert ... ... ... ... 26 „
Ric̃ Holland fi: Hugh ... ... ... ... ... 27 „
Ector Westhead fi: Edw: ... ... ... ... 29 „
Henry Talior fi: Wiƚƚm ... ... ... ... ... „ „
Tomazon Jollie fi: Tho: ... ... ... ... ... „ „
Edward Peeterson fi: Peeter ... ... ... ... 16 Januarie
Margerie Cropp̃ fi: Tho:... ... ... ... ... ... „ „
Henry Browne Jamis ... ... ... ... ... ... 17 „
Jaine Traves fi: Wiƚƚm ... ... ... ... ... 19 „
Gilbert Sutton fi: Robert ... ... ... ... 20 „
Margaret & Alis Peeter fi: John ... ... ... 21 „
Joanie Orte fi: Omfrey ... ... ... ... ... „ „
Margaret Hankin fi: Wiƚƚm ... ... ... ... 24 „
Jamis ffletcher fi: Hugh ... ... ... ... ... 26 „
Hugh Morecrofte fi: Cuthbert ... ... ... 3 ffebruarie
Anne Goare fi: Ric̃ ... ... ... ... ... ... 7 „
Alis Wholey fi: Robert ... ... ... ... ... 14 „
Alis Allerton fi: Tho: de Laƭ [? Lat] ... ... 17 „
Alis Allerton fi: Ric̃ ... ... ... ... ... ... 20 „
spū Marie Rainforth fi: Peeter ... ... ... ... 27 „

Joaine Holland fi: John ... ... ... ... 28 ffebruarie
Jaine ffrith fi: Gilberte ... ... ... ... ... 2 Martche
Alis Spuner fi: Wittm ... ... ... ... ... ... 3 „
Elizabeth Windrow fi: Ric ... ... ... ... 5 „
Tho: Skinner fi: John ... ... ... ... ... 6 „
Wittm Hey fi: Ric ... ... ... ... ... ... 7 „
Thomas Haughton fi: George ... ... ... „ „
Phillip Skete fi: Ric ... ... ... ... ... 8 „
Rodger Barton fi: Wittm ... ... ... ... 10 „
Loare Haughton fi: Homfrey ... ... ... ... 14 „
Jaine Hoolme fi: Edw: ... ... ... ... 15 „
Marie Morecroft fi: Ric ... ... ... ... ... 16 „
Marie Thorne fi Tho: ... ... ... ... ... „ „
Alis Toppinge fi: Homfrey ... ... ... ... 24 „

## 1605.

Alis Jamis fi: Ric ... ... ... ... ... ... ... 27 Martche
Ellin Blundell fi: Edward ... ... ... ... „ „
Margaret Shawe fi: Gabriell ... ... ... ... 28 „
Raffe Cropp fi: Peeter ... ... ... ... ... ... 1 Aprill
Katherin Smoulte fi: Tho: ... ... ... ... 2 „
Ellin Tyrer fi: Jamis ... ... ... ... ... ... 6 „
Alis Towne fi: Robert ... ... ... ... ... 12 „
Grace Kocket fi: Robert ... ... ... ... 13 „
Wittm Ambrose fi: Thomas ... ... ... ... „ „
Henry Hunter fi: Thomas ... ... ... ... 21 „
Hugh Toppinge fi: John ... ... ... ... 28 „
Richard Ambrose fi: George ... ... ... ... 2 Maye
Marie Halsall fi: Henry ... ... ... ... ... „ „
Peeter Presket fi: Henry ... ... ... ... 9 „
Steven Haughton fi: Richard ... ... ... 10 „
Elizabeth Barton fi: Hugh ... ... ... ... „ „
Marie Lyon fi: Jamis ... ... ... ... ... 12 „
Wittm Kewquicke fi: Robert ... ... ... 15 „
Ellene Gill fi: Richard ... ... ... ... ... 17 „
Anne Mawdisley fi: Henry ... ... ... ... 18 „
Wittm Gibbonson fi: Witt ... ... ... ... 30 „
George Waynewright fi: Ric ... ... ... ... 3 June
Thomas Armestronge fi: John ... ... ... 6 „
Ellen Scarsbrecke fi: Tho: ... ... ... ... 8 „
Richard Tyrer fi: Ric ... ... ... ... ... 9 „
Jamis Willson fi: John ... ... ... ... ... 11 „
Katherin Charles fi: Peeter ... ... ... ... „ „
Dorethie Luskin fi: Sacarie ... ... ... ... 13 „
Alis Mollinex fi: Tho: ... ... ... ... ... 17 „
Ric Whytstones fi: George ... ... ... ... 25 „
Elizabeth Rigbie fi: John ... ... ... ... „ „
Ellin Wholey fi: Henry ... ... ... ... ... 26 „

Fo. 116 Robert Weltch fi: Gilbert ... ... ... ... 6 July
Richard Lathom fi: Ric̃ ... ... ... ... ... ... 7 „
Jamis Tomson fi: Tho: ... ... ... ... ... ... 11 „
Tho: Scarsbrecke fi: Henry ... ... ... ... 25 „
Katherin Gerrerd fi: Tho: ... ... ... ... ... 30 „
Jamis Blundell fi: Robert ... ... ... ... 31 „
Margaret Davie fi: John ... ... ... ... ... 1 Auguste
Ellin Aspinwall fi: Peeter ... ... ... ... „ „
Willm Johnson fi: Ric̃ ... ... ... ... ... 8 „
Henry Morecrofte fi: Ric̃ ... ... ... ... 11 „
Marierie Blackeledge fi: John ... ... ... 18 „
Ric̃ & Ellen Tuson fi: John ... ... ... ... 21 „
Marie Gleaste fi: Ellise ... ... ... ... ... „ „
Anne Sanke fi: Willm ... ... ... ... ... 24 „
Lawrance Halliwall fi: Robert ... ... ... 25 „
Rodger Sanke fi: Ric̃ ... ... ... ... ... 29 „
Margaret Lithom fi: Omfrey ... ... ... ... 1 September
Jamis Rethrop fi: Edw: ... ... ... ... ... 5 „
Anne Mollinex fi: Henry ... ... ... ... ... 8 „
Alis Tomson fi: Willm ... ... ... ... ... „ „
Elizabeh Blundell fi: Edw: ... ... ... ... 12 „
George Craine fi: Robert ... ... ... ... 22 „
Edward Craine fi: Willm ... ... ... ... 29 „
Willm Mawdisley fi: John ... ... ... ... 13 October
Hugh Swyfte fi: Jamis ... ... ... ... ... „ „
Elizabeth Westhead fi: Rodger ... ... ... 21 „
Marie Hartleye fi: Jamis ... ... ... ... ... 23 „
Ric̃ Sutch fi: Silvester ... ... ... ... ... 27 „
Margaret Mawdisley fi: Richard ... ... ... 4 November
Thomas Alker fi: Jamis ... ... ... ... ... 10 „
Peeter Lathwhat fi: Robert ... ... ... ... 13 „
Marie Sutch fi: John ... ... ... ... ... „ „
Alis Westhead fi: Henrie ... ... ... ... 24 „
Robert Cowp fi: Ric̃ ... ... ... ... ... 28 „
Fo. 117 Jaine Blundell fi: Gilbert ... ... ... ... 1 December
Willm Eccleston fi: John ... ... ... ... „ „
Henrie Ascrofte fi: Johne ... ... ... ... 5 „
Willm Anderton fi: Henrie ... ... ... ... 6 „
Richard Ireland fi: Charles ... ... ... ... 11 „
Elizabeth Gorsutch fi: Nicolas ... ... ... 14 „
Willm Neale fi: Pease ... ... ... ... ... 25 „
Grace ffrithe fi: Hugh ... ... ... ... ... 1 Januarie
Anne Stopforth fi: Henry ... ... ... ... 3 „
Margaret Stananought fi: Thurstan de bispam 4 „
Elizabeth Morecrofte fi: Emanuell ... ... 8 „
Tho: Hiton fi: John ... ... ... ... ... ... 10 „
Tho: Sefton fi: John ... ... ... ... ... ... 12 „
Jamis Waringe fi: Cristopher ... ... ... 15 „
Richard Smulte fi: Robert ... ... ... ... 24 „

Katherin Cropp fi: Rodger ... ... ... ... 26 Januarie
Richard Whittle fi: Raffe ... ... ... ... 28 „
George Martin fi: John ... ... ... ... ... 31 „
Anne Aspinwall fi: Peeter ... ... ... ... 5 ffebruarie
Wiłłm Sutch fi: Tho: ... ... ... ... ... 6 „
Dorethie Rainforth fi: Ja: ... ... ... ... 11 „
Richard Wainewright fi: Tho: ... ... ... 13 „
Wiłłm Gill fi: Ric̃ ... ... ... ... ... ... „ „
Jaine Morecroft fi: Cuthbert ... ... ... ... 14 „
Mildred Haughton fi: Jamis ... ... ... ... 21 „
Abigall Harison fi: Tho: ... ... ... ... 23 „
John Hey fi: Jamis ... ... ... ... ... ... 25 „
Richard Spencer fi: John ... ... ... ... 26 „
Katherin Walker fi: George ... ... ... ... 28 „
Ellen Sumner fi: Alexander ... ... ... ... 1 Martch
Johne Huton fi: Rich ... ... ... ... ... 5 „
Homfrey Goulbron fi: ffrances ... ... ... 10 „
Edw: Aiscroft fi: John ... ... ... ... ... „ „
Richard Mason fi: Tho: ... ... ... ... 11 „
Amy Medow fi: Tho ... ... ... ... ... 16 „
Katherin Lea fi: Rodger ... ... ... ... 17 „
Tho: Morecroft fi: Tho: ... ... ... ... 21 „
Marie Voce fi: Hugh ... ... ... ... ... „ „

## 1606.

Ellin Ambrose fi: Ric̃ ... ... ... ... ... 30 Martch
Anne Webster fi: Henrie ... ... ... ... 31 „
Gowther Morecroft fi: Edw: ... ... ... ... 9 Aprill
John Preskot fi: Jamis ... ... ... ... ... 20 „
Anne Windrow fi: Richard ... ... ... ... 21 „
Jamis Hunter fi: Cristopher ... ... ... ... 27 „
Grace Lailand fi: Tho: ... ... ... ... ... 28 „
Marie Woosey fi: Gowther ... ... ... ... 30 „
Marie Mawdisley fi: Hector ... ... ... ... 14 Maye
Wiłłm Rimmer fi: Hugh ... ... ... ... 16 „
Anne Ambrose fi: John talior ... ... ... 21 „
John Sefton fi: Edmund ... ... ... ... 1 June
Gabriell Woodes fi: Henrie ... ... ... ... 5 „
Anne Sumner fi: Edw: ... ... ... ... ... 15 „
Margreat Gill fi: . . . ... ... ... ... 29 „
Marie Lea fi: Tho: de Aughton ... ... ... 1 July
Gabriell Haughton fi: Gabriell ... ... ... 2 „
Elizabeth Sutch fi: George ... ... ... ... 10 „
Jaine & Margreat Shawe fi: Nicolas ... ... 13 „
Margreat Cropp fi: fi: [*sic*] Hugh... ... ... 18 „
Marierie Lyon fi: Peeter ... ... ... ... 20 „
Margreat Cosey fi: Edw: ... ... ... ... 21 „
Margreat Lunt fi: Wiłłm ... ... ... ... 24 „

| | | | |
|---|---|---|---|
| | Peeter Westhead fi: Ric̃ | 7 | August |
| | Katherin Morecrofte fi: Hector | 13 | " |
| | Izabell Molinex fi: Ric̃ | 14 | " |
| | Jaine Cocket fi: Tho: | " | " |
| | Margreat Parre fi: Edmund | 17 | " |
| | Margreat Barton fi: Ro: | 20 | " |
| | Elizabeth Hey fi: John | 28 | " |
| | Gabriell Windrow fi: Rodger | 1 | September |
| | Tho: Derbie fi: John | 3 | " |
| | Margreat Smyth fi: John | 5 | " |
| | John Garstange fi: Tho: | 7 | " |
| | Hugh Sanforth fi: Henry | 8 | " |
| | Wiłłm Scarsbrecke fi: Hugh | 14 | " |
| | Jamis Scarsbrecke fi: Mr Thomas | 20 | " |
| | Bartholomew ffletcher fi: Hugh | 22 | " |
| Fo. 119 | Richard Brighowse fi: Peeter | 23 | " |
| | Jamis Barton fi: Wiłłm | " | " |
| | Henry Scarsbrecke fi: Henry | 24 | " |
| | Alis Walliner fi: Homfrey | " | " |
| | Margreat Cotton fi: Ro: | 25 | " |
| | Elizabeth Spencer fi: Tho: | 26 | " |
| | Marie Mawdisley fi: Robert | " | " |
| | Peeter Barton fi: Wiłł | 28 | " |
| | Elizabeth Swifte fi: Jamis | 2 | October |
| | Marie Kenion fi: Henry | " | " |
| | Richard Morecrofte fi: Henry | 7 | " |
| | Katherin Ashursts fi: John | 9 | " |
| | Anne Westhead fi: Peeter | 12 | " |
| | Henry Nelson fi: Henry | 19 | " |
| | Tho: Asmall fi: Edw: | 22 | " |
| | John Blundell fi: Henry | 26 | " |
| | Thomas Poole fi: Raufe | 29 | " |
| | Jaine Kekewicke fi: Wiłłm | 2 | November |
| | Genet Mercer fi: Robert | 5 | " |
| | John Barton fi: Gilbert | " | " |
| | Margreat Chadocke fi: Adame | 8 | " |
| | Margerie Spencer fi: Jamis | 9 | " |
| | Jaine Wholey fi: Robert | 12 | " |
| | Marie Sankey fi: Ric̃ | 14 | " |
| | Jaine Langley fi: Tho: | 17 | " |
| | Robert Cowp fi: Hugh | 18 | " |
| | Anne Marclough fi: John | " | " |
| | Katherin Harden fi: Wiłłm | 22 | " |
| | Edmund Smulte fi: Tho: | " | " |
| | Jaine Shawe fi: Peeter | 03 | " [*sic*] |
| | Elizabeth Spencer fi: Peeter | 7 | December |
| | Anne Hankin fi: Wiłłm | " | " |
| | John Killshaw fi: Wiłł | 14 | " |
| | Anthoney Parker fi: Tho: | " | " |

Jamis fforster fi: Edw: ... ... ... ... ... 16 December
Jaine Hoolme fi: Anthoney ... ... ... ... 19 „
Anne Rydinge fi: John ... ... ... ... ... „ „
John Lea fi: Jamis ... ... ... ... ... ... 21 „
Robert Clapam fi: Rodger ... ... ... ... 24 „
Henry Ashton fi: Tho: ... ... ... ... ... 26 „
Robert Gill fi: Henry ... ... ... ... ... 31 „
Thomas Wallis fi: Hector ... ... ... ... „ „
Margreat Westhead fi: Edw: ... ... ... 1 Januarie
Anne Woodes fi: Tho: ... ... ... ... ... 2 „
Jaine Stanley fi: Witłm ... ... ... ... ... 3 „
Henry Ambrose fi: John ... ... ... ... 7 „
Homfrey Morecroft fi: Ric̃ ... ... ... ... 10 „
John Withingeton fi: Robert ... ... ... ... 12 „
Margerie Lancaster fi: John ... ... ... ... 22 „
Margreat Barton fi: Tho: ... ... ... ... 23 „
ffrances Sutton fi: Robert ... ... ... ... 25 „
ffrances Walworke fi: Rodger ... ... ... 28 „
Anne Miller fi: Witłm ... ... ... ... ... 31 „
Bartholomew Asmall fi: Witłm ... ... ... „ „
Witłm Cowp fi: Witłm ... ... ... ... ... 2 ffebruarie
Ellin Eimund fi: John ... ... ... ... ... 5 „
Richard Kekewicke fi: Edw: ... ... ... 9 „
Jaine Sumner fi: Witłm ... ... ... ... ... „ „
Katherin Whytestones fi: Ric̃ ... ... ... 16 „
Ellin Haythiway fi: John ... ... ... ... 20 „
Thomas Swifte fi: Phillipe ... ... ... ... 21 „
John Wright fi: Witłm ... ... ... ... ... 25 „
Tho: Brighowse fi: Witł ... ... ... ... 1 Martch
John Peeter fi: John ... ... ... ... ... „ „
Margerie Cropp fi: Raphe ... ... ... ... „ „
John Barton fi: Ric̃ ... ... ... ... ... ... 2 „
Joanie Ambrose fi: George ... ... ... ... 4 „
Marie Barton fi: Hugh ... ... ... ... ... 7 „
Henry Hill fi: Tho: ... ... ... ... ... ... 8 „
John Allerton fi: Ric̃ ... ... ... ... ... ... 11 „
Izabell Coockeson fi: Silvester ... ... ... „ „
Robert Welles fi: Symund ... ... ... ... 15 „
Robert fforshaw fi: Witłm ... ... ... ... 16 „
Elizabeth Ambrose fi: Antho: de Aughton ... 21 „
Anne Tyrer fi: Jamis ... ... ... ... ... 22 „
Katherin Withingeton fi: Robert ... ... ... 24 „

## 1607.

Jaine Howcrofte fi: John ... ... ... ... 27 Martch
Tho: Westhead fi: Rodger ... ... ... ... 29 „
Ellin Ambrose fi: Ellis ... ... ... ... ... 4 Aprill
Edward Barton fi: John ... ... ... ... ... 5 „

Ellin Smyth fi: Thomas ... ... ... ... ... ... 7 Aprill
Jamis Sutch fi: Rodger ... ... ... ... ... ... 25 Maye
Fo. 121 Tho: Hill fi: Wittm ... ... ... ... ... ... 14 „
Anne Sankey fi: Will ... ... ... ... ... ... 24 „
Hugh Lathom fi: Ric ... ... ... ... ... ... 25 „
Anne Traves fi: Wittm ... ... ... ... ... ... 26 „
Katherin ffletcher fi: Thomas ... ... ... 31 „
Anne Greaves fi: Tho: ... ... ... ... ... ... 10 June
sp: Margerie Gill fi: Tho: ... ... ... ... ... ... 14 „
Wittm Lea fi: Jamis ... ... ... ... ... ... 16 „
John Rainforth fi: Jamis de Aughton ... ... 18 „
Margaret Hey fi: Jamis ... ... ... ... ... ... 28 „
Elizabeth Scarsbrecke fi: ffardinando ... ... 30 „
Margreat Lyon fi: Jamis ... ... ... ... ... ... 5 July
Elizabeth Mosse fi: John ... ... ... ... ... „ „
Rodger Balie fi: Raffe bastard ... ... ... 22 „
Hugh Spencer fi: John ... ... ... ... ... ... 23 „
Margreat Armistronge fi: John ... ... ... 29 „
sp: Margaret Speakeman fi: Henr ... ... ... 2 August
Anne Sutch fi: Henry ... ... ... ... ... ... 7 „
Jaine Davie fi: Tho: ... ... ... ... ... ... 11 „
Richard Stanley fi: Mr Thomas of Marton ... 12 „
Richard Breykell fi: Wittm ... ... ... ... ... 17 „
Thomas Barton fi: Wittm ... ... ... ... ... 19 „
Katherin Ormishaw fi: Tho: ... ... ... 24 „
John Hodgekinson fi: Ric ... ... ... ... ... 26 „
Silvester Halsall fi: Edw: ... ... ... ... ... 6 September
Anne Brates* fi: Robert stranger ... ... ... 9 „
Richard Holland fi: Hugh ... ... ... ... ... 20 „
Gilbert † Gobbin fi: Henry ... ... ... ... 3 October
Katherin Barton fi: Rodger ... ... ... ... ... 6 „
Marie Cropp fi: ffardinando ... ... ... ... 9 „
Elizabeth Lathwhat fi: Wittm ... ... ... 22 „
Hugh Barton fi: Henrie ... ... ... ... ... 24 „
Richard Lathwhat fi: Robert ... ... ... ... 28 „
Gabriell Gelder fi: Michall ... ... ... ... 29 „
Elizabeth Greaves fi: John ... ... ... ... „ „
Richard Walker fi: Gabriell ... ... ... ... 30 „
Richard Cropp fi: Wittm ... ... ... ... „ „
George Leister fi: Nicolas A gipsie ... ... „ „
Fo. 122 Gilbert Woosey fi: Hugh of Aughton ... ... 7 November
Alis Aspinwall fi: Edw: ... ... ... ... ... „ „
Marie Smoolte fi: Robert ... ... ... ... ... 22 „
Alis Jackeson fi: Henrie ... ... ... ... ... „ „
Homfrey Morecroft fi: Cuthbert ... ... ... 24 „
John ‡ Piningeton fi: Homfrey ... ... ... „ „

* Bates in Chester Transcript.
† William in Chester Transcript.
‡ Janie in Chester Transcript.

Margaret Aspinwall fi: Peeter ... ... ... 11 December
Richard Haughton fi: Hoomfrey ... ... ... 13 „
Margreat Hunt fi: John ... ... ... ... ... „ „
Katherin Killshaw fi: Gilbert ... ... ... ... 15 „
Thomas Craine fi: Edw: ... ... ... ... 21 „
Elizabeth Wainewright fi: Tho: ... ... ... 23 „
Ellin Tomson fi: Williñ [*sic*] ... ... ... 3 Januarie
Wiñm Golbron fi: Alex: ... ... ... ... 4 „
Katherin Cropp fi: Hugh ... ... ... ... „ „
Robert Morecroft fi: Henrie ... ... ... ... „ „
Richard Westhead fi: Wiñm ... ... ... ... 5 „
Anne Smith fi: Rich ... ... ... ... ... 14 „
Anne Sanforth fi: Henrie ... ... ... ... 15 „
Margreat Hey fi: John ... ... ... ... ... 17 „
Anne Neale fi: Pease ... ... ... ... ... 23 „
Richard Morecroft fi: Riĉ ... ... ... ... 25 „
Peeter Blundell fi: Jamis ... ... ... ... „ „
Elizabeth Lithom fi: Homfrey ... ... ... 3 ffebruarie
Margreat Butler fi: Mr Henrie de Raclif ... „ „
Jain & Alis Lathwhat fi: Wiñm ... ... ... 4 „
Jamis Eccleston fi: John ... ... ... ... 7 „
Margreat Penketh fi: Henrie ... ... ... ... „ „
Ellin Martindaile fi: Hugh ... ... ... ... 11 „
Margreat Voce fi: Hugh ... ... ... ... ... 12 „
Claris Haughton fi: Samwell ... ... ... ... 14 „
Margreat Willson fi: John ... ... ... ... „ „
Silvester Bootle fi: ffardinandow ... ... ... „ „
John Blundell fi: Edw: ... ... ... ... ... 21 „
Alis Ireland fi: Riĉ ... ... ... ... ... „ „
Hugh Halliwan fi: John A stranger ... ... „ „
Marierie Gillibrund fi: Riĉ ... ... ... ... 27 „
Tho: Hallsall fi: Jamis ... ... ... ... ... 24 „
Marie Preskot fi: Tho: ... ... ... ... ... 4 Martch
Robert Morecroft Hector ... ... ... ... 8 „
Alis Preskot fi: Jamis ... ... ... ... ... 10 „
Wiñm Barton fi: John ... ... ... ... ... „ „
Alis Kennion fi: Henrie ... ... ... ... ... 11 „
Bartholomew Harsnep fi: Jamis ... ... ... „ „
Edw: Sankey fi: Riĉ ... ... ... ... ... 14 „
Peeter Ambrose fi: Tho: ... ... ... ... „ „
Wiñm Killshaw fi: Riĉ ... ... ... ... ... 19 „
Gabriell Haughton fi: George ... ... ... 20 „
Ellin Kirkebie fi: Homfrey ... ... ... ... 22 „

## 1608.

Elizabeth Shaw fi: Nicolas ... ... ... ... 25 Martch
Elizabeth Sutch fi: John ... ... ... ... 28 „
Riĉ ffrith fi: Hugh ... ... ... ... ... ... 29 „

| | | | |
|---|---|---|---|
| | Ric̃ Haiton fi: John | 31 | Martch |
| | Ellin Scarsbrecke fi: Edw: | 2 | Aprill |
| | Katherin Wallis fi: Hector | 3 | „ |
| | Robert Swift fi: Jamis | 6 | „ |
| | Emlin Spencer fi: Tho: | 7 | „ |
| | Gabriell Thornall fi: Tho: | 8 | „ |
| | Willm Ridinge fi: Rowland | 10 | „ |
| | Tho: ffletcher fi: Hugh | 16 | „ |
| | John Cropp fi: Raphe | 21 | „ |
| | John Withingeton fi: Henr̃ | „ | „ |
| | Martha Gowlbrond fi: ffrances | 22 | „ |
| | Ric̃ Asmall fi: Thurstan | „ | „ |
| | Tho: Rimmer fi: Hugh | 24 | „ |
| | Elizabeth Holland fi: Robert | „ | „ |
| | Margreat Tuson fi: John | 26 | „ |
| | Robert Wildinge fi: Henrie | 2 | Mayee |
| | Alis Mawdisley fi: R: | 3 | „ |
| | Tho: Sefton fi: Tho: | „ | „ |
| | Elin Mawdisley fi: Jamis | 8 | „ |
| | Thomas Asshort fi: John | 10 | „ |
| | Peeter Woosey fi: Gouther | „ | „ |
| | Ellin Chadocke fi: Adam | „ | „ |
| | John Lathwhat fi: Henrie | „ | „ |
| | Margreat Ambrose fi: Ric̃ | 12 | „ |
| sp: | Richard & Margreat Ledbeter fi: Peete | 16 | „ |
| | Marie Gleast fi: Ellis | 20 | „ |
| | Anne Charnocke fi: Rodger | 4 | June |
| | Margreat Barton fi: Willm | 7 | „ |
| | Marie Cropp fi: Peeter | 9 | „ |
| | Tho: Waringe fi: Cristopher | „ | „ |
| | Ellin Kekewicke fi: Ed: | 19 | „ |
| sp: | Margreat Balshaw fi: Jamis | 21 | „ |
| | Elizabeth Mawdisley fi: Willm | 27 | „ |
| | Elizabeth Ashton fi: Tho: | 29 | „ |
| Fo. 124 | Willm Hesketh fi: Mr Gabriell de Aught | 4 | July |
| | Richard Derbie fi: John | 6 | „ |
| | Tho: Barton fi: Hathor | 7 | „ |
| | Tho: Weltch fi: Gilbert | 12 | „ |
| | Marie Mawdisley fi: Henrie | 18 | „ |
| | Richard Hoolme fi: Ric̃ | „ | „ |
| | Henrie Windrowe fi: George | 1 | August |
| | Tho: Ambrose fi: Anthoney de Augton | 5 | „ |
| sp: | James Sumner fi: Gilbert | 11 | „ |
| | Marie Cosey fi: Edw: | 14 | „ |
| | Marie Browne fi: Jamis | 16 | „ |
| | Willm Westhead fi: Gabriell | 18 | „ |
| | Robert Henrieson fi: Henrie | 21 | „ |
| | Katherin Clapam fi: Rodger | 28 | „ |
| | Edw: Morecroft fi: Ric̃ | „ | „ |

... ... ... 4 September
... ... ... 7 "
... ... ... 14 "
... ... ... " "
... ... ... 18
... ... ... 22 "
... ... ... 27 "
... ... ... 1 October
... ... ... 6 "
... ... ... 8 ..
... ... ... 9 . "
... ... ... 13 "
... ... ... 21 "
... ... ... 2 November
... ... ... 8 "
... ... ... 13
... ... ... 18
... ... ... 19
... ... ... " ..
... ... ... 24 "
... ... ... " "
... ... ... 30 "
... ... ... 1 December
... ... ... 7 "
... ... ... 8
... ... ... " "
... ... ... 12
... ... ... 13
... ... ... "
... ... ... 21
... ... ... 23
... ... ... 24
... ... ... 25
... ... ... 26
... ... ... 31 "
... ... ... " "
... ... ... 2 Januarie
... ... ... 6 "
... ... ... 7
... ... ... 8
... ... ... 10
... ... ... 13
... ... ... 22
... ... ... 26 "
... ... ... 29 "
... ... ... 2 ffebruary
... ... ... 3 "
... ... ... 7
... ... ... 8

Tho: Alker fi: John ... ... ... ... ... ... 8 ffebruary
Gilbert Barton fi: Willm ... ... ... ... ... 9 „
Izabell Web fi: Richard ... ... ... ... ... ... 12 „
Alis Howton fi: Richard ... ... ... ... ... 14 „
Edw: Morecroft fi: Henry ... ... ... ... ... 15 „
Henry Talior fi: Richard ... ... ... ... 19 „
Thomas Alerton fi: Richard ... ... ... ... ... „ „
Rodger Skinner fi: Tho: ... ... ... ... ... 27 „
Genet Longton fi: Gabriell . ... ... ... 6 Martch
Mr Edward Scarsbrecke fi: Henry Esqr of Scarsbrecke ... ... ... ... ... ... 9 „
Gabriell Smoolte fi: Robert ... ... ... ... ... 12 „
Richard Howcroft fi: John ... ... ... ... ... 17 „
Robert Willmson fi: Robert ... ... ... ... ... 18 „
Ellin Anglesdaile fi: John ... ... ... ... ... 19 „
Ellene Woofall fi: Christopher ... ... ... ... 22 „

## 1609.

Willm Tyrer fi: Jamis ... ... ... ... ... ... 26 Martch
Marie Halsall fi: Richard ... ... ... ... ... 1 Aprill
Anne ffletcher fi: Hugh ... ... ... ... ... ... 2 „
Jaine Mason fi: Arthor ... ... ... ... ... ... 12 „
Tho: Alcocke fi: Nicolas ... ... ... ... ... 30 „
Tho: Hunter fi: Tho: ... ... ... ... ... ... 5 Maye
Jaine Wallis fi: Hector ... ... ... ... ... ... 6 „
Izabell Talior fi: Peeter ... ... ... ... ... ... 11 „
Peeter Cropp fi: Edmund ... ... ... ... ... 19 „
Richard Butler fi: Mr Henrie Buler of Raclif 22 „
Margaret Morecroft fi: Cuthbert ... ... ... 26 „
Katherine Swifte fi: John ... ... ... ... ... 4 June
Jaine Sorton fi: Tho: ... ... ... ... ... ... 11 „
sp: Ellin Chorley fi: Edward ... ... ... ... ... 14 „
Thomas & Izabell Lancaster ... ... ... ... ... 15 „
Elizabeth Brighowse fi: Will ... ... ... ... ... „ „
Susan Lyon fi: Jamis ... ... ... ... ... ... 25 „
Myles Barton fi: Rodger ... ... ... ... ... 26 „
Henry Lathwhat fi: Willm ... ... ... ... ... 2 July
Catherin Scarsbrecke fi: ffardinand ... ... 4 „
Richard Sankey fi: Richard ... ... ... ... ... 6 „
Katherin Haughton fi: Ric̃ ... .. ... ... ... 8 „
Ellener Gerrarde fi: Myles de Aughton ... 10 „
Anne Ashton fi: Richard ... ... ... ... ... 17 „
sp: Ellin Worthingeton fi: Edw: ... ... ... ... 25 „
Anne Mawdisley fi: Robert ... ... ... ... ... 26 „
Mawde Blundell fi: Robert ... ... ... ... ... 28 „
Henry Whittill fi: Richard ... ... ... ... ... 10 August
Adam Voce fi: John ... ... ... ... ... ... 24 „
Ellin Sutch fi: Henry ... ... ... ... ... ... 28 „

Witłm Asley fi: Thomas ... ... ... ... 10 September
John Gilbertson fi: Gilbert ... ... ... ... 29 „
Agnes Parre fi: Edmund ... ... ... ... 1 October
Jaine Hey fi: Jamis ... ... ... ... ... 4 „
Ellin Willson fi: John ... ... ... ... ... 7 „
Richard Holland fi: Robert ... ... ... ... 10 „
Richard Cropp fi: Hugh... ... ... ... ... 15 „
Robert Halsall fi: Henry ... ... ... ... 19 „
Dorethie Sutch fi: Silvester ... ... ... ... 23 „
Jaine Roades fi: Tho: ... ... ... ... ... 28 „
Phillip Medowe fi: Tho: ... ... ... ... 29 „
Robert Mawdisley fi: Henry ... ... ... ... 31 „
Margaret Marser fi: John ... ... ... ... 1 November
Anne Clarkeson fi: Witłm ... ... ... ... 2 „
Grace Henryson fi: Tho: ... ... ... ... 3 „
Cuthber Kekewicke fi: Edw: ... ... ... 10 „
Ellin Darbie fi: John ... ... ... ... ... 12 „
Catherin Gill fi: Gilbert ... ... ... ... „ „
Marie Halsall fi: Edw: ... ... ... ... 15 „
Claris Lathwhat fi: Jamis ... ... ... ... 19 „
Witłm Lea fi: Rodger ... ... ... ... ... 21 „
Geffrey Gill fi: Richard ... ... ... ... ... 1 December
Marie Davie fi: Thomas ... ... ... ... „ „
Jaine Walne fi: Hugh ... ... ... ... ... 4 „
Bartholomew Windrow fi: Tho: ... ... ... 5 „
Tho: Scarsbrecke fi: Edw: ... ... ... ... 17 „
Ellin Asmall fi: Witłm ... ... ... ... ... 23 „
Ellin Mollinex fi: Richard ... ... ... ... 26 „
Claris Charnocke fi: Rodger ... ... ... ... 9 Januarie
Gilbert Scarsbrecke fi: Hugh ... ... ... 14 „
Anne Waynewright fi: Tho: ... ... ... ... 20 „
Richard Smyth fi: Tho: ... ... ... ... „ „
Edmund Westhead fi: Witłm ... ... ... 25 „
Richard Killshaw fi: Tho: ... ... ... ... 5 ffebruarie
Robert Cowp fi: Witłm ... ... ... ... ... 9 „
Ellin Withingeton fi: Robert ... ... ... 13 „
Witłm Aiscroft fi: John ... ... ... ... ... 18 „
Johne Abott fi: Witłm ... ... ... ... ... 21 „
Henry Knowles fi: Witł precher ... ... ... 23 „
Anne Walworth fi: Rodger ... ... ... ... 24 „
Jaine Henrison fi: Richard ... ... ... ... „ „
John Walker fi: Gabriell ... ... ... ... 25 „
Myles Kirkebie fi: Homfrey ... ... ... ... „ „
Elizabeth Heaton fi: Ewaine ... ... ... ... „ „
Witłm Smyth fi: Edward ... ... ... ... 27 „
Witłm ffletcher fi: Tho: ... ... ... ... 1 Martch
Witłm Woodes fi: Henry ... ... ... ... 3 „
Anne Waringe fi: Robert ... ... ... ... 5 „
Jaine Spencer fi: Peeter ... ... ... ... ... 6 „

Thomas Spencer fi: Hugh ... ... ... ... 17 Martch
Tomasin Sandes fi: Tho: ... ... ... ... 18 „
Ellis Ireland fi: Charles ... ... ... ... ... 21 „
Anne Blundell fi: John ... ... ... ... ... 22 „
sp: Anne Walker fi: George ... ... ... ... „ „

## 1610.

Richard Haughton fi: Samuell ... ... ... 28 Martch
Thomas Barton fi: Richard ... ... ... ... ... „ „
Hector Mawdisley fi: Thomas ... ... ... „ „
Thomas Blundell fi: Robert ... ... ... ... 1 Aprill
Alis Ridinge fi: John ... ... ... ... ... ... „ „
Thomas Smyth fi: Richard ... ... ... ... 4 „
Thomas & Marie Sefton fi: Edmund ... ... 5 „
Jaine Willdinge fi: Henry ... ... ... ... ... 6 „
Hamlet Rethrope fi: Edw: ... ... ... ... ... 7 „
Margaret & Jenet Shaw fi: Nicoles ... ... 10 „
Ranould Mason fi: Witłm ... ... ... ... ... 11 „
sp: Ellin Hoolme fi: Thomas ... ... ... ... ... 16 „
Thomas Gall fi: Robert ... ... ... ... ... ... 17 „
Alexsander Hesketh fi: Gabriell Esq^r de Aughton ... ... ... ... ... ... ... ... ... 20 „
Edward Ambrose fi: Tho: ... ... ... ... ... 25 „
Jaine Hey fi: John ... ... ... ... ... ... ... 26 „
Witłm Cockesonne fi: Silvester ... ... ... 27 „
Richard Hey fi: Tho: ... ... ... ... ... ... 2 Maye
Thomas Kenion fi: Henry ... ... ... ... ... 8 „
Thomas Withingeton fi: Robert ... ... ... 9 „
Cuthbert Neale fi: Peas ... ... ... ... ... ... 20 „
Fo. 129 Robert Deye fi: John ... ... ... ... ... ... 22 „
Cuthbert Ambrose fi: Ric̃ ... ... ... ... ... 29 „
sp: John Lea fi: Tho: ... ... ... ... ... ... ... 3 June
Nicolas ffletcher fi: Hugh ... ... ... ... ... 4 „
Twoo base Children of Tho: Huton ... ... 8 „
Elin Greaves fi: John ... ... ... ... ... ... 10 „
Gilbert Waringe fi: Cristopher ... ... ... 13 „
Edward Winstanley fi: Tho: ... ... ... ... 28 „
Robert Mason fi: Thomas ... ... ... ... ... 2 July
Katherin Lithom fi: Homfrey ... ... ... 8 „
Richard Garstange fi: John ... ... ... ... „ „
Katherin Smalshaw fi: Tho: ... ... ... ... „ „
Elizabeth Tuson fi: John ... ... ... ... ... 22 „
Robert Egikar fi: Hugh ... ... ... ... ... 2 August
Marie Lemman fi: Ric̃ A stranger ... ... „ „
Elizabeth Sumpner fi: John ... ... ... ... 3 „
Raffe Barton fi: Witłm ... ... ... ... ... 5 „
Ellin Parker fi: Tho: ... ... ... ... ... ... „ „
Hector Lea fi: Jamis ... ... ... ... ... ... 10 „

Alis Lathom fi: Richard ... ... ... ... 14 August
Peeter Voce fi: Hugh ... ... ... ... ... 15 „
Elizabeth Kilshaw fi: John ... ... ... ... 18 „
Ellen Haiton fi: John ... ... ... ... ... 19 „
: Katherin Blundell fi: John ... ... ... ... 23 „
John Kilshaw fi: Witłm ... ... ... ... ... 26 „
Alis ffrith fi: Hugh ... ... ... ... ... 29 „
John Mortmeer fi: Andrew a stranger ... ... 30 „
Margaret Aimun fi: John ... ... ... ... 4 September
Henry Woosey fi: Gouther ... ... ... ... 7 „
Richard Willes fi: Rodger ... ... ... ... „ „
Thomas Aspinwall fi: Peeter ... ... ... 9 „
. . . Barton fi: Henry ... ... ... ... „ „
Alis Burscough fi: Tho: ... ... ... ... 15 „
Emaniwell Stanley fi: George ... ... ... 16 „
John Rimmer fi: Hugh ... ... ... ... ... 22 „
Rodger Morecroft fi: Ric̃ ... ... ... ... 26 „
Anne Barton fi: Hugh ... ... ... ... ... 29 „
Grace Gelder fi: Micaell ... ... ... ... „ „
o Henry Hurst fi: Ellis ... ... ... ... ... 5 October
: Elizabeth Lunt fi: Peeter ... ... ... ... 7 „
Hugh Cosey fi: Edw: ... ... ... ... ... 8 „
John Cropp fi: Witłm ... ... ... ... ... 9 „
Ellin Aspinwall fi: Thurstan ... ... ... ... 15 „
Ellin Westhead fi: Tho: ... ... ... ... 22 „
: Elizabeth Smith fi: Edw: de Croston ... ... 24 „
Ellin Bursko mg⁹ [*sic*] fi: Edw: de Croston... „ „
Elizabeth Spencer fi: Ja: ... ... ... ... 28 „
: Alis Barton fi: Rowland ... ... ... ... 1 November
Jamis Smulte fi: Robert ... ... ... ... ... 9 „
Jamis Blackledge fi: Ric̃ ... ... ... ... 11 „
Katherin Trves fi: Witłm ... ... ... ... „ „
Margaret Modisley fi: Ja: ... ... ... ... 16 „
Elizẽ Wolsey fi: Hugh de Aughton ... ... 19 „
George Lathom fi: Goulter ... ... ... ... 28 „
Edw: & Elizabeth Morecroft fi: Cuthbert ... 7 December
Jamis* Sankey fi: Ric̃ ... ... ... ... ... 9 „
Peeter Parre fi: Edmund ... ... ... ... 16 „
Alis Windrow fi: George ... ... ... ... „ „
Anne Aspinwall fi: Ric̃ ... ... ... ... ... 17 „
Jamis Poolle fi: Raffe ... ... ... ... ... 18 „
Joanie Sowerbutes fi: John ... ... ... ... 22 „
Richard Marclough fi: Witłm ... ... ... 29 „
Marie Halsall fi: Jamis ... ... ... ... ... 31 „
Jamis Henryson fi: Henry ... ... ... ... 2 Januarie
Margaret Holden fi: George ... ... ... ... „ „
Katherin Barton fi: Tho: ... ... ... ... 4 „
Gregorie Mason fi: Gowther ... ... ... ... „ „

* Written over Thomas struck through.

| | | | |
|---|---|---|---|
| | Margaret Blundell fi: Edw: ... ... ... ... | 6 | Januarie |
| | Alis Davies fi: John ... ... ... ... ... | „ | „ |
| | Robert Carre fi: Ric̃ .. ... ... ... ... | 10 | „ |
| | Margaret Stopford fi: Hugh ... ... ... ... | „ | „ |
| | Cislie Abraham fi: Matthew ... ... ... ... | 11 | „ |
| | Katherin Aiscroft fi: Jamis ... ... ... ... | 14 | „ |
| | Richard Wainewright fi: Ric̃ ... ... ... ... | 19 | „ |
| | Marie Ashton fi: Tho: bap at latho: Chap ... | 21 | „ |
| | Alis fforster fi: Edw: ... ... ... ... ... | 25 | „ |
| Fo. 131 | Richard Kekewicke fi: Wiłłm ... ... ... | 27 | „ |
| | Elizabeth Lathwhat fi: Wiłłm ... ... ... | „ | „ |
| | Elizabeth Westhead fi: Ric̃ ... ... ... ... | 28 | „ |
| | Elis Hodgeson fi: Ric̃ ... ... ... ... ... | 31 | „ |
| | Eline Preskot fi: Jamis ... ... ... ... ... | „ | „ |
| | Wiłłm Aspinwall fi: Anthoney ... ... ... | „ | „ |
| | John Barton fill: Wiłłm ... ... ... ... ... | 7 | ffebruarie |
| | Wiłłm Knowles fi: Wiłł ... ... ... ... ... | 8 | „ |
| | Katherin Johnson fi: Rich: ... ... ... ... | 9 | „ |
| | Margreat Millner fi: Wiłłm ... ... ... ... | 11 | „ |
| | John Lailand fi: Tho: ... ... ... ... ... | 14 | „ |
| sp: | Elizabeth Barton fi: Wiłłm a stranger ... ... | 15 | „ |
| | Edward Skinner fi: Tho: ... ... ... ... ... | 17 | „ |
| | Marie Aspinwall fi: Tho: ... ... ... ... ... | 19 | „ |
| | Jaine Sutch fi: Hugh ... ... ... ... ... | 22 | „ |
| | Oliver Atherton fi: Godfrey ... ... ... ... | 27 | „ |
| | Margreat ffarclough fi: Thurstan ... ... ... | 28 | „ |
| | Jaine Cropp fi: Rodger ... ... ... ... ... | 3 | Martch |
| | Cislie Harsnep fi: Robert ... ... ... .. | 4 | „ |
| | Grace Scarsbrecke fi: Mr Tho: ... ... ... | 6 | „ |
| | Alis Woofall fi: Cristopher ... ... ... ... | 10 | „ |
| | John Thornton fi: Tho: ... ... ... ... ... | „ | „ |
| | Katherin Swift fi: James ... ... ... ... | 12 | „ |
| | Margreat Whytestones fi: George ... ... ... | 14 | „ |

## 1611.

| | | | |
|---|---|---|---|
| | Tho: Waringe fi: Wiłłm ... ... ... ... ... | 29 | Martch |
| | Katherin Wholey fi: Robert ... ... ... . | 3 | Aprill |
| | Elizabeth Preskot fi: Jamis ... ... ... ... | 7 | „ |
| | Emlin Barton fi: Peeter ... ... ... ... ... | 10 | „ |
| | Jaine Chadocke fi: Ric̃ ... ... ... ... ... | 12 | „ |
| | Hugh Gilbertson fi: Edw: ... ... ... ... ... | 16 | „ |
| | Alis Kekewicke fi: Robert ... ... ... ... | 1 | Maye |
| | Gabriell Morecroft fi: Edw: ... ... ... | 7 | „ |
| | Elline Scarsbrecke fi: Henry ... ... ... ... | 13 | „ |
| | Edward Westhead fi: Peeter ... ... ... ... | 23 | „ |
| | Jaine Lunt fi: Wiłłm ... ... ... ... ... | 27 | „ |
| Fo. 132 | Robert Maudisley fi: Richard ... ... ... | 1 | June |
| | Margreat Waineright fi: Tho: ... ... ... | 4 | „ |

| | | |
|---|---|---|
| Margreat and Elizabeth Stanley fi: Willm ... | 11 | June |
| Anne Brough fi: Willm ... ... ... ... ... ... | 12 | „ |
| Rodger Gill fi: Willm ... ... ... ... ... ... | 23 | „ |
| Jane Cowdocke fi: Edmund ... ... ... ... ... | 30 | „ |
| Alis Kilshaw fi: John ... ... ... ... ... ... | 3 | July |
| Thomas Barker fi: Henry ... ... ... ... ... | 7 | „ |
| Ellin Lathwhat fi: Robert ... ... ... ... ... | 8 | „ |
| Marie Howcroft fi: John ... ... ... ... ... | 10 | „ |
| Elizabeth & Jaine Knowles fi: Henry ... ... | „ | „ |
| Elizabeth Irland fi: Jamis ... ... ... ... ... | 14 | „ |
| Rodger Shawe fi: John ... ... ... ... ... ... | 17 | „ |
| Alis Allerton fi: Raffe ... ... ... ... ... ... | 21 | „ |
| Jonne Mawdisley fi: Tho: ... ... ... ... ... | 31 | „ |
| . . . Grine fi: John ... ... ... ... ... ... | 5 | August |
| Richard Killshaw fi: John ... ... ... ... ... | 6 | „ |
| Richard Smult fi: Tho: ... ... ... ... ... ... | 7 | „ |
| Ellin Thornton fi: Robert ... ... ... ... ... | „ | „ |
| Willm Talior fi: Peeter ... ... ... ... ... ... | 8 | „ |
| Elizabeth Roades fi: Tho: ... ... ... ... ... | 24 | „ |
| John Woods fi: Richard ... ... ... ... ... ... | 31 | „ |
| Alis Hill fi: Willm ... ... ... ... ... ... ... | 12 | September |
| Margreat Cocket fi: Tho: ... ... ... ... ... | 13 | „ |
| Jaine Aspinwall fi: Edward ... ... ... ... ... | 27 | „ |
| Thomas Mawdisley fi: Rodger ... ... ... | 5 | October |
| Richard Hoolme fi: Raffe ... ... ... ... ... | 20 | „ |
| Richard Balshaw fi: Jamis ... ... ... ... ... | 25 | „ |
| Lawrance Willson fi: John ... ... ... ... ... | 3 | November |
| Elizabeth Lunt fi: Peeter ... ... ... ... ... | „ | „ |
| Margreat Stanley fi: George ... ... ... ... ... | 8 | „ |
| Margreat Swift fi: James ... ... ... ... ... | 10 | „ |
| Katherin Craine fi: Robert ... ... ... ... ... | 21 | „ |
| Thomas Halsall fi: Edw: ... ... ... ... ... | 28 | „ |
| Rodger Ridinge fi: Jamis ... ... ... ... ... | „ | „ |
| Willm Kilshaw fi: Willm ... ... ... ... ... | 29 | „ |
| Richard Haughton fi: John ... ... ... ... ... | 30 | „ |
| . . . Garstange fi: John ... ... ... ... ... | 3 | December |
| Margreat Charnocke fi: Rodger ... ... ... | 5 | „ |
| Margreat Smulte fi: Tho: ... ... ... ... | 8 | „ |
| Thomas Sumner fi: Allexander ... ... ... | 18 | „ |
| Hugh Worthingeton fi: Richard ... ... ... | 24 | „ |
| Thomas Barton fi: Robert ... ... ... ... ... | 26 | „ |
| Alis Wallis fi: Hector ... ... ... ... ... ... | 4 | Januarie |
| Raphe Withingeton fi: Robert ... ... ... ... | 6 | „ |
| Anne Brighowse fi: Willm ... ... ... ... ... | 9 | „ |
| Jaine & Margreat Sankey fi: Ric ... ... ... | „ | „ |
| Claris Parker fi: Tho: ... ... ... ... ... ... | 13 | „ |
| Gilbert Scarsbrecke fi: Edw: ... ... ... ... | 16 | „ |
| Robert Poole fi: Raffe ... ... ... ... ... ... | 22 | „ |
| Elizabeth Knowles fi: Willm ... ... ... ... | „ | „ |

Margreat Sephton fi: Raffe ... ... ... ... 24 Januarie
Thomas Mason fi: Wittm ... ... ... ... 14 ffebruarie
Thomas Stopforth fi: Tho: ... ... ... ... 11 „
Thomas Simkin fi: Edw: ... ... ... ... 16 „
Jamis Spenser fi: Hugh ... ... ... ... ... „ „
Marie Yate fi: Thomas ... ... ... ... ... „ „
Gilbert Voce fi: Tho: ... ... ... ... ... 17 „
Hugh Parker fi: Tho: ... ... ... ... ... 18 „
Richard Ambros fi: Richard ... ... ... ... „ „
Richard Sowerbutes fi: John ... ... ... ... 24 „
Thomas Sephton fi: Hugh ... ... ... ... „ „
Marie Gill fi: Tho: ... ... ... ... ... 27 „
Henry Tasker fi: Tho: ... ... ... ... ... „ „
Joane Chadocke fi: Rich ... ... ... ... 28 „
Richard Simkin fi: Thomas ... ... ... ... 29 „
Thomas Kekewicke fi: John ... ... ... ... 8 Martch
Elin Kilshaw fi: Richard ... ... ... ... 9 „
Anne Voce fi: John ... ... ... ... ... 12 „
Ellin Morecroft fi: Gabriell ... ... ... ... 13 „
Jamis Preskot fi: Jamis ... ... ... ... ... 15 „
Margreat Morecroft fi: Homfrey ... ... ... „ „
Gabriell Gill fi: Henry ... ... ... ... ... 17 „
Jenet Shepard fi: Wittm de Aught ... ... „ „
Gilbert Ormishaw fi: Tho: ... ... ... ... 19 „

## 1612.

Fo. 134 Ellis Chadocke fi: Adam ... ... ... ... 4 Aprill
Richard Talior fi: Wittm ... ... ... ... 5 „
Richard Morecrofte fi: Ric̃ ... ... ... ... 23 „
Elizabeth Talior fi: Ric̃ ... ... ... ... ... 26 „
Joanie Hurst fi: Ellis ... ... ... ... ... „ „
Gilbert Barton fi: Gilbert ... ... ... ... 29 „
Raffe Langley fi: Tho: ... ... ... ... ... 7 Maye
Jaine Barton fi: Wittm ... ... ... ... ... „ „
Elizabeth Cropp fi: Edmund ... ... ... ... 8 „
Tho: Armetridinge fi: John ... ... ... ... 9 „
Robert Hunter fi: Edw: ... ... ... ... 11 „
Hugh Aspinwall fi: Homfrey ... ... ... ... 14 „
Marie Westhead fi: Gabriell ... ... ... ... „ „
Gabriell Westhead fi: Wittm ... ... ... ... 15 „
Margreat Kilshaw fi: Wittm ... ... ... ... 18 „
Margreat Windrow fi: Tho: ... ... ... ... „ „
John Clarkeson fi: Wittm ... ... ... ... 24 „
Raffe Ashton fi: Richard ... ... ... ... 1 June
. . . Blundell fi: Robert ... ... ... ... 7 „
John Ambrose fi: Henry ... ... ... ... 11 „
sp: Jamis Rethrope allis Mossocke hen̄ ... ... 20 „
Elizabeth Phillipes fi: Wittm ... ... ... ... 26 „

| | | |
|---|---|---|
| Henry Sutch fi: Hugh ... ... ... ... ... ... | 29 | June |
| Jaine Blundell fi: Edw: ... ... ... ... ... ... | 3 | July |
| Robert Jumpe fi: Tho: ... ... ... ... ... ... | 14 | „ |
| Margerie Holland fi: Richard ... ... ... | 18 | „ |
| Cuthbert Thorneton fi: Robert ... ... ... | 21 | „ |
| Marie Haughton Allis Rannould ... ... ... | „ | „ |
| Myles Skiñer fi: Tho: ... ... ... ... ... ... | 31 | „ |
| Alis Parker fi: Tho: ... ... ... ... ... ... | 2 | August |
| Ellin Sephton fi: Tho: ... ... ... ... ... ... | „ | „ |
| Jamis Steele fi: Jamis ... ... ... ... ... ... | 7 | „ |
| Richard Gill fi: Gilbert ... ... ... ... ... ... | 11 | „ |
| Alis Blackledge fi: John ... ... ... ... ... | 13 | „ |
| John Haughton fi: Samuell ... ... ... ... ... | „ | „ |
| Wittm Shaw fi: Nicolas ... ... ... ... ... ... | 14 | „ |
| Edmund Walker fi: Gabriell ... ... ... ... ... | 15 | „ |
| Jaine Heaton fi: Ewaine ... ... ... ... ... | 16 | „ |
| Anne Killshaw fi: Ric̃ ... ... ... ... ... ... | 26 | „ |
| Edward Hankinson fi: Robert ... ... ... | 1 | September |
| Jamis Cropp fi: ffardinandow ... ... ... ... | 3 | „ |
| Jane Barton fi: Rowland ... ... ... ... ... | 4 | „ |
| John Smyth fi: Tho: ... ... ... ... ... ... | 5 | „ |
| Elizabeth Morecroft fi: Henry ... ... ... | 10 | „ |
| Anne Marcer fi: John ... ... ... ... ... ... | 14 | „ |
| Henry Asley fi: Tho: de Aughton ... ... | 17 | „ |
| Tho: Page fi: Cristopher ... ... ... ... | „ | „ |
| Wittm Toppinge fi: Homfrey ... ... ... | 18 | „ |
| Jamis Shires fi: Richard ... ... ... ... ... | 1 | October |
| Izabell Mawdisley fi: Tho: ... ... ... ... ... | 2 | „ |
| Thomas Killshaw fi: Wittm ... ... ... ... ... | 6 | „ |
| Jamis Mawdisley fi: Henry ... ... ... ... ... | 8 | „ |
| Thomas Alerton fi: Edward ... ... ... ... ... | „ | „ |
| Jefferey Lea fi: Ric̃ sp: ... ... ... ... ... ... | 18 | „ |
| Margreat Sutch fi: Henry ... ... ... ... ... | 26 | „ |
| Thomas Lea fi: Rodger ... ... ... ... ... ... | 27 | „ |
| Myles ffletcher fi: Richard ... ... ... ... ... | 30 | „ |
| Thomas ffasacarley fi: Rodger ... ... ... | 7 | November |
| Margreat Howcroft fi: John ... ... ... ... ... | 25 | „ |
| Wittm Ambrose fi: Tho: ... ... ... ... ... | 26 | „ |
| Wittm Gobin fi: Henry ... ... ... ... ... ... | „ | „ |
| Thomas Windgrow fi: George ... ... ... | 30 | „ |
| Anne Sowerbutes fi: John ... ... ... ... | 1 | December |
| Ellin Gleast fi: Ellis ... ... ... ... ... ... | 2 | „ |
| Jamis Morecroft fi: Richar̃ ... ... ... ... | 6 | „ |
| John Sworton fi: Tho: A stranger ... ... | 30 | „ |
| Elizabeth Gore fi: Henry ... ... ... ... ... | 31 | „ |
| Ellin Balshaw fi: Jamis ... ... ... ... ... ... | 3 | Januarie |
| Margreat Brough fi: Wittm ... ... ... ... ... | 10 | „ |
| Elizabeth Chadocke fi: Ric̃ ... ... ... ... ... | 12 | „ |
| Wittm Sumner fi: John ... ... ... ... ... ... | 14 | „ |

| | | | |
|---|---|---|---|
| | Edward Croft fi: Edward | 17 | Januarie |
| | Claris Barton fi: Thomas | „ | „ |
| | John Irland fi: Jamis | 19 | „ |
| sp: | Thomas Wilkinsonn fi: George | „ | „ |
| | Edward Mollinex fi: Richard | 21 | „ |
| | John Aiscroft fi: John | 22 | „ |
| Fo. 136 | Thomas Tuson fi: John | 7 | ffebruarie |
| | Jamis Waringe fi: Wiłłm | 8 | „ |
| | Margreat Craine fi: John | 11 | „ |
| | Alis Barton fi: Hugh | „ | „ |
| | Anne Gore fi: Henry | 18 | „ |
| | Ellin More fi: Jamis | 19 | „ |
| | Richard Kirkebie fi: Homfrey | 21 | „ |
| | Richard Traves fi: Wiłłm | 23 | „ |
| | Henry Blackledge fi: Richard | 25 | „ |
| | Rodger Lathwhat fi: Wiłłm | 26 | „ |
| | Margreat Scarsbrecke fi: Henry | 27 | „ |
| | Grace Garrerd fi: Mr Myles of Aughton | 2 | Martch |
| | Margreat Smyth fi: Edw: de Snap | 4 | „ |
| | Thomas Abraham fi: Matthew | „ | „ |
| | John Roades fi: Thomas | 10 | „ |
| | Margreat Worthingeton fi: Ric̃ | „ | „ |
| | Wiłłm Mawdisley fi: John | 12 | „ |
| | Robert Hesketh fi: Richard | 13 | „ |
| | Izabell Corbay fi: Joseph | 14 | „ |
| | Wiłłm Killshaw fi: Thomas | 21 | „ |

## 1613.

| | | | |
|---|---|---|---|
| | Lawrance Wilson fi: John | 26 | Martch |
| | Wiłłm Lathwhat fi: Henry | „ | „ |
| sp: | Richard Lathwhat fi: Jamis | 28 | „ |
| | Elizabeth Moone fi: Anthoney | 30 | „ |
| | Thomas Smalshaw fi: George | 5 | Apriłł |
| | Elizabeth Neale fi: Peaze | „ | „ |
| | Edward Sitch fil: Thomas | 9 | „ |
| | Dorithie Barker fi: Henrie | 13 | „ |
| | Homphrie Morcrofte fił Gabriell | 26 | „ |
| sp: | Ellen Shawe fił Wiłłm | „ | „ |
| | Katherine Aspinwall fił Richard | 27 | „ |
| | Rob̃te Shawe fił Richard | 30 | „ |
| | Jane Aspinwall fił Peeter | 16 | May |
| | Elizabeth Kilshawe fił Henry | 21 | „ |
| | Katherine Causey fił Edward | 30 | „ |
| | Ellen Blundiłł fił Edward | „ | „ |
| | James Wainwright fił Thomas | 1 | June |
| sp: | Margrett Rutter fił Roger | 4 | „ |
| | John Wilson fił Wiłłm de Aughtõ | 13 | „ |
| sp: | James Gorsatch fił James | 18 | „ |

137 Thomas Sankie fil Richard ... ... ... ... 20 June
sp: Willm Hadocke fil Thomas ... ... ... ... „ „
Anne Aspinwall fil Thurstan ... ... ... ... 23 „
Elizabeth Whalley fil Robte ... ... ... ... 26 „
Elizabeth Westhead fil Richard ... ... ... 4 Julie
Henrie Gilder fil Michaell ... ... ... ... 9 „
Willm Lathwaitt fil Henrie ... ... ... ... 7 August
John Shawe fil John a stranger ... ... ... 13 „
Katherine Barton fil Richard ... ... ... ... 24 „
Jane Knowles fil Willm Clarke ... ... ... 27 „
John Brookes fil Charles a stranger ... ... 29 „
Henry Aspinwall fil Hugh ... ... ... ... 30 „
Anne Soothworth fil Robt ... ... ... ... 31 „
Margrett Cowp fil Willm ... ... ... ... 3 September
Margrett Aspinwall fil Willm ... ... ... ... 12 „
Thomas Sumner fil Willm ... ... ... ... „ „
sp: Marie Cottam fil Edward ... ... ... ... „ „
Roger Parke fil Edmund ... ... ... ... 17 „
William Walker fil George ... ... ... ... 23 „
Elizabeth Jackson fil John ... ... ... ... 2 October
Thomas Diconson fil Edward ... ... ... 3 „
Ellyn Lyon fil James ... ... ... ... ... 7 „
Katherine Sowerbutts fil John de Aughton ... 16 „
James Westhead fil Thomas ... ... ... ... 19 „
Elizabeth Barton fil Henry ... ... ... ... 24 „
Willm Modisley fil James ... ... ... ... 4 November
Margrett Ambrose fil Edward ... ... ... 20 „
John Tasker fil Thomas ... ... ... ... ... 23 „
James Jackson fil Richard ... ... ... ... 8 December
Hugh Ratheram fil Edward ... ... ... ... 9 „
Marie Smult fil Thomas ... ... ... ... ... 19 „
Anne Crofte fil Edward ... ... ... ... ... 22 „
sp: Elizabeth Bennett fil John ... ... ... ... 29 „
John Kilshawe fil John ... ... ... ... ... 31 „
138 Edward & William Spencer fil James ... ... 2 Januarie
Willm Keakwick fil John ... ... ... ... 6 „
sp: Ellen Smyth fil Cuthbert ... ... ... ... 9 „
Elizab: Robtson fil Henry ... ... ... ... 16 „
Clarice Parker fil Thomas ... ... ... ... 18 „
Hugh Ascroft fil James ... ... ... ... ... 20 „
Thomas Miller fil James ... ... ... ... ... 26 „
Anne Barton fil George ... ... ... ... ... 3 ffebruarie
Robt Hunter fil Edward ... ... ... ... 9 „
Thomas Keakwicke fil Robte ... ... ... ... 11 „
John Prescott fil John ... ... ... ... ... 13 „
Alice Hey fil James ... ... ... ... ... ... 16 „
sp: Margrett Melling fil Rauffe ... ... ... ... 17 „
Katherine Gill fil Willm ... ... ... ... ... 19 „
Elizabeth Couldock fil Edmund ... ... ... 20 „

Ellen Riding fiƚ James ... ... ... ... ... 21 ffebruarie
James Barton fiƚ Peeter ... ... ... ... ... 22 „
James Shires fiƚ Richard ... ... ... ... ... 27 „
Henrie Davie fiƚ John ... ... ... ... ... 1 March
Elizabeth Traveise fiƚ Wiƚƚm ... ... ... ... 3 „
Marie Martinscroft fiƚ Thomas ... ... ... 16 „
John Marclew fiƚ Richard ... ... ... ... 18 „
sp : Sisley Spencer fiƚ William ... ... ... ... 19 „
Jane Heies fiƚ Thomas ... ... ... ... ... 20 „
Elizabeth Wroe fiƚ Peter ... ... ... ... „ „
Anne Lea fiƚ James ... ... ... ... ... 24 „
Richard Charnock fiƚ Roger ... ... ... ... „ „

## 1614.

Henry Modisley fiƚ Henry ... ... ... ... ... 25 March
John Ambrose fiƚ Anthony de Aughtō ... ... 28 „
Jennett Bullocke fiƚ Wiƚƚm ... ... ... ... ... 31 „
Hugh Vace fiƚ Hugh ... ... ... ... ... ... „ „
Jane ffidler fiƚ James ... ... ... ... ... ... 2 Apriƚƚ
Margrett ffidler fiƚ Robt ... ... ... ... ... 6 „
Jane Mason fiƚ Thomas ... ... ... ... ... „ „
Thomas Angesdale fiƚ John ... ... ... ... 10 „
Edward Scarisbrick fiƚ Edward ... ... ... 19 „
Isabell fforster fiƚ Edward ... ... ... ... 23 „
Fo. 139 Elizabeth ffairclough fiƚ Thurstan ... ... ... 28 „
Clarice Barton fiƚ Wiƚƚm ... ... ... ... ... 1 Maie
Hugh Baron fiƚ Gilbert ... ... ... ... ... 3 „
sp : Elizabeth Tarlton fiƚ Edward ... ... ... ... 11 „
Wiƚƚm Lythom fiƚ Homphrie ... ... ... ... 20 „
sp : Rauffe Whitestones fiƚ Hugh ... ... ... ... 21 „
Elizabeth Thornall fiƚ Robte ... ... ... ... 25 „
Marie Sutch fiƚ Hugh ... ... ... ... ... 31 „
Margrett Halsall fiƚ James ... ... ... ... 6 June
Ranald Gille fiƚ Thomas ... ... ... ... ... 19 „
Edward Stanley fiƚ George ... ... ... ... 20 „
Gilbte Taylor fiƚ Peter ... ... ... ... ... 23 „
Anne Lee fiƚ Alexander ... ... ... ... ... 26 „
Alice Crane fiƚ Wiƚƚm ... ... ... ... ... 30 „
Henrie Hawarth fiƚ Wiƚƚm ... ... ... ... 4 Julie
Henrie Tyrer fiƚ Robte ... ... ... ... ... 10 „
Judeth Scarisbricke fiƚ Thomas ... ... ... 11 „
Anne Swyfte fiƚ James ... ... ... ... ... 15 „
George Symkin fiƚ Edward ... ... ... ... 24 „
Ellen Kilshaw fiƚ Henrie ... ... ... ... 26 „
Henrie Woofall fiƚ Xpofer ... ... ... ... 1 August
Elizabeth Morcroft fiƚ James ... ... ... ... 7 „
Henrie Hale fiƚ James ... ... ... ... ... 9 „
Hugh Shawe fiƚ Nicolas ... ... ... ... ... 13 „

... ... ... 14 August
... ... ... 16 „
... ... ... 25
... ... ... „
... ... ... 27
... ... ... „
... ... ... 29 „
... ... ... 30 „
... ... ... 5 September
... ... ... 8 „
... ... ... 13
... ... ... 17
... ... ... 18
... ... ... 21
... ... ... 25
... ... ... „ „
... ... ... 30 „
... ... ... 1 October
... ... ... 9 „
... ... ... „
... ... ... 11 „
... ... ... 20 „
... ... ... 3 November
... ... ... „ „
... ... ... 6
... ... ... „
... ... ... 12
... ... ... „
... ... ... 17 „
... ... ... 18 „
... ... ... 26 „
... ... ... 3 December
... ... ... 4 „
... ... ... 5
... ... ... 6
... ... ... 8
... ... ... 9
... ... ... 12
... ... ... „
... ... ... 16 „
... ... ... 29 „
... ... ... 4 Januarie
... ... ... 13 „
... ... ... 19 „
... ... ... 20 „
... ... ... „ „
... ... ... 22
... ... ... 23 „

afterwards struck through.

Jennett Clearkson fil Willm ... ... ... ... ... 25 Januarie
Katherine & Alice Brighouse fil Willm ... 26 „
Henrie Phillipps fil Willm ... ... ... ... 28 „
Myles Rymmer fil Hugh ... ... ... ... ... 30 „
Fo. 141 Richard Croft fil Edward ... ... ... ... 3 ffebruarie
spu William Reader fil Cuthbert ... ... ... ... 6 „
Alice Vauce fil John ... ... ... ... ... 7 „
Thomas Roades fil Thomas ... ... ... ... 9 „
spu Robte Gille fil James ... ... ... ... ... 10 „
Emlin Sourbutts fil John ... ... ... ... 12 „
spu Peregrina Scarisbricke filia Anthonie ... ... 14 „
Thomas Wilkinson fil George ... ... ... 15 „
William Weatherbie fil Robte ... ... ... „ „
Margrett Swyfte fil Henrie ... ... ... ... 23 „
Thomas Smult fil Thomas ... ... ... ... 26 „
Thomas Lassell fil Hugh ... ... ... ... 3 March
Henrie Walker fil Gabriel ... ... ... ... 4 „
sp: Alice Lunt fil Peter de Aughton ... ... ... „ „
Hector & James Kilshawe filij Willm ... ... 14 „
Margrett Robinson fil Richard ... ... ... 16 „
Ellen Jackson fil Richard ... ... ... ... „ „
Ellen Crapper fil Willm ... ... ... ... ... 17 „
Jane Maudisley fil Roger ... ... ... ... 18 „
Elizabeth ffletcher fil Richard ... ... ... 19 „
Margrett Wainwright fil Thomas ... ... ... 21 „
Elizabeth Jackson fil Gilbte ... ... ... ... „ „

## 1615.

Elizabeth Whitestones fil Thomas ... ... ... 2 Aprill
Jony Morcrofte fil Richard ... ... ... ... 3 „
Thomas Haughton fil Samuel ... ... ... 30 „
Ellen Waring fil Willm ... ... ... ... ... 16 May
Jane Barton fil Hugh ... ... ... ... ... 18 „
Elizabeth Lyon fil James ... ... ... ... 21 „
Dorithie Smalshawe fil Richard ... ... ... 24 „
Alice Waon* fil Hugh ... ... ... ... ... 30 „
Katherine Walton fil Richard ... ... ... „ „
Anne Haughton fil Richard ... ... ... ... 1 June
Edward Thornton fil Thomas ... ... ... ... 19 „
Roger Ormishawe fil John ... ... ... ... 20 „
Elizabeth Brough fil Willm ... ... ... ... 27 „
Ellen Aspinwall fil Richard ... ... ... ... 29 „
Fo. 142 James Smalshaw fil George ... ... ... ... 5 Julie
sp: James Lathwaitt fil James ... ... ... ... „ „
Richard Ryding fil James ... ... ... ... 13 „
Cuthbert Kilshawe fil Richard ... ... ... 14 „
Thomas Willmson fil Willm ... ... ... ... 18 „

* Waan in Chester Transcript.

Barton Morcroft fil Gabriell ... ... ... ... 18 Julie
Elizabeth Davie fil Thomas ... ... ... ... 25 „
Willm Barton fil Rowland ... ... ... ... „ „
Anne Leigh fil Alexander ... ... ... ... 2 August
Ellen Ashton fil Thomas ... ... ... ... 6 „
Dave Haughton fil George ... ... ... ... 10 „
Henry Allerton fil Richard ... ... ... ... „ „
Robte Hooton fil Richard ... ... ... ... 15 „
Edward Hawarth fil James ... ... ... ... 17 „
Katherine Winder fil George ... ... ... ... 19 „
Anne Lunt fil Willm ... ... ... ... ... „ „
Marie Lunt fil Thomas ... ... ... ... ... „ „
Thomasson Aughton fil Willm ... ... ... 22 „
Jane Miller fil Willm ... ... ... ... ... „ „
Anne Golborne fil Alexander ... ... ... ... 26 „
Richard Jackson fil John ... ... ... ... 30 „
Elizabeth Melling fil Rauffe ... ... ... ... 3 September
Edith Edggiker fil Hugh ... ... ... ... 7 „
Emlin Barton fil fil [*sic*] Thomas ... ... ... 9 „
William Houlme fil Richard ... ... ... ... 10 „
Robte Sephton fil Thomas ... ... ... ... „ „
Dorithie Ratcliffe fil Henry ... ... ... ... 11 „
Ellice Ambrose fil Edward ... ... ... ... 15 „
Roger Jollybrand fil Richard ... ... ... ... 16 „
Jane Prescott fil John ... ... ... ... ... 17 „
Richard Rainforth fil James ... ... ... ... „ „
Anne Marclewe fil Richard ... ... ... ... 18 „
Ellen Melling fil Willm ... ... ... ... ... 21 „
John Halsall fil Edward ... ... ... ... ... 28 „
Richard Aspinwall fil Anthony ... ... ... „ „
Henry Atherton fil Gotfrey ... ... ... ... 1 October
Dorithie Parke fil Edmund ... ... ... ... 6 „
Richard Hill fil Thomas ... ... ... ... ... 7 „
Thomas Davie fil John ... ... ... ... ... 8 „
Margrett ffenton fil Thomas ... ... ... ... 10 „
ffardinand Stanly fil Willm ... ... ... ... 12 „
John Wallice fil Hector ... ... ... ... ... 17 „
Anne Clapham fil Richard ... ... ... ... 20 „
Clarice Holcroft fil John ... ... ... ... 21 „
Rowland Barton fil Willm ... ... ... ... 25 „
Katherine Tuson fil John ... ... ... ... „ „
Jane Cowper fil Hugh ... ... ... ... ... 29 „
Elizabeth Ascroft fil Henry ... ... ... ... 6 November
Anne Prescott fil James ... ... ... ... ... „ „
James Page fil Jeffrey ... ... ... ... ... 7 „
Edward Par fil Edmund ... ... ... ... ... „ „
Alice Stanley fil George ... ... ... ... ... 12 „
John Blundill fil James ... ... ... ... ... 17 „
Elizabeth Barton fil Richard ... ... ... ... 18 „

Katherine Banke fil Robte ... ... ... ... 24 November
Elizabeth Croston fil Edward ... ... ... 28 „
Ellen Chadocke fil Richard ... ... ... ... 30 „
Jane Modisley fil Thomas ... ... ... ... 3 December
Henry Rutter fil John ... ... ... ... ... 7 „
Henry Letherbarrow fil Roger ... ... ... 14 „
John Crapp fil Edmund ... ... ... ... ... 15 „
George Scarisbrick fil Hugh ... ... ... ... 21 „
Christopher Sutch fil Peter ... ... ... ... 25 „
Alice Woodhouse fil Richard ... ... ... ... 26 „
Richard Streete fil George ... ... ... ... 28 „
Thomas Lathom fil Robte ... ... ... ... „ „
Alexander Abraham fil Mathewe ... ... ... „ „
Alice Moone fil Anthony ... ... ... ... 5 January
John Pemberton fil James ... ... ... ... „ „
ffleetwoode Causey fil Edward ... ... ... „ „
James Blundill fil Edward ... ... ... ... 6 „
James Rimer fil Hugh ... ... ... ... ... „ „
Fo. 144 Willm Ashton fil Richard ... ... ... ... 7 „
Josua Rose fil Richard ... ... ... ... ... „ „
Edward Westhead fil Richard ... ... ... 8 „
Elizabeth Sutch fil James ... ... ... ... 9 „
Elizabeth Ambrose fil Henry Vicar ... ... 12 „
John Lea fil Hector ... ... ... ... ... 13 „
Henry Morecrofte fil Rich de Aughtō ... ... 15 „
Myles Abbott fil Willm ... ... ... ... ... 21 „
Thomas Soothwoorth fil Anthony ... ... ... 22 „
Elizabeth Roiston* fil James ... ... ... ... 23 „
Jennett Spencer fil Thomas ... ... ... ... 28 „
Margrett Prescott fil John ... ... ... ... 29 „
Henry Charnocke fil Roger ... ... ... ... 2 ffebruary
Thomas Blundill fil Gilbte ... ... ... ... 4 „
Katherine Croston fil Henry ... ... ... ... „ „
Henry Shires fil Richard ... ... ... ... 8 „
James Laithwaitt fil William ... ... ... ... 13 „
James Smult fil Thomas ... ... ... ... ... 14 „
George Hurst fil Ellice ... ... ... ... ... 15 „
Bright Holden fil George ... ... ... ... 17 „
sp: Robte Keakwicke fil Edward ... ... ... ... 19 „
ffrancis Lea fil Roger ... ... ... ... ... 22 „
Richard Aspinwall fil Peter ... ... ... ... „ „
Roger Haughton fil Robte ... ... ... ... 23 „
Elizabeth Hale fil James ... ... ... ... 24 „
Richard Oston fil Robte *or* Roger ... ... ... 25 „
Richard Winder † fil Richard ... ... ... „ „
Margery Layland fil Xpofer ... ... ... ... 26 „
Thomas Modisley fil Henry ... ... ... ... „ „

* Roistron in Chester Transcript.

† Windrow in Chester Transcript.

| | |
|---|---|
| Wittm Lathwaitt fil Henry ... ... ... ... | 2 March |
| Wittm Gill fil Henry ... ... ... ... ... | 3 " |
| Wittm Tyrer fil Robte ... ... ... ... ... | " " |
| Lettice Kilshawe fil Thomas ... ... ... ... | 4 " |
| Richard Tayler fil Peter ... ... ... ... ... | 6 " |
| Thomas Bank* fil Thomas ... ... ... ... | 7 " |
| George Woodes fil Richard ... ... ... ... | 9 " |
| Henry Topping fil Raphe ... ... ... ... | 18 " |
| Elizabeth Ploumbe † fil Henry ... ... ... | 21 " |
| Thomas Gore fil Henry ... ... ... ... ... | 22 " |
| James ffletcher fil Richard ... ... ... ... | " " |

## 1616.

| | |
|---|---|
| Thomas Balshawe fil John ... ... ... ... | 25 March |
| Wittm Scarisbrick fi: Edward ... ... ... | " " |
| Thomas Rigby fil Myles ... ... ... ... | 26 " |
| Edward Gill fil Wittm ... ... ... ... ... | 28 " |
| Martha Modisley fil John ... ... ... ... | 2 Aprill |
| Ellen Robteson fil Henry ... ... ... ... | " " |
| Alexand Smyth fil Edward ... ... ... ... | " " |
| Margrett Johnson fil Wittm ... ... ... ... | 4 " |
| Maria Aspinwall fil Edward ... ... ... ... | 11 " |
| Roger Ireland fil James ... ... ... ... ... | 12 " |
| Ellen Hunter fil Edward ... ... ... ... | 13 " |
| Edward Wilding fil Peter ... ... ... ... | " " |
| Anne Stopford fil Wittm ... ... ... ... | 14 " |
| Jane Tyrer fil James ... ... ... ... ... | " " |
| Thomas Greaues fil John ... ... ... ... | " " |
| Jane Sutton fil John ... ... ... ... ... | 15 " |
| Richard Hodson fil Richard ... ... ... ... | " " |
| Anne Stopford fil Thomas ... ... ... . | 16 " |
| Katheryne Hey fil James ... ... ... .. | 20 " |
| Jane fforshawe fil Richard ... ... ... ... | 21 " |
| Alice Warde fil John ... ... ... ... ... | " " |
| William Marcer fil John ... ... ... ... ... | 28 " |
| Elizabeth Sephton fil Thomas ... ... ... | " " |
| Marie Sutch fil Henry ... ... ... ... ... | 29 " |
| Anne Rigbie fil Peter ... ... ... ... ... | 30 " |
| Elizab: Dale fil Henry de Aughton ... ... | 2 May |
| Hugh Dodde fil Hugh ... ... ... ... ... | " " |
| Mary Kenion fil Robte ... ... ... ... . | 12 " |
| Katheryne ffarclough fil Wittm ... ... ... | 19 " |
| Isabell Crane fil John ... ... ... ... ... | " " |
| Grace Marcer fil Robte ... ... ... ... .. | " " |

* Blanke in Chester Transcript.

† Prombe in Chester Transcript.

Gabriell Ratherā fil Edward ... ... ... ... 24 May
Wiłłm Morcroft fil Thom̃ ... ... ... ... 26 „
Anne Jackson fil John ... ... ... ... ... 28 „
Hugh Layland fil Thom̃ ... ... ... ... ... 1 June
Elizabeth ffidler fil Robte ... ... ... ... 2 „
Anne Hesketh fil Richard ... ... ... ... 3 „
Wiłłm Wilding fil Peter ... ... ... ... ... 10 „
John Houlme fil Henry ... ... ... ... ... 14 „
Emlin Withington fil Robte ... ... ... ... 18 „
Margery Aspinwall fil Peter ... ... ... ... 20 „
Clarice Haughton fil Roger ... ... ... ... 26 „
Thomas Modisley fil James ... ... ... ... 30 „
Fo. 146 John Pye fil George ... ... ... ... ... 10 Julie
Anne Woofall fil Xpofer ... ... ... ... ... 21 „
Ellen Shawe fil John ... ... ... ... ... „ „
Thomas Spencer fil James ... ... ... ... 22 „
Margrett Crapp fil Wiłłm ... ... ... ... 23 „
Thomas Rigbie fil Hugh ... ... ... ... 4 August
John Cowp fil Richard ... ... ... ... ... 5 „
Gabriell Barton fil Peter ... ... ... ... ... 7 „
Jonie Mason fil Thomas ... ... ... ... ... 8 „
Isabell Houlme fil Thomas ... ... ... ... 11 „
Edward Craffts fil Edward ... ... ... ... „ „
Jennett Hawarth fil Wiłłm ... ... ... ... 12 „
sp: Clarice Bower fil Robte ... ... ... ... ... 13 „
sp: Margrett Whitestones fil Hugh ... ... ... 14 „
Anne Wainwright fil John ... ... ... ... 26 „
Thomas Ambrose fil Ellice ... ... ... ... 27 „
John Shawe fil Richard ... ... ... ... ... 30 „
Richard Atherton fil Gotfrey ... ... ... ... 3 September
Hugh Cowp fil Edward ... ... ... ... ... 5 „
Elizabeth Tasker fil Thom̃ ... ... ... ... 6 „
Susan Thornall fil Robte ... ... ... ... 8 „
Jane Scarisbrick fil Homphry ... ... ... 9 „
William Bartō fil George ... ... ... ... 21 „
Margrett Whalley fil Henry ... ... ... ... 25 „
Margrett Thorton fil Robte ... ... ... ... „ „
John Rethrope fil James ... ... ... ... ... „ „
Thomas Allerton fil Henry ... ... ... ... 28 „
Dorithy Dickett fil John ... ... ... ... 6 October
Margery Dicconson fil Edward ... ... ... 19 „
Mr Tho: Stanley fil Edward Esqr ... ... 22 „
Alice Gille fil Henry ... ... ... ... ... ... 27 „
Robte Hesketh fil George ... ... ... ... 4 November
Thomas Garrard fil Tho: de Eccleston ... 5 „
Hector Kilshawe fil Raphe ... ... ... ... 12 „
Henry Crane fil Wiłłm ... ... ... ... ... 13 „
Edward Taylor fil Wiłłm ... ... ... ... 15 „
Henry Kilshawe fil John ... ... ... ... ... 16 „

|  |  |  |
|---|---|---|
| Margret Hesketh fil Edward | 16 | November |
| Willm Harrison fil Henry Willmson | „ | „ |
| Anne Carby fil Joseph | 21 | „ |
| James Sheppd fil Willm | 26 | „ |
| Henry Spencer fil John | 10 | December |
| Thomas Crapp fil James | 11 | „ |
| Henry Swifte fil James | 12 | „ |
| Thomas Brighouse fil Peter | „ | „ |
| Margrett Swyfte fil Huan | 14 | „ |
| Elizabeth Robinson fil Rich: de Aughtō | 17 | „ |
| Cisley Whitestones fil George | 23 | „ |
| John Mollyneux fil Richard | 27 | „ |
| William Westhead fil Richard | 5 | January |
| Anne Sutch fil Thomas | 8 | „ |
| Peter Sutch fil James | 11 | „ |
| Jennett Lythom fil Homphry | 12 | „ |
| Sisley Chadocke fil Richard | 14 | „ |
| Jane ffforshawe fil Arthur | „ | „ |
| Richard Rose fil Richard | 17 | „ |
| James Swyft fil James | 24 | „ |
| Margrett Gleast fil Ellice | 28 | „ |
| Edward Poole fil Raphe | 4 | ffebruary |
| Grace Woorthington } Anne Woorthington } fil Edward | „ | „ |
| Robte Sturbacre fil Phillip et Maria Scarisbricke | 5 | „ |
| Thomas Ambrose fil Edward | 8 | „ |
| Thomas More fil James | 10 | „ |
| Margrett Modesley fil George | 12 | „ |
| James Cowp fil Ranald | 15 | „ |
| James Topping fil Raph | 17 | „ |
| Thomas Woodes fil Robte | 24 | „ |
| Katheryne Wainwright fil Tho: | „ | „ |
| Elizabeth Pemberton fil James | 25 | „ |
| Anne Kilshawe fil Willm | „ | „ |
| William Halsall fil Richard gent: | 26 | „ |
| Myles Thrope fil Hugh | 1 | March |
| Henry Cockett fil Thomas | „ | „ |
| Henry ffairclough fil Thurstan | 2 | „ |
| Elizabeth Adamson fil Thomas | 3 | „ |
| Ellen Tompson fil John | 6 | „ |
| Roger & Alice Rim̄er fil Hugh | 7 | „ |
| Huan Swyfte fil Thomas | 9 | „ |
| Edward Ascough fil Huan | „ | „ |
| Thomas Scarisbricke fil ffardinando | „ | „ |
| Alice Baron fil Gilbte | 11 | „ |
| Hugh Whitestones fil Thomas | 17 | „ |
| Hugh Whitestones fil Thomas | 18 | „ |
| Henry Henry [*sic*] Hesketh fil John de Aughtō | 19 | „ |
| James Ashton fil Hugh de Bispam | 20 | „ |

## 1617.

| |  |  |  |
|---|---|---|---|
| | . . . Rodes fil Thomas | 27 | March |
| | Gilbte Hilham fil John | 28 | „ |
| | Margrett Parker fil Thomas | 31 | „ |
| | Dorithie Laithwaitt fi: Thom̃ | 4 | Aprill |
| | Anne Ormeshawe fi: Edmund | 10 | „ |
| | Anne Bullocke fi: Willm | 11 | „ |
| | Anne Neale fil Peaze Curat: | „ | „ |
| | Richard Sephton fil Hugh | 14 | „ |
| | Margery Shyres fil Richard | 20 | „ |
| | Margrett Soothworth fil Anthony | 23 | „ |
| sp: | Dorithy Gille fil Edward | 24 | „ |
| | Jane Swyfte fil Lyonell | 25 | „ |
| | Hugh Smyth fil Richard | „ | „ |
| sp: | Anne Spencer fil Rich | 27 | „ |
| | Ellinor Charles fil Hugh | „ | „ |
| | Elizabeth James Daughter | 30 | „ |
| | Willm Mason fil Thomas | 1 | May |
| | Thomas Kilshawe fil John | 7 | „ |
| | John ffletcher fil Richard | 9 | „ |
| | John Scarisbricke fil Henry | 11 | „ |
| | Katheryne Hurst fil Ellice | 12 | „ |
| | James Morcrofte fil Homphrey | 16 | „ |
| sp: | Ellen Lunt fil John de Sephton pishe | 17 | „ |
| | Anne Burscough fil Thomas | 20 | „ |
| | Willm Leadbetter fil John | 25 | „ |
| | Anne Woodes fil Richard | 8 | June |
| | Willm Spencer fil Thom̃ | 12 | „ |
| sp: | Jennett Lunt fil Tho: de Aughtō | 14 | „ |
| | Anthony Ranold fil John | 15 | „ |
| | Willm Haughton fi: Samuell | „ | „ |
| | Richard Corneforth fil Thomas | 22 | „ |
| | Elizabeth Cowper fil Willm | 24 | „ |
| | John Dunkon fil John | 26 | „ |
| | John Letherbarrowe fil Roger | 10 | July |
| sp: | George More fil Willm | „ | „ |
| | Anne Jackson fil John | 13 | „ |
| | Thomas Melling fil Raph | „ | „ |
| | Thomas Sumner fil John | 17 | „ |
| Fo. 149 | Thomas Gille fil Gilbte | 24 | „ |
| | Anne Marclewe fil Peter | 25 | „ |
| | Margery Prescott fil James | 27 | „ |
| | Grace Warde fil John | 29 | „ |
| | Anne Sutch fil Hugh | 31 | „ |
| | James Keakwicke fil Robte | „ | „ |
| | Hugh Smult fil Robte | 1 | August |
| | Willm Rowley fil Thomas | 6 | „ |

| | | | |
|---|---|---|---|
| | Anne Sharples als Warde fil Richard ... ... | 9 | August |
| | Isabell Alte fil Homphry ... ... ... ... ... ... | 18 | „ |
| | Mary Blundill fil James ... ... ... ... ... ... | 20 | „ |
| | Jane Prescott fil James ... ... ... ... ... ... | 23 | „ |
| | Ellen Ashurst fil Edward ... ... ... ... ... | 27 | „ |
| | Cisley Winder fil Thomas ... ... ... ... ... | 30 | „ |
| | Elizabeth Torbocke fil Thom̃ ... ... ... | „ | „ |
| | Alice Clarkson fil Willm ... ... ... ... ... | 2 | September |
| | Roger Aspinwall fil Thurstan ... ... ... ... ... | „ | „ |
| | Edward Parker fil Thom̃ ... ... ... ... ... | 3 | „ |
| | Henry Stanley fil Edw: Esq[r] ... ... ... | „ | „ |
| | Elizabeth Ascroft fil James ... ... ... ... ... | 11 | „ |
| | Jony Ascroft fil John ... ... ... ... ... ... | 12 | „ |
| | Ellen Thornton fil Thurstan ... ... ... ... ... | „ | „ |
| | John Caritam fil Rich ... ... ... ... ... ... | 21 | „ |
| sp: | Peter Marclewe fil Hugh ... ... ... ... ... | 25 | „ |
| | Henry Houlme fil Richard ... ... ... ... ... | 28 | „ |
| | Mary Leigh fil Alexander ... ... ... ... ... | 2 | October |
| | Richard Hadocke fil Thom̃ ... ... ... ... ... | „ | „ |
| | Anne Heaton fil Huan ... ... ... ... ... ... | 5 | „ |
| | Richard Gille fil Thom̃ ... ... ... ... ... ... | „ | „ |
| | Margrett Westhead fil Willm ... ... ... ... ... | „ | „ |
| | Richard Miller fil James ... ... ... ... ... | „ | „ |
| | Thomas Hey fil Phillip ... ... ... ... ... ... | „ | „ |
| | Elizab: Woodes fil Henry de Aughtō ... ... | 7 | „ |
| | Katheryne Holland fil Willm ... .. ... ... | 15 | „ |
| | Martha & Elizabeth Haughton fil Richard ... | 17 | „ |
| | Cisley Carre fil Rich ... ... ... ... ... ... | 18 | „ |
| sp: | Richard Marclewe fil Thom̃ ... ... ... ... ... | 19 | „ |
| | Thomas Morcroft fil Willm ... ... ... ... ... | 20 | „ |
| | Anne Mathewe fil Henry ... ... ... ... ... | 21 | „ |
| | Jane Hesketh fil Tho: de Aughtō ... ... ... | 26 | „ |
| | Margrett Modsley fil Roger ... ... ... ... ... | 27 | „ |
| 150 | John Balshawe fil James ... ... ... ... ... ... | 2 | November |
| | Robte Gille fil Edward ... ... ... ... ... ... | 13 | „ |
| | Cisley Tyrer fil Robte ... ... ... ... ... ... | 16 | „ |
| | Anne Butler fil Willm ... .. ... ... ... ... | 18 | „ |
| | Bartholomewe Keakwicke fil John de Aughton | 20 | „ |
| | Ellen Brough fil Willm ... ... ... ... ... ... | 24 | „ |
| | Willm Rigmaden fil George ... ... ... ... ... | 27 | „ |
| | John Waring fil Willm ... ... ... ... ... ... | „ | „ |
| | James Jackson fil Gilbte ... ... ... ... ... | 1 | December |
| sp: | Margrett Swyft fil Rich ... ... ... ... ... ... | 2 | „ |
| | Henry Leadbetter fil Peter ... ... ... ... ... | 3 | „ |
| | Anne Shawe fil Rich ... ... ... ... ... ... | 11 | „ |
| sp: | Homphry Tayler fil Thom̃ ... ... ... ... ... | 17 | „ |
| | Ellen Brighouse fil Willm ... ... ... ... ... | 19 | „ |
| | Richard Davy fil Thomas ... ... ... ... ... | 20 | „ |
| | Edith Arnolde fil Rich de Aughtō ... ... ... | 21 | „ |

Anne Ascroft fil Henry ... ... ... ... ... 26 December
Edith Spencer fil Hugh ... ... ... ... ... 27 „
Alice Allon fil Edward ... ... ... ... ... 1 January
Willm Houlding fil George ... ... ... ... 3 „
ffrancis Carby fil Joseph ... ... ... ... ... 10 „
Peregrine . . . . . . . ... ... ... ... „ „
Margrett Johnson fil Richard ... ... ... ... 18 „
Robte Shorlakers fil John ... ... ... ... 21 „
Willm Rigbie fil Peter ... ... ... ... ... 25 „
Anne Steele fil George ... ... ... ... ... 29 „
Katheryne Symkin fil Edward ... ... ... 1 ffebr:
Elizabeth Smalshawe fil Rich ... ... ... 2 „
Edward Halsall fil James ... ... ... ... ... 7 „
sp: Thomas Jackson fil Rich: ... ... ... ... 8 „
Thom Lathom fil Edward ... ... ... ... „ „
Jane Croocke fil Edward ... ... ... ... 9 „
Henry Barton fil Hugh ... ... ... ... ... „ „
John Bower fil Thom ... ... ... ... ... ... 12 „
Thom Kilshawe fil Henry ... ... ... ... 13 „
M'grett Hesketh fil Thomas ... ... ... ... „ „
Katheryne Kilshawe fil Willm ... ... ... 14 „
Edward Smult fil Thom ... ... ... ... ... 15 „
Elizab: Brighouse fil Thom ... ... ... ... „ „
John Withingtō fil Robte ... ... ... ... 20 „
sp: Thom Ormeshaw fil Willm ... ... ... ... 24 „
M'gery Vauce fil John ... ... ... ... ... „ „
Elizab: Clapam fil Richard ... ... ... ... 27 „
John Layland fil Xpofer ... ... ... ... ... 28 „
Fo. 151 Margrett Gille fil John ... ... ... ... ... 1 March
Elizabeth Aspinwall fil Homphry ... ... ... 5 „
Ellen Sutch fil James ... ... ... ... ... 6 „
Henry Barton fil Willm ... ... ... ... ... 9 „
Jane Thrope fil Hugh ... ... ... ... ... 10 „
James Kilshawe fil Richard ... ... ... ... 15 „
Elizab: Halsall fil Richard ... ... ... ... 22 „
Elizabeth Garrard fil Myles ... ... ... ... „ „

## 1618.

Elizabeth Ascrofte fil John ... ... ... ... 29 March
Ellen Morcrofte fil Phillip ... ... ... ... „ „
Elizab: Jackson fil Rich ... ... ... ... 31 „
Margrett Blundill fil Roger ... ... ... ... 2 Aprill
Cisley Wilding fil Peter ... ... ... ... ... 5 „
Ranalde Allerton fil Raph ... ... ... ... „ „
Rich Spencer fi: Edward ... ... ... ... 11 „
Anne Barton fi: Rowland ... ... ... ... 12 „
Raphe Allerton fi: Rich ... ... ... ... ... 13 „
Peter Aspinwall fi: Rich ... ... ... ... ... 19 „

Henry Orme fi: John ... ... ... ... ... 20 Aprill
Thomas Stopford fi: Peter ... ... ... ... 26 „
Margrett ffairclough fi: Willm ... ... ... 5 May
Jane Darby fi: John ... ... ... ... ... 10 „
Huan Langeley fi: Raphe ... ... ... ... 19 „
Rich Parke fi: Edmund ... ... ... ... „ „
Elizabeth Blundill fi: Alexander ... ... ... 2 June
Gawther Barton fi: Rich ... ... ... ... 7 „
Rich Melling fi: Willm ... ... ... ... ... 11 „
Mariery Smalshawe fi: George ... ... ... „ „
Willm Ascough fil Huan ... ... ... ... 14 „
Willm Dickett fi: John ... ... ... ... ... 18 „
sp: Thomas Whalley fi: James ... ... ... ... 21 „
sp: Mary Parre fi: Edward ... ... ... ... ... 25 „
Anne & Alice Crapper fi: Edmund ... ... 27 „
Thomas Nelson fi: Rich ... ... ... ... 2 July
Henry Tasker fi: Thom̃ ... ... ... ... ... 3 „
Richard Ambrose fi: Thom̃ ... ... ... ... 5 „
Elizab: Halsall fi: Rich gent ... ... ... 6 „
Katheryne Swyfte fi: Henry ... ... ... ... 9 „
Edward Dod fi: Hugh ... ... ... ... ... 11 „
John Rostron fi: James ... ... ... ... ... 13 „
Anne Cowp fi: Homphry ... ... ... ... 14 „
Elizab: Keakwicke fi: Edward ... ... ... 17 „
Willm Houlme fi: Thom̃ ... ... ... ... 25 „
John Smyth fi: Edward ... ... ... ... ... „ „
Katheryne Wainwright fi: John ... ... ... „ „
Edward Modesley fi: Rich ... ... ... ... 29 „
Anne Bower fi: Willm ... ... ... ... ... 30 „
Thomas Hawarth fi: Willm ... ... ... ... 31 „
0152 Elizab: Houlme fi: John sp: ... ... ... 1 August
Rich Westhead fi: Thom̃ ... ... ... ... 2 „
Thomas Ashurst fil Edw: ... ... ... ... 3 „
Margrett Prescott fi: Hamlett ... ... ... 9 „
Mary Haughtō fi: Gabriell ... ... ... ... 15 „
James Blundill fi: Rich: de Aughtō ... ... 17 „
John Scarisbricke fi: Hugh ... ... ... ... 18 „
Mariery Cowp fi: Edward ... ... ... ... „ „
John Woan fi: Hugh ... ... ... ... ... 23 „
Rich Kilshawe fi: Willm ... ... ... ... 26 „
sp: Jane Davy fi: Thom̃ ... ... ... ... ... 12 September
Katheryne Woorthingtō fi: Edw: ... ... ... 13 „
Anne Sephtō fil Thom̃ ... ... ... ... ... 14 „
Margrett Rathwell fi: James ... ... ... ... 15 „
James Hey fi: Thom̃ ... ... ... ... ... 17 „
Anne Blundell fi: Edward ... ... ... ... 18 „
John Peter fi: Thom̃ ... ... ... ... ... 20 „
Anne Sephtō fi: Thom̃ ... ... ... ... ... „ „
Margrett Lea fi: Hector ... ... ... ... ... „ „

| | | | |
|---|---|---|---|
| | Edward Rigby fil Hugh ... ... ... ... ... ... | 21 | September |
| | Henry Jackson fi: John ... ... ... ... ... ... | 24 | „ |
| | Henry Burscough fi: Thom ... ... ... ... ... | 27 | „ |
| | Jane Dale fi: Henry ... ... ... ... ... ... | „ | „ |
| | Jane Spopford fi: Wiltm ... ... ... ... ... | 1 | October |
| | Anne Rainforth fi: Rich ... ... ... ... ... | „ | „ |
| | Adam Chadocke fi: Rich ... ... ... ... ... | 5 | „ |
| | Katheryne Thorton* fi: Robte ... ... ... ... | 7 | „ |
| | Edward Holland fi: Wiltm ... ... ... ... ... | 9 | „ |
| | Margrett Woodhouse fi: Rich: ... ... ... ... | „ | „ |
| | Wiltm Robinson fi: Rich: de Aughtō ... ... | 11 | „ |
| | Henry Gille fi: Gilbte ... ... ... ... ... ... | 13 | „ |
| | Katheryne Bonell fi: John ... ... ... ... ... | 18 | „ |
| | Richard Swyft fi: Huan ... ... ... ... ... ... | „ | „ |
| | Edward Balshawe fi: John ... ... ... ... ... | 22 | „ |
| | Margrett Modesley fi: Thomas ... ... ... ... | 23 | „ |
| | Edward Marbeck fi: Emanuel ... ... ... ... | 25 | „ |
| | Huan Allerton fi: Henry ... ... ... ... ... | 28 | „ |
| | John Hayton fi: Thomas ... ... ... ... ... | 29 | „ |
| | Anne ffidler fi: Robte ... ... ... ... ... ... | 15 | November |
| sp: | James Townley fi: Wiltm ... ... ... ... ... | 16 | „ |
| | Katheryne Swyft fi: Lyonell ... ... ... ... ... | „ | „ |
| | Jeremy Evans a Stranger ... ... ... ... ... | 23 | „ |
| | Thomas Harrison fi: Henry ... ... ... ... ... | 25 | „ |
| | Homphrey Wetherby fi: Robte ... ... ... | „ | „ |
| | Huan Westhead fi: Richard ... ... ... ... ... | 28 | „ |
| | Margrett Modesley John ... ... ... ... ... ... | 30 | „ |
| Fo. 153 | Raph Whitestones fi: Thomas ... ... ... ... | 1 | December |
| | John Hodson fi: ffardinando ... ... ... ... ... | 3 | „ |
| | Emlin Scarisbrick fi: Edward ... ... ... ... | 10 | „ |
| | Thomas Lyon fi: James ... ... ... ... ... | „ | „ |
| | Isabell Marclewe fi: Hugh ... ... ... ... ... | 16 | „ |
| | James Laithwaitt fi: Thom ... ... ... ... ... | 20 | „ |
| | Hugh Warde fi: John ... ... ... ... ... ... | 29 | „ |
| | James Woodes fi: Henry ... ... ... ... ... | 30 | „ |
| sp: | Agnes Weerden fi: John ... ... ... ... ... ... | 1 | January |
| sp: | Mary Wignall fi: John ... ... ... ... ... ... | 2 | „ |
| | John Holland fi: Hugh ... ... ... ... ... ... | 5 | „ |
| | Wiltm Wallice fi: Hector ... ... ... ... ... | 7 | „ |
| sp: | Jane Houlme fi: Raph ... ... ... ... ... ... | 9 | „ |
| | Jennett Baron fi: Gilbte ... ... ... ... ... | 12 | „ |
| | Elizabeth Rigby fi: Mayles ... ... ... ... ... | 15 | „ |
| | Gotfrey Atherton fi: Andrewe ... ... ... ... | 20 | „ |
| | Anne Barton fi: Wiltm ... ... ... ... ... ... | „ | „ |
| | Henry Hale fi: James ... ... ... ... ... ... | 21 | „ |
| | Thomas Spencer fi: John ... ... ... ... ... | 22 | „ |
| | Henry Ledbetter fi: John ... ... ... ... ... | „ | „ |
| | Dorithy Mollyneux fi: Richard ... ... ... ... | 24 | „ |

* Thornton in Chester Transcript.

Alice Gille fi: Henry ... ... ... ... ... 28 January
Emlin Page fi: Jeffrey ... ... ... ... ... " "
Thomas Babot fi: Richard ... ... ... ... 30 "
Anne Ambrose fi: Edward ... ... ... ... " "
Alice Holcroft fi: John ... ... ... ... ... 2 ffebruary
Elizabeth Gille fi: Edward ... ... ... ... 7 "
James Cartmer fi: James ... ... ... ... " "
Sara Greenough fi: Henry ... ... ... ... 10 "
Margrett Hodson fi: Richard ... ... ... ... 12 "
Richard Whalley fi: Thomas ... ... ... 13 "
Robte Lathom fi: Willm ... ... ... ... 14 "
Ann Morcroft fi: Richard ... ... ... ... " "
John Swyft fi: Richard ... ... ... ... ... 17 "
Willm Smult fi: Thom ... ... ... ... ... 24 "
Robte Modesley fi: Henry ... ... ... ... " "
Richard Winstanley fi: Thom ... ... ... 25 "
John Marclewe fi: Richard ... ... ... ... 1 March
Willm fforshawe fi: Richard ... ... ... ... " "
James Stanley fi: Edward Armig: ... ... 3 "
Alice Leadbetter fi: Robte ... ... ... ... 4 "
Ranald Wainwright fi: Thom ... ... ... 7 "
Thomas Hunter fi: Edward ... ... ... ... 9 "
Ellen Melling fi: Raph ... ... ... ... ... 11 "
Margrett Prescott fi: John ... ... ... ... " "
. . . Whalley fi: Henry ... ... ... ... 19 "

## 1619.

Alexander Scotfeild* fi: John ... ... ... 25 March
Peter Shawe fi: John ... ... ... ... ... 31 "
Thomas Mossocke fil Hen: ... ... ... ... " "
Jane Rose fi: Richard ... ... ... ... ... 4 Aprill
Ellen Pemberton fi: . . . . ... ... ... ... 9 "
Myles Hesketh fi: George ... ... ... ... 15 "
Elizab: Cowp fi: Willm ... ... ... ... ... 20 "
Anne Wetherby fi: John ... ... ... ... 22 "
Elizabeth Barton fi: Gowther ... ... ... 23 "
Hugh Swyft fi: Willm ... ... ... ... ... 30 "
Edith Westhead fi: Edward ... ... ... ... 1 May
John Whitestones fi: Hugh ... ... ... ... 2 "
James Bower fi: Robte ... ... ... ... ... 16 "
Richard Sootwoorth fi: Robte ... ... ... 17 "
Richard Spencer fi: James ... ... ... ... 18 "
Elizabeth Kilshawe fi: Richard ... ... ... 28 "
ffleetwood Woorthington fi: Edward ... ... 29 "
Henry Mercer fi: John ... ... ... ... ... 30 "
Anne Rainforth fi: Peter ... ... ... ... 31 "
Thomas Sutch fi: James ... ... ... ... ... 3 June

* Scoefeild in Chester Transcript.

John Ryding fi: James ... ... ... ... ... 10 June
Henry Scarisbricke fi: ffardinand ... ... ... " "
Isabell Barton fi: Peter ... ... ... ... .... 13 "
Anne Cockett fi: Thomas ... ... ... ... 17 "
Henry Robinson fi: John ... ... ... ... 20 "
Elizabeth Rutter fi: John ... ... ... ... 27 "
Dorithy Neale fi: Peaze ... ... ... ... ... " "
Henry Gille fi: Wittm ... ... ... ... ... 29 "
Cysley Longley Raph ... ... ... ... ... 4 July
Robte Hesketh fi: Edward ... ... ... ... 5 "
Richard Sutton fi: John ... ... ... ... 7 "
Thomas Rodes fi: Thomas ... ... ... ... 8 "
Hugh Morcroft fi: Gabriell ... ... ... ... 16 "
John Banke fi: Robte ... ... ... ... ... 18 "
Raph Scath fi: James ... ... ... ... ... 22 "
sp: Thomas Hunter fi: Rich ... ... ... ... 27 "
Margrett Stopford fi: Thom ... ... ... ... 29 "
Richard Moorcroft s. of Humprey* ... ... " "
Idithe Modesley fi: James ... ... ... ... 1 August
Katheryne Barton fi: Rowland ... ... ... " "
Roger Modesley fi: Henry ... ... ... ... 3 "
Anne Harrison fi: John ... ... ... ... ... 5 "
Ellen Webster fi: Henry ... ... ... ... 6 "
John Martin fi: James his maties preach9 ... ... 8 "
Ellen ffarclough fi: Thurstan ... ... ... ... " "
Peter Hesselden fi: James ... ... ... ... 10 "
James Prescott fi: Henry ... ... ... ... " "
John † Ascroft fi: Thomas ... ... ... ... 11 "
James Blundill fi: Alexander ... ... ... ... 15 "
Mary fforshawe fi: Arthur ... ... ... ... 26 "
Fo. 155 Anne Parker fi: Thomas ... ... ... ... 3 September
Anne Banke fi: Thomas ... ... ... ... ... 5 "
Katheryne Myller fi: James ... ... ... ... 9 "
Edward Yate fi: Thom: ... ... ... ... ... 12 "
Ellen Walker fi: Gabriel ... ... ... ... 14 "
Wittm Clarkson fi: Wittm ... ... ... ... 16 "
Nicolas Hey fi: James ... ... ... ... ... " "
Walter Munck fi: Rich: ... ... ... ... 18 "
Wittm Rathram fi: Edward ... ... ... ... 21 "
Ellen Sumner fi: James ... ... ... ... ... 25 "
Thomas Houlme fi: Henry ... ... ... ... 26 "
Anne Thornton fi: Robte ... ... ... ... " "
Ellen Gille fi: John ... ... ... ... ... " "
Ellen Marclewe fi: Wittm ... ... ... ... 29 "
Anne Cheetam fi: James ... ... ... ... 5 October
sp: Margrett Holland fi: Edward ... ... ... " "
Richard Crane fi: Wittm ... ... ... ... 6 "

* This is an interlineation in a different hand at a much later date.

† Anne in Chester Transcript.

Ellen Prescott fi: John ... ... ... ... ... ... 14 October
John Tayler fi: Willm ... ... ... ... ... ... „ „
Elizabeth Rigby fi: Peter ... ... ... ... ... „ „
Anne Steenson fi: Henry ... ... ... ... ... 5 November
Isabell Hey fi: Phillip ... ... ... ... ... ... „ „
Elizabeth Abraham fi: Mathew ... ... ... 9 „
John Claytō fi: Adā de Layland ... ... ... 12 „
Dorithy Halsall fi: Richard gent ... ... ... 17 „
. . . Rayfornth fi: Hugh ... ... ... ... 18 „
Robte Allerton fi: Henry ... ... ... ... 24 „
James Berry fi: Homphry de Rainforth ... 25 „
Roger Poole fi: Raphe ... ... ... ... ... 7 December
p: Edward Winstanley fi: Edward ... ... ... 8 „
Jane Kilshawe fi: Willm ... ... ... ... ... 11 „
Richard Smalshawe fi: James ... ... ... 20 „
Anne Dunkon fi: John ... ... ... ... ... ... „ „
John Barton fi: Roger ... ... ... ... ... ... 21 „
Anne Morcroft fi: Phillip ... ... ... ... ... 23 „
Agnes Barton* ... ... ... ... ... ... ... ...
p: Thomas Butterfeild fi: Roger ... ... ... 25 „
Thomas Halsall fi: Richard ... ... ... ... 28 „
Katheryne Stopford fi: Hugh ... ... ... 4 January
Willm Melling fi: John ... ... ... ... ... ... 6 „
Margrett Alcar fi: Willm ... ... ... ... ... 8 „
Richard Jarman fi: James ... ... ... ... ... „ „
Henry Barker fi: Alexander ... ... ... ... 16 „
Willm Topping fi: Raphe ... ... ... ... ... 17 „
Ellice Barton fi: Edward ... ... ... ... ... „ „
Elizabeth Tyrer fi: Robte ... ... ... ... ... 18 „
Thomas Hurst fi: Ellice ... ... ... ... ... 21 „
Elizabeth Smyth fi: Edward ... ... ... ... 22 „
56 Richard Soothwoorth fi: Anthony ... ... ... 7 ffebruary
Edmund Kilshawe fi: Willm ... ... ... ... 12 „
Anne Robinson fi: Henry ... ... ... ... ... 14 „
Christopher † Sumner fi: John ... ... ... 18 „
Thomas Garrard fi: Myles ... ... ... ... 27 „
Richard Houlme fi: Willm ... ... ... ... 28 „
sp: Anne Hughson fi: Thom̃ de Magehull ... ... „ „
Isabell Brighouse fi: Willm ... ... ... ... 1 March
ffrances Morcroft fi: Thomas ... ... ... ... 10 „
James Jackson fi: Henry ... ... ... ... ... 17 „
Jane Steele fi: George ... ... ... ... ... ... 22 „
Elizabeth ‡ & Willm } John Johnson fi Gilbte :... ... 23 „
Willm Brighouse fi: John ... ... ... ... ... „ „

* This entry in Chester Transcript only.
† Cisley in Chester Transcript.
‡ Isabell in Chester Transcript.

## 1620.

| |  |  |  |
|---|---|---|---|
| | James Spencer fi: Thom̃ | 25 | March |
| | Edward Scarisbricke fi: Henry | 26 | " |
| | George Haughton fi: Samuel | 28 | " |
| | Robte Briggs fi: John a Stranger | 30 | " |
| sp: | Anne Lunt fi: Henry | 2 | Aprill |
| | Richard Hallywell fi: Robte | " | " |
| | Katheryne Lowe fi: Thomas | 4 | " |
| | Richard Cowp fi: Richard | " | " |
| | Mary Atherton fi: Andrew | 7 | " |
| | Jenett Hey fi: James | 9 | " |
| | Mary Dickett fi: John | 13 | " |
| | Elizabeth Prescott fi: John | 14 | " |
| | Margery Barton fi: George | 15 | " |
| | Anne Chadocke fi: Richard | " | " |
| | Henry Wallice fi: Hector | 17 | " |
| | Ellen Bury fi: Willm | " | " |
| | George Mathew fi: Henry | 27 | " |
| | Thomas Shawe fi: Richard | 30 | " |
| | Peter Aspinwall fi: Anthony | 1 | May |
| | Willm Jackson fi: John | " | " |
| | Katheryne Py fi: George | 2 | " |
| | Margrett Breers fi: Alexandr | 7 | " |
| | Robte Coale* fi: Anthony | 11 | " |
| | Homphry Aspinwall fi: Peter | " | " |
| sp: | Alice Keakwicke fi: Richard | 13 | " |
| | Sara Rozaway fi: Abraham | 15 | " |
| | Hugh Woorthington fi: Edward | 16 | " |
| | ffrancis Whitestones fi: George | 25 | " |
| | Thomas Butler fi: Robte | 27 | " |
| | Anne Rose fi: Richard | 28 | " |
| Fo. 157 | Margrett Hesketh fi: George | 3 | June |
| | Robte Moone fi: John | 14 | " |
| | Ellen Greenhaugh fi: John | 16 | " |
| | Thomas Swyft fi: Thomas | 18 | " |
| | Hugh Jollybrand † fi: Richard | 19 | " |
| | Katherine & Margrett Higham fi: John | 22 | " |
| | Willm Ascrofte fi: John | 29 | " |
| | Thomas Henryson | 1 | July |
| | Jane Rigbie fi: Myles | " | " |
| | James Scarisbricke fi: John | 5 | " |
| | Jane Haughton fi: Gabriell | 6 | " |
| | Richard Houlme fi: Willm | 8 | " |
| | Alice Lunt fi: Homphry | 9 | " |
| | Myles Barton fi: Willm | " | " |

* Jollie in Chester Transcript.

† Goldborne in Chester Transcript.

... ... ... 9 July

... ... ... 14 ,,

... ... ... 15

... ... ... 30 ,,

... ... ... ,, ,,

... ... ... 2 August

... ... ... 17 ,,

... ... ... ,,

... ... ... ,,

... ... ... 21

... ... ... 27 ,,

... ... ... ,,

... ... ... 28

... ... ... 29 ,,

... ... ... 31 ,,

... ... ... 6 September

... ... ... ,, ,,

... ... ... 17 ,,

... ... ... ,,

... ... ... 18

... ... ... 19

... ... ... 22

... ... ... 24

... ... ... 26

... ... ... 28

... ... ... ,, ,,

... . ... 29 ,,

... ... ... 1 October

... ... ... ,, ,,

... ... ... 3

... ... ... 4

... ... ... 7

... ... ... 8

... ... ... ,,

... ... ... ,,

... ... ... ,,

... ... ... 10

... ... ... 11 ,,

... ... ... ,,

... ... ... 15

... ... ... 16

... ... ... 22

... ... ... 23

... ... ... 25

... ... ... 26

... ... ... 29 ,,

... ... ... 31 ,,

... ... ... 2 November

... ... ... ,, ,,

sp: Margrett Rothwell fi: Robte ... ... ... ... 3
Elizabeth Barton fi: James ... ... ... ... 4
Wittm Kilshawe fi: John ... ... ... ... 5
Thomas ffairclough fi: Wittm ... ... ... ... „
Elizab: & Ellen Barton fi: Hugh ... ... ... „
. . . Marclewe fi: Hugh ... ... ... ... 6
John Haworth fi: Wittm ... ... ... ... 7
Thomas Robinson fi: John ... ... ... ... 12
Thomas Holcroft fi: John ... ... ... ... 15
Richard Burgh fi: Wittm ... ... ... ... 23
Elizabeth Rothwell fi: James ... ... ... 25
Peter dale fi: Henry de Aughtō ... ... ... 26
John Hille fil: Thomas ... ... ... ... ... 27
Margrett Kilshawe fi: John ... ... ... ... 28
Ellen Page fi: John ... ... ... ... ... 10
Elizab: Vauce fi: Peter ... ... ... ... ... „
Jane Woofall fi: Lawrence de Aughton ... ... 13
Homphry Houlme fi: Rich ... ... ... ... „
Robte Holland fi: Richard ... ... ... ... „
Katheryne Croock fi: Edward ... ... ... 16
Anne Kilshawe fi: Henry ... ... ... ... „
Elizabeth Sutch fi: Hugh ... ... ... ... 17
Anne Nelson fi: Richard ... ... ... ... „
Margery Carby fi: Josephe ... ... ... ... 18
Joane Houlme fi: Henry de Croston ... ... 19
Richard Smalshawe fi: George ... ... ... 26
Ellen Shawe fi: Wittm ... ... ... ... ... „
Huan Swyfte fi: Richard ... ... ... ... 31
Fo. 159 Jane Aspinwall fi: Edward ... ... ... ... 2
Rychard Vaudrie fi: John ... ... ... ... 3
Margrett Swyft fi: Huan ... ... ... ... ... „
Elizabeth Bower fi: Wittm ... ... ... ... 7
Katheryne Spencer fi: Edward ... ... ... 10
Thomas Sutch fi: Peter ... ... ... ... ... 11
Jane Clapham fi: Richard ... ... ... ... 12
Arthur Lea fi: James ... ... ... ... ... 14
Ellen Shawe fi: Thomas ... ... ... ... 16
James Holland fi: Hugh ... ... ... ... ... 19
Margrett Kilsh* fi: Richard ... ... ... ... 21
Wittm Stopford fi: Wittm ... ... ... ... 22
Margrett Kilshawe fi: Wittm ... ... ... ... 27
Mariery † Masson fi: Lawrence ... ... ... 28
Elizabeth Nyclason fi: Xpofer ... ... ... 1
sp: Hugh Woorthington fi: Richard ... ... ... 4
Wittm Ashurst fi: Edward ... ... ... ... 5
Richard Chadocke fi: Cuthbert ... ... ... 6
Ellen Aspinwall fi: Homphry ... ... ... ... 10

* Kilshshawe in Chester Transcript.

† Margrett in Chester Transcript.

| | | |
|---|---|---|
| Thomas Olyverson fi: Ellice | 11 | ffebruary |
| Mary Robinson fi: Henry | 16 | „ |
| Robte Walsh fi: John | 17 | „ |
| Alice Holte fi: Witlm | 18 | „ |
| Richard Leadbetter fi: John | 19 | „ |
| James Smalshawe fi: James | 23 | „ |
| Henry Crapp fi: Hamlett fi: Hamlett [*sic*] | „ | „ |
| Mary Wynstanley fi: Thom | 24 | „ |
| Mary Page fi: Geffrey | 25 | „ |
| Richard Waynwright fi: Thom | 27 | „ |
| Anne Sephton fi: Witlm | „ | „ |
| Henry Halsall fi: Richard | 4 | March |
| Ellen Scofelt fi: John | „ | „ |
| Ideth Raynforth fi: James de Aughtō | 5 | „ |
| George Sephton fi: Thom | 11 | „ |
| Thomas Leyland* | | |
| Jane † ffydler fi: Robte | „ | „ |
| Dorithie Houlme fi: Thom | 13 | „ |
| James Houlme fi: Hugh | 17 | „ |
| Alice Westhead fi: Thom | 18 | „ |
| Katheryne Melling fi: Raph | 24 | „ |

## 1621.

| | | |
|---|---|---|
| Gabriel Haughtō fi: Samuel | 25 | March |
| Hugh Sumner fi: John | 27 | „ |
| Ellen Mollyneux fi: Richard | 3 | Aprill |
| Robte Py fi: George | 6 | „ |
| Thom Robinson fi: Rich de Aughtō | 9 | „ |
| George Longely fi: Raphe | 12 | „ |
| Jane Stopford fi: Peter | „ | „ |
| Myles Barton fi: Edward | 13 | „ |
| Anne Layland fi: Xpofer | „ | „ |
| Henry Symkin fi: Edward | 15 | „ |
| Jennett Ormeshawe fi: Witlm | 19 | „ |
| Witlm Pemberton fi: James | 22 | „ |
| Myles More fi: James | 25 | „ |
| Anne Jolly fi: Henry | 26 | „ |
| Robte Ambrose fi: Rich | 29 | „ |
| Robte Haughtō fi: Robte | 30 | „ |
| Margrett Ashton fi: Rich | 1 | May |
| Jane Smult fi: Thomas | 3 | „ |
| Henry Blundill fi: Edward | 13 | „ |
| Edward Waynwright fi: Thom | 21 | „ |
| Richard Johnson fi: Witlm | „ | „ |
| Alexander Smyth fi: Rich | 23 | „ |
| Anne Tasker fi: Thom | 13 | „ |

* This entry in Chester Transcript only.

† Anne in Chester Transcript.

Henry Westhead fi: Rich ... ... ... ... 13 May
James Greenhaugh fi: John ... ... ... ... 7 June
Margrett Barton fi: Peter ... ... ... ... 11 „
Margrett Johnson fi: James ... ... ... ... „ „
Thomas Hale fi: James ... ... ... ... ... „ „
George Swyfte fi: Thom̃ ... ... ... ... 18 „
John Whatton fi: James ... ... ... ... ... „ „
Elizabeth Barton fi: Peter ... ... ... ... 19 „
Katheryne fforshawe fi: Rich ... ... ... ... 24 „
Wiłłm Swyft fi: Henry ... ... ... ... ... 27 „
John Percivalson ... ... ... ... ... ... 4 July
Anne Hodson fi: ffardinand ... ... ... ... 5 „
Jennett Barton fi: Rowland ... ... ... ... 9 „
Margrett Sutton fi: John ... ... ... ... „ „
Xpofer Morcroft fi: Gabriel ... ... ... ... 15 „
Hugh Crapper fi: Peter ... ... ... ... ... 19 „
sp: Wiłłm Hallywell fi: Lawrence de Ecclestone... „ „
Thomas Gille fi: Edwarde ... ... ... ... 23 „
Jane Modesley fi: Henry ... ... ... ... 30 „
sp: Thomas Weston fi: Thom̃ ... ... ... ... 2 August
Thomas Gobben fi: Robte ... ... ... ... 3 „
Katheryne Hale fi: James ... ... ... ... 4 „
Edward Rodes fi: Thom̃ ... ... ... ... 9 „
Isabell Vauce fi: John ... ... ... ... ... 10 „
Richard Taylor fi: Thomas ... ... ... ... 19 „
Sylvester Laythwaitt fi: Thom̃ ... ... ... 20 „
Robte Smult fi: Thom̃ ... ... ... ... ... „ „
Fo. 161 Margrett Hille fi: John ... ... ... ... ... 21 „
Bellafront Carritam fi: Rich ... ... ... ... 23 „
Bartholomew Rym̃er fi: Rich ... ... ... ... 24 „
Ellen Orme fi: John ... ... ... ... ... „ „
Margrett Whalley fi: Thom̃ ... ... ... ... 31 „
sp: Henry Worthingtõ fi: Rich ... ... ... ... „ „
Margrett Hey fi: Phillipp ... ... ... ... 5 Septembe
Thomas Smyth fi: Edward ... ... ... ... 6 „
Silvester Ryding fi: James ... ... ... ... 9 „
Richard Ireland fi: James ... ... ... ... 19 „
Wiłłm Robinson fi: James ... ... ... ... 22 „
James Peter fi: Thom̃ ... ... ... ... ... 23 „
Alice Webster fi: Wiłłm ... ... ... ... ... „ „
James Rostorne fi: James ... ... ... ... 4 October
John Blundill fi: Rich de Aughton ... ... 7 „
Ellen Haughton fi: Gabriel ... ... ... ... „ „
Alexander Hesketh fi: George ... ... ... 10 „
James Hayton fi: Thom̃ ... ... ... ... ... 11 „
Thomas Whalley fi: Henry ... ... ... ... „ „
Thomas Watkinson fi: Henry de Rufforth ... 14 „
John Jollybrand fi: Rich ... ... ... ... 17 „
Elizab: Whetherby fi: John ... ... ... ... „ „

| | | |
|---|---|---|
| Ellen Breers fi: Alexand: ... ... ... ... | 21 | October |
| Cysley Mollyneux fi: Robte ... ... ... ... | 22 | " |
| Thomas Astley fi: Cuthbte ... ... ... ... | 24 | " |
| Jane Gyles fi: Henry de Aughton ... ... ... | " | " |
| Anne Westhead fi: Edward ... ... ... ... | 25 | " |
| Edith Miller fi: James ... ... ... ... ... | 27 | " |
| Robte Marcer fi: John ... ... ... ... ... | 1 | November |
| Huan Swyft fi: Lyonell ... ... ... ... ... | 2 | " |
| Thomas Woan fi: Hugh ... ... ... ... ... | " | " |
| Jane Shorlokers fi: John ... ... ... ... | 4 | " |
| Anne Topping fi: Raphe ... ... ... ... | 6 | " |
| Anne Houlme fi: Thomas ... ... ... ... | 7 | " |
| John Ackers fi: Wiltm ... ... ... ... ... | 10 | " |
| Edward Kilshawe fi: John ... ... ... ... | 14 | " |
| James Halsall fi: Rich gent ... ... ... ... | " | " |
| Henry Morcrofte fi: Phillippe ... ... ... | 18 | " |
| Homphry Lythom fi: Homphry ... ... ... | 19 | " |
| Richard Lea fi: Roger ... ... ... ... ... | 23 | " |
| Nicolas Hunt fi: Thom ... ... ... ... ... | " | " |
| Elizabeth Parke fi: Edmund ... ... ... ... | 30 | " |
| John Raynforth fi: Hugh ... ... ... ... | 2 | December |
| Henry Atherton fi: Andrewe ... ... ... ... | 5 | " |
| Henry Laithwaitt fi: Henry ... ... ... ... | 14 | " |
| Richard Wetherby fi: Robte ... ... ... ... | 18 | " |
| John Stanley fi: Edward Armig[r] ... ... ... | 19 | " |
| Thomas Chadocke fi: Richard ... ... ... | 22 | " |
| Anne Modesley fi: Rich ... ... ... ... ... | " | " |
| Jony Morcrofte fi: Wiltm ... ... ... ... | 31 | " |
| Katheryne Mason fi: Ranald ... ... ... ... | " | " |
| Randall Johnson fi: Wiltm ... ... ... ... | 3 | January |
| Richard Baron fi: Gilbte ... ... ... ... | " | " |
| Anne Tomlinson fi: Richard ... ... ... ... | 5 | " |
| Thomas Bore fi: Robte ... ... ... ... ... | " | " |
| Katheryne Atherto fi: Wiltm de Dalton ... | 8 | " |
| Margrett Jarman fi: James ... ... ... ... | 22 | " |
| Richard Clarkson fi: Wiltm ... ... ... ... | 1 | ffebruary |
| Anne Symkin fi: Henry ... ... ... ... ... | " | " |
| Margrett Houlme fi: Wiltm ... ... ... ... | 4 | " |
| . . . Woorthingtō fi: Edward ... ... ... | 7 | " |
| James Yate fi: Thomas ... ... ... ... ... | 10 | " |
| Peter Morcroft fi: Roger ... ... ... ... | " | " |
| Thomas Gobben fi: Gilbte ... ... ... ... | 12 | " |
| Henry Johnson fi: Wiltm ... ... ... ... | 13 | " |
| Wiltm Hunter fi: Edward ... ... ... ... | 14 | " |
| Elizabeth Prescott fi: James ... ... ... ... | " | " |
| John Keakwicke fi: Richard ... ... ... ... | 15 | " |
| Wiltm Woodhouse fi: Rich ... ... ... ... | 19 | " |
| Elizabeth Page fi: John ... ... ... ... ... | 26 | " |
| Henry ffletcher fi: Richard ... ... ... ... | 28 | " |

sp: Jane Kerfoote fi: Thomas ... ... ... ... 4 March
Peter Aspinwall fi: Edward ... ... ... ... 5 „
Thomas Houlme fi: George ... ... ... ... 9 „
Thomas Cowper fi: Wittm ... ... ... ... 11 „
Elizabeth Kilshawe fi: Raphe ... ... ... 14 „
Maude Wignall fi: Thom̃ ... ... ... ... „ „
Thomas Letherbarrowe fi: Roger ... ... ... 16 „
John Nicolson fi: Xpofer ... ... ... ... „ „
Henry Sutch fi: James ... ... ... ... ... 20 „
James Keakwicke fi: Edward ... ... ... ... 21 „
Hugh Ascroft fi: John ... ... ... ... ... „ „

## 1622.

John Modesley fi: Thomas ... ... ... ... 26 March
Thom̃ Wythingtō fi: Henry ... ... ... ... 27 „
Fo. 163 Ellen Wallice fi: Hector ... ... ... ... ... ... 2 Aprill
Jane Melling fi: Raph ... ... ... ... ... 4 „
Anne Stopford fi: Thom̃ ... ... ... ... „ „
Edward Barton fi: Gowther ... ... ... ... 5 „
Margrett Aspinwall fi: Homphry ... ... ... 7 „
James Alcar fi: Thomas .. ... ... ... ... 11 „
Margrett Keakwicke fi: John de Aughton ... 12 „
Raphe ffforshawe fi: Arthur ... ... ... ... 14 „
sp: Thomas Hille fi: Thom: de Marton in Cheshire „ „
Elizabeth Percy fi: ffardinand a Stranger ... 18 „
sp: James Atherton fi: Phillip ... ... ... ... 19 „
Ellen Soothwoorth fi: Robte ... ... ... ... 22 „
Elizabeth Houlme fi: Hugh ... ... ... ... 23 „
Mary Cowp fi: Hugh ... ... ... ... ... 25 „
Emlin Cowbron fi: Thom̃ ... ... ... ... 27 „
sp: James Wilding fi: Peter ... ... ... ... ... 30 „
Thomas Blessing fi: Wittm ... ... ... ... 8 May
Elizabeth Webster fi: Henry ... ... ... ... 9 „
Margrett Stopford fi: John ... ... ... ... 12 „
John Billinge fi: Peter ... ... ... ... ... „ „
Roger Barton fi: Edward ... ... ... ... 14 „
Sara Waynwright fi: Henry ... ... ... ... 20 „
Cisley Smalshawe fi: James ... ... ... ... „ „
Susan Thornton fi: Robte ... ... ... ... 26 „
James Edwardson ... ... ... ... ... ... 30 „
James Marclewe fi: Wittm ... ... ... ... 2 June
Thomas Hodson fi: Richard ... ... ... ... 8 „
Richard Halsall fi: Richard ... ... ... ... 14 „
Margrett Kilshawe fi: Richard ... ... ... 27 „
Jane Barton fi: Roger ... ... ... ... ... 2 July
Margrett Martindale fi: Hugh ... ... ... 4 „
sp: Ellen Hynley fi: Robte ... ... ... ... ... „ „
James Yate fi: John ... ... ... ... ... 11 „

Thomas Rigby fi: Myles ... ... ... ... ... ... 18 July
Richard Hunter fi: John ... ... ... ... ... ... 19 „
Mary Modesley fi: James ... ... ... ... ... 30 „
Margrett Modesley fi: Rich ... ... ... ... ... „ „
Thomas Cowp fi: Edward ... ... ... ... 3 August
Joseph Waynwright fi: Thom ... ... ... 13 „
John Jackson fi: Henry ... ... ... ... ... ... 15 „
Margrett Smyth fi: Symon ... ... ... ... ... 23 „
Ellen Taylor fi: Witłm de Aughton ... ... 29 „
Anne Bonnell fi: John ... ... ... ... ... ... 9 September
Thomas Rathrā fi: Edward ... ... ... ... „ „
Elizabeth Letherbarrowe fi: Henry de Halsall pishe ... ... ... ... ... ... ... ... ... ... 12 „
George Rothwell fi: Robte ... ... ... ... ... „ „
Jane Blundill fi: James ... ... ... ... ... ... 16 „
Thomas Barker fi: Alexand ... ... ... ... ... 22 „
Witłm Modesley fi: George ... ... ... ... ... 23 „
Edith Gill fi: Gabriel ... ... ... ... ... ... 28 „
Edward Swyft fi: Rich: ... ... ... ... ... ... 29 „
Thomas Whatton fi: James ... ... ... ... 3 October
Thom̃ Shawe fi: Witłm ... ... ... ... ... ... 5 „
Cisley & Isabell Swyft fi: Lyonel ... ... ... 19 „
Witłm Hesketh fi: Edward ... ... ... ... ... 22 „
Mary Breers fi: Alexand gent ... ... ... ... ... 26 „
Ellen Ascroft fi: Witłm ... ... ... ... ... ... 29 „
Emlin Jackson fi: Gilbte ... ... ... ... 31 „
Thomas Rose fi: Richard ... ... ... ... 8 November
Anne Spencer fi: Thom̃ ... ... ... ... ... ... 10 „
Ellen Dickett fi: John ... ... ... ... ... ... „ „
Margrett Topping fi: Raph ... ... ... ... ... 16 „
Anne Layland fi: Richard ... ... ... ... ... 17 „
Margrett Vaudry fi: John ... ... ... ... ... 18 „
Anne Alcar fi: Witłm ... ... ... ... ... ... „ „
Katheryne Swyft fi: Huan ... ... ... ... ... 23 „
ffrancis Stanley fi: Edw Esq^r ... ... ... ... 5 December
Edward Symkin fi: Henry ... ... ... ... ... „ „
Mary Steele fi: George ... ... ... ... ... ... 7 „
Lewes Ashurst fi: Richard ... ... ... ... ... 12 „
Mary Shawe fi: Witłm ... ... ... ... ... ... 13 „
Cuthbte Garrard fi: Myles ... ... ... ... ... „ „
Henry Mollyneux fi: Robte ... ... ... ... ... 18 „
Ellen Kilshawe fi: Witłm ... ... ... ... ... 20 „
Elizabeth Bartō fi: Andrew ... ... ... ... ... 21 „
Edward Walsh fi: John ... ... ... ... ... ... 26 „
Anne Adamson fi: Thom̃ ... ... ... ... ... 27 „
Alice Vauce fi: Peter ... ... ... ... ... ... 1 January
Jane Moncke fi: Richard ... ... ... ... ... 3 „
Thomas Bretherton fi: Rich ... ... ... ... ... 5 „
Thom̃ Laithwaitt fi: Thom̃ ... ... ... ... ... „ „

| | | | |
|---|---|---|---|
| | Robte Clarkson fi: Willm ... ... ... ... | 16 | January |
| | Thomas Ascough fi: Willm ... ... ... ... | 17 | „ |
| | . . . Ascough fi: George ... ... ... ... | 18 | „ |
| | Henry Page fi: Geffrey ... ... ... ... ... | 24 | „ |
| | Margrett Rodes fi: Thomas ... ... ... ... | 31 | „ |
| | Hugh Hurst fi: Ellice ... ... ... ... ... | 2 | ffebruary |
| | Edward Houlme fi: Henry ... ... ... ... | „ | „ |
| | Willm Walker fi: Gabriel ... ... ... ... | 5 | „ |
| | Ellen Chadocke fi: Cuthbte ... ... ... ... | 7 | „ |
| | Margrett Parre fi: Alexander ... ... ... ... | 9 | „ |
| | Margrett Barton fi: Roger ... ... ... ... | „ | „ |
| | Hugh Hodson fi: Huan ... ... ... ... ... | 11 | „ |
| | Isabell Hawarth fi: Willm ... ... ... ... | 13 | „ |
| | Thomas Ascroft fi: Phillip ... ... ... ... | 14 | „ |
| | Elizabeth Scarisbricke fi: Henry ... ... ... | 16 | „ |
| | Alice Modesley fi: Roger ... ... ... ... | 17 | „ |
| | Alice Prescott fi: Richard ... ... ... ... | 24 | „ |
| | Judeth Atherton fi: Andrew ... ... ... ... | 25 | „ |
| | Ellen Harryson fi: John ... ... ... ... ... | „ | „ |
| | Richard Stopford fi: Willm ... ... ... ... | 4 | March |
| | Richard Dale fi: Henry ... ... ... ... ... | 9 | „ |
| | Jane Waynwright fi: John ... ... ... ... | 13 | „ |

## 1623.

| | | | |
|---|---|---|---|
| | Richard Wynder fi: Raphe ... ... ... ... | 25 | March |
| | Gilbte Robteson ... ... ... ... ... ... | 28 | „ |
| | George Nayler fi: Thomas ... ... ... ... | 30 | „ |
| | Jennett Barton fi: George ... ... ... ... | 3 | Aprill |
| | Robte Seddon fi: John ... ... ... ... ... | 6 | „ |
| | Cisley Coockson fi: Henry ... ... ... ... | 10 | „ |
| | Katheryne Butler fi: Robte ... ... ... ... | „ | „ |
| sp: | George Worthington fi: Richard ... ... ... | 13 | „ |
| | Willm Crapp fi: Edmund ... ... ... ... | 20 | „ |
| | Henry Hille fi: John ... ... ... ... ... | 30 | „ |
| | John Tasker fi: Hugh ... ... ... ... ... | 4 | May |
| | John Shawe fi: Thom̄ ... ... ... ... ... | „ | „ |
| | John Hille fi: Willim ... ... ... ... ... | 8 | „ |
| | Elizabeth Wilding fi: Thurstan ... ... ... | „ | „ |
| | Ellen Abbott fi: Willim ... ... ... ... ... | 15 | „ |
| | Ellen & Jane Leadbetter fi: Peter ... ... ... | „ | „ |
| | John Barton fi: Peter ... ... ... ... ... | 18 | „ |
| | Thomas Robinson fi: Henry ... ... ... ... | „ | „ |
| | Katheryne Hodson fi: ffardinand ... ... ... | 22 | „ |
| Fo. 166 | Margery Kerfoote fi: Thom̄ ... ... ... ... | 1 | June |
| | Bartholomew Houlme fi: Thom̄ ... ... ... | 2 | „ |
| | Margrett Houlme fi: Raphe ... ... ... ... | 6 | „ |
| | Randale Johnson fi: Willim ... ... ... ... | 9 | „ |
| | Elizab: Kendale fi: Thom̄ ... ... ... ... | 11 | „ |

|  |  |  |
|---|---|---|
| Anne Whitestones fi: Thom̃ | 11 | June |
| Katheryne Ashurst fi: Thom̃ | 16 | „ |
| Anne Holcroft fi: John | 20 | „ |
| Rob̃te Crapp fi: Hamlett | 22 | „ |
| Katheryne Prescott fi: John | „ | „ |
| Richard Ambrose fi: Peter | „ | „ |
| Henry Ascroft fi: James | 26 | „ |
| Anne Laithwaitt fi: Henry | 10 | Julie |
| John Hey fi: John | 16 | „ |
| Raphe Crane fi: Wiłłim | 19 | „ |
| Margrett Ascroft fi: Henry | 20 | „ |
| Anne Bootle fi: ffardinand | 22 | „ |
| Thomas Walton fi: John | 1 | August |
| Katheryne Blundill fi: James | „ | „ |
| Anne Marclewe fi: Hugh | 17 | „ |
| James Smyth fi: Edward | „ | „ |
| Jane Worthingtō fi: Edward | 24 | „ |
| Elizab̃: Arnold de Aughtō | „ | „ |
| Thom̃ Smyth fi: Symon | „ | „ |
| Alexander Scarisb̃r fi: Homphrey | 30 | „ |
| Alexander Jollybrand fi: Rich̃ | 5 | Septemb̃ |
| James Houlme fi: George | 7 | „ |
| Hugh Barton fi: Peter | 9 | „ |
| Anne Woorthingtō fi: Rich | 11 | „ |
| Henry Dunkon fi: John | „ | „ |
| Jane Stopford fi: Roger | 14 | „ |
| Thomas Wynstanley fi: Arthur | 16 | „ |
| Elizabeth Whittle fi: Hugh | 18 | „ |
| : Huan Swyft fi: Hugh | 29 | „ |
| Thom̃ Hooton fi: Rich | 5 | October |
| Homphrey Greaues fi: John | „ | „ |
| Jane Ashtō fi: Thom̃ | 3 | Novemb |
| Margery Langley fi: Raph | 4 | „ |
| Ellice Mason fi: Thom̃ | 6 | „ |
| James Swyft fi: Lyonell | 11 | „ |
| Mary Houlme fi: Hugh | 17 | „ |
| Richard Edwardsō fi: Wiłłm | „ | „ |
| John Ollyverson fi: Ellice | 19 | „ |
| Joane Carbee fi: Joseph | 20 | „ |
| Richard Kilshawe fi: Wiłłim | 25 | „ |
| 7 Emlin* Hunt fi: Thomas | 30 | „ |
| Nicolas Spencer fi: Thom̃ | 1 | December |
| Isabell ffoster fi: Henry | 8 | „ |
| : Nicolas Morcroft fi: John | „ | „ |
| Henry Westhead fi: Tho: | 15 | „ |
| Katheryne Georgson fi: Wiłłm | 27 | „ |
| Alice Westhead fi: Wiłłim | 29 | „ |
| Elizabeth Modesley fi: Wiłłim | 2 | January |

* Ellen in Chester Transcript.

| | | | |
|---|---|---|---|
| | Elizabeth Breers fi: Alexander | 6 | January |
| | Wiłłim Sutch fi: Peter | 13 | „ |
| | Margery Masson fi: Lawrence | 31 | „ |
| | Elizabeth Jackson fi: James & | 2 | ffebruary |
| | Elizab̄: Swabricke de Aughtō | „ | „ |
| | Henry Rose fi: Richard | 15 | „ |
| | Thomas Melling fi: Wiłłim | 16 | „ |
| | Beniamin Lewis fi: Mr̄i Johnis | 17 | „ |
| sp: | Edward Lyon fi: Rich: | 18 | „ |
| | Katheryne Hayton fi: Thom̄ | 19 | „ |
| | Cisely Swyft fi: Richard | „ | „ |
| | Cuthb̄te Chadocke fi: Richard | „ | „ |
| | . . . Jarman fi: James | 25 | „ |
| | Margret Ascroft fi: John | 26 | „ |
| | Elizabeth Rainforth fi: Hugh | 29 | „ |
| | Edward Morcroft fi: James | 6 | Martch |
| | Elizabeth Gore fi: Homphrey | 11 | „ |
| | Alice Barton fi: Roger | 18 | „ |
| | Huan Swyft fi: Henry | 22 | „ |

## 1624.

| | | | |
|---|---|---|---|
| | Edward Melling fi: John | 25 | Martch |
| | Gabriel Rim̄er fi: Richard | 29 | „ |
| | Alice Kilshawe fi: Henry | 4 | Aprill |
| | Elizabeth Haughton fi: George | 8 | „ |
| | Richard Layland fi: Richard | 13 | „ |
| | Margrett Holland fi: Hugh | 18 | „ |
| sp: | Elizabeth Atherton fi: Phillip | 23 | „ |
| | Rob̄te Swyft fi: Huan | 27 | „ |
| Fo. 168 | John Swyft fi: Huan | 2 | May |
| | Katheryne Blundill fi: James | 15 | „ |
| | Mary Brighouse fi: Thom̄ | 16 | „ |
| | Henry Melling fi: Raph | 20 | „ |
| | Katheryne Smult fi: Edmund | 30 | „ |
| | Isabell Rostorne fi: James | 31 | „ |
| | Elizabeth Crooke fi: Edward | 13 | June |
| | Rob̄te Gyles fi: Wiłłim | 15 | „ |
| | Wiłłim Hodson fi: Richard | 20 | „ |
| | Margrett Coockson fi: Henry | 21 | „ |
| | Ellen Hoole fi: Rich: de Aughtō | „ | „ |
| | Ellen Wignall fi: Thom̄ | 1 | July |
| | Peter Wainwright fi: Thom̄ | 7 | „ |
| | Ellen Modesley fi: Henry | 15 | „ |
| | Ellen Stopford fi: James | 16 | „ |
| sp: | Wiłłim Clapā fi: John | 18 | „ |
| | Anne Wainwright fi: Henry | 23 | „ |
| | Elizabeth Shawe fi: John | 25 | „ |
| | Henry Gill fi: Edward | 1 | August |

| | | |
|---|---|---|
| Elizab̄ Aspinwall fi: Edward | 4 | August |
| Anne Atherton fi: Andrew | 15 | " |
| Anne Kilshawe fi: Rich̄ | 17 | " |
| James Chadocke fi: Cuthb̄te | 18 | " |
| Edward Dickett fi: John | 22 | " |
| Peter Tayler fi: Thom̄ | 25 | " |
| Katheryne Blundill fi: Gilb̄te | 26 | " |
| Alice Robinson fi: James | " | " |
| Susan Morcroft fi: Phillip | " | " |
| Thom̄ Marcer fi: Roger | 2 | Septemb |
| Alice Otie fi: John de Rufforth | " | " |
| John Gilb̄teson fi: Edward | 8 | " |
| Alice Smyth fi: Henry | 11 | " |
| Mary Scarisbrick fi: John | 12 | " |
| Ellen Jackson fi: John | 17 | " |
| Joane Peter fi: Thom̄ | 19 | " |
| Hugh Prescott fi: James | 26 | " |
| Anna Duckenfeild fi: Rich: gent | 21 | " |
| Alice Kilshawe fi: John | 4 | October |
| John Turner fi: John | 6 | " |
| Margrett Morcroft fi: Wiƚƚm | 7 | " |
| Emlin Houlme fi: Wiƚƚim | 8 | " |
| Richard Boure fi: Rich dec̄ | 27 | " |
| Margrett Jolly fi: Henry | 28 | " |
| Wiƚƚim Mollyneux fi: Rob̄te | 30 | " |
| Wiƚƚim Kilshawe fi: Rich | 31 | " |
| Katheryne Clapā fi: Rich̄ | 1 | November |
| Richard Smoult fi: Thom̄ | " | " |
| James Jolly fi: Thom̄ | 4 | " |
| Wiƚƚim Massey fi: Thom̄ | 10 | " |
| Homphrey Barton fi: Arthur | 11 | " |
| Rob̄te Wallice fi: Hector | " | " |
| Andrewe & John Cowborne fi: Thom̄ | 26 | " |
| John Webster fi: Wiƚƚim | 30 | " |
| George Throppe fi: Hugh | 2 | December |
| Anne Tyldsley fi: Gilb̄te | 5 | " |
| Wiƚƚim Whatton fi: James | 8 | " |
| Edward Hille fi: Thom̄ | 9 | " |
| Margrett Morcroft fi: Gabrieƚ | 12 | " |
| Alice Sutch fi: James | 14 | " |
| Margrett Morcroft fi: Rich̄ | 22 | " |
| Thomas Keakwicke fi: Rich̄ | 23 | " |
| Dorithie Alcar fi: Wiƚƚim | 25 | " |
| Henry Robinson fi: Rich de Aughtō | 26 | " |
| Bartholomewe Scarisbricke fi: Homphrey | 16 | January |
| Alexander Shorlokers fi: John | 17 | " |
| Margrett Butler fi: Rob̄te | 20 | " |
| Mary Barton fi: Gowther | 31 | " |
| Alice Smyth fi: Gilb̄te | 1 | ffebruary |

Elizabeth Ashurst fi: Richard ... ... ... 3 ffebruary
Jeffrey Clarkson fi: Willim ... ... ... ... 4 „
James Houlme fi: John ... ... ... ... ... „ „
Edward Hale fi: James ... ... ... ... ... 5 „
James Topping fi: Raphe ... ... ... ... 6 „
Thomas Robinson fi: John ... ... ... ... 9 „
John Bartõ fi: George ... ... ... ... ... 18 „
Richard Ollyverson fi: Henry ... ... ... 19 „
Anne Modesley fi: Thom̃ ... ... ... ... 20 „
Peter Symkin fi: Edward ... ... ... ... 21 „
sp: Willm Smyth fi: Henry ... ... ... ... ... 22 „
Jennett Dunkon fi: John ... ... ... ... 24 „
Alice Sourbutts fi: John ... ... ... ... ... 25 „
Fo. 170 Ellen Kilshawe fi: Richard ... ... ... ... 3 Martch
Anne Modesley fi: John ... ... ... ... ... „ „
Hugh ffletcher fi: Richard ... ... ... ... 13 „
Margrett Scofelt fi: John ... ... ... ... „ „
Richard Billinge fi: Peter ... ... ... ... 16 „
Phillipp Hey fi: James ... ... ... ... ... 20 „
Anne Johnson fi: Willim ... ... ... ... 24 „

## 1625.

Phillippe Swyft fi: Willim ... ... ... ... 29 Martch
Ellen Barton fi: Willim ... ... ... ... ... 1 Aprill
Mary Kendale fi: Thomas ... ... ... ... 3 „
John Johnson fi: John ... ... ... ... ... 4 „
Richard Symkin fi: Henry ... ... ... ... 5 „
sp: John Biccursteth fi: Thom̃ ... ... ... ... 15 „
Joseph Rigby fi: Peter ... ... ... ... ... 16 „
Joane fforshawe fi: George ... ... ... ... 21 „
Henry Hesketh fi: George ... ... ... ... 24 „
sp: James Hunt fi: Henry ... ... ... ... ... 26 „
Anne Croock fi: Thomas ... ... ... ... 7 May
Jane Hankinson fi: Robte ... ... ... ... 8 „
Henry Stopford fi: Thom̃ ... ... ... ... „ „
Mary Ollyverson fi: Ellice ... ... ... ... 11 „
Richard Abraham fi: Mathew ... ... ... 12 „
Elizab: Woodes fi: Henry ... ... ... ... 21 „
Jennett Smyth fi: James ... ... ... ... 26 „
Margrett Barton fi: Edward ... ... ... ... „ „
sp: James Parker fi: Willim ... ... ... ... 28 „
Richard Smoult fi: Raph ... ... ... ... 31 „
George Page fi: John ... ... ... ... ... 5 June
John Shackshaft fi: Henry ... ... ... ... 6 „
Thomas Banester fi: Richard ... ... ... 7 „
Thomas Hunter fi: Robte ... ... ... ... 10 „
Margrett Shawe fi: Thom̃ de Aughtõ ... ... 11 „
Willim Lawrenson fi: Tho ... ... ... ... 12 „

| | | |
|---|---|---|
| Hugh Athertō fi: Phillipp ... ... ... ... ... | 29 | June |
| Anne Breers fi: Alexand ... ... ... ... | 8 | July |
| Anne Parke fi: Edmund ... ... ... ... ... ... | 13 | „ |
| Anne Halsall fi: Richard Armig ... ... ... | 16 | „ |
| Margrett Sumner fi: Hugh ... ... ... ... ... | 19 | „ |
| Trymer Swyft fi: Henry ... ... ... ... ... | 22 | „ |
| John Blacowe fi: John ... ... ... ... ... | 1 | August |
| James Westhead fi: Richard ... ... ... ... ... | 13 | „ |
| Margrett Ormeshaw fi: Wiłłim ... ... ... | 18 | „ |
| Wiłłim Hill fi: John ... ... ... ... ... ... | 21 | „ |
| Roger Tomlinson fi: James ... ... ... ... | „ | „ |
| Ellen Prescott fi: Rob̄te ... ... ... ... ... | 24 | „ |
| Ellen Hallywell fi: Nicolas ... ... ... ... | 25 | „ |
| Wiłłim Hunt fi: Thom̄ ... ... ... ... ... | 28 | „ |
| Anne Barton fi: Roger ... ... ... ... ... | 9 | September |
| John Vauce fi: John ... ... ... ... ... ... | 25 | „ |
| Margrett Greaues fi: John ... ... ... ... ... | 26 | „ |
| Henry Whitehead fi: John ... ... ... ... | 27 | „ |
| Thomas Webster fi: Richard ... ... ... ... | 2 | October |
| Thomas Jamson fi: Edward ... ... ... ... | 5 | „ |
| Anne Ireland fi: James ... ... ... ... ... | 9 | „ |
| Jane Smalshawe fi: James ... ... ... ... | 10 | „ |
| Trinity Crookoe fi: Wiłłim ... ... ... ... | 16 | „ |
| Elizab̄: Smyth fi: Edward ... ... ... ... | 18 | „ |
| Ellen Berry fi: James ... ... ... ... ... ... | 22 | „ |
| Richard Shawe fi: Richard ... ... ... ... | 25 | „ |
| Elizab̄: Lunt fi: John ... ... ... ... ... ... | 27 | „ |
| Henry Sutton fi: John ... ... ... ... ... | „ | „ |
| Henry Jollie fi: Wiłłim ... ... ... ... ... | „ | „ |
| Thom̄ Vauce fi: Peter ... ... ... ... ... | „ | „ |
| Mary Aspinwall fi: James ... ... ... ... | 6 | November |
| Mary Hooton fi: Richard ... ... ... ... | 7 | „ |
| Elizab̄ Modesley fi: Thom̄ ... ... ... ... | 16 | „ |
| Thomas Scarisbr̄ fi: John ... ... ... ... | 20 | „ |
| Ellen Crapper fi: Hamlett ... ... ... ... | 25 | „ |
| Rob̄te Bartō fi: Gilb̄te ... ... ... ... ... | 7 | December |
| Henry Rose fi: Rich̄ ... ... ... ... ... | 11 | „ |
| Margrett Ram̄er fi: John... ... ... ... ... ... | „ | „ |
| Rob̄te Turner fi: John ... ... ... ... ... ... | 24 | „ |
| Margrett Hoomle fi: George ... ... ... ... | 27 | „ |
| Tho: Nayler fi: Nicolas ... ... ... ... ... | 30 | „ |
| John Westhead fi: Tho: ... ... ... ... ... | „ | „ |
| James Gobben fi: Rob̄te ... ... ... ... | 6 | January |
| Margery Keakwicke fi: Rich ... ... ... ... | „ | „ |
| Ellen Ashurst fi: Tho ... ... ... ... ... | 8 | „ |
| Edward Rylons fi: Rob̄te ... ... ... ... | 10 | „ |

[*At this point there are two blank pages not numbered.*]

| | | |
|---|---|---|
| Wiłłim Houlme fi: Hugh ... ... ... ... ... | 13 | „ |
| Mary Gerrard fi: Tho: de Aughtō ... ... | „ | „ |

Katheryne Spencer fi: Tho ... ... ... ... 22 January
sp: Jennett Halsall fi: Tho: de Halsall and of Mary Walsh ... ... ... ... ... ... 25 ,,
Thomas Waynwright fi: Henry ... ... ... 26 ,,
Edward Hesketh fi: Tho: ... ... ... ... 28 ,,
Ellen Rothwell fi: Robte ... ... ... ... ,, ,,
Ciceley Georgsō fi: Willim ... ... ... ... 30 ,,
George Durham fi: Robte ... ... ... ... 2 ffebruary
James Rigby fi: Myles ... ... ... ... ... 4 ,,
Mary Scarisbr fi: Henry ... ... ... ... ... 5 ,,
Mary Longley fi: Raph ... ... ... ... ... 11 ,,
Richard Swyft fi: Lyonell ... ... ... ... ,, ,,
Cicely Wynstanley fi: Arthur ... ... ... ... ,, ,,
Elizab Alcar fi: Thomas ... ... ... ... 14 ,,
Edward Masson fi: Lawrence ... ... ... 15 ,,
Thomas Walsh fi: Rich ... ... ... ... ... 16 ,,
Thomas Croocke fi: John ... ... ... ... ,, ,,
Willim Hoole fi: Rich ... ... ... ... ... 17 ,,
James Ascroft fi: James ... ... ... ... ... 19 ,,
Willim Bartō fi: Peter ... ... ... ... ... ,, ,,
Richard Symkin fi: Edward ... ... ... ... ,, ,,
John Ascroft fi: . . . ... ... ... ... 20 ,,
Huan Lee fi: Hector ... ... ... ... ... 21 ,,
James Bartō fi: Rich: ... ... ... ... ... ,, ,,
Robte Kerfoote fi: Tho: ... ... ... ... 26 ,,
Edward Adamson fi: Tho: ... ... ... ... ,, ,,
Edward Houlme fi: Hugh ... ... ... ... ,, ,,
sp: Anne Shawe fi: Gabriel ... ... ... ... ... ,, ,,
Thomas Molyneux fi: Richard ... ... ... 27 ,,
Isaacke Ashton fi: Tho: ... ... ... ... 5 Martch
Elize Longe fi: Elize gent ... ... ... ... 7 ,,
Edward Hale fi: James ... .. ... ... ... ,, ,,
Richard & Alice Nayler fi: Thom ... ... ... 8 ,,
Edward Swyft fi: Rich: ... ... ... ... ... 9 ,,
Jane Crapp fi: Edmund ... ... ... ... ... 13 ,,
Henry Morcroft fi: Willim ... ... ... ... 14 ,,
Margrett Bower fi: Willim ... ... ... ... 16 ,,
Margrett Layland fi: Rich ... ... ... ... 17 ,,
Fo. 173 Mary Leadbetter fi: Peter ... ... ... ... 20 ,,
sp: Jane Sephtō fi: Willim ... ... ... ... ... 21 ,,
Ellen Chadocke fi: Richard ... ... ... ... 23 ,,

## 1626.

Alice Aspinwall fi: John ... ... ... ... 25 Martch
Alice Stopford fi: Willim ... ... ... ... ,, ,,
sp: Margrett Keele fi: John de Aughtō ... ... 29 ,,

[*Next in Original follow Marriages, but preserving the order followed generally in the Society's publications, the Burials here follow.*]

**be regester booke** of sutche as haue bine Buried withine perishe of Ormis$^{k}$ since the begininge of her ma$^{tis}$ moste happie Raignė (whiche did begine to Englands Joye And Comforte) y$^{e}$ Seventinthe daye of Novembere Anno dni 1557

---

## BURIALS.

### 1557.

| | | |
|---|---|---|
| Robert Richardson buried | 17 | November |
| Robert Harison In eccłia | 20 | ,, |
| Adam Woosey in Eccłia | ,, | ,, |
| Eliz$^{th}$ Kekuicke | 21 | ,, |
| Marget Kekuicke | 23 | ,, |
| Marget Woodhowse in ecclia | ,, | ,, |
| George Blvndell | ,, | ,, |
| Margerie Weaver | ,, | ,, |
| Peeter Preskot | 25 | ,, |
| John Burscough | ,, | ,, |
| Robert Smute | 27 | ,, |
| Tho: Blvndell | ,, | ,, |
| Ellin Svmner vx$^{9}$ Gilb̄ in eccłia | ,, | ,, |
| Marie Bruckefeelde in eccłia | ,, | ,, |
| vx$^{9}$ Hector Jumpe | 29 | ,, |
| John Prescot | 2 | December |
| John Prescot | 10 | ,, |
| Jenet Andrew in ecclia | 13 | ,, |
| Gilb̄ Burscough in eccłia | 16 | ,, |
| Wiłłm Prescot in eccłia | 17 | ,, |
| Richard Butterie in ecclia | 28 | ,, |
| vx$^{9}$ Edmund Burscough | ,, | ,, |
| vx$^{9}$ Edmund Alerton | ,, | ,, |
| Marie Waynewright | 3 | Januarie |
| Anne Mellinge | ,, | ,, |
| vx$^{9}$ Cristopher Sherringeton | 7 | ,, |
| Tho: Svtton in eccłia | 8 | ,, |
| vx$^{9}$ Robert Hiłł | 11 | ,, |
| Wiłłm Shawe | 13 | ,, |
| Sibell Johnes doughter | 15 | ,, |

Hugh Spencer in ecclia ... ... ... ... ... ... 16 Januarie
George Martindaile ... ... ... ... ... ... 20 „
Eliz^th Robins doughter ... ... ... ... ... 21 „
Elin Henrison ... ... ... ... ... ... ... „ „
Ladie Dorethie Stanley doughter to the Right
Honerable Edw: Earle of Derbie was bur̄ 22 „
John Breykell ... ... ... ... ... ... ... ... „ „
Hugh Butchard ... ... ... ... ... ... 23 „
Henrie Blackledge in eccl̄ia ... ... ... ... 24 „
Tho: Mosse ... ... ... ... ... ... ... „ „
Marget Leadbetter ... ... ... ... ... ... 27 „
Margerie Winde ... ... ... ... ... ... 28 „
Alis Adamson ... ... ... ... ... ... ... 31 „
Marget vx^9 Tho: Chadocke in ecc ... ... 5 ffebruarie
John Moscropp in eccl̄ia ... ... ... ... 8 „
Jenet Scarsbricke in eccl̄ia ... ... ... ... „ „
Edw: Bootle ... ... ... ... ... ... ... ... 10 „
Edw: Prescot ... ... ... ... ... ... ... ... „ „
Rob̄t Smallshaw in eccl̄ia ... ... ... ... 13 „
Alis Henrison in ecclia ... ... ... ... ... 15 „
Eliz^th Crosse ... ... ... ... ... ... ... 21 „
Jaine Mason ... ... ... ... ... ... ... 6 March
Eliz^th Tho: doughter in eccl̄ia ... ... ... 9 „
Katherin Chadocke ... ... ... ... ... ... 10 „
Marget vx^9 Hugh Burscough ... ... ... ... 11 „
Elin Webster vx^9 hen: ... ... ... ... ... 17 „
Eliz^th Bellsha vx^9 Robart... ... ... ... ... 18 „
Ric̄ Mollinex ... ... ... ... ... ... ... 19 „

## 1558.

Elin vx^9 Gilb̄ Johnson ... ... ... ... ... ... 27 March
Jamis Bylinge ... ... ... ... ... ... ... 31 „
Fo. 271 Jaine Charles ... ... ... ... ... ... ... 1 Aprill
Jamis Smallshey in ecclia ... ... ... ... 3 „
Alis Werrall in ecclia ... ... ... ... ... 5 „
Roffe Marclough ... ... ... ... ... ... „ „
Robart Killshaw ... ... ... ... ... ... 6 ,
vx^9 Peeter Haughton ... ... ... ... ... 8 „
A stranger buried ... ... ... ... ... ... 9 „
Margerie Leigh in ecclia ... ... ... ... ... 12 „
John Wallis ... ... ... ... ... ... ... 18 „
Margerie Bucher ... ... ... ... ... ... 20 „
Wiłłm Mowdie ... ... ... ... ... ... ... 21 „
Izabell Catrall ... ... ... ... ... ... ... „ „
Edw: Buchard in eccl̄ia ... ... ... ... ... 25 „
Anne Morecrofte in eccl̄ia ... ... ... ... 26 „
Ser Hugh Huckesley Pryor of Burscough in
ecclia ... ... ... ... ... ... ... 2 Maye

|  |  |  |
|---|---|---|
| Sir Willm Burscough Clarke bur In ecclia ... | 3 | Maye |
| Nicolas Jackeson ... ... ... ... ... ... ... | 4 | „ |
| vx$^9$ Henrie Gore in ecclia ... ... ... .. | 9 | „ |
| Jaine Barton ... ... ... ... ... ... ... ... | „ | „ |
| John Greaves ... ... ... ... ... ... ... ... | 10 | „ |
| Alis Gill ... ... ... ... ... ... ... ... ... | 13 | „ |
| Alis Collinson ... ... ... ... ... ... ... ... | 15 | „ |
| Ellin Osbaston ... ... ... ... ... ... ... ... | „ | „ |
| Jenet vx$^9$ Tho: Edmund ... ... ... ... ... | 17 | „ |
| Ric Mowldie ... ... ... ... ... ... ... ... | 19 | „ |
| Marget Gill ... ... ... ... ... ... ... .. | „ | „ |
| John Sadler in ecclia ... ... ... ... ... ... | 22 | „ |
| John Barker ... ... ... ... ... ... ... ... | 29 | „ |
| Edw: Bradshaw ... ... ... ... ... ... ... | „ | „ |
| John Jump ... ... ... ... ... ... ... ... | 30 | „ |
| Rodger Henrieson ... ... ... ... ... ... ... | „ | „ |
| Ric Gellibrund ... ... ... ... ... ... ... ... | 13 | June |
| vx$^9$ Ric Barke ... ... ... ... ... ... ... ... | „ | „ |
| Ric Barker ... ... ... ... ... ... ... ... ... | 14 | „ |
| 72 Izabell late wyfe of Ja: Scarsbreck Esqr bur | 22 | „ |
| Tho: Stopforth ... ... ... ... ... ... ... | 26 | „ |
| Jamis Moscrop ... ... ... ... ... ... ... ... | „ | „ |
| Symond Towne ... ... ... ... ... ... ... | „ | „ |
| Izabell Crosse ... ... ... ... ... ... ... ... | „ | „ |
| Willm Spencer ... ... ... ... ... ... ... ... | „ | „ |
| Henrie Oliverson ... ... ... ... ... ... ... | 1 | July |
| Tho: Hunt in ecclia ... ... ... ... ... ... | 3 | „ |
| vx$^9$ Willm Gowbron in ecclia ... ... ... | 8 | „ |
| Randall Lvskin in ecclia ... ... ... ... ... ... | 13 | „ |
| vx$^9$ George Kekuicke ... ... ... ... ... ... | 17 | „ |
| Oliver Prescot ... ... ... ... ... ... ... ... | 18 | „ |
| Jenet Blvndell ... ... ... ... ... ... ... ... | „ | „ |
| Robt Gorsutch ... ... ... ... ... ... ... ... | 20 | „ |
| John Halsall in ecclia ... ... ... ... ... ... | 22 | „ |
| Jaine Sadler in ecclia ... ... ... ... ... ... | „ | „ |
| Willm Aspinwall in ecclia ... ... ... ... ... | 24 | „ |
| Willm Craine in ecclia ... ... ... ... ... ... | „ | „ |
| Eliz$^{th}$ vx$^9$ Robert Haile ... ... ... ... ... ... | 25 | „ |
| Ellin Bould in ecclia ... ... ... ... ... ... | 26 | „ |
| Ric Shaw ... ... ... ... ... ... ... ... ... | „ | „ |
| Ser John Dolland Preeste in ecclia ... ... | 30 | „ |
| Parsivall Shurlicars ... ... ... ... ... ... ... | „ | „ |
| Henrie Cropp in ecclia ... ... ... ... ... ... | 1 | Auguste |
| George Perker ... ... ... ... ... ... ... ... | 2 | „ |
| Eliz$^{th}$ vx$^9$ Ric Mowdisley ... ... ... ... ... ... | „ | „ |
| Ewan Aiscrofte ... ... ... ... ... ... ... | 3 | „ |
| Mathew Lunte ... ... ... ... ... ... ... ... | „ | „ |
| Cristopher Worthington at Stand ... ... ... | „ | „ |
| Marget Picavance at Aughton ... ... ... ... | „ | „ |

| | | | |
|---|---|---|---|
| | John Orrell et Eius vxꝰ in eccl̄ia | 4 | |
| | Homfrey Jackeson | 6 | |
| | Douse vxꝰ Ellis Longe in eccl̄ia | 7 | |
| | Ellin vxꝰ Will̄m Toppinge in eccl̄ia | „ | |
| | vxꝰ Hugh Bycarstaffe | 8 | |
| | Gefferey Clapa in eccl̄ia | „ | |
| | Edmund Killshaw | „ | |
| | George Kekuike | „ | |
| Fo. 273 | vxꝰ Ric̃ Woodes in ecclia | 9 | |
| | vxꝰ Edmund Macon at Halsall | „ | |
| | Will̄m Jump | 10 | |
| | Sꝰ John Parsivall in eccl̄ia | 14 | |
| | vxꝰ Hugh Aiscroft in eccl̄ia | „ | |
| | Rob̄t Wythingeton in eccl̄ia | 15 | |
| | Marget vxꝰ Edw: Yate | 16 | |
| | Tho: Shurlicars | 17 | |
| | Jamis Withingeton in eccl̄ia | „ | |
| | George Preskot | 21 | |
| | Sꝰ Gilb̄ Shurlicars Pꝰ in ecclia | „ | |
| | Jaine Blvndell | 25 | |
| | Ric̃ Mellinge | 28 | |
| | Tho: Haiton in eccl̄ia | 29 | |
| | Henrie Lathwhat | 31 | |
| | Ric̃ Allerton | 2 | S |
| | Agnes vxꝰ Edw: Whyte | „ | |
| | Ric̃ Anderton | 3 | |
| | Jamis Leland in ecclia | „ | |
| | Marget vxꝰ Tho: Blvndell | „ | |
| | Gilb̄ Kilshaw | „ | |
| | Gilb̄ Bycarstaff in eccl̄ia | 6 | |
| | Ric̃ Mowdisley | 8 | |
| | John Prescot | „ | |
| | Anne vxꝰ Jam: Gregson | 12 | |
| | Jamis Talior | 21 | |
| | Elizth Sutch in eccl̄ia | 22 | |
| | John Withingeton in eccl̄ia | „ | |
| | Robert Hoolme | 23 | |
| | Trymor Irland | 26 | |
| | Agnes Martindaile in eccl̄ia | 28 | |
| | John fformbie | 1 | O |
| | John Jackeson | „ | |
| | Ric̃ Holland | „ | |
| | Will̄m Blvndell | 3 | |
| | vxꝰ Raffe Haille | 4 | |
| Fo. 274 | Ric̃ Barton in eccl̄ia | 7 | |
| | Ric̃ Lathwhat | „ | |
| | Jamis Mellinge | 8 | |
| | Symond Mowdisley in eccl̄ia | 11 | |
| | Jaine vxꝰ Ranoldie Marrall | „ | |

| | | |
|---|---|---|
| Alis vx$^{9}$ Thō: Stopforth | 14 | October |
| Jenet vx$^{9}$ Ric̃ ffrith | 15 | „ |
| Rob̄t A Stranger | 16 | „ |
| Ottuwell Blvndell | 17 | „ |
| Henrie Asmall | 20 | „ |
| Jamis Rutter | 21 | „ |
| Alis Mowdisley in ecclia | „ | „ |
| Sislie vx$^{9}$ Gilb̄ Cropp | 22 | „ |
| Alis vx$^{9}$ Rodg Scarsbreck | 25 | „ |
| Willm Bower | 29 | „ |
| Ellin vx$^{9}$ Hughe Hoolme in ecclia | 30 | „ |
| vx$^{9}$ Waterworth | „ | „ |
| vx$^{9}$ Jamis Spencer | 4 | November |
| Jamis Hawet | 7 | „ |
| Hugh Leech | 10 | „ |
| Eideth ffrances | 18 | „ |
| Ric̃ Brigehowse | 20 | „ |
| Willm Shelton | 24 | „ |
| Katherin Rainforth | 29 | „ |
| Eideth Hill | 7 | December |
| John Haiton | 8 | „ |
| John Hoolme | 13 | „ |
| Anne vx$^{9}$ Ric̃ Wrightinton in ecclia | 15 | „ |
| John Spencer | 17 | „ |
| Eliz$^{th}$ vx$^{9}$ Ric̃ Carre | 21 | „ |
| Jenet Halworth | 1 | Januarie |
| Harrie Hulme | 2 | „ |
| Mowde Greaves | 3 | „ |
| Tho: Paver | 5 | „ |
| Margerie Haughton | 10 | „ |
| Eliz$^{th}$ Woodhowse | 18 | „ |
| John Mellinge in ecclia | 21 | „ |
| Godferey Kewquicke in ecclia | „ | „ |
| 75 Robert Prescot | 25 | „ |
| Peeter Shaw | 29 | „ |
| . . . Prescot | 2 | ffebruarie |
| Eliz$^{th}$ Hill | 4 | „ |
| Tho: Sutch theldest | 11 | „ |
| Hector Jumpe | 14 | „ |
| John Swifte | „ | „ |
| Ric̃ Hill | 17 | „ |
| Elis Anderton | „ | „ |
| Katherin vx$^{9}$ Hugh Banke | 21 | „ |
| Jinet vx$^{9}$ Tristram Ascroft* | 24 | „ |
| John Cropp | 3 | Martch |
| Marget vx$^{9}$ Ric̃ ffletcher in ecclia | 4 | „ |
| Alis Rainforth | „ | „ |
| Edw: Eccleston | 8 | „ |

* Written over Haughton.

Ellinor Gill ... 8 Martch
Rob̄t Garrerd in ecclia ... 11 „
vxꝰ Clapam ... 17 „
A Childe of Ric̃ Lancaster ... „ „
A childe of one Bowers ... 19 „
A Childe of Jamis Bankes ...
Ric̃ Crofte ... 23 „
John Cropp ... 25 „
vxꝰ Peeter Preskot ... „ „

## 1559.

Jaine Parker ... 7 Aprill
Katherin Gill ... 8 „
Jaine Nalior in ecclia ... „ „
John Smyth in ecclia ... 14 „
Hugh Burscough ... 17 „
Jenet vxꝰ Lav: Savag ... „ „
Edw: Parre in eccłia ... „ „
Wiłłm Banke in eccłia ... 19 „
Dorethie vxꝰ Ric̃ Ormishaw in ecclia ... 21 „
Jaine Preskot ... 23 „
Ric̃ Hodgeson in ecclia ... 26 „
Margerie Ashton ... 27 „
Fo. 276 Hector Lea in eccłia ... 4 Maye
Adam Elizth [*sic*] in eccłia ... 19 „
Jamis Hoolme ... 26 „
John Ploumbe ... 28 „
Tho: Swifte in eccłia ... 1 June
Alis Hoolme in eccłia ... 3 „
Tho: Banke in eccłia ... „ „
vxꝰ Wiłłm Barker ... 6 „
Rodger Mowdisley in eccłia ... 13 „
Ric̃ Burscough ... 14 „
Jamis Scarsbrecke in eccłia ... 18 „
Elizth Muldie ... „ „
John ffryth bast ... 25 „
Arthor Groue in eccłia ... 5 July
George Hill ... 6 „
Jamis Banke In eccłia ... 10 „
Tho: Ormishaw ... 16 „
Jamis Kidd ... 17 „
Eadē Elizth Crosse in eccłia pur̃ ... 19 „
Margerie Mowdisley ... „ „
Jamis Gill ... 20 „
Jamis Hunt fi: Ja: ... 26 „
Tho: Breykell ... 31 „
Elizth Holland in eccłia ... 1 Auguste
Margerie Tasker ... „ „

... ... ... ... 1 Auguste
... ... ... ... 5 „
... ... ... ... 6 „
... ... ... ... 21 „
... ... ... ... „ „
... ... ... ... 23 „
... ... ... ... 24 „
... ... ... ... 25 „
... ... ... ... 26 „
... ... ... ... 28 „
... ... ... ... „ „
... ... ... ... 2 September
... ... ... ... 4 „
... ... ... ... „ „
... ... ... ... 5 „
... ... ... ... „ „
... ... ... ... 7 „
... ... ... ... 8 „
... ... ... ... 9 „
... ... ... ... 10 „
... ... ... ... 13 „
... ... ... ... „ „
... ... ... ... 14 „
... ... ... ... 20 „
... ... ... ... 21 „
... ... ... ... 24 „
... ... ... ... 1 October
... ... ... ... 3 „
... ... ... ... 10 „
... ... ... ... 17 „
... ... ... ... 21
... ... ... ... 22 „
... ... ... ... „ „
ia ... ... ... „ „
... ... ... ... 26 „
... ... ... ... „ „
... ... ... ... 3 Nvember
... ... ... ... 4 „
... ... ... ... 7
... ... ... ... 16 „
... ... ... ... „ „
... ... ... ... 30 „
... ... ... ... „ „
... ... ... ... 15 December
... ... ... ... 30 „
... ... ... ... 31 „
... ... ... ... 5 Januarie
ecc̃ ... ... ... 10 „

Wittm Bradshaw in ecctia ... ... ... ... 20 Januarie
Margerie Robinson ... ... ... ... ... ... 25 „
Rodger Alker ... ... ... ... ... ... ... 4 ffebruarie
Oliver Atherton ... ... ... ... ... ... „ „
Wittm Adamson in ecctia ... ... ... ... 13 „
Wittm Henrieson ... ... ... ... ... ... 15 „
John Butler in ecctia ... ... ... ... ... 26 „
Annes vx⁹ Rañ Morcrofte ... ... ... ... 8 March
John Parker ... ... ... ... ... ... ... „ „
John Ditton ... ... ... ... ... ... ... 11 „
Jamis Gill ... ... ... ... ... ... ... ... „ „
Wittm Alker ... ... ... ... ... ... ... 12 „
Anne Hill ... ... ... ... ... ... ... ... „ „
Ewan Mowdisley ... ... ... ... ... ... 14 „
Peeter Rimmer ... ... ... ... ... ... 19 „

## 1560.

Jamis Watkinson in ecctia ... ... ... ... 28 March
Margerie Wilson ... ... ... ... ... ... 1 Aprill
Katherin Kirvin in ecctia ... ... ... ... 2 „
Anne vx⁹ Homfrey Gill señ ... ... ... ... 5 „
Hugh Coockeson ... ... ... ... ... ... 6 „
Marget Windrow ... ... ... ... ... ... 7 „
Edward Richardson ... ... ... ... ... ... 8 „
Margerie Banke ... ... ... ... ... ... 15 „
Eliz^th vx⁹ Wittm Tarleton ... ... ... ... 16 „
Marge Webster in ecctia ... ... ... ... ... 22 „
Hugh Sutch in ecctia ... ... ... ... ... 24 „
Marget Scarsbrecke in ecctia ... ... ... ... 9 Maye
Kathẽ vx⁹ Johanine [*sic*] Ashorst in ecctia ... 14 „
Jaine Whytestons in ecctia ... ... ... ... 19 „
Fo. 279 vx⁹ Rog Ascrofte ... ... ... ... ... ... 8 June
Lawrence Breckell in ecctia ... ... ... ... 24 „
Egle Blundell ... ... ... ... ... ... ... 26 „
pu: Eliz^th Breckell in ecctia ... ... ... ... ... 7 Julye
Alis Haiton ... ... ... ... ... ... ... 10 „
Robt Breckell in ecctia ... ... ... ... ... 14 „
pu: Wittm Shawe in ecctia ... ... ... ... ... 17 „
Eliz^th Aiscrofte ... ... ... ... ... ... ... 18 „
Anas Sutche ... ... ... ... ... ... ... 23 „
Homfray Locker in ecctia ... ... ... ... 25 „
John Ambrose in ecctia ... ... ... ... ... „ „
Nicolas Worsley ... ... ... ... ... ... 29 „
pu: Eliz^th Shawe in ecctia ... ... ... ... ... 5 Auguste
Margerie Hardman ... ... ... ... ... ... „ „
pu: Robt Shawe in ecctia ... ... ... ... ... 6 „
Alis Jolibrone in ecctia ... ... ... ... ... 17 September
pu: Tho: Sele in ecctia ... ... ... ... ... „ „

| | | | |
|---|---|---|---|
| | Jaine Breckell | 5 | October |
| | Hughe Shawe | 11 | ” |
| | Margerie Hardman | 2 | November |
| | Hugh Beconsall | 6 | ” |
| | John Ambrose in eccl̄ia | 15 | ” |
| | John Gill in eccl̄ia | 20 | ” |
| | Will̄m Wildinge in eccl̄ia | 30 | ” |
| | vx Ric̃ Blundell in ecclia | 4 | December |
| pu: | Peeter Chadocke in eccl̄ia | 28 | ” |
| | Alis Taskere | ” | ” |
| | Edw: Keckwicke in eccl̄ia | 30 | ” |
| Fo. 280 | Gefray fformbie | 3 | Januarie |
| | Hamlet Leadbeter in eccl̄ia | 7 | ” |
| | *[No entries for ffebruarie]* | | |
| puer | Elin Ambrose in eccl̄ia | 3 | Marche |
| | Katherin Smyth in ec̃ | 4 | ” |
| | John Lowrance | 16 | ” |

## 1561.

| | | | |
|---|---|---|---|
| | Elizth Barton in ecclia | 27 | Marche |
| | John Swyft in eccl̄ia | 1 | Aprill |
| | Mrs Elizth Stanley | 12 | ” |
| | Sybyll Shurlekers | 13 | ” |
| | Rob̄t Leadbeter in eccl̄ia | 21 | ” |
| | Dovse Charles | 26 | ” |
| | Ric̃ Woodes in eccl̄ia | 29 | ” |
| | *[No entries for Maye]* | | |
| | vxꝰ Adam Cockson | 2 | June |
| | Katherine Tatlocke | 14 | ” |
| | Adam Aspinwall in eccl̄ia | 16 | ” |
| | Ellin Jackeson | 17 | ” |
| | Ellin Maner vxꝰ Tho: | 5 | Julye |
| | Homfraye Gill | 6 | ” |
| | Elizth Whitstonse | 11 | ” |
| | John Mowdisley | ” | ” |
| | Gilbert Gerard in eccl̄ia | 19 | ” |
| | Emlin Kilshawe | 1 | Auguste |
| | Cristopher Crosbie | 3 | ” |
| | Ric̃ Barker | 14 | ” |
| | Sislie Ashton | ” | ” |
| Fo. 281 | Gemet *[sic]* Smyth in eccl̄ia | 23 | ” |
| | John ffarclough in eccl̄ia | ” | ” |
| | John Gilb̄son | ” | ” |
| | Margerie Whytestones | 24 | ” |
| | George Swyfte | 25 | ” |
| | Henrie ffarclough | 5 | September |
| | Ric̃ Lea | 9 | ” |
| | Tho: Hunter | 13 | ” |

Wiłł Shaw ... ... ... ... ... ... ... ... ... 24 October
George Manne ... ... ... ... ... ... ... ... 26 „
Eliz[th] Swifte in ecclia ... ... ... ... ... ... 31 „
Jaine Morecrofte ... ... ... ... ... ... ... 8 November
Wiłłm Asshurst ... ... ... ... ... ... ... 13 „
Robert Livesey in ecclia ... ... ... ... ... ... 3 December
John Whatton in ecclia ... ... ... ... ... ... 11 „
Alis Sheppord ... ... ... ... ... ... ... ... 15 „
Marget Blvndell ... ... ... ... ... ... ... 21 „
Alis Wildinge in ecclia ... ... ... ... ... ... 13 Januarie
pu: Ric Cowp in ecclia ... ... ... ... ... ... ... 15 „
Robert Gobin in ecclia ... ... ... ... ... ... 17 „
puer Tho: Shawe in ecclia ... ... ... ... ... ... 8 ffebruarie
Tho: Browne ... ... ... ... ... ... ... ... 19 „
Gilb Smyth in ecclia ... ... ... ... ... ... 1 March
Tho: Barker ... ... ... ... ... ... ... ... 2 „
Margerie Chadocke in ecclia ... ... ... ... ... „ „
Johne Hodgeson in ecclia ... ... ... ... ... 5 „
Margerie Ball Alias Talior ... ... ... ... ... 7 „
Margerie Lee in the chancell ... ... ... ... ... 12 „

## 1562.

Fo. 282 Marget Cvtune *or* Cvbane ... ... ... ... ... 7 Aprill
puer . . . Cropp in ecclia ... ... ... ... ... ... „ „
Margerie Mathew ... ... ... ... ... ... ... 16 „
Ideth Leadbetter ... ... ... ... ... ... ... 19 „
Jaine Colinson ... ... ... ... ... ... ... ... 9 Maye
Jenet Mosse in ecclia ... ... ... ... ... ... 17 „
Alis Jackeson ... ... ... ... ... ... ... ... „ „
Johne Cosey in ecclia ... ... ... ... ... ... 1 June
Robt Craine ... ... ... ... ... ... ... ... 7 „
Margerie Pecocke ... ... ... ... ... ... ... 18 July
Lionell Hoolme ... ... ... ... ... ... ... 20 „
puer John Loccar in ecclia ... ... ... ... ... ... 30 „
Marget Mosse in ecclia ... ... ... ... ... ... 3 Auguste
Marget Butchard ... ... ... ... ... ... ... 10 „
Robert Hawet ... ... ... ... ... ... ... ... 16 „
Wiłłm Swifte in ecclia ... ... ... ... ... ... 3 September
Tho: Hatton ... ... ... ... ... ... ... ... 5 „
Hugh Westhead ... ... ... ... ... ... ... 9 „
Athor Parbot ... ... ... ... ... ... ... ... 10 „
Wiłłm ffisher ... ... ... ... ... ... ... ... 18 „
Parret Waringe ... ... ... ... ... ... ... 29 „
Jenet Atherton in ecclia ... ... ... ... ... ... 12 October
Se[9] John Mouldie parson of Eccleston ... ... 16 „
Tho: Waringe ... ... ... ... ... ... ... ... 20 „
Hugh Worthingeton in chancel ... ... ... ... 28 „
puer Henrie Werall in ecclia ... ... ... ... ... ... 29 „

| | Name | Day | Month |
|---|---|---|---|
| | Margerie Waring ... ... ... ... ... ... ... | 29 | October |
| | *[No entries for November]* | | |
| 283 | Ellin Hunter ... ... ... ... ... ... ... ... | 1 | December |
| | Jamis Manor ... ... ... ... ... ... ... ... | ” | ” |
| | Ewan Hoolme ... ... ... ... ... ... ... ... | 18 | ” |
| | S$^{9}$ Wiłłm Aspinwall ... ... ... ... ... ... | 25 | ” |
| | Jenet Harison ... ... ... ... ... ... ... ... | 26 | ” |
| | Richard Morecroft ... ... ... ... ... ... ... | 28 | ” |
| | Ric̄ Cadicke ... ... ... ... ... ... ... ... | ” | ” |
| | Cristopher Sumner ... ... ... ... ... ... ... | 29 | ” |
| | . . . Blvndell ... ... ... ... ... ... ... | 30 | ” |
| | Eliz$^{th}$ Mason in the chansell ... ... ... ... ... | 1 | Januarie |
| | Marget Mowdisley in eccl̄ia ... ... ... ... ... | 3 | ” |
| | Izabell Morcrofte ... ... ... ... ... ... ... | ” | ” |
| | Gilb̄ Woodfall in eccl̄ia ... ... ... ... ... ... | 4 | ” |
| | Marget Haughton ... ... ... ... ... ... ... | 14 | ” |
| | Izabell Swifte in eccl̄ia ... ... ... ... ... ... | 16 | ” |
| | Nicolas Tasker ... ... ... ... ... ... ... ... | 17 | ” |
| | Jenet Mowdisley in eccl̄ia ... ... ... ... ... | 19 | ” |
| | Threstram Swifte in eccl̄ia ... ... ... ... ... | 30 | ” |
| puer | Henrie Lvskin in eccl̄ia ... ... ... ... ... ... | 2 | ffebruarie |
| puer | Ellin Hill in eccl̄ia ... ... ... ... ... ... ... | 6 | ” |
| puer | Peeter Barrow in eccl̄ia ... ... ... ... ... ... | 12 | ” |
| | Anne Cropp ... ... ... ... ... ... ... ... | 13 | ” |
| | Ric̄ the porefelow ... ... ... ... ... ... ... | 19 | ” |
| | Ric̄ Mason ... ... ... ... ... ... ... ... | 21 | ” |
| | Wiłłm Traves ... ... ... ... ... ... ... ... | 25 | ” |
| | Adam Hunter ... ... ... ... ... ... ... ... | 29 | ” |
| | Marget Westhead ... ... ... ... ... ... ... | 6 | Marche |
| | Emlin Holton ... ... ... ... ... ... ... ... | 8 | ” |
| | Jamis Waringe ... ... ... ... ... ... ... ... | 10 | ” |
| | Marget Mason ... ... ... ... ... ... ... ... | 17 | ” |
| | Marget Carter ... ... ... ... ... ... ... ... | ” | ” |
| | Eliz$^{th}$ Massie in the Chancell ... ... ... ... ... | 19 | ” |
| | John Nalior in eccl̄ia ... ... ... ... ... ... | 22 | ” |
| | Gilb̄ Baner ... ... ... ... ... ... ... ... | 23 | ” |

## 1563.

| | Name | Day | Month |
|---|---|---|---|
| | Alis Ascroft ... ... ... ... ... ... ... ... | 30 | Marche |
| | . . . Hallworth ... ... ... ... ... ... ... | ” | ” |
| 284 | Hector & Katherin Mowdisley ... ... ... ... | 3 | Aprill |
| | John Mason ... ... ... ... ... ... ... ... | 11 | ” |
| | Izabbell Scarsbreck in eccl̄ia ... ... ... ... ... | 13 | ” |
| | Jaine Ambrose in saint nicolas chan: ... ... | 20 | ” |
| | Cristopher Hallworth ... ... ... ... ... ... | 21 | ” |
| | Jamis Gorsutch ... ... ... ... ... ... ... | 23 | ” |
| | Sislie Mason ... ... ... ... ... ... ... ... | 25 | ” |
| | Peeter Ormishaw ... ... ... ... ... ... ... | 27 | ” |

| | Name | Day | Month |
|---|---|---|---|
| | Alis Banet | 30 | Aprill |
| | Nicolas Aspinwell in eccl̄ia | 6 | Maye |
| | Lowrance Sage | „ | „ |
| | Tho: Banke | 8 | „ |
| | . . . Woodes | 11 | „ |
| | Izabbell Jackeson | 19 | „ |
| | John Price alias Showen in eccl̄ia | „ | „ |
| | Eliz$^{th}$ Ormishaw in eccl̄ia | 24 | „ |
| | Jenet Mowdisley | 26 | „ |
| | Jenet the northeren woman | 1 | June |
| | Jenet Hoolton | 2 | „ |
| | Anas Colinson | „ | „ |
| | Grace Barker | 3 | „ |
| | Alis Symond in the Channsell | 7 | „ |
| | Ric̄ Holland | 13 | „ |
| | Janie Holland | 18 | „ |
| | Henrie Wilson alias Palmer | 22 | „ |
| | Eliz$^{th}$ Scarsbreck in eccl̄ia | 29 | „ |
| | . . . Morecrofte | „ | „ |
| | Alis Edw: doughter | 30 | „ |
| | Athoney Mellinge | 2 | July |
| | Edw: Hunter | „ | „ |
| | Gilb̄ Gilb̄son | 3 | „ |
| | Margerie Arton | 4 | „ |
| | Hugh Preskot | 10 | „ |
| | George Waynewright | 11 | „ |
| | Alis Crofte in eccl̄ia | 12 | „ |
| | Elnor Crofte | 14 | „ |
| | Willm̄ ffletcher | 15 | „ |
| Fo. 285 | Ellin Allerton | 16 | „ |
| | Margerie Hodgekinson | 26 | „ |
| | John Whytestones | 30 | „ |
| | John Mason | „ | „ |
| | Eliz$^{th}$ Hadocke | „ | „ |
| | George Prescot in eccl̄ia | 3 | Auguste |
| | John Prescot | 7 | „ |
| | Hamlet Brigehowse | 11 | „ |
| | John Shervingeton | 13 | „ |
| | John Whytestones in eccl̄ia | 30 | „ |
| | Martin Morecrofte in eccl̄ia | 6 | September |
| | Jamis Wright | „ | „ |
| | Margerie Becarstath | 7 | „ |
| | Margerie Nalior vx$^9$ John in eccl̄ia | 22 | „ |
| | Alis Lunte | 24 | „ |
| | Elin Makon | 25 | „ |
| | Jaine Rutter | 26 | „ |
| | Elin Bycarstaff in eccl̄ia | 29 | „ |
| | Katherin Cropp in eccl̄ia | „ | „ |
| | Jenet Asmall | „ | „ |

| | | |
|---|---|---|
| Jenet Hey | 1 | October |
| . . . Lathom | 14 | „ |
| Elizth Halworth | 15 | „ |
| Marget Dicket | 19 | „ |
| Phillip Hey in eccłia | 9 | November |
| John Walne in saint nic̃ Chancell | 15 | „ |
| Tho: Aspinwall | 19 | „ |
| Margerie Hoolme in eccłia | „ | „ |
| Ewan Ashton | 27 | „ |
| Marget Edw:son | 8 | December |
| Ellin Shaw | 10 | „ |
| Wiłłm Mason | 13 | „ |
| Marget Warriner | 18 | „ |
| Jamis Shepard | 21 | „ |
| Alis Blvndell | 28 | „ |
| Nicolas Waringe | 1 | Januarie |
| Alis Shurlicars | 3 | „ |
| Elizth Sounse | 27 | „ |
| Wiłłm Rylans | 30 | „ |
| Hugh ffletcher in eccłia | 1 | ffebruarie |
| Edmund Shurlicars | 13 | „ |
| Ellin the wyfe Ewan Hoolme | 14 | „ |
| Jenet Jolibrond in ecclia | 20 | „ |
| Rob̄t Preskot | 13 | March |
| Marie Haselgreave | 17 | „ |

## 1564.

| | | |
|---|---|---|
| Edw: Sadler in eccłia | 28 | March |
| John Pemberton | 6 | Aprill |
| Parsiuall Shurlicars | 7 | „ |
| . . . Higham | 28 | „ |
| Alis Standishe | 25 | Maye |
| Jamis Smyth in eccłia | 26 | „ |
| Jaine Barker fi: Ric̃ in eccłia | 31 | „ |
| Xpꝰofer Mason in Sat nicõ chancell | 10 | June |
| Edm: Smulte in ecclia | 11 | „ |
| Ric̃ Gorsutch | 4 | July |
| John Traves | 15 | „ |
| Lyonell Swifte | 17 | „ |
| Blanch Aspinwall | 30 | „ |
| Jenet Aspinwap [*sic*] in eccłia | 4 | August |
| Emlin Pecocke | 24 | „ |
| Wiłłm Aspinwall | „ | „ |
| Ellin Waringe | 14 | September |
| . . . Smyth | 29 | „ |
| 7 Tho: Johnson | 2 | October |
| Richard the muxeman̄ | 7 | „ |
| vxꝰ Rodger Sutch in eccłia | 11 | „ |

| | | | |
|---|---|---|---|
| | Ellin Cadicke ... ... ... ... ... ... ... | 16 | October |
| | Jenet Tomes ... ... ... ... ... ... ... | 22 | „ |
| | Tho: Shawe ... ... ... ... ... ... ... | 7 | November |
| | Marget Scarsbrecke ... ... ... ... ... ... | 11 | „ |
| | Tho: Wainwright in ecclia ... ... ... ... | 13 | „ |
| | Edw: Killshaw ... ... ... ... ... ... | 29 | „ |
| | Tho: Gyles ... ... ... ... ... ... ... | 30 | „ |
| | Eliz^th^ Rutter ... ... ... ... ... ... ... | „ | „ |
| puer | Tho: Hodgeson ... ... ... ... ... ... | 3 | December |
| | John Marclife ... ... ... ... ... ... ... | 6 | „ |
| puer | Jamis Banke in ecclia ... ... ... ... ... | 29 | „ |
| | Witm Gowlbron in Sant nicol chan: ... ... | 30 | „ |
| | Hugh Bycarstaff in ecclia ... ... ... ... | 1 | Januarie |
| | vx' Tho: Draper ... ... ... ... ... ... | 4 | „ |
| | Henrie Morecrofte ... ... ... ... ... ... | „ | „ |
| | Nicolas fformbey ... ... ... ... ... ... | 11 | „ |
| | Ellin vx' Ja: Waringe ... ... ... ... ... | 17 | „ |
| | Tho: fformby ... ... ... ... ... ... ... | 29 | „ |
| | Anne Asmall in S^t^ ni: Chancell ... ... ... | „ | „ |
| | . . . Ambrose ... ... ... ... ... ... | 1 | ffebruarie |
| | vx' Peeter Shaw in ecclia ... ... ... ... | 4 | „ |
| | Marget Shurlicars ... ... ... ... ... ... | 5 | „ |
| | vx' John fformbey ... ... ... ... ... ... | 12 | „ |
| | Ric Harker ... ... ... ... ... ... ... | 15 | „ |
| | vx' Ade Aspinwall in ecclia ... ... ... ... | 20 | „ |
| | George Haughton ... ... ... ... ... ... | 23 | „ |
| | Myles Sadler in ecclia ... ... ... ... ... | „ | „ |
| | Witm Marclough ... ... ... ... ... ... | 27 | „ |
| | Emlin Prescot ... ... ... ... ... ... ... | „ | „ |
| | Jaine Robertson ... ... ... ... ... ... | „ | „ |
| | Cristopher Hoolme ... ... ... ... ... ... | 28 | „ |
| | Marget Toppinge ... ... ... ... ... ... | „ | „ |
| Fo. 288 | Omfrey Towne in ecclia ... ... ... ... ... | 1 | March |
| | Tho: Gorsutch ... ... ... ... ... ... | 5 | „ |
| pur | Jaine Barow in ecclia ... ... ... ... ... | 6 | „ |
| | Jenet Hodgson ... ... ... ... ... ... ... | „ | „ |
| | . . . Wignall ... ... ... ... ... ... | 9 | „ |
| | vx' Ric Witter ... ... ... ... ... ... ... | 13 | „ |
| | Parsivell Shurlicars ... ... ... ... ... ... | 18 | „ |
| | vx' Ric Marclew ... ... ... ... ... ... | „ | „ |

## 1565.

| | | |
|---|---|---|
| vx' Edm: Smlte in ecclia ... ... ... ... ... | 31 | March |
| Grace Burscough ... ... ... ... ... ... | 3 | Aprill |
| Ellin Gowlbron ... ... ... ... ... ... | „ | „ |
| Tho: Whytestones ... ... ... ... ... ... | 4 | „ |
| . . . Burie ... ... ... ... ... ... ... | 10 | „ |
| Ric Rigmaden ... ... ... ... ... ... ... | 11 | „ |

| | | |
|---|---|---|
| . . . Colinson ... ... ... ... ... ... | 21 | Aprill |
| Jaine Atherton ... ... ... ... ... ... ... | „ | „ |
| John Irland in ecctia ... ... ... ... ... | 22 | „ |
| Edw: Carre ... ... ... ... ... ... ... | 2 | Maye |
| Katherin Hunter ... ... ... ... ... ... | 4 | „ |
| Karker [*sic*] ... ... ... ... ... ... ... | 5 | „ |
| John Werall in ecctia ... ... ... ... ... | 11 | „ |
| . . . Croffte ... ... ... ... ... ... | „ | „ |
| Ric̃ Hutton ... ... ... ... ... ... ... | 19 | „ |
| Jamis Kirvin in ecctia ... ... ... ... ... | 24 | „ |
| Katherine Clarke Alias man ... ... ... ... | „ | „ |
| Tho: Clarke Alias man in ecctia ... ... ... | 28 | „ |
| Jam: Duncon ... ... ... ... ... ... ... | „ | „ |
| vx[9] Tho: Clarke ... ... ... ... ... ... | 31 | „ |
| Ellin Ambrose in ecctia ... ... ... ... ... | 1 | June |
| . . . Woolsey ... ... ... ... ... ... | „ | „ |
| Eliz[th] vx[9] John Hoolme in ecctia ... ... ... | 4 | „ |
| Alis Wignall ... ... ... ... ... ... ... | 7 | „ |
| Wittm Lathwhat in ecctia ... ... ... ... | 10 | „ |
| Jaine vx[9] Wittm ffarclough ... ... ... ... | „ | „ |
| Ellin Morris vx[9] in ecctia ... ... ... ... | 14 | „ |
| Margerie Cropp in ecctia ... ... ... ... | 26 | „ |
| Edw: Smyth in Sa[t] nic̃ Chan: ... ... ... ... | 28 | „ |
| Seth Svmner ... ... ... ... ... ... ... | 29 | „ |
| Godferey Bycarstaff ... ... ... ... ... ... | 3 | July |
| Jaine Prescot in ecctia ... ... ... ... ... | 9 | „ |
| Marie Haselgreave ... ... ... ... ... ... | 12 | „ |
| Tho: Kekuicke in ecctia ... ... ... ... | 14 | „ |
| Izabell Westhead ... ... ... ... ... ... | 16 | „ |
| Wittm Rydinge ... ... ... ... ... ... | 25 | „ |
| Tho: Westhead ... ... ... ... ... ... | 26 | „ |
| Tho: Hardman ... ... ... ... ... ... | 28 | „ |
| Marget Halsall in ecctia ... ... ... ... ... | 2 | August |
| Marget Crosbie ... ... ... ... ... ... | 6 | „ |
| Ellice Coockeson ... ... ... ... ... ... | 7 | „ |
| Gilƀ Barton in ecctia ... ... ... ... ... | 12 | „ |
| Gilƀ Jump ... ... ... ... ... ... ... | 17 | „ |
| Wittm Tarleton ... ... ... ... ... ... | 24 | „ |
| Jamis Asshorst in ecctia ... ... ... ... ... | 7 | September |
| John Mosse ... ... ... ... ... ... ... | 29 | „ |
| vx[9] George Wildinge ... ... ... ... ... | „ | „ |
| Marget Macon ... ... ... ... ... ... ... | 3 | October |
| . . . Mossocke in ecctia ... ... ... ... | 4 | „ |
| Hugh Hey in ecctia ... ... ... ... ... | 19 | „ |
| Jamis She ... ... ... ... ... ... ... ... | „ | „ |
| Jaine Tasker ... ... ... ... ... ... ... | „ | „ |
| Margerie Lathom ... ... ... ... ... ... | 20 | „ |
| John Smalshaw ... ... ... ... ... ... | 30 | „ |
| Ellin vx[9] Peet[9] Rigbie in ecctia ... ... ... | 11 | November |

| | | | |
|---|---|---|---|
| | Rob̄t Holonde ... ... ... ... ... ... ... ... | 13 | November |
| | Homfray Jumpe ... ... ... ... ... ... ... | 2 | December |
| | George Witere ... ... ... ... ... ... ... ... | 5 | ,, |
| | Margerie Preskot ... ... ... ... ... ... ... | 16 | ,, |
| | Elizth Aerton ... ... ... ... ... ... ... ... | ,, | ,, |
| | John Mowdisley ... ... ... ... ... ... ... | 22 | ,, |
| | Eline Bourskoughe ... .. ... ... ... ... | 24 | ,, |
| | Elizth Mason ... ... ... ... ... ... ... ... | 29 | ,, |
| Fo. 290 | Jenet Waringe ... ... ... ... ... ... ... ... | 5 | Januarie |
| | Margreat Shurlecars ... ... ... ... ... ... ... | 8 | ,, |
| | Alis Whalese vxꝰ Hec ... ... ... ... ... ... | 12 | ,, |
| | vxꝰ Rog Tomson ... ... ... ... ... ... ... | ,, | ,, |
| | Edw: Ridgbie in eccl̄ia ... ... ... ... ... ... | 13 | ,, |
| | Jenete Brescotte ... ... . . ... ... ... | 19 | ,, |
| | Kathrrin vx: Ric̄ Jolibran in the high chansell | 31 | ,, |
| | Eline Lathwhat ... ... ... ... ... ... ... | 4 | ffebruarie |
| | Margreat Eccelston ... ... ... ... ... ... ... | 6 | ,, |
| | Grace Atherton ... ... ... ... ... ... ... | 7 | ,, |
| | vxꝰ Adam Hunter ... ... ... ... ... ... ... | 11 | ,, |
| | Adame Morcrofte ... ... ... ... ... ... ... | 15 | ,, |
| | Henrie Hodgkinson ... ... ... ... ... ... ... | ,, | ,, |
| | vxꝰ Radulfie Marcer ... ... ... ... ... ... | 4 | Marche |
| | Tho: Will̄mson in eccl̄ia ... ... ... ... | 12 | ,, |
| | Emline Sephton in the high chansell ... ... | 14 | ,, |
| | Ewan Wainwrighte in eccl̄ia ... ... ... ... | 18 | ,, |
| | James Hunter ... ... ... ... ... ... ... | 23 | ,, |

## 1566.

| | | | |
|---|---|---|---|
| | Jenete Barton ... ... ... ... ... ... ... ... | 28 | Marche |
| pure | Emline Lockere in eccl̄ia ... ... ... ... ... ... | 29 | ,, |
| | Will̄m Shawe ... ... ... ... ... ... ... | 27 | Aprill |
| | Alis vxꝰ Tho: Heskethe ... ... ... ... ... ... | 4 | Maye |
| | Tho: Mawthrowe ... ... ... ... ... ... ... | 28 | ,, |
| | John Ascrofte ... ... ... ... ... ... ... ... | 10 | June |
| | Emline Greaves ... ... ... ... ... ... ... | 11 | ,, |
| | Hughe Woodwordthe ... ... ... ... ... ... | 29 | ,, |
| | Jaine vxꝰ Thur̄ Aspinwall ... ... ... ... ... | 30 | ,, |
| | Margerie Vrmston ... ... ... ... ... ... ... | 13 | Julye |
| | Eline Smalshawe ... ... ... ... ... ... ... | ,, | ,, |
| | Edw: Garstange ... ... ... ... ... ... ... | 18 | ,, |
| Fo. 291 | Jenete Morcrofte in eccl̄ia ... ... ... ... ... | 7 | Auguste |
| puer̄ | Rob̄t Haslgreave in eccl̄ia ... ... ... ... ... | 11 | ,, |
| | Jenet Gleaste ... ... ... ... ... ... ... ... | 13 | ,, |
| | vxꝰ Jo: Ridgbie in eccl̄ia ... ... ... ... ... | 3 | October |
| | John Tandanoughte in St niclo chansell ... ... | 11 | ,, |
| | John Wainwrighte in eccl̄ia ... ... ... ... | 16 | ,, |
| | vxꝰ Tho: Jumpe ... ... ... ... ... ... ... | 22 | ,, |
| | Pure Tho: Whitstons ... ... ... ... ... ... | 7 | November |

| | | |
|---|---|---|
| Jenet Veale | 13 | November |
| vxꝰ Henrie Mason in eccl̄ia | 18 | „ |
| Emline vxꝰ Tho: Baricke in eccl̄ia | 31 | December |
| Arth: Cropp | 13 | Januarie |
| Johne Topping | 25 | „ |
| Ewan Blackledge in eccl̄ia | 26 | „ |
| Margaret Banke | „ | „ |
| Sr Denize Stanleye pꝰt | 4 | ffebruarie |
| Ric̄ Cropp | 5 | „ |
| Gilb̄t Holond in eccl̄ia | 7 | „ |
| Will̄m Banister in eccl̄ia | 10 | „ |
| Anne Ric[r]son | 13 | „ |
| Ane Davie | „ | „ |
| Ric̄ Smyth | 14 | „ |

## 1567.

| | | |
|---|---|---|
| George Hill | 28 | Marche |
| Jamis Movdisley | 26 | „ |
| Mris Jenet Grenwode | „ | „ |
| Tho: Hesкethe | 4 | Aprill |
| vxꝰ Hnrie [*sic*] Sutche | 9 | „ |
| Izabell Ascoght | 20 | „ |
| Margreat Boutle | 21 | „ |
| Tho: Ambrose | 26 | „ |
| Rodger Smith | 13 | Maye |
| Will̄m Gorsuche in eccl̄ia | 26 | „ |
| Sr Homfry Jackson pꝰst in ecc̄ | 29 | „ |
| Thurstan Aspinwall in ecclia | 1 | June |
| . . . Haughton | „ | „ |
| Eline Taskar | 2 | „ |
| Gabriell White | 6 | „ |
| Eline Windrawe | 13 | „ |
| Rodger Clapham | 22 | „ |
| James Shawe in ecclia | 23 | „ |
| . . . vxꝰ Hugh in eccl̄ia | „ | „ |
| Jenet Aspinwall | | |
| Anne Towne | 7 | Julye |
| John Sutche | 11 | „ |
| Rodger Sutche | „ | „ |
| Jaine Ashurste in eccl̄ia | 16 | Auguste |
| Ranolde Garstange | 30 | „ |
| Alis Coupp | „ | „ |
| Jane Ambrose vid | 4 | September |
| Ric̄ Whitt | 12 | „ |
| Kath: Gill | 18 | „ |
| Rob̄t: ffarclough in eccl̄ia | 29 | „ |
| Alis Blacklee vxꝰ Ewā in ecc̄ | 3 | October |
| Margaret Stopford vxꝰ Hen: in ecc̄ | 27 | „ |

| | | | |
|---|---|---|---|
| | Tho: Hoolme | 7 | November |
| Fo. 293 | Jaine Gobbin in ecclia | 5 | December |
| | Eline Shakledie | 6 | „ |
| | Rodger Ormishawe | 20 | „ |
| pur | Willm Barton | 23 | „ |
| | Tho: Ruttere | „ | „ |
| puere | Margrate Whitstons | „ | „ |
| | ffardinando Garrard | 26 | „ |
| pu: | Tho: Cowdreye in ecclia | 26 | Januarie |
| | Mi's Margreate Veale | „ | „ |
| | Elin Rowe | „ | „ |
| | Peeter Leye | 6 | ffebruarie |
| | Richard Cocket | 19 | Marche |

## 1568.

| | | | |
|---|---|---|---|
| | Eliz^th Ascrofte in ecclia | 30 | Marche |
| | Margreate Heskethe | 4 | Aprill |
| | Ric Gill | 5 | „ |
| | Phillip Mowdisley | 26 | „ |
| | Robt Cowp in ecclia | 8 | Maye |
| | Siline Alker | 14 | „ |
| pur | John Sutch | 19 | „ |
| pur | Alis Asshurst | 20 | „ |
| pur | John Lancaster | 19 | June |
| | Jaine Robinson vx9 Ja: | 25 | „ |
| | Eliz^th Jackeson vx9 | 6 | July |
| | Alis Asshurst in ecclia | „ | „ |
| | Ric Cawdrey in ecclia | 10 | „ |
| | Ric Blackeledge | 11 | „ |
| | Tho: Smyth fi: Jo: | 16 | „ |
| | John Aspinwall | 18 | „ |
| | Ellin Sutch vx9 George in ecclia | „ | „ |
| Fo. 294 | Eliz^th Cropp fi: Godfrey in ecclia | „ | „ |
| | Jaine Alke | 23 | „ |
| | Willm Wright fi: Tho: | 30 | „ |
| | Gilb Shawe | 16 | August |
| | Jaine Gorsutch fi: Rob | 21 | „ |
| | Jaine Cowp in ecclia | 14 | September |
| | Jamis Cowp in ecclia | 22 | „ |
| | Marget Hoolme vx9 Will in ecclia | 29 | „ |
| | Marget Cowp vx9 John in ecclia | 15 | October |
| | Andrue Blvndell | 20 | „ |
| | Godfrey Jackeson in ecclia | 24 | „ |
| | Ric Lathom Junior in ecclia | 9 | November |
| | John Smyth in ecclia | „ | „ |
| | Marget Longley vx9 Tho: | 19 | „ |
| | Jaine Marclew vx9 Ric | 20 | „ |
| | Elline Sutch vx9 in ecclia | 23 | „ |

| | | |
|---|---|---|
| Mi'rs Sislie Stanley vx⁹ Peeter ar̄ ... ... ... | 28 | November |
| Ellin Ley ... ... ... ... ... ... ... ... | 14 | December |
| Jaine Jumpe vx⁹ Rob̄ ... ... ... ... ... ... | 15 | " |
| vx⁹ Hector Sutton ... ... ... ... ... ... | 18 | " |
| Eliz^th Wright vx⁹ Tho: ... ... ... ... ... | 27 | " |
| Alis Hesketh ... ... ... ... ... ... ... | 3 | Januarie |
| Ellin Robinson fi: Tho: ... ... ... ... | 18 | " |
| Margerie & Eideth Gardiner ... ... ... ... | 24 | " |
| Ric̄ Towne fi: Wil̄l ... ... ... ... ... ... | 27 | " |
| Jenet Smallshaw in ecc̄lia ... ... ... ... | 28 | " |
| Eliz^th Willson fil: Tho ... ... ... ... ... | 12 | ffebruarie |
| Susanna Mossocke fi: Hen: in ecclia ... ... | 20 | " |
| Eliz^th Croston fi Edw: ... ... ... ... ... | 22 | " |
| Eliz^th Aspinwall fi Elis ... ... ... ... ... | 26 | " |
| Hector Whytestons fi: Tho: ... ... ... ... | 1 | March |
| Wil̄lm Webster ... ... ... ... ... ... | 7 | " |
| Anne Prescot fi: Rob̄t ... ... ... ... ... | 9 | " |

## 1569.

| | | |
|---|---|---|
| Davie Ideth ... ... ... ... ... ... ... | 25 | March |
| Margerie Mvdie ... ... ... ... ... ... | 27 | " |
| Johne Prescot fi: Wil̄l ... ... ... ... ... | " | " |
| Tho: Morgan̄ ... ... ... ... ... ... ... | 7 | Aprill |
| Eliz^th Lathom ... ... ... ... ... ... ... | " | " |
| Eliz^th Anderton in ecc̄lia ... ... ... ... ... | 11 | " |
| Peeter Hunter in ecc̄lia ... ... ... ... ... | 12 | " |
| John Marrow fi: Tho: ... ... ... ... ... | 20 | " |
| John Balshaw ... ... ... ... ... ... ... | 21 | " |
| Ranovld Waynewright in ecc̄lia ... ... ... | 3 | Maye |
| Peeter Houghton ... ... ... ... ... ... | " | " |
| Rodger Morecrofte ... ... ... ... ... ... | 29 | " |
| Richard Marclew ... ... ... ... ... ... | 31 | " |
| Lawrance Aspinwall fi Ranould ... ... ... | 4 | June |
| John Pendleburie ... ... ... ... ... ... | 11 | " |
| Jaine Blvndell ... ... ... ... ... ... ... | 12 | " |
| Anne Cowley ... ... ... ... ... ... ... | " | " |
| Ric̄ Henrieson ... ... ... ... ... ... ... | 19 | " |
| Jaine Mosocke vx⁹ Hen: in ecclia ... ... ... | 28 | " |
| Alis Smyth fi: Tho: ... ... ... ... ... | 15 | Julye |
| Eliz^th Browne fi: Wil̄l ... ... ... ... ... | 27 | " |
| Jamis Sutch in the high chancell ... ... ... | 10 | August |
| Edw Veale fi: M⁹ ffrances in the high chancell | 13 | " |
| Rob̄t Cawsey in ecc̄lia ... ... ... ... ... | 24 | " |
| John Gobin fi: Tho: ... ... ... ... ... | 1 | September |
| Tho: Houghton fi: Ewan ... ... ... ... | 7 | " |
| Edw: Brighowse ... ... ... ... ... ... | 14 | " |
| Wil̄lm Buchard fi Lyonell ... ... ... ... | 18 | " |
| Anne Whytestones fi: Wil̄l ... ... ... ... | 22 | " |

Margerie Sutton vx⁹ Hector ... ... ... ... 25 September
Ric̃ Mason in eccl̃ia ... ... ... ... ... 27 „
John Barton fi: John ... ... ... ... ... 12 October
Jaine Gill fi: Tho: ... ... ... ... ... ... 14 „
Margerie Eliot fi: Ja: ... ... ... ... ... 23 „
Izabell Wane fi: Ja: ... ... ... ... ... 30 „
Alis Blvndell vx⁹ Ja: in eccl̃ia ... ... ... 28 November
Peeter Carre fi: Edm: ... ... ... ... ... „ „
Willm Johnson fi: Cristopher ... ... ... 6 December
Edmund Haidocke ... ... ... ... ... ... 8 „
Elizth Mullinex fi Will ... ... ... ... ... 19 „
Anne Haughton Relic̃ Tristrom ... ... ... 25 „
Ellin ffletcher ... ... ... ... ... ... ... 28 „
John Barton ... ... ... ... ... ... ... 30 „
Jaine Willson in eccl̃ia ... ... ... ... ... 5 Januarie
Alis Eideth vx⁹ Davie ... ... ... ... ... 8 „
Agnes Shaw Reli Peeter ... ... ... ... ... 18 „
Eideth Blvndell fi: Cristopher ... ... ... 20 „
Jenet Thomasson Relic̃ Jo: ... ... ... ... 27 „
Ric̃ Tasker ... ... ... ... ... ... ... 28 „
Johne Killshaw fi: Witl ... ... ... ... ... 2 ffebruarie
Elizth Orton Relic̃ Jo: in ecclia ... ... ... 5 „
Jaine Hallworth fi: Will ... ... ... ... 10 „
Marget Gobin in eccl̃ia ... ... ... ... ... 16 „
Katherin Holland fi: Ric̃ in eccl̃ia ... ... 27 „
Homfrey Parker ... ... ... ... ... ... 1 March
Ellin Jackeson ... ... ... ... ... ... ... 6 „
Nicolas Marten ... ... ... ... ... ... 11 „
Alis Lathwhat vx⁹ Hen: in the High chan ... 13 „
Fo. 297 Emlin Lvskin fi: Will ... ... ... ... ... ... 15 „
Anne Hunter Relic̃ Tho ... ... ... ... ... 16 „
John Burscough fi: Tho: ... ... ... ... ... 20 „
Hugh Lailand ... ... ... ... ... ... ... 24 „
Peeter Hunter ... ... ... ... ... ... ... „ „

## 1570.

Ric̃ Blondell in eccl̃ia ... ... ... ... ... 27 March
Jenet Blvndell Relic̃ Barthõ ... ... ... ... 3 Aprill
Emlin Whytestones fi: Hec̃ ... ... ... ... 5 „
Elizth Tarbut ... ... ... ... ... ... ... 11 „
Jaine Hesketh fi: Tho: ... ... ... ... ... 15 „
Willm Hankick ... ... ... ... ... ... „ „
Homfrey Hey ... ... ... ... ... ... ... 16 „
Anes Mollinex Relic̃ Ric̃ ... ... ... ... 21 „
Hugh Lockeye in eccl̃ia ... ... ... ... ... 2 Maye
Jaine Barker fi: Alex in eccl̃ia ... ... ... 3 „
Ric̃ Alerton fi John ... ... ... ... ... ... 5 „
Izabell Grosier vx⁹ Ric̃ ... ... ... ... ... 10 „

Ellin Mowdisley fi : Ja : ... ... ... ... ... ... 25 Maye
Margerie Mollinex vx⁹ Tho : in the high chañ 1 June
Silvester Halworth fi : Witt ... ... ... ... ... 13 „
Dorethie Mowdisley fi : Ja : ... ... ... ... ... 15 „
Ric̃ Hunter fi : Tho : ... ... ... ... ... ... „ „
Henrie Halsall fi : Silvester in ecc̃lia ... ... 27 „
Marget Golibrond vx⁹ Ric̃ in ye high cha̅ ... 29 „
Emlin Howghton vx⁹ Witt̃m ... ... ... ... ... 6 July
Anne Hardman fi : Tho : ... ... ... ... ... 14 „
Marget Curtes ... ... ... ... ... ... ... ... 15 „
Hugh Hulme fi : Tho : ... ... ... ... ... ... 20 „
Eliz^th Mowdisley vx⁹ Ja : ... ... ... ... ... 25 „
Eliz^th Brandocke in ecc̃lia ... ... ... ... ... 5 August
Marget Whytestones vx⁹ Hen : in ecc̃lia ... 8 „
Anne Letherbarow fi : Jo : ... ... ... ... ... 18 „
John Henrieson fi : Myles in ecc̃lia ... ... 20 „
Raffe Winder ... ... ... ... ... ... ... ... 4 September
Ric̃ Lathom fi Witt ... . ... ... ... ... ... 15 „
Silvester Kekeuicke fi John ... ... ... ... 27 „
Henrie Speakeman ... ... ... ... ... ... ... 2 October
Jaine Gill ... ... ... ... ... ... ... ... ... 11 „
Witt̃m Ley fi : Hugh ... ... ... ... ... ... 12 „
Jaine Ley fi : John ... ... ... ... ... ... 21 „
Marget ffletcher fi : Tristram ... ... ... ... 24 „
Sislie Aughton fi Witt̃m ... ... ... ... ... 2 November
John Hoolme fi : Peeter ... ... ... ... ... 3 „
Ellin Hey vx⁹ Witt̃m in ecclia ... ... ... 7 „
ffrances Sankey fi : Rod : in ecc̃lia ... ... 9 „
Ellin Wainewright Relic̃ Tho : in ecclia ... 10 „
Elin Cropp fi : Ric̃ Senior... ... ... ... ... 11 „
Margerie Hunter vx⁹ Jo : ... ... ... ... ... 14 „
Marget Prescot Relic̃ Jo : ... ... ... ... ... 23 „
George Howlden fi : Hen : ... ... ... ... ... 28 „
ffrances Rylance fi : Rob̃ ... .. ... ... 6 December
S⁹ George Stanley Knight in the high Chancel 8 „
. . . Cosey fi : Ja : ... ... ... ... ... ... 10 „
Anne Ambrose in ecc̃lia ... ... ... ... ... 11 „
Ellis Mvniley in ecc̃lia ... ... ... ... ... „ „
Marget Oliverson Relic̃ Tho : ... ... ... 12 „
Ewan Westhead ... ... ... ... ... ... ... „ „
Witt̃m Sulbie fi : Ranould in ecc̃lia ... ... 14 „
Marget Jumpe Relic Witt̃m ... ... ... ... 19 „
Robert Herdman fi : Tho : ... ... ... ... ... 21 „
Marget Gilbertson vx⁹ Will : ... ... ... ... 28 „
Marget Cropp fi Ric̃ ... ... ... ... ... ... 4 Januarie
Ric̃ Breykill in eccletia [*sic*] ... ... ... ... 8 „
Margerie Mvlie [?] Relic̃ Hugh ... ... ... 10 „
Gabrell Lathom fi : Tho : ... ... ... ... ... 18 „
Eliz^th Jackeson Relic Nicolas ... ... ... ... 20 „

Hugh Lathom in eccl̄ia ... ... ... ... ... 22 Januarie
Jaine Jumpe vx⁹ Edw: ... ... ... ... ... 26 „
Edw: Aiscroft ... ... ... ... ... ... ... 29 „
Tho: Woodhowse in ecclia ... ... ... ... 7 ffebruarie
Tho: Cropp in ecclia... ... ... ... ... ... „ „
Agnes Ormishaw Relic Rodge ... ... ... 8 „
Eme Grove Relic Arthor ... ... ... ... ... 10 „
Marie Mason fi: Hugh in eccl̄ia ... ... ... 17 „
Alexander Barker in ecclia ... ... ... ... 9 March
Eliz^th^ Carter Relic Henrie... ... ... ... ... 10
Tho Aiscroft fi Raffe ... ... ... ... ... „ „
Parsevall Jumpe fi: Edw: ... ... ... ... 12 „
Elin Waynewright fi Hen: ... ... ... ... 13 „
John Barton Junior ... ... ... ... ... ... 14 „
Marget Gill vx⁹ Parsevall ... ... ... ... „ „
Marget Webster Relic Edmund in ecclia ... 17 „
Hamlet Spencer fi Edmund ... ... ... ... 18 „
Eliz^th^ Waynewright vx⁹ Tho: in eccl̄ia ... ... 19 „
Jenet Lathwhat vx⁹ Richard ... ... ... ... „ „
Anne Gill fi Parcevall ... ... ... ... ... 24 „

## 1571.

Marget Smyth fi: Will ... ... ... ... ... 26 March
Jaine Richardson fi: Edw: ... ... ... ... 29 „
Mores Johnson in ecclia ... ... ... ... ... 5 Aprill
Marget Sutch Ric̃ Hugh in eccl̄ia ... ... 7 „
Eliz^th^ ffooler ... ... ... ... ... ... ... ... 8 „
Ric̃ Waringe ... ... ... ... ... ... ... ... 9 „
Katherin Butcher vx⁹ John in eccl̄ia ... ... 14 „
Wiłłm Hallworth ... ... ... ... ... ... ... 21 „
John Charles in ecl̄ia ... ... ... ... ... 23 „
Gilbart Morcroft in eccl̄ia ... ... ... ... „ „
Fo. 300 Jamis ffranfeman [*sic* probably Franseman] ... 24 „
Hugh Woosey fi Ric̃ ... ... ... ... ... „ „
Ric̃ Morecroft fi: Wiłł ... ... ... ... ... „ „
Elin Barton ... ... ... ... ... ... ... ... 5 Maye
Kath Wainewright fi: Georg ... ... ... ... 12 „
Gabrell Killshaw fi: Wiłł ... ... ... ... 16 „
Anne Barton fi: Wiłł ... ... ... ... ... 25 „
Eliz^th^ Stopforth fi: John ... ... ... ... ... 28 „
Eliz^th^ Aiscroft ... ... ... ... ... ... ... 1 June
Eliz^th^ Bonke fi: Hen: ... ... ... ... ... 8 „
John Golibrond in the high Chañ ... ... ... 17 „
Jamis Lawranson alis Robertson ... ... ... 2 July
Alis Ley ... ... ... ... ... ... ... ... 10 „
Cuthbrt Butle in the high chanc̃ ... ... ... 27 „
Rodger Hankin in eccl̄ia ... ... ... ... 2 August
John Mowdisley fi: Ja: ... ... ... ... ... 7 „

vx' Jamis Waringe ... ... ... ... ... ... ... 13 August
Peeter Barton fi: Gilb ... ... ... ... ... ... 4 September
Elizth Aspinwall Relic George in ecclia ... ... 8 "
Tho Toppinge fi: John ... ... ... ... ... ... 14 "
Marget Prescot Relic John ... ... ... ... ... 26 "
Elizth Sefton fi: Tho: in ecclia ... ... ... 29 "
Tho: Aspinwall fi: Jamis ... ... ... ... ... " "
Tho: Swifte In ecclesia ... .. .. ... ... 4 October
Elizth Stopforth vx' Tho: in the high chanc ... " "
Marget Sefton vx' Tho: in ecclia ... ... ... 5 "
Katherin Eliot Relic Edw: ... ... ... ... ... 13 "
Robart Shawe fi: Rodge ... ... ... ... ... ... 18 "
John & Jenet Orton ... ... ... ... ... ... 31 "
John Eliot fi: Tho: ... ... ... ... ... ... 1 November
Jeenet Westhead Relic Ewan ... ... ... ... ... " "
John Cosey fi: Hugh ... ... ... ... ... ... 3 "
Rodger Kekeuicke fi: John in ecclia ... ... 7 "
John Tasker ... ... ... ... ... ... ... ... ... 13 "
Xpopher Shirvingeton ... ... ... ... ... ... 6 December
Ric Kilshawe ... ... ... ... ... ... ... ... ... 23 "
Elizth Mowdie ... ... ... ... ... ... ... ... ... 15 Januarie
Anne Care ... ... ... ... ... ... ... ... ... 18 "
Jaine Hatton fi: Tho: ... ... ... ... ... ... 1 ffebruarie
Margerie Gill ... ... ... ... ... ... ... ... ... 4 "
Grace Holonde vx' Hu: in ecclia ... ... 5 "
Caris Webster fi: Hen ... ... ... ... ... ... 13 "
Ric Blundell ... ... ... ... ... ... ... ... ... 15 "
Elizth Rydinge vx' Willm ... ... ... ... ... ... " "
Mathew Hesketh in ecclia ... ... ... ... ... 14 Marche
Elin Bonnde ... ... ... ... ... ... ... ... ... 16 "
Margreat Kenione fi: Edw: ... ... ... ... ... 22 "
Robt Wilson ... ... ... ... ... ... ... ... ... 23 "

## 1572.

John Care ... ... ... ... ... ... ... ... ... ... 28 Marche
Elin Haskene Relict Tho: ... ... ... ... ... 7 Aprill
Tho: Parker fi: Richard ... ... ... ... ... 20 "
Margreat Barker vx' Ric ... ... ... ... ... 22 "
Katherin Pavor ... ... ... ... ... ... ... 1 Maye
Milis Scarsbricke ... ... ... ... ... ... ... 3 "
Anne Aspinwall fi: Tho: ... ... ... ... ... 9 "
Elin Scarsbricke ... ... ... ... ... ... ... 10 "
Godfraie Cropp fi: Pet ... ... .. ... ... 11 "
Elin Longton fi: Ric ... ... ... ... ... ... 12 "
Izabell Asmole ... ... ... ... ... ... ... ... " "
Margrat Morcrofte ... ... ... ... ... ... ... 17 "
Tho Morcrofte fi Willm ... ... ... ... ... ... 18 "
John Stophford fi Raph ... ... ... ... ... ... 21 "

|  |  |  |
|---|---|---|
| Robt Lathwate in ecclia | 25 | Maye |
| Elin Mowdisley in ecclia | 27 | „ |
| Elin Wainwright | 28 | „ |
| John Ttyem [*sic*] fi: Jo: | 29 | „ |
| Ellis Ambrose Late Vicar of O[k] in ecclia | 1 | June |
| Elin Hardman | „ | „ |
| John Leyland fi: Jo: | 2 | „ |
| John Leyland fi: Jo: | „ | „ |
| Elin Pinington | 4 | „ |
| George Jumpe fi: Robt | 5 | „ |
| Willm Sephton fi: Georg | 12 | „ |
| Edw: Bridghouse fi: Ric̃ | 14 | „ |
| Margerie Crofte Relicte Ric̃ | 17 | „ |
| John Hankin fi: Jo: in ecclia | 20 | „ |
| Eliz[th] Hatton fi Ric̃ | 22 | „ |
| Katherine Halworth fi: Lynell | 23 | „ |
| Jaine Ascrofte vx[9] Hen: | 24 | „ |
| Margreat Leadbeater | 2 | Julye |
| Henrie Bathe | 4 | „ |
| Jaine Rutter fi: Tho: | 22 | „ |
| Edmund Hatton | 29 | „ |
| Katherin Charles in ecclia | 1 | Auguste |
| Margreat Morcrofte | 6 | „ |
| Anne Whetstones fi Robt in ecclia | 9 | „ |
| John Prescote in ecclia | 16 | „ |
| Ellin Ainsworthe vx[9] Edw: in ecclia | 17 | „ |
| John Kilshawe fi: Willm | 18 | „ |
| John Mawdisleye fi Ector | „ | „ |
| Ane Wilson fi Xpo: | 21 | „ |
| Willm Whitwell in ecclia | 28 | „ |
| Tho: Draper in ecclia | 29 | „ |
| Fo. 303 Ric̃ Lathom in the highe Chansell | 2 | September |
| Emlin Wariner fi Tho: | 23 | „ |
| Willm Buler in the high chancell | 1 | October |
| Anne Ashton | „ | „ |
| Jaine Molinex | 24 | „ |
| Alis Tasker fi: Tho: | 6 | November |
| Robert Shaw | 11 | „ |
| Bartholomew Hoolme | 12 | „ |
| Homfrey Hill fi: John in ecclia | 21 | „ |
| filia Rodger Stanley in ecclia | „ | „ |
| Alis Hill | 28 | „ |
| Edwarde Late Earle of Derbie in the high Chancell | 4 | December |
| Anne Swifte Relic̃ Tho: in ecclia | 7 | „ |
| Katherin Crofte fi: Tho: in ecclia | „ | „ |
| Hugh Woodhowse in ecclia | 11 | „ |
| Jamis Waringe | „ | „ |
| Jamis Jackeson fi: Hugh | 16 | „ |

| | | |
|---|---|---|
| Marget Batersbie | 18 | December |
| Ric̃ Norres | 6 | Januarie |
| Alis Yate | 8 | ” |
| Margerie Mason | 9 | ” |
| Izabell Johnson Relic̃ | 11 | ” |
| Katherin Hankin | 18 | ” |
| Gilb̃ Blvndell | 22 | ” |
| Ellin Swyfte in ecclia | ” | ” |
| Edw: Garret | ” | ” |
| Henrye Lathwhat in St. Nicolas Chañ | 26 | ” |
| Margerie Haughton | 28 | ” |
| Jaine Haworth vx⁹ Lyonell | 8 | ffebruarie |
| Katherin Gowlb̃ fi: John de Halsal | 10 | ” |
| John Batersbie in eccl̄ia | 11 | ” |
| Jamis Moscrop | 12 | ” |
| Tho: Scarsbricke in ecclia | 13 | Marche |
| Rodger Such in the high Chansell | 15 | ” |
| Sislie Parker | 17 | ” |
| Jamis Swifte in eccl̄ia | 20 | ” |
| Will̄m Carre | 21 | ” |
| Marget Woodes vx⁹ George in eccl̄ia | 24 | ” |

## 1573.

| | | |
|---|---|---|
| Will̄m Barton | 29 | March |
| Nicolas Holliwall | 5 | Aprill |
| vx⁹ Holland in eccl̄ia | ” | ” |
| Jaine Prescott | 14 | ” |
| Jaine Mowdisley | 16 | ” |
| Jaine Easthead | 18 | ” |
| Henrie Swifte fi: Ja: in eccl̄ia | 21 | ” |
| Eliz^th fformbie | 22 | ” |
| Anne Precott | 28 | ” |
| Marget Luskin in eccl̄ia | 29 | ” |
| Hugh Cropp | ” | ” |
| Peeter Morecroft | 5 | Maye |
| Margerie Swifte | ” | ” |
| Gilb̃t Morecroft | 13 | ” |
| Marget Moscrop in eccl̄ia | ” | ” |
| Jenet Hallworth | 23 | ” |
| Henrie Burie | 29 | ” |
| Eliz^th Morcroft vx⁹ Tho: in eccl̄ia | 2 | June |
| Gilbart Blvndell in St nic̃ chañ | 6 | ” |
| Hector Whytestones | 26 | ” |
| Marget Sutton | 27 | ” |
| Katherin Clapam in eccl̄ia | 28 | ” |
| Anne Ambrose vx⁹ Elis in eccl̄ia | 5 | July |
| Jaine Gobin | 6 | ” |
| Edw: Yate | 7 | ” |

| |  |  |  |
|---|---|---|---|
| | Anne Ley fi: Hector in eccl̄ia ... ... ... | 11 | July |
| | Jaine Hankin vxꝰ Tho: ... ... ... ... ... ... | 13 | „ |
| | John Whytestons fi: Rob̄ in eccl̄ia ... ... | 19 | „ |
| | Robert Lenard in mr Scarsbreckes Chancell ... | 22 | „ |
| Fo. 305 | Elizth Blundell in Sain nicolas chansell ... ... | 23 | „ |
| | Ric̃ Preskot ... ... ... ... ... ... ... ... | 26 | „ |
| | John Longley fi: John ... ... ... ... ... ... | 9 | August |
| | Eme Anderton vxꝰ Edw: in ecclia ... ... | 10 | „ |
| | Marget Speakeman ... ... ... ... ... ... ... | 16 | September |
| | Jenet Morecrofte ... ... ... ... ... ... ... | 20 | „ |
| | John Rigbie in eccl̄ia ... ... ... ... ... ... | 28 | „ |
| | Eideth Hill ... ... ... ... ... ... ... ... | 30 | „ |
| | Marget Hoolme ... ... ... ... ... ... ... | 19 | October |
| | Tho: Craine ... ... ... ... ... ... ... ... | 24 | „ |
| | Elizth Hunter fi: Rob̄ in eccl̄ia ... ... ... | 27 | „ |
| | Gilb̄ Lancaster in eccl̄ia ... ... ... ... ... ... | 26 | November |
| | Marget Cosey Relic̃ Robert in eccl̄ia ... ... | 4 | December |
| | Tho: Scarsbrecke fi: Peeter in eccl̄ia ... ... | 18 | „ |
| | Katherin Aiscrofte Relic Wil̄l ... ... ... | 22 | „ |
| | Nicolas Prescot fi: Peet ... ... ... ... ... ... | „ | „ |
| | Ric̃ Jumpe fi: Edw: ... ... ... ... ... ... ... | 23 | „ |
| | Peeter Shaw in ecclia ... ... ... ... ... ... | 18 | Januarie |
| | John Bower in the high chancell ... ... ... | 19 | „ |
| | Eideth Haliwell in eccl̄ia ... ... ... ... ... | „ | „ |
| | Elin Leech Relic̃ Hugh ... ... ... ... ... ... | 3 | ffebruarie |
| | John Asshorst in eccl̄ia ... ... ... ... ... ... | 15 | „ |
| | Margerie Halliwell ... ... ... ... ... ... ... | „ | „ |
| | Elizth Spencer in eccl̄ia ... ... ... ... ... ... | 22 | „ |
| | Tho: Morecroft ... ... ... ... ... ... ... | 24 | „ |
| | John Skelton ... ... ... ... ... ... ... ... | 28 | „ |
| | John Barton ... ... ... ... ... ... ... ... | 4 | March |
| | Jenet Mowdisley ... ... ... ... ... ... ... | 21 | „ |

## 1574.

| |  |  |  |
|---|---|---|---|
| | Henrie Webster in eccl̄ia ... ... ... ... ... | 13 | March |
| Fo. 306 | John Barton fi: Lewes ... ... ... ... ... ... | 3 | Aprill |
| | Alis Blvndell ... ... ... ... ... ... ... ... | 7 | „ |
| | Anne Asmall fi: Elis ... ... ... ... ... ... | 8 | „ |
| | Katherin Prescot ... ... ... ... ... ... ... | „ | „ |
| | Ric̃ Stopforth fi: George ... ... ... ... ... | 9 | „ |
| | John Westhead ... ... ... ... ... ... ... ... | 10 | „ |
| | Peeter ffletcher in eccl̄ia ... ... ... ... ... ... | 19 | „ |
| | Jaine Brigehowse ... ... ... ... ... ... ... | 22 | „ |
| | Tho: Morcroft in eccl̄ia ... ... ... ... ... ... | 23 | „ |
| | Alis Barton ... ... ... ... ... ... ... ... | 25 | „ |
| | Will̄m Holland fi: John ... ... ... ... ... ... | 5 | Maye |
| | Marget Barton vxꝰ Hector ... ... ... ... | „ | „ |

| | | |
|---|---|---|
| Eliz$^{th}$ Kocket fi : Hen : ... ... ... ... ... ... | 7 | Maye |
| John Far fi : Rob̄ ... ... ... ... ... ... ... | „ | „ |
| Edmund Smult . ... ... ... ... ... ... ... | 9 | „ |
| . . . Elizabeth ... ... ... ... ... ... ... | „ | „ |
| Katherin Garrerd in eccl̄ia ... ... ... ... ... | 16 | „ |
| Elin Hey ... ... ... ... ... ... ... ... ... | 24 | „ |
| Dowse Loccar Relic̃ Law : ... ... ... ... ... | 2 | June |
| Gabriell Croft fi : Tho : ... ... ... ... ... ... | 4 | „ |
| Will̄m Mowdisley in eccl̄ia ... ... ... ... ... | 14 | „ |
| Jaine Atherton fi : Ja : in eccl̄ia ... ... ... ... | 17 | „ |
| vxꝰ Rodger Alker ... ... ... ... ... ... ... | 29 | „ |
| Jamis Beconso ... ... ... ... ... ... ... ... | 30 | „ |
| Vrsvla Aspinwall fi : Wil̄l in eccl̄ia ... ... | 3 | July |
| Will̄m Waynewright ... ... ... ... ... ... | 4 | „ |
| Jamis Winder fi : Tho : ... ... ... ... ... ... | 7 | „ |
| Alis vxꝰ Richardson ... ... ... ... ... ... | 19 | „ |
| Rodger Gill ... ... ... ... ... ... ... ... | 22 | „ |
| Anne Richardson fi : Lawranc̃ ... ... ... ... | 29 | „ |
| Ric̃ Jackeson ... ... ... ... ... ... ... ... | 3 | August |
| Marget Sutch fi : Geof̄ in eccl̄ia ... ... ... | 2 | September |
| Alis Hill ... ... ... ... ... ... ... ... ... ... | 4 | „ |
| Margerie Wilson Relic̃ Ric̃ ... ... ... ... ... | 15 | „ |
| Elizabeth Coockeson fi : Adam ... ... ... ... | 16 | „ |
| Alis Smyth Relic Gilb̄ in ecclia ... ... ... ... | „ | „ |
| 7 John Hunte fi : Ja : ... ... ... ... ... ... ... | 25 | „ |
| Alis ffarclough in eccl̄ia ... ... ... ... ... ... | 26 | „ |
| Wil̄l Aiscroft ... ... ... ... ... ... ... ... | 29 | „ |
| Robert Ambrose ... ... ... ... ... ... ... | 1 | October |
| Jaine Ambrose ... ... ... ... ... ... ... ... | 4 | „ |
| Hector Whytestones ... ... ... ... ... ... | 12 | „ |
| Ric̃ Kekuicke fi : Ja : ... ... ... ... ... ... | 15 | „ |
| Edw : Waliner ... ... ... ... ... ... ... ... | 17 | „ |
| Tho : Heicclif in ecclia ... ... ... ... ... ... | 4 | November |
| Edw : Orton ... ... ... ... ... ... ... ... | 9 | „ |
| Anne Smyth fi : Hugh ... ... ... ... ... ... | 15 | December |
| vxꝰ Raffe Ashton in eccl̄ia ... ... ... ... ... | 16 | „ |
| Jaine Brickefeeld vxꝰ Ric̃ ... ... ... ... ... | 23 | „ |
| Gilb̄ Lancaster in eccl̄ia ... ... ... ... ... ... | 2 | Januarie |
| Anthoney Morcroft ... ... ... ... ... ... ... | 4 | „ |
| John Gill fi : Ric̃ in eccl̄ia ... ... ... ... ... | 8 | „ |
| Ric̃ Banke in eccl̄ia ... ... ... ... ... ... | 22 | „ |
| Will̄m Hey in eccl̄ia ... ... ... ... ... ... | 1 | ffebruarie |
| Peeter Scarsbrecke in eccl̄ia ... ... ... ... ... | 8 | „ |
| John Bawthe ... ... ... ... ... ... ... ... | „ | „ |
| Marget Jackeson fi : Rob̄ in eccl̄ia ... ... ... | 12 | „ |
| Ewan Waynewright in eccl̄ia ... ... ... ... ... | 16 | „ |
| John Ocar ... ... ... ... ... ... ... ... ... | 19 | „ |
| John Norres ... ... ... ... ... ... ... ... | 21 | „ |
| Robert Byram in eccl̄ia ... ... ... ... ... ... | 27 | „ |

Ric̃ Howlden fi: Henrie ... ... ... ... ... ... 16 March
Marget Jackeson vx⁹ Pet̃ in eccl̃ia ... ... 19 „
Ottuwell Blvndell in eccl̃ia ... ... ... ... 22 „

## 1575.

Elin Gowbron ... ... ... ... ... ... ... ... 26 March
John Blackledge in eccl̃ia ... ... ... ... 27 „
Marget Hawoth ... ... ... ... ... ... ... 28 „
Fo. 308 Katherin Morecroft ... ... ... ... ... ... ... 2 Aprill
vx⁹ Henrie Ambrose in eccl̃ia ... ... ... 4 „
Jenet Breykell vx⁹ Wilt ... ... ... ... ... 8 „
Alis Jumpe vx⁹ pcevell ... ... ... ... ... 11 „
Elizth Burscough in eccl̃ia ... ... ... ... „ „
Isabell Redfurthe Relic̃ Rawffe ... ... ... 15 „
Tho: Windraie ... ... ... ... ... ... ... 3 Maye
Jenet Richardson ... ... ... ... ... ... ... „ „
Hector Sutton in eccl̃ia ... ... ... ... ... 16 „
Jaine Rob̃tson ... ... ... ... ... ... ... ... „ „
Katherin Cropp Relic Jo: in eccl̃ia ... ... 18 „
Alis Molinex ... ... ... ... ... ... ... ... 21 „
John Westhead fi: Gilb̃ ... ... ... ... ... 25 „
Elin Blvndell vx⁹ Peeter in eccl̃ia ... ... ... 28 „
Tho: Gobin in eccl̃ia ... ... ... ... ... ... 2 June
Tho: Hankin ... ... ... ... ... ... ... ... 4 „
Margerie Porter fi: Peeter in eccl̃ia ... ... 14 „
Marget Kidd Relic̃ Ja: ... ... ... ... ... ... 16 „
Charles Eccleston ... ... ... ... ... ... ... 17 „
Marget Parker vx⁹ John ... ... ... ... ... 25 „
Jamis Rigbie in eccl̃ia ... ... ... ... ... ... 3 Julye
Henrie Whytestones ... ... ... ... ... ... „ „
Izabell Smallshaw fi: Witt ... ... ... ... ... 5 „
Elin Mawdisley vx⁹ John ... ... ... ... ... 21 „
Peeter Scarsbrecke in eccl̃ia ... ... ... ... 6 August
John Anglesdaile fi: Homfrey ... ... ... ... 19 „
Katherin Smyth Relic Witt in eccl̃ia ... ... 23 „
Tho: Hill ... ... ... ... ... ... ... ... ... 25 „
Tho: Mawdisley ... ... ... ... ... ... ... 30 „
Ja: Morecrofte in eccl̃ia ... . ... ... ... 4 September
John Longe ... ... ... ... ... ... ... ... 9 „
Ellin Scarsbrecke vx⁹ Witt in eccl̃ia ... ... 13 „
Tho: Lathom ... ... ... ... ... ... ... ... 14 „
Fo. 309 John Sutch fi: George in eccl̃ia ... ... ... 19 October
Cristopher Swifte fi: Tho: ... ... ... ... ... 12 November
Jaine Henrieson fi: Hugh ... ... ... ... ... 27 „

[*No entries for December*]

Katherin Martindaile fi: Phillip in eccl̃ia ... 7 Januarie
Jamis Prescot in ecclia ... ... ... ... ... ... 28 „

| | | |
|---|---|---|
| Robert Cowp | 2 | ffebruarie |
| John Burscough in eccl̄ia | 18 | „ |
| Ric̄ Gill | 28 | „ |
| Izabeƚƚ Henrison in eccl̄ia | „ | „ |
| John Sutch | 3 | March |
| Byhan [*sic*] Swyfte | 13 | „ |

## 1576.

| | | |
|---|---|---|
| Tho: Crofte | 26 | March |
| Hugh Ascrofte in eccl̄ia | 5 | Aprill |
| Wiƚƚm Bootle in ecclia | 6 | „ |
| Hugh Henrison | 15 | „ |
| Eliz[th] Westhead in eccl̄ia | 23 | „ |
| Wiƚƚm Toppinge in eccl̄ia | 26 | „ |
| Edw: Hesketh | „ | „ |
| Tho: Smvlte in eccl̄ia | 14 | Maie |
| Parsivall Mossocke in eccl̄ia | 18 | „ |
| Henrie Morecroft in eccl̄ia | 23 | „ |
| Alis Leadbetter | 24 | „ |
| Ewan Cropp | 10 | June |
| Marget Dolland | 15 | „ |
| John Gill in eccl̄ia | 2 | Julye |
| Elin Morecroft in eccl̄ia | 13 | „ |
| Eliz[th] Martindaile | 20 | „ |
| ffrances Gorsutch | 8 | August |
| John Kewquicke in eccl̄ia | 28 | „ |
| Margerie Barker | 30 | „ |
| Wiƚƚm Sailes in eccl̄ia | 8 | September |
| Margerie Whatton | 10 | „ |
| Matthew Waringe | 11 | „ |
| Ric̄ Kekuicke in eccl̄ia | 14 | „ |
| Eliz[th] Diconson in Chonc̄ | „ | „ |
| George Ormishaw | 15 | „ |
| Peeter Rigbie in eccl̄ia | 25 | „ |
| Alis Halworth in ecclia | 28 | „ |
| Peeter Blvndell | 11 | October |
| Jaine Svtch in eccl̄ia | 17 | „ |
| Alis Voce | 18 | „ |
| Tho: Eccleston | 21 | „ |
| Jaine Hesketh | 31 | „ |
| Alis Whytestones in eccl̄ia | 6 | November |
| Elin Waringe | 8 | „ |
| Gilb̄t Jackeson | 11 | „ |
| Bartholomew Whytestones | 18 | „ |
| Rodger Lea | 30 | „ |
| Raffe Monne | „ | „ |
| Margerie Spenser in eccl̄ia | 5 | December |
| Henrie Atherton in eccl̄ia | 12 | „ |

| | | | |
|---|---|---|---|
| | Marie Billinge ... ... ... ... ... ... ... | 13 | December |
| | Eliz$^{th}$ Rylanse in ecclia ... ... ... ... ... | 14 | „ |
| | George Sutch in ecclia ... ... ... ... ... | 17 | „ |
| | John Sefton fi: George in ecclia ... ... ... | 3 | Januarie |
| | Katherin Hatton ... ... ... ... ... ... | 19 | „ |
| | Marget Hesketh in choro ... ... ... ... ... | „ | „ |
| | S$^{9}$ John Rainforth priste in ecclia ... ... ... | 1 | ffebruarie |
| | Jaine Barton in ecclia ... ... ... ... ... | 5 | „ |
| Fo. 311 | Charles Hadocke ... ... ... ... ... ... | 7 | „ |
| | Godfrey Ormishaw ... ... ... ... ... ... | „ | „ |
| | Jaine Hesketh ... ... ... ... ... ... ... | 15 | „ |
| | John Worrolle ... ... ... ... ... ... ... | 24 | March |

## 1577.

| | | | |
|---|---|---|---|
| | Margreat Spenser fi Ric in ecclia ... ... ... | 6 | Aprill |
| | Jaine Scarsbricke fi: Gulielmi in ecclia ... | 11 | „ |
| | Tho: Berie in ecclia ... ... ... ... ... | 12 | „ |
| | Jaine Robinson ... ... ... ... ... ... | 14 | „ |
| | Peeter Mowdisley ... ... ... ... ... ... | 26 | „ |
| | Margreat Moscrofte vx$^{9}$ Rodg ... ... ... | „ | „ |
| | Rodger Alker ... ... ... ... ... ... ... | 23 | May |
| | Jaine Mowdisley ... ... ... ... ... ... | 31 | „ |
| | Richard ffrithe ... ... ... ... ... ... ... | 11 | June |
| | Eliz$^{th}$ Halworthe... ... ... ... ... ... ... | 22 | „ |
| | Ellis Longe in ecclia ... ... ... ... ... | „ | „ |
| | John Sutche ... ... ... ... ... ... ... | 24 | „ |
| | Willm Gorsutch ... ... ... ... ... ... | 14 | Julye |
| | John Garnet ... ... ... ... ... ... ... | 25 | „ |
| | Emlin ffinche ... ... ... ... ... ... ... | 3 | Auguste |
| | Jaine Standishe ... ... ... ... ... ... | 9 | „ |
| | John Shorlokars ... ... ... ... ... ... | 29 | „ |
| | Emlin Collinson ... ... ... ... ... ... | 4 | September |
| | Eliz$^{th}$ Aspinwall ... ... ... ... ... ... ... | 9 | „ |
| | Elin Rydinge fi: fi: Robt in ecclia ... ... | 11 | „ |
| | John Alerton ... ... ... ... ... ... ... | 13 | „ |
| | Eliz$^{th}$ Anderton ... ... ... ... ... ... ... | 14 | „ |
| Fo. 312 | Margerie Blundell ... ... ... ... ... ... | 4 | October |
| | Margreat Blacklidg Elidg East ... ... ... | 5 | „ |
| | Margrat Aspinwall in ecclia ... ... ... ... | 16 | „ |
| | Jaine Harson ... ... ... ... ... ... ... | 21 | „ |
| | Willm Burdges ... ... ... ... ... ... ... | 24 | „ |
| | Robt Owtie ... ... ... ... ... ... ... | 30 | „ |
| | Margerie Prescott ... ... ... ... ... ... | 14 | November |
| | John Barton fi Adam ... ... ... ... ... | 24 | „ |
| | John Lea in ecclia ... ... ... ... ... ... | 24 | December |
| | Alis Cocker in ecclia ... ... ... ... ... | „ | „ |
| | John Martindaill in ecclia ... ... ... ... .... | 25 | „ |
| | Katherin Mason in ecclia ... ... ... ... | 28 | „ |

Jonie ffarclough in ecclia ... ... ... ... 1 Januarie
Edm: Hallworth in eccl̄ia ... ... ... ... 6 „
Alis Howforth in eccl̄ia ... ... ... ... ... 12 „
Alis Halword ... ... ... ... ... ... ... 13 „
Eliz[th] Halsall in eccl̄ia ... ... ... ... ... 18 „
Maria Atkinson ... ... ... ... ... ... 20 „
Elin Lathum in eccl̄ia ... ... ... ... ... 23 „
Nicolas Marow in eccl̄ia ... ... ... ... ... „ „
Ric̃ Svmner ... ... ... ... ... ... ... 28 „
Homfrey Waynewright ... ... ... ... ... 4 ffebruarie
Elin Chadocke ... ... ... ... ... ... ... 19 „
Eliz[th] Mason ... ... ... ... ... ... ... 22 „
Ellin Halton ... ... ... ... ... ... ... 25 „
Anne Kilshaw ... ... ... ... ... ... ... 9 March
Gilb̄ Asshurst ... ... ... ... ... ... ... „ „
Eliz[th] ffarrer eleg... ... ... ... ... ... ... „ „
Ric̃ Brickefilde ... ... ... ... ... ... ... „ „
Alis Gill ... ... ... ... ... ... ... ... 11 „
Eliz[th] Westhead ... ... ... ... ... ... ... 12 „
Jaine Byggot ... ... ... ... ... ... ... „ „
John Litherland ... ... ... ... ... ... 19 „
Humfrey Morcrofte ... ... ... ... ... ... 24 „

## 1578.

Joane Blvndell in eccl̄ia ... ... ... ... ... 25 March
Marget Bower ... ... ... ... ... ... ... 26 „
Ellin Whytestones ... ... ... ... ... ... 16 Aprill
Anne Jackeson ... ... ... ... ... ... ... 20 „
Eliz[th] Tasker ... ... ... ... ... ... ... 21 „
Eliz[th] Robinson ... ... ... ... ... ... ... 24 „
Jamis Crosse ... ... ... ... ... ... ... 26 „
Eliz[th] Blvndell ... ... ... ... ... ... ... 28 „
John Precott fi: Ja: elig ... ... ... ... ... „ „
Katherin Mellinge ... ... ... ... ... ... 29 „
Thomas ffarer ... ... ... ... ... ... ... 1 Maye
Hen: Waynewright in eccl̄ia ... ... ... ... 2 „
Emlin Morecrofte in ecclia ... ... ... ... 6 „
Anne ffarer ... ... ... ... ... ... ... 14 „
Ric̃ Cobon in ecclia ... ... ... ... ... ... 30 „
Tho: Waringe ... ... ... ... ... ... ... 1 June
Eliz[th] Mosse ... ... ... ... ... ... ... 21 „
Elin Chadocke ... ... ... ... ... ... ... 30 „
Ric̃ Masson in eccl̄ia ... ... ... ... ... 3 Julie
Ellin Cowp... ... ... ... ... ... ... ... 22 „
Eliz[th] Barton ... ... ... ... ... ... ... 25 „
Margerat Woodes fi Rob̄ in eccl̄ia ... ... ... 28 „
John Hamerson in eccl̄ia ... ... ... ... 3 Auguste
Joanie Cocket ... ... ... ... ... ... ... 11 „

Marie Barton ... ... ... ... ... ... ... ... 11 Auguste
Jaine Edw: son in ecclia ... ... ... ... 13 „
Henrie Lathwhat in ecclia ... ... ... ... „ „
Willm Gill ... ... ... ... ... ... ... ... 15 „
Anne Barton ... ... ... ... ... ... ... ... 24 „
Alis Atherton in ecclia ... ... ... ... ... ... 27 „
Jaine Sutch in ecclia ... ... ... ... ... ... 29 „
Fo. 314 Henrie Asshurst in ecclia ... ... ... ... 7 September
Hugh Morecrofte ... ... ... ... ... ... ... 30 October
Marie Mowdisley ... ... ... ... ... ... ... 1 November
Katherin Kekeuicke in ecclia ... ... ... 2 „
Anne Coockeson in ecclia ... ... ... ... ... 18 „
. . . Mawdisley in ecclia ... ... ... ... ... 23 „
Tho: Prescot ... ... ... ... ... ... ... ... 24 „
Marget Banke in ecclia ... ... ... ... ... 8 December
Edw: Charnley in ecclia ... ... ... ... ... 24 „
Anne Barton ... ... ... ... ... ... ... ... 26 „
Gotfrey Cropp in ecclia ... ... ... ... ... 1 Januarie
Alison Woodworte in ecclia ... ... ... ... 9 „
Jaine Cartrowe ... ... ... ... ... ... ... 12 „
Ric Mason in ecclia ... ... ... ... ... ... 24 „
Willm Barton ... ... ... ... ... ... ... ... „ „
John Chadocke in ecclia ... ... ... ... ... 25 „
Jaine Hunte in ecclia ... ... ... ... ... ... „ „
Elline Ormishaw in ecclia ... ... ... ... ... 27 „
Peter Preskot in ecclia ... ... ... ... ... ... 16 ffebruarie
Tho: Knowles in ecclia ... ... ... ... ... ... „ „
Marget Whytestones ... ... ... ... ... ... 21 „
Elizabeth Mosse ... ... ... ... ... ... ... 29 „
Eliz[th] Jackeson in ecclia ... ... ... ... ... 5 March
Marget Asmall in ecclia ... ... ... ... ... „ „
Alis Smalshaw ... ... ... ... ... ... ... ... 9 „
Robt Whytestones in ecclia ... ... ... ... 11 „
Eliz[th] Haide Lathō in ecclia ... ... ... ... 13 „
George Haughton ... ... ... ... ... ... ... 15 „
Ellin Barton ... ... ... ... ... ... ... ... 20 „
Anne Cosey ... ... ... ... ... ... ... ... „ „
Tho: Cadicke ... ... ... ... ... ... ... ... 23 „

## 1579.

Fo. 315 Katherin Orton ... ... ... ... ... ... 25 March
George Mowdisley in ecclia ... ... ... ... ... 27 „
Peeter Blundell ... ... ... ... ... ... ... „ „
John Burscough in ecclia ... ... ... ... ... 30 „
Tho: Pemerton in ecclia ... ... ... ... ... 3 Aprill
Phillip Mawdisley ... ... ... ... ... ... ... 4 „
Genet Morecroft ... ... ... ... ... ... ... 5 „
Elin Hill in ecclia ... ... ... ... ... ... ... 7 „

| | Name | Day | Month |
|---|---|---|---|
| | John Aiscrofte | 9 | Aprill |
| | Joanie Aerre | 11 | „ |
| | Tho: Ascough | 19 | „ |
| | John Sumner in eccſia | 23 | „ |
| | Tho: Goodes | „ | „ |
| | Marget Prescot | 28 | „ |
| | Emlin Barton | 29 | „ |
| | Ellin Parker | 5 | Maye |
| | Margerie Preskot | „ | „ |
| | Nicolas ffornbie | 8 | „ |
| | John Jackeson in eccſia | 9 | „ |
| | Alis Bootle in eccſia | 14 | „ |
| | vx⁹ Phillip Mawdisley | „ | „ |
| | Elin Orton | 30 | „ |
| | Tho Lailon in eccſia | 3 | June |
| | Margerie ffarrer | 6 | „ |
| | Elin Bucher | 9 | „ |
| | Alis Mawdisley | 18 | „ |
| | Tho: Jamson | 22 | „ |
| | Joanie Beconsall fi: Ric̃ | 23 | „ |
| | Lawrance Robertson | 24 | „ |
| | Alis Plume | 30 | „ |
| | Henrie Allerton | 5 | July |
| | Jamis Wiłłmson | „ | „ |
| | Marget Kekuicke in eccletia | 7 | „ |
| | Grace Stopforth in eccſia | „ | „ |
| c 316 | Henrie Aspinwall | 8 | „ |
| | George Barton | „ | „ |
| | Wiłłm Lathwhat Peetro | 13 | „ |
| | Jaine Berrye | „ | „ |
| | Jaine Chadocke fi: Hugh bap et buř | „ | „ |
| | Alis Chrouchley in ecclia | 14 | „ |
| | Eliz^th^ Goare Alias Butrie in eccſia | „ | „ |
| | ffrances Smalshey | 29 | „ |
| | John Jonson fi: Alexand bap et buř | „ | „ |
| | John Chadocke | 30 | „ |
| | Robert Jumpe | 5 | Auguste |
| | Alis Woodfall in eccſia | 10 | „ |
| | Henrie Blundell | 11 | „ |
| | Tho: fferrer | 13 | „ |
| | Katherin Doubabyn in eccſia | 15 | „ |
| | Henrie Littler | 20 | „ |
| | Edmund Oarton in ecclia | 21 | „ |
| | John Rydinge fi: Rob̃t in eccſia | 24 | „ |
| | Bartholomew Worthingeton in eccſia | 25 | „ |
| | Richard Gille | 28 | „ |
| puer | John Edwardson in eccſia | 29 | „ |
| | Elin Hancocke | 8 | September |
| puř | Nicolas Shawe in eccſia | 12 | „ |

Marget Hoolme in ecctia ... ... ... ... 17 September
Thomas Hatton [?] ... ... ... ... ... ... „ „
Tho: Stopforth in ecctia ... ... ... ... 1 October
Eliz^th Prescot ... ... ... ... ... ... ... „ „
Wittm Stopforth in ecctia ... ... ... ... 1 November
Wittm Morecroft in ecctia ... ... ... ... 9 „
Marget Kekeuicke in ecctia ... ... ... ... 13 „
pur Elin Aiscroft in ecctia ... ... ... ... ... 17 „
Grace Edwardson in ecctia ... ... ... ... 19 „
Elin Richardes doughter ... ... ... ... ... 20 „
Fo. 317 Marget Blvndell In ecctia ... ... ... ... 2 December
Alis Clapom in ecctia ... ... ... ... ... 8 „
Jenet Barton ... ... ... ... ... ... ... 10 „
John Kilshaw fi: Tho: ... ... ... ... ... „ „
John Preskot ... ... ... ... ... ... ... 18 „
Elin Alerton ... ... ... ... ... ... ... 21 „
Alis Hollond ... ... ... ... ... ... ... 9 Januarie
John & Ric̃ Alerton ... ... ... ... ... ... 13 „
Jamis Formby ... ... ... ... ... ... ... 14 „
Jaine Cropp fi: Tho: ... ... ... ... ... 18 „
John Barker fi: Tho: ... ... ... ... ... „ „
Wittm Naliar fi Hen: ... ... ... ... ... „ „
Jaine Cropp ... ... ... ... ... ... ... 19 „
Anne Gore ... ... ... ... ... ... ... 21 „
Jaine Brigehowse ... ... ... ... ... ... 23 „
Margerie Sutch in ecctia ... ... ... ... 24 „
Jaine Lathom ... ... ... ... ... ... ... 28 „
Marget Kilshaw in ecctia ... ... ... ... 29 „
Katherin Law ... ... ... ... ... ... ... 30 „
John Marclew ... ... ... ... ... ... ... 10 ffebruarie
Emlin Morcroft ... ... ... ... ... ... 12 March
Jaine Scarsbrecke ... ... ... ... ... ... 14 „
Tho: Cropp in ecctia ... ... ... ... ... 24 „

## 1580.

. . . Holm ... ... ... ... ... ... ... ... 1 Aprill
Robert Bycarstafe ... ... ... ... ... ... 24 „
Ric̃ Hesketh ... ... ... ... ... ... ... 4 Maye
Genet Modisley ... ... ... ... ... ... 13 „
Wittm Cocket ... ... ... ... ... ... ... 16 „
Jamis Whytestones ... ... ... ... ... ... 18 „
Henrie Stopforth in ecctia ... ... ... ... 21 „
Blanch Smyth in ecctia ... ... ... ... ... 28 „
Fo. 318 Elin Rigbie ... ... ... ... ... ... ... 4 June
Wittm Rainforth ... ... ... ... ... ... „ „
Ric̃ Mason fi: Hugh in ecctia ... ... ... 6 „
Marget Livisley ... ... ... ... ... ... 3 July
John Wilson ... ... ... ... ... ... ... 9 „

| Name | Day | Month |
|---|---|---|
| Tho: Barton in eccłia | 27 | July |
| Wiłłm Gilbertson in eccłia | ,, | ,, |
| Wiłłm Smyth in eccłia | 31 | ,, |
| Marget Kocket | 3 | August |
| Eliz[th] Smyth | 5 | ,, |
| Wiłłm Mossocke of Haiton in eccl | 10 | ,, |
| Izabell Jackeson | 11 | ,, |
| Marget Halsall in eccłia | 13 | ,, |
| Ellin Mulinex | 14 | ,, |
| Eliz[th] Arnould | ,, | ,, |
| Eliz[th] Burscough | 17 | ,, |
| Anne Gill | 20 | ,, |
| Alis Prescot | ,, | ,, |
| Robert Howlden | 4 | September |
| Peeter Lea in eccłia | 10 | ,, |
| Marget Allerton | ,, | ,, |
| Wiłłm Bradley in eccłia | 14 | ,, |
| Tho: Woodhowse in ecclia | ,, | ,, |
| Adam Asshurst in eccłia | 16 | ,, |
| Eliz[th] Morecroft in eccłia | 28 | ,, |
| Claris Sanderson in eccłia | 3 | October |
| Margerie fforshaw | 9 | ,, |
| Marget Sutch in eccłia | 11 | ,, |
| John Mosse | 12 | ,, |
| Tho: Blundell | 20 | ,, |
| Margerie Sutton | ,, | ,, |
| John Swifte | ,, | ,, |
| Eliz[th] Swifte | 22 | ,, |
| Anne Molinex | ,, | ,, |
| 9 Gowther Lunte | 2 | November |
| Wiłłm Aiscough | 7 | ,, |
| Marget Barker | 12 | ,, |
| Jaine Kekuicke in eccłia | 28 | ,, |
| Marget Hodgeson | 7 | December |
| Tho: Byrch | 11 | ,, |
| Emlin Lathwhat | 12 | ,, |
| Robert Butler | 17 | ,, |
| Will Morecrofte fi: Homfrey in eccłia | 26 | ,, |
| John Bucke | 28 | ,, |
| John Verguse | 2 | Januarie |
| Emlin Irland | 8 | ,, |
| Marget Walker | 15 | ,, |
| Jamis Blvndell | 19 | ,, |
| Marget Talior | 25 | ,, |
| Alis Mawdisley fi: Tho: in eccłia | 26 | ,, |
| Wiłłm Morecrofte | 27 | ,, |
| Marget Allerton | ,, | ,, |
| Tho: Eccleston | 30 | ,, |
| Wiłłm Aspinwall | 6 | ffebruarie |

| | | | |
|---|---|---|---|
| | Ewan Mosse ... ... ... ... ... ... ... | 9 | ffebruarie |
| | Katherin Rainforth ... ... ... ... ... ... | ,, | ,, |
| | Raffe Leadbetter alis Cocket ... ... ... ... | ,, | ,, |
| | Henrie Ambrose in ecc̄lia ... ... ... ... | 10 | ,, |
| | Izabell Banke fi: Henr̄: in ecc̄lia ... ... | 15 | ,, |
| | Marget Parker fi: Edw: in ecc̄lia ... ... ... | 16 | ,, |
| | Eliz^th^ Marclough ... ... ... ... ... ... | 17 | ,, |
| | Eliz^th^ Blundell ... ... ... ... ... ... ... | 25 | ,, |
| | Izabell Mawdisley in ecc̄lia ... ... ... ... | 27 | ,, |
| | Marget Mowdisley ... ... ... ... ... ... | 28 | ,, |
| Fo. 320 | Marget Gill ... ... ... ... ... ... ... | 5 | March |
| | Margerie Ainsworth ... ... ... ... ... ... | ,, | ,, |
| | Marget Coventrie in ecc̄lia ... ... ... ... | 6 | ,, |
| | Margerie Preskot ... ... ... ... ... ... | 7 | ,, |
| | Hugh Scarsbrecke ... ... ... ... ... ... | 11 | ,, |
| | Peeter Scarsbrecke fi: Gabrell in ecclia ... | 23 | ,, |

## 1581.

| | | | |
|---|---|---|---|
| | Wil̄lm Shawe in the high Chanc̃ ... ... ... | 7 | Aprill |
| | Anne Shawe ... ... ... ... ... ... ... | ,, | ,, |
| | . . . Houghton ... ... ... ... ... ... | ,, | ,, |
| | Alis Lea ... ... ... ... ... ... ... ... | 11 | ,, |
| | Katherin Marrall in ecc̄lia ... ... ... ... | 15 | ,, |
| | Margerie Sheppord ... ... ... ... ... ... | 23 | ,, |
| | George Wildinge ... ... ... ... ... ... | 26 | ,, |
| | Jenet Lithom ... ... ... ... ... ... ... | 20 | Maye |
| | Ric̃ Bebot fi: Tho: ... ... ... ... ... | 7 | June |
| | Roase Swifte in ecc̄lia ... ... ... ... ... | ,, | ,, |
| | Ric̃ Stopford in ecc̄lia ... ... ... ... | 8 | ,, |
| | Margerie Butrie in the high chañ ... ... ... | 15 | ,, |
| | Izabell Barker ... ... ... ... ... ... ... | 17 | ,, |
| | Lionell Vrmston ... ... ... ... ... ... | 29 | ,, |
| | Jaine Lathom ... ... ... ... ... ... ... | 4 | July |
| | Henrie Mason fi: Gabriell in ecclia ... ... | 10 | ,, |
| | John Lea in ecc̄lia ... ... ... ... ... ... | 14 | ,, |
| | Eliz^th^ Garrard ... ... ... ... ... ... ... | ,, | ,, |
| | Jamis Mowdisley ... ... ... ... ... ... | 16 | ,, |
| | Tho: Millner ... ... ... ... ... ... ... | 17 | ,, |
| | Jamis Spencer ... ... ... ... ... ... ... | 21 | ,, |
| | Jenet Richardson ... ... ... ... ... ... | 28 | ,, |
| | Marget Tomson ... ... ... ... ... ... | 11 | August |
| | Claris Waynewright in ecc̄lia ... ... ... ... | ,, | ,, |
| | Wil̄lm Gilb̄tson ... ... ... ... ... ... | 14 | ,, |
| | John Traves ... ... ... ... ... ... ... | ,, | ,, |
| | Marie Kekuicke ... ... ... ... ... ... | 17 | ,, |
| | Eliz^th^ Bebot ... ... ... ... ... ... ... | ,, | ,, |
| Fo. 321 | Wil̄lm Jackeson in ecclia ... ... ... ... | 19 | ,, |
| | Agnes Kekuicke ... ... ... ... ... ... | ,, | ,, |

Peeter Jackeson in ecclia ... ... ... ... 25 August
Alis Haughton in ecclia ... ... ... ... ... ... 1 September
Jaine Mason in ecclia ... ... ... ... ... ... 5 „
John Prescot ... ... ... ... ... ... ... 13 „
Marget Burie ... ... ... ... ... ... ... 14 „
Jenet Winde ... ... ... ... ... ... ... „ „
Margerie Sadler in ecclia ... ... ... ... 18 „
Agnes Cowp in ecclia ... ... ... ... ... 23 „
Margerie Burie in ecclia ... ... ... ... ... 24 „
Ric̃ Scarsbrecke in ecclia ... ... ... ... 2 October
Eliz$^{th}$ Wignall ... ... ... ... ... ... ... „ „
Jaine Tomson ... ... ... ... ... ... ... 3 „
Jaine Killshaw ... ... ... ... ... ... ... 14 „
Eliz$^{th}$ Pendleburie ... ... ... ... ... ... 17 „
Jaine Spencer ... ... ... ... ... ... ... 30 „
Joane Spencer ... ... ... ... ... ... ... 3 November
Anne Woodhowse ... ... ... ... ... ... 4 „
Margerie Bispam in ecclia ... ... ... ... 14 „
Mi$^{rs}$ Margett Scarsbreck in St nic̃ Chancell ... 16 „
John Killshaw ... ... ... ... ... ... ... 17 „
John Mollinex in ecclia ... ... ... ... ... 19 „
Claris Homfrey in ecclia ... ... ... ... 24 „
Margerie Sutch in ecclia ... ... ... ... ... 2 December
Tho: Killshaw in ecclia ... ... ... ... ... 4 „
Eliz$^{th}$ Anderton ... ... ... ... ... ... .. 10 „
Tho: Livesley ... ... ... ... ... ... ... 12 „
Katherin Balshaw ... ... ... ... ... ... 16 „
Katherin Waynewright in ecclia ... ... ... 26 „
Jenet Jumpe ... ... ... ... ... ... ... 11 Januarie
Raffe Cadicke ... ... ... ... ... ... ... 17 „
Willm Harwood in ecclia ... ... ... ... 19 „
Tho: Oliverson ... ... ... ... ... ... 24 „
Elin Anderton ... ... ... ... ... ... ... 26 „
22 Elin Burscough ... ... ... ... ... ... 6 ffebruar
Thomas Gill ... ... ... ... ... ... ... 12 „
Katherin Blundell in ecclia ... ... ... ... 13 „
Marget Swifte in ecclia ... ... ... ... ... 14 „
Margerie Ploumbe ... ... ... ... ... ... 17 „
Jamis Crucke ... ... ... ... ... ... ... 20 „
. . . Stananought fi: Edw: ... ... ... 21 „
John Barton ... ... ... ... ... ... ... 1 March
Jaine Awtie ... ... ... ... ... ... ... „ „
Jamis Lunte ... ... ... ... ... ... ... 3 „
Alis Collison ... ... ... ... ... ... ... 4 „
Thomas Shaw in ecclia ... ... ... ... ... 5 „
Willm Holland ... ... ... ... ... ... ... 6 „
Marget Prescot ... ... ... ... ... ... ... 13 „
Tho: Swifte ... ... ... ... ... ... ... 15 „
Abraham Prescot in ecclia ... ... ... ... „ „
Margerie Gill ... ... ... ... ... ... ... 22 „

## 1582.

Margerie Kekuicke ... ... ... ... ... ... ... 30 March
Izabell Pyke ... ... ... ... ... ... ... ... 2 Aprill
John Parker ... ... ... ... ... ... ... ... ,, ,,
Cudbert Shaw in eccl̃ia ... ... ... ... ... ... 3 ,,
John Shurlecars ... ... ... ... ... ... ... ,, ,,
Eliz[th] Mowdisley... ... ... ... ... ... ... ... 5 ,,
John Parker ... ... ... ... ... ... ... ... 7 Maye
Jane Smyth fi: Tho: ... ... ... ... ... ... 10 ,,
Tho: Burie in eccl̃ia ... ... ... . ... 20 ,,
Dame Izabell Stanley vx[9] Je militis in the high
Chañ ... ... ... ... ... ... ... ... ... 25 ,,
Anne Knowles in eccl̃ia ... ... ... ... ... ... 26 ,,
Jaine Swifte in eccl̃ia ... ... ... ... ... ... ,, ,,
Alis Ashton ... ... ... ... ... ... ... ... 27 ,,
Jenet Allerton ... ... ... ... ... ... ... ... 3 June
Jaine Smulte in eccl̃ia ... ... ... ... ... ... 12 ,,
Robert Moscrop ... ... ... ... ... ... ... ,, ,,
Marie Duncon in eccl̃ia ... ... ... ... ... ... 13 ,,
Fo. 323 Margerie Mellinge ... ... ... ... ... ... ... 4 July
Eliz[th] Worthington in the high Chañ ... ... 11 ,,
Margrat Annderton ... ... ... ... ... ... ... 20 ,,
Robert Cosey ... ... ... ... ... ... ... ... 22 ,,
George Gill ... ... ... ... ... ... ... ... 3 Auguste
Joaine Orrell ... ... ... ... ... ... ... ... 3 September
Henrie Mawdisley ... ... ... ... ... ... ... 11 ,,
Henrie Mullinex ... ... ... ... ... ... ... 29 ,,
Eliz[th] Waynewright ... ... ... ... ... ... ... 14 October
Ric̃ Witter ... ... ... ... ... ... ... ... 19 ,,
Ric̃ Badger ... ... ... ... ... ... ... ... 25 ,,
Robert Croocke ... ... ... ... ... ... ... 9 November
Grace Worall in eccl̃ia ... ... ... ... ... ... 11 ,,
Jaine Henrison ... ... ... ... ... ... ... ... 13 ,,
Hugh Mason in eccl̃ia ... ... ... ... ... ... 19 ,,
Anne Mason in eccl̃ia ... ... ... ... ... ... 20 ,,
Ric̃ Preskot in eccl̃ia ... ... ... ... ... ... 27 ,,
Eliz[th] Allerton ... ... ... ... ... ... ... ... 28 ,,
Elin Sankey in eccl̃ia ... ... ... ... ... ... 18 December
Alis Beconso ... ... ... ... ... ... ... ... 19 ,,
Jhon Byspam in eccl̃ia ... ... ... ... ... ... 22 ,,
Marget Mowdisley ... ... ... ... ... ... ... 27 ,,
Ellin Aspinwall in eccl̃ia ... ... ... ... ... ,, ,,
George Stopforth in eccl̃ia ... ... ... ... ... 29 ,,
Mowde Talior in eccl̃ia ... ... ... ... ... 3 Januarie
Jenet Blvndell ... ... ... ... ... ... ... ... ,, ,,
Marget Penket ... ... ... ... ... ... ... ... ,, ,,
Agnes Prescot in eccl̃ia ... ... ... ... ... ... 5 ,,

| | | | |
|---|---|---|---|
| | Anne Mowdisley in eccl̃ia | 10 | Januarie |
| 324 | Barthollomew Carr | 12 | „ |
| | Eliz[th] Hey in eccl̃ia | „ | „ |
| | Agnes Aspinwall in ecclia | 13 | „ |
| | Tho: Butchart in ecclia | 18 | „ |
| | Jaine Jackeson in eccl̃ia | 8 | ffebruarie |
| | Anne Mason in eccl̃ia | 13 | „ |
| | Henrie Scarsbrecke geñ in eccl̃ia | 21 | „ |
| | Cristopher Jump | 15 | March |
| | Jaine Bootle in eccl̃ia | 19 | „ |
| | Ric̃ Mosse in the high Chancell | 22 | „ |
| | Alis Barton | „ | „ |

## 1583.

| | | | |
|---|---|---|---|
| | Anne Aiscroft | 25 | March |
| | Tho: Halworth in eccl̃ia | 26 | „ |
| pur̃ | Katherin ffarclough in eccl̃ia | 30 | „ |
| pur | Johne Aspinwall | 31 | „ |
| pu | Tho: Lowe | 6 | Aprill |
| pu | John ffisher | „ | „ |
| | Eline fformbie | 7 | „ |
| | James Sumner | 9 | „ |
| | M[r] ffransis Stanley sone to the Righte Honorable Henrie Earle of Derbie | 16 | „ |
| | Izabell Scarsbricke in eccl̃ia | 17 | „ |
| pu | Elin Scarsbricke | 26 | „ |
| | Margerie Prekott | 29 | „ |
| | Ally Shawe | 4 | Maye |
| | Parsevell Jumpe | 15 | „ |
| | John Hoolme in eccl̃ia | 20 | „ |
| | Wiłłm Oliverson | 22 | „ |
| | Cislye White | 30 | „ |
| 325 | Marye Worthington in the high chan | 1 | June |
| | Alis Cockett | 7 | „ |
| | Tho: Thorton | „ | „ |
| | Wiłłm Gill in eccl̃ia | 8 | „ |
| | Eline Blvndell in eccl̃ia | 11 | „ |
| | Margrate Worthington in the high chañ | 20 | „ |
| | Adame Bartone | 24 | „ |
| | Hughe Houghton | 28 | „ |
| | Katherin Lea in eccl̃ia | 8 | July |
| | Eline Sefton in eccl̃ia | 22 | „ |
| pu: | John Leylande in eccl̃ia | 29 | „ |
| | Joane Preskott fi: Hug | 30 | „ |
| | Wiłłm Smyth in eccl̃ia | 2 | Auguste |
| | Ric̃ Barton in eccl̃ia | 5 | „ |
| | Margaret Molinex in eccl̃ia | „ | „ |
| | Rodger Scarsbricke | 23 | „ |

| | | | |
|---|---|---|---|
| | Elene Sutche | 25 | Auguste |
| | Ric̃ Johnson | 1 | October |
| | Phelis Lea in eccl̄ia | 18 | „ |
| | Eliz[th] Harison in eccl̄ia | „ | „ |
| | Jaine Skeltone | 21 | „ |
| | Margaret Laylande | 26 | „ |
| | John Swifte | 4 | November |
| | Peeter Spackman in eccl̄ia | 12 | „ |
| | Wiłłm Hill | 13 | „ |
| | Alison Preskott | „ | „ |
| | Anne Hill | 26 | „ |
| Fo. 326 | Jane Kelett fi: Ric̃ | 10 | December |
| | Hugh Morcrofte in eccl̄ia | 11 | „ |
| | Elene Heye | 23 | „ |
| pu: | Wiłłm Cadicke in eccl̄ia | 27 | „ |
| | filij Rob̄ti Blackledge | 11 | Januarie |
| pu: | Jaine Morcrofte | 25 | „ |
| | Peeter Care | 26 | „ |
| | Wiłłm Whitstons | 3 | ffebruarie |
| | Wiłłm Killshawe in eccl̄ia | 12 | „ |
| | E . . Preskott in eccl̄ia | 20 | „ |
| | Alis Swyfte in eccl̄ia | 10 | March |
| | One Cropp | „ | „ |
| | Clares Brighouse | 12 | „ |

## 1584.

| | | | |
|---|---|---|---|
| pure | James Morcrofte in ecclia | 3 | Aprill |
| | Elene Smythe in eccl̄ia | 4 | „ |
| pũ | Ric̃ Melinge | 23 | „ |
| puer | Anne Cowson | 18 | Maye |
| | Rob̄te Mowdisley in ecclia | 22 | „ |
| | Philipe Martandall in ecclia | 3 | June |
| | Gilberte Mosse in ecclia | 11 | „ |
| | John Swifte in eccl̄ia | 17 | „ |
| | Rob̄te Blundell | 18 | „ |
| | Jams Taylior fi: Jo: | 19 | „ |
| | Clemans Shawe in eccl̄ia | 27 | „ |
| pure | . . . Shurlekars | 30 | „ |
| Fo. 327 | Katherin Asmall in ecclia pur | 7 | July |
| | Ric̃ Cropp in eccl̄ia | 8 | „ |
| | John Banister whoe was slaine in eccl̄ia | 10 | „ |
| | Jamis Killshaw | 13 | „ |
| pur | Anne Gollibrand in eccl̄ia | „ | „ |
| | Tho: Martindaile | 30 | „ |
| | Cristopher Barton | 3 | Auguste |
| | Henrie Yate | 8 | „ |
| | Em Ascrofte | „ | „ |
| | Katherin Yate | 11 | „ |

| | | | |
|---|---|---|---|
| | Katherin Bradley in eccl̄ia ... ... ... ... ... | 15 | Auguste |
| | Ric̃ Jollie in the high Chancell ... ... ... | 19 | „ |
| pur | Marget ffodge in eccl̄ia ... ... ... ... ... ... | 20 | „ |
| | Jamis Blundell in eccl̄ia ... ... ... ... ... ... | „ | „ |
| | Jaine Preskot in eccl̄ia ... ... ... ... ... ... | 23 | „ |
| pur | Tho: Burie ... ... ... ... ... ... ... ... | 10 | September |
| | Margerie Gorsutch ... ... ... ... ... ... ... | 14 | „ |
| | Marie Mason in eccl̄ia ... ... ... ... ... ... | 18 | „ |
| | Katherin Blvndell in eccl̄ia ... ... ... ... | 9 | October |
| | Wil̄lm Rimmer ... ... ... ... ... ... | 10 | „ |
| | Marget Barton ... ... ... ... ... ... ... ... | 30 | „ |
| | Ellin Butcherd fi: Edw: in eccl̄ia ... ... ... | 8 | November |
| | Joanie ffarbrother A stranger ... ... ... | 14 | „ |
| | Wil̄lm Woofall ... ... ... ... ... ... ... ... | 18 | „ |
| | Jaine Aspinwall in eccl̄ia ... ... ... ... ... | 19 | „ |
| | Margerie Cattrall in eccl̄ia ... ... ... ... ... | „ | „ |
| | Ric̃ Robinson de Scarsbreck ... ... ... ... ... | 21 | „ |
| | Eliz^th^ Mollinex ... ... ... ... ... ... ... ... | 3 | December |
| | Margerie Gorsutch in ecclia ... ... ... ... ... | 11 | „ |
| | Rob̄t Everingeam in ecclia ... ... ... ... ... | „ | „ |
| pur | Jaine Morecrofte in eccl̄ia ... ... ... ... ... | 13 | „ |
| | Margerie Mowdsley in eccl̄ia ... ... ... ... ... | „ | „ |
| | Rodger ffidler ... ... ... ... ... ... ... ... | 20 | „ |
| | Sislie Matthew ... ... ... ... ... ... ... ... | 21 | „ |
| pur | Katherin Gilbertson in eccl̄ia ... ... ... ... | 23 | „ |
| 328 | Marie Abraham in eccl̄ia ... ... ... ... ... ... | 3 | Januarie |
| pur | Marget Hunt in ecclia ... ... ... ... ... ... | „ | „ |
| | Jenet Lancaster ... ... ... ... ... ... ... | 12 | „ |
| | Eliz^th^ Aspinwall in the high Chañ de aughton | 13 | „ |
| | Jaine Waringe in eccl̄ia ... ... ... ... ... ... | 15 | „ |
| | Izabell Barton in eccl̄ia ... ... ... ... ... ... | 20 | „ |
| | John Preskot bast ... ... ... ... ... ... ... | „ | „ |
| pur | John Cosey ... ... ... ... ... ... ... ... | „ | „ |
| | Henrie Morecroft ... ... ... ... ... ... ... | 22 | „ |
| | . . . Barton ... ... ... ... ... ... ... | 23 | „ |
| | Edm: Walker ... ... ... ... ... ... ... ... | 24 | „ |
| | Marget Lowe in eccl̄ia ... ... ... ... ... ... | 28 | „ |
| | Jaine Burscough in eccl̄ia ... ... ... ... ... | 3 | ffebruarie |
| | Robert Gobin ... ... ... ... ... ... ... ... | „ | „ |
| | Tho: Sumner ... ... ... ... ... ... ... ... | „ | „ |
| pur | Thurstan ffarclough ... ... ... ... ... ... ... | „ | „ |
| | Margerie Barton ... ... ... ... ... ... ... | 9 | „ |
| | Marget Waringe ... ... ... ... ... ... ... | 10 | „ |
| | Thomazin Mowdisley ... ... ... ... ... ... | 15 | „ |
| | Ellin Morecroft ... ... ... ... ... ... ... | „ | „ |
| | George Blackelege in eccl̄ia ... ... ... ... ... | 17 | „ |
| | John Billinge ... ... ... ... ... ... ... ... | 19 | „ |
| | Jaine Worthingeton in y^e^ high Chañ ... ... | 20 | „ |
| | Jaine Waringe ... ... ... ... ... ... ... ... | 21 | „ |

| | | | |
|---|---|---|---|
| | Alis Hill | 26 | ffebruarie |
| | Ric̃ Worthingeton in y^e^ high Chanc̃ | " | " |
| | Anne Tomson | 1 | March |
| | Joanie Halsall in y^e^ high Chanc̃ | 9 | " |
| | Hugh Lathom in eccl̃ia | 11 | " |
| | Anne Matthew | 13 | " |

## 1585.

| | | | |
|---|---|---|---|
| | Hugh Smyth in eccl̃ia | 25 | March |
| | Hen: Worthingeton in y^e^ high Chañ | 5 | Aprill |
| pur̃ | Alis Omfrey in eccl̃ia | 7 | " |
| | Agnes Shaw in eccl̃ia | 18 | " |
| | Alis Morcroft in ecclia | " | " |
| | Eliz^th^ Cocket | 19 | " |
| pur | Wiłłm Jackeson in eccl̃ia | " | " |
| | Marget Gill | 23 | " |
| | Ellin Jackeson in ecclia | " | " |
| Fo. 329 | Hugh Holland in eccl̃ia | 26 | " |
| | Gabrell Hockenell | " | " |
| puer | Marget Mowdisley in eccl̃ia | 1 | Maye |
| | Ellin Awtye | 10 | " |
| pur | Eliz^th^ Morecroft in eccl̃ia | 13 | " |
| | Robert Cowp | 14 | " |
| | Margerie Prescot | 15 | " |
| | Lowrance Marche in eccl̃ia | 16 | " |
| | Jaine Balshaw | " | " |
| | Joanie Stopforth in eccl̃ia | 18 | " |
| | Eliz^th^ Spencer in y^e^ high Chanc̃ | 22 | " |
| pur | Henrie A stranger from Bycarstafe in eccl̃ia | 23 | " |
| | Jenet Balshaw | 26 | " |
| | John Jackeson in eccl̃ia | 5 | June |
| | John Swifte in eccl̃ia | 9 | " |
| | Tho: Huton in eccl̃ia | 11 | " |
| | Eliz^th^ Werall in eccl̃ia | 18 | " |
| | Anne Lathom | 20 | " |
| pur | Hugh Mason in eccl̃ia | 29 | " |
| | George Aspinwall in eccl̃ia | 4 | Julye |
| | Eliz^th^ Mundie | 5 | " |
| | Katherine Scarsbrecke in eccl̃ia | 7 | " |
| | Wiłłm Garrard in eccl̃ia | 11 | " |
| | Henrie fformbie | 18 | " |
| pur | Richard Golibrand in ecclia | " | " |
| | Rodger Barton in eccl̃ia | 23 | " |
| | Anne Stopforth in y^e^ high Chañ | 26 | " |
| | Eliz^th^ Harison | 6 | August |
| | Henrie Gill in eccl̃ia | 10 | " |
| | Tho: Eccleston fi: Wiłl in eccl̃ia bast | 12 | " |
| | Sislie Talier in eccl̃ia | 13 | " |

| |  |  |  |
|---|---|---|---|
| | Ranould Alerton | 14 | August |
| | Agnes Walne | 30 | ,, |
| 330 | Jaine Shawe in eccl̃ia | 5 | September |
| | Henrie Gollie | 6 | ,, |
| | John Porter in eccl̃ia | 14 | ,, |
| | Elenor Shawe in eccl̃ia | 16 | ,, |
| | John Walne | 22 | ,, |
| | Katherin Harison | 27 | ,, |
| | Elizth Worthingeton in eccl̃ia | 3 | October |
| pur̃ | . . . Diket fi: Will̃m in ecclia | ,, | ,, |
| | Jaine Hunter | 20 | ,, |
| | Marget Waringe | 12 | November |
| | Rodger Barton in eccl̃ia | 19 | ,, |
| | Henrie Penket | 22 | ,, |
| | Anne Waynewright in eccl̃ia | 23 | ,, |
| | George Clarkeson A stranger | 29 | ,, |
| | Sibell Westhead in eccl̃ia | 4 | December |
| | Elin Butler | ,, | ,, |
| | Izabell Westhead in ecclia | 7 | ,, |
| pur | Will̃m Whytestones in eccl̃ia | 15 | ,, |
| | Izabell Scarsbrecke | 21 | ,, |
| | Tho: Prescot | 25 | ,, |
| | Henrie Barker | 30 | ,, |
| | . . . Barton | 3 | Januarie |
| pur̃ | Jaine Killshaw | ,, | ,, |
| | Jaine Whytestones in eccl̃ia | 8 | ,, |
| | Tho: Blundell | 9 | ,, |
| | Will̃m Cobann | 10 | ,, |
| | Elin Mowdisley in eccl̃ia | ,, | ,, |
| | Jamis ffidler | 11 | ,, |
| pur̃ | Ric̃ Stanley in eccl̃ia | 12 | ,, |
| | Gefferey Burie in eccl̃ia | 17 | ,, |
| | Elizth Killshaw | 22 | ,, |
| | Anne Tomson | 24 | ,, |
| pur̃ | Hugh Cosey in eccl̃ia | 26 | ,, |
| pur̃ | Jaine Mowdisley | 30 | ,, |
| | Elizth Bycarstaff | 31 | ,, |
| 331 | Jamis Cowp in eccl̃ia | 6 | ffebruarie |
| | Marget Waynewright in eccl̃ia | 13 | ,, |
| pur̃ | Ric̃ Mellinge | ,, | ,, |
| | Tho: & Elinor Aman bast | 24 | ,, |
| | Marget Lea in eccl̃ia | ,, | ,, |
| | Alis Rigbie | 25 | ,, |
| pur̃ | Marget Morcrofte in eccl̃ia | 27 | ,, |
| | Will̃m Mowdisley in eccl̃ia | 28 | ,, |
| stanger | John Gorsutch | 2 | March |
| | Marget Lythom | 12 | ,, |
| | Will̃m Lythom | 13 | ,, |
| | Rob̃t Bower | 14 | ,, |

Em Woosey in ecctia ... ... ... ... ... 18 March
Jamis Oliverson ... ... ... ... ... ... 19 „
Marget Shawe ... ... ... ... ... ... ... 23 „
Jaine Morcroft ... ... ... ... ... ... ... 24 „

## 1586.

Anne Waynewright in ecctia ... ... ... ... 25 March
Alis Blvndell ... ... ... ... ... ... ... ... 26 „
Margerie Mellinge in ecctia ... ... ... ... 28 „
Marget Whalleye ... ... ... ... ... ... ... 29 „
Elin Ascroft ... ... ... ... ... ... ... ... 1 Aprill
Tho: Hunt in ecctia ... ... ... ... ... ... 3 „
Tho: Mellinge ... ... ... ... ... ... ... 8 „
Wittm Haughton ... ... ... ... ... ... ... 10 „
James Gill ... ... ... ... ... ... ... ... 13 „
John Preskott ... ... ... ... ... ... ... „ „
Alis & Elene Bradshawe ... ... ... ... ... 15 „
Eline Sutche in ecctia ... ... ... ... ... 17 „
Wittm Waynewright in ecctia ... ... ... 18 „
Tho: Whithington ... ... ... ... ... ... ... 19 „
pu Jaine Jackson in ecctia ... ... ... ... ... 2 Maye
pu: Homfray Gill ... ... ... ... ... ... ... ... 3 „
Henrie Bekonsall ... ... ... ... ... ... ... „ „
Margerie Sedone ... ... ... ... ... ... ... 4 „
James Beconsall ... ... ... ... ... ... ... „ „
Anne Ambrose in ecctia ... ... ... ... ... 18 „
Jaine Layland in ecctia ... ... ... ... ... 28 „
Fo. 332 Alis Mullinex ... ... ... ... ... ... ... ... 1 June
Marget Asshurst in ecctia ... ... ... ... ... 5 „
Jaine Barker ... ... ... ... ... ... ... ... „ „
Richard Barton ... ... ... ... ... ... ... 8 „
Robert Pwsey ... ... ... ... ... ... ... ... 10 „
Robt Jolibrond in ecctia ... ... ... ... ... „ „
Jaine Asshurst ... ... ... ... ... ... ... 11 „
Elizth Peeter in ecctia ... ... ... ... ... 16 „
pur Henrie Mowdisley in ecctia ... ... ... ... 18 „
Marget Kekuicke in ecctia ... ... ... ... 27 „
Marget Mudie ... ... ... ... ... ... ... ... 6 July
pur Marie Scarsbrecke in the nue chañ ... ... 3 August
Anne Waynewright in ecctia ... ... ... ... 16 „
Ellin Woofall ... ... ... ... ... ... ... ... „ „
Alis Croocke ... ... ... ... ... ... ... ... 20 „
Wittm Jackeson in ecctia ... ... ... ... ... „ „
Jaine Morecroft in ecctia ... ... ... ... ... „ „
Tho: Hesketh ... ... ... ... ... ... ... ... 27 „
. . . Mowdisley ... ... ... ... ... ... ... 29 „
John Westhead ... ... ... ... ... ... ... 1 September
Henrie Whytestones ... ... ... ... ... ... 4 „

| | | |
|---|---|---|
| Anne Morecrofte ... ... ... ... ... ... | 22 | September |
| Janat Jumpe ... ... ... ... ... ... ... | 26 | „ |
| Anne Hodgeson in eccl̄ia ... ... ... ... | 14 | October |
| Hector Barton ... ... ... ... ... ... ... | 25 | „ |
| Ellin Prescot ... ... ... ... ... ... ... | 30 | „ |
| Anne Rigbie in eccl̄ia ... ... ... ... ... | 14 | November |
| Alis Haidocke ... ... ... ... ... ... ... | 22 | „ |
| Tho: Haiworth ... ... ... ... ... ... | „ | „ |
| Sislie Prescot in eccl̄ia ... ... ... ... ... | „ | „ |
| Peeter Longe in eccl̄ia ... ... ... ... ... | 27 | „ |
| Robert Dwarihows ... ... ... ... ... ... | 2 | December |
| Ric̃ Burscough ... ... ... ... ... ... ... | 3 | „ |
| Tho: A stranger ... ... ... ... ... ... | 5 | „ |
| Eliz$^{th}$ Marrow in eccl̄ia ... ... ... ... ... | 15 | „ |
| Ric̃ Lathwhat in ecclia ... ... ... ... ... | 20 | „ |
| Custan Atherton in eccl̄ia ... ... ... ... | „ | „ |
| Marget Ambrose in eccl̄ia ... ... ... ... | 27 | „ |
| Emlin Kekuicke in ecclia ... ... ... ... | 28 | „ |
| Eliz$^{th}$ Aspinwall ... ... ... ... ... ... ... | 2 | Januarie |
| Katherin Gregson in eccl̄ia ... ... ... ... | 9 | „ |
| Mrs Marḡet Mollinex in eccl̄ia ... ... ... | 12 | „ |
| Margaret Sutch ... ... ... ... ... ... | 24 | „ |
| Eliz$^{th}$ Kekuicke ... ... ... ... ... ... ... | „ | „ |
| Ric̃ Westhead in ecclia ... ... ... ... ... | 2 | ffebruarie |
| Tho: Prescot in eccl̄ia ... ... ... ... ... | 22 | „ |
| Alis Brighowse ... ... ... ... ... ... ... | 27 | „ |

[*No entries for March*]

## 1587.

[*No entries for Aprill*]

| | | |
|---|---|---|
| Ellin Swifte in eccl̄ia ... ... ... ... ... | 7 | Maye |
| Margaret Lathom in eccl̄ia ... ... ... ... | „ | „ |
| Hugh Halsall ... ... ... ... ... ... ... | 25 | „ |
| Elin Traves ... ... ... ... ... ... ... | 26 | „ |
| Ellin Barton in eccl̄ia ... ... ... ... ... | 29 | „ |
| George Waynewright in eccl̄ia ... ... ... | 30 | „ |
| Eliz$^{th}$ Lancaster ... ... ... ... ... ... ... | 31 | „ |
| John Stonton ... ... ... ... ... ... ... | 3 | June |
| Tho: Morcroft ... ... ... ... ... ... ... | 6 | „ |
| Anne Burie in eccl̄ia ... ... ... ... ... | 21 | „ |
| Margerie ffarclough in eccl̄ia ... ... ... ... | „ | „ |
| Tho: Huton in eccl̄ia ... ... ... ... ... | 25 | „ |
| Agnes Garrard ... ... ... ... ... ... ... | 2 | Julye |
| Sislie Hoolme ... ... ... ... ... ... ... | 9 | „ |
| Jenet Jackeson in eccl̄ia ... ... ... ... | 11 | „ |
| Margaret Spakeman in eccl̄ia ... ... ... ... | 15 | „ |
| Ellin Sefton ... ... ... ... ... ... ... | 28 | „ |
| Eliz$^{th}$ Eccleston ... ... ... ... ... ... ... | 9 | August |

| | | | |
|---|---|---|---|
| | Jaine Carr | 30 | August |
| | . . . Egle | ” | ” |
| | Elizth Barton in eccłia | 1 | September |
| | Margaret Lathom | 4 | ” |
| | Wiłłm Kilshaw | ” | ” |
| | John Stopforth | ” | ” |
| | Ric̃ Aiscroft | 6 | ” |
| | Tho: Asmall | 7 | ” |
| | Jamis Blvndell in eccłia | 12 | ” |
| | Jamis Gill | ” | ” |
| pur̃ | Tho: Cowsey in eccłia | 21 | ” |
| pur̃ | Thomas Smulte in eccłia | 2 | October |
| | Gilƀ Sumner | 12 | ” |
| | ffrances fformbie | ” | ” |
| | Margaret Ascrofte | 20 | ” |
| | Edm: Killshaw | 23 | November |
| | Wiłłm Gyles in eccłia | 5 | December |
| | Izabell Coockeson in eccłia | 7 | ” |
| | Margaret Oliverson in eccłia | ” | ” |
| | Wiłłm Mowdisley in eccłia | 13 | ” |
| | Elin Harison | ” | ” |
| | Peeter Marrow in eccłia | 14 | ” |
| | Hugh Mason in eccłia | ” | ” |
| | Elin Harison | 28 | ” |
| | Margaret Shaw in ye high chañ | 29 | ” |
| | Peter Lunt | ” | ” |
| | Margaret Brigehowse | ” | ” |
| Fo. 335 | Hugh Holland in eccłia | 5 | Januarie |
| | John Makin in eccłia | 19 | ” |
| | Tho: Haword in eccłia | 23 | ” |
| | John Matthew in eccłia | 28 | ” |
| | Jamis Earle | 31 | ” |
| | Margaret Gaskin in eccłia | 4 | ffebruarie |
| | Tho: Crucke | 8 | ” |
| | Wiłłm Harison | ” | ” |
| | Margerie Shervington | 17 | ” |
| | Tho: Killshaw | 18 | ” |
| | Margaret Heskeine in eccłia | 26 | ” |
| | Elizth Shurlicars in eccłia | 28 | ” |
| | Edw: Haughton | 2 | March |
| | Alis Shaw in eccłia | 4 | ” |
| | Jaine Scarsbreck in eccłia | ” | ” |
| | Peeter Hunter | 13 | ” |
| | Jamis Morecroft in eccłia | 16 | ” |
| | Jaine Waynewright | 18 | ” |
| | John Bore | ” | ” |
| | Ric̃ Scarsbrecke | 21 | ” |
| | Izabell Gill | ” | ” |
| | Alis Lufkin | 23 | ” |

## 1588.

| | | |
|---|---|---|
| John Gobbin in eccl̃ia ... ... ... ... ... | 6 | Aprill |
| James Cropp ... ... ... ... ... ... ... | ,, | ,, |
| Elin Davie ... ... ... ... ... ... ... | ,, | ,, |
| Tho: Gill ... ... ... ... ... ... ... | 9 | ,, |
| . . . . Rotherope ... ... ... ... ... ... | 10 | ,, |
| Jamis Barton ... ... ... ... ... ... ... | 11 | ,, |
| ffrances Locker in eccl̃ia ... ... ... ... | 14 | ,, |
| Gilbarte Gill ... ... ... ... ... ... ... | 19 | ,, |
| John Peckvance ... ... ... ... ... ... | 21 | ,, |
| Margerie White ... ... ... ... ... ... | 26 | ,, |
| Margrat fformbie ... ... ... ... ... ... | 29 | ,, |
| Margery Plumbe ... ... ... ... ... ... | 30 | ,, |
| Alis Smythe in ecclia ... ... ... ... ... | 1 | Maye |
| Tho Rutter in eccl̃ia ... ... ... ... ... | 6 | ,, |
| Ric̃ Swifte in ecclia ... ... ... ... ... ... | 10 | ,, |
| Tho: Beconsall ... ... ... ... ... ... | 11 | ,, |
| Alis Makin in ecclia ... ... ... ... ... | 16 | ,, |
| Katherin Stopforth in eccl̃ia ... ... ... ... | 18 | ,, |
| Jenet Haughton ... ... ... ... ... ... | 20 | ,, |
| Katherin Gerrerd ... ... ... ... ... ... | 22 | ,, |
| Margerie Lyvesley in eccl̃ia ... ... ... ... | ,, | ,, |
| Elene Golbrane in eccl̃ia ... ... ... ... | 24 | ,, |
| Will̃m Omfray in eccl̃ia ... ... ... ... ... | ,, | ,, |
| Elizth Aiscrofte in eccl̃ia ... ... ... ... ... | 28 | ,, |
| Philipe Martindall in eccl̃ia ... ... ... ... | 29 | ,, |
| Elizth Coockson ... ... ... ... ... ... | 30 | ,, |
| Tho: Watkinson ... ... ... ... ... ... | 31 | ,, |
| James Morcrofte in ecclia ... ... ... ... | 1 | June |
| Eline Barton in ecclia ... ... ... ... ... | ,, | ,, |
| Ewan Swifte in ecclia .. ... ... ... ... ... | ,, | ,, |
| Ric̃ Golbron in the high Chañ ... ... ... | 5 | ,, |
| Jenet Jackson in eccl̃ia . . ... ... ... ... | ,, | ,, |
| Edw: Anderton in the high Chañ ... ... ... | 7 | ,, |
| Jane Holande in eccl̃ia ... ... ... ... ... | 9 | ,, |
| Elizth Morcrofte in eccl̃ia ... ... ... ... | 12 | ,, |
| Katherin Wilson ... ... ... ... ... ... | 13 | ,, |
| Eline Morcrofte in eccl̃ia . ... ... ... ... | 14 | ,, |
| Edmund Specer in the high Chañ ... ... ... | 18 | ,, |
| Katherin Whitstons in eccl̃ia ... ... ... ... | 24 | ,, |
| Margaret Morcrofte in eccl̃ia ... ... ... | ,, | ,, |
| Tho: Toppinge in eccl̃ia ... ... ... ... | ,, | ,, |
| Ric̃ Aspinwall in eccl̃ia ... ... ... ... ... | 29 | ,, |
| Tho: Robinson ... ... ... ... ... ... | 30 | ,, |
| John Aspinwall in eccl̃ia pu: ... ... ... ... | 9 | Julye |
| Jaine Houlme in eccl̃ia ... ... ... ... ... | 16 | ,, |
| Elizth Harison ... ... ... ... ... ... ... | 24 | ,, |

| | | | |
|---|---|---|---|
| | Rob̄t Raynforthe | 29 | Julye |
| | Alis Gilbertson | 2 | Auguste |
| | Hugh Holonde in eccl̄ia | 6 | „ |
| | Jaine Shepard | 8 | „ |
| | Raynolde Aspinwall | 21 | „ |
| | Alis Plommbe | „ | „ |
| | Edw: Morcrofte in eccl̄ia | 6 | September |
| | Margratt Harison in eccl̄ia | 9 | „ |
| | Jaine Boothe | 15 | „ |
| | Anne Shurlikars | 16 | „ |
| | Ric̃ Hooulme | 18 | „ |
| | Alis Harkar | 24 | „ |
| | Alis Walkare | 10 | October |
| | Jony Preskott | 11 | „ |
| | Elizth Swifte in eccl̄ia | 12 | „ |
| | Margerie Irlande | 13 | „ |
| pu: | Hughe Marson in eccl̄ia | „ | „ |
| | Edmund Waringe | 24 | „ |
| | Anne Ambrose | 30 | „ |
| | Tho: Mosse | 1 | November |
| | Jaine Martandall | 14 | „ |
| | filij Cuthberte Gerrard in eccl̄ia | 23 | „ |
| | Alis Bruche | „ | „ |
| | Edw: Lunte | 29 | „ |
| | Katherin Garrard | 5 | December |
| | Rodger Scarsbricke in eccl̄ia | 10 | „ |
| | Henrie Aspinwall | 22 | „ |
| | Cislie Weaver | 24 | „ |
| pu: | Gabriell Cropp in eccl̄ia | „ | „ |
| | Alis Gill | 30 | „ |
| Fo. 338 | Claris Lathom | 4 | Januarie |
| | Raffe Shawe in eccl̄ia | 6 | „ |
| pur̃ | John Kellet in eccl̄ia | 15 | „ |
| | Nicolas Collins in ye high Chanc̃ | 16 | „ |
| | John Aiscroft | 1 | ffebruarie |
| | Elizth Vrmiston | 11 | „ |
| | Jamis Prescot | 17 | „ |
| pur̃ | George Holland in eccl̄ia | 20 | „ |
| pur̃ | Raffe Holland in eccl̄ia | 24 | „ |
| | Elizth Morecroft | 27 | „ |
| | John Wadington | 5 | March |
| | Katherin Withington in eccl̄ia | 7 | „ |
| | Elizth Asmall in eccl̄ia | 16 | „ |
| | Jaine Halworth in eccl̄ia | 19 | „ |

## 1589.

| | | |
|---|---|---|
| Margerie Hoolme in eccl̄ia | 29 | March |
| Ric̃ Ambrose Senior in eccl̄ia | 30 | „ |

| | | |
|---|---|---|
| John Rydinge ... ... ... ... ... ... ... ... | 1 | Aprill |
| . . . Waringe ... ... ... ... ... ... ... | " | " |
| Ric̃ Ambrose Junior in ecctia ... ... ... ... ... | 2 | " |
| Jaine Scarsbrecke ... ... ... ... ... ... ... | 6 | " |
| Marie Prescot ... ... ... ... ... ... ... ... | 14 | " |
| Emlin Morecrofte ... ... ... ... ... ... ... | 15 | " |
| Henrie Todde ... ... ... ... ... ... ... ... | 23 | " |
| Anne Oliverson ... ... ... ... ... ... ... | 28 | " |
| Alis ffarrer ... ... .. . ... ... ... | 4 | Maye |
| Wiłłm Worthingeton in ye high Chanc̃ ... ... | 7 | " |
| Jenet Voce ... ... ... ... ... ... ... ... | 9 | " |
| Izabell Carre ... ... ... ... ... ... ... ... | " | " |
| Jamis Hunte in ecctia ... ... ... ... ... ... | 13 | " |
| Rodger Kewquicke in ecctia ... ... ... ... ... | " | " |
| Ewan Ascough in ecctia ... ... ... ... ... ... | 19 | " |
| Tho: Ambrose in ecctia ... ... ... ... ... | 24 | " |
| Elizth Scarsbrecke in the new chap ... ... | 28 | " |
| Elizth Gollie ... ... ... ... ... ... ... ... | 30 | " |
| Elizth Talior in ecctia ... ... ... ... ... ... | 2 | June |
| Tho: Hooten ... ... ... ... ... ... ... ... | 4 | " |
| Ric̃ Martindaile ... ... ... ... ... ... ... | " | " |
| Izabell Lancaster ... ... ... ... ... ... ... | 5 | " |
| Robrt Bebot ... ... ... ... ... ... ... ... | 17 | " |
| Jaine Rimer ... ... ... ... ... ... ... ... | 24 | " |
| Lawrance Asmall ... ... ... ... ... ... ... | " | " |
| Elizth Stopforth in ecctia ... ... ... ... ... | 16 | Julye |
| Maria Mason in ecctia ... ... ... ... ... ... | " | " |
| Alis Scarsbrecke in ye new chappl ... ... ... | 17 | " |
| Katherin Jackeson ... ... ... ... ... ... ... | 18 | " |
| Gilb̃ Waynewright ... ... ... ... ... ... | 19 | " |
| Gowther Hodgkinson ... ... ... ... ... ... | 26 | " |
| Tho: Hankin in ecctia ... ... ... ... ... ... | 2 | August |
| Jenet Hawton ... ... ... ... ... ... ... ... | 12 | " |
| John Lea in ecctia ... ... ... ... ... ... ... | 22 | " |
| Marie Hill in ecctia ... ... ... ... ... ... ... | " | " |
| John Spencer ... ... ... ... ... ... ... ... | 25 | " |
| Elizth Smult in ecctia ... ... ... ... ... ... | 28 | " |
| Alis Westhead in ecctia ... ... ... ... ... ... | 4 | September |
| Anne Walker ... ... . ... ... ... ... ... | 7 | " |
| Alis Richardson ... ... ... ... ... ... ... | " | " |
| Douse Babott ... ... ... ... ... ... ... ... | 16 | " |
| Ranould Blvndell ... ... ... ... ... ... ... | 17 | " |
| Izabell Cropp in ecctia ... ... ... ... ... ... | 26 | " |
| Jaine Martindaile in ecctia ... ... ... ... ... | 27 | " |
| Henrie Gill ... ... ... ... ... ... ... ... | " | " |
| Peeter Cropp ... ... ... ... ... ... ... ... | 5 | October |
| Wiłłm Bower ... ... ... ... ... ... ... ... | " | " |
| Rob̃t Stopforth in ecctia ... ... ... ... ... | 31 | " |
| George Preskot ... ... ... ... ... ... ... | 24 | November |

| | | | |
|---|---|---|---|
| | Henrie Knowles in eccłia ... ... ... ... | 25 | November |
| | Henrie Leadbetter in eccłia ... ... ... ... | 26 | " |
| | Alis Hesketh ... ... ... ... ... ... ... ... | 27 | " |
| Fo. 340 | Claris Voce ... ... ... ... ... ... ... ... | 8 | December |
| | Katherin Kellet vx⁹ Ric̃ in eccłia ... ... ... | 10 | " |
| | Sislie Smalshaw ... ... ... ... ... ... ... | 11 | " |
| | Anne Marclough ... ... ... ... ... ... ... | 13 | " |
| | Joanie Aiscroft ... ... ... ... ... ... ... | 22 | " |
| pur̃ | Ric̃ Dutton in eccłia ... ... ... ... ... | " | " |
| | Margaret Swifte in eccłia ... ... ... ... ... | " | " |
| | John Stopforth ... ... ... ... ... ... ... ... | 23 | " |
| | Alis Shaw ... ... ... ... ... ... ... ... | 27 | " |
| | Eliz^th Atherton ... ... ... ... ... ... ... ... | 6 | Januarie |
| | Margerie Sutch in the Chancell ... ... ... | 7 | " |
| | Henrie Ascall ... ... ... ... ... ... ... ... | 9 | " |
| pur̃ | Wiłłm Garret fi: Cuthbart in eccłia ... ... | 10 | " |
| | M^r Edw: Scarsbrecke fi: Edw: Esqr ... ... | 17 | " |
| | Eliz^th Clapam in eccłia ... ... ... ... ... ... | 20 | " |
| | Maria Swifte ... ... ... ... ... ... ... ... | 24 | " |
| | Hector Whytestones ... ... ... ... ... ... | 27 | " |
| infant | Hugh Bennet ... ... ... ... ... ... ... ... | " | " |
| | Adam Martindaile fi: Hugh in eccłia ... ... | 3 | ffebruarie |
| | Katherin Mellinge vx⁹ Jo: ... ... ... ... ... | 5 | " |
| | Marie Baron fi: Gilƀ ... ... ... ... ... ... | 6 | " |
| | Eliz^th Adamsoñ in eccłia ... ... ... ... ... | 20 | " |
| | Bryhan Morecrofte ... ... ... ... ... ... ... | 25 | " |
| | Jenet Killshaw vid in eccłia ... ... ... ... | 9 | March |
| | Ewan Traves ... ... ... ... ... ... ... ... | 10 | " |
| | John Langley ... ... ... ... ... ... ... ... | 13 | " |
| | Mi^rs Jenet Scott in y^e Chansell ... ... ... ... | 21 | " |
| | A Srvant of Ri: Worthington wch was drownt | " | " |
| | Margerie Halworth ... ... ... ... ... ... ... | 22 | " |

## 1590.

| | | | |
|---|---|---|---|
| | Gilƀ Lathom ... ... ... ... ... ... ... ... | 26 | March |
| | Edw: Standanought in eccłia ... ... ... | 27 | " |
| pur̃ | Elin Holland fi: Tho: in eccłia ... ... ... | 2 | Aprill |
| | Ric̃ Parpointe fi: Raffe ... ... ... ... ... ... | 4 | " |
| pur̃ | John Haile in eccłia ... ... ... ... ... ... | 23 | " |
| pur̃ | Marget Ambrose fi: Ric̃ in eccłia ... ... ... | 24 | " |
| | ffardinandow Hutchin in eccłia ... ... ... | 27 | " |
| Fo. 341 | Jaine Barton vx⁹ Gabriell ... ... ... ... | 8 | Maye |
| | Wiłłm Gorton in ecclia ... ... ... ... ... ... | 17 | " |
| | Northren Roƀin ... ... ... ... ... ... ... | 18 | " |
| | Peeter Hill ... ... ... ... ... ... ... ... | 21 | " |
| | Joanie Marrow in eccłia ... ... ... ... ... | 1 | June |
| | Alis Hankin in eccłia ... ... ... ... ... ... | 2 | " |
| | Eliz^th Corker fi: John ... ... ... ... ... ... | 21 | " |

| | | | |
|---|---|---|---|
| | Henrie Smyth fi: Symond in ecclia | 30 | June |
| | John Greene | 1 | July |
| | Robert Jackeson in ecclia | 10 | ,, |
| pur | Tho: Woodes in ecclia | 11 | ,, |
| | Gilb Westhead in ecclia | 13 | ,, |
| | Tho: Ormishaw in ecclia | 16 | ,, |
| | Alis Voce vx' Peeter in ecclia | 19 | ,, |
| | Willm Marclough | 23 | ,, |
| | Hugh Lea fi: Will ... aste | 25 | ,, |
| | Marget Mason vid in ecclia | ,, | ,, |
| | John Gilbertson | 27 | ,, |
| | Alis Dunkon vx' John in ecclia | ,, | ,, |
| | Hugh Holte in ecclia | ,, | ,, |
| | Maria Asmali vx' Hugh in Chapell | 28 | ,, |
| | Hector Mowdisley in ecclia | ,, | ,, |
| | John Prescot | ,, | ,, |
| | Gabriell Gill fi: Gilb | ,, | ,, |
| | George Blvndell | 29 | ,, |
| | Elin Holland vx' Raffe in ecclia | ,, | ,, |
| | Jenet Blundell vx' Ottwell in ecclia | ,, | ,, |
| | John Diconson in ye Chancell | 30 | ,, |
| | Richard Marclough | 1 | Auguste |
| | Alis Gill vid | 2 | ,, |
| | Homfrey Gill | 3 | ,, |
| pur | Mrgerie Holland in ecclia | ,, | ,, |
| | Anne Marclough vx' Ric | ,, | ,, |
| | Ellin Toppinge vid in ecclia | 4 | ,, |
| 342 | Margaret Rigmaden vx' Ric in ecclia | 5 | ,, |
| | Gilb Ormishaw in ecclia | 8 | ,, |
| | Willm Wane de Presto in ecclia | ,, | ,, |
| | John Stopforth | 9 | ,, |
| | Elizth Swifte vx' Lyonell in ecclia | ,, | ,, |
| | Ric Mowdisley in ecclia | ,, | ,, |
| | Marget Bycarstaf vid | 11 | ,, |
| pur | John Woodworth fi John | 12 | ,, |
| | Willm Griffie fi: Davie | ,, | ,, |
| | Jaine Parker vx' Ri: | 15 | ,, |
| | Robt Hunter Scolm | ,, | ,, |
| | Margerie Longe vx' Ellis in ecclia | 16 | ,, |
| pur | George Ploumbe fi: Ja: | 17 | ,, |
| | George Croocke | ,, | ,, |
| | Katherin Lithom fi: Ric | 18 | ,, |
| | Robert Swifte | 20 | ,, |
| | . . . Mason vx' Ric | 21 | ,, |
| | Eideth Gill vx' Hen: in ecclia | 23 | ,, |
| | Tho: Barton | 24 | ,, |
| | George Howlden in ecclia | 25 | ,, |
| pur | Henrie Voce in ecclia | ,, | ,, |
| | Hugh Cowsey in ecclia | 28 | ,, |

| | | | |
|---|---|---|---|
| | Henrie Ashton in eccꝉia | 28 | Auguste |
| | Ellin Ormishaw vxꝰ Peeter | ” | ” |
| | Mrs Katherin Stanley vxꝰ Edw: | ” | ” |
| | Hen: Houlme fi: Peeter in eccꝉlia | 5 | September |
| | Edw: Aspinwall fi Hugh | 13 | ” |
| | Roƀt Westhead fi: Tho: in eccꝉia bast | 19 | ” |
| | Mꝰ Henrie Stanley de crosse hall in the chancell | 20 | ” |
| | Katherin Ashton vxꝰ Oliver in eccꝉia | 24 | ” |
| | Elin Seale vxꝰ John in eccꝉia | 25 | ” |
| | Alis Low vxꝰ Tho: in eccꝉia | 29 | ” |
| | Jaine Elis vxꝰ Jo: | 30 | ” |
| Fo. 343 | Wiꝉꝉm Harvie in eccꝉia | 3 | October |
| | Margaret Anderton in eccꝉia | 6 | ” |
| | Edm: Carre | 7 | ” |
| | Ric̃ Rigemaden fi: Wiꝉꝉ bast | 9 | ” |
| | Ellin Rimmer in eccꝉia | 11 | ” |
| | Eliz$^{th}$ Ormishaw vxꝰ Roƀt | 13 | ” |
| | Marie Penketh vxꝰ Henrie in eccꝉia | ” | ” |
| | Katherin Killshaw fi Jo: in eccꝉia | 16 | ” |
| | Myles Harison in eccꝉia | 19 | ” |
| | Eliz$^{th}$ Prescot vxꝰ Ja: in eccꝉia | 22 | ” |
| | John Mason in ecclia | 4 | November |
| | Hen: Lea in eccꝉia | 7 | ” |
| | Izabell Scarsbrecke vid in eccꝉia | 19 | ” |
| | Sislie Wainewright fi: Wiꝉꝉ | 26 | ” |
| | Katherin Socknell fi: ffrances bast | 27 | ” |
| | Mꝰ George Scarsbreck fi: Edw: Esq$^r$ | 29 | ” |
| pur̃ | A chyld of Ric̃ Cropp in eccꝉia | 10 | December |
| | Wiꝉꝉm Waringe | 19 | ” |
| pur̃ | John Lea fi: Rodger | ” | ” |
| | Eliz$^{th}$ Sands | 21 | ” |
| | John Blackeledge in eccꝉia | 30 | ” |
| | John Hoolme fi: Tho: in eccꝉia | 30 | Januarie |
| | Agnes Bowtell vid in eccꝉia | 1 | ffebruarie |
| | Margaret Nalior vxꝰ Georg in eccꝉia | 3 | ” |
| | Dowse Ormishaw | 8 | ” |
| | Eliz$^{th}$ Whytestones vxꝰ John | 12 | ” |
| | Margerie Westhead vxꝰ Wiꝉꝉ in ecc̃ | 13 | ” |
| | Ewan Beconsall fi: Gilƀ in eccꝉia | ” | ” |
| | Katherin Wainewright vxꝰ Georg in eccꝉia | 14 | ” |
| | Ellin Becconsall vxꝰ Gilƀ | 15 | ” |
| | Tho: Huton in eccꝉia | 27 | ” |
| Fo. 344 | Ewan Hodgeson in eccꝉia | 3 | March |
| | Eliz$^{th}$ Houlme vxꝰ Phillip in eccꝉia | ” | ” |
| | Katherin Hallworth in eccꝉia | 5 | ” |
| pur̃ | John Worthington fi: in the high chañ | 16 | ” |
| | Rodger Alker | 20 | ” |
| | Gowther Scarsbrecke in eccꝉia | ” | ” |
| | Margerie Scarsbrecke | ” | ” |
| pur̃ | Alis Lea in eccꝉia | 23 | ” |

## 1591.

| |  |  |  |
|---|---|---|---|
| | Ellin ffletcher in ecclia | 29 | March |
| | Eliz[th] Hankin | 31 | „ |
| | Eliz[th] Prescot | 9 | Aprill |
| | Margaret Holland in ecclia | 16 | „ |
| | Anne Asmall in ecclia | 22 | „ |
| | Sibell Sutch | „ | „ |
| | Eliz[th] Westhead | 23 | „ |
| pur | Edw: Martindaile | 25 | „ |
| | Jaī Gill vidua | 26 | „ |
| | Gilб Allerton | „ | „ |
| | Jaine Beconsall vid | 28 | „ |
| | Henrie Killshaw | 9 | Maye |
| | Ellin Withington in ecclia | 12 | „ |
| | Gabriell Scarsbrecke in ecclia | 13 | „ |
| | Tho: Poape | 18 | „ |
| | Izabell Butcherd in ecclia | 19 | „ |
| | Homfrey Anglesdaile in ecclia | „ | „ |
| | Richard Martin in ecclia | 20 | „ |
| | John Kinge in the high Chancell | 21 | „ |
| | Jamis Asmall in y[e] new chancell | „ | „ |
| | Willm ffarclough | 30 | „ |
| | Alis Coventrie | 3 | June |
| | Alis Waringe | 11 | Julie |
| | Marget Webster in eclia | 12 | „ |
| | John Billinge | 15 | „ |
| | Jony Orm̃ | 22 | „ |
| | Eliz[th] Marclough | „ | „ |
| | Robert Mowdisley in ecclia | 23 | „ |
| p. 345 | Tho: Asshurst in ecclia | 2 | Auguste |
| | George Woodes in ecclia | „ | „ |
| | Anne Greaves vid in ecclia | 3 | „ |
| | Tho: Barton | 7 | „ |
| | George Mason in ecclia | „ | „ |
| pur̃ | Marget Prescot in ecclia | „ | „ |
| | Gilб Tyrer | 11 | „ |
| | Eliz[th] Mowdisley | „ | „ |
| | Jamis Mowdisley in ecclia | 12 | „ |
| pur̃ | Peeter Aspinwall in ecclia | „ | „ |
| | Margerie Ascough in ecclia | 13 | „ |
| pur̃ | John Preskot | 15 | „ |
| | Eliz[th] Preskoth | 16 | „ |
| | Ellin Blackeledge in ecclia | 20 | „ |
| | Alis Lathom | 23 | „ |
| | Eliz[th] Stopforth | „ | „ |
| | A Child of Ewan Longley | 24 | „ |
| | Margerie Barton | 25 | „ |

| | | | |
|---|---|---|---|
| | Jaine Martin vid | 25 | Auguste |
| | Katherin Gyles vid | 27 | „ |
| | Jaine fforshaw | „ | „ |
| Juuenis | Tho: Henrieson | 2 | September |
| | Margaret Billinge vid | 3 | „ |
| pur̄ | Jam Killshaw | 5 | „ |
| | Alis Wainewright in eccl̄ia | 9 | „ |
| Juvenis | Ric̄ Chadocke in eccl̄ia | 10 | „ |
| | Wil̄lm Kadicke | 13 | „ |
| | Ric̄ Chadocke | „ | „ |
| | Tristrom Haughton | „ | „ |
| | Sislie Eccleston et pur̄ Eius | 15 | „ |
| | Elizth Preskoth vid | 17 | „ |
| | Elizth Mason vid | „ | „ |
| | Joanie Cropp | 22 | „ |
| | A child of Rodger Lea in eccl̄ia | „ | „ |
| | Wil̄lm Lucas A stranger in eccl̄ia | 23 | „ |
| | Jaine Bower vid | 24 | „ |
| | Ellin Gill vid in eccl̄ia | „ | „ |
| | Jenet Scarsbrecke in eccl̄ia | 26 | „ |
| | Tho: Aiscroft | 27 | „ |
| Fo. 346 | Katherin Spencer in eccl̄ia | 3 | October |
| | Elizth Woodes | 5 | „ |
| Juuē | Ewan Gill | 6 | „ |
| | Margerie Sefton | 10 | „ |
| | Hector Killshaw | 13 | „ |
| | Margerie Chadocke in eccl̄ia | 17 | „ |
| | John Ainsworth in the new chancel | 19 | „ |
| pur̄ | John Peningeton | „ | „ |
| | pur̄ Margaret Barton | 24 | „ |
| | Izabell Aiscrofte | 25 | „ |
| | pur̄ Edw: Jolibrand in ecclia | 28 | „ |
| | Margaret Shurlicars | 29 | „ |
| | Elizth Pendleburie vxꝰ Tho: | 31 | „ |
| | Margerie Coockeson vxꝰ Hen: in eccl̄ia | 1 | November |
| | Claris Killshaw | 2 | „ |
| | Robert Cowp in eccl̄ia | „ | „ |
| | Alis Pickvance | 6 | „ |
| | Margerie Waynewright fi: Gorg | 14 | „ |
| | John Brighows fi: Ric̄ | 18 | „ |
| | Ellin Woodes vxꝰ John | 19 | „ |
| | Wil̄lm Orte | „ | „ |
| | Elizth fferiman vid | 24 | „ |
| | Jaine Kilshaw vid | 25 | „ |
| | John Aiscroft | „ | „ |
| pur̄ | Elizth Mowdisley | 27 | „ |
| | Robert Woodes | 28 | „ |
| pur̄ | Gilb̄ Garrard fi: Cuth: in ecc lata | 30 | „ |
| pur̄ | Hugh Barton fi: John | „ | „ |

| | | | |
|---|---|---|---|
| | Willm Hoolme in ecclia | 2 | December |
| | Eliz$^{th}$ Marclough vid | 4 | „ |
| pur | Ewan Hodgeson fi: John in ecclia | 8 | „ |
| | A Chylde of Willm Sutch | 9 | „ |
| pur | Raffe Killshaw | 15 | „ |
| | John Shurlicars in ecclia | 16 | „ |
| | Margerie Gobin in ecclia | 23 | „ |
| | Thurstan Gobin in ecclia | 24 | „ |
| | John Hardman | 29 | „ |
| | Eliz$^{th}$ Hoolme in ecclia | „ | „ |
| 347 | Alis Lathom vx$^{9}$ | 5 | Januarie |
| | Ellin Watkinson vid | 15 | „ |
| pur | Emlin Barton | 17 | „ |
| | Eliz$^{th}$ Lathwhat vx$^{9}$ Tho: | 30 | „ |
| | Izabell Bagilay | „ | „ |
| pur | Edw: Prescot | 2 | ffebruarie |
| | Emlin Smallsha vx$^{9}$ Rob | 3 | „ |
| | A Chyld of Mhill Scarsbreck | 22 | „ |
| | Margeret Haide vx$^{9}$ in ecclia | 26 | „ |
| nster | Emlin Mowdisley | 28 | „ |
| | Jaine Bycarstaffe vx$^{9}$ Hugh in ecclia | 1 | March |
| | Peeter Haughton in ecclia | 8 | „ |
| | Tho: Hardman | „ | „ |
| pur | Ellin Traves | 13 | „ |
| | A Chyld of Water Lathom | 15 | „ |
| pur | Tho: Lathom in ecclia | 17 | „ |
| | Jamis Aspinwall | 19 | „ |

## 1592.

| | | | |
|---|---|---|---|
| | Tho: Burscough | 25 | March |
| | Jaine Preskot | „ | „ |
| | Henrie Atherton in ecclia | 8 | Aprill |
| pur | Symond Turner | 16 | „ |
| | Margaret Henrieson | 28 | „ |
| | Peeter Aiscroft | „ | „ |
| | Raffe Burscough | 11 | Maye |
| pur | John Higham | 17 | „ |
| | Eliz$^{th}$ Mason vid in ecclia | 18 | „ |
| | A stranger | 21 | „ |
| | Jamis Barton in ecclia | 22 | „ |
| pur | Ric Butler | 27 | „ |
| | Ja: Ascroft | 31 | „ |
| 348 | Margreat Cropp in ecclia | 7 | June |
| | A Chyld of Ric Cropp in ecclia | 11 | „ |
| pur | Sislie Rigbie in ecclia | 14 | „ |
| | Tho: Partingeton | 19 | „ |
| pur | John Smyth in ecclia | 29 | „ |
| | George Nalior in ecclia | 30 | „ |
| | Alis Kellet in ecclia | 4 | July |

John Butler in ecclia ... ... ... ... ... 6 July
Peeter Stanley of Bycarstaf esq^r bur in his chancell ... ... ... ... ... ... ... 24 „
pur Margaret Barton ... ... ... ... ... ... „ „
pur Katherin Mason ... ... ... ... ... ... 8 August
A child of Robt Cowps ... ... ... ... ... 10 „
Tho: Wetherbie ... ... ... ... ... ... 20 „
pur Margaret Shervington ... ... ... ... ... 22 „
. . . Singleton butler at Scarsb in ecclia ... 25 „
. . . Mosse vx[9] John ... ... ... ... ... 28 „
John Orrell in ecclia ... ... ... ... ... „ „
Oliver Ashton in ecclia ... ... ... ... ... 29 „
George Matthew ... ... ... ... ... ... „ „
Anne Chadocke vid in ecclia ... ... ... ... 4 September
Anne Morecroft ... ... ... ... ... ... 5 „
Anne Smyth vid in ecclia ... ... ... ... 6 „
Sislie Allerton vid ... ... ... ... ... 7 „
Katherin Goliebrand in ecclia ... ... ... „ „
Margerie Parker vid ... ... ... ... ... 11 „
Marget Barton vx[9] in ecclia ... ... ... ... 12 „
Alis Taune [?] vx[9] in ecclia ... ... ... ... „ „
Izabell Barker ... ... ... ... ... ... 14 „
Sislie Haile vx[9] in ecclia ... ... ... ... 16 „
Peeter Rigbie in ecclia ... ... ... ... ... 17 „
A chyld of Tho: Jolie ... ... ... ... ... 20 „
Peeter Westhead in ecclia ... ... ... ... 21 „
Jun John Towne ... ... ... ... ... ... „ „
Katherin Sanforth ... ... ... ... ... ... 27 „
Fo. 349 Jamis Shaw ... ... ... ... ... ... 6 October
pur Arther Lowe ... ... ... ... ... ... „ „
A Chyld of Ric Preskot ... ... ... ... ... 8 „
pur Robert Hodgekinson ... ... ... ... ... 9 „
Robert Smulte senior in ecclia ... ... ... 10 „
Jun John Harieson ... ... ... ... ... ... 15 „
Margaret Donkon vx[9] ... ... ... ... ... „ „
pur Robart Gill ... ... ... ... ... ... 23 „
pur Anne Sanforth ... ... ... ... ... ... „ „
Henrie Mollinex ... ... ... ... ... ... 28 „
Tho: Ascroft in ecclia ... ... ... ... ... 31 „
Katherin Sutch in ecclia ... ... ... ... ... 4 November
Izabell Hankin vx[9] ... ... ... ... ... ... 5 „
pur Margaret Coockeson ... ... ... ... ... 8 „
Jenet Stopforth in ecclia ... ... ... ... „ „
pur Margerie Dowber in ecclia ... ... ... ... 16 „
Tho: Whitefeld ... ... ... ... ... ... „ „
pur Hen: Sankey in ecclia ... ... ... ... ... 25 „
Anne Sankey vx[9] in ecclia ... ... ... ... 26 „
pur Ric Hodgeson ... ... ... ... ... ... 3 December
pur Jamis Jackeson ... ... ... ... ... ... 6 „

| | | |
|---|---|---|
| Alis Windrow ... ... ... ... ... ... ... | 24 | December |
| John Swifte in ecclia ... ... ... ... ... | 30 | " |
| Eliz[th] Cockeson vid ... ... ... ... ... ... | 1 | Januarie |
| Jaine Whytestons in ecclia ... ... ... ... | 3 | " |
| Expõ Biggbie in ecclia ... ... ... ... ... | 6 | " |
| Marget Pendleburie vx[9] ... ... ... ... ... | 19 | " |
| Gilbert Beconsaw ... ... ... ... ... ... | 22 | " |
| Lenord Tatum in the chancell ... ... ... | 28 | " |
| Margerie Talior fi: Witt in ecclia ... ... ... | 30 | " |
| Tho: Ascough in ecclia ... ... ... ... ... | 10 | ffebruarie |
| Eliz[th] Whytestones in ecclia ... ... ... ... | 11 | " |
| Anne Morecroft ... ... ... ... ... ... ... | 18 | " |
| Margaret Pawsey ... ... ... ... ... ... ... | 23 | " |
| Eliz[th] Preskoth vx[9] ... ... ... ... ... ... | 1 | March |
| Witłm Sutch ... ... ... ... ... ... ... ... | 3 | " |
| A chyld of Tho: ffidler ... ... ... ... ... | 6 | " |
| Rodger Haughton ... ... ... ... ... ... ... | " | " |
| Hector Mowdisley in ecclia ... ... ... ... | 9 | " |
| Phillip Mowdisley ... ... ... ... ... ... | 19 | " |

## 1593.

| | | |
|---|---|---|
| A Chyld of Jamis Jackeson in ecclia ... ... | 30 | March |
| Peeter Care ... ... ... ... ... ... ... | 6 | Aprill |
| Alis Farcloughe vid: in ecclia ... ... ... | 7 | " |
| Thrustram Barton ... ... ... ... ... ... | 14 | " |
| Tho: Keckwicke ... ... ... ... ... ... ... | 16 | " |
| Peeter Lathfott ... ... ... ... ... ... ... | 17 | " |
| Robt Woodes ... ... ... ... ... ... ... ... | 22 | " |
| Katherin Butler vx[9] Tho: in ecclia ... ... | 25 | " |
| Raph Melinge vido in ecclia ... ... ... ... | 29 | " |
| Howcrofte Watkinson fi: Hughe ... ... ... | 1 | Maye |
| Hughe Askrofte in ecclia ... ... ... ... | 5 | " |
| Anne Whitstons in ecclia ... ... ... ... | 8 | " |
| A child of Tho: Pendleberis ... ... ... ... | 26 | " |
| Tho: Askrofte ... ... ... ... ... ... ... | 29 | " |
| Margreat Morecrofte vx[9] Ric in ecclia ... ... | 30 | " |
| A child of James Barton ... ... ... ... ... | 3 | June |
| Tho: Sutche in ecclia ... ... ... ... ... | 13 | " |
| Hugh Aspinwall in chañ ... ... ... ... ... | 20 | " |
| Genatt Blackledge vx[9] ... ... ... ... ... | 1 | Julye |
| Anne Barton ... ... ... ... ... ... ... | " | " |
| Witłm Mosoke in ecclia ... ... ... ... | 12 | " |
| Hughe Turnebridge ... ... ... ... ... ... | " | " |
| Edeth fforshawe vx[9] In ecclia ... ... ... | 15 | " |
| Margerie Hollande ... ... ... ... ... ... | " | " |
| Izabell Hayton vido in ecclia ... ... ... ... | 24 | " |
| John Mosse in ecclia ... ... ... ... ... | 28 | " |
| Katherine Haill fi: Ellis in ecclia ... ... ... | 31 | " |

| | | | |
|---|---|---|---|
| | Margerie Stophford fi: | 6 | Auguste |
| | Tho: Wallas | 12 | ” |
| | John Wareinge | 18 | ” |
| | Anne Hill vx$^9$ Hen: | ” | ” |
| Juve | John Barton | 26 | ” |
| | A child of George Croppes | 31 | ” |
| | Ric̃ Eccleston | 6 | September |
| | James Lancaster in eccl̃ia | 15 | ” |
| | Anne Cropp in eccl̃ia | 18 | ” |
| | Elene Rachdaill | 19 | ” |
| vx$^9$ | Anne Ascrofte in eccl̃ia | 23 | ” |
| | James Hey in eccl̃ia | ” | ” |
| vido | Jaine Sutton | 30 | ” |
| sp: | Jonie Waynwright fi: Georg in eccl̃ia | 14 | October |
| vx$^9$ | Katherin Martindayle in eccl̃ia | ” | ” |
| Pu: | Alis Lathom in eccl̃ia | 18 | ” |
| | Tho: Swifte in eccl̃ia | 28 | ” |
| | Willm Aspinwall late clarke in ecclia | 19 | November |
| | Henrie Mosocke gent in eccl̃ia | 22 | ” |
| pu: | John Preskotte | 26 | ” |
| Fo. 352 | Robert Gill | 3 | December |
| | The funerall of the Right Honerable Henrie late Earle of Derbie in the new Chancell* | 4 | ” |
| | A childe of Tho: Gilles | 6 | ” |
| | Tho: ffishe | 7 | ” |
| | Tho: Sefton gent in eccl̃ia | ” | ” |
| | Jaine Swifte vid in eccl̃ia | ” | ” |
| | Claris vx$^9$ Jamis Sutch in eccl̃ia | 11 | ” |
| pur | Margaret Gollie | 13 | ” |
| | Anthoney Gill | 15 | ” |
| | . . . Haidon vid in eccl̃ia | ” | ” |
| | Alis Prescot fi: Tho: | 16 | ” |
| | Tho: Gill | ” | ” |
| | Margaret Westhead | 19 | ” |
| Juũ | Margaret Alerton | 22 | ” |
| | Margaret Kenion | 23 | ” |
| | A child of Boothes | ” | ” |
| | A childe of Hen: Barkers in ecclia bast | 24 | ” |
| | John Lea in eccl̃ia | 31 | ” |
| | Gabrell Barton | 3 | Januarie |
| | Katherin Haughton vx$^9$ Antho: in eccl̃ia | 12 | ” |
| | Jam: Morecroft fi: Ric̃ in eccl̃ia | 15 | ” |
| | Jaine Hoolme vid | 22 | ” |
| | Eliz$^{th}$ Shaw | 30 | ” |
| pur̃ | Henrie Hesketh fi: Tho: | ” | ” |
| | Jaine Killshaw fi: John in eccl̃ia | 9 | ffebruarie |
| | Izabell Whytstones | 10 | ” |

* In the left hand margin of the original there is written in pencil the following:—“1st Earl in the Derby Chapel.”

|  |  |  |
|---|---|---|
| John Hill fi : Ric̄ | 10 | ffebruarie |
| A Childe of Homfrey Goulbron | 15 | „ |
| Anne Hill vid | 16 | „ |
| George fforshae in ecc̄lia | 22 | „ |
| Willm̄ Halworth in ecc̄lia | 25 | „ |
| John Hey fi : Tho : in ecc̄lia | 26 | „ |
| John Sutch fi : George pur̄ | 5 | March |
| Hugh Mowdisley fi : Hen : | 10 | „ |
| Margerie Jackeson vid in ecc̄lia | 14 | „ |
| Jaine Vackeffeeld fi : Rob̄t | 15 | „ |
| Raffe Ashton | 18 | „ |

## 1594.

|  |  |  |
|---|---|---|
| Jamis Stopforth in ecc̄lia | 28 | March |
| John Baker | 5 | Aprill |
| Anne Alerton vx$^{9}$ Tho : | 7 | „ |
| Elin ffarer | 13 | „ |
| Jaine Sutch fi : Lucke | 26 | „ |
| Eliz$^{th}$ Cubon vx$^{9}$ John in ecc̄lia | 11 | Maye |
| Margaret Whitffelde | 16 | „ |
| A Chyld of Tho : Killshawes | 17 | „ |
| Margerie Allerton | 18 | „ |
| Margaret Ascough fi : Tho : in ecc̄lia | 24 | „ |
| The funerall of the Right honorable Fardnand late Earle of Derbie | 28 | „ |
| Eliz$^{th}$ Howte | 3 | June |
| Tho : Burscough gent in ecc̄lia | 15 | „ |
| Emlin Woosey vx$^{9}$ Hen : in ecc̄lia | 17 | „ |
| Jenet Huton | 18 | „ |
| Alis Swifte vid in ecc̄lia | 26 | „ |
| Agnes Cocket | 29 | „ |
| Jaine Garrerd in ecc̄lia | 2 | Julye |
| Margerie Cropp | 13 | „ |
| Henrie Hill in ecc̄lia | 20 | „ |
| Catherin Smallshaw in ecc̄lia | „ | „ |
| Margerie Sutch in ecc̄lia | „ | „ |
| Jaine Sutch vid in ecc̄lia | 24 | „ |
| Jaine Plomb̄e | 27 | „ |
| Rob̄t Butler in ecclia | 28 | „ |
| Tho : Cocket | 4 | August |
| A pore child | 15 | „ |
| A Child of Rob̄t Harisons | 16 | „ |
| A pore wooman | 23 | „ |
| Jonie Robinson | 28 | „ |
| Jaine Woosey fi : Hen : in ecc̄lia | 29 | „ |
| A Child of Ewans Lea | 6 | September |
| Margaret Hoolme in ecclia | 12 | „ |
| Alis Abraham in ecc̄lia | 13 | „ |

| | | | |
|---|---|---|---|
| | Eliz[th] Robinson ... ... ... ... ... ... | 17 | September |
| | Izabell Stanton ... ... ... ... ... ... | ,, | ,, |
| | A Childe of Jam: Coockesons ... ... ... | 22 | ,, |
| pur̃ | John Greaves ... ... ... ... ... ... ... ... | 26 | ,, |
| | Hen: ffletcher fi: Myles ... ... ... ... ... ... | 9 | October |
| Ju: | Jon Withingeton in ecclia ... ... ... ... | 27 | ,, |
| | A chyld of M[r] Edw: Stanley of y[e] more hall... | 10 | November |
| | Tho: Barwicke ... ... ... ... ... ... | ,, | ,, |
| pur̃ | Jaine Preskot ... ... ... ... ... ... ... ... | 12 | ,, |
| Juũ | Anne Mowdisley in ecclia ... ... ... ... | 15 | ,, |
| | Izabell Cropp in ecclia ... ... ... ... ... ... | 21 | ,, |
| | A Chyld of Peeter Rowes in ecclia ... ... | ,, | ,, |
| | A Chyd of Byhan Webster ... ... ... ... | 24 | ,, |
| | Alis Cowp vx[9] Hugh in ecclia ... ... ... | 6 | December |
| | Willm Breykell in ecclia ... ... ... ... ... | 14 | ,, |
| | Margerie Marclough vid ... ... ... ... ... | 20 | ,, |
| pur̃ | Hugh Wildinge fi: Hen: ... ... ... ... ... | 23 | ,, |
| | Anne Cropp fi: Raffe ... ... ... ... ... | 26 | ,, |
| | Raffe Mercer ... ... ... ... ... ... ... | 28 | ,, |
| | Trymor Leadbetter in ecclia ... ... ... ... | 4 | Januarie |
| Juũ | Tho: Haide in ecclia ... ... ... ... ... | 7 | ,, |
| | Emlin Shaw vx[9] Jo: in ecclia ... ... ... | 8 | ,, |
| | Izabell Mowdisley vid ... ... ... ... ... | 15 | ,, |
| spinst | Ellin Key in ecclia ... ... ... ... ... ... | 20 | ,, |
| | Jam: Cropp in ecclia ... ... ... ... ... | 22 | ,, |
| | A child of Ric̃ Preskote ... ... ... ... ... | 26 | ,, |
| | John Whytestones in ecclia ... ... ... ... | 27 | ,, |
| | A child of John Rutters ... ... ... ... ... | ,, | ,, |
| Juũ | Tho: Lunte ... ... ... ... ... ... ... ... | 30 | ,, |
| | Gabrell Ambrose fi: Ri: vic: in ecclia ... | 6 | ffebruarie |
| | A pore wooman ... ... ... ... ... ... | ,, | ,, |
| | A Childe of Robrt Hollanes ... ... ... ... | 8 | ,, |
| | Henrie Smyth fi: Tho: ... ... ... ... ... | ,, | ,, |
| Fo. 355 | Mowde Townley vid in ecclia ... ... ... ... | 9 | ,, |
| | Katherin Haid vx[9] Ric̃ in ecclia ... ... ... | 11 | ,, |
| | Two Children of John Ascough ... ... ... | 13 | ,, |
| | Anne Killshaw fi: Jo: in ecclia ... ... ... | 14 | ,, |
| | Izabell Blundell vid ... ... ... ... ... ... | 15 | ,, |
| | Elin Ellam fi: Raffe ... ... ... ... ... | 16 | ,, |
| | Jaine Cowdocke fi: Will ... ... ... ... | 19 | ,, |
| | A Chylde of Tho: Buklers ... ... ... ... | 21 | ,, |
| | Margaret Lathom vid ... ... ... ... ... | 23 | ,, |
| Juũ | Edw: Haide in ecclia ... ... ... ... ... | 24 | ,, |
| | Tho: fformbey ... ... ... ... ... ... ... | 25 | ,, |
| | Jamis Swift fi: John ... ... ... ... ... | 26 | ,, |
| | Richard ffletcher in ecclia ... ... ... ... | ,, | ,, |
| | Towe Children of Will Sutch ... ... ... ... | 2 | March |
| | Eliz[th] Swifte vid ... ... ... ... ... ... | 3 | ,, |
| | Ric̃ Haid in ecclia ... ... ... ... ... ... | 8 | ,, |

| | | |
|---|---|---|
| Henrie Hunter fi: Tho: in ecclia ... ... ... | 8 | March |
| Ja: Gill ... ... ... ... ... ... ... ... | 9 | „ |
| Gualter Haide in ecclia ... ... ... ... ... | „ | „ |
| Will Waynewright in ecclia ... ... ... ... | 11 | „ |
| Sislie Wetherbie In eclia ... ... ... ... | „ | „ |
| Jaine Halworth vid ... ... ... ... ... ... | 14 | „ |
| Ellin Killshaw fi: Ja: ... ... ... ... ... | „ | „ |
| Silvester Wailch ... ... ... ... ... ... | 18 | „ |
| Ric Layland ... ... ... ... ... ... ... | 24 | „ |

## 1595.

| | | |
|---|---|---|
| Peeter Blundell in ecclia ... ... ... ... ... | 31 | March |
| Alis Stopforth vid in ecclia ... ... ... ... | „ | „ |
| Anne Watkinson vid ... ... ... ... ... ... | 1 | Aprill |
| Alis Lea vid in ecclia ... ... ... ... ... | 3 | „ |
| Hugh Whitestones ... ... ... ... ... ... | 4 | „ |
| Maria Withingeton in ecclia ... ... ... ... | 7 | „ |
| Katherin Richards doughter ... ... ... ... | 11 | „ |
| A Childe of Willm Hoolms y<sup>e</sup> yonger ... ... | 16 | „ |
| A Chyld of Tho: Westhead of Bycar tanner in ecclia ... ... ... ... ... ... ... | 19 | „ |
| A Chyld of Tho: Heyes in ecclia ... ... ... | 21 | „ |
| A Chyld of John Aiscrofte in ecclia ... ... | „ | „ |
| Robert Gyles ... ... ... ... ... ... ... | 26 | „ |
| A Child of Charles Ireland base gotten ... ... | 27 | „ |
| Richard Smulte in ecclia ... ... ... ... ... | 28 | „ |
| Anne Cowsan fi: John ... ... ... ... ... ... | 3 | Maye |
| Robert ffarclough ... ... ... ... ... ... | 4 | „ |
| Ric Atherton fi: John ... ... ... ... ... | 6 | „ |
| Alis Croocke ... ... ... ... ... ... ... | 7 | „ |
| Ric Aiscrofte in ecclia ... ... ... ... ... | 10 | „ |
| Tho: ffrannce in ecclia ... ... ... ... ... | 12 | „ |
| Ric Aspinwall in ecclia ... ... ... ... ... | 15 | „ |
| Tho: Smyth in ecclia ... ... ... ... ... | 25 | „ |
| Ric Bower ... ... ... ... ... ... ... | 5 | June |
| Ellin Gill vx<sup>9</sup> Cristopher ... ... ... ... ... | 12 | „ |
| . . . Lailond in ecclia ... ... ... ... | 13 | „ |
| Willm Nalior in ecclia ... ... ... ... ... | „ | „ |
| Homfrey Crowsley in ecclia ... ... ... ... | „ | „ |
| Ellin Simkin ... ... ... ... ... ... ... | 18 | „ |
| Tho: ffletcher in ecclia ... ... ... ... ... | 27 | „ |
| Margaret Traves ... ... ... ... ... ... | 29 | „ |
| Ja: Ascough in ecclia ... ... ... ... ... | 30 | „ |
| Robert Talior in ecclia ... ... ... ... ... | „ | „ |
| Elin Mosse vid in y<sup>e</sup> Chancell ... ... ... ... | 2 | Julye |
| Willm Spencer in ecclia ... ... ... ... ... | 4 | „ |
| Peeter Pinner ... ... ... ... ... ... ... | 9 | „ |
| vx<sup>9</sup> Jaine Aiscough in ecclia ... ... ... ... | 10 | „ |

| | | | |
|---|---|---|---|
| | Marget Stanley fi: Edw: Junnor gent in his Chancell | 11 | Julye |
| pur | Tho: Haughton in eccl̄ia | 29 | „ |
| | Katherin Barton vid | 3 | August |
| pur̄ | Eliz$^{th}$ Aspinwell fi: Ric̄ bast | 5 | „ |

Fo.*357 * A blank of two inches left at the top of this page.

| | | | |
|---|---|---|---|
| | Ellin Aiscough | 5 | September |
| sp: | Jaine Mowdisley in eccl̄ia | 10 | „ |
| pur̄ | Margaret Burscough | 25 | „ |
| sp: | A chyld of Will̄ Mollinex in eccl̄ia | 26 | „ |
| | Jenet ffarer vx$^{9}$ Maye [*sic*] | 29 | „ |
| | Anne Gobin vx$^{9}$ in ecclia | 7 | October |
| | George Penketh | 8 | „ |
| | Edw: ffloyd | 18 | „ |
| | A Chylde of Homfrey Piningeton | 19 | „ |
| | Sislie Windrow vid | 21 | „ |
| | Ottuwall Bower | 1 | November |
| | Richard Sutch | 5 | „ |
| | A Chyld of Gilb̄ Killshaw | 6 | „ |
| | A Chyld of Cristopher Waringes bast | 12 | „ |
| | Margerie Kocket | 19 | „ |
| | Jaine Scarsbrecke vx$^{9}$ | 23 | „ |
| | Henrie Showe | 4 | December |
| | Robart Wardeman | 8 | „ |
| | John Spencer in eccl̄ia | 9 | „ |
| | Katherin Hey fi: John in eccl̄ia | 13 | „ |
| | Margaret Scarsbrecke fi: | 19 | „ |
| | Robert Goare fi Jo: in ecclia | 25 | „ |
| | Marget Shaw vx$^{9}$ Hugh in ecclia | 2 | Januarie |
| pur̄ | Alis Gollie fi: Tho: | „ | „ |
| | Alic Lanc̄ fi: Jo: in eccl̄ia | 8 | „ |
| | A poare man | 10 | „ |
| | A Chylde of Rodger Lea | 26 | „ |
| Fo. 358 | Rob̄t Lay fi Ewan in ecclia | 4 | ffebruarie |
| | Tho: Butler in eccl̄ia | „ | „ |
| | vx$^{9}$ Rob̄t Shawe in eccl̄ia | 15 | „ |
| | Eliz$^{th}$ ffletcher vx$^{9}$ Rob̄t in eccl̄ia | 18 | „ |
| | Hugh Chadoke in ecclia | 22 | „ |
| | Rob̄t Rylandes | 23 | „ |
| | A childof Tho: ffidlers | 24 | „ |
| | Margreat Wrighte vx$^{9}$ Jo: in eccl̄ia | 25 | „ |
| | A child of Rob̄rt ffletchers in eccl̄ia | „ | „ |
| | Rob̄t Haslgreaue in eccl̄ia | 27 | „ |
| | M$^{r}$ Tho: Mossocke in eccl̄ia | 3 | Marche |
| | Jone & Joanie Banckes fi Ja: bast | 6 | „ |
| | Jaine Preskott | 15 | „ |

## 1596.

| | | |
|---|---|---|
| Joanie Sankie fi : Ric̃ in eccl̃ia ... ... ... | 30 | Marche |
| Joanie Wilkinson fi : Ric̃ bast ... ... ... ... ... | 2 | Aprill |
| Alexander Tomson ... ... ... ... ... ... ... | 6 | „ |
| Alis Atherton ... ... ... ... ... ... ... ... | 17 | „ |
| Robert Whytestones fi : Ric̃ ... ... ... ... ... | 18 | „ |
| Margreat Lathom fi : Ric̃ ... ... ... ... ... | 21 | „ |
| Mr Alexander Scarsbrecke in his ffathers chancell ... ... ... ... ... ... ... ... ... | 28 | „ |
| Katherin Aspinwall vid ... ... ... ... ... ... | 4 | Maye |
| Will̃m Westhead ... ... ... ... ... ... ... | 9 | „ |
| Raffe Withingeton ... ... ... ... ... ... ... | 10 | „ |
| Elizth Turner fi : Omfrey ... ... ... ... ... ... | 15 | „ |
| Elizth Prescot fi : Hugh ... ... ... ... ... ... | 23 | „ |
| Myles Mawdisley fi : Rob̃t ... ... ... ... ... | 10 | June |
| Ellin Asshorst fi : Tho : ... ... ... ... ... ... | 12 | „ |
| Jenet Houghton in eccl̃ia ... ... ... ... ... | 18 | „ |
| Elizth Mowdisley vx9 in ecclia ... ... ... ... | 21 | „ |
| Batholomew Hoolme ... ... ... ... ... ... | 24 | „ |
| Robert Bonnde ... ... ... ... ... ... ... ... ... | 7 | July |
| Margerie Cropp vid in eccl̃ia ... ... ... ... ... | 8 | „ |
| A Chyld of Mat Lathoms ... ... ... ... ... | 9 | „ |
| Nicolas Shawe in eccl̃ia ... ... ... ... ... ... | 12 | „ |
| Ric̃ Coockeson in eccl̃ia ... ... ... ... ... ... | „ | „ |
| Margerie Mowdisley vid in eccl̃ia ... ... ... ... | 23 | „ |
| Will̃m Griffin ... ... ... ... ... ... ... ... | 24 | „ |
| Ellin Killshaw fi : Jam : ... ... ... ... ... ... | 27 | „ |
| John Werall in eccl̃ia ... ... ... ... ... ... | 28 | „ |
| John Barnes fi : Hug in eccl̃ia ... ... ... ... | 30 | „ |
| Elizth Dowber fi : Will̃ ... ... ... ... ... ... | „ | „ |
| Tho Hoolme fi : Ric̃ ... ... ... ... ... ... | 3 | Auguste |
| Cuthbart Garthife ... ... ... ... ... ... ... | 17 | „ |
| Jamis Robinson in eccl̃ia ... ... ... ... ... | 21 | „ |
| Lettis Holland vid in eccl̃ia ... ... ... ... ... | 23 | „ |
| Margerie Martindaile vx9 ... ... ... ... ... | 2 | September |
| Tho : Gill in eccl̃ia ... ... ... ... ... ... ... | 5 | „ |
| A Childe of Edw : Halsall ... ... ... ... ... | „ | „ |
| A Child of George Haughton in eccl̃ia ... ... | 7 | „ |
| Margerie Smyth in eccl̃ia ... ... ... ... ... | 12 | „ |
| John Yate ... ... ... ... ... ... ... ... | 19 | „ |
| Margaret Gill ... ... ... ... ... ... ... | 25 | „ |
| Anne Wright vid in eccl̃ia ... ... ... ... ... | 30 | „ |
| Tho : Dughtie fi : Nical in eccl̃ia ... ... ... | 9 | October |
| Elizth Rycrofte fi Will̃ ... ... ... ... ... ... | 6 | November |
| Edw : Blackeledge fi : Ewan in eccl̃ia ... ... | 7 | „ |
| Ric̃ Werall fi : Ric̃ in eccl̃ia ... ... ... ... ... | 16 | „ |
| Will̃m Longeworth in eccl̃ia ... ... ... ... ... | 20 | „ |

| | | | |
|---|---|---|---|
| | Wiłłm Mollinex | 24 | November |
| | Alis Wildinge fi: Wiłł in eccłia | 25 | „ |
| | A doughter of Sr Jamis Martindaill | 26 | „ |
| | Agnes Bynson | 27 | „ |
| | Amis Garnet | 29 | „ |
| Fo. 360 | John Lathom in eccłia | 1 | December |
| | A Chylde of Henrie Drapers | 3 | „ |
| | Wiłłm Aspinwall in eccłia | „ | „ |
| | Ric̃ Tomson fi Wiłł | 6 | „ |
| | Margerie Breykell in eccłia | 9 | „ |
| | Marget Leadbetter | 13 | „ |
| Juū | Tho: Hill | 18 | „ |
| | Elizth Jackeson vxꝰ Ric̃ in eccłia | 25 | „ |
| | Tho: Harison in eccłia | 30 | „ |
| | Peeter Barton fi: Rob̃ in eccłia | „ | „ |
| | John Mowdisley in eccłia | 1 | Januarie |
| | A pore wooman | „ | „ |
| | Emlin Higham fi: Wiłł | 6 | „ |
| | Alis Plumbe vid | 11 | „ |
| | Margaret Gollie fi: Rob̃ in eccłia | 16 | „ |
| | Anne Martindaile fi: Hugh in eccłia | 17 | „ |
| | Sislie Eccleston | 26 | „ |
| | Jamis Smyth | 21 | „ |
| | Anne Lancaster fi: Jo: in eccłia | 31 | „ |
| | Agnes Graystocke | 5 | ffebruarie |
| | vxꝰ Henrie Arnould | 8 | „ |
| | Henrie Barton fi: Gilb̃ | 14 | „ |
| | Wiłłm Swifte in eccłia | 15 | „ |
| | Edw: Masonn fi: Ja: | 17 | „ |
| | Katherin Greave vxꝰ Ric̃ | 20 | „ |
| | Ellin Barton fi: Peeter | „ | „ |
| | John Coban in eccłia | 22 | „ |
| | George Lathwhat fi: Hen: in eccłia | 25 | „ |
| | Margaret Ormishaw in eccłia | „ | „ |
| | Jaine Swifte vxꝰ Phillip in ecclia | 26 | „ |
| | Anne Ascrofte | 27 | „ |
| | Elizth Alcker | 28 | „ |
| | Anne Traves fi: Ric̃ | 4 | March |
| | Elis Burie | 6 | „ |
| | Jaine Kocket fi: Henrie | 9 | „ |
| Fo. 361 | Symond Towne in eccłia | 10 | „ |
| | Marie Kocket | 13 | „ |
| | Margaret Sutch vid | „ | „ |
| | Anne Powsey fi Ric̃ | „ | „ |
| | Peeter Porter in eccłia | 14 | „ |
| | Ric̃ Gill fi: Hen: in eccłia | „ | „ |
| | Widow Shaw | 15 | „ |
| | Marget Haughton vid | 17 | „ |
| | A Chylde of Rodger Rydinges | 20 | „ |

| | | | |
|---|---|---|---|
| | vx$^{9}$ Hugh Morecroft vid | 22 | March |
| | Henrie Alker | 24 | ” |
| | Anne Irland fi : John | ” | ” |

## 1597.

| | | | |
|---|---|---|---|
| | Jaine Bowker | 31 | March |
| | Margerie Gill vid | 2 | Aprill |
| | Eliz$^{th}$ Cowldocke fi : Wiłł | 4 | ” |
| | Mathew ffarer | 5 | ” |
| | John Harison | 6 | ” |
| | Symond Mowdisley | 10 | ” |
| | George Woodes fi : Wiłł | 11 | ” |
| | Edw : Mowdisley in ecc̄lia | 13 | ” |
| | Eliz$^{th}$ Cropp vid | 14 | ” |
| | Eliz$^{th}$ Hey | 26 | ” |
| | Ellin Blundell | 29 | ” |
| | John Aiscroft fi : Hugh | ” | ” |
| | George Craine et vx$^{9}$ eius in ecc̄lia | 1 | Maye |
| | John Letherbarow | 3 | ” |
| | John Gleaste | 4 | ” |
| | Henrie Diket fi : Wiłł in ecc̄lia | 7 | ” |
| | Edw : Hill in ecc̄lia | 8 | ” |
| | Marget Rob̄in vid in ecc̄lia | 13 | ” |
| | Edw : Plumbe | ” | ” |
| | Izabell Hoolme | ” | ” |
| | A chyld of Davies Gill | 15 | ” |
| | Ric̃ Mellinge | ” | ” |
| | Anne Stanley vx$^{9}$ Wiłł in ecc̄lia | 21 | ” |
| | Ric̃ Kewquicke fi : Wiłł | 31 | ” |
| | Jamis Hatton | ” | ” |
| 362 | Jaine Lathwhat fi Robert in ecc̄lia pur̃ | 2 | June |
| pur̃ | Marie Lathwhat fi : Jam̃ in ecc̄lia | 4 | ” |
| | Anne Hoolme in ecc̄lia | 14 | ” |
| | A chyld of Ric̃ Vooe | 21 | ” |
| | Jaine Robinson | ” | ” |
| | Nicolas Darwayne fi : John | ” | ” |
| pur̃ | Katherin Preskoth | 22 | ” |
| | George Stopforth fi : Wiłł in ecc̄lia | 25 | ” |
| | Eliz$^{th}$ Kellet vx$^{9}$ Ric̃ in ecc̄lia | 29 | ” |
| pur̃ | Margaret Cropp in ecc̄lia | 2 | July |
| | Katherin Sutch vx$^{9}$ Wiłł in ecc̄lia | ” | ” |
| | Jaine Morecrofte vid | 10 | ” |
| pur̃ | Margerie Skelton | 14 | ” |
| | Hugh Cropp fi : George in ecc̄lia | ” | ” |
| | Jienet Smyth vid in ecc̄lia | 17 | ” |
| pur̃ | Jaine Preskot | 26 | ” |
| | George Cropp | ” | ” |
| pur̃ | Jamis Hulme | 29 | ” |

o

| | | | |
|---|---|---|---|
| | Margaret Jackeson xꝰ [*sic*] Ja : in ecclia ... | 5 | August |
| | Gilƀ Barton ... | 8 | „ |
| pur | Wiłłm Jackeson in eccłia ... | 18 | „ |
| | A Chyld of Tho : Jolies ... | „ | „ |
| | Godfrey Atherton ... | 20 | „ |
| Juū | Anne Blvndell ... | 24 | „ |
| | Ewan Langley in ecclia ... | 28 | „ |
| | Alis Prescot vid ... | „ | „ |
| pur̃ | Wiłłm Jackeson ... | 29 | „ |
| pur̃ | Hugh Mason ... | 30 | „ |
| pur̃ | Ric̃ Mason ... | 31 | „ |
| pur̃ | Henrie and Elnor Milner ... | 3 | September |
| | A pore manne ... | 4 | „ |
| pur̃ | Alis Blundell ... | 6 | „ |
| | Alis Mollinex ... | 7 | „ |
| | Alis Lunte vxꝰ Hen ... | 8 | „ |
| | Jaine Milner vxꝰ ... | 16 | „ |
| | Dorethie Milner fi : Tho : ... | 18 | „ |
| Fo. 363 | Gabriell Lithom pur̃ ... | „ | „ |
| | Anne Mollinex vxꝰ in eccłia ... | 21 | „ |
| pur̃ | John Mason ... | 22 | „ |
| | Peeter Cropp in eccłia ... | 23 | „ |
| | Charles Droning in eccłia ... | 25 | „ |
| | Katherin Smulte vid in eccłia ... | 26 | „ |
| | Margaret Waringe vxꝰ ... | 6 | October |
| | Hugh ffarclough ... | 7 | „ |
| | A pore chylde ... | 9 | „ |
| | Ja : Jackeson in eccłia ... | 10 | „ |
| | Ric̃ Irland in eccłia ... | 12 | „ |
| | Marie Abraham vxꝰ in eccłia ... | 13 | „ |
| Juū | John Gorsutch in eccłia ... | 14 | „ |
| | A pore chyld ... | „ | „ |
| | Ellin Alerton pawp ... | 15 | „ |
| | Margaret Bootle vxꝰ Roƀt in y$^e$ high Chañ ... | 16 | „ |
| Juū | Tho : Westhead ... | 24 | „ |
| pur̃ | Henrie Windrow ... | 27 | „ |
| pur̃ | ffrances ffarer ... | „ | „ |
| | Ellin Smyth in eccłia ... | „ | „ |
| | Margerie Blvndell vxꝰ ... | 29 | „ |
| | Eideth Holland in ecclia ... | 31 | „ |
| | A doughter of Raffe mason in ecclia ... | „ | „ |
| | Edm : Smulte in eccłia ... | 3 | November |
| | Margaret ffletcher vxꝰ Hugh in eccłia ... | 5 | „ |
| | Katherin Hesketh ... | 8 | „ |
| | Alis Ascroft vid ... | „ | „ |
| | ffrances Scarsbrecke vid in eccłia ... | 10 | „ |
| | Gilƀ Greene ... | „ | „ |
| | Eliz$^{th}$ Scarsbreck vxꝰ ... | „ | „ |
| | Jenet Wright vid ... | 18 | „ |

| | | | |
|---|---|---|---|
| | A Child of Rodger Lea in eccl̄ia | 22 | November |
| | Alis Craine fi: Ranould | ” | ” |
| | Ellin Lea vx⁹ in eccl̄ia | 24 | ” |
| | A Childe of Tho: Allerton | 29 | ” |
| | Tho: Hallworth in eccl̄ia | 30 | ” |
| 364 | Godfrey Atherton in ecclia | 2 | December |
| | Robert Garerd | 3 | ” |
| pur̄ | Anne Walworth fi: Rodge in eccl̄ia | 5 | ” |
| | A pore wooman | ” | ” |
| | Tho: Robinson in eccl̄ia | 6 | ” |
| | A Chyld of Wil̄l̄m Robinsons | 8 | ” |
| | Hugh Wright | 9 | ” |
| | Anne Adamson vid in eccl̄ia | ” | ” |
| | A pore Chylde of one Lea | 12 | ” |
| | Edw: Morcroft fi: Tho: | 15 | ” |
| | Claris Cropp and her Chyld in the high Chancell | 18 | ” |
| | Another pore chylde of one Lea | ” | ” |
| | Katherin Westhead vx⁹ in eccl̄ia | ” | ” |
| | A wench of Symonde Mawdisley | 21 | ” |
| | A chyld of John Bal̄shaw | ” | ” |
| | A chyld of Symond Modisley | 24 | ” |
| | Margerie Robinson fi: Wil̄l̄ | 30 | ” |
| | Ellen Griffith vid | ” | ” |
| | Hugh Martindaile in eccl̄ia | 31 | ” |
| | Ellin Lea fi: Wil̄l̄ | 1 | Januarie |
| | Hen: Robinson in eccl̄ia | 4 | ” |
| | Sislie Smyth fi: Tho: in eccl̄ia | 6 | ” |
| | Ja: Reade | 10 | ” |
| | Ja: Blundell fi: John | 20 | ” |
| | vx⁹ Wil̄l̄m Kekuicke | ” | ” |
| Juū | John Blundell | 22 | ” |
| | Margaret Manninge | 25 | ” |
| | Izabell Rimmer vid | 26 | ” |
| | Eliz^th Hoolme in eccl̄ia | ” | ” |
| | Eliz^th Burie vx⁹ | 28 | ” |
| | A Chyld of Hugh Chadocke | 2 | ffebruarie |
| | Ric̄ Hill | 7 | ” |
| | Katherin Aiscroft fi: Wil̄l̄ in eccl̄ia | ” | ” |
| | Genet Rimmer | ” | ” |
| 365 | A chyld of Symond Mowdisley | 8 | ” |
| | Eliz^th Stopforth fi: Tho: in y^e high Chañ | ” | ” |
| | Cristopher Barton | 11 | ” |
| | George Preskot in eccl̄ia | 13 | ” |
| | Margaret Howlden | ” | ” |
| | Makes Abraham in eccl̄ia | 20 | ” |
| | Eliz^th Marow vx⁹ in eccl̄ia | 21 | ” |
| | Katherin Haide fi: Wil̄l̄ | 22 | ” |
| Juū | Richard Eccleston | 23 | ” |

| | | | |
|---|---|---|---|
| | Henrie Withingtons wyfe ... ... ... ... | 26 | ffebruarie |
| | Jaine Morecroft vx$^{9}$ ... ... ... ... ... ... | 28 | „ |
| | Ellin Croston fi: Hen: ... ... ... ... ... | 1 | March |
| | Marie Shepord fi Hen: ... ... ... ... ... | „ | „ |
| | Alis Wariner vx$^{9}$ ... ... ... ... ... ... | 3 | „ |
| | John Tyrer ... ... ... ... ... ... ... | 4 | „ |
| | Tho: Haughton ... ... ... ... ... ... | 5 | „ |
| Juū | Ric̃ Mowdisley ... ... ... ... ... ... ... | 19 | „ |
| | Emlin Whytesaide vx$^{9}$ in eccłia ... ... ... | 23 | „ |

## 1598.

| | | | |
|---|---|---|---|
| | Ellin Tunstall vx$^{9}$ ... ... ... ... ... ... ... | 29 | March |
| | vx$^{9}$ Henrie Whitstones ... ... ... ... ... | 3 | Aprill |
| Jū | Raphe Badger ... ... ... ... ... ... ... | 5 | „ |
| pu: | Rodger Sutche ... ... ... ... ... ... | 8 | „ |
| | Barbarie Barton vid ... ... ... ... ... ... | 9 | „ |
| | A poore mann ... ... ... ... ... ... ... | 16 | „ |
| | Ranete Kilshawe ... ... ... ... ... ... | 17 | „ |
| | Sislie Mowdinge vido ... ... ... ... ... | 20 | „ |
| | Jaine Edwardson vx$^{9}$ Peeter ... ... ... ... | „ | „ |
| | John Kockett ... ... ... ... ... ... ... | 23 | „ |
| | Eliz$^{th}$ Standnoughte in eccłia ... ... ... ... | 29 | „ |
| Fo. 366 | Margerie Croston ... ... ... ... ... ... | 6 | Maye |
| | Tho: Burskoughe fi: Jo: ... ... ... ... | 7 | „ |
| Ju: | James Alker ... ... ... ... ... ... ... | 9 | „ |
| | Bryhan Webster ... ... ... ... ... ... | 12 | „ |
| | Wiłłm Barton fi: Gilb̃t ... ... ... ... ... | 14 | „ |
| | Tho: Burie ... ... ... ... ... ... ... | „ | „ |
| | A childe of Ric̃ Cowp ... ... ... ... ... | 15 | „ |
| | A child of Wiłłm Dobers in eccłia ... ... ... | 30 | „ |
| | Arthor Styham ... ... ... ... ... ... ... | „ | „ |
| | John Spencer in eccłia ... ... ... ... ... | 6 | June |
| | Anne Haughton vid ... ... ... ... ... ... | 7 | „ |
| pu: | George Prescotte ... ... ... ... ... ... | 10 | „ |
| | Elene Burscough vid ... ... ... ... ... | 18 | „ |
| | Sislie Lathom vx$^{9}$ ... ... ... ... ... ... | 22 | „ |
| pu: | George Swifte ... ... ... ... ... ... ... | 3 | Auguste |
| | Tho: Sutton in eccłia ... ... ... ... ... | 4 | „ |
| | Ric̃ Cropp in ecclia ... ... ... ... ... ... | 14 | „ |
| | Tho: Warinere ... ... ... ... ... ... | 15 | „ |
| | Henrie Stanley of Bicarstafe Esquire bu$^{r}$ 23$^{th}$ of July whose funearl was the 16 Auguste 1598 | | |
| | Anne Cowdocke vx$^{9}$ Wiłł ... ... ... ... ... | 31 | „ |
| | One Kewquicke ... ... ... ... ... ... | 4 | September |
| | Anne Cumberbache vx$^{9}$ in eccłia ... ... ... | 12 | „ |
| pu: | Jo: Crayne in eccłia ... ... ... ... ... | 29 | „ |
| | Marie Jollie vx$^{9}$ ... ... ... ... ... ... | 3 | October |

| | | | |
|---|---|---|---|
| | Jaine Barton vx$^{9}$ in eccl̄ia ... ... ... ... | 6 | October |
| Ju: | Margerie Eues ... ... ... ... ... ... ... ... | ,, | ,, |
| Ju: | Alis Yeatt ... ... ... ... ... ... ... ... ... | 9 | ,, |
| pu: | Eliz$^{th}$ Hollonde bast ... ... ... ... ... ... | 15 | ,, |
| Ju: | Margaret Smyth ... ... ... ... ... ... ... | 19 | ,, |
| | Eline Sankey fi: Ric̄ in eccl̄ia ... ... ... | ,, | ,, |
| | Margrie Alker ... ... ... ... ... ... ... ... | 23 | ,, |
| | Genett ffletcher vid ... ... ... ... ... ... ... | 29 | ,, |
| 367 | Jenet Hvnt vid ... ... ... ... ... ... ... ... | 3 | November |
| | Ann Hodgkinson vx$^{9}$ ... ... ... ... ... ... | 11 | ,, |
| | Rob̄t Shawe in eccl̄ia ... ... ... ... ... ... | 16 | ,, |
| Ju: | Alis Sutche ... ... ... ... ... ... ... ... | 17 | ,, |
| Ju: | Eliz$^{th}$ Lathom ... ... ... ... ... ... ... ... | 20 | ,, |
| pu: | Elene Kewqkeicke ... ... ... ... ... ... ... | 25 | ,, |
| pu: | Ric̄ ffletche in eccl̄ia ... ... ... ... ... ... | 27 | ,, |
| | Tho: Lowe in eccl̄ia ... ... ... ... ... ... | 8 | December |
| pu: | John Blundell ... ... ... ... ... ... ... ... | 9 | ,, |
| Jū | Jaine Swifte in eccl̄ia ... ... ... ... ... ... | 14 | ,, |
| | Rob̄t Hunter ... ... ... ... ... ... ... ... | 15 | ,, |
| | Eliz$^{th}$ Morecrofte fi: Tho: ... ... ... ... ... | 18 | ,, |
| | Alis Harison vx$^{9}$ in eccl̄ia ... ... ... ... | 6 | Januarie |
| | Hughe Gleaste fi: Ellis ... ... ... ... ... ... | 7 | ,, |
| | Rob̄t Blundell in eccl̄ia ... ... ... ... ... ... | 11 | ,, |
| | Eliz$^{th}$ Robinsone vid in eccl̄ia ... ... ... ... | 12 | ,, |
| | A poore woman ... ... ... ... ... ... ... ... | 13 | ,, |
| | Wil̄lm Mosse in eccl̄ia ... ... ... ... ... ... | 16 | ,, |
| Jū | Jenette Mylner in eccl̄ia ... ... ... ... ... ... | 18 | ,, |
| | Anne Hoolme vx$^{9}$ ... ... ... ... ... ... ... | 20 | ,, |
| | Peeter Mason fill gau: in eccle ... ... ... | ,, | ,, |
| | Ann ffetcher widow ... ... ... ... ... ... ... | 22 | ,, |
| | Ellin Byrchwood vx$^{9}$ eccl: ... ... ... ... ... | 27 | ,, |
| | Hugh Bartō fil Ja: ... ... ... ... ... ... ... | ,, | ,, |
| pu: | James Banester ... ... ... ... ... ... ... | 30 | ,, |
| | John Hunt in ecl: ... ... ... ... ... ... ... | 3 | ffebruarie |
| pu: | Alis Cropp in eccl̄ia ... ... ... ... ... ... | 5 | ,, |
| | Margerie Tumson ... ... ... ... ... ... ... | 17 | ,, |
| pu: | Ric̄ Cropp in eccl̄ia ... ... ... ... ... ... | 18 | ,, |
| | Margarett Scarsbricke vid in ecclia ... ... | 23 | ,, |
| 368 | Ann Gill pu ... ... ... ... ... ... ... ... | 2 | Marche |
| | Margaret Plumbe vx$^{9}$ ... ... ... ... ... ... | 7 | ,, |
| | Margaret Gill vx$^{9}$ ... ... ... ... ... ... ... | 8 | ,, |

## 1599.

| | | | |
|---|---|---|---|
| | Anne Ormishawe fi: Tho: ... ... ... ... | 26 | Marche |
| pu: | Ric̄ Ormishawe ... ... ... ... ... ... ... | ,, | ,, |
| Ju: | Izabell Carre ... ... ... ... ... ... ... ... | ,, | ,, |
| | Rob̄t Haliwell ... ... ... ... ... ... ... ... | 30 | ,, |
| pu: | James Greaves ... ... ... ... ... ... ... ... | ,, | ,, |

| | | | |
|---|---|---|---|
| pu: | Tho: Duncon in ecclia ... ... ... ... ... ... | 30 | Marche |
| | Gilbert Aiscroft ... ... ... ... ... ... | 5 | Aprill |
| | Katherin Wering [? Worthington] vid ... ... | 7 | " |
| | Ric̃ Lanc̃ ... ... ... ... ... ... ... ... ... | 14 | " |
| | Alis Preskot vid ... ... ... ... ... ... | 16 | " |
| | Alis Woodhowse vid ... ... ... ... ... | 21 | " |
| | George Waynewright in ecclia ... ... ... ... ... | 23 | " |
| | Mꝰ Edw: Scarsbrecke of Scarsbrecke burid in his owne Chapell . ... ... ... ... | 28 | " |
| | Tho: Stopford in the high chan ... ... ... | 3 | Maye |
| Juñ | Margaret Balshaw ... ... ... ... ... ... ... | 10 | " |
| | A Chyld of John Mowdisley ... ... ... ... | 16 | " |
| | Hugh Cowp in eccl̃ia ... ... ... ... ... | 19 | " |
| | Margerie Rigmaden in eccl̃ia ... ... ... ... | " | " |
| | Mrs. Jaine Scarsbrecke bur̃ in her father his Chappell ... ... .. . ... ... ... | 16 | " |
| | Eideth Shawe vid in y$^{e}$ high Chañ ... ... ... | 5 | June |
| | Ric̃ Becconson ... ... ... ... ... ... ... ... | 20 | " |
| | A Chyld of Edw: Blundell ... ... ... ... | 5 | July |
| | Jaine Sankey fi: Ric̃ in eccl̃ia ... ... ... ... | 7 | " |
| | Elizabeth Garard vid ... ... ... ... ... ... | 9 | " |
| Juū | Margerie Whytstones ... ... ... ... ... ... | 11 | " |
| | Margaret Gleaste fi: Eline ... ... ... ... | 12 | " |
| | Tho: Garrard fi: Chuthbart in eccl̃ia ... ... | 14 | " |
| Fo. 369 | Edw: Wardman ... ... ... ... ... ... | 6 | August |
| | Tho: Munkes ... ... ... ... ... ... ... ... | 10 | " |
| | Silvester Aiscrofte in ecclia ... ... ... ... ... | 14 | " |
| | Grace Henrison in eccl̃ia ... ... ... ... ... | 17 | " |
| | A chyld of John Pyes bast ... ... ... ... ... | 26 | " |
| | Eliz$^{th}$ Hodgekinson vxꝰ ... ... ... ... ... ... | 10 | September |
| | Davie Westhead in eccl̃ia ... ... ... ... ... | 12 | " |
| | Edmund Haide in eccl̃ia ... ... ... ... ... | 21 | " |
| | Eliz$^{th}$ Roase vxꝰ in eccl̃ia ... ... ... ... | 5 | October |
| | Eliz$^{th}$ Crotchley vxꝰ ... ... ... ... ... ... | 10 | " |
| | Ellin Smyth in eccl̃ia ... ... ... ... ... ... | 14 | " |
| pur̃ | Anne Eliverson ... ... ... ... ... ... | " | " |
| pur̃ | John Cropp ... ... ... ... ... ... ... | 17 | " |
| | Homfrey Henrison in eccl̃ia ... ... ... ... | 24 | " |
| | A pore chyld ... ... ... ... ... ... ... ... | 2 | November |
| | Jamis Blackeledge in eccl̃ia ... ... ... ... | 4 | " |
| | John Blvndell̃ in eccl̃ia ... ... ... ... ... ... | 17 | " |
| pur̃ | John Eastehead fi Jo: ... ... ... ... ... | 9 | December |
| | Eliz$^{th}$ Hodgekinson vid in eccl̃ia ... ... ... | 29 | " |
| | Tho: Lanc̃ fi: Jo: in eccl̃ia ... ... ... ... | 30 | " |
| | Wiłłm Lathom ... ... ... ... ... ... ... ... | 2 | Januarie |
| | Tho: Waynewright ... ... ... ... ... ... ... | 11 | " |
| | Ellin Mowdisley vid in eccl̃ia ... ... ... | 12 | " |
| | Margaret Craine vxꝰ ... ... ... ... ... ... | 16 | " |
| | Cristopher Oliverson ... ... ... ... ... | 21 | " |

| | | | |
|---|---|---|---|
| | Willm Barton | 21 | Januarie |
| puř | Elin Ormishawe | „ | „ |
| 370 | Willm Hoolme | 3 | ffebruarie |
| | Humfrey Morecroft fi: Edw: | 5 | „ |
| | Jam: Jackeson in ecclia | 8 | „ |
| | Eline Asmall | 9 | „ |
| | Henrie Lunte | „ | „ |
| | Alis Cropp fi: George in ecclia | 10 | „ |
| Juū | Gabrell Gorsutch in ecclia | 12 | „ |
| | Margaret Sutton | 15 | „ |
| | Ric̃ Mason in ecclia | 24 | „ |
| | John Marclow | 28 | „ |
| | Eliz$^{th}$ Tavenar vx$^{9}$ | 29 | „ |
| | Jenet Mowdisley vid | 3 | March |
| | Eliz$^{th}$ ffarclough | 9 | „ |
| | Mrs. Blanch ffallowes vid in ecclia | 12 | „ |
| Juū | Jaine ffarclough | 18 | „ |
| | A Chyld of Tho: ffletcher | 22 | „ |

## 1600.

| | | | |
|---|---|---|---|
| | Jamis Harison in ecclia | 26 | March |
| Juū | Willm Ormishaw in ecclia | 27 | „ |
| | A Chyld of Hugh Standish | „ | „ |
| | Robert Killshaw fi: Aleñ | 31 | „ |
| | Anne Howlden vid in ecclia | 9 | Aprill |
| | Anne Diconson fi: Edw: in y$^{e}$ Chanc̃ | 10 | „ |
| | Margerie Spencer vx$^{9}$ | 13 | „ |
| | Eliz$^{th}$ Lathom | 16 | „ |
| | Elis Swifte | 18 | „ |
| | Eliz$^{th}$ Howlden vx$^{9}$ | „ | „ |
| puř | Raffe Whytestones | 19 | „ |
| | Willm Holton | 5 | Maye |
| | A Chyld of Willm Sutton | 8 | „ |
| | John Blundell | 11 | „ |
| | Margaret Gowlbron fi: Homfrey in m$^{9}$ Scarsbreckes chapell | 13 | „ |
| | Robert Hunter | „ | „ |
| | Henrie Parker | 15 | „ |
| | Jam: Kewquicke | 16 | „ |
| 371 | Tho: Gleast | 18 | „ |
| | Peeter Precot [*sic*] in ecclia | 21 | „ |
| | A Chyld of Ric̃ Sankeyes in ecclia | 24 | „ |
| | Tho: Weshead [*sic*] fi: Davie | 26 | „ |
| | A Chyld of Henrie Ormishaw | 30 | „ |
| | Willm Wadingeton | 11 | June |
| | Parre Gill vid | 6 | July |
| puř | Margaret Traves in ecclia | 14 | „ |
| | Jamis Harwood in ecclia | 30 | „ |

| | | | |
|---|---|---|---|
| | Anne Atkinson vx⁹ in ecclia ... ... ... ... ... | 20 | August |
| | Margaret Croston vid ... ... ... ... ... | 23 | „ |

[*No entries for September*]

| | | | |
|---|---|---|---|
| pur | Jenet Westhead fi: in ecclia ... ... ... ... ... | 20 | October |
| | Ellin Barker fi: Hen: in ecclia ... ... ... | 26 | „ |
| | A Chyld Tho: Rigbies ... ... ... ... ... | „ | „ |
| | Eliz^th Talior vx⁹ in ecclia ... ... ... ... | 29 | „ |
| | Edw: Windrow ... ... ... ... ... ... | 10 | November |
| | Willm Rydinge ... ... ... ... ... ... ... ... | „ | „ |
| | Katherin Macristie vid ... ... ... ... ... | 29 | „ |
| | Katherin Shaw vx⁹ in ecclia ... ... ... ... | 8 | December |
| | Margerie Kewquicke vid ... ... ... ... ... | 10 | „ |
| | A stranger slayne by one of the glassemen beinge A ffrenchman then workinge at Bycarstaff and bur ... ... ... ... ... ... | „ | „ |
| | Anne Gobin vid in ecclia ... ... ... ... | 14 | „ |
| | Tho: Smallshaw in ecclia ... ... ... ... | 15 | „ |
| | Hugh Bycarstaf in ecclia ... ... ... ... | 24 | „ |
| | Marie Hunter fi: Tho: in ecclia ... ... ... | 25 | „ |
| | pur Joane Prescot fi: Ric ... ... ... ... ... | 31 | „ |
| Fo. 372 | Thomas Mylner ... ... ... ... ... ... ... ... | 3 | Januarie |
| | Izabell Haughton vx⁹ Ja: in ecclia ... ... | 6 | „ |
| Juu | Willm Bate ... ... ... ... ... ... ... ... | 25 | „ |
| | Ric Waringe fi: Robert in ecclia ... ... ... | 26 | „ |
| Ju | Robert Barton in ecclia ... ... ... ... ... ... | 29 | „ |
| | Izabell Haille vx⁹ James ... ... ... ... ... | 30 | „ |
| | Alis Craine fi: Edw: ... ... ... ... ... | 2 | ffebruarie |
| | Anne Mawdisley vx⁹ Robert in ecclia ... ... | 4 | „ |
| | Otewell Blundell in ecclia ... ... ... ... ... | 7 | „ |
| | Anne Abraham ... ... ... ... ... ... ... ... | „ | „ |
| | Jaine Jollie ... ... ... ... ... ... ... ... | 13 | „ |
| | Marie Brigehowse fi: Tho: ... ... ... ... ... | „ | „ |
| | Peeter Barton fi: Hugh in ecclia ... ... ... | 22 | „ |
| | Jamis Sutch bur in the high chancell ... ... | 26 | „ |
| | Catherin Hoolme vx⁹ in ecclia ... ... ... | 27 | „ |
| | Tho: Sefton in ecclia ... ... ... ... ... | 1 | March |
| | George Cropp in ecclia ... ... ... ... ... | 2 | „ |
| | Izabell Gill fi Ric ... ... ... ... ... ... | 6 | „ |
| | Mowde Waringe fi: Henrie ... ... ... ... | 12 | „ |
| | Ric ffidler fi: Tho: ... ... ... ... ... ... | 23 | „ |
| | A Chyld of John Eastheades ... ... ... ... | 24 | „ |

## 1601.

| | | |
|---|---|---|
| Izabell Atherton sen in ecclia ... ... ... ... | 26 | March |
| A Chyld of George Lyons ... ... ... ... | 1 | Aprell |
| Rodger Lathwhat in ecclia ... ... ... ... | 2 | „ |

|  |  |  |
|---|---|---|
| Myles Lathwhat in eccl̄ia ... ... ... ... | 3 | Aprell |
| A Chyld of Will̄m Brykell ... ... ... ... | " | " |
| Tho Cadicke in Eccl̄ia ... ... ... ... ... | 4 | " |
| A pore Chylde ... ... ... ... ... ... ... ... | 12 | " |
| A Chylde of Ric̃ Whytestones ... ... ... ... | 17 | " |
| Tho: Crosse ... ... ... ... ... ... ... ... | 22 | " |
| Jaine Blundell vxꝰ Edw: in eccl̄ia ... ... ... | 23 | " |
| Hugh Worthingeton Juū bur̃ in the high Chancell ... ... ... ... ... ... ... ... | 1 | Maye |
| John Barton fi: Henery ... ... ... ... ... | 16 | " |
| Henrie Haille in eccl̄ia ... ... ... ... ... | 20 | " |
| George Oliverson ... ... ... ... ... ... | " | " |
| Ellen Killshaw fi: Gilbert ... ... ... ... | 2 | June |
| Bryhan Barton ... ... ... ... ... ... ... | 4 | " |
| Katherin Banester ... ... ... ... ... ... | 5 | " |
| Tho: Molinex ... ... ... ... ... ... ... | 6 | " |
| Margaret Kenion ... ... ... ... ... ... | 9 | " |
| Raffe Rosse in eccl̄ia ... ... ... ... ... | 10 | " |
| Rodger Sankey fi: Ric̃ in eccl̄ia ... ... ... | 23 | " |
| Ric̃ Marcer fi: Rodger ... ... ... ... ... | 28 | " |
| Elizabeth Stanley fi: Edw: de more hall bur̃ in Mꝰ Stanleys Chancell ... ... ... ... | 5 | July |
| Lore Gill ... ... ... ... ... ... ... ... ... | 8 | " |
| Jamis Blundell fi: Edw: ... ... ... ... ... | 14 | " |
| Sibell Woodhowse vid in eccl̄ia ... ... ... | 9 | Auguste |
| Izabell Clarke ... ... ... ... ... ... ... | 12 | " |
| Alis Burscough vxꝰ Gilbert in eccl̄ia ... ... | 13 | " |
| Ewan Waringe ... ... ... ... ... ... ... | 19 | " |
| Will̄m Adamson fi: Will̄ in eccl̄ia ... ... ... | 25 | " |
| Margerie Shawe vxꝰ Rodger ... ... ... ... | 1 | September |
| Alis Morecrofte fi: Ric̃ in eccl̄ia ... ... ... | 10 | " |
| Margerie Rutter vid ... ... ... ... ... ... | 23 | " |
| Gilbert Hoton ... ... ... ... ... ... ... | 28 | " |
| ffardinando Tomson fi: John ... ... ... ... | 30 | " |
| Anne Smallshaw vxꝰ Will̄ in eccl̄ia ... ... | " | " |
| Margaret Coockeson fi: Silvester ... ... ... | 1 | October |
| Loare Tarior pur̃ ... ... ... ... ... ... | 11 | " |
| Thomas Cropp fi: Hugh in eccl̄ia ... ... ... | 19 | " |
| A chyld of Ric̃ Cowpers in eccl̄ia ... ... ... | 25 | " |
| Jamis Haughton in eccl̄ia ... ... ... ... | 13 | November |
| Sislie Bromley vxꝰ Peeter ... ... ... ... | " | " |
| Rodger Weltch fi: Gilbert ... ... ... ... | 19 | " |
| Margaret Mawdisley fi: Tho: in eccl̄ia ... ... | 21 | " |
| Jamis Sutch pur̃ ... ... ... ... ... ... | 24 | " |
| A chyld of Gilbert Burscough in ecclia ... ... | 5 | December |
| Eliz$^{th}$ Alker vxꝰ Tho: in eccl̄ia ... ... ... | 8 | " |
| Tho: Windrow fi: Ric̃ ... ... ... ... ... | 12 | " |
| Tho: Killshaw fi: Gilbert ... ... ... ... | 19 | " |
| A Chyld of Bryhan Websters ... ... ... ... | 20 | " |

A Chyld of Tho: Mollinex ... ... ... ... 28 December
Eliz^th Tobie vx^9 Ric̃ in eccl̃ia ... ... ... 2 Januarie
Ranould Grosier ... ... ... ... ... ... 7 „
A Chyld of Tho: Preskot ... ... ... ... 8 „
Elizbeth Blundell vid in ecclia ... ... ... 12 „
Brichet Sefton vx^9 John in eccl̃ia ... ... ... 13 „
Jū Margaret Ashton ... ... ... ... ... ... 19 „
Hugh Lathwhat fi: Wil̃lm in eccl̃ia ... ... 24 „
Wil̃lm Smyth in M^9 Scarsbrecks chansell ... 26 „
pur̃ Katherin Scarsbrecke ... ... ... ... ... ... 27 „
Henrie Henrison fi: Tho: ... ... ... ... 1 ffebruarie
John Carre ... ... ... ... ... ... ... 4 „
Margaret Wythingeton fi: Robert in ecc̃ ... 7 „
pur̃ Robert Toppinge ... ... ... ... ... ... ... 13 „
Ric̃ Mason fi: Gowther ... ... ... ... ... 27 „
Margaret Allerton fi: John ... ... ... ... 1 Martch
Adam Barton ... ... ... ... ... ... ... 7 „
Tho: Jackes ... ... ... ... ... ... ... 10 „
Ellin Kocket vx^9 Tho: ... ... ... ... ... „ „
Elin Worthingeton vid in eccl̃ia ... ... ... 12 „
Anne Butchert vx^9 Edw: ... ... ... ... 13 „
Alis Tomson vx^9 Hugh in eccl̃ia ... ... ... 16 „
ij Children of Tho: Skinners in eccl̃ia ... ... „ „
spū Tho: Morecroft fi: Henrie in eccl̃ia ... ... 17 „
Elizabeth Mores vx^9 Rob̃t in eccl̃ia ... ... 18 „
Jayne Barker bur̃ in M^9 Scarsbreckes chansell 22 „
Catherin Loccar vid In eccl̃ia ... ... ... 24 „

## 1602.

Jayne Winde vid ... ... ... ... ... ... 26 Martch
Tho: Holey fi: John ... ... ... ... ... 30 „
Jamis Chadocke pur̃ ... ... ... ... ... 26 „
Robert Preskot in eccl̃ia ... ... ... ... ... 2 Aprill
Homfrey Greaves fi: Tho: ... ... ... ... 4 „
Ric̃ Aspinwall in eccl̃ia ... ... ... ... ... 7 „
Ellin Adamson fi: Wil̃lm in eccl̃ia ... ... 21 „
Fo. 375 Anthoney Cadicke ... ... ... ... ... ... 2 Maye
Anne Barton vx^9 Wil̃lm ... ... ... ... ... 3 „
Elin Mollinex ... ... ... ... ... ... „ „
Eliz^th Morecroft fi: Edw: ... ... ... ... 7 „
Ric̃ Preskot in eccl̃ia ... ... ... ... ... 8 „
Anne Alker fi: Jamis ... ... ... ... ... 10 „
Jaine Tomson vx^9 Wil̃lm ... ... ... ... 19 „
Anne Gleaste fi: Ellis ... ... ... ... ... 22 „
Ju Jaine Mossocke in eccl̃ia ... ... ... ... 3 June
Henrie Stopforth in the high Chansell ... ... 18 „
Hamlet Dayle fi: Wil̃lm ... ... ... ... ... 20 „
Hector Westhead in eccl̃ia ... ... ... ... 25 „

| | | |
|---|---|---|
| Anne Killshaw fi: Jamis ... ... ... ... ... ... | 1 | July |
| A Chyld of Ric̃ Voce ... ... ... ... ... ... | 25 | „ |
| Ric̃ Ormishaw in eccl̃ia ... ... ... ... ... ... | 27 | „ |
| Elin Shaw ... ... ... ... ... ... ... ... | 6 | August |
| Catherin Asmall vx° Will̃ ... ... ... ... ... | 7 | „ |
| George Sefton in eccl̃ia ... ... ... ... ... ... | 22 | „ |
| Ellizabeth Speakeman vx° Ric̃ in eccl̃ia ... | 27 | „ |
| Henry Yate fi: Henry ... ... ... ... ... ... | 24 | September |
| Eliz[th] Morecrofte vid ... ... ... ... ... ... | 28 | „ |
| Ellin Prescot vx° John in eccl̃ia ... ... ... | 6 | October |
| A Chylde of Will̃m Breykel ... ... ... ... ... | 23 | „ |
| Jenet Blessinge fi: Raffe ... ... ... ... ... | 24 | „ |
| A Chylde of M° fferis ... ... ... ... ... ... | 25 | „ |
| Another Chylde of M° ffrris [*sic*] ... ... ... | 27 | „ |
| A Chylde of Henry Aiscrofte in eccl̃ia ... ... | 28 | „ |
| Margaret Wildinge vx° ... ... ... ... ... ... | 1 | November |
| Alis Briscow fi: Humfrey ... ... ... ... ... | 10 | „ |
| Peinbiall [*sic*] fferie fi: Rowland ... ... ... | 12 | „ |
| Margaret Sankey vx° Ric̃ in eccl̃ia ... ... ... | 14 | „ |
| Will̃m Jackeson fi: Ric̃ in eccl̃ia ... ... ... | „ | „ |
| Henry Lutman ... ... ... ... ... ... ... | 15 | „ |
| Tho: Ludgate fi: Will̃ ... ... ... ... ... ... | 19 | „ |
| Hugh Smyth fi: John ... ... ... ... ... ... | 22 | „ |
| ffrancis Waringe fi: Cristopher ... ... ... | 1 | December |
| Ellin Lathwhat fi: Henry in eccl̃ia ... ... | 6 | „ |
| Eliz[th] Hoolme ... ... ... ... ... ... ... ... | 12 | „ |
| Ric̃ Jackeson in eccl̃ia ... ... ... ... ... ... | 14 | „ |
| Homfrey Talior fi: Ric̃ in eccl̃ia ... ... ... | 15 | „ |
| Emlin Bycarstaffe in eccl̃ia ... ... ... ... ... | 21 | „ |
| Tho: Gobin in eccl̃ia ... ... ... ... ... ... | 22 | „ |
| Margaret Holland vx° Robert ... ... ... | 3 | Januarie |
| Tho: Roughley fi: Tho: ... ... ... ... ... | 14 | „ |
| Anne Kewquicke fi: Hugh ... ... ... ... ... | 16 | „ |
| A Chyld of John Easteheades ... ... ... ... | 19 | „ |
| Ric̃ Ashton fi: Rodger ... ... ... ... ... ... | 31 | „ |
| Eideth Ormishaw vx° Rodger in eccl̃ia ... ... | 5 | ffebruarie |
| Will̃m Cowsey ... ... ... ... ... ... ... ... | 8 | „ |
| Elin Jackeson vid in eccl̃ia ... ... ... ... ... | 15 | „ |
| Ric̃ Stryker fi: Micall ... ... ... ... ... ... | 18 | „ |
| A Chylde of Tho: Prescot ... ... ... ... ... | 22 | „ |
| A Chylde of Tho: Smyth in eccl̃ia ... ... | 23 | „ |
| Martha Smyth fi: Tho: in eccl̃ia ... ... ... | 24 | „ |
| Margaret Anglesdaile fi: John ... ... ... | 28 | „ |
| Ellizabeth Lee bur̃ in M° Scarsb̃ Chappell ... | 5 | Martch |
| Marierie Hunter vx° Ric̃ in eccl̃ia ... ... ... | 6 | „ |
| Elizabeth Asmall vid in eccl̃ia ... ... ... | 12 | „ |
| Will̃m Smyth in eccl̃ia ... ... ... ... ... ... | 16 | „ |
| Jane Clapam ... ... ... ... ... ... ... ... | 17 | „ |

## 1603.

Henry Smyth in ecclia ... ... ... ... ... 25 Martch
Cuthbert Gerrerd in ecclia ... ... ... ... 1 Aprill
A poare Chyld ... ... ... ... ... ... ... ... „ „
Elizabeth Woodes fi: Witm ... ... ... ... 4 „
Agnes Barton vid in ecclia ... ... ... ... 6 „
Jamis Cadicke puer ... ... ... ... ... ... „ „
Hugh Jackeson ... ... ... ... ... ... ... 8 „
Jũ John Barker ... ... ... ... ... ... ... 13 „
Jamis Anglesdaile fi: John in ecctia ... ... 14 „
Eliz[th] Holland vid in ecctia ... ... ... ... 18 „
Ellin Ellam vx[9] Raffe in ecctia ... ... ... 21 „
Eliz[th] Killshawe fi John in ectia ... ... ... 23 „
Jũ Tho: Jackeson in ecctia ... ... ... ... ... 29 „
Fo. 377 Anne Brygehowse vx[9] Hamlet ... ... ... 3 Maye
Margarett Blundell in ecctia ... ... ... ... „ „
Jaine Tomson fi: John ... ... ... ... ... 5 „
Marie Brigehowse ... ... ... ... ... ... „ „
Catherin Stopforth vid ... ... ... ... ... „ „
Jayne Worthingeton fi: Hugh in the high chañ 15 „
Robert Leadbetter in ecctia ... ... ... ... 17 „
Jamis Ascrofte in ecctia ... ... ... ... ... 25 „
Ellin Kenion fi: Henry ... ... ... ... ... 28 „
Twoo Children of Jamis Barton ... ... ... 29 „
Jayne Daron vx[9] ... ... ... ... ... ... ... 31 „
Robert Gill fi: Ric̃ ... ... ... ... ... ... 1 June
Margaret Morecrofte fi: Gabriell in ecclia ... 2 „
Tho: Swyfte fi: Phillipe in ecclia ... ... ... 11 „
Anne Asmall vid ... ... ... ... ... ... ... 14 „
Alis Windrow fi: Ric̃ ... ... ... ... ... 17 „
Tho: Eccleston ... ... ... ... ... ... ... 18 „
Alis Mollinex fi: John ... ... ... ... ... 19 „
Anne Stanley fi: M[9] Henry buř in Scarsbř
Chappell ... ... ... ... ... ... ... ... 23 „
Alis Marrall vx[9] Hamlet in ecctia ... ... ... 2 Julye
Marierie Mawdisley vx[9] Tho: in ecctia ... ... 7 „
Alis Whitefild ... ... ... ... ... ... ... 11 „
Margaret Morecrofte pueř ... ... ... ... 23 „
Jaine Armetrydinge vx[9] ... ... ... ... ... „ „
Margaret Whytstones vx[9] ... ... ... ... 27 „
Witm Boothe ... ... ... ... ... ... ... 28 „
Tho: Coockeson ... ... ... ... ... ... ... 30 „
Margaret Hey fi: John ... ... ... ... ... 31 „
Anne ffogge fi John ... ... ... ... ... ... 2 August
Elizabeth Windrow fi: George ... ... ... 4 „
sp: A chyld of Hugh Cropp in ecctia ... ... ... 8 „
Catherin Morecrofte fi: Ric̃ in ecctia ... ... „ „

Tho: Rigbie in ecclia ... ... ... ... ... ... 17 August
Ric̃ Hunter in ecclia ... ... ... ... ... ... 21 „
Tho: Hodgeson in ecclia ... ... ... ... 3 September
Ric̃ Kellet in ecclia ... ... ... ... ... ... ... 4 „
Sislie Douhtie vx[9] Micall in ecclia ... ... ... 6 „
ū Tho: Piningeton ... ... ... ... ... ... ... 17 „
Phillip Hoolme ... ... ... ... ... ... ... ... „ „
Hugh Prescotte ... ... ... ... ... ... ... ... 26 „
8 A chyld of . . . . ... ... ... ... ... ... ... 1 October
Agnes Whytestones in ec̃ ... ... ... ... ... 2 „
John Leigh fil Von ... ... ... ... ... ... ... 3 „
Elizabeth Sumner fil John in ec̃ ... ... ... 7 „
Thomas Brighouse fil Will ... ... ... ... ... 22 „
Elizabeth Barton vx[9] Hugh in ec̃ ... ... ... 23 „
Marie Aiscroft vx[9] Raffe in ecclia ... ... ... 27 „
Richard Webster ... ... ... ... ... ... ... 7 November
A chyld of Ric̃ Hooton ... ... ... ... ... ... 12 „
Gabriell Shawe fi: Tho: ... ... ... ... ... ... 16 „
Robert Mawdisley in ecc ... ... ... ... ... ... 18 „
Ellin Wignall vx[9] in ecc ... ... ... ... ... ... 24 „
Katherin Holland vx[9] Edw: in ecc ... ... 9 December
Willm Lvskin in ecc ... ... ... ... ... ... 14 „
Ellin Eccleston vx[9] John ... ... ... ... ... 17 „
A chylde of Robert Cocketes ... ... ... ... 21 „
Claris Preskot vid ... ... ... ... ... ... ... 9 Januarie
A chylde of Tho: Yate in eccl ... ... ... 11 „
Mawde Scarisbrecke bur in m[9] Scarsbreck his chappel ... ... ... ... ... ... ... ... 13 „
Jaine Lea fi: Willm in ecc ... ... ... ... ... 18 „
Rodger Rydinge ... ... ... ... ... ... ... 27 „
Jayne Grosier ... ... ... ... ... ... ... ... 6 ffebruarie
Ellin Eccleston ... ... ... ... ... ... ... 13 „
Hamlet Brighowse [*seems to have been altered from* Rithrope] ... ... ... ... ... ... ... 18 „
Margaret Killshaw ... ... ... ... ... ... ... 22 „
Hugh Holland fi: Hugh in ecc ... ... ... ... „ „
A chyld of John Asshort in eccl ... ... ... „ „
Alis Leadbetter in eccl ... ... ... ... ... ... 25 „
Elizabeth ffrith vx[9] ... ... ... . ... ... „ „
M[9] Edward Stanley bur in the high Chansell 2 Martch
Margaret Morecroft vx[9] in eccli ... .. ... 9 „
Mrs Anne Scarsbrecke vid bur in Scarb chan... 17 „
Elizabeth Shaw vid ... ... ... ... ... ... ... 20 „
pū Rodger Barton in ecclia ... ... ... ... ... 24 „

## 1604.

pū James Barton in ecclia ... ... ... ... ... 26 Martch
A childe of Ric̃ Gill ... ... ... . ... 28 „
79 Tho: Stopforth fi: Henry in the high chanc̃... 4 Aprill

| | | | |
|---|---|---|---|
| | Marie Toppinge fi: Omfrey in ecclia | 7 | Aprill |
| | A Chyld of Henry Penketh | 8 | „ |
| | Elizabeth Doughtie fi Micall in ecclia | 16 | „ |
| | Margaret Cropp vxꝰ Hugh shumaker in ecclia | 27 | „ |
| | A man wch dwet [*sic*] wth Ric̃ Macon wch was drowned | 29 | „ |
| | Denis Vlster | 30 | „ |
| | Anne Aspinwall vid in ecclia | 25 | Maye |
| | Ellin Morecrofte fi: Cuthber in ecclia | 7 | June |
| | Thomas Jumpe | 9 | „ |
| | Britchet Whytestones fi: George | 11 | „ |
| Jū | Homfrey Gill | 30 | „ |
| | Catherin Davie fi: John | 8 | July |
| Jū | John Woode | 10 | „ |
| sp: | Richard Smalshaw fi: Tho | 22 | „ |
| | Willm Asmall in ecclia | 24 | „ |
| | Nicholas Sumner in ecclia | 27 | „ |
| | Elizabeth Spenser vid in ecclia | 28 | „ |
| | Margaret Barker vxꝰ Henry in ecclia | 1 | August |
| | John Bycarstafe | 2 | „ |
| pū | John Piñiton | 20 | „ |
| | Henry Traves | 24 | „ |
| | Sꝰere Edward Stanley bur in my Lords Chapi | 4 | September |
| | A Chyld of Ric̃ Morecroft in ecclia | 6 | „ |
| | John Sumner in ecclia | 14 | „ |
| | Jaine Mawdisley vxꝰ Rodger in ec̃ | 6 | October |
| | Jaine Stopforthe vid in ec̃c | 9 | „ |
| | Jaine Barton | „ | „ |
| Jū | Izabell Jameson in ecclia | 17 | „ |
| Jū | Thomas Sumner in ecclia | 28 | „ |
| Jū | Joanie Whytestones | 4 | November |
| sp: | Johne Lea fi: Ewan | 7 | „ |
| | A Chylde of Raffe Blessinge | 10 | „ |
| | Jaine Longeworth vid in ecclia | 12 | „ |
| | A chyld of John Eccleston | 18 | „ |
| | Joanie Eccleston fi: John | 20 | „ |
| | Rodger Shawe | 24 | „ |
| | John Scarsbrecke | 26 | „ |
| Fo. 380 | Tho: Modisley in ecclia | 3 | December |
| | Jamis Modisley | 7 | „ |
| | Gilbert Hulme in ecclia | 9 | „ |
| | Elizabeth Traves vid | 10 | „ |
| | Jaine ffletcher fi: Hugh in ecclia | 30 | „ |
| | Hugh Sharrocke fi: John | 2 | Januarie |
| | Tho: Smyth in ecclia | 4 | „ |
| | Ric̃ Wyet | „ | „ |
| | Margreat Peeter in ecclia | 1 | ffebruarie |
| | Alis Peeter in ec̃c | 6 | „ |
| | Elizabeth Smyth vxꝰ Tho: in eccl | 11 | „ |

| | | | |
|---|---|---|---|
| | Richard Gollibrond gent in ecclia | 19 | ffebruarie |
| | Barbarie Bobbin* vid in ecclia | „ | „ |
| | Ellin Mowdisley vx' John & her Chyld in eccl | 28 | „ |

## 1605.

| | | | |
|---|---|---|---|
| | A Chyld of George Shawe in ecclia | 26 | Martch |
| | Homfrey Morecrofte fi: Gabriell in eccl | 4 | Aprill |
| | Margaret Hoolme vx' Ric in ecclia | 6 | „ |
| | Mowde Aiscrofte | 9 | „ |
| | A Chylde of John Asshort in ecclia | 11 | „ |
| | Thomas Marrow in ecclia | 18 | „ |
| | Anne Talior pū | 19 | „ |
| | Peeter Bromiley | 22 | „ |
| | A Chylde of Willm Barton in ecclia | 24 | „ |
| | John Whytestones in ecclia | 25 | „ |
| | Elizabeth Walne vx' Henrie | 26 | „ |
| | Alis Bower vx' Tho: in ecclia | 5 | Maye |
| | George Waynewright in ecclia | 8 | „ |
| | Alis Irland in ecclia | „ | „ |
| | Robert Lunt in ecclia | 9 | „ |
| | Elizabeth Windrow fi: Ric | „ | „ |
| | Marie Moare vx' John bur in m' Scarsbreckes Chancell | 10 | „ |
| | Edward Sefton fi: Tho: in ecclia | 12 | „ |
| | Tho: Alker | 16 | „ |
| | Margaret Mowdisley vid | 18 | „ |
| | John Prescot in ecclia | „ | „ |
| Jū | Henrie Lea in ecclie [*sic*] | 26 | „ |
| | Katherin Henrieson vid in ecclia | 28 | „ |
| | Elizabeth Preskot vx' Gilb in ecclia | „ | „ |
| | Margaret ffarrer vx' Robert | 31 | „ |
| 81 | Hugh Morecrofte fi: Cuth: in ecclia | 4 | June |
| | Alis Leadbetter | 5 | „ |
| | Hugh Morecroft fi: Edw: in ecclia | 19 | „ |
| | A Chylde of Gabriell Haughton in eccl | 17 | July |
| | Alis Rigbie vx' John in ecclia | 24 | „ |
| Jū | Jaine Burie in ecclia | 27 | „ |
| | A Chylde of Richard Mollinex | 28 | „ |
| | Ellin Scarsbrecke fi: M' Tho: in the new Chansell | 31 | „ |
| | Anne Cropp vid in ecclia | 7 | Auguste |
| | Elllin [*sic*] Woofall vx' Cris in ecclia | „ | „ |
| | Willm Ambrose fi: Tho: in ecclia | 29 | „ |
| | Marierie Mollinex vx' Ric | 10 | September |
| Jū | Anne Scarsbrecke | 12 | „ |
| | Gabriell Mason [*or* Muson] m' of arts in ecclia | 15 | „ |
| | Alis Hadocke vx' Tho: | 19 | „ |

* Gobbin *in Chester Transcript.*

Catherin Carre vid in ecclie [*sic*] ... ... ... 20 September
Tho: Sillcocke ... ... ... ... ... ... 22 „
Raffe Stanley A stranger ... ... ... ... ... 16 October
Wittm Browne ... .. ... ... ... ... ... 17 „
Elizabeth Rigbie fi: Jo: in ecctia ... ... 18 „
Alis Sumner vid ... ... ... ... ... ... 23 „
Elizabeth Leadbetter vid in ecctia ... ... ... 2 November
Jũ Jaine Atherton ... ... ... ... ... ... ... ... 8 „
Jenet Hallworth vx[9] Hen: in ecctia ... ... 9 „
Jaine Walles vid in ecctia ... ... ... ... ... 11 „
Jũ Gilbert Babot ... ... ... ... ... ... ... ... „ „
Emlin Read vid ... ... ... ... ... ... ... 13 „
Jamis Towne in ecctia ... ... ... ... ... ... 14 „
Ellin Talior vid ... ... ... ... ... . . 18 „
A Childe of m[9] Tho: Stanley bur in in [*sic*] lord his Chancell ... ... ... ... ... ... 21 „
Elizabeth Cocket vid ... ... ... ... ... ... 25 „
Elizabeth Whitfilde ... ... ... ... ... ... ... 28 „
Margreat Barton vx[9] Henrie ... ... ... . . 4 December
Gabriell Brighowse fi: Peeter ... ... ... 11 „
Ann Lunte vx[9] Wittm in ecctia ... ... ... 15 „
John Mellinge ... ... ... ... ... ... ... ... 21 „
Jenet Carre vx[9] John ... ... ... ... ... 25 „
Alis Mawdisley vid in ecctia ... ... ... ... 28 „
Fo. 382 Edw: Letherbarow in ecctia ... ... ... ... 1 Januarie
. . . Barton vid ... ... ... ... ... ... 12 „
Rodger Sankey fi: Ric in ecctia ... ... ... 14 „
Genet Huton vid in ecc ... ... ... ... ... ... 18 „
Jane Carre vid ... ... ... ... ... ... ... 27 „
A Childe of John Easthead in ecc ... ... ... 2 ffebruarie
A Childe of Rodger Walworth in ecc ... ... 7 „
Wittm Barton ... ... ... ... ... ... ... ... 13 „
Elizabeth Barton vx[9] Cristopher ... ... ... 14 „
A Chylde of Wittm Sumner ... ... ... ... 23 „
Tho: Scarsbrecke bur in m[9] Scarsbrecke his Chappell ... ... ... ... ... ... ... 27 „
Homfrey Talior Jũ: in ecctia ... ... ... „ „
Edw: Marrow Jũ in ecctia ... ... ... ... 3 Martch
Jaine Miller fi: Wittm ... ... ... ... ... 14 „
Alis Morecroft vx[9] ... ... ... ... ... ... 21 „
Richard Parker ... ... ... ... ... ... ... 22 „
Jamis Gregson in ecctia ... ... ... ... .... „ „

## 1606.

Tho: Dvmcon in ecctia ... ... ... ... ... ... 28 Martch
Lyonell Swifte in ecctia ... ... ... ... ... 30 „
A childe of Wittm Mellinge ... ... ... ... 1 Aprill
Katherin Mawdisley vid in ecc ... ... ,.. 6 „

| | | |
|---|---|---|
| Alis Bromiley vid ... ... ... ... ... ... | 12 | Aprill |
| John Rigbie in ecclia ... ... ... ... ... | 13 | „ |
| Margreat Rydinge vx⁹ in ecc ... ... ... ... | 24 | „ |
| Katherin Swift in ecc ... ... ... ... ... | 26 | „ |
| A Chyld of Willm Breykell ... ... ... ... | 1 | Maye |
| Cristopher Sumner ... ... ... ... ... ... | 2 | „ |
| Anne Ormishaw vid in ecclia ... ... ... ... | 3 | „ |
| Elloner Aiscroft vx⁹ Jamis ... ... ... ... | „ | „ |
| Ellin Morecroft vx⁹ Ric in ecclia ... ... ... | 5 | „ |
| Jaine Windrow vx⁹ Ric ... ... ... ... ... | 7 | „ |
| A base Chylde of Ewan Lea in ecclia ... ... | 10 | „ |
| Margerie Hill Ju: ... ... ... ... ... ... | 11 | „ |
| A chyld of Willm Hoolme ... ... ... ... ... | 15 | „ |
| Elizabeth Robinson fi: Raffe ... ... ... | „ | „ |
| Katherin Lea fi: Ewann in ecclia ... ... ... | 16 | „ |
| Marierie Swift vx⁹ Tho: in ecclia ... ... ... | 18 | „ |
| Ellin Aiscroft vid in ecclia ... ... ... ... | „ | „ |
| Grace Modisley vid in ecclia ... ... ... ... | 21 | „ |
| Katherin Walker fi: George ... ... ... ... | 25 | „ |
| Katherin Stanley fi: M⁹ Tho: bur in my lo: his Chappell ... ... ... ... ... ... | 28 | „ |
| Richard Holland fi: Hugh in ecclia ... ... | 30 | „ |
| Elizabeth Swifte in ecclia ... ... ... ... | 2 | June |
| John Hey fi: Jamis in ecclia ... ... ... ... | 13 | „ |
| Jaine Perker vx⁹ Henrie in ecclia ... ... ... | 16 | „ |
| Elizabeth Whytestones vid in ecclia ... ... | 18 | „ |
| Richard Ligh bur in m⁹ Scarsbr his chappell | 25 | „ |
| Richard Waynewright fi :Tho: in ecc ... ... | 8 | July |
| Lyonell Jackeson in ecclia ... ... ... ... | 1 | August |
| Marie Rainforth in ecclia ... ... ... ... | 2 | „ |
| Gabriell Haughton fi: Gabriell in ecclia ... | 3 | „ |
| Margaret Gill puer ... ... ... ... ... ... | 7 | „ |
| Marie Norres ... ... ... ... ... ... ... | „ | „ |
| Jenet Westhead in ecclia ... ... ... ... | 23 | „ |
| A Child of Robert Holland ... ... ... ... | 27 | „ |
| Willm Stanley fi: m⁹ Edw: de Morehall bur in m⁹ Stanleys Chappell ... ... ... | 8 | September |
| Hugh Tomson in ecclia ... ... ... ... ... | 9 | „ |
| Alis Voce in ecclia ... ... ... ... ... ... | „ | „ |
| A Chyld of Tho: Yate ... ... ... ... ... | 10 | „ |
| John Bury ... ... ... ... ... ... ... ... | 21 | „ |
| Eideth Morecroft in ecc ... ... ... ... ... | 25 | „ |
| A Childe of Hugh Lailand in ecclia ... ... | 29 | „ |
| Jaine Edwardes vid in ecclia ... ... ... ... | 30 | „ |
| Willm Hallsall pur ... ... ... ... ... ... | 6 | October |
| Jaine Kenion vx⁹ Henry ... ... ... ... ... | 10 | „ |
| Margerie Mawdisley vx⁹ in ecclia ... ... ... | 13 | „ |
| Peeter Charles in ecclia ... ... ... ... ... | 30 | „ |
| Marie Barton ... ... ... ... ... ... ... | 4 | November |

A Child of Nicolas Shaw in ecclia ... ... ... 8 November
Tho Asmall fi : Edw : in ecclia ... ... ... 10 „
Jū Alis Lea Jū in ecclia ... ... ... ... ... ... 14 „
Anne Sumner vx⁹ Ric̃ in ecc̃ ... ... ... ... 17 „
Jaine Morecroft fi : Cuthbert in ecc̃ ... ... „ „
Margreat Westhead fi : Ric̃ in ecc̃ ... ... ... 25 „
John Aiscroft fi : John in ecclia ... ... ... 27 „
Richard Lathom fi : Ric̃ in ecclia ... ... ... 6 December
Hugh Standishe bur̃ in the high chancell ... 10 „
Ric̃ Traves ... ... ... ... ... ... ... ... „ „
Jaine Hoolme fi : Anthoney ... ... ... ... 21 „
Hugh Sutch ... ... ... ... ... ... ... ... 26 „
Peeter Lathwhat fi : Robert in ecclia ... ... 27 „
Jamis Lathom fi : Henry in ecclia ... ... ... 29 „
Robert Clapam in ecclia ... ... ... ... ... 30 „
Fo. 384 Homfrey Morecroft in ecclia ... ... ... ... 5 Januarie
A Childe of Ellis Gleast ... ... ... ... ... 6 „
Jū Edmund Swifte in eccl ... ... ... ... ... 7 „
Elizabeth Hey fi : John in ecclia ... ... ... 21 „
Anne Brigehohwse [*sic*] fi : Tho : ... ... ... 22 „
Elizabeth Morecroft fi : Ema : in eccla ... ... 28 „
Tho : Babot ... ... ... ... ... ... ... ... 30 „
Robert Gerrerd ... ... ... ... ... ... ... 31 „
Marie Cropp fi : George in ecclia ... ... ... 2 ffebruarie
Margerie Lancaster fi : John in ecclia ... ... 5 „
Ellin Scarsbrecke fi : ffard : in ecclia ... ... 6 „
Margaret Hunter fi : Tho : in ecclia ... ... 9 „
Elizabeth Breykell fi : Willm ... ... ... ... „ „
John Allerton ... ... ... ... ... ... ... ... 19 „
Hugh Sanforth fi : Henry in ecclia ... ... ... 20 „
Margaret Blundell vx⁹ John in ecc̃ ... ... ... 22 „
George Smyth fi : Tho : in ecclia ... ... ... 28 „
Symund Smyth in ecc̃ ... ... ... ... ... ... 1 Martch
Marie Sanforth fi : John ... ... ... ... ... „ „
Willm Jackeson ... ... ... ... ... ... ... 4 „
Willm Lathwhat fi : Willm in ecclia ... ... 12 „
Margerie Cropp fi : Raffe ... ... ... ... ... 16 „
Margreat Orrell vid in ecclia ... ... ... ... 17 „
Jaine Haughton fi : Jamis in ecclia ... ... „ „
Robert Haughton in ecclia ... ... ... ... ... 18 „

## 1607.

Jū Katherin Hesketh ... ... ... ... ... ... ... 29 Martch
Margaret Hesketh vx⁹ Robert ... ... ... 5 Aprill
Margaret Chadocke fi : Adam in eccl ... ... 27 „
Jū Hugh Garret Jū in eclia ... ... ... ... ... 5 Maye
Jū John Aiscroft in ecclia ... ... ... ... ... 8 „
Margerie Hey vx⁹ Tho : in ecclia ... ... ... 14 „

| | | |
|---|---|---|
| Sislie Westhead vid in eccłia | 15 | Maye |
| Tho: Aiscroft fi: John in eccl | 16 | „ |
| A Childe of Tho: Cropp in eccł | 27 | „ |
| Margaret Morecroft vid in eccłia | 29 | „ |
| Katherin Hoolton fi Ric̄ in eccłia | 7 | June |
| Elloner Toppinge fi: John | 12 | „ |
| Margerie Alker vid | 22 | „ |
| Jenet Boothe vid | 1 | July |
| Elizabeth Morecroft in eccłia | 3 | „ |
| Claris Stopforth fi: Henrie | 9 | „ |
| Izabell Garret vxꝰ Tho: | 10 | „ |
| Katherin Hatton vid | 11 | „ |
| Margaret Whytstons vxꝰ Raffe in ecc̄ | 14 | „ |
| John Blundell | 18 | „ |
| Margaret Nalior vid in eccłia | 25 | „ |
| Jaine Barton vxꝰ Tho: | 3 | August |
| John Cropp in eccłia | 6 | „ |
| Margerie Whytestones | 11 | „ |
| A Childe of Tho: Medowes | „ | „ |
| Hugh Haughton in eccłia | 12 | „ |
| Wiłłm Whatton in eccłia | 19 | „ |
| John Cowson | 26 | „ |
| Tho: Hill fi: Wiłłm in eccłia | 29 | „ |
| Richard Gill in eccłia | 11 | September |
| Wiłłm Kekewicke fi: Robert in eccłia | 13 | „ |
| John Cottrell A stranger | 16 | „ |
| Margaret Leivers vid in eccłia | 23 | „ |
| John Halworth fi: Edw: | 26 | „ |
| Wiłłm Lea fi: Jamis | 7 | October |
| A child of Peeter Talior | 13 | „ |
| Ellin Westhead vid | 15 | „ |
| Richard Werall in eccłia | 16 | „ |
| Margaret Smyth fi: John | 23 | „ |
| Margaret Lea vxꝰ in eccłia | 25 | „ |
| Jamis Sutch in eccłia | 29 | „ |
| Randle Sailes in eccłia | 30 | „ |
| Genet Beconson vid | 1 | November |
| Emlin Wood fi: Ric̄ | 12 | „ |
| Silvester Halsall fi: Edw: | „ | „ |
| Mꝰ Geffrey Rishton bur̄ in the high chancell | 15 | „ |
| Raffe Elam in ecclia | 16 | „ |
| Alis Aspinwall fi: Edw: in eccłia | „ | „ |
| Margaret Askroft vid | 17 | „ |
| Thomas Butler in eccłia | 18 | „ |
| Jamis Smalshaw in eccłia | 22 | „ |
| Marierie Preskot fi: ffardinandoe | 29 | „ |
| Jamis Blundell | 1 | December |
| Brichet Marshall fi: John in eccłia | 2 | „ |
| Wiłłm Mollinex in eccłia | 15 | „ |

| | | | |
|---|---|---|---|
| | Gabriell Thornall fi: Tho: ... ... ... ... | 22 | December |
| | Margaret Croston vx⁹ Edw: in eccl̄ia ... ... | 25 | „ |
| Jū | Anne Cowp in eccl̄ia ... ... ... ... ... ... | 26 | „ |
| | A child of Armetridinges in eccl̄ia ... ... ... | 3 | Januarie |
| Jū | Margerie Walliner in eccl̄ia ... ... ... ... ... | 8 | „ |
| | Elizabeth Stopforth vid in eccl̄ia ... ... ... | 10 | „ |
| | Ellin Hoolme vid in eccl̄ia ... ... ... ... ... | 17 | „ |
| | A childe of Gabriell Morecroft in eccl̄ia ... | 18 | „ |
| | A child of Wil̄lm Aiskroft in eccl̄ia ... ... | 19 | „ |
| | Ellin Yate vid in eccl̄ia ... ... ... ... ... ... | 24 | „ |
| | Marie Smulte fi: Robert in eccl̄ia ... ... ... | 28 | „ |
| | Thurston Woodworth ... ... ... ... ... ... | „ | „ |
| | Jamis Orte fi: John in eccl̄ia ... ... ... ... | 31 | „ |
| | Robert Balie fi: John in eccl̄ia ... ... ... | 2 | ffebruarie |
| | James and Alis Lathwhat fi: Wil̄lm in eccl̄ia... | 6 | „ |
| | Ellin Eccleston vx⁹ in eccl̄ia ... ... ... ... | 7 | „ |
| Jū | Grace Wainewright in eccl̄ia ... ... ... ... | 9 | „ |
| | Jamis Cawsey ... ... ... ... ... ... ... ... | 12 | „ |
| | Anne Asmall vid ... ... ... ... ... ... ... | 22 | „ |
| Jū | John Jackeson in eccl̄ia ... ... ... ... ... | 23 | „ |
| | Elizabeth Cosey in eccl̄ia ... ... ... ... ... | 6 | Martch |
| | ffrances Spencer in eccl̄ia ... ... ... ... ... | 12 | „ |
| | Wil̄lm Morecroft ... ... ... ... ... ... ... | 13 | „ |
| | Gilbert Sutton pur̄ ... ... ... ... ... ... ... | 16 | „ |
| | Wil̄lm Aspinwall ... ... ... ... ... ... ... | 20 | „ |
| | Wil̄lm Killshaw fi: Ric̄ ... ... ... ... ... | 21 | „ |
| Jū | Nicolas Scarsbreske [*sic*] in eccl̄ia ... ... ... | 23 | „ |
| Jū | Marie Rainforth ... ... ... ... ... ... ... | „ | „ |

## 1608.

| | | | |
|---|---|---|---|
| | Richard Asshorst ... ... ... ... ... ... ... | 9 | Aprill |
| | Jaine Griffie vid in eccl̄ia ... ... ... ... ... | 17 | „ |
| | Margreat Barton vid in eccl̄ia ... ... ... ... | 18 | „ |
| | Raffe Byrtchwood in eccl̄ia ... ... ... ... ... | 19 | „ |
| | Tho: Harwood in eccl̄ia ... ... ... ... ... | 24 | „ |
| | Alis Hodgeson vid in eccl̄ia ... ... ... ... ... | 25 | „ |
| | John Cropp fi: Raffe ... ... ... ... ... ... | 26 | „ |
| | Alis Craine fi: Wil̄lm ... ... ... ... ... ... | 28 | „ |
| | Tho: ffletcher fi: Hugh in eccl̄ia ... ... ... | 1 | Maye |
| | Jaine Tomson vx⁹ John ... ... ... ... ... | 7 | „ |
| | Alis Stopforth ... ... ... ... ... ... ... ... | 16 | „ |
| | Homfrey Morecroft fi: Cuth: in eccl̄ia ... | 24 | „ |
| | Ric̄ Leadbetter fi: Peeter in ecc̄ ... ... ... | 26 | „ |
| | Hamlet Brigehows ... ... ... ... ... ... ... | 28 | „ |
| | Margreat Ledbetter fi: Peeter in ecc̄ ... ... | 29 | „ |
| | Gowther Bicarstaff in ecclia ... ... ... ... | 30 | „ |
| Fo. 387 | Ric̄ Tobie ... ... ... ... ... ... ... ... ... | 1 | June |
| | Richard Barton fi: Gilbert ... ... ... ... ... | 8 | „ |

Katherin Wallis fi: Hector in eccl̄ia ... ... 18 June
Jaine Cadicke vid in eccl̄ia ... ... ... ... 26 „
Tho: Sefton fi: Tho: in eccl̄ia ... ... ... 7 July
sp: Richard Dughtie fi: Michall in eccl ... ... 8 „
Ellin Coockeson vx⁹ Jamis in eccl̄ia ... ... 12 „
Jenet Lathwhat vid in eccl̄ia ... ... ... ... 20 „
Edward Morecroft ... ... ... ... ... ... „ „
Wil̄l̄m Willdinge in eccl̄ia ... ... ... ... 1 August
Blantch Hodgeson vx⁹ John in ecc̄ ... ... ... 8 „
Anne Hankin fi: Wil̄l̄m in eccl̄ia ... ... ... 10 „
Jaine Sankey fi: Rodger in eccl̄ia ... ... ... 14 „
Tho: Anderton fi: Henry ... ... ... ... 15 „
Hugh Gillibrond in eccl̄ia ... ... ... ... 24 „
Jaine Hey vx⁹ John in eccl̄ ... ... ... ... 25 „
A child of Silvester Sutch in eccl ... ... ... 28 „
Elizabeth Ashton fi: Tho in Ecclia ... ... 5 September
Margreat Crooke vx⁹ John ... ... ... ... 7 „
Margaret Gillibrond fi: Ric̄ in eccl̄ia ... ... 14 „
A Childe of Robert Holland ... ... ... ... 15 „
Hugh Asmall in eccl̄ia ... ... ... ... ... 28 „
Jū Saraie Morecroft in eccl̄ia ... ... ... ... 29 „
Ladie Elizabeth Stanley fi: Wil̄l̄m Earle of derbie was bur̄ in my lo: his Chappell ... 17 October
M⁹ Henry Scarsbrecke of Scarsbrecke Esq[r] was bur̄ in his owne Chappell ... ... 19 „
A Child of John Mason in eccl̄ia ... ... ... 2 November
sp: Tho: Smalshaw fi: Tho: in ec̄ ... ... ... 3 „
Thomas Koket ... ... ... ... ... ... ... ... 5 „
Marie Kennion fi: Henry... ... ... ... ... 12 „
Rodger ffine ... ... ... ... ... ... ... ... 19 „
Ellin Gill vx⁹ Henry in eccl̄ia ... ... ... ... „ „
Henry Lunt ... ... ... ... ... ... ... ... 20 „
Jaine Lunt fi: Wil̄l in eccl̄ia ... ... ... ... 23 „
A Child of Geffrey Page ... ... ... ... ... 24 „
388 Elin Sutch fi: John in eccl̄ia ... ... ... ... 1 December
Richard Orme fi: John ... ... ... ... ... 9 „
Ellin Sumner fi: Ric̄ ... ... ... ... ... „ „
Margreat Leae fi: Rodger in ecc̄ ... ... ... 12 „
Thomas Disley ... ... ... ... ... ... ... 21 „
Alis Mawdisley vid in eccl̄ia ... ... ... ... 26 „
Margerie Cropp vx⁹ ... ... ... ... ... ... 31 „
Grace Gill vx⁹ ... ... ... ... ... ... ... „ „
Marie Morecroft fi: Tho: ... ... ... ... 8 Januarie
Izabell Marser fi: Robert ... ... ... ... 12 „
Wil̄l̄m Kocket fi: Robert ... ... ... ... 13 „
John Allerton in eccl̄ia ... ... ... ... ... 14 „
Henry Ormishaw in eccl̄ia ... ... ... ... 17 „
Alis Westhead fi: Henry ... ... ... ... 19 „
Elizabeth Halsall vx⁹ Robert in eccl̄ ... ... 23 „

| | | | |
|---|---|---|---|
| | Tho: Mawdisley in eccl̃ia | 30 | Januarie |
| | A Child of John Eccleston | 31 | „ |
| | Edward Sankey fi: Richard in eccl̃ia | 1 | ffebruarie |
| | Elizabeth Hey vxꝰ Nicolas | 4 | „ |
| | Eideth Lea in eccl̃ia | 6 | „ |
| | Mirs Dorethie Scarsbrecke fi: Edw: in mꝰ Scarsbrecke his Chappell | 13 | „ |
| | Hugh Sumner in eccl̃ia | 15 | „ |
| | Jamis Wainewright in eccl̃i | 17 | „ |
| | Josephe Marclew fi: Will̃m | „ | „ |
| Jū | Lawrance Haughton in eccl̃ia | 19 | „ |
| Jū | Peeter ffloyde | 21 | „ |
| | Will̃m Mawdisley in eccli | 28 | „ |
| | Henry Cropp fi: Raffe | „ | „ |
| | Will̃m Smalshaw in eccl̃a | 3 | Martch |
| | A Child of Tho: Swift in eccl̃ | 7 | „ |
| | Margaret Holland vid | 19 | „ |
| | John Hodgekinson | 20 | „ |
| | Elizabeth Ambrosse vid in eccl̃i | 21 | „ |
| | Jaine Lea spinster in eccl̃ia | 22 | „ |
| | Margaret Mollinex vid | 23 | „ |
| | Elizabeth ffisher vxꝰ Ric̃ in eccl̃ia | „ | „ |
| | Richard Mason | „ | „ |

## 1609.

| | | | |
|---|---|---|---|
| | Margerie Allerton vxꝰ Tho: | 26 | Martch |
| | Margaret Rimmer vxꝰ Tho: in eccl̃ | 30 | „ |
| Fo. 389 | Sislie Mason fi: Gowther in eccl̃ia | 1 | Aprill |
| | Ellin Scarsbrecke vxꝰ Hugh in eccli | „ | „ |
| | Anne Morecroft vxꝰ Henry bur̃ in the high chañ | 6 | „ |
| | Jamis Blundell | 12 | „ |
| | Elizabeth Morecroft vxꝰ in eccl̃ia | 17 | „ |
| | Richard Morecroft in eccl̃ia | 20 | „ |
| | Jaine Barton vxꝰ | 21 | „ |
| | Raffe Croppe in eccl̃ia | 23 | „ |
| | Alis Halworth vid in eccl̃ia | „ | „ |
| | Anne Killshaw vxꝰ in eccli | 26 | „ |
| Jū | Ewan Allerton | 1 | Maye |
| | Jaine Harden vxꝰ Will̃m | 3 | „ |
| | Ellin Sumner vid in eccl̃ia | 5 | „ |
| | John Sanforth | 12 | „ |
| Jū | Brichet Hughsdoughter in eccl̃i | 15 | „ |
| | Ellin Asmall vid | 20 | „ |
| | Thomas Sutch | 31 | „ |
| | Nicolas Hey | 7 | June |
| | Thomas Cropp Jū in eccl̃ia | 11 | „ |
| | Katherin Kilshaw fi: Gilbert | 21 | „ |

Wiłłm Kilshaw ... ... ... ... ... ... ... ... 22 June
A Child of Tho: Ormishaw in eccłia ... ... 26 „
Ellin Waringe vid ... ... ... ... ... ... ... 7 July
Alis Henryson vid in eccłia ... ... ... ... 11 „
Hector Lea in eccłia ... ... ... ... ... ... 19 „
Edw: Morecroft fi: Henry in ecciła ... ... 30 „
Henry Goulbron Jũ ... ... ... ... ... ... ... 4 August
Thomas Barker fi: Henry in eccłia ... ... 11 „
Elizabeth Mawdisley fi: Wiłłm in eccłia ... 13 „
A Childe of Peeter Rowe in eclia ... ... ... 18 „
Hugh Ashton fi: Jamis in eccłia ... ... ... 25 „
Alis Stanley fi: vx⁹ in eccłia ... ... ... ... 28 „
Elizabeth Barton vid... ... ... ... ... ... ... 29 „
Anne Traves fi: Richard ... ... ... ... ... ... 30 September
Anne Mawdisley fi: Robert in eccłia ... ... 5 October
A Child of Robert Stopforth ... ... ... ... 12 „
Hugh Dvncon ... ... ... ... ... ... ... ... 16 „
Margaret More Croft fi: Cuthbeř in ecc̃ ... ... 19 „
Wiłłm Woodes ... ... ... ... ... ... ... ... 25 „
Ellis Ambrose in eccłia ... ... ... ... ... ... 3 November
Elizabeth Longley vx⁹ ... ... ... ... ... ... 17 „
John Killshaw ... ... ... ... ... ... ... ... „ „
A Child of Wiłłm Sumner ... ... ... ... 30 „
Henry Mawdisley ... ... ... ... ... ... ... „ „
A Child of Thomas Brigehowse ... ... ... 1 December
Elizabeth Smyth vx⁹ George in eccli ... ... 2 „
Anne Mawdisley vid in eccłia ... ... ... „ „
Anne Burscough ... ... ... ... ... ... ... „ „
Margerie Blundell Ju: ... ... ... ... ... ... 9 „
Richard Holland in eccłia ... ... ... ... ... 13 „
Ellin Aspinwall vx⁹ Henry in eccłia ... ... 18 „
Margaret Westhead vx⁹ Tho: in ecc̃ ... ... 20 „
Tho: Gill Jũ in eccłia ... ... ... ... ... ... 21 „
Jaine Shawe vx⁹ Peeter in eccłi ... ... ... 27 „
A Child of Jamis Aiscroft in eccłia ... ... „ „
Silvester Sutch in eccłia ... ... ... ... ... 31 „
Agnes Parre fi: Edmund... ... ... ... ... ... „ „
Mawde Blundell vid in eccłia ... ... ... ... 4 Januarie
Ellis Haile in eccłia ... ... ... ... ... ... 8 „
Elizabeth Smyth vx⁹ John ... ... ... ... ... 16 „
Elizabeth Voce vx⁹ Gilbert in eccłi ... ... 20 „
A Child of Elis Gleast ... ... ... ... ... ... 22 „
Margerie Bower vx⁹ Robert in ecc̃ ... ... ... 2 ffebruarie
Izabell Lancaster fi: John in eccli ... ... ... 15 „
Peeter Hoolme in eccłia ... ... ... ... ... 17 „
John Tomson ... ... ... ... ... ... ... ... 18 „
Jaine Accristie vid ... ... ... ... ... ... „ „
Thomas Morecroft fi: Richard in ecc̃ ... ... 23 „
Jaine Barton vx⁹ Rodger in eccłia ... ... „ „

Jaine Oliverson vid ... ... ... ... ... ... 26 ffebruarie
A Child of Richard Killshaw ... ... ... ... ... 27 „
Fo. 391 Dorethie Sutch fi: Silvester in eccl ... ... 1 Martch
Thomas Hunter in ecclia ... ... ... ... 3 „
Nicolas Ranal ... ... ... ... ... ... ... 10 „
Hugh Badger ... ... ... ... ... ... ... 20 „
Elizabeth Allerton in ecclia ... ... ... ... 21 „

## 1610.

Edward Stanley de Morehall bur in M9 Stanley his Chappell ... ... ... ... ... ... ... 1 Aprill
Margaret Longley vx9 Tho: ... ... ... ... ... 3 „
Henry Halworth in ecclia ... ... ... ... 9 „
ffrances Sutton fi: Robert ... ... ... ... 10 „
Jaine Sutton fi: Robert ... ... ... ... ... 11 „
Jaine Cropp vid in ecclia ... ... ... ... 15 „
Elizabeth Preskot vid ... ... ... ... ... 16 „
Edward ffogge fi: John in ecclia ... ... ... 20 „
Mawde Croston vx9 Henry in ecclia ... ... 25 „
Ozed Ranould pur ... ... ... ... ... ... 26 „
Anne Walker fi: George ... ... ... ... ... 29 „
Join Wardman vxor ... ... ... ... ... ... 2 Maye
Jaine Mason fi: Arthor in ecclia ... ... ... 3 „
Rowland Ridinge in ecclia ... ... ... ... „ „
Thomas Aspinwap in ecclia ... ... ... ... 14 „
Henry Woofall in ecclia ... ... ... ... ... 31 „
Alis Gilbertson *alias* Johnson vid in eccl ... 12 June
Ric Mason in ecclia ... ... ... ... ... 29 „
Margaret Jackeson vid in ecclia ... ... ... 6 July
Edmund Aspinwall fi: buried in m9 Scarsbreckes Chancell ... ... ... ... ... . „ „
Ellin Hunter vid ... ... ... ... ... ... 7 „
Jenet Shawe fi: Nicolas in ecclia ... ... ... 10 „
Margaret Shawe fi: Nicolas in ecclia ... ... 4 August
Elizabeth Aiscroft pur ... ... ... ... ... 21 „
Willm Prescot ... ... ... ... ... ... ... 29 „
John Mortimer fi: Andrew a stranger ... ... 30 „
Rodger Shaw fi: Juvenis ... ... ... ... ... „ „
Elizabeth ffrith vx9 Hugh ... ... ... ... 31 „
Fo. 392 A Child of Gilbert Jackeson in ecl ... ... ... 1 September
Willm Tyrer fi: Jamis ... ... ... ... 3 „
Willm Woodes fi: Ric bur in the high Chancell „ „
Genet Huton puer ... ... ... ... ... ... 5 „
Alis ffrith fi: Hugh ... ... ... ... ... ... 8 „
Henrye Draper Juvenis ... ... ... ... ... 18 „
Edmund Winstanley fi: Tho: ... ... ... 19 „
Richard Wainewright in ecclia ... ... ... 20 „
John Kilshaw fi: Willm in eclia ... ... ... 21 „

| | | |
|---|---|---|
| . . . Mawdisley fi: Tho: in ecclia | 23 | September |
| Margerie Blundell pur | 25 | „ |
| Emaniwell Stanley fi: George in ec | 28 | „ |
| Ellin Gill | „ | „ |
| Elizabeth Kilshaw fi: John in eccl | 17 | October |
| Jaine Swifte vx⁹ Trymour in ec | 15 | November |
| Elizabeth Ormishaw in ecla | 18 | „ |
| Jenet Yate vx⁹ John | 19 | „ |
| Gilbert Kilshaw | 29 | „ |
| Edward Morecroft fi: Cuthbert in ecclia | 9 | December |
| Alis Allerton vid | 11 | „ |
| Elizabeth Morecroft vx⁹ Tho: | 18 | „ |
| A Child of Henry Gobbin in ecclia | „ | „ |
| Henry Hurst fi: Elis | 20 | „ |
| . . . Sumner vx⁹ Willm | „ | „ |
| Joanie Sowerbutes | 2 | Januarie |
| John Killshaw fi: Willm | 4 | „ |
| Alis Hawwet vid | 5 | „ |
| Katherin Barton fi: Tho: | 6 | „ |
| Henry Coockeson in eccli | 8 | „ |
| Elizabeth Vrmiston | 12 | „ |
| Izabell Jolibrond vid in ecclia | 13 | „ |
| John Duncon *alias* Seall in ecclia | 15 | „ |
| Ranould Mason in ecclia | 28 | „ |
| Anne Ince vx⁹ Hamlet in ecclia | „ | „ |
| 3 Katherin Goulbron vx⁹ ffrances in ecclia | 4 | ffebruarie |
| Thomas Huton in ecclia | 5 | „ |
| Robert Bower in eccl | 9 | „ |
| John Lancaster in eccl | 11 | „ |
| John Hesketh | 16 | „ |
| Anne Scarsbrecke Ju | 21 | „ |
| Marie Aspinwall fi: Tho: | 22 | „ |
| A Child of Raffe Bullocke | „ | „ |
| Oliver Atherton in eccli | 27 | „ |
| Margreat Burie vid | 28 | „ |
| Tho: Kenion fi: Henry in ec | 5 | Martch |
| Robert Brighows fi: Ric in eccl | „ | „ |
| A Child of Edmund Cropp in eccli | 10 | „ |
| Ellin Westhead fi: Tho: in eccl | 13 | „ |
| Cuthbert Morecroft in eccli | 18 | „ |
| Katherin Balshaw vx⁹ John | 24 | „ |

## 1611.

| | | |
|---|---|---|
| A Child of Jamis Preskot in ecclia | 7 | Aprill |
| . . . Gill vx⁹ Willm | 8 | „ |
| Elizabeth Preskot fi: Jamis in eccli | 9 | „ |
| Jaine Chadocke fi: Ric | 14 | „ |
| Willm Woodes in eccli | 15 | „ |

Jaine Hey fi: John in eccli ... ... ... ... 19 Aprill
John Rothwell in eccła ... ... ... ... ... 23 „
Edward Barton fi: John in eccli ... ... ... 26 „
Marie Hey vx⁹ John in ecclia ... ... ... 29 „
George Mawdisley in ecclia ... ... .. ... „ „
Witłm Knowles fi: Witłm bur in the high Chansell ... ... ... ... ... ... ... ... ... 3 Maye
Robert Williamson fi: Robert ... ... ... 15 „
Richard Lathwhat fi: Witłm in eccli ... ... 19 „
Jenet Langley vid ... ... ... ... ... ... ... 3 June
Anne Holland vx⁹ Hugh in eccłi ... ... ... „ „
Richard Martinscroft in ecclia ... ... ... 19 „
Elizabeth Holland vx⁹ John in eccl ... ... 20 „
Emlin Withingeton vx⁹ Tho: in ecclia ... ... 25 „
Jaine Sutch fi: Hugh in eccl ... ... ... ... 28 „
Edw: Gorsutch fi: Edw: in eclia ... ... 1 July
Robert Egicar fi: Hugh in ecclia ... ... ... 6 „
Jaine Knowles fi: Henr ... ... ... ... 12 „
Margreat Whitstons fi: George ... ... ... 21 „
Alis Smulte vid in eccłi ... ... ... ... ... „ „
Anne Morcroft vx⁹ Hector ... ... ... ... 22 „
Robert Woodworth in eccli ... ... ... ... 28 „
Elizabeth Knowles fi: Henrie ... ... ... ... „ „
Tho: Hey in ecclia ... ... ... ... ... 30 „
Fo. 394 Joane Mawdisley fi: Tho: in eccli ... ... 1 August
Joane Killshaw fi: Ric̃ ... ... ... ... ... 8 „
A bace Child of Tho: Hutons ... ... ... 9 „
Trymower Swift in eccłi ... ... ... ... ... 10 „
Ranould Craine in eccłi ... ... ... ... ... 12 „
Elizabeth Irland fi: Jamis ... ... ... ... 25 „
Anne Shawe vx⁹ John ... ... ... ... ... 12 September
John Dod fi: Hugh gentlman in eccłi ... ... „ „
Gilbert Smith in ecclia ... ... ... ... ... 15 „
Sislie Worthingeton Jũ in the high Chancell ... „ „
Anthoney Haughton ... ... ... ... ... 27 „
Henry Breykell in ecclia ... ... ... ... 29 „
A Child of Peeter Westhead in eccłi ... ... 3 October
Margreat Wainewright fi: Tho: in eccłi ... 7 „
John Peeter in eccłi ... ... ... ... ... 9 „
Loare Haughton Jũ in eccłi ... ... ... ... „ „
Katherin Burmiston vx⁹ Raffe in eccłi ... ... 14 „
John Woodes fi: Ric̃ in the high Chañ ... ... 15 „
Jaine Parker vid ... ... ... ... ... ... 23 „
A Child of Thomas Wholeis in ec̃ ... ... ... 25 „
Jenet Gregson vx⁹ Rodger in eccłi ... ... ... 27 „
Emlin Scarsbrecke in m⁹ Scarsbr̃ Chap ... 28 „
Jaine Johnson in eccli ... ... ... ... ... 1 November
Jaine Tarbocke vx⁹ Robert in eccli ... ... 3 „
Ellin Wholey vx⁹ Tho: in ecclia ... ... ... 8 „

Lawrance Willson fi: John ... ... ... 8 November
Elizabeth Morecrofte Jū ... ... ... ... ... ... 11 „
Izabell Leadbetter vx⁹ Robert in eccl̄ia ... 13 „
Anne Waringe fi: Robert ... ... ... ... 16 „
Claris Swift Jū in eccl̄ia ... ... ... ... ... 28 „
Thomas Halsall fi: Edward in eccl̄ia ... ... 6 December
Parsevell Gill ... ... ... ... ... ... ... ... 10 „
Rodger Ridinge fi: Jamis ... ... ... ... 11 „
Jenet Davie vx⁹ Bryhan ... ... ... ... ... 16 „
Henry Halsall in eccl̄ia ... ... ... ... ... „ „
Emlin Westhead vx⁹ Peeter in eccl̄ia ... ... 31 „
5 Elizabeth Hoton fi: Robert ... ... ... ... 7 Januarie
A Child of Edw: Crofte ... ... ... ... 19 „
Rodger Shawe Shawe [*sic*] fi: John ... ... 24 „
Alis Dronninge fi: Richard in eccl̄ia ... ... 27 „
Katherin Gleast vid ... ... ... ... ... ... 31 „
A Child of John Mawd̄isley in eccl̄ia ... ... 3 ffebruarie
Ewaine Blackeledge in eccl̄ia ... ... ... ... 4 „
A Child of Gilbert Jackeson in eccl̄ia ... ... 6 „
Hugh Worthingeton fi: Ric̃ in the high Chansell ... ... ... ... ... ... ... „ „
Margreat Sephton fi: Raffe in eccl̄ia ... ... 16 „
Anne Cropp fi: Tho: in eccl̄ia ... ... ... „ „
Tho: Willson in eccl̄ia ... ... ... ... ... 20 „
Richard Sowerbutes fi: John in ecclia ... ... 25 „
Rodger Gill ... ... ... ... ... ... ... ... 26 „
A Child of Henry Gill ... ... ... ... ... 27 „
Joane Chadocke fi: Richard ... ... ... ... 29 „
Elizabeth Hodgeson pū in eccl̄ia ... ... ... 2 Martch
A Child of Tho: Medowes ... ... ... ... 5 „
Henry Tasker fi: Tho: ... ... ... ... ... 6 „
Hugh Hodgeson in ecclia ... ... ... ... 8 „
Elizabeth Knowles fi: Wil̄l̄m in the high Chansell ... ... ... ... ... ... ... 19 „
Margreat Bispam in ecclia ... ... ... ... 20 „

## 1612.

Ellin Morecroft fi: Gabriell in eccl̄ia ... ... 25 Martch
Anne Mann vx⁹ John in eccl̄ia ... ... ... 26 „
Elizabeth Cowp fi: Ranould in eccl̄ia ... ... 28 „
Elizabeth Westhead fi: Ric̃ in eccl̄ia ... ... „ „
Wil̄l̄m Oudam pū in ecclia ... ... ... ... 31 „
Margerie Litherland ... ... ... ... ... ... 4 Aprill
Jaine Nelson fi: Wil̄l̄m in eccl̄ia ... ... ... 6 „
Elizabeth Asshorst vid in eccl̄ia ... ... ... 9 „
. . . Preskot vid ... ... ... ... ... ... 11 „
Raffe Burmiston in eccl̄ia ... ... ... ... 17 „
Thomas Pendleburie in eccl̄ia ... ... ... 24 „

Izabell Henryson* ... ... ... ... ... ... 24 Aprill
Hamlet Marrow ... ... ... ... ... ... 27 „
Myles Preskot ... ... ... ... ... ... ... 18 Maye
Wiłłm Moscrop ... ... ... ... ... ... „ „
Grace Cowp fi: Ric in eccłia ... ... ... ... „ „
. . . Hadocke ... ... ... ... ... ... 19 „
Elizabeth Hoolme vx[9] Wiłłm ... ... ... ... 27 „
Tho: Mason fi: Will in eccłia ... ... ... 30 „
Fo. 396 Jaine Aiscroft puř in eccłia ... ... ... ... 3 June
Margeri Jackeson vid ... ... ... ... ... 11 „
Grace Lailand fi: Tho: in eccłia ... ... ... 12 „
Jamis Robertson fi: Robert ... ... ... ... 16 „
Elin Kilshaw vx[9] Wiłłm in eccłia ... ... 2 July
John Sutch in eccłia ... ... ... ... ... ... 7 „
Elizabeth Wildinge vx[9] in ecclia ... ... ... 10 „
John Holland fi: Robert ... ... ... ... ... 19 „
Tho: Armetridinge fi: John ... ... ... ... 25 „
A Child of Wiłłm Talior in eccłia ... ... 26 „
Margreat Henryson* vid in eccłia ... ... ... 29 „
Henry Sutch fi: Hugh in eccłia ... ... ... „ „
Elizabeth Hoolme vid ... ... ... ... ... 13 August
Huan Hadocke ... ... ... ... ... ... ... ... 31 „
Jamis Coockeson ... ... ... ... ... ... 10 September
Alis Smyth vid in eccłia ... ... ... ... ... 12 „
John Withingeton in eccłia ... ... ... ... 13 „
Anne Stananought vid in eccłia ... ... ... 14 „
John Smyth fi: Tho: in eccłia ... ... ... „ „
A Child of George Whitstons ... ... ... 19 „
Anthoney Wardman ... ... ... ... ... ... 2 October
Katherin Craine fi: Robert in eccł ... ... 5 „
Tho: Whytestons ... ... ... ... ... ... 7 „
Izabell Moscrop ... ... ... ... ... ... 8 „
Jamis Steele peř ... ... ... ... ... ... 11 „
Jū Richard Adamson in eccła ... ... ... ... 14 „
Hugh Haughton ... ... ... ... ... ... 18 „
Thomas Garrard ... ... ... ... ... ... 19 „
Peeter Swift ... ... ... ... ... ... ... 22 „
Jenet Jumpe vid ... ... ... ... ... ... 26 „
Dowse Cowp vid in eccłia ... ... ... ... 29 „
Jū Gefferey Kindsley in eccłia ... ... ... ... 31 „
Lettis Crooke vid bur in eccłia ... ... ... 6 November
Robert ffar ... ... ... ... ... ... ... „ „
John Balshaw fi: Jamis bur ... ... ... ... 10 „
Margerie Jackeson vid: buř ... ... ... ... 11 „
Thomas Killshaw in eccłia ... ... ... ... 27 „
Thomas Withingeton in eccłia ... ... ... 28 „
Richard Cropp ... ... ... ... ... ... 29 „
Jaine Holland vid ... ... ... ... ... ... „ „

* Harryson *in Chester Transcript.*

| Fo. | | Name | Day | Month |
|---|---|---|---|---|
| 397 | | Henry Howldinge fi: George bur̃ ... ... ... | 8 | December |
| | | Richard Tuson fi: John in eccl̃a ... ... ... | 9 | „ |
| | | Margreat Marclew ... ... ... ... ... ... ... | „ | „ |
| | | John Bankes in eccl̃ia ... ... ... ... ... | 13 | „ |
| | | Margerie Matthew fi: Henry ... ... ... ... | 20 | „ |
| | | Elizabeth Lathwhat fi: Will̃m in ecc̃ ... ... | 23 | „ |
| | Jũ | Edward Scarsbrecke ... ... ... ... ... ... | „ | „ |
| | | Nicolas Morecroft ... ... ... ... ... ... ... | 27 | „ |
| | | Will̃m Scarsbrecke ... ... ... ... ... ... | 29 | „ |
| | | Elizabeth Mollinex fi: John in eccl̃i ... ... | 7 | Januarie |
| | | Will̃m Plumpton ... ... ... ... ... ... ... | 8 | „ |
| | Jũ | Alis Sutch in eccl̃ia ... ... ... ... ... ... ... | 12 | „ |
| | | Margerie Whitfeeld ... ... ... ... ... ... ... | 15 | „ |
| | | Jamis Shires fi: Ric̃ in eccl̃ia ... ... ... ... | 19 | „ |
| | | Richard Hall fi: Robert in eccl̃ia ... ... ... | „ | „ |
| | | Will̃m Mason in eccl̃ia ... ... ... ... ... ... | 21 | „ |
| | | Edward Croft fi: Edw: in eccl̃ia ... ... ... | 25 | „ |
| | | Ellin Groger ... ... ... ... ... ... ... ... | 28 | „ |
| | | A Child of Robert ffidler ... ... ... ... ... | 29 | „ |
| | | Anne Anglesdaile in eccl̃ia ... ... ... ... ... | „ | „ |
| | | Ewan Blackeledge in eccl̃ia ... ... ... ... ... | 1 | ffebruarie |
| | | Katherin ffarclough ... ... ... ... ... ... ... | 2 | „ |
| | | Robert Morecroft ... ... ... ... ... ... ... | 3 | „ |
| | | Gabriell Darbie fi: John ... ... ... ... ... | 5 | „ |
| | | Rodger Morecroft fi: Ric̃ in eccl̃ia ... ... | 6 | „ |
| | | Richard Hadocke fi: Rober ... ... ... ... ... | „ | „ |
| | | Richard Ambrose Clarke Vicar of Ormisk: bur̃ in the high chansell ... ... ... ... ... ... | 7 | „ |
| | | Jamis Haughton in eccl̃ia ... ... ... ... ... | 10 | „ |
| | | Jamis Waringe fi: Will̃m ... ... ... ... ... | 14 | „ |
| | | Thomas Darbie fi: John ... ... ... ... ... | 16 | „ |
| | | Thomas Winder fi: George ... ... ... ... ... | 18 | „ |
| | | Margerie Gill Spinster ... ... ... ... ... ... | 19 | „ |
| | | Ellin Sutch vx⁹ Cristopher ... ... ... ... ... | „ | „ |
| | | Henry Mawdisley in ecclia ... ... ... ... ... | 25 | „ |
| | | Peete Westhead in eccl̃ia ... ... ... ... ... | 26 | „ |
| | Jũ | Christopher Cropp in eccl̃ia ... ... ... ... ... | 27 | „ |
| | | Elizabeth Alker Spinster ... ... ... ... ... ... | „ | „ |
| 398 | | Elizabeth Rilans vid ... ... ... ... ... ... | 1 | Martch |
| | | John Longley ... ... ... ... ... ... ... ... | 4 | „ |
| | | Richard Swift fi: Tho: in eccl̃i ... ... ... ... | 5 | „ |
| | | Edward Barton fi: in eccl̃ia ... ... ... ... ... | 8 | „ |
| | | Thomas Lathwhat in eccl̃ia ... ... ... ... ... | 9 | „ |
| | | Jamis Preskot ... ... ... ... ... ... ... ... | „ | „ |
| | | Alis Allerton Infance in ecc̃ ... ... ... ... ... | 11 | „ |
| | | Gilbert Gobin fi: Henry in ecc̃ ... ... ... ... | 13 | „ |
| | | Margreat Scarsbrecke fi: Hen̄r in ecc̃ ... ... | „ | „ |
| | | Tho: Aimond fi: John ... ... ... ... ... ... | 16 | „ |
| | | Sislie Whitstons vx⁹ Hugh in ec̃ ... ... ... ... | „ | „ |

| | | | |
|---|---|---|---|
| | Alis Barton Infanc̄ | 20 | Martch |
| | Hugh Whitestons in ecclia | 21 | ,, |
| | John Eccleston | 23 | ,, |

## 1613.

| | | | |
|---|---|---|---|
| | Katherin Smulte vid in eccl̄ia | 25 | Martch |
| | Ellin Carr fi: Ric̄ | 26 | ,, |
| | Izabell Haughton vxꝰ Ric̄ | 28 | ,, |
| | Margrett Morecroft vid in eccl̄ia | 9 | Aprill |
| | Anne Neale fil Peaze | ,, | ,, |
| | Jane Winder vxꝰ Richard | 11 | ,, |
| | Margrett Alcar vxꝰ Hector | 13 | ,, |
| | Rob̄te Ireland | ,, | ,, |
| | Margrett Garrard Inf: | 18 | ,, |
| | Rob̄te Morecroft fil Henrie in the highe Chancell | 19 | ,, |
| | Margrett Hey fil James in eccl̄ia | 21 | ,, |
| | Homphrie Haughton | ,, | ,, |
| | Thomas Laland Inf fil Christo in eccl̄ia | ,, | ,, |
| | Jennett Burrie | 25 | ,, |
| | Elizabeth Shaw fil Peeter in eccl̄ia | 26 | ,, |
| | Sisley Carre vid | 28 | ,, |
| | Richard Sannes the ... | 1 | May |
| | Anne Wythingtō vxꝰ Rob̄t in eccl̄ia | ,, | ,, |
| | Nicolas Aspinwall in eccl̄ia | 2 | ,, |
| | Elizabeth Maudisley fil Huan in ecclia | 5 | ,, |
| Fo. 399 | Jane Barker | 9 | ,, |
| | Henrie Whitcliffe fil Richard | ,, | ,, |
| | Ellen More fil James | 11 | ,, |
| | . . . Ascough vxꝰ Huan in eccl̄ia | ,, | ,, |
| | Richard Kirkbie fil Homphry | 14 | ,, |
| | Katherine Marclew vxꝰ Thomas in ecclia | 15 | ,, |
| | Richard Traves fil Willm | 16 | ,, |
| | Thomas Mollyneux | 18 | ,, |
| | Isabell Smyth vid in eccl̄ia | 22 | ,, |
| | James Elliot | 24 | ,, |
| | Anne Garrard vid in eccl̄ia | ,, | ,, |
| | Margrett Butcher spinster in ecclia | 29 | ,, |
| | Thomas Keakwick fil John in eccl̄ia | 7 | June |
| | Thomas Bennett Juvenis | 8 | ,, |
| | Isabell Carbie fil Joseph | 17 | ,, |
| | Ellen Holland fil Willm in eccl̄ia | 19 | ,, |
| | Margrett Crane vxꝰ Edward | 20 | ,, |
| | Marie Davie fil Thomas in eccl̄ia | 25 | ,, |
| | Thomas Sefton fil Edmund in eccl̄ia | 27 | ,, |
| | Ellin Gill vid | 3 | Julie |
| | Claris Westhead fi: Rodger in ecc̄ | 4 | ,, |
| | Slslie Mason fi: Gowther in eccl̄ia | 14 | ,, |

| | | |
|---|---|---|
| Edward Haughton Jū | 18 | Julie |
| John Sephton fi: Edmund in eccl̄ia | 19 | „ |
| Ellin ffletcher in eccl̄ia | 22 | „ |
| Thomas Jollie | 25 | „ |
| Gilbert Preskot Jū in eccl̄ia | „ | „ |
| Robert Shaw in eccl̄ia | 27 | „ |
| A Child of Tho: Davies in eccl̄a | 31 | „ |
| Wil̄l̄m Sumner puer̄ | 6 | August |
| Robert Rutter in eccl̄ia | 7 | „ |
| Richard Lathwhat fi: Jamis | 10 | „ |
| Ellin Sephton fi: Tho: in eccl̄ia | 11 | „ |
| Elizabeth Killshaw fi: Henr̄ | 14 | „ |
| Elizabeth Moscrop Jū | 31 | „ |
| Jaine Morecroft fi: Edw: in eccl | 1 | September |
| Jaine Knowles fi: Wil̄l̄m Clarke bur̄ in the high chansell | 3 | „ |
| Elizabeth Neale fi: Peaze Clarke | „ | „ |
| Anne Mawdisley vid in eccl̄ia | 6 | „ |
| A Child of Edw: Kekewicke | 7 | „ |
| Anne Lailand fi: Tho: in eccl̄ia | „ | „ |
| Margaret Goare Spinster in eccl̄ia | 8 | „ |
| A child of John Aimund | 11 | „ |
| Izabell Luskin Jū in eccl̄ia | „ | „ |
| Thomas Smyth in eccl̄ia | 13 | „ |
| Anne Weaver | 15 | „ |
| Jaine Marcer Jū | „ | „ |
| Katheryne Jumpe wyddow* | 30 | „ |
| Ellis Chadocke fi: Adam in eccl̄ia | 1 | October |
| Wil̄l̄m Lathwhat fi: Henry in eccl̄ia | 5 | „ |
| Alexander Shurliker Jū in eccl̄ia | 7 | „ |
| Robert Halsall in eccl̄ia | 10 | „ |
| John and Anthoney Whiclife in ecclia | „ | „ |
| Henry Gill in eccl̄ia | 12 | „ |
| Elizabeth Morecroft Infanc̄ in eccl̄ia | „ | „ |
| Thomas Haughton fi: Robert | 15 | „ |
| Jamis Stopforth in the high Chansell | 27 | „ |
| Rodger Sankey in ecclia | 2 | November |
| Thomas Hunter fi: Tho: in eccl̄ia | 3 | „ |
| Mrs Margaret Stanley of Bycarstaff vid bur̄ in her owne Chappell | „ | „ |
| John Hayton fi: Tho: in eccl̄ia | 8 | „ |
| Thomas ffidler | 9 | „ |
| Rodger Lathwhat fi: Wil̄l̄m in eccl̄ia | 11 | „ |
| Ellis Haile fi: Robert in eccl̄ia | 14 | „ |
| Jaine Sankey vid in eccl̄ia | 18 | „ |
| Anne Soothworth fil̄ Rob̄t | 25 | „ |

* *This is an interlineation in another hand. In the margin opposite the entry is the following* "note y[t] shee was a Recusant & bur wthout consent of y[e] vicar."

Mrs Katherine Stanley vx⁹ Edward of Beccursteth Esquire bur̄ in theire high Chancell ... 27 November
James Cowp in ecctia ... ... ... ... ... ... 1 December
Henry Modisley Jū in ecctia ... ... ... ... ... 6 „
Wittm Walker fit George ... ... ... ... ... „ „
Fo. 401 William Stopford in ecclia ... ... ... ... ... 17 „
George Haughton ... ... ... ... ... ... ... ... 22 „
ffrances Hamlett in the high Chancell ... ... 26 „
Robt Hunter fit Edward ... ... ... ... ... ... 27 „
Margrett Mason vx⁹ Cuthbert in ecctia ... ... 30 „
Ellen Lyon fit James in ecctia ... ... ... 8 Januarie
Ranald Gill ... ... ... ... ... ... ... ... ... 12 „
Elizab: Ascroft vx⁹ James in ecclia ... ... 29 „
James Westhead Inf: in ecclia ... ... ... 1 ffebruary
Edith Masō vid in ecctia ... ... ... ... ... 3 „
A child of Gowther Mason in ecctia ... ... „ „
Joanie Holland vid ... ... ... ... ... ... ... 5 „
Anne Croft fit Edward ... ... ... ... ... ... 10 „
Elizab: Biccursteth ... ... ... ... ... ... ... „ „
John Rhodes Inf ... ... ... ... ... ... ... 11 „
Edward fforster ... ... ... ... ... ... ... 13 „
Gilbt Ormishawe Inf: bur in ecctia ... ... „ „
Jane Simson Inf: in ecclia ... ... ... ... ... 16 „
James Harrison in ecctia ... ... ... ... ... 18 „
Nicolas Walthew in ecctia ... ... ... ... „ „
Anne Caudery vx⁹ Wittm ... ... ... ... ... 27 „
Elizabeth Wardman vid ... ... ... ... ... ... 1 March
Elizab: Halton spinster ... ... ... ... ... ... 5 „
Xpofer Gill ... ... ... ... ... ... ... ... ... 6 „
A Childe of Edmund Parr ... ... ... ... ... „ „
Thomas Wilkinson fit George in ecctia ... ... 8 „
Ellen Johnson vx⁹ Wittm ... ... ... ... ... 12 „
Margrett Hill fit Thomas ... ... ... ... ... 16 „
John Holland fit Richard in ecctia ... ... 17 „
Thomas Haslie ... ... ... ... ... ... ... ... ... „ „
Thomas Smyth in ecctia ... ... ... ... ... 19 „
Edw: Spencer fit James in ecctia ... ... ... „ „
Ellen Smyth fit Cuthbert in ecctia ... ... ... „ „
Margery Laland vx⁹ John in ecctia ... ... 21 „

## 1614.

Huan Hawarth fit James in ecctia ... ... ... 29 March
Jane Prescott Jū in ecclia ... ... ... ... ... „ „
Elizab: Weend ... ... ... ... ... ... ... ... ... 31 „
Margrett Hill spinster ... ... ... ... ... ... 2 Aprill
Jennett Woode vid ... ... ... ... ... ... ... 6 „
Maude Blundill fill Robt ... ... ... ... ... 13 „
George Rigmaden in ecctia ... ... ... ... ... 19 „

| | | |
|---|---|---|
| Katherine Prynne a stranger ... ... ... ... ... | 23 | Aprill |
| Richard Glasburrow ... ... ... ... ... ... ... | 24 | „ |
| Mꝰgerie Webster vxꝰ John in eccl̄ia ... ... | 25 | „ |
| Henry Jackson inf: fil̄ Richard ... ... ... ... | „ | „ |
| 02 . . . Woodhouse vxꝰ Hugh in ecclia... ... | 28 | „ |
| Gilb̄te Burscough in eccl̄ia ... ... ... ... ... | „ | „ |
| Ellen Shawe infans in eccl̄ia ... ... ... ... ... | 29 | „ |
| Thomas Gilb̄tson in eccl̄ia ... ... ... ... ... | 1 | Maie |
| A Childe of Rob̄te Crane in eccl̄ia ... ... ... | 3 | „ |
| Will̄m Rigmaden in eccl̄ia ... ... ... ... ... | 5 | „ |
| Roger Haughton ... ... ... ... ... ... ... | „ | „ |
| Will̄m Godbeere ... ... ... ... ... ... ... | 6 | „ |
| Rob̄te ffarrer ... ... ... ... ... ... ... ... | 12 | „ |
| Jane Davie fil̄ Thome in ecclia ... ... ... | 13 | „ |
| Margerie Lea vid in ecclia ... ... ... ... | 16 | „ |
| Agnes ffenton vid in eccl̄ia ... ... ... ... ... | „ | „ |
| sp: John Marclew fil̄ Thome in eccl̄ia ... ... ... | „ | „ |
| John ffarre Juvenis ... ... ... ... ... ... ... | 20 | „ |
| A Childe of John Sowrbutts in ecclia ... ... | 22 | „ |
| sp: Rauffe Whitestones infans in eccl̄ia ... ... | 23 | „ |
| Margrett Mollynex vid ... ... ... ... ... ... | 1 | June |
| Jennett Marrall vid in eccl̄ia ... ... ... ... ... | 8 | „ |
| Jane Rose Jū in ecclia ... ... ... ... ... ... | 12 | „ |
| Henrie Leiusley ... ... ... ... ... ... ... | 18 | „ |
| Jane Blundill fil̄ Edward in eccl̄ia ... ... ... | „ | „ |
| Richard Charnocke fil̄ Roger in eccl̄ia ... ... | 21 | „ |
| Henrie Davie fil̄ John in eccl̄ia ... ... ... ... | 26 | „ |
| Elizabeth Tarlton infans ... ... ... ... ... ... | 1 | Julie |
| Anne Lee infans in eccl̄ia ... ... ... ... ... | 5 | „ |
| James Smalshawe in eccl̄ia ... ... ... ... ... | 7 | „ |
| Albanie Butler bur̄ in mꝰ Scarisbricke his chancell ... ... ... ... ... ... ... ... ... | 9 | „ |
| James Becconsall ... ... ... ... ... ... ... | 10 | „ |
| Hector Morcrofte Juven ... ... ... ... ... ... | 12 | „ |
| Hugh Baron Infans in eccl̄ia ... ... ... ... | 14 | „ |
| John Lancaster Juven in eccl̄ia ... ... ... ... | 15 | „ |
| Will̄m Nayler in eccl̄ia ... ... ... ... ... ... | 21 | „ |
| Dorithie Stanley virg: ... ... ... ... ... ... | 22 | „ |
| Edward Balle the ... ... ... ... ... ... ... | 23 | „ |
| Sisley Spencer infans ... ... ... ... ... ... | 26 | „ |
| John Sallett ... ... ... ... ... ... ... ... | 29 | „ |
| Clarice Barton infans in eccl̄ia ... ... ... ... | 30 | „ |
| 403 John Marclewe infans ... ... ... ... ... ... | 12 | August |
| Margrett Ashurst vid ... ... ... ... ... ... | 16 | „ |
| Henrie Hale infans in eccl̄ia ... ... ... ... ... | 17 | „ |
| Anne Swyfte inf ... ... ... ... ... ... ... | 20 | „ |
| Thomas Mollyneux ... ... ... ... ... ... ... | 26 | „ |
| John Ascrofte infan: in eccl̄ia ... ... ... ... | 3 | September |
| A childe of Richard Modisley ... ... ... ... ... | 5 | „ |

Richard Leegh Juven bur m[9] Scarisbricks Chappell ... 10 September
Xpofer Sutch ... 17 „
Anne Withington vx[9] George ... 20 „
James Hankin in ecclia ... 24 „
A Childe of Jeffrey Parye ... 28 „
Arthur Marclew fil Willm ... 29 „
Richard Shawe ... 5 October
Alice Barton vx[9] Pet: in ecclia ... 31 „
John A stanger [*sic*] ... 3 November
Margrett Jollie Spinster ... 8 „
Jane Prescott vx[9] Thomas ... 9 „
Ellen Jumpe ... 10 „
Katherine Marclewe vx[9] Willm in ecclia ... „ „
Thomas Houlme fil Richard ... 11 „
Peter Vauce Inf in ecclia ... 18 „
Edward Jones fil Roger ... „ „
Huan Wainwright ... 21 „
Betridge Gill vx[9] Hugh ... 22 „
Jennite Morcrofte vx[9] James ... 30 „
Richard Smult fil Robte in ecclia ... 1 December
Richard Ashton fil Rich ... 15 „
Henry Crapper fil Edm̃ in ecclia ... 22 „
Edward Stanley fil George in ecclia ... 25 „
Roger Winder the ... 8 Januarie
Jenett Haughtō vid in ecclia ... „ „
Marie Tyrer fil James ... „ „
John Ascrofte in ecclia ... „ „
Edward Hutchin in ecclia ... 10 „
Hugh ffletcher in ecclia ... 17 „
Clarice Hodgkinson virg: in ecclia ... 19 „
A Childe of Anthonie Soothwoorth ... 23 „
Hugh Gill ... 25 „
Roger Scarisbricke Inf: ... 27 „
John Hurst infans ... 31 „
Fo. 404 Anne Ambrose vx[9] Henrie ... 3 ffebruarie
Katherine Meadowe vx[9] Thom̃ ... 5 „
Willm Reades Inf: ... 9 „
Anne Houlme vx[9] Edward ... 10 „
A Childe of M[9] Willm Knowles Vicar bur in the highe chancell ... 11 „
Elizabeth Shawe spinster ... „ „
Alice Ascrofte vid in ecclia ... 12 „
Luke Sutch in ecclia ... 15 „
Jonie Sutch vid ... „ „
Amery Sumner vid in ecclia ... 22 „
Rauffe Ascrofte in ecclia ... 26 „
Alice Vauce vx[9] Rich: in ecclia ... 27 „
John Maudisley in ecclia ... 28 „

|  |  |  |
|---|---|---|
| Wiłłm Sankie infans in eccłia ... ... ... | 1 | March |
| Marie Maudisley fił : Tho : in eccłia ... ... | 4 | „ |
| Nic̃ ffořbie Juven in eccłia ... ... ... ... | „ | „ |
| Lawrence Rylans Jū ... ... ... ... ... | 5 | „ |
| Thomas Mason fił Ranald in eccłia ... ... | 6 | „ |
| Thomas Sutton infan in eccłia ... ... ... | 9 | „ |
| Katherine Lythom infans ... ... ... ... ... ... | „ | „ |
| Thomas Roades infans ... ... ... ... ... ... | 22 | „ |
| Jane Bale vid ... ... ... ... ... ... ... ... | „ | „ |
| James Lathwaitt Juvenis in eccłia ... ... ... | 23 | „ |

## 1615.

|  |  |  |
|---|---|---|
| Elizabeth ffletcher infans ... ... ... ... ... | 26 | March |
| Elizab : Mason vx⁹ Gawther in eccłia ... ... | 3 | Aprill |
| Elizab : Brigghouse vx⁹ Thom in eccłia ... | 4 | „ |
| John Webster in eccłia ... ... ... ... ... ... | 9 | „ |
| Anne Gliasburrow vid ... ... ... ... ... ... | 14 | „ |
| Anne Martin vid ... ... ... ... ... ... ... ... | 16 | „ |
| William Ascroft fił : John in eccłia ... ... | 17 | „ |
| Myles Rimmer infans in eccłia ... ... ... | 19 | „ |
| Wiłłm Lea de Aughtō in eccłia ... ... ... | 20 | „ |
| Wiłłm Coockson in eccłia ... ... ... ... ... | 23 | „ |
| Richard Croft infans ... ... ... ... ... ... | 24 | „ |
| Jennett Jackson vid ... ... ... ... ... ... ... | 25 | „ |
| Sisley Holden fił George ... ... ... ... ... ... | 20 | „ |
| Richard Marclew Juven in ecclia ... ... ... | 9 | Maie |
| Richard Ploumbe Inf : in ecclia ... ... ... | 10 | „ |
| Mrs Elizabeth Cotton p̱egrina in the high Chancell ... ... ... ... ... ... ... ... | 13 | „ |
| James Laithwaitt Juven in eccłia ... ... ... | „ | „ |
| Anne Elliot spinster ... ... ... ... ... ... ... ... | „ | „ |
| Ellen Crapper Infans ... ... ... ... ... ... | 3 | June |
| Katherine Butler vid in eccłia ... ... ... | 10 | „ |
| Ellen Parker fił Thomas ... ... ... ... ... ... | 14 | „ |
| A Childe of John Sumner ... ... ... ... ... | 16 | „ |
| Richard Holland de Aughton ... ... ... | 23 | „ |
| Rob̄te Maudisley in eccłia ... ... ... ... | 28 | „ |
| Elizabeth Browne vid ... ... ... ... ... | 2 | July |
| Jane Prescott Spinster ... ... ... ... ... ... | 3 | „ |
| Anne Carbee Infans ... ... ... ... ... ... ... | 17 | „ |
| A Childe of Henry Scarisbricke ... ... ... | 30 | „ |
| Wiłłm Whickliffe ... ... ... ... ... ... ... | 4 | August |
| Gilb̄t Swyft fił James in eccłia ... ... ... | 5 | „ |
| Margret Wainwright vx⁹ Hugh in eccłia ... | 11 | „ |
| Sisley Wroe vx⁹ Peter in eccła ... ... ... | 25 | „ |
| Richard Allerton fił Rauffe in eccłia ... ... | 26 | „ |
| Richard Jackson Inf in eccłia ... ... ... | 31 | „ |

Edward Holland in ecclia ... ... ... ... 2 September
Margrett Ireland vx⁹ Robt ... ... ... ... 14 „
Margret Haughton vid ... ... ... ... ... 16 „
Grace Morcroft virg in ecclia ... ... ... ... 17 „
Hugh Hesketh in ecclia ... ... ... ... ... 20 „
Jane Ascough virgo ... ... ... ... ... ... 29 „
Jennett Scarisbrick vid ... ... ... ... ... 4 October
Elizabeth Gleast vx⁹ Ellice ... ... ... ... 5 „
Henry Atherton infans in ecclia ... ... ... 8 „
John Wright Infans in ecclia ... ... ... ... 9 „
Richard Brighouse yeoman ... ... ... ... „ „
Homphry Garrard Juven ... ... ... ... ... 14 „
Isabell Prescott vx⁹ Richard in ecclia ... ... „ „
Jane vx⁹ Henry Stopford in ecclia... ... ... 15 „
Robte Prescott ... ... ... ... ... ... ... 16 „
Grace Melling vx⁹ Rauffe ... ... ... ... 20 „
Robte Button A stranger ... ... ... ... ... „ „
Edward Causey in ecclia ... ... ... ... 27 „
A child of Lewes Hewsō A stranger ... ... „ „
Jane Cowp vx⁹ Willm in ecclia ... ... ... 30 „
Fo. 406 Gilbte Balshewe ... ... ... ... ... ... 2 November
Edward Yate ... ... ... ... ... ... ... 3 „
Willm Cawdery ... ... ... ... ... ... 4 „
Emlin Shell in ecclia ... ... ... ... ... 5 „
Richard Mosse in ecclia ... ... ... ... ... 7 „
Michaell Geldard de Aughtō ... ... ... ... 9 „
Alice Esthead* vx⁹ John ... ... ... ... ... 10 „
Thomas Sutch in ecclia ... ... ... ... ... 16 „
Ellen Ireland vid in ecclia ... ... ... ... „ „
John Gobben Infans in ecclia ... ... ... ... 18 „
Hector Morecroft ... ... ... ... ... ... 21 „
Edward Thornall Infans ... ... ... ... ... „ „
Elizabeth Woodes vx⁹ Willm in ecclia ... ... 22 „
Clarice Sankie vx⁹ Richard in the highe Chancell ... ... ... ... ... ... ... ... 25 „
Margrett Welsh spinster ... ... ... ... ... „ „
Alice Tompson fil Willm ... ... ... ... 27 „
Thomas Modisley in ecclia ... ... ... ... 1 December
Margrett Stopford spinster ... ... ... ... 14 „
Robte Cockett ... ... ... ... ... ... ... 22 „
Silvester Coockson ... ... ... ... ... ... 23 „
Elizabeth Waring vid ... ... ... ... ... 25 „
James Morcroft ... ... ... ... ... ... ... 26 „
Barton Morcoft [*sic*] Inf in ecclia ... ... ... „ „
Jane Allerton vid ... ... ... ... ... ... 27 „
Margrett Mason Spinster in ecclia ... ... ... 28 „
Margrett Hale virg in ecclia ... ... ... ... 29 „

* Asshorst *in Chester Transcript.*

Henry ffairclough ... ... ... ... ... ... 2 January
James Rym̄er Inf: in eccl̄ia ... ... ... ... 7 „
John Pemberton Infans ... ... ... ... ... „ „
Richard ffysher ... ... ... ... ... ... 8 „
Will̄m Towne Juvenis in eccl̄ia ... ... ... 9 „
Rob̄te Gille Infans ... ... ... ... ... ... 10 „
Edward Westhead Inf: in eccl̄ia ... ... ... 15 „
Henry Aspinwall in eccl̄ia ... ... ... ... „ „
Jane Crapper vxꝰ Raphe ... ... ... ... ... 16 „
Elizabeth Stananought vxꝰ Thom: in eccl̄ia ... 19 „
John Esthead ... ... ... ... ... ... ... „ „
Grace Bartō vxꝰ John in eccl̄ia ... ... ... 22 „
Thomas Soothwarth fil̄ Anthony ... ... ... 29 „
407 Mary Gregson vxꝰ Thomas in ecclia ... ... 6 ffebruarie
Jennett Spencer Inf in eccl̄ia ... ... ... ... 12 „
Mary Knowles vxꝰ Will̄m the Kinges preacher in the high Chancell ... ... ... ... 17 „
James Smult fil̄ Thomas in eccl̄ia ... ... ... „ „
George Hurst Inf ... ... ... ... ... ... 20 „
George Sutch ... ... ... ... ... ... ... 25 „
Rob̄te Keakwicke Inf ... ... ... ... ... 28 „
Ellen Chadock Inf ... ... ... ... ... ... 5 March
Ellen vxꝰ Rob̄ti Whalley ... ... ... ... ... 6 „
Mary Woorthington vxꝰ Rich in eccl̄ia ... ... 7 „
Anne Aspinwall vid in eccl̄ia ... ... ... ... 11 „
Edward Barton Juv in eccl̄ia ... ... ... ... 18 „
Margrett Blundill vxꝰ Edward in eccl̄ia ... ... 21 „

## 1616.

Sisley Chadock vxꝰ Rich ... ... ... ... 28 March
Thomas Rigbie Infans ... ... ... ... ... „ „
Anne Prescott Inf in eccl̄ia ... ... ... ... 1 Aprill
Rob̄te Woodes in the highe chancell ... ... 4 „
Alice Blundill vid ... ... ... ... ... ... 5 „
James ffletcher Inf ... ... ... ... ... ... 6 „
John Greaues ... ... ... ... ... ... ... „ „
Thomas Lea in eccl̄ia ... ... ... ... ... „ „
Edmunde Shawe in eccl̄ia ... ... ... ... 11 „
Margrett vxꝰ Homphry Greaues ... ... ... 15 „
Richard Gille ... ... ... ... ... ... ... „ „
Elizabeth Greene vid ... ... ... ... ... 27 „
A childe of Henry Dale de Aughton ... ... 2 May
Henry Shires Infans in eccl̄ia ... ... ... ... 5 „
Peter Morcroft fil̄ Thomas ... ... ... ... 6 „
. . . Shawe vid in eccl̄ia ... ... ... ... 8 „
Henry Allerton fil̄ Richard ... ... ... ... 13 „
Gilb̄te Scarisbricke in ecclia ... ... ... ... „ „
Katheryne Rym̄er vid ... ... ... ... ... 19 „

| | | | |
|---|---|---|---|
| | Robte Marrall in ecclia ... ... ... ... ... ... | 20 | May |
| | Margrett Traves fil Wm ... ... ... ... ... | 24 | „ |
| | Elizab: Keakwick vxꝰ Hugh in ecclia ... ... | 27 | „ |
| | Katheryne Barton vxꝰ Myles in ecclia ... ... | 29 | „ |
| | George Woodes Infans in the high chancell ... | 3 | June |
| | Emlin Laythwaitt vid in ecclia ... ... ... | 9 | „ |
| | Ellen vxꝰ Rich Kilshawe ... ... ... ... ... | 25 | „ |
| Fo. 408 | William Barton ... ... ... ... ... ... ... | 10 | Julie |
| | Edward Billinge Infans ... ... ... ... ... ... | 20 | „ |
| | Emlin Sephton vid in ecclia ... ... ... ... | 2 | August |
| | Alice Warde Infans ... ... ... ... ... ... ... | 9 | „ |
| | Margery Barton vxꝰ Lewes ... ... ... ... ... | 16 | „ |
| | Maude Blundill vxꝰ Henry ... ... ... ... | 22 | „ |
| | Gotfrey Atherton ... ... ... ... ... ... ... | 27 | „ |
| | Jane vxꝰ Richard Shawe in ecclia ... ... ... | 30 | „ |
| | Anne Blundill vxꝰ Gilbte ... ... ... ... | 2 | September |
| | Ellen Blundill vxꝰ Alexand in ecclia ... ... | „ | „ |
| | John Parker ... ... ... ... ... ... ... ... | 12 | „ |
| | Willm Woodes in ecclia ... ... ... ... ... ... | 16 | „ |
| | Richard Prescott ... ... ... ... ... ... ... | „ | „ |
| | Vere Marshall fil John gent in ecclia ... ... | 17 | „ |
| | Elizabeth Higham Inf ... ... ... ... ... ... | 19 | „ |
| | A Childe of Maij of Athertō in ecclia ... ... | 30 | „ |
| | Margery Waring Spinster ... ... ... ... ... ... | 9 | October |
| | A Childe of Thomas Gille ... ... ... ... ... | 11 | „ |
| | Jane Atherton vid in ecclia ... ... ... ... ... | 12 | „ |
| | Margery Aspinwall Inf: in ecclia ... ... ... | 25 | „ |
| | John Aingsdale in ecclia ... ... ... ... ... | 6 | November |
| | Margrett vxꝰ James Lathom in ecclia ... ... | 15 | „ |
| | Margrett Marclewe vid in ecclia ... ... ... | 16 | „ |
| | Margrett Prescott vxꝰ ffardinand in ecclia ... | 17 | „ |
| | Margrett Kilshawe vid ... ... ... ... ... | 25 | „ |
| | Xpofer Blundill ... ... ... ... ... ... ... | 1 | December |
| | Thomas Bore ... ... ... ... ... ... ... ... | 2 | „ |
| | Willm Smult in ecclia ... ... ... ... ... ... | 3 | „ |
| | Ellen Hunter vid in ecclia ... ... ... ... | 7 | „ |
| | Jane Dukes A stranger ... ... ... ... ... ... | 8 | „ |
| | Willm Hopwoode ... ... ... ... ... ... ... | 14 | „ |
| | Phillip vxꝰ Homphry Berry ... ... ... ... | 15 | „ |
| | Margrett Swyft Inf in ecclia ... ... ... ... | „ | „ |
| | Anne Morcroft vid ... ... ... ... ... ... ... | 17 | „ |
| | A Childe of Robte Hollywell ... ... ... ... | 19 | „ |
| | Margrett Crapp vid in ecclia ... ... ... ... | 25 | „ |
| | Clarce Car vxꝰ Thom: in ecclia ... ... ... | 26 | „ |
| Fo. 409 | Elizab: Haughtō vid ... ... ... ... ... | 5 | January |
| | Richard Ormeshawe de Aughtō ... ... ... | 8 | „ |
| | Peter Sutch Inf in ecclia ... ... ... ... ... | 17 | „ |
| | Willm Westhead Inf in ecclia ... ... ... | 19 | „ |
| | John Dixon ... ... ... ... ... ... ... | 23 | „ |

|  |  |  |
|---|---|---|
| Thomas Adamson ... ... ... ... ... ... | 28 | „ |
| Maud Hunt vid in eccl̄ia ... ... ... ... | 1 | ffebruary |
| Margrett Sharples Spinster ... ... ... ... | 7 | „ |
| Elizabeth Ploumbe vxꝰ James in eccl̄ia ... ... | 9 | „ |
| Alice Carre spinster in eccl̄ia ... ... ... ... ... | 14 | „ |
| Ellen Webster vid in eccl̄ia ... ... ... ... ... | 28 | „ |
| Gowther Woosie in eccl̄ia ... ... ... ... ... | 2 | March |
| Anne Kilshawe Inf ... ... ... ... ... ... ... | 6 | „ |
| Alice Barton Inf ... ... ... ... ... ... ... | 13 | „ |
| Gilb̄te Barton ... ... ... ... ... ... ... ... | „ | „ |
| Elizabeth Webster vid in eccl̄ia ... ... ... ... | 19 | „ |
| Margrett Whitestones vxꝰ Rich : in eccl̄ia ... | 20 | „ |
| Margery Layland Infans in eccl̄ia ... ... ... | „ | „ |

## 1617.

|  |  |  |
|---|---|---|
| Anne Kilshawe Infans in eccl̄ia ... ... ... | 26 | March |
| Elizabeth Preston Inf : a stranger ... ... ... | 28 | „ |
| A Childe of James Morcrofte ... ... ... ... | 1 | Aprill |
| Jennett Johnson vid ... ... ... ... ... ... | 3 | „ |
| Margrett Gleast Inf : ... ... ... ... ... ... | 6 | „ |
| James Blundill Junior ... ... ... ... ... ... | „ | „ |
| Margery Snape Spinster ... ... ... ... ... ... | „ | „ |
| Myles Thrope Inf : ... ... ... ... ... ... ... | 12 | „ |
| Elizabeth Jolly vid ... ... ... ... ... ... ... | 14 | „ |
| Myles ffletcher in eccl̄ia ... ... ... ... ... ... | „ | „ |
| . . . Ascroft Inf : in eccl̄ia ... ... ... | 20 | „ |
| A childe of John Sourbutts in eccl̄ia ... ... | „ | „ |
| Thomas Meadowe ... ... ... ... ... ... ... | 21 | „ |
| Rob̄te Skirbacre [*sic*] Inf : ... ... ... ... ... | 22 | „ |
| George Prescott Juvē in eccl̄ia ... ... ... | 24 | „ |
| Jane Swyfte Inf : in ecclia ... ... ... ... | 30 | „ |
| Will̄m Kilshawe in eccl̄ia ... ... ... ... ... | 2 | Maye |
| Ellen Whalley virgo in eccl̄ia ... ... ... ... | 6 | „ |
| Henry Harrison Juvenis in eccl̄ia ... ... ... | 7 | „ |
| Margrett Cockett vxꝰ Henry ... ... ... ... | „ | „ |
| Jane Walker Infans in eccl̄ia ... ... ... ... | 10 | „ |
| James Topping Inf ... ... ... ... ... ... ... | 11 | „ |
| John Crapp in eccl̄ia ... ... ... ... ... ... | 12 | „ |
| Elizab : Ryding vxꝰ Will̄m ... ... ... ... | 23 | „ |
| Anne Morcroft vid in eccl̄ia ... ... ... ... | 25 | „ |
| Mary Sutch Inf in eccl̄ia ... ... ... ... ... | 27 | „ |
| F. 410 ffardinand Wardman ... ... ... ... ... | 7 | June |
| Elizab : Balle vid in eccl̄ia ... ... ... ... ... | 8 | „ |
| Will̄m Langeley gent : in the Erle of Derbies Chappell ... ... ... ... ... ... ... | 9 | „ |
| Margrett Parker Infans ... ... ... ... ... ... | 11 | „ |
| Richard Houlme in eccl̄ia ... ... ... ... ... | 15 | „ |
| Ellen Tompson fil̄ John ... ... ... ... ... ... | „ | „ |

Edward Gille in Mr Scarisbricks Chancell ... 15 June
Katheryne Wardman vid ... ... ... ... ... ... 16 „
John Spencer Inf ... ... ... ... ... ... ... 18 „
Martha Sutch virgo in ecclia ... ... ... ... ... 19 „
Thomas Winder the ... ... ... ... ... ... 22 „
Rob̄te Hatherwoode ... ... ... ... ... ... 24 „
Margrett Gilb̄tson vid in eccłia ... ... ... 1 Julie
Wiłłm Robinson de Aughtō in ecclia ... ... 6 „
Mary Stryker ... ... ... ... ... ... ... ... „ „
Anne Woodes Infans in ye high chancell ... 7 „
Richard Marclew fił Wiłłm ... ... ... ... 13 „
Anne Jackson fił John in eccłia ... ... ... 16 „
Elizab: vx9 Georgij Haughtō ... ... ... ... ... 19 „
Lawrence Mathewe Inf: a stranger ... ... 27 „
Gilb̄te Higham Infans ... ... ... ... ... ... 29 „
Henry Burscough Juvenis ... ... ... ... ... 2 August
Jane Crapp virgo in the high chancell ... ... 7 „
James Hawett Juveñ in eccłia ... ... ... 15 „
Anne Burscough Inf: in eccłia ... ... ... 16 „
Katheryne vx9 Henry Winder ... ... ... „ „
Raph Crapp ... ... ... ... ... ... ... ... „ „
Richard Brookes inf: in eccłia ... ... ... „ „
Elizabeth Barker spinster ... ... ... ... „ „
Ellen Coppall spinster ... ... ... ... ... 19 „
A man childe of James Lyon in eccłia ... ... 2 September
Anne Kilshawe vx9 Allon ... ... ... ... 5 „
Katheryne Haughton spinster ... ... ... ... „ „
John Rose fił Rich: in eccłia ... ... ... ... 6 „
Roger Aspinwall fił Thurstā in eccłia ... ... 8 „
Henry Mountieson in my Lord of Derbies Chancell ... ... ... ... ... ... ... ... 10 „
Rich: Sharples ałs Warde in eccłia ... ... 11 „
Ellen Ashurst Inf in eccłia ... ... ... ... 13 „
Dorithy Sharples ałs Ward in eccłia ... ... 14 „
Rob̄te Wilson ... ... ... ... ... ... ... ... 16 „
Hugh Hey Bacheler ... ... ... ... ... ... 29 „
Fo. 411 Mr Wm Knowles in the high chancell ... ... 2 October
Peter Marclewe Inf: ... ... ... ... ... ... 5 „
George Winder the ... ... ... ... ... ... 7 „
Margrett vx9 Gilb̄te Gille in eccłia ... ... ... 9 „
Jane Smyth vid in eccłia ... ... ... ... ... „ „
Alice Morcroft spinster in eccłia ... ... ... 12 „
Rob̄te ffryth Bacheler ... ... ... ... ... „ „
Cisley vx9 Gilb̄ti Blundill ... ... ... ... 14 „
Hugh Crapp in eccłia ... ... ... ... ... 15 „
Grace Warde Inf: ... ... ... ... ... ... 4 November
Martha Haughton inf: ... ... ... ... ... „ „
Roger Gregson in eccłia ... ... ... ... ... 5 „
A childe of Peter Deanes of Wigan in eccłia ... 8 „

Richard Spakeman in ecclia ... ... ... ... ... 14 November
Mꝰgrett Rigby vxꝰ John in eccłia ... ... ... 17 „
Wiłłm Walley infans ... ... ... ... ... 21 „
Margrett White vid ... ... ... ... ... ... 22 „
Thomas Hey Inf: ... ... ... ... ... ... 23 „
Margrett Morcroft virgo in eccłia ... ... ... 24 „
Hugh ffazacharley ... ... ... ... ... ... 26 „
Elizab: Abrahā spinster in eccłlia ... ... 27 „
Cisley Winder Inf: ... ... ... ... ... ... 3 December
A child of Raph Pale in eccłia ... ... ... 6 „
Jane Moscrop vid ... ... ... ... ... ... „ „
Elizab: vxꝰ Arthur Bartō in eccłia ... ... 7 „
Rob̄te Gille Infan ... ... ... ... ... ... 8 „
Isabell Parker virgo generosa in Mꝰ Scarisbricks chancell ... ... ... ... ... ... ... ... 9 „
Emlin Martindale spinster ... ... ... ... 12 „
Alice vxꝰ Henric̄ Sutch in the High Chancell 14 „
Hugh Jollybrand fił Rich: gent: in eccłia ... 28 „
Anne Maundy spinster ... ... ... ... ... „ „
Elizab: Hopwoode widowe ... ... ... ... 3 January
A childe of John Prescott in ecclia ... ... 4 „
Ellice Gleast ... ... ... ... ... ... ... 5 „
Ellen Gilder vid de Aughtō ... ... ... ... „ „
Katheryne Smult Spinster ... ... ... ... „ „
Jane Gille vxꝰ John ... ... ... ... ... ... 10 „
Sara vxꝰ Henry Wythingtō in eccłia ... ... 12 „
Jane Atherton vid in eccłia ... ... ... ... 20 „
Ellen Gleast Infan ... ... ... ... ... ... „ „
2 . . . Barton Juveñ in ecclia ... ... ... 24 „
A childe of James Steele ... ... ... ... ... 26 „
Jennett Ascroft vid ... ... ... ... ... ... „ „
Hugh Lathom puer in eccłia ... ... ... ... 29 „
Jennett vxꝰ Raph Morcroft ... ... ... ... 1 ffebruary
. . . Shakstaffe a stranger ... ... ... 2 „
Katheryne Keakwick vid ... ... ... ... ... 6 „
Jennett Hunter vid in eccłia ... ... ... ... 8 „
Margery Harryson vxꝰ Rob̄t in eccłia ... ... 11 „
Thomas Wright Labourer ... ... ... ... 23 „
James Ashton ... ... ... ... ... ... ... 4 March
A childe of John Sowerbuts in eccłia ... ... 8 „
Margrett vxꝰ George Steele ... ... ... ... 12 „
Elizabeth Mason vid in Mꝰ Scarisbricks Chancell ... ... ... ... ... ... ... ... 17 „
Richard Miller Infans ... ... ... ... ... 18 „
Alice vxꝰ Raph Houlme in eccłia ... ... ... 21 „
Alice Davie Inf: in eccłia ... ... ... ... 22 „

## 1618.

| |  |  |  |
|---|---|---|---|
| | John Wallice Infan in eccl̄ia ... ... ... ... ... | 2 | Aprill |
| | Thomas Adlington ... ... ... ... ... ... ... ... | 4 | „ |
| | Ellen Melling vxꝰ John in eccl̄ia ... ... ... | 5 | „ |
| | Elizab: Brighouse Inf: ... ... ... ... ... ... | 9 | „ |
| | Alice vxꝰ Tho: Wiswald in eccl̄ia ... ... ... | 12 | „ |
| | Katheryne Prescott vid ... ... ... ... ... ... | 16 | „ |
| | Wil̄l̄m Scarisbricke in eccl̄ia ... ... ... ... | 17 | „ |
| | Gilb̄te Morcroft ... ... ... ... ... ... ... | 18 | „ |
| | Margrett Blundill Inf: ... ... ... ... ... ... | „ | „ |
| | John Davy in eccl̄ia ... ... ... ... ... ... | „ | „ |
| | Xpofer Gilbertson and Ellen Thorntō Inf: ... | 20 | „ |
| | Elizab: vxꝰ James More ... ... ... ... ... | 22 | „ |
| | A stranger the ... ... ... ... ... ... ... ... | 23 | „ |
| | Wil̄l̄m Waring ... ... ... ... ... ... ... ... ... | „ | „ |
| | Isabell vxꝰ James Waring ... ... ... ... | 30 | „ |
| | Elizab: Barton vid ... ... ... ... ... ... ... ... | 2 | May |
| | Gilb̄t Gille ... ... ... ... ... ... ... ... ... | 8 | „ |
| | Ellen Blundill spinster ... ... ... ... ... ... | „ | „ |
| | Mathewe Athertō in eccl̄ia ... ... ... ... ... | 9 | „ |
| | . . . Hartley Inf: ... ... ... ... ... ... | „ | „ |
| | Jane Garrard vid ... ... ... ... ... ... ... | 27 | „ |
| | Peter Shawe in eccl̄ia ... ... ... ... ... ... | „ | „ |
| | Margrett vxꝰ Thꝰstā Aspinwall in eccl̄ia ... | 29 | „ |
| | John Morcrofte ... ... ... ... ... ... ... | „ | „ |
| Fo. 413 | Martha Goldborne Inf in eccl̄ia ... ... ... | 3 | June |
| | Anne Topping ... ... ... ... ... ... ... ... | 7 | „ |
| | Ellen Brough Inf: ... ... ... ... ... ... ... | 9 | „ |
| | Henry ffairclough Inf: ... ... ... ... ... ... | 10 | „ |
| | Anne Barton Infans ... ... ... ... ... ... ... | 15 | „ |
| | Anne Gilder Inf ... ... ... ... ... ... ... | 22 | „ |
| | Elizab: Py spinster ... ... ... ... ... ... ... | 24 | „ |
| | . . . Barton in eccl̄ia ... ... ... ... ... | 27 | „ |
| | Peter Barton in eccl̄ia ... ... ... ... ... ... | „ | „ |
| | Rob̄te Burscough fi: Tho: in eccl̄ia ... ... | 12 | July |
| | Henry Cockett ... ... ... ... ... ... ... ... | 17 | „ |
| | Rich Gore Inf: in eccl̄ia ... ... ... ... ... | 19 | „ |
| | Isabell Gille spinster ... ... ... ... ... ... | 29 | „ |
| | Rich Ryding fi: James ... ... ... ... ... ... | 6 | August |
| | Ellen Sutch Inf in ecclia ... ... ... ... ... | 13 | „ |
| | Hugh Ascroft in eccl̄ia ... ... ... ... ... ... | „ | „ |
| | A childe of Gabriell Walker in eccl̄ia ... ... | 14 | „ |
| | Anne Barker vid ... ... ... ... ... ... ... | 15 | „ |
| | Rich Longe a stranger ... ... ... ... ... ... | 20 | „ |
| | Mariery ffryth spinster ... ... ... ... ... ... | 23 | „ |
| | George Prescott in eccl̄ia ... ... ... ... ... | 29 | „ |
| | Elizab: Blundill Inf: in eccl̄ia ... ... ... | „ | „ |

Katheryne Holland Inf: in ecclia ... ... ... 31 August
Willm Dickett in ecclia ... ... ... ... ... 5 September
Robte Hadocke Inf ... ... ... ... ... ... ... 8 „
Jennett Lythom Inf ... ... ... ... ... ... 9 „
ffrances vxꝰ Cuthbti Garrard in ecclia ... ... 10 „
Jane Davy Inf ... ... ... ... ... ... ... 14 „
John Hey in ecclia ... ... ... ... ... ... 17 „
Jane Haughton spinster ... ... ... ... ... „ „
A man childe of Tho: Lowe ... ... ... ... 19 „
Margrett vxꝰ Henry Lathom ... ... ... ... 28 „
Edward Dod Inf in ecclia ... ... ... ... 3 October
A childe of Willm Crane ... ... ... ... ... 8 „
A childe of Arthur Whalley ... ... ... ... 9 „
Ellen Greaues viꝰgo... ... ... ... ... ... 19 „
John Portman Inf: fi: Sꝰ Henry Knight bur in the Right Hoble Therle of Derby his Chancell ... ... ... ... ... ... ... 16 „
Thomas Sankie Inf: in ecclia ... ... ... 20 „
Edward Holland Infans in ecclia ... ... ... „ „
Anne Hynde vxꝰ Willm ... ... ... ... ... „ „
Elizab: Jollybrand Infans in ecclia ... ... 21 „
Elizab: Thornton Infa: ... ... ... ... ... 23 „
Anne Coockson vid ... ... ... ... ... ... 25 „
Sannel [*sic*] Kenion Adolesc ... ... ... ... „ „
4 Gilbte Houlme Adolesc ... ... ... ... ... 3 November
. . . Withington Inf in ecclia ... ... ... 8 „
Elizab: Houlme Inf: ... ... ... ... ... ... 13 „
Allon* Kilshawe ... ... ... ... ... ... 15 „
Ellen Kilshawe fi: Henry ... ... ... ... 19 „
James Alcar ... ... ... ... ... ... ... 4 Decemb
Anne vxꝰ Robte Hankin ... ... ... ... ... 6 „
Henry Jackson Inf: in ecclia ... ... ... ... 9 „
Cuthbte Sharples gent: in ecclia ... ... ... 21 „
Willm Modesley Adoles: in ecclia ... ... 28 „
Richard Aspinwall ... ... ... ... ... ... „ „
John Scarisbrick Inf ... ... ... ... ... 1 January
Anne a stranger ... ... ... ... ... ... 6 „
Ellinor Holden ... ... ... ... ... ... 10 „
Ellen Hunt vid ... ... ... ... ... ... 16 „
Huan Allerton Inf ... ... ... ... ... ... „ „
Margery Stopford vid in ecclia ... ... ... 18 „
Jherome Barrowes Bacheler in ecclia ... ... 22 „
Richard Whitestones in ecclia ... ... ... 24 „
James Kenion Inf ... ... ... ... ... ... 29 „
Jane Houlme Inf ... ... ... ... ... ... „ „
Lewes Holland Adolesc ... ... ... ... ... 6 ffebruary
Ellen Rigby vid in ecclia ... ... ... ... 12 „

* Ellen *in Chester Transcript.*

| | | | |
|---|---|---|---|
| | Wiłłm Garrard adol: in eccłia | 13 | ffebruary |
| | Elizab: Higham vx$^{9}$ John | 15 | " |
| | Katherine Morcroft spin: in eccłia | 17 | " |
| | Ellen Garnett spin: in eccłia | 20 | " |
| | Richard Houlme | 28 | " |
| | ffardinando Crapp in eccłia | 7 | March |
| | Ellen Ambrose virgo in eccłia | " | " |
| | John Goldborne | 10 | " |
| | Thomas Wainwright in eccłia | 13 | " |
| | Lewes Barton | 17 | " |
| | . . . Westhead | 22 | " |

## 1619.

| | | | |
|---|---|---|---|
| | Margery Carre vid | 27 | March |
| | Edmund Carre | 4 | Aprill |
| | Susan Thornton | " | " |
| | James Cartmer Inf | 5 | " |
| | Thom̃ Wiswald in the High chancell | 11 | " |
| | A child of Edw: Blundill in eccłia | " | " |
| | Katheryne Lathom spinster | 13 | " |
| | Margrett Marclewe spinster | " | " |
| | Anne Mason Inf in eccłia | " | " |
| | Ellen Tayler Widdowe in eccłia | 14 | " |
| | John Smyth | 15 | " |
| | Thom̃ Butler Adolesc̃ in eccłia | 19 | " |
| | Thom̃ Wything* fi: Rob̃t in eccłia | 20 | " |
| | Thomas Stanley in eccłia | " | " |
| | Homphry Greaues | 27 | " |
| | Henry Alcar Adolesc̃ | 28 | " |
| Fo. 415 | John Swyft Inf: | 1 | May |
| | Myles Hesketh Inf | 7 | " |
| | Thomas Whitstones | 11 | " |
| | Richard Symkin | 14 | " |
| | Jane Wythington vid in eccłia | 17 | " |
| | Mary Wignall Inf: | 18 | " |
| | Peter Edwardson the | 19 | " |
| | Henry Topping fi: Raph | " | " |
| | Wiłłm Harden the | 20 | " |
| | Henry Soothwoorth Inf | 21 | " |
| | Peter Brighouse | " | " |
| | ffardinando Crapper Bacheler | 22 | " |
| | Rob̃te Modesley Inf: in eccłia | 23 | " |
| | A man childe of Hugh Crapp in eccłia | " | " |
| | Ellen vx$^{9}$ John Bore alias Man | 25 | " |
| | Mary Modesley Widdowe | 26 | " |
| | James Stanley Inf: in M$^{9}$ Stanles chancell | 28 | " |
| | Gotfrey Atherton Inf: in eccłia | 31 | " |

* Wythington *in Chester Transcript.*

| | | |
|---|---|---|
| Henry Allerton ... ... ... ... ... ... ... | 7 | June |
| Dothery Mollyneux Inf ... ... ... ... ... | 9 | „ |
| Jennett Spencer Inf: ... ... ... ... ... | 10 | „ |
| Margrett Lea vxꝰ Hector in eccl̃ia ... ... ... | 16 | „ |
| Jane Swyft ... ... ... ... ... ... ... | 17 | „ |
| Richard Holland in eccl̃ia ... ... ... ... | „ | „ |
| Edward Crane fil̃ Will̃m ... ... ... ... ... | 19 | „ |
| Elizab: Kilshaw Inf: in eccl̃ia ... ... ... | 23 | „ |
| Hugh Ward Inf ... ... ... ... ... ... | 25 | „ |
| John Hyton Inf in eccl̃ia ... ... ... ... | 8 | July |
| A woman child of George Haughton ... ... | 9 | August |
| A man childe of Thomas Ascroft in eccl̃ia ... | 11 | „ |
| John Ascorft Inf in eccl̃ia ... ... ... ... ... | 18 | „ |
| Richard Brighouse adolesc̃ ... ... ... ... ... | 19 | „ |
| John ffoster ... ... ... ... ... ... ... | 24 | „ |
| Tyldesley Breers in eccl̃ia ... ... ... ... | 25 | „ |
| A child of Arthur Greenells in eccl̃ia ... ... | 31 | „ |
| Isabell Bartō Inf ... ... ... ... ... ... ... | 1 | September |
| Alice Holcroft Inf ... ... ... ... ... ... ... | 7 | „ |
| Alice vxꝰ Hamlet Prescot ... ... ... ... | 12 | „ |
| Raph Scath Inf ... ... ... ... ... ... ... | 16 | „ |
| Thomas Davie in eccl̃ia ... ... ... ... ... ... | 28 | „ |
| Richard Cowp in eccl̃ia ... ... ... ... ... | 18 | October |
| Henry Dunkon in eccl̃ia ... ... ... ... ... | „ | „ |
| Henry Robinson in eccl̃ia ... ... ... ... | 23 | „ |
| . . . Crapp fi: James ... ... ... ... ... | 27 | „ |
| John Atherton in eccl̃ia ... ... ... ... ... | 28 | „ |
| A poore Childe ... ... ... ... ... ... | 31 | „ |
| Richard Winstanley ... ... ... ... ... ... ... | 5 | November |
| Katheryne Barton Inf: ... ... ... ... ... ... | 15 | „ |
| William Modesley Inf: in eccl̃ia ... ... ... | 23 | „ |
| Margrett Woods spinster in eccl̃ia ... ... ... | 24 | „ |
| Hugh Morcroft ... ... ... ... ... ... ... | 28 | „ |
| A childe of Will̃m Will̃m [*sic*] Blessing ... | 30 | „ |
| Thomas Jackson Inf: in eccl̃ia ... ... ... | 2 | December |
| Thomas Ormeshawe ... ... ... ... ... ... | 5 | „ |
| John Houlme Inf: ... ... ... ... ... ... ... | 21 | „ |
| Anne Dunkon Inf: in eccl̃ia ... ... ... ... | 24 | „ |
| Martha Stopford spinster in eccl̃ia ... ... ... | 29 | „ |
| Ciceley Stopford spinster in eccl̃ia ... ... ... | 4 | January |
| A childe of Edward Winstanley ... ... ... | 5 | „ |
| George Stopford in eccl̃ia ... ... ... ... | 9 | „ |
| Elizabeth Dunkon vid ... ... ... ... ... | „ | „ |
| Joseph Parke Inf ... ... ... ... ... ... | „ | „ |
| John Gobben in eccl̃ia ... ... ... ... ... | 19 | „ |
| Jane Lowe in eccl̃ia ... ... ... ... ... ... | 20 | „ |
| Thomas Halsall* ... ... ... ... ... ... | | |

* *This entry in Chester Transcript only.*

Jane vx[9] Hector Alty in ecctia ... ... ... 21 January
Margrett Duddill vx[9] Joh in ecctia... ... ... 25 „
Robte Hankin ... ... ... ... ... ... ... 4 ffebruar
Jane vx[9] Robte Anderton ... ... ... ... 6 „
Trystram Haughton Juv: ... ... ... ... 15 „
Alice Jolly Inf in ecctia ... ... ... ... ... „ „
Ellen Eves in ecctia ... ... ... ... ... 16 „
John Bore ... ... ... ... ... ... ... „ „
Anne vx[9] Rich Westhead in ecctia ... ... ... 17 „
Anne Morcroft spinster in ecctia ... ... ... „ „
John Kilshawe in ecctia ... ... ... ... ... 22 „
Witlm Alcar ... ... ... ... ... ... ... „ „
Thomas Parker ... ... ... ... ... ... 23 „
Thom Westhead Bacheler in ecctia ... ... 27 „
Fo. 417 Anne Barton spinster in M[9] Scarisbricks chancell ... ... ... ... ... ... ... 1 March
Symond Westhead in ecctia ... ... ... ... 7 „
Bryan Davy in ecctia ... ... ... ... ... 9 „
Katherine Davie* ... ... ... ... ... ...
John Alcar in ecctia ... ... ... ... ... 21 „

## 1620.

Grace Standish in the high Chancell ... ... 29 March
Anne Lea vid in ecctia ... ... ... ... ... 30 „
Ellen Scarisbricke ... ... ... ... ... ... „ „
Mary Atherton Inf in ecctia ... ... ... ... 13 Aprill
Elizabeth Cowp vid in ecctia ... ... ... „ „
Xpofer Barton ... ... ... ... ... ... ... 17 „
Hugh Ascroft Inf: ... ... ... ... ... ... 19 „
Cycely Sumner Inf ... ... ... ... ... ... 20 „
Katheryne vx[9] Huan Lea in ecctia ... ... 21 „
George Haughtons Inf ... ... ... ... ... „ „
Agnes Pendleton vid in ecctia... ... ... ... 23 „
Jane Scarisbr vid in ecctia ... ... ... ... „ „
Ellen vx[9] Thomas Houlme ... ... ... ... 26 „
John Higham in ecctia ... ... ... ... ... 30 „
Richard Jackson in ecctia ... ... ... ... 3 May
Mary Wallener ... ... ... ... ... ... 4 „
Homphry Goldborne in M[9] Scarisbricks Chancell ... ... ... ... ... ... ... 10 „
Alexander Smyth Inf: in M[9] Scarisbricks Chancell ... ... ... ... ... ... ... 13 „
Margery vx[9] Hugh Crapper in ecctia ... ... 19 „
Ellen vx[9] Gowther Barton in ecctia ... ... 23 „
Homphry Topping in ecctia ... ... ... ... 25 „
Henry Gille ... ... ... ... ... ... ... 10 June
Witlm Morcrofte ... ... ... ... ... ... 11 „

* *This entry in Chester Transcript only.*

|  |  |  |
|---|---|---|
| Willm Adamson in ecclia | 19 | June |
| Margery Gille fi: Thomas | ,, | ,, |
| Alice Mathewe vid | 24 | ,, |
| John Smyth inf: | 1 | July |
| Hugh Harryson in ecclia | 5 | ,, |
| Robt Towne | 6 | ,, |
| A childe of Willm Houlme in ecclia | 8 | ,, |
| A man childe of John Hille in ecclia | 28 | ,, |
| A man childe of Thomas Hyton in ecclia | ,, | ,, |
| Henry Babott Adolesc̃ | 30 | ,, |
| Richard Crapp in the high Chancell | 5 | August |
| Margrett Prescott Inf: | 14 | ,, |
| Alice Parker fi: Thomas | 29 | ,, |
| Ellen Garrard vid in ecclia | ,, | ,, |
| Henry Hille Bacheler | 6 | September |
| Jane Haughton Infant | 18 | ,, |
| James Carrytam Inf: | 20 | ,, |
| Huan Modesley de Daltō in ecclia | ,, | ,, |
| James Carby fi: Joseph | 23 | ,, |
| Jane Johnson Infant | 26 | ,, |
| Sara Rozaway Inf: | ,, | ,, |
| Edward Smyth in ecclia | 5 | October |
| Richard Carre | 15 | ,, |
| Katheryne Miller fi: Willm | 20 | ,, |
| Ellen Harrison vid in ecclia | ,, | ,, |
| Richard Barton | 23 | ,, |
| Jane vx[9] Willm Sutton | 24 | ,, |
| Robte Morcrofte Inf: in ecclia | 25 | ,, |
| Jane Swyfte vid in ecclia | 30 | ,, |
| Richard Houlme Bacheler in ecclia | 10 | November |
| Jane Burscough vid | 14 | ,, |
| Ellen vx[9] Hugh Barton in ecclia | 15 | ,, |
| Thomas Stopford Bacheler in ecclia | 17 | ,, |
| Elizab: Barton Inf: in ecclia | 1 | December |
| Anne Parke Inf: in ecclia | 2 | ,, |
| Cysley Whytestones Inf: in ecclia | 9 | ,, |
| Katheryne Lathom vid | 24 | ,, |
| Alice Stopford Inf in ecclia | 28 | ,, |
| Roger Modesley Inf: in ecclia | 29 | ,, |
| . . . Stopford Inf: in ecclia | 2 | January |
| Joane Aspinwall Inf: in ecclia | 3 | ,, |
| Ellell* Kilshawe vid in ecclia | 5 | ,, |
| Peter Dale Inf: | 7 | ,, |
| Margrett Swyfte Inf: in ecclia | 10 | ,, |
| Ellen Wyndle Inf: | 15 | ,, |
| Roger Ormeshawe in ecclia | 16 | ,, |
| John Layland in ecclia | ,, | ,, |
| Elizab: Rigmaden Inf: in ecclia | 18 | ,, |

* Ellen *in Chester Transcript.*

James Halle in M^ris Scarisbricks Chancell ... 28 January
Alice Atherton vid in ecc̃lia ... ... ... ... ... 31 „
A childe of Wiłłm Blessing ... ... ... ... 5 ffebruary
Thomas Marclewe ... ... ... ... ... ... ... 19 „
Ellen Marclewe vx^r Peter w^th her childe in ecc̃lia ... ... ... ... ... ... ... ... 6 March
Katheryne Henryson vid in ecc̃lia ... ... ... 7 „
Jane fforshawe vid in ecc̃lia ... ... ... ... ... 20 „
Richard Hey in ecc̃lia ... ... ... ... ... ... „ „
Henry Stopford in ecc̃lia... ... ... ... ... ... 22 „
Richard Vauce in ecc̃lia ... ... ... ... ... „ „

## 1621.

Fo. 419 Ellen ffletcher Inf: ... ... ... ... ... ... 25 March
John Deane Inf: a stranger ... ... ... ... ... 29 „
Thomas Hesketh Inf: ... ... ... ... ... ... 1 Aprill
Hugh Monck Inf: ... ... ... ... ... ... ... 4 „
Anthony Lawrenson in ecc̃lia ... ... ... ... ... 6 „
Ellen Barton Inf: in ecc̃lia ... ... ... ... ... 8 „
Robte Walsh Inf ... ... ... ... ... ... ... 9 „
Wiłłm Ratherã Inf ... ... ... ... ... ... 13 „
Phillip Swyft in ecc̃lia ... ... ... ... ... ... „ „
Richard Marcer puer ... ... ... ... ... ... „ „
Margrett Athertõ* vid in ecc̃lia ... ... ... 15 „
Thomas Wynstanley Inf: ... ... ... ... ... 19 „
Alice Keakwicke Inf ... ... ... ... ... ... „ „
Elizab: Nicolson Inf ... ... ... ... ... ... 20 „
Thomas Melling ... ... ... ... ... ... ... 24 „
Gilbte Vauce in ecclia ... ... ... ... ... ... 25 „
Thom̃ Strongarme Inf: ... ... ... ... ... ... 26 „
Mary Page Inf ... ... ... ... ... ... ... ... „ „
Margrett Hesketh ... ... ... ... ... ... ... „ „
Robte Blackledge ... ... ... ... ... ... ... 27 „
Margery Cowp spinster in ecc̃lia ... ... ... 29 „
Ellen Page Inf: ... ... ... ... ... ... ... „ „
John Ambrose in ecc̃lia ... ... ... ... ... 2 May
Anne vx^r George Stanley in ecc̃lia ... ... 18 „
Alice Westhead Inf . ... ... ... ... ... ... 19 „
A man childe of Hugh Houlme ... ... ... 20 „
Ciceley vx^r Thomas Westhead ... ... ... 21 „
Richard Halsall Inf: in the High Chancell ... 24 „
Myles Barton Inf ... ... ... ... ... ... ... 25 „
ffrancis Mossocke Inf: ... ... ... ... ... ... 31 „
Alice Iddon vx^r Thomas ... ... ... ... 1 June
Edward Waynwright Inf ... ... ... ... ... „ „
Richard Leadbetter Inf: in ecc̃lia ... ... ... 2 „
James Smalshawe Inf in ecclia ... ... ... „ „

* Ackers *in Chester Transcript.*

| | | |
|---|---|---|
| A woman Chylde of Hugh Whittell | 3 | June |
| James Plowmbe | 5 | ,, |
| Ellen Aspinwall Inf in eccl̄ia | 7 | ,, |
| Margrett Lawrenson Inf in ecclia | 9 | ,, |
| Margrett Hawarth in eccl̄ia | 11 | ,, |
| Anne Whalley Inf in eccl̄ia | 12 | ,, |
| Elizab: vxꝰ Rob̄te Anderton | 14 | ,, |
| Kathery Barton Inf: in eccl̄ia | 16 | ,, |
| Ellen vxꝰ Will̄m Laithwaitt in eccl̄ia | 21 | ,, |
| James Laithwaitt Inf: in eccl̄ia | 28 | ,, |
| Katheryne Melling Inf | 1 | July |
| Alice Waynwright vid in eccl̄ia | 20 | ,, |
| Hugh Cowp Inf: in eccl̄ia | 23 | ,, |
| Anne Stanley virgo et generoso in her fathers Chancell | 28 | ,, |
| Ellen Layland vid in eccl̄ia | 29 | ,, |
| Gilb̄te Prescott in eccl̄ia | 30 | ,, |
| Ellen vxꝰ Johanis Shawe in ecclia | 1 | August |
| Henry Garnett de Aughtō in eccl̄ia | 2 | ,, |
| Henry Halsall Inf: | 4 | ,, |
| Alice vxꝰ Thurstan Heskeyne de Writhington | 5 | ,, |
| Ellen Tompson virgo | 12 | ,, |
| Anne Hitchin vid in eccl̄ia | 19 | ,, |
| Hugh Jollybrand Inf in eccl̄ia | 29 | ,, |
| Katheryne Hale Inf | 2 | September |
| Anne Taberner | 3 | ,, |
| Thomas Prescott Inf | 6 | ,, |
| Ellen Sutch virgo | ,, | ,, |
| A man chylde of Alexandꝰ Barker in eccl̄ia | 7 | ,, |
| Houmphry Turner | 9 | ,, |
| Jennett Ascroft vid in eccl̄ia | 14 | ,, |
| A man childe of James Robinson | 20 | ,, |
| Henry Symkin Inf | 2 | October |
| Will̄m Brighouse | 6 | ,, |
| John Hodson in eccl̄ia | 8 | ,, |
| Raphe Allerton in eccl̄ia | 14 | ,, |
| Elizab: Rigmaden vid in ecl̄ia | 2 | ,, |
| A woman Chylde of Henry Prescott in eccl̄ia | 20 | ,, |
| Will̄m Hallywell Inf | 1 | November |
| Huan Swyft Inf in eccl̄ia | 3 | ,, |
| A man childe of Hugh Throppe | 13 | ,, |
| Margery Aynswoorth in the High Chancell | 14 | ,, |
| Anne Woods virgo in eccl̄ia | 19 | ,, |
| Thomas Barton | 23 | ,, |
| Raphe Melling | 24 | ,, |
| Will̄m Sutton | 2 | December |
| Gilb̄te Ormeshawe in eccl̄ia | 3 | ,, |
| Thomas Whitacre Inf | 4 | ,, |
| Elizabeth Johnson spinster | 8 | ,, |

| | | | |
|---|---|---|---|
| | Margrett Caritā Inf ... ... ... ... ... ... | 8 | December |
| | Richard Hille ... ... ... ... ... ... ... ... | 12 | „ |
| | Anne Spencer Inf ... ... ... ... ... ... | „ | „ |
| | Margrett Hille vid ... ... ... ... ... ... | 21 | „ |
| | John Jollybrand fi : Rich : in ecclia ... ... | 23 | „ |
| | John Hollywell Infant ... ... ... ... ... ... | 27 | „ |
| Fo. 421 | Anne Johnson virgo ... ... ... ... ... ... | 5 | January |
| | Anne Topping Inf ... ... ... ... ... ... | 10 | „ |
| | Jane Tompson Inf ... ... ... ... ... ... | 14 | „ |
| | Witlm Halton Juveñ ... ... ... ... ... | 19 | „ |
| | Anne Garnett de Aughton in ecclia ... ... | 23 | „ |
| | Henry Morcrofte Infant ... ... ... ... ... | „ | „ |
| | A childe of John Shawe in ecclia ... ... ... | 24 | „ |
| | Thom̃ Gobben fi : Rob̃te in ecclia ... ... ... | 29 | „ |
| | Thomas Whitestones the ... ... ... ... ... | 31 | „ |
| | A man childe of Thom̃ : Ashurst ... ... ... | „ | „ |
| | Hugh Gilb̃tson ... ... ... ... ... ... ... | 1 | ffebruary |
| | Witlm Gille Adolescens ... ... ... ... ... ... | 2 | „ |
| | Elizabeth Pembertō virgo ... ... ... ... | 3 | „ |
| | Margrett Woods Inf in ecclia ... ... ... | „ | „ |
| | Margery Burry vid in ecclia ... ... ... ... | 9 | „ |
| | Richard Clarkson Inf ... ... ... ... ... | „ | „ |
| | Jane* Hale vid in ecclia ... ... ... ... ... | 16 | „ |
| | Anne Symkin Inf in ecclia ... ... ... ... | 19 | „ |
| | Anne Adamson vid ... ... ... ... ... ... | 24 | „ |
| | Myles Barton Inf : in the high Chancell ... | 28 | „ |
| | Anne Barton Inf : in the high Chancell ... | 3 | March |
| | Henry Modesley Inf : in ecclia ... ... ... | 4 | „ |
| | Margrett Mathewe spinster ... ... ... ... | 7 | „ |
| | Emlin Page Inf : ... ... ... ... ... ... | 8 | „ |
| | Richard Adamson Inf : ... ... ... ... ... | „ | „ |
| | Silvester Laithwaitt Inf : in ecclia ... ... ... | 10 | „ |
| | Anne Woodhouse virgo in ecclia ... ... ... | 13 | „ |
| | Henry Georgson Inf : in ecclia ... ... ... | 14 | „ |
| | Richard Wo$^9$thingtō in y$^e$ high Chancell ... | 16 | „ |
| | John Ireland in ecclia ... ... ... ... ... | „ | „ |
| | John Cartwright in ecclia ... ... ... ... | 18 | „ |
| | Witlm Marrall ... ... ... ... ... ... ... | 20 | „ |
| | Mary Rob̃tson† Inf : in ecclia ... ... ... | 24 | „ |
| | Jane Shorloker Inf : in ecclia ... ... ... | „ | „ |

## 1622.

| | | |
|---|---|---|
| Richard Monke Inf : in ecclia ... ... ... | 28 | March |
| Henry Parker ... ... ... ... ... ... ... ... | 31 | „ |
| Thomas Wythingtō Infant ... ... ... ... | 1 | Aprill |
| Margrett Woorthingtō vid in the high Chancell | 5 | „ |

* Anne *in Chester Transcript.*

† Robinson *in Chester Transcript.*

|  |  |  |
|---|---|---|
| Margrett Hille Infant in ecclia | 8 | Aprill |
| Elizab: . . . vid | 16 | „ |
| Elizabeth Kenyon Inf | 17 | „ |
| Thomas Mason | 19 | „ |
| Myles Harryson in ecclia | 24 | „ |
| George Stanley in ecclia | „ | „ |
| Ranald Johnson Inf | 25 | „ |
| Jennett Shawe vid in ecclia | „ | „ |
| Anne Cowp vid in ecclia | 28 | „ |
| Margrett Kirkham vxꝰ Thom̃ | 4 | May |
| Bryan Mathewe Bacheler | „ | „ |
| Anne Alte vid | 16 | „ |
| Jane Dale Inf | 18 | „ |
| James Carter | 19 | „ |
| Thom̃ Houlme Inf | 20 | „ |
| Henry Longewoorth | 27 | „ |
| Anne Oldam vxꝰ Thom̃ in ecclia | 30 | „ |
| Mary Cawsey virgo in ecclia | 31 | „ |
| Raphe Stopford Inf: in ecclia | 2 | June |
| Richard Keakwicke in ecclia | 3 | „ |
| Raphe Whytestones in ecclia | 4 | „ |
| Margrett Hankinson vxꝰ Rob̃te in Mꝰ Scarisbricks Chancell | 15 | „ |
| Arthur Mason in ecclia | 29 | „ |
| Katheryne vxꝰ Willmi Stanley | „ | „ |
| Alice Crane virgo | „ | „ |
| Jane Scott a stranger | 4 | July |
| James Wilding Inf | 12 | „ |
| Cisley Wynstanley Inf: in ecclia | 13 | „ |
| Edward Aspinwall in ecclia | 16 | „ |
| Anne Chaundler vxꝰ Hugh in ecclia | 22 | „ |
| A woman childe of Peter Cowp in ecclia | 29 | „ |
| Willm Ryding Inf | „ | „ |
| Margrett Prescott vid | 3 | August |
| Alice vxꝰ Henry Hawett in ecclia | „ | „ |
| Margrett Mathewe virgo | 8 | „ |
| Thomas Allerton | 14 | „ |
| Isabell Ryding vid | 22 | „ |
| Thom̃ Slippd fi: W$^{m}$ a stranger | 1 | September |
| Thom̃ Moody* | 2 | „ |
| John Gille in ecclia | 7 | „ |
| Margrett Smyth Inf: in ecclia | „ | „ |
| Grace Blundill vxꝰ John | 9 | „ |
| Anne Mollyneux spinster | 15 | „ |
| Ellen Spakman spiñ in ecclia | 11 | „ |
| Jane Blundill | 23 | „ |
| Thomas Shawe | 8 | October |
| Rob̃te Leadbetter in ecclia | 9 | „ |

* Meadowe *in Chester Transcript.*

Jony Blundill Inf ... ... ... ... ... ... 10 October
Richard Morcroft in eccl̄ia ... ... ... ... 19 „
Fo. 423 Cecely Swyft Inf: in eccl̄ia ... ... ... ... 1 November
Ellen ffarre vid ... ... ... ... ... ... ... ... 9 „
Dorithy Shawe vx$^{9}$ Hugh in eccl̄ia ... ... 10 „
Edward Swyft Inf ... ... ... ... ... ... ... „ „
Jane Hesketh vid gen̄ in M$^{9}$ Stanley his chancell ... ... ... ... ... ... ... ... 17 „
Thom̄ Stanynought in eccl̄ia ... ... ... ... 19 „
Katheryne Swyfte Inf: in eccl̄ia ... ... ... 26 „
Katheryne Blackledge in eccl̄ia ... ... ... 3 December
Alice Bartō Inf: in eccl̄ia ... ... ... ... 5 „
Jennett Blundill spinster ... ... ... ... ... ... 9 „
Homphrey Tayler Inf ... ... ... ... ... ... 11 „
Edward Peterson Inf ... ... ... ... ... ... 15 „
Anne Layland Inf in eccl̄ia ... ... ... ... ... 21 „
Elizabeth* Bartō Inf ... ... ... ... ... ... 29 „
Henry Sandforth in eccl̄ia ... ... ... ... ... 30 „
Alice Layland vid in eccl̄ia ... ... ... ... ... 31 „
Homphrey Berry ... ... ... ... ... ... ... 2 January
Edith Gille Inf ... ... ... ... ... ... ... ... „ „
Alice Mason vid in eccl̄ia ... ... ... ... ... 3 „
Thom̄ Hodgkinson ... ... ... ... ... ... ... 5 „
Katheryne Walker vid ... ... ... ... ... ... 12 „
Richard Gille Infant ... ... ... ... ... ... „ „
Ellen Waynwright in eccl̄ia ... ... ... ... ... 13 „
Xpofer Woofall ... ... ... ... ... ... ... „ „
Hugh Shawe in eccl̄ia ... ... ... ... ... ... 15 „
A man childe of W$^{m}$ Ascough in eccl̄ia ... ... 17 „
Barnaby Mason ... ... ... ... ... ... ... 20 „
Thurstan Tompson ... ... ... ... ... ... ... 21 „
Will̄m Ambrose in ecclia ... ... ... ... ... 22 „
Susan Thornton Inf: ... ... ... ... ... ... „ „
sp: Thomas Weston Inf: ... ... ... ... ... ... 26 „
Will̄m Vallentyne ... ... ... ... ... ... ... 30 „
Raphe Morcroft ... ... ... ... ... ... ... „ „
Elizabeth Kenion vx$^{9}$ Rob̄te ... ... ... ... ... 5 ffebruary
Alice Allerton virgo ... ... ... ... ... ... ... 6 „
Katheryne Gille vx$^{9}$ Will̄m ... ... ... ... ... 13 „
Katheryne Halsall vx$^{9}$ Richard in the high Chancell ... ... ... ... ... ... ... ... „ „
John Haughton ... ... ... ... ... ... ... 16 „
Margrett Parre fi: Alexander ... ... ... ... ... 17 „
Will̄m Robinson Inf: ... ... ... ... ... ... 19 „
Elizabeth Shawe vid in eccl̄ia ... ... ... ... „ „
Jane Stanynought vid ... ... ... ... ... ... „ „
Will̄m Hodson Inf: in eccl̄ia ... ... ... ... 21 „

* Isabel *in Chester Transcript.*

| | | |
|---|---|---|
| . . . Robinson fi: John ... ... ... ... | 21 | ffebruary |
| Richard Walker in eccl̄ia ... ... ... ... | 22 | „ |
| . . . Bowker Inf: ... ... ... ... ... | 23 | „ |
| Will̄m Hynde ... ... ... ... ... ... ... | 24 | „ |
| Margery Ashton ... ... ... ... ... ... | „ | „ |
| Hugh Woodhouse in eccl̄ia ... ... ... ... | 4 | March |
| Anne Steele Inf ... ... ... ... ... ... | 14 | „ |
| Ellen Mollynex vid ... ... ... ... ... ... | 15 | „ |
| . . . Whytestones Juveñ ... ... ... ... | 17 | „ |
| Margrett More vx$^9$ Will̄m ... ... ... ... | „ | „ |
| Margery Abram̄ vx$^9$ Tho: in eccl̄ia ... ... | 18 | „ |
| Alice Robinson spinster ... ... ... ... ... | 20 | „ |

## 1623.

| | | |
|---|---|---|
| Thomas Ambrose Ludim$^9$ in eccl̄ia ... ... | 27 | March |
| Gabriel̄ Haughtō ... ... ... ... ... ... | 8 | Aprill |
| Anne Sandforth vid .. ... ... ... ... ... | 9 | „ |
| Alice Jollybrand vx$^9$ Rich: ... ... ... ... | 10 | „ |
| Rob̄te Riding ... ... ... ... ... ... ... | 11 | „ |
| Anne Allertō ... ... ... ... ... ... ... | 12 | „ |
| Katheryne Ascough virgo ... ... ... ... | 13 | „ |
| Jennett Bartō Inf ... ... ... ... ... ... | 15 | „ |
| Homphrey Wetherby Inf: ... ... ... ... | 16 | „ |
| Ellen Wynder vid ... ... ... ... ... ... | 20 | „ |
| Ellen Chadocke Inf ... ... ... ... ... | 23 | „ |
| Hugh Hurst Inf ... ... ... ... ... ... | „ | „ |
| Henry Tasker Inf: ... ... ... ... ... ... | 25 | „ |
| Emlin Wynstanley vid ... ... ... ... ... | „ | „ |
| Anne vx$^9$ Hugh Rigby in eccl̄ia ... ... ... | 26 | „ |
| Rich: Walmsley Inf: a stranger ... ... ... | 29 | „ |
| Jennett Parker Inf ... ... ... ... ... ... | 3 | May |
| Elizab: Lancaster vid ... ... ... ... ... | „ | „ |
| Margrett Gill vx$^9$ Gilb̄te ... ... ... ... ... | 7 | „ |
| Thomas Skinner ... ... ... ... ... ... | 13 | „ |
| A man childe of Henry Woodes ... ... ... | „ | „ |
| Alice Lunt vid ... ... ... ... ... ... ... | 15 | „ |
| Huan Lea in eccl̄ia ... ... ... ... ... | „ | „ |
| Edith Edggeker Inf ... ... ... ... ... ... | 16 | „ |
| Mary Ambrose spinster ... ... ... ... ... | 22 | „ |
| John Ascogh the ... ... ... ... ... ... | 23 | „ |
| Ellice Ambrose in eccl̄ia ... ... ... ... ... | 25 | „ |
| Margrett Tuson virg ... ... ... ... ... ... | „ | „ |
| Agnes Molyneux vid in eccl̄ia ... ... ... | 26 | „ |
| Richard Stopford Inf in eccl̄ia ... ... ... | 2 | June |
| Richard Coop in eccl̄ia ... ... ... ... ... | 6 | „ |
| Edward Waynwright puer ... ... ... ... | „ | „ |
| Henry Woan in eccl̄ia ... ... ... ... ... | 11 | „ |
| James Lathom ... ... ... ... ... ... ... | „ | „ |

| |  |  |  |
|---|---|---|---|
| | Wiłłm Ascroft in eccłia ... ... ... ... ... ... | 19 | June |
| | Ellen Agnesdale vid in eccłia ... ... ... ... ... | ” | ” |
| Fo. 425 | Elizab: Croston virg in eccłia ... ... ... | 21 | ” |
| | John Barton in eccłia ... ... ... ... ... | 22 | ” |
| | Edith Gleast ... ... ... ... ... ... ... | 23 | ” |
| | Margrett Wright vid ... ... ... ... ... ... | ” | ” |
| | A man childe of James Such in eccłia ... ... | 26 | ” |
| | Raphe Lyngley ... ... ... ... ... ... ... | 27 | ” |
| | Henry Molyneux ... ... ... ... ... ... | 29 | ” |
| | Blanch Wetherby virg ... ... ... ... ... | 4 | July |
| | Ellen Scofelt Infant ... ... ... ... ... ... | 6 | ” |
| | Elizab: Holcroft spinster ... ... ... ... | 8 | ” |
| | Elizab: Lunt vx[9] W[m] in eccłia ... ... ... | 11 | ” |
| | Katheryne Butler Inf ... ... ... ... ... | 13 | ” |
| | Alice vx[9] Ro: Letherbarr̄ in eccłia ... ... | 17 | ” |
| | John Tasker Inf ... ... ... ... ... ... | ” | ” |
| | Thom̃ Abrahā in eccłia ... ... ... ... ... | 18 | ” |
| | Thom̃ Swyft in eccłia ... ... ... ... ... | 23 | ” |
| | A strange boy ... ... ... ... ... ... ... | 26 | ” |
| | Elizab: ffairclough vid ... ... ... ... ... | 30 | ” |
| | Margrett Hunt Inf ... ... ... ... ... ... | 31 | ” |
| | Gilb̄te Scarisbr̄ puer ... ... ... ... ... | 1 | August |
| | Thom̃ Tomlinson in eccłia ... ... ... ... | 5 | ” |
| | Jane Haughtō vx[9] Rob̄te ... . ... ... | 8 | ” |
| | George Worthingtō Inf: ... ... ... ... | 9 | ” |
| | Anne Traves vid ... ... ... ... ... ... | 13 | ” |
| | Susan Marclew fi: Peter ... ... ... ... ... | 20 | ” |
| | Margrett Houlme vx[9] W[m] ... ... ... ... | 22 | ” |
| | Judith Athertō Inf in eccłia ... ... ... ... | 29 | ” |
| | Elizab: vx[9] Rich Hadocke ... ... ... ... | 3 | Septemb̄ |
| | Thomas Rathram Bacheler ... ... ... ... | 6 | ” |
| | Thomas Hawarth puer in eccłia ... ... ... | 7 | ” |
| | Anne Mosse vid in eccłia . . ... ... ... | 11 | ” |
| | Margrett Garstange vid in the high Chancell... | 13 | ” |
| | James Lea ... ... ... ... ... ... ... | 14 | ” |
| | Huan Westhead puer in eccłia ... ... ... | 15 | ” |
| | Katheryne Mason vid ... ... ... ... ... | 17 | ” |
| | Anne Marclew vid ... ... ... ... ... ... | ” | ” |
| | Anne Shawe virg ... ... ... ... ... ... | ” | ” |
| | Hamlet Prescott ... ... ... ... ... ... | 18 | ” |
| | Rich: Steele puer ... ... ... ... ... ... | 23 | ” |
| | Henry Dunkon Inf: in eccłia ... ... ... ... | 24 | ” |
| | A woman child of Edw: Symkin in eccłia ... | 26 | ” |
| | Rich: Cootō in y[e] High Chancell ... ... ... | 28 | ” |
| | Henry Mathewe ... ... ... ... ... ... | 12 | Octob: |
| | Rich: Ambrose Inf: in eccłia ... ... ... | ” | ” |
| | John Modesley in eccłia ... ... ... ... ... | 17 | ” |
| | Ellen Walker vx[9] Edm̃: in eccłia ... ... ... | 18 | ” |
| | Wiłłm Marclew ... ... ... ... ... ... | 21 | ” |

| | | | |
|---|---|---|---|
| | Edward Blundill ... ... ... ... ... ... | 25 | Octob: |
| p. 426 | Ellen Marclew vid ... ... ... ... ... ... | 27 | " |
| | Anne Smult vxꝰ Rich: in eccl̄ia ... ... ... | 28 | " |
| | John Croocke ... ... ... ... ... ... ... | 31 | " |
| | Mꝰgery Ollyverson vxꝰ Thom̄ ... ... ... | 14 | Novemb̄: |
| | Clarice Dickett vid in eccl̄ia ... ... ... ... | 20 | " |
| | Anne Jacksō vxꝰ Hen: in eccl̄ia ... ... ... | 23 | " |
| | Henry Waynwright in eccl̄ia ... ... ... ... | " | " |
| | Ellen Babott ... ... ... ... ... ... ... | " | " |
| | Alice Burscough spinster ... ... ... ... | 25 | " |
| | Elizab: Scarisbr̄: vxꝰ Edward in eccl̄ia ... | 26 | " |
| | Neale Bay ... ... ... ... ... ... ... ... | 27 | " |
| | Emlin Modesley vid in eccl̄ia ... ... ... ... | 29 | " |
| | Will̄m Ashton puer ... ... ... ... ... ... | 30 | " |
| | Alice Rigmaden vxꝰ George ... ... ... ... | 2 | December |
| | John Ollyverson Inf: ... ... ... ... ... | " | " |
| | Elizabeth Ascough vid ... ... ... ... ... | 6 | " |
| | ffrances Asley spinster ... ... ... ... ... | 7 | " |
| | Myles Barton Inf: the high Chancell ... ... | 8 | " |
| | Jane Shawe vxꝰ Will̄m ... ... ... ... ... | 10 | " |
| | George Wackfeild in eccl̄ia ... ... ... ... | 11 | " |
| | Margery* Blundill spinster ... ... ... ... | 14 | " |
| | James Barton ... ... ... ... ... ... ... | 15 | " |
| | Thomas Whalley in eccl̄ia ... ... ... ... | " | " |
| | Alice Spencer vxꝰ Peter ... ... ... ... ... | 17 | " |
| | Isabell Hodges spinster ... ... ... ... ... | " | " |
| | Hector Altie in eccl̄ia ... ... ... ... ... | 22 | " |
| | Edward Hunter ... ... ... ... ... ... ... | 24 | " |
| | Agnes Eccleston ... ... ... ... ... ... | 26 | " |
| | Thomas Wardman ... ... ... ... ... ... | 28 | " |
| | Elizab: Haytō a stranger ... ... ... ... | " | " |
| | Rob̄te Modesley in eccl̄ia ... ... ... ... | 30 | " |
| | Richard Spencer and Henry Spencer Inf: in eccl̄ia ... ... ... ... ... ... ... | " | " |
| | Elizabeth Ryding vxꝰ John ... ... ... ... | " | " |
| | Jane Smalshawe vid ... ... ... ... ... | " | " |
| | Rowland Barton ... ... ... ... ... ... | 1 | January |
| | Margery Masson Inf ... ... ... ... ... | 2 | " |
| | Ellen Spencer Inf ... ... ... ... ... ... | " | " |
| | Anne Masson Inf ... ... ... ... ... ... | 4 | " |
| | Cicely Lancaster vxꝰ John in eccl̄ia ... ... | 5 | " |
| p. 427 | Elizabeth Brighouse vxꝰ Rich: ... ... ... | 6 | " |
| | Anne Woodes vxꝰ Thom̄: in eccl̄ia ... ... | 12 | " |
| | John Hawarth Inf ... ... ... ... ... ... | 13 | " |
| | Anne ffletcher vid in eccl̄ia ... ... ... ... | 15 | " |
| | Hugh Hochkinson Inf ... ... ... ... ... | " | " |
| | John Spencer in eccl̄ia ... ... ... ... ... | " | " |
| | Peter Spencer puer in eccl̄ia ... ... ... ... | " | " |

* Marie *in Chester Transcript*

Mariery Modesley vxꝰ Rich in eccl̄ia ... ... 18 January
Thomas Molyneux Juven ... ... ... ... „ „
Jane Pinnington vxꝰ Homphrey ... ... ... 19 „
Ellen Bennett vid ... ... ... ... ... ... 20 „
Jane Prescott vid ... ... ... ... ... ... 24 „
Anne Laithwait Inf in eccl̄ia ... ... ... ... 31 „
John Rigby in eccl̄ia ... ... ... ... ... „ „
Margrett Ollyverson spinster ... ... ... ... 1 ffebruary
Hugh Keakwicke in eccl̄ia ... ... ... ... 3 „
Richard Marclewe ... ... ... ... ... ... „ „
Jane Whalley virgo ... ... ... ... ... ... 5 „
Margery Ascough vxꝰ Tho: in eccl̄ia ... ... 11 „
Jennett Dunkon vid in eccl̄ia ... ... ... ... „ „
Elizabeth Gobben spinster in eccl̄ia ... ... 12 „
Ellen ffazakerley vid ... ... ... ... ... 13 „
Elizabeth Rothwell Inf: ... ... ... ... ... „ „
Alice Banerster vid in Mꝰ Stanley his Chancell „ „
John Rutter in eccl̄ia ... ... ... ... ... 14 „
. . . Aspinwall in my Lo: Chancell ... 15 „
Anne Houlme vxꝰ Wil̄lm in eccl̄ia ... ... ... „ „
Jennett Cadwell a stanger [*sic*] ... ... ... 17 „
James Marclewe puer in eccl̄ia ... ... ... „ „
Judith Lewis vxꝰ Mr̄i Johañis in the high chancell ... ... ... ... ... ... ... „ „
Ellen Ambrose virg in eccl̄ia ... ... ... ... „ „
Wil̄lm Tayler in eccl̄ia ... ... ... ... ... 18 „
Gilb̄te Blundill ... ... ... ... ... ... 21 „
Mary Ambrose spinster in eccl̄ia ... ... ... 22 „
Hector Lea Juveñ in eccl̄ia ... ... ... ... „ „
Ellice Mason Inf: ... ... ... ... ... ... 25 „
Thomas Ollyverson ... ... ... ... ... ... „ „
Jennett Ormeshawe vid ... ... ... ... ... 27 „
Ellen Ormeshawe spinster ... ... ... ... 29 „
Katheryne Melling vid ... ... ... ... ... 3 Martch
Ellen Prescott vxꝰ Thom̄ in eccl̄ia ... ... ... 4 „
Ellizab: ffrance a stranger ... ... ... ... „ „
George Wythington ... ... ... ... ... ... 8 „
Fo. 428 A strange man ... ... ... ... ... ... „ „
Richard Hodson in eccl̄ia ... ... ... ... „ „
Margery Westhead spin: ... ... ... ... 9 „
Elynor Hunter vxꝰ Thom̄ in eccl̄ia ... ... „ „
Homphrev Pinningtō ... ... ... ... ... 12 „
Margrett Drap vxꝰ Henry ... ... ... ... „ „
Clarice Lathom vxꝰ Rob̄te ... ... ... ... 18 „
Edward Morcroft Inf ... ... ... ... ... „ „
Wil̄lm Shawe ... ... ... ... ... ... ... „ „

## 1624.

| | | |
|---|---|---|
| Alice Towne spinster | 29 | Martch |
| Martha Brighouse vxꝰ John | 3 | Aprill |
| Mary Whitestones vid | 9 | „ |
| Margery Willimson vid | 14 | „ |
| Thomas Ascough in ecclia | 15 | „ |
| Bridgett fformby vxꝰ John | „ | „ |
| Anne Scarisbricke vid | 18 | „ |
| Anne Boyer vid | 22 | „ |
| Margery Barton vid | 29 | „ |
| James Kilshawe puer | 1 | May |
| Gabriel Lunt Juvenis | 2 | „ |
| Katheryne Lowe Inf | 3 | „ |
| James Halsall Bacheler in the high Chancell | 13 | „ |
| Anne Clapū vxꝰ Rogeri in ecclia | 21 | „ |
| Margery Cockett vid | 6 | June |
| Elizabeth Tyrer Inf | 11 | „ |
| Margrett Ascroft Inf in ecclia | 14 | „ |
| Gabriel Rim̄er Inf | 18 | „ |
| Leonard Smethly Herald in the high Chancell | 24 | „ |
| . . . Modesley vxꝰ Rob̄ti | 4 | July |
| Henry Ormshawe Inf | 7 | „ |
| Roger Barton Inf | 8 | „ |
| John Amonde | 11 | „ |
| A man childe of p̄civall Peterson | 14 | „ |
| Huan Swyft Inf: in ecclia | 18 | „ |
| 9 Richard Hodson puer in ecclia | 29 | „ |
| Margrett Coockson Inf in ecclia | 5 | August |
| Willm Burscough puer in ecclia | 7 | „ |
| James Scarisbricke | 9 | „ |
| Margrett Scarisbricke virgo in ecclia | 13 | „ |
| Henry Rose Inf in ecclia | 28 | „ |
| Katheryne Bradshawe Inf in ecclia | 31 | „ |
| Willm Hodson Inf in ecclia | 5 | September |
| Thomas Sutch in ecclia | 13 | „ |
| Jony Smyth Inf | 14 | „ |
| Mary Scarisbricke Inf | 23 | „ |
| Margrett Woan vid | 26 | „ |
| Isabell Lathom Spinster | 4 | October |
| Elizabeth Sutch vid | 5 | „ |
| Jane Sephton vxꝰ Thō: in ecclia | 11 | „ |
| Elizab̄: Ormshaw vxꝰ Thom̄: in ecclia | 22 | „ |
| Elizab̄: Cubban vxꝰ Thom̄ in ecclia | 92 | „ [*sic*] |
| Margrett Dale vid | 10 | November |
| Margrett Hunter vid | 6 | Decemb̄ |
| Alice Gille vid | 13 | „ |
| Rob̄te Gille Bacheler in ecclia | 14 | „ |

| | Name | Day | Month |
|---|---|---|---|
| | Thom̄ Prescott | 15 | Decemb̄ |
| | Henry Blundill | 16 | „ |
| | Richard Masō Juven in eccl̄ia | 17 | „ |
| | Alice Cowp vxꝰ Rob̄ti | 26 | „ |
| | Andrewe Cowborne Inf | 28 | „ |
| | Margrett Ascroft vxꝰ John in eccl̄ia | 12 | January |
| | Mary Prescott vid | 17 | „ |
| | Richard Lathō in eccl̄ia | 21 | „ |
| | Will̄im Massey Inf | 28 | „ |
| | Will̄im Rigby Inf in eccl̄ia | 2 | ffebruary |
| | Will̄im Houlme in ecclia | 4 | „ |
| | Margrett Lawrensō vid in eccl̄ia | 9 | „ |
| | Richard Brighouse | 11 | „ |
| | Arthur Lea puer in eccl̄ia | 15 | „ |
| | Jane Carbee vxꝰ Josephe | „ | „ |
| | George Throppe Inf | 17 | „ |
| | Alice Ascroft vid | 19 | „ |
| Fo. 430 | Margrett Morcroft Inf | 10 | Martch |
| | Jane Thornton vxꝰ Rob̄te | 11 | „ |
| | Cicely fforshaw vxꝰ Henry de Daltō | 14 | „ |
| | Thomas Wynstanley in eccl̄ia | 15 | „ |
| | George Mathewe puer | 16 | „ |
| | Anne Symkin Inf in eccl̄ia | 23 | „ |
| | Richard Lea Inf in ecclia | „ | „ |

## 1625.

| Name | Day | Month |
|---|---|---|
| Henry Jackson in eccl̄ia | 26 | Martch |
| Edward Kilshawe Inf in eccl̄ia | 27 | „ |
| Katheryne Mason vid in eccl̄ia | 30 | „ |
| Ellen Tasker vxꝰ Henry | 2 | Aprill |
| Ellen Moscrop vxꝰ ffardinand | 3 | „ |
| Martha Brighouse vxꝰ John | 7 | „ |
| Judith Scarisbricke in Mꝰ Scarisbr̄ Chancell | 14 | „ |
| Ellen Barton Inf: in the High Chancell | „ | „ |
| Rob̄te Garnett in eccl̄ia | 24 | „ |
| Richard Hochkinson in eccl̄ia | 30 | „ |
| A woman childe of John Kilshawe in ecclia | 3 | May |
| Edward Hale Inf in eccl̄ia | 9 | „ |
| James Ormeshawe Bacheler in eccl̄ia | 10 | „ |
| Richard Walker Juven in eccl̄ia | 11 | „ |
| Will̄m Hunter Inf: in eccl̄esia | 17 | „ |
| John Worthingtō in eccl̄ia | 18 | „ |
| Anne Coocksō spinster | 21 | „ |
| Joane Peter Inf: | „ | „ |
| Roger Scarisbr̄ in eccl̄ia | 22 | „ |
| Anne fformby spinster | 23 | „ |
| George Westhead puer in eccl̄ia | 25 | „ |
| Ellen Modesley Inf | 27 | „ |

| | Name | Day | Month |
|---|---|---|---|
| | Gilb̄te Robinson Inf in eccl̄ia | 28 | May |
| | Jane Bowker Wyddowe | 29 | " |
| | Thom̄ Houlme | 2 | June |
| | Margrett Hatherwood vid | 6 | " |
| | Alice Sourbutts Inf in ecclia | 9 | " |
| | James Parker Inf: | 17 | " |
| | Margrett Stanley vid | " | " |
| 1 | Rob̄te Leadbetter | 19 | " |
| | John Biccursteth Inf | " | " |
| | Katheryne Carre vid | 21 | " |
| | Margrett Halsal̄ Inf: in the High Chancell | " | " |
| | John Ambrose in eccl̄ia | 23 | " |
| | Margery Ormshawe vxꝰ Rob̄te | 26 | " |
| | Margery Kerfoote Inf | 29 | " |
| | Anne vxꝰ Richi Halsall Armigr̄ in Mꝰ Scarisbr̄ Chancell | 7 | July |
| | Henry Houlme Inf | 8 | " |
| | Thomas Ormeshawe in eccl̄ia | 22 | " |
| | Gabriel Thorntō puer | " | " |
| | Thom̄ Aspinwall | 23 | " |
| | Dorithy Alcar Inf | " | " |
| | Elizab̄ Ambrose vxꝰ Thomas in eccl̄ia | 24 | " |
| | A woman child of Rob̄t ffidler | 28 | " |
| | Richard Harryson in eccl̄ia | 5 | August |
| | Jane Hesketh vxꝰ George | 9 | " |
| | Ellen Houlme vxꝰ Wil̄l̄im in eccl̄ia | " | " |
| | Margrett Sumner Inf | 10 | " |
| | Jane Hankinsō Inf | 11 | " |
| | Richard Waynwright | 28 | " |
| | Richard Henrysō Inf | 3 | September |
| | Peter Crane Bacheler | " | " |
| | John Cowborne Inf | 5 | " |
| | A womā childe of Henry Laithwaitt in ecclia | 6 | " |
| | Wil̄l̄im Hunt Infant in eccl̄ia | 8 | " |
| | A man child of Thom̄ Peter | 9 | " |
| | Margrett Rainforth Inf | 14 | " |
| | Thom̄ Morcroft Bacheler in eccl̄ia | 19 | " |
| | Richard Sowter Inf | 3 | October |
| | Hugh Woodes puer in the high Chancell | 15 | " |
| | Ellen Woofall spinster | 20 | " |
| | Wil̄l̄m Henrison puer | " | " |
| | Anne Chadocke Inf | " | " |
| | Anne Halsal̄ Inf: in Mꝰ Scarisbr̄ chancell | 29 | " |
| 32 | Thom̄ Melling Inf | 7 | November |
| | A woman Childe of Silvester Laithwaitt in eccl̄ia | 8 | " |
| | Mary Thorntō vxꝰ Rob̄te | 13 | " |
| | Elizab̄ Modesley Inf: in eccl̄ia | 1 | Decemb̄ |

| | | |
|---|---|---|
| A woman childe of Tho: Whitestones ... ... | 16 | Decemƀ |
| John Sutch Infant ... ... ... ... ... ... ... | 19 | „ |
| Katheryne Laithwaitt vx⁹ Willim in ecclia ... | 24 | „ |
| Richard Robinsō Inf ... ... ... ... ... ... | 27 | „ |
| Elizabeth Bartō virgo ... ... ... ... ... ... | 29 | „ |
| A man childe of John Seddon in ecclia ... ... | 7 | January |
| John Westhead Inf ... ... ... ... ... ... ... | 8 | „ |
| Margrett Whitestones vid ... ... ... ... ... | 16 | „ |
| Henry Whitehead Inf ... ... ... ... ... ... | 19 | „ |
| Margery Martindale vid in ecclia ... ... ... | 28 | „ |
| Phillip Hey in ecclia ... ... ... ... ... | 29 | „ |
| Ciceley Ormshawe vid in ecclia ... ... ... | „ | „ |
| Tho: Waynwright Inf in ecclia ... ... ... | 8 | ffebruary |
| Rich: Boore Inf ... ... ... ... ... ... ... | 10 | „ |
| Edw:* Potter Gent: in my Lords chancell... | 18 | „ |
| Richard Swyft Inf in ecclia ... ... ... ... | 19 | „ |
| Elizaƀ: Blackledge virgo in ecclia ... ... | 20 | „ |
| Rich: Symkin Inf in ecclia ... ... ... ... | 21 | „ |
| Henry Prescott ... ... ... ... ... ... ... | 22 | „ |
| Richard Brighouse ... ... ... ... ... ... ... | „ | „ |
| Henry Holden in ecclia ... ... ... ... ... | 23 | „ |
| George Nayler Inf ... ... ... ... ... ... | 27 | „ |
| Mary Modeslev virgo in ecclia ... ... ... | 7 | Martch |
| James Bartō Inf ... ... ... ... ... ... ... | 8 | „ |
| Fo. 433 Henry Croston in ecclia ... ... ... ... ... ... | 20 | „ |
| Edward Houlme ... ... ... ... ... ... ... | „ | „ |
| Ellen Kilshawe vx⁹ John in ecclia ... ... ... | 23 | „ |

## 1626.

| | | |
|---|---|---|
| Anne Greaues vid ... ... ... ... ... ... | 6 | Aprill |

* Thomas *in Chester Transcript.*

175 **The Regester booke** of sutch as haue bene Maried within the parishe of Ormis$^{k}$ Churche Since the Beginninge of hir Ma$^{tes}$ most happie Raigne whiche did begine (to Englands Joye and Comforte) the 17$^{th}$ daye of November Anno dni 1557

---

## MARRIAGES.

### 1557.

| | | |
|---|---|---|
| John Herryson Margerie Mossocke mariede... | 25 | November |
| Henrie Whitstons Margreat Radley ... ... | 27 | „ |
| Gilberte Sonnes Alis Cawe ... ... ... ... | „ | „ |
| Peeter Jackson Margreat Rydde ... ... ... | „ | „ |
| [*No entries for December*] | | |
| Hughe Lea Eliz$^{th}$ Coockson ... ... ... | 16 | Januarie |
| Thomas Jahnson Jahn Gill ... ... ... ... | „ | „ |
| Henrie Balard Margreat Charles ... ... ... | „ | „ |
| Ric̃ Cropp Margerie Alerton ... ... ... | 23 | „ |
| Roberte Mowdisley Margreat Aynsworth ... | 30 | „ |
| Adam Ashords Anne Woodfall ... ... ... | „ | „ |
| Tho: Ambrose Eliz$^{th}$ Gerrard ... ... ... | 5 | ffebruarie |
| James Watkinson Margery C adocke ... ... | „ | „ |
| Rob̄t Whitstons Eliz$^{th}$ Wolsie ... ... ... | „ | „ |
| Ric̃ Arnold Anne Mossocke ... ... ... ... | 18 | Aprill |
| Wil̄lm Mulinxe Margret Cattrall ... ... ... | 24 | „ |

### 1558.

| | | |
|---|---|---|
| Wil̄lm Hoolme Anne Tockeholes ... ... | 5 | June |
| Thomas Keykwicke Margerie Preskot ... | „ | „ |
| Hugh Henrieson Alis Rainforth ... ... ... | 12 | „ |
| Robert Haile Eliz$^{th}$ Prescot ... ... ... ... | 19 | „ |
| Henrie Winder Jaine Moscroppe ... ... ... | „ | „ |
| Edmund Holland Ellin Waringe ... ... ... | 3 | July |
| Edmunde Alerton Ellin Hutchen ... ... | „ | „ |
| Edward Barker Alis Berye ... ... ... ... | 17 | „ |
| Wil̄lm Cophull Katherin Ascroft ... ... ... | 31 | „ |
| Henrie Webster Eliz$^{th}$ Butchard ... ... ... | 9 | October |

Willm Pryce Jaine Jackeson ... ... ... 23 October
Richard Maken Jaine Leadbetter... ... ... „ „
Willm ffarscarre Margerie Blundell ... ... 6 November
Tho: Knowles Anne Hatton ... ... ... „ „
Fo. 177 Willm Waynewright Marget Moscrop ... ... 20 „
John Cubbon Eliz[th] Musker ... ... ... ... „ „
Willm Bradshaw Jaine Prescott ... ... ... 26 „
Thomas Burie Eliz[th] Walker ... ... ... 15 Januarie
Hugh Jackeson Margerie Spencer ... ... „ „
Symond Banburie Ellin Hodgeson ... ... „ „
George Woodes Marget Buchard ... ... ... „ „
Thomas Haale Ellin Craine ... ... ... ... „ „
Ric̃ Stophford Grace Savage ... ... ... 21 „
John Wolfall Alis Skaresbricke ... ... ... „ „
Ric̃ Ambrose Jane Morcrofte ... ... ... „ „

[*No entries for ffebruarie*]

## [1559.]

Tho: Crofte Margerye Waynwright ... ... 9 Aprill
Ellis Hall Cislie Kadicke ... ... ... ... „ „
Fo. 178 Edward Blundell Eliz[th] Shurlacars ... .. 16 „
George Suche Jane Withington ... ... . 22 „
Homfray Gill Margat Woodhouse ... ... 26 „
Rodger Smyth Claris Hallsall ... ... ... 28 Maye
Anthoney Haughton Katherin Webster ... 11 June
Jamis Asmall Ellin Tatlocke ... ... ... 18 „
Hugh Lunte Katherin Swifte ... ... ... „ „
Willm Boockefilde Ellin Killshaw ... ... „ „
Richard Lailand Ellin Savage ... ... ... 25 „
Peeter Woosey Eliz[th] Ambrose ... ... ... 30 July
Henrie Richardsoñ Eliz[th] Arnould ... ... 6 Auguste
Richard Clapam Eliz[th] Houghton ... ... „ „
Fo. 179 Robert Waythmā Eliz[th] Hoolme ... ... ... 15 „
Willm Smyth Alis Woolfall ... ... ... ... 24 September
Thomas Leadbetter Alis Baines ... ... ... 1 October
Henrie Mowdisley Anne Waynewright... ... 8 „
Edward Whyte Sislie Sutch ... ... ... ... 29 „
Willm Cadicke Jaine Haughton ... ... ... 3 November
Rodger Scarsbrecke Sibell Blundell ... ... „ „
Jamis Goulbron Emlin Dwarrehowse ... ... 12 „
John Lea Margerie Longley ... ... ... ... „ „
Willm Luskin Alis Woodfall ... ... ... 19 „
Randall Saile Jaine Scarsbrecke ... ... ... 26 „
Hugh Loccar Katherin ffletcher ... ... ... „ „
Ellin Longe . . . Margerie [*sic*] ... ... „ „
Fo. 180 Willm Jumpe Jaine Smyth ... ... ... ... 7 Januarie
John Werrall . Ellin Woodfall ... ... ... 28 „

| | Names | Day | Month |
|---|---|---|---|
| | Thomas ffryth Margerie Clapam | 28 | Januarie |
| | Gilbart Asshorst Izabell Scarsbrecke | 5 | ffebruarie |
| | Robert Rylanes Elizabeth Garrard | „ | „ |
| | Charles Le Margerie Smyth | „ | „ |
| | George Burie Izabell Talior | „ | „ |
| | George Cropp Agnes Thomson | „ | „ |
| | Willm Butler Margerie Holland | 11 | „ |
| | Willm Worthingeton Elin Smoolte | „ | „ |
| | Tho: Holland Anne Waringe | „ | „ |
| | Robart ffarclough Alis Hunte | „ | „ |
| | Lawrance Gasken Margat Buler | 19 | „ |
| | Ranolde Waynewright Marget Bower | „ | „ |

## 1560.

| | Names | Day | Month |
|---|---|---|---|
| | Ranould Craine Marget Ormishaw | 21 | Aprill |
| 181 | John fforshaw Ellin Eritage | 6 | Maye |
| | Willm Pecocke Grace Banke | 12 | „ |
| | Tho: Jamson Margerie Sutton | 19 | „ |
| | Thomas Asmall Eliz^th^ Jump | 23 | June |
| | Jamis Swyfte Eliz^th^ Carre | „ | „ |
| | Nicolas ffornby Ellen Smoolte | 14 | July |
| | John Tysinge Marget Cowp | 30 | „ |
| | Willm Smallshaw Anne Lea | 11 | August |
| | Thomas Byrtch Jaine Anderton | 1 | September |
| | John Ashorst Anne Ashton | 22 | „ |
| | Richard Cropp . . . . . | „ | „ |
| | Richard Mowdisley Ellin Lea | 29 | „ |
| | Thomas Gill Marget Sumner | 6 | October |
| | Willm Morecroft Jaine Burie | 13 | „ |
| 182 | John Thornton Alis Gobbin | 20 | „ |
| | John Gill Eliz^th^ Sutch | 26 | „ |
| | John Aiscroft Alis Swyfte | 27 | „ |
| | Jamis Blundell Alis Arnould | „ | „ |
| | Hugh Lathom Jaine Tasker | 17 | November |
| | Alexander Thackerow Jine Coockeson | „ | „ |
| | Hugh Sutch Isabell Spencer | 1 | December |
| | Rodger She Margerie Morecroft | 8 | „ |
| | Gefferey Burie Margerie Mellinge | 15 | „ |
| | Hugh Hoolme Alis Aspinwall | 26 | Januarie |
| | Richard Asshorst Eliz^th^ Lancaster | „ | „ |
| | Willm Sutch Marget Toccolles | 27 | „ |
| | Peeter Morecrofte Jenet Holleworth | 1 | ffebruarie |
| | Ranould Mason Eideth Gill | 2 | „ |
| | Edmunde Spencer Eliz^th^ Lunge [*or* Lune] | 8 | „ |
| | Gilbert Westhead Sislie Haughton | „ | „ |

## 1561.

| Fo. | Names | Day | Month |
|---|---|---|---|
| Fo. 183 | Henrie Woofall Ellin Tockholes | 12 | Aprill |
| | Raffe Burscough Ellin Lathom | 27 | " |
| | Hugh Bycarstaf Elizth Burie | 28 | " |
| | Tho Ambrose Elizth Holland | 4 | Maye |
| | Parsevall Gill Margerie Sutch | 11 | " |
| | Rodger Scarsbrecke Marget Greene | 18 | " |
| | Richard Lithom Alis Waterworth | " | " |
| | Tho: Hardman Elizth Irland | 25 | " |
| | Edward Blundell Ellin Carre | 8 | June |
| | Tho: Burton Jaine . . | 17 | " |
| | Robert Shurlicars Marget Jamisdoughter | 27 | July |
| | Richard Bucke Jaine Burie | 18 | Auguste |
| | Robert Haile Jenet Barker | 24 | " |
| | Richard Gorsutch Marget Shurlicars | 31 | " |
| Fo. 184 | Henrie Parre Elizth Cropp | 14 | September |
| | Henrie Dobson Jaine Blundell | 28 | " |
| | John Waringe Marget Gineson | 5 | October |
| | Thomas Hutton Katherin Scarsbrecke | 12 | " |
| | Bryhan Morecrofte Elizth Sage | 19 | " |
| | Rodger Smyth Izabell Asmall | 26 | " |
| | Cristopher Gill Ellin Lea | 9 | November |
| | Willm Bootle Elizth Nelson | " | " |
| | Edmund Carre Jaine Preskot | 16 | " |
| | Lucke Sutch Margerie Mawdisley | 7 | December |
| | Symond Smyth Izabell Chadocke | " | " |
| | Thomas Preston Izabell Woodes | 4 | Januarie |
| | Edw: Holland Katherin Acocke | 8 | " |
| | George Harieson Elizth ffeetewood [*sic*] | 11 | " |
| | John Sumner Ellin Kidd | 18 | " |
| | Adam Coockeson Elizth Scath | 25 | " |
| Fo. 185 | Willm ffarclough Alis Werrall | 1 | ffebruarie |
| | John Knowles Ellin Haslam | " | " |

## 1562.

| Names | Day | Month |
|---|---|---|
| Gilbart Barton Margerie Carre | 5 | Aprill |
| Nicolas Werall Margerie Watkinson | 13 | " |
| George Morgan Elizth Cocket | 26 | " |
| George Barton Jaine Gill | " | " |
| Willm Killshaw Jaine Scarsbrecke | 27 | " |
| Ottuwell Blundell Ellin Spencer | " | " |
| Nicolas fformby Blanch Blundell | 10 | Maye |
| Jamis Spencer Marget Hunter | " | " |
| Richard Rutter Jaine Jumpe | 24 | " |
| John Diconson Elizth Holland | " | " |
| Hamle Bygehowse Ann Scarsbreck | " | " |

| No. | Groom | Bride | Day | Month |
|---|---|---|---|---|
| | John Hunter | Margerie Barton | 7 | June |
| | George Blundell | Margerie Shurlicars | „ | „ |
| | Richard Waringe | Ellin Sumner | „ | „ |
| | Johne Yate | Jenet Smyth | 24 | „ |
| | Edward Stevenson | Alis Shepord | 26 | „ |
| 86 | John Richardson | Margerie Barton | 12 | July |
| | Henrie Garrerd | Elizth Barwicke | 19 | „ |
| | Thomas Waynewright | Elizth Preskot | 2 | Auguste |
| | Robert Cosey | Marget Rydinge | 31 | „ |
| | Ellis Ambrosse | Anne Ormishaw | 6 | September |
| | Peeter Shawe | Jaine Rutter | „ | „ |
| | Robert Parre | Alis Cropp | 20 | „ |
| | Thomas Whytestones | Marget Pye | 4 | October |
| | Ewan Blackeledge | Anne Stopforth | „ | „ |
| | John Kakewicke | Marget Sutch | 13 | „ |
| | Richard Gowlbron | Ellin Scarsbrecke | 19 | „ |
| | Edmund Smulte | Katherin Stopforth | 9 | November |
| | Richard Breykell | Marget Hoolme | 10 | „ |
| | Henrie Lea | Jaine Mawdisley | 12 | „ |
| | Richard Woode | Katherin Ball | „ | „ |
| 87 | Henrie Drap . . . . . . | | 29 | „ |
| | Robert Shaw | Alis Lennard | „ | „ |
| | Thomas Seale alies Duncon | Catherin Withingeton | 30 | „ |

*[No entries for December—blank space left]*

## 1563.

| No. | Groom | Bride | Day | Month |
|---|---|---|---|---|
| | Robert Smyth | Alis Carr | 18 | Aprill |
| | Raffe Burscough | Jaine Jackeson | 25 | „ |
| | Thomas Morton | Katherin Morecrofte | 2 | June |
| | Rob̄t Hunter | Elline Cowsey | 6 | „ |
| | John Hawghton | Margerie ffornbie | 13 | „ |
| | Ric̄ Keickwicke | Katharen Haughton | „ | „ |
| | John Abbot | Ellin Seddon | 27 | „ |
| 88 | Peeter Cropp | Margreat Barton | 4 | Julie |
| | Gilb̄t Sumner | Alis Yeate | „ | „ |
| | Henrie Stanley Esquire | Mrs Margreat Stanley | 26 | September |
| | Edw: Westhead | Margreat Worthington | „ | „ |
| | Ric̄ Ball | Jaine Waringe | „ | „ |
| | Hector Lea | Margreat Jumpe | 3 | October |
| | Thomas Aspinwall | Elizth Worthington | 11 | „ |
| | Thomas Gobine | Anas Wilson | 7 | November |
| | Richard Wackenson | Jane Halle | 30 | „ |
| | Henrie Halworthe | Jenet Ambrose | 2 | Januarie |
| | James Smythe | Sislie Heaton | 3 | „ |
| | Rob̄t Halsall | Elizth Moscrop | 6 | „ |
| | Henrie Banke | Katharin Pye | 10 | „ |

| | | | |
|---|---|---|---|
| | John David Anne Jumpe ... ... ... ... | 25 | Januarie |
| | James Jackson Katherin Hunter ... ... ... | 30 | " |
| | Tho: Wethington Emlin Halworth ... ... | " | " |
| Fo. 189 | Edw: Johnson Jane Asheton ... ... ... | " | " |
| | Edmond Richardson Anne Mowdisley ... | 31 | " |
| | Thomas Morcrofte Jane Beconsall ... ... | 2 | ffebruarie |
| | Peeter Barton Alis Locker ... ... ... ... | 6 | " |

## 1564.

| | | | |
|---|---|---|---|
| | Willm Cothere Anne Berye ... ... ... ... | 28 | Maye |
| | John Westhed Margerie Barker ... ... ... | 18 | June |
| | Willm Morcrofte Katharin Morcrofte ... ... | 25 | " |
| | John Mathewe Grace Gill ... ... ... ... | 4 | Julye |
| | Thomas Winstanley Eliz^th^ Longe ... ... | 3 | September |
| | Willm Asmoll Katherine Barker ... ... ... | 10 | " |
| | John Spencer Jaine Shepert ... ... ... ... | 8 | October |
| | . . . Pedder Anne Arton ... ... ... | 29 | " |
| Fo. 190 | Richard Barton Jaine Mowdisley ... ... ... | 19 | November |
| | Willm Wariner Marget Shurlicars ... ... | 26 | " |
| | . . . Smallshaw Ellin Cubannes ... ... | " | " |
| | Godferey Atherton Eliz^th^ . . . ... ... | 3 | December |
| | Robert Hunter Ellin Blundell ... ... ... | 10 | " |
| | John Lea Anne Robinson ... ... ... ... | 7 | Januarie |
| | Peeter Bromilay Sislie Sones ... ... ... | 29 | " |
| | John Prescot Sislie Rutter ... ... ... ... | 4 | ffebruarie |
| | Nicolas Smyth Blanch fformby ... ... ... | 5 | March |

## 1565.

| | | | |
|---|---|---|---|
| | Gowther Tunstall Ellin Stonton ... ... ... | 30 | Aprill |
| | Lawrance Richardson Marget Gorsutch ... | 13 | Maye |
| | Hugeh Gill Kat.edge [*sic*] Medow ... ... | 3 | June |
| | Peeter Holland Eliz^th^ Preskot ... ... ... | " | " |
| | Jamis Blundell Katherin Scarsbrecke ... ... | 17 | " |
| | Edw: Alerton Jaine Seale ... ... ... ... | " | " |
| Fo. 191 | Robert Bower Margerie Ryesse ... ... ... | 8 | Julye |
| | Richard Mowdisley Tomazin Preskot ... ... | 15 | " |
| | Tho: Whatton Eliz^th^ Gorsutch ... ... ... | " | " |
| | Tho: Bisshell Marget Gill ... ... ... ... | 22 | " |
| | Johne Webster Marget Sharpus ... ... ... | 19 | Auguste |
| | Ewan Hodgeson Eliz^th^ Hunte ... ... ... | " | " |
| | John Styhan Jaine Chadocke ... ... ... | 25 | " |
| | Jamis Burie Anne Whitworth ... ... ... | " | " |
| | Peeter Hoolme Eliz^th^ Cocket ... ... ... | 2 | September |
| | John Hoolme Margerie Cooke ... ... ... | 16 | " |
| | Richard Martclife Jaine Clarke ... ... ... | 7 | October |
| | Tho: Tasker Ellin Parker ... ... ... ... | 11 | November |
| | John Carre Jenet Sumner ... ... ... ... | " | " |

Edwarde Blundell Alis Tomson ... ... ... 9 December
Thomas Jumpe Margerie Blundell ... ... 13 Januarie
Willm ffarclough Jaine Shackledie ... ... 20 „
Willm Barton Anne Ruter ... ... ... ... 9 ffebruarie
Rodger ffarclough Alis Sankey ... ... ... 10 „
Tho: ffletcher Katheren Sutch ... ... ... 25 „

## 1566.

Edmund Awtie Genet Blundell ... ... ... 2 Aprill
Jamis Aspinwall Eliz$^{th}$ ffarclough ... ... 26 Maye
Raffe Marcer Genet Shurlicars ... ... ... 23 June
Homfrey Harison Marget Dober ... ... ... „ „
Willm Lithom Marget ffarclough ... ... ... 30 „
Jamis Henrieson Alis Burscough ... ... ... 28 Julye
George Sefton Emlin Barton ... ... ... 27 November
Edmund Bispam Eliz$^{th}$ Bispam ... ... ... 15 December
Thomas Woodhowse Alis Preskot ... ... 5 Januarie
Tho: Scarsbrecke Marget Shurlicars ... ... 29 „
John Aiscrofte . . . . . ... ... ... 6 ffebruarie

## 1567.

Robert Mowdisley Elin Aiscrofte ... ... 12 Maie
Edward Richardson Elizabeth Sedon ... ... 16 June
Cristopher Mowdinge Sislie Carr ... ... ... 20 Julye
M$^{r}$ Robert Hesketh Mrs Marie Stanley ... 29 September
Henrie Howlden Eliz$^{th}$ Macon ... ... ... 4 October
George Ormishaw Dawse Hill ... ... ... 23 November
Robert Morecrofte Anne Sumner ... ... 7 December
John Gowlbroñ Anne Gill ... ... ... ... 11 Januarie
Tho: Croston Eliz$^{th}$ Butchart ... ... ... 8 ffebruarie
John Batersbie Jenet Wrennall ... ... ... 9 „
Willm Preskot Alice Sutch ... ... ... ... 15 „
Tho: Barton Alis Dughtie ... ... ... ... 23 „

## 1568.

Richard Ambrose Marget Bowker ... ... 16 Maye
John Hill Eliz$^{th}$ Sutch ... ... ... ... ... „ „
Ellis Aspinwall Anne Kekiwicke ... ... ... 30 „
John Burscough Eliz$^{th}$ Gill ... ... ... ... „ „
John Cropp Jaine Molinex ... ... ... ... „ „
Hugh fforshaw Eliz$^{th}$ Lei ... ... ... ... 13 June

[*No entries for July*]

John Gobbin Anne Thornton ... ... ... 6 Auguste
Richard Banke Marget Morecroft ... ... „ „
Richard Irland Elin Hancocke ... ... ... „ „
Tho: Marrall Ellin Lea ... ... ... ... 13 „

| Fo. | Names | Day | Month |
|---|---|---|---|
| | Hugh Woofall Eliz$^{th}$ Morcroft ... ... ... | 13 | Auguste |
| Fo. 195 | Ranould Aspinwall Margerie Cockeson ... | 5 | September |
| | Johne Letherbarow Izabell Soracowle ... ... | 26 | „ |
| | Jamis Turner Anne Ambrose ... ... ... | „ | „ |
| | Jamis Sutch Claris Kilshaw ... ... ... ... | 26 | October |
| | Henrie Winder Catherin Wilkinson ... ... | 7 | November |
| | Tho: Asshorst Jaine Standanough ... ... | 15 | „ |
| | Hugh Holland Grace Leadbetter ... ... ... | 23 | Januarie |
| | Hugh Bycarstaffe Jaine Ainesworth ... ... | 6 | ffebruarie |
| | John Peeter Eliz$^{th}$ Preskot ... ... ... ... | 21 | „ |

## 1569.

| Fo. | Names | Day | Month |
|---|---|---|---|
| | Richard Marclough Eliz$^{th}$ Alke ... ... ... | 17 | Aprill |
| | Raffe Cropp Jaine ffrith ... ... ... ... | 8 | Maye |
| | John Allerton Alis Hill ... ... ... ... | 22 | „ |
| | George Bow Marget Jackeson ... ... ... | „ | „ |
| | Willm Walshe Eliz$^{th}$ Haughton ... ... ... | „ | „ |
| | Willm Hoolme Jaine Ormishaw ... ... ... | 26 | June |
| Fo. 196 | Tho: Holland Catherin Cowp ... ... ... | 30 | October |
| | Hugh Cowp Alis Killshaw ... ... ... ... | 22 | Januarie |
| | John Clarke Anne Asmall ... ... ... ... | 29 | „ |
| | Richard Holland Ellin Mellinge ... ... ... | „ | „ |
| | Richard Swifte Eliz$^{th}$ Howden ... ... ... | „ | „ |

## 1570.

| Fo. | Names | Day | Month |
|---|---|---|---|
| | Henrie Rimmer Ellin Babot ... ... ... ... | 13 | Aprill |
| | Rodger Tomson Anne Marceland ... ... | 30 | „ |
| | Willim Allerton Katherin Ormishaw ... ... | 28 | Maye |
| | George Ball Alis Blundell ... ... ... ... | 5 | June |
| | John Smyth Eliz$^{th}$ Ormishaw ... ... ... | 25 | „ |
| | Henrie Morecrofte Emlin Livessey ... ... | 9 | July |
| | Hugh Lathom Marget Rimmer ... ... ... | 16 | „ |
| | Robert Jump Eliz$^{th}$ Dreage ... ... ... ... | „ | „ |
| Fo. 197 | Robert Richardson alis Jackeson Ellin Richardesdoughter ... ... ... ... ... | 5 | Auguste |
| | Henrie Blundell Eliz$^{th}$ Watkinson ... ... | 10 | September |
| | Tho: Brwicke Emlin Barton ... ... ... | 8 | October |
| | Richard Gill Eliz$^{th}$ Blackeledge ... ... ... | „ | „ |
| | John Allcar Ellin Eccleston ... ... ... | „ | „ |
| | Jaims Bycarstafe Anne Westhead ... ... | 22 | „ |
| | Trymour Lunte Genet Tomson ... ... ... | „ | „ |
| | John Sheill Alis Ambrose ... ... ... ... | 12 | November |
| | Ewan Swyfte Katherin Livsey ... ... ... | „ | „ |
| | Richard Brigehowse Elizabeth Preskot ... | 19 | „ |
| | Robert Rydinge Marget Mowdisley ... ... | „ | „ |
| | Phillip Mowdisley Katherin Alcocke ... ... | 27 | „ |

| | Names | Day | Month |
|---|---|---|---|
| | John Shawe Emlin Westhead | 10 | December |
| | Richard Westhead Anne Shawe | ” | ” |
| | Robert Bycarstafe Marget Brigehowse | 18 | January |
| 198 | Thomas Killshaw Alis Robertesdoughter | 4 | ffebruarie |
| | Richard Killshaw Elizth Barton | ” | ” |
| | Jamis Beconsall Emlin Kekuicke | 11 | ” |
| | Tho: Cowsey Marget Mowdisley | 18 | ” |
| | Gilbart Martin Jaine Morecroft | ” | ” |

## 1571.

| | Names | Day | Month |
|---|---|---|---|
| | Edward Fenes Eideth Barton | 29 | Aprill |
| | Parsivell Gill Marget Talier | ” | ” |
| | Robert Hesketh Marget Breykell | 1 | Maye |
| | Tho: Mollinex Marget Croocke | 1 | Julye |
| | Richard Whytesaid Margerie* Cropp | 25 | ” |
| | John Atkinson Anne Mellinge | 16 | September |
| | Willm Gill Margerie Lea | 7 | October |
| | Jamis Blundell Marget Blundell | 3 | December |
| | Henrie Mawdisley Elizth Shaw | 16 | ” |
| 199 | Jamis Elliett Elizth Shaw | 20 | Januarie |
| | Hugh Preskot Katherin Maile | 27 | ” |
| | Tho: Hey Katherin Swifte | 3 | ffebruarie |
| | David Letherbarow Elizth Morecroft | ” | ” |
| | Lyonet [*sic*] Vrmeston Elizth Talior | 4 | ” |
| | Jamis White Anne Whatton | 10 | ” |
| | Raffe Claiton Katherin Morecroft | 17 | ” |

## 1572.

| | Names | Day | Month |
|---|---|---|---|
| | Phillip Swifte Jaine Gorsutch | 18 | Maye |
| | Levis Barton Margerie Shirdley | 25 | ” |
| | Thomas Ric̃son Jenet Blundell | 22 | June |
| | Nicolas fforshawe Jane Tho: doughter | ” | ” |
| | Peeter Blundell Margreat Bashawe | 6 | Julye |
| | Ric̃ Garnet Elizth Ascrofte | 19 | Auguste |
| | John Jamson Izabell Longe | ” | ” |
| 200 | Cuthbart Mason Marget Burgas | 19 | October |
| | Tho: fformbey ffraces Lathom | ” | ” |
| | Willm Scarsbrecke Jaine Richardson | ” | ” |
| | Thomas Picavance Elizth Spencer | ” | ” |
| | Henrie Aspinwall Anne Hesketh | 18 | Januarie |
| | Willm Goare Margaret † Gill | ” | ” |
| | Cuthbart Harrson Ellin Haughton | ” | ” |

* *This may be* Marget. *An alteration has been made, but it is not quite clear which is the substantive name.*

† *This may be* Margerie.

## 1573.

Ewan Waringe Eliz$^{th}$ Stopforth ... ... ... 5 Aprill
George Mowdisley Margerie Ashton ... ... 12 „
Thomas Whicke Jaine Woodes ... ... ... 3 Maye
Jamis Haile Izabell Mollinex ... ... ... 17 „
Jamis Sutton Sislie Pemberton ... ... ... 21 June
Henrie Standanought Ellin Ashton ... ... „ „
Omfray Morecroft Izabell Stanton ... ... 25 Julie
John Burie Marget Barton ... ... ... ... 26 „
Fo. 201 George Stopforth Jaine Preskot ... ... ... 9 Auguste
Peeter Spakeman Marget Richardesdoughter 23 „
Cristopher Willmson Anne Henrieson ... „ „
Willm Marcer Anne Marcer ... ... ... 30 „
Robert Shawe Marget Cowp ... ... ... 27 September
Willm Shawe Marget Swifte ... ... ... ... 18 October
Jamis Adderton Izabell Webster ... ... ... 25 „
John Ainesworth Margerie ffarrer ... ... 3 November
Willm Spencer Eliz$^{th}$ Mowdisley ... ... ... 8 „
Henrie Lathom Ellin Butler ... ... ... 22 „
Gilbart Butler Dowse Smyth ... ... ... „ „
Raffe Mellinge Grace Sutch ... ... ... ... 29 „
Myles Barton Katherin Ormishaw ... ... 2 December
Raffe Boockefeelde Anne Whytestones ... 3 „
Adame Barton Marget Prescot ... ... ... 13 „
John Guddes Ellin Marclough ... ... ... „ „
Edw: Anderton Marget Charles ... ... ... 15 „
Fo. 202 Tho: Ambrose Eliz$^{th}$ Leadbetter ... ... 10 Januarie
Edw: Worthington Loare Haughton ... ... 17 „
George Stanley Alis Killshaw ... ... ... 24 „
Johne ffarclough Margerie Prescot ... ... „ „
Edmunde Smulte Katherin Whytestones ... 31 „
John Marclough Anne Crosbie ... ... ... „ „
George Kocket Anne Woolsey ... ... ... 14 ffebruarie
Jamis Sutch Marget fforster ... ... ... ... „ „

## 1574.

Jamis Sanderson Claris Smolte ... ... ... 25 Aprill
Raffe Allerton Eliz$^{th}$ Spakeman ... ... ... „ „
Tho: Sutton Jaine Ballshaw ... ... ... 9 Maye
Robert Tatlocke Anne Jump ... ... ... 23 „
Phillip Hoolme Eliz$^{th}$ Barker ... ... ... 14 June
Jamis Cruick Lettis Harwood ... ... ... „ „
Henrie ffarclough Eliz$^{th}$ Gilbartson ... ... 20 „
Jamis Arnould Anne Killshaw ... ... 8 August
Elis Ambrose Ellin Westhead ... ... ... 22 „
Fo. 203 Willm Henrieson Margerie Hoolme ... ... 10 October

Phillip Martindaile Jaine Millingeton ... ... 7 November
Ric̃ Lathom Marget Rutter ... ... ... ... 20 „
Tho: Mowdisley Elin Lathwhat ... ... ... 21 „
Willm Aspes Marget Martindaile ... ... 28 „
Willm Waynewright . . . ... ... ... 9 Januarie
Robert Shawe Eliz Lennard ... ... ... ... „ „
Ric̃ Crucke Marget Howlden ... ... ... 27 „
Jamis Cowp Anne Shawe ... ... ... ... 28 „
Tho: Abraham Marget Worthington ... ... 29 „
Tho: Barker Eliz[th] Crvcke ... ... ... ... „ „
Cristopher Harison Jaine Mowdisley ... ... 31 „
Jamis Asshorst Marget Haughton ... ... „ „
Edmond Richardson Alis Ormishaw ... ... 7 ffebruarie
Tho: Burie Alis Holland ... ... ... ... „ „
Gefferey Haiton Izall Arker ... ... ... ... „ „
Tho: Prescott Marget Mowdisley ... ... „ „
Tho: Swifte Margerie Ireland ... ... ... 8 „
Jamis Plumbe Margerie Blageborne ... ... „ „

## 1575.

Ric̃ Marclough Anne Burscough ... ... ... 7 Aprill
Robert Shurlicars Jaine Hill... ... ... ... „ „
Robart Banister Alis Barton ... ... ... ... 10 „
Ric̃ Gill Marget Kekuicke ... ... ... ... 24 „
George Waynewright Ellin Smulte ... ... 8 Maye
Lawrance Yate Ellin Spencer ... ... ... 12 June
Robart Bootle Marget Stopforth ... ... ... „ „
Peeter Jackeson Jaine Tasker ... ... ... 13 „
Henrie ffarclough Margerie Sutton ... ... 19 „
Johe Litherland Margerie Wingrow ... ... 20 „
Willm Haide Anne Holland ... ... ... ... 29 „
Hugh Gilbartson Emlin Ambrose ... ... 17 July
John Blvndell Marget Hallworth ... ... ... 4 Auguste
Robert Monkey Ellin Gill ... ... ... ... 18 October
Hugh Shawe Alis Morecroft ... ... ... 26 „
Jamis Beconsaw Jenet Sutch ... ... ... 3 December
Richard Hill Marget Killshaw ... ... ... 7 „
John Cocket Eliz[th] Barton ... ... ... ... „ „
Willm Ormie Katherin Withingeton ... ... 19 „
Robart Anderton Anne Halsall ... ... ... 28 „
John Barker Anne Mawdisley ... ... ... 12 ffebruarie
John Goulbron Alis Shepord ... ... ... 26 „

## 1576.

Edw: Sutton gent: Anne Stanley gent ... 14 Maye
John Hunt Jaine Morecroft ... ... ... ... 20 „
Robart Ball Katherin Claton ... ... ... 31 „

Jamis Willson Margerie Pendleburie ... ... 3 June
Tho: Aiscroft Genet Ormisha ... ... ... „ „
Myles Skipton Roafe Martindaile ... ... 30 „
Fo. 206 Wiƚƚm Scarsbrecke Katherin Allerton ... ... 5 July
Rowland Lee Jaine Smyth ... ... ... ... 26 August
Jamis Edw:son Blanch Blvndell ... ... ... 2 September
Robert Rimmer Eliz$^{th}$ Shurlicars ... ... ... 16 „
Peeter Westhead Alis Halworth ... ... ... 17 „
Jamis Sutch Marget Mawdisley ... ... ... 9 October
Cristopher Richardson Ellin Gill ... ... 21 November
Henrie Lvnt Alis Kekuicke ... ... ... ... 25 „
John Cowson Jaine Cocket ... ... ... ... 9 December
Tho: Burscough Alis Sumner ... ... ... 23 „
Hugh Cowp Ellin Gilbertson ... ... ... 13 Januarie
Myles Hughson Alis Gill ... ... ... ... 27 „
Tho: Thorpe Alis Swifte ... ... ... ... „ „
Homfrey Winstanley Katherin Parbould ... 30 „
Fo. 207 Jhon Burgas Jaine Hallworth ... ... ... 3 ffebruarie
Jamis Waringe Jaine Jackeson ... ... ... „ „
Tho: Morecroft Agnes Shaw ... ... ... 4 „
Raffe Whytestones Marget Morecrofte ... „ „
John Weshead Jenet Sumner ... ... ... 11 „
Omfrey Morecroft Marget Garrard ... ... „ „

## 1577.

Wiƚƚm Killshaw Anne Hill ... ... ... ... 14 Aprill
Henrie Hodgeson Marget Gill ... ... ... 28 „
Gilbart Lathome Jaine Milner ... ... ... 19 Maye
Robart Darwaine Jaine Mvsketh ... ... ... 23 June
Bryan Henrison Ellin Simkinson ... ... ... 14 July
Robert Rylans Eliz$^{th}$ Barton ... ... ... 23 December

## 1578.

Tho: Halworth Eliz$^{th}$ Bootle ... ... ... 17 Aprill
Ric̃ Swifte Jaine Robertesdoughter ... ... „ „
Fo. 208 Henrie Houghton Marget Macon ... ... ... 10 Maye
Robert Hoolme Jaine Gill ... ... ... ... 25 „
Wiƚƚm Morecroft Marget Bootle ... ... ... „ „
Wiƚƚm Morcroft Anne Walker ... ... ... 6 June
[*No entries*] July
Wiƚƚm Withingeton Jaine Preskot ... ... 27 August
Hugh Asmall Margerie Wiƚƚmdoughter ... 22 October
Wiƚƚm Barton Eliz$^{th}$ Lea ... ... ... ... 26 Januarie

## 1579.

Tho: Alerton Anne Ric̃doughter ... ... 14 June
Henrie Martindaile Margerie Kekuicke ... 19 Julye

| | | | |
|---|---|---|---|
| Ric̃ Longeton | Genet Rodgerson | 23 | Auguste |
| John Hill | Alis Toppinge | 24 | „ |
| Richard Morecroft | . . . . | 26 | „ |
| John Blvndell | Elizth Mowdisley | 11 | October |
| Richard Walkar | Elizth Barton | 25 | „ |
| Peeter Edwardson | Grace Barton | 8 | November |
| Robart ffarrer | Margete Scarsbrecke | „ | „ |
| Richard Sharpus | Alis Rydinge | 10 | „ |
| Robert Talior | Ellin Harwood | 22 | „ |
| John Pye | Grace Halsall | 21 | Januarie |
| Allen Kilshaw | Anne Kilshaw | 22 | „ |
| Richard Preskot | Izabell Willson | 23 | „ |
| Robart Tarleton | Jaine Aspinwall | 1 | ffebruarie |
| Ric̃ Bycarstaffe | Marget Crosse | 7 | „ |
| Raffe Withingeton | Katherin Mowdisley | „ | „ |
| Tho: Waynewright | Alis Rithrope | 14 | „ |
| Richard Spakeman | Elizth Burie | 15 | „ |

## 1580.

| | | | |
|---|---|---|---|
| Lawrance Garrard | Jaine Martindaile | 2 | Julye |
| George Wainewright | Katherin Morecrofte | 17 | „ |
| Xpopher Preskot | Ellin Howlden | 24 | „ |
| Jamis Mowdisley | Mowde Byrtchwood | 31 | „ |
| Ric̃ Whytestones | Marget Morecroft | 7 | August |
| Tho: Hill | Alis Hodgeson | 19 | „ |
| Hugh Haughton | Elizth Kekuicke | 21 | „ |
| Tho: Sutch | Jaine Tasker | 16 | September |
| Henrie Leadbetter | Alis Lithom | 7 | October |
| Robert Aluin | Mawde Boer | 28 | November |
| John Willson | Margerie Scarsbrecke | „ | „ |
| Hamlet Rithrop | Marie Bolton | 29 | Januarie |
| Jamis Henrison | Katherin fformbey | 30 | „ |
| Tho: Westhead | Anne Starkey | 6 | ffebruarie |

## 1581.

| | | | |
|---|---|---|---|
| Willm Mollinex | Anne Asshorst | 4 | Aprill |
| 1 Jamis Smulte | Jaine Hodgeson | 21 | Maye |
| Peeter Bradshaw | Alis Waringe | 22 | „ |
| Robert Marrall | Elizth Abraham | 28 | „ |
| Robert Whytesaid | Margerie Preskot | 4 | June |
| Willm Plumton | Alis Aspinwall | „ | „ |
| Jamis Jackeson | Jaine Ambrose | „ | „ |
| Richard Mason | Alis Yate | 19 | „ |
| Ric̃ Balle | Elizth Cropp | 2 | Julye |
| Homfrey Swifte | Eloner Gilbertson | 16 | „ |
| Cristopher Page | Emlin Morecroft | 21 | „ |
| Alexander Shackeleydie | Jaines Barnes | 24 | „ |

| Fo. | Husband | Wife | Day | Month |
|---|---|---|---|---|
| | John Weltche | Elizth Preskot | 13 | Auguste |
| | Robert Smalshaw | Emlin Kekuiwicke | 16 | „ |
| | Jamis Jackeson | Marget ffletcher | 27 | „ |
| | Wiłłm Sefton | Margerie Woodhows | 3 | September |
| | Gilbart Greene | Elizth Weltch | 25 | „ |
| Fo. 212 | Gabriell Barton | Jaine Asmall | 8 | October |
| | Richard . . . | Eme Haughton | 2 | November |
| | Wiłłm Wright | Margerie Mowdisley | 5 | „ |
| | | *[No entries]* | | December |
| | Hector Killshaw | Elizth fforshaw | 28 | Januarie |
| | Jamis Killshaw | Marget Clapam | 4 | ffebruarie |
| | Tho: Nalior | Marie Holland | 18 | „ |
| | Robert Anderton | Jaine Mowdisley | „ | „ |
| | Lawrance Yate | Izabell Talior | „ | „ |
| | Wiłłm Barton | Anne Ormishaw | 25 | „ |
| | Tho: Bower | Ellin Banke | „ | „ |
| | Stven Livinge | Ellin Tasker | 26 | „ |
| | Robart Balshaw | Marget Spencer | „ | „ |

## 1582.

| Fo. | Husband | Wife | Day | Month |
|---|---|---|---|---|
| | Tho: Walles | Katherin Killshaw | 20 | Maye |
| | John Barton | Elizth Westhead | 4 | June |
| | John Stanley | Mowde Mowdisley | 6 | „ |
| Fo. 213 | Jamis Barton | Jaine Lathom | 15 | July |
| | Symond Mawdisley | Katherin Henrieson | 5 | August |
| | Wiłłm Ratclife | Jaine Holland | 19 | „ |
| | Richard Haughton | Izabell Aspinwall | „ | „ |
| | John Gobbin | Alis Dobson | 26 | „ |
| | Gilbart Haile | Marget Westhead | 3 | September |
| | Jamis Yate | Margerie Mowdisley | 16 | „ |
| | Henry Waringe | Margerie Holland | 28 | October |
| | Wiłłm Allerton | Jaine Whytestones | 10 | November |
| | Peeter Longe | Elizth Lunt | „ | „ |
| | Henrie Holland | Marget Morecroft | „ | „ |
| | Wiłłm Porter | Elizth Mason | 12 | „ |
| | Richard Kadicke | Anne Jackson | 10 | „ |
| | Robert Irland | Marget Parker | 20 | „ |
| Fo. 214 | John Walne | Jaine Dey | 20 | Januarie |
| | Tho: Morecrofte | Elizth Scarsbrecke | 27 | „ |
| | John Hervie | Margerie Barton | „ | „ |
| | Tho: Hunter | Genet Debdell | 3 | ffebruarie |

## 1583.

| Fo. | Husband | Wife | Day | Month |
|---|---|---|---|---|
| | Wiłłm Booth | Genet Gill | 9 | Maye |
| | Richard Henrison | . . . Blvndell | 12 | „ |
| | Robert Haughton | Marget Haughton | 7 | June. |

George Pye ffrances Blackeledge ... ... ... 8 July
Robert Garrard Anne Shaw ... ... ... ... 14 „
John Whytestones Elizth Preskot ... ... ... 9 August
Edward Whyte Marget Mowdisley ... ... 20 November
Alexander Tomson Katherin Hatton ... ... 24 „
215 John Blvndell Jaine Hill ... ... ... ... 8 December
Richard Breykell Margerie Jump ... ... ... 19 „
John Sharocke Izabell Barton ... ... ... 10 Januarie
James Mowdisley Margreat Asmolle ... ... 20 „
Willm Wainwright Margrat Pye ... ... ... 26 „
Henrie Cropp Margreat Stophford ... ... „ „
Henrie Haill Jaine Lockker ... ... ... ... 18 ffebruarie
Trayamore Swyfte Jaine Blacklidge ... ... 20 „
Willm Swifte Alis Blackledge ... ... ... „ „
Hughe Scarsbricke Jaine Woodhovse ... ... 27 „
Tho: Willson Katherine Keckwicke ... ... 1 Marche
Tho: Borskoughe Jaine Traves ... ... ... „ „

## 1584.

Willm Haughton Alis Cobane ... ... ... 20 Aprill
Tho: Rimmere Margreat Blundell ... ... 3 Maye
James Reade Emlin Adamsone ... ... ... 30 „
216 Ric̃ Jackson Elizth Wainwrighte ... ... ... 14 June
Milis Hesketh Jenete Westhed ... ... ... 21 „
Willm Halworth Katherin Hardman ... ... 24 „
John White Jane ffazacarley ... ... ... ... 5 Julye
Henrie Stopford Jaine fforshawe ... ... ... 2 Auguste
George Penkett Izabell Swifte ... ... ... 9 „
Hughe Rgerson Alis Claton ... ... ... ... 10 „
Tho: Shawe Elizth Harison ... ... ... 6 December
Rodgere Sankie Anne Pickett ... ... ... 8 „
Henrie Hill Anne Haidocke ... ... ... 19 Januarie
217 Nicolas Charles Alis Buchard ... ... ... 8 ffebruarie
Randill Sailes Christian Smyth ... ... ... 21 „
John Goye Marie Longe ... ... ... ... „ „
Rodger Hallsall Anne Holonde ... ... ... 23 „

## 1585.

James Waringe Izabell Kilshawe ... ... ... 13 Aprill
Rodger Andisdaill Jane Balshawe ... ... 18 „
Henrie Gill Ellin Golbrone ... ... ... ... „ „
Tho: Aspinwall Anne Westhead ... ... ... 9 Maye
Nicolas Whaley Anne Scarsbricke ... ... 21 „
Rodgere . . . Jaine Balshawe ... ... 29 „
Nicolas Aspinwal Anne Traves ... ... ... 6 June
Henrie Ambrose Anne Swifte ... ... ... 23 „
Ric̃ fformbie Edeithe Tomson ... ... ... 18 July

| | | | | |
|---|---|---|---|---|
| Fo. 218 | Willm Preskote | Margreat Shawe ... ... ... | 1 | September |
| | Tho: Alerton | Margery Askough ... ... ... | 21 | October |
| | Ric̃ Marson | Katherin Preskot ... ... ... | 20 | „ |
| | David Letherbarowe | Jenet Jackson ... ... | 2 | December |
| | Rob̃t Letherbarowe | Elizth Jackson ... ... | „ | „ |
| | Henrie Mulinxe | Margreat Huson ... ... ... | 17 | Januarie |

## 1586.

| | | | | |
|---|---|---|---|---|
| | Lawrance Woodes | Margreat Lathon ... ... | 2 | Maye |
| | Ric̃ Kidde | Jenet Norris ... ... ... ... | 15 | „ |
| | James Spenser | Katherine Yeatte ... ... ... | 9 | June |
| | George Watt | Margrat fferrer ... ... ... | 28 | Julye |
| | John Gernere | Anne Cokkett ... ... ... ... | 1 | Auguste |
| Fo. 219 | Homfray Rosheye | Alis Biycye ... ... ... | 1 | September |
| | Ric̃ Voce | Alis Preskott ... ... ... ... ... | 9 | October |
| | Rob̃t Ball | Jaine Cropp ... ... ... ... ... | 29 | Januarie |
| | Rob̃t Cadicke | Margreat Parker ... ... ... | „ | „ |
| | John Bell | Marie Whitstons ... ... ... ... | 6 | ffebruarie |
| | Willm Holden | Margerie Prescot ... ... ... | „ | „ |
| | James Scarsbricke | Margerie Lea ... ... ... | 7 | „ |
| | Hugh Ascrofte | Katherin Ashurste ... ... | 8 | „ |

## 1587.

| | | | | |
|---|---|---|---|---|
| | Ewan Doson | Margreat Kilingworth ... ... | 17 | Aprill |
| | James Keckwicke | Katherine Ryse ... ... | 28 | Maye |
| | Bryane Cockett | Margerie Mason ... ... ... | 30 | „ |
| | John Hesketh | Margrat Barton ... ... ... | 8 | June |
| | Hugh Aspinwall | Marie Stanley ... ... ... | 11 | „ |
| Fo. 220 | Ellis Ambrose | Elizth Aspinwall ... ... ... | 29 | Auguste |
| | Tho: ffarclough | Alis Mowdisley ... ... ... | 24 | September |
| | Robert Willson | Marget Craine ... ... ... | 2 | October |
| | Robert Lyon | Katherin Asimall ... ... ... | 15 | „ |
| | Tho: Stanley | Marget Marrow ... ... ... | 31 | „ |
| | Ewan Swyfte | Izabell Coockeson ... ... ... | „ | „ |
| | Raffe Marcer | Margerie Coocke ... ... ... | „ | „ |
| | Robert Blvndell | Katherin Balshaw ... ... | 10 | ffebruarie |
| | George Smalshaw | Katherin Marrall ... ... | 18 | „ |
| | George Preskot | Elizth Whytestones ... ... | „ | „ |
| | Cuthbart Garrerd | Ellin Burton ... ... ... | 4 | Martch |

## 1588.

| | | | | |
|---|---|---|---|---|
| | Ric̃ Arnould | Katherin Abraham ... ... ... | 14 | Aprill |
| | Hugh Backestonden | Katherin Wainewright... | 15 | May |
| | John Willson | Elizth Mollinex ... ... ... | 2 | June |
| Fo. 221 | Henrie Lathom | Ellinn Rimmer ... ... ... | 15 | Julye |

Richard Swyfte Eliz$^{th}$ Holland ... ... ... 13 October
Jamis Waynewright Alis Preskot ... ... ... 20 „
Hugh Kewquicke Eliz$^{th}$ Clapam ... ... ... 27 „
George Watkinson Marget Beconso ... ... 4 November
Jamis Crosse Izabell Holland ... ... ... 10 „
John Barton Eliz$^{th}$ Cropp ... ... ... ... 24 „
Peeter Charles Ellin Asmall ... ... ... 8 December
Tho: Robinsoñ Elliz$^{th}$ Holland ... ... ... „ „
George Sutch Emlin Morecrofte ... ... ... 15 „
Elis Sumner Katherin Macon ... ... ... 21 „
Willm Gorhson [?] Alis Wignall ... ... ... 4 Januarie
Nicolas Hey Eliz$^{th}$ Shell ... ... ... ... 18 „
Raffe Holland Elin Webster ... ... ... 26 „
John Hunt Ellin Haile ... ... ... ... ... „ „
Henrie Wolfall Katherin Svmner ... ... ... 10 ffebruarie

## 1589.

John Peeter Eliz$^{th}$ Blackeledge ... ... ... 20 Aprill
Richard Hodgeson Anne Dobsoñ ... ... 27 „
Davie Griffeth Eliz$^{th}$ Holland ... ... ... 1 Maye
John Jackeson Marget Gill ... ... ... ... 12 „
Henrie Lathom Katherin Scarsbrecke ... „ „
Raffe Withingeton Margerie Alker ... ... 22 „
Robert Gill Eliz$^{th}$ Wythingeton ... ... ... 31 August
Tho: Hallworth Marget Walliner ... ... 21 September
Hector Killshaw Margerie Cropp ... ... 26 October
Willm Woodes Anne Rutter ... ... ... ... 3 November
John Kekuicke Katherin Scarsbrecke ... ... 16 „
Tho: Hoolme Ellin Loccar ... ... ... ... 24 Januarie
Tho: Skinner Marget Wadingeton ... ... 25 „
Rodger Lea Ellin Sollam ... ... ... ... 12 ffebruarie
Nicolas Morecrofte Jaine Hadocke ... ... 15 „
Johne Hoolme Katherin Blvndell ... ... „ „
Thomas Jolie Margerie Macon ... ... ... 17 „
John Marclough Eline Daron ... ... ... 18 „
Homfrey Lyon Jaine Smallshaw ... ... ... 26 „

## 1590.

Jaine [*sic*] Lathom Marget Worthingeton ... 26 Aprill
Gowther Barton Ellin Scarsbrecke ... ... 1 June
Richard Clapam Jenet Worthingeton ... ... 24 „
Jamis Sutton Anne Smallshey ... ... ... 29 „
George Cropp Ellin Garrard ... ... ... 12 July
Tho: Henrieson Katherin Stanley ... ... 24 „
Rodger Rydinge Eliz$^{th}$ Kewquicke ... ... 2 Auguste
Peeter Voce Ellin Houghton ... ... ... 29 „
Cristopher Johnsoñ Marie Blvndell ... ... 9 September

| | | | |
|---|---|---|---|
| | Richard Holland Elizth Shepord | 18 | October |
| | Peeter Shawe Katherin Hodgeson | 20 | November |
| | John ffaringeton gent Marget Hodgeson | „ | „ |
| Fo. 224 | John Seale Johne Withingeton | 1 | December |
| | John Gill Jaine Barton | 3 | „ |
| | Willm Lailand Katherin Kidd | 27 | „ |
| | Hugh Thorston Anne Leadbetter | 28 | Januarie |
| | Robart Patricke Katherin Nelson | 7 | „ |
| | Tho: Carre Claris Cropp | 27 | „ |
| | Henrie Morecrofte Elin Mowdisley | 2 | ffebruarie |
| | Peeter Specer Margerie Woosey | „ | „ |
| | Gilbart Barton Jaine Mason | 4 | „ |
| | Tho: Allerton Anne Gobbin | 7 | „ |
| | Henrie Croston Marget Letherbarow | 11 | „ |
| | Tho: Asshorste Annes Swifte | 14 | „ |

## 1591.

| | | | |
|---|---|---|---|
| | Cristopher Woofall Ellin Jumpe | 18 | Aprill |
| | Raffe Cropp Jaine Jackeson | 9 | Maye |
| | John Ormishaw Elizth Sutch | 16 | „ |
| | John Allisage Elizth Lewes | 25 | „ |
| Fo. 225 | Hugh Preskot Elizth Marclough | 6 | September |
| | Robert Gyles Elizth Mowdisley | 8 | „ |
| | Phillipe Hoolme Ellin Blvndell | 28 | „ |
| | John Sutch Marget fforshaw | 29 | „ |
| | Tho: Greaves Grace Asmall | 5 | October |
| | Tho: Sutch Marget Mather | 17 | „ |
| | Robert Haliwell Margerie Croocke | 18 | November |
| | Ather Barton Elizth Aspinwall | 30 | „ |
| | Hughe Sutche Elizth Oliverson | 9 | December |
| | Water Lathom Margreat Preskot | 14 | „ |
| | Peeter Blundell Alice Bimson | 19 | „ |
| | Willm Tatlocke Margreat Smalshawe | 23 | Januarie |

## 1592.

| | | | |
|---|---|---|---|
| | Herie Garnet Anne Rydinge | 9 | Aprill |
| | Tho: Gill Margreat Gobin | 10 | „ |
| | Silvester Coockeson Ellin Cutler | 16 | „ |
| Fo. 226 | Willm Johnson Anne Haughton | 23 | „ |
| | Willm Luskin Jaine parbot [*sic*] | 24 | „ |
| | Gilbert Weltch Anne Tasker | 6 | Maye |
| | Robert Blackeledge Genet Gollie | 21 | „ |
| | Robert Witon Genet Sumner | 5 | July |
| | Robart Palmer Elizth Lowrance | 9 | „ |
| | Rodger March Marget Baner | 12 | „ |
| | Tho: Hey Katherin Aiscroft | 30 | „ |

| Husband | Wife | Day | Month |
|---|---|---|---|
| Thomas Medowes | Katherin Ormishaw ... | 20 | Auguste |
| Ric̃ ffletcher | Dorethie Spencer ... ... ... | 12 | September |
| Edmunde Carre | Katherin Morecrofte ... ... | 24 | " |
| Homfrey Greaves | Marget Gill ... ... ... | 9 | October |
| Tho: Wiswall | Alis Picket ... ... ... ... | 20 | " |
| Tho: Mawdisley | Marget Yate ... ... ... | 21 | " |
| Edw: Bankes | Marget Shawe ... ... ... | 30 | " |
| Gilbart Lathom | Sislie Ashton ... ... ... | 6 | November |
| Wiſłm Mosse | Eliz[th] Ormishaw ... ... ... | 9 | " |
| 27 Richard . . . | Jaine Garrerd ... ... ... | 24 | December |
| Homfrey Harrison | Marget Westhead ... ... | 29 | Januarie |
| Jamis Burie | Grace Croockes ... ... ... | 31 | " |
| Gowther Woosey | Izabell Chadocke ... ... | 11 | ffebruarie |
| Tho: Carter | Ellen Hunte ... ... ... ... | 18 | " |

## 1593.

| Husband | Wife | Day | Month |
|---|---|---|---|
| Gilbert Blvndell | Eliz[th] Sutch ... ... ... | 13 | Maye |
| Richard Whytestones | Eliz[th] Alerton ... ... | 15 | " |
| Richard Voce | Margerie Rutter ... ... ... | 5 | June |
| Hugh Cropp | Marget Osbaston ... ... ... | 16 | " |
| Wiſłm Tomson | Katherin Johnson ... ... | 17 | " |
| John Makin | Marget Gaskin ... ... ... ... | 24 | " |
| Henrie Woosey | Emlin Jumpe ... ... ... | 8 | July |
| Tho: Hey | Margerie Garrard ... ... ... | " | " |
| Tho: Hesketh | Anne Lea ... ... ... ... | 15 | " |
| Richard Gill | Alis fforster ... ... ... ... | 29 | August |
| 228 Edmund Carter | Marget Mellinge ... ... ... | 23 | September |
| Tho: Holcrofte | Anne Brookefilde ... ... | 26 | " |
| Gabriell Hesketh gẽt | Jaine Stanley gent ... | 30 | October |
| John Taylior | Eliz[th] Craine ... ... ... ... | 5 | November |
| Edw: Lythom | Jaine Barton ... ... ... | 11 | " |
| John Parker | Eliz[th] Hervie ... ... ... ... | 12 | " |
| Robert Holland | Marget Asmall ... ... ... | 25 | " |
| Raffe Burmiston | Katherin Hebleforth ... ... | 9 | December |
| Henrie . . . | Elizabeth . . . ... ... | 23 | " |
| Richarde Tatlocke | Eliz[th] Chadocke ... ... | " | " |
| Hugh Martindaile | Margerie Woodes ... ... | 24 | " |
| Ewan Blackeledge | Margerie Whytestones ... | 20 | Januarie |
| Adame Barton | Eliz[th] Bootle ... ... ... ... | 21 | " |
| Henrie Lathwhat | Marget Puye ... ... ... | 24 | " |
| Edw: Hoolme | Anne ffarclough ... ... ... | 3 | ffebruarie |
| John Robertson | Alis Aspinwall ... ... ... | 4 | " |
| John Stanley | Jaine Cropp ... ... ... ... | " | " |

## 1594.

| Husband | Wife | Day | Month |
|---|---|---|---|
| 229 Robert Blackeledge | Katherin Smyth ... ... | 8 | Aprill |
| Tho: Sefton | Ellin Aiscroft ... ... ... ... | 9 | " |

| | | | | |
|---|---|---|---|---|
| | Henrie Barton | Marget Gill | 22 | Aprill |
| | Rodger Heskeyn | Genet Yate | 5 | Maye |
| | Gilbert Killshaw | Anne Loccar | 12 | „ |
| | Henrie Hesketh | Eliz$^{th}$ Hoolme | 13 | „ |
| | Richard Barnes | Elizabeth Gobin | 2 | June |
| | Henrie Kenion | Jaine Barton | „ | „ |
| | Edward Plumbe | Anne Morecroft | 16 | „ |
| | Ric̃ Barton | Brichet Penketh | 30 | „ |
| | Henrie Lunte | Alis Mowdisley | 1 | July |
| | Wiłłm fforshaw | Margerie Sutch | 7 | „ |
| | Tho: Parker | Anne Killshaw | 21 | „ |
| | Henrie Puye | Ellin Bretton | 22 | September |
| | Peeter Cropp | Margerie Marcer | 1 | October |
| | Wiłłm Rigmaden | . . . . | 5 | „ |
| | John Bradshaw | Alis Stivenson | 28 | „ |
| Fo. 230 | Tho: Smyth | Anne Barton | 4 | November |
| | Wiłłm Hoolme | Anne Waringe | 7 | „ |
| | Tho: Mulinexe | Ellin Blundell | 1 | December |
| | John Nixsone | Margerie Marser | 15 | „ |
| | Ric̃ Gleaste | Emblin Bawige | 22 | Januarie |
| | James Blundell | Eliz$^{th}$ Parkere | 2 | Marche |

## 1595.

| | | | | |
|---|---|---|---|---|
| | Ric̃ Sankie | Margrat Ascrofte | 1 | Maye |
| | Edw: Spenser | Alis Blundell | 11 | „ |
| | Hugh ffletcher | Margret Aspinwall | 6 | „ |
| | Thursten Wolsie | Katherin Codreye | 1 | June |
| | Rodgere ffinne | Eline Dowren | 15 | „ |
| | John Eastheade | Alĩs Heye | „ | „ |
| | Edw: Yeatte | Eliz$^{th}$ Sutche | 22 | „ |
| | Nicalas Hamson | Ellin Mason | 29 | „ |
| | Tho: Lathwhat | Alis Luskine | 30 | „ |
| | James Blundell | Jenett Blundell | „ | „ |
| Fo. 231 | Robt Awtie | Sislie Harison | 27 | July |
| | Gilbearte ffrithe | Eliz$^{th}$ Jackson | 13 | Auguste |
| | Ric̃ Morcrofte | Eliz$^{th}$ Hatton | 11 | September |
| | Wiłłm Sutche | Katherine Backstendeyle | 21 | October |
| | Henrie Sutche | Ellin Spenser | 22 | „ |
| | Robt Mowdisley | Anne Garrard | 9 | November |
| | Davie Westheade | Ellin Morcrofte | 16 | „ |
| | Wiłłm Breckell | Margreat Shawe | 7 | December |
| | Hector Sutche | Alis Walas | 14 | „ |
| | Edw: Blundell | Jaine Shurliker | 18 | „ |
| | Edw: Crayne | Ellin Alker | 1 | Januarie |
| | Rodger Westhead | Jaine Asmoll | 1 | ffebruarie |
| | Edw: Kilshawe | Anne Mowdisley | 2 | „ |
| | Ric̃ Irelande | Margreat Traves | 8 | „ |

Silvester Ascrofte Anne Worthington ... ... 8 ffebruarie
32 Thomas Longhey Marget Gorsuth [*sic*] ... 17 „
Peeter Aspinwall Elizabeth ffletcher ... ... 18 „

## 1596.

Willm Hopwood Eliz^th^ Aiscroft ... ... ... 12 Aprill
John Aiscrofte Eliz^th^ Spencer ... ... ... 20 Maye
Bryhan Kocket Elinn Hunte ... ... ... 23 „
Tho: Hunter Ellin Butler ... ... ... ... 9 June
Rodger Wallworth Sibell Barton ... ... ... 12 September
Richard Windrow Jaine Morecroft ... ... 14 „
Tho: Ambrose Katherin Smyth ... ... ... 19 December
Henrie Smyth Alis Haide ... ... ... ... 27 Januarie
Edw: Clarke Katherin Waynewright ... ... 30 „
Robert Rainforth Margerie Atherton ... ... „ „
Ric̃ Bolle Katherin Parker ... ... ... ... 31 „

## 1597.

Ric̃ Burie Ellin Whytestones ... ... ... 12 Aprill
Jamis Blvndell Anne Sutch ... ... ... ... 24 „
233 Tho: Cubon Marget Dobson ... ... ... 30 Maye
Phillip Swifte Anne Cropp ... ... ... ... 4 August
Hugh Aiscrofte Katherin Waynewright ... 7 „
Edw: Croston Marget Layland ... ... ... 15 „
Henrie Wallne Eliz^th^ Kewquick ... ... ... 26 September
Robert Wythingeton Eliz^th^ Preskot ... ... 24 October
Ric̃ Ball Sislie Allerton ... ... ... ... ... ... „ „
Tho: Barton Anne Withingeton ... ... ... 14 November
Willm Coockeson Sislie Holland ... ... ... 10 December
Hugh Barton Eliz^th^ Mowdisley ... ... ... 15 Januarie
Ric̃ Holland Ellin Marrow ... ... ... ... 22 „
John Ambrose Marie Sadler ... ... ... ... 29 „
Tho: ffletcher Anne Whytestones ... ... 12 ffebruarie
Ric̃ Haile Anne Asmall ... ... ... ... ... 27 „

## 1598.

Edw: Edwardson Anne Jhnesdoughter ... 12 Aprill
Willm Tomson Jaine Morecrofte ... ... 23 „
234 Henrie Blvndell Mowde Blvndell ... ... ... 8 Maye
Jamis Chadocke Ellin Morecrofte ... ... 15 „
John Mowdisley Ellin Killshaw ... ... ... „ „
Robart Shaw Eliz^th^ Longley ... ... ... 25 „
Hamlet Marrall Alis Crowshey ... ... ... 13 September
Jamis Swifte Genet Ormishaw ... ... ... 19 October
Willm Aiscrofte Eliz^th^ Aspinwall ... ... ... „ „

Henrie Penketh Margerie Hand ... ... ... 12 November
Hugh ffletcher Ellin Dandie ... ... ... ... „ „
Edw: Tarbocke gent Anne Stanley gent ... 16 „
Willm Brigehowse Genet Cropp ... ... ... „ „
Ric̃ Kellet Katherin Kekuicke ... ... ... 4 December
Tho: Gollie Elizth Ascough ... ... ... ... 3 Januarie
Willm Hoolme Mowde Smyth ... ... ... 4 ffebruarie
Johne Parker Izabell Gyles ... ... ... ... 12 „
John Smyth Alis Tyrer ... ... ... ... 13 „

## 1599.

Raffe Byrtchwood Marget Whytestones ... 9 Aprill
Ric̃ Greene Eideth Gleaste ... ... ... ... 10 „
Fo. 235 Gilbart Morecroft Katherin Ambrose ... ... 17 „
Willm Cowdocke Elizth Lathwhat ... ... 22 „
Ric̃ Fisher Elizth Woollen ... ... ... ... 6 Maye
Raffe Poole Ellin Morecroft ... ... ... ... 20 „
Henrie Anderton Anne Woode ... ... ... 28 „
Anthoney Cadicke Marget Shawe... ... ... 29 „
Willm Mollinex Anne Toppinge ... ... ... 18 June
Richard Beconsawe Anne Ambrose ... ... „ „
Tho: Lawranson Marie Whatton ... ... 1 July
Richard Garstange Alis Scarsbrecke ... ... 16 „
Robert Towne Marget Barker ... ... ... 29 „
Edmund Osbaston Ellin Haughton ... ... 20 August
Robert Sutton Elizth Barton ... ... ... ... 27 „
Henrie Mowdisley Marget Preskot ... ... 2 October
Cristopher Waringe Jaine Hesketh ... ... 6 November
Richard Goare Jaine Sefton ... ... ... ... 17 „
Fo. 236 Willm Ballshaw Alis Scarsbreck ... ... ... 16 December
Tho: Johnson Anne Hunter ... ... ... „ „
Richard Talior Alis Aspinwall ... ... ... 30 Januarie

## 1600.

Edmund Cropp Marget Swifte ... ... ... 4 Maye
John Davie Eme Woodes ... ... ... ... 13 „
Willm fformbie Elizth Morecrofte ... ... 22 June
Tho: Aiscrofte Elizth Gill ... ... ... ... 13 Julye
John Atherton Alis Ainsworth ... ... ... 14 „
Silvester Sutch Marie ffletcher ... ... ... 16 „
Tho: Coockeson Anne Gardner ... ... ... 19 August
Henrie Longley Jaine Lea ... ... ... ... 1 September
Omfrey Toppinge Marie Morecroft ... ... „ „
John Anglesdaile Anne Aimund ... ... ... 22 „
Henrie Barton Anne Plvmbe ... ... ... 28 „
Ric̃ Houghton Margerie Gill ... ... ... „ „

Gabriell Morecroft Eliz$^{th}$ Parbould ... ... 13 October
Richard Jackeson Anne Burscough ... ... 21 „
Robert Waringe Eliz$^{th}$ Coockeson ... ... 23 „
John Platte Izabell Barton ... ... ... ... 26 „
Wiłłm Hollonde Eliz$^{th}$ Ambrose ... ... ... 18 December
Peeter Sefton Anne Smalshaw ... ... ... 21 „
Rodger Hodgkinson Margaret Ryce ... ... 27 „
Wiłłm Blundell Grace Gill ... ... ... ... 15 Januarie
Nicolas Hollande Margerie Smallshaw ... 22 „
Peeter Spencer Alis Aspinwall ... ... ... 5 ffebruarie
John Sefton Brychet Blundell ... ... ... 9 „

## 1601.

Robert Mowdisley Emllin Westhead ... ... 11 June
Wiłłm Dalle Margare Ballert ... ... ... 31 August
John Marsher Alis Karre ... ... ... ... 1 September
Robert Lunte Jaine Scarsbrecke ... ... ... 8 „
Richard Sefton Anne Coockeson ... ... ... 10 „
Thomas Thornow Anne Accristie ... ... 4 October
Ric̃ Hall Marie Sumner ... ... ... ... 1 November
John Blundell Grace Savige ... ... ... ... 5 „
John Hesketh Margaret Lathom ... ... ... 15 „
George Barrow Alis Breykell ... ... ... 30 „
Tho: Waynewright Izabbell Gleaste ... ... 21 December
George Ambrose Elizabeth Hunter ... ... 5 Januarie
Peeter Bromley Alis Killshaw ... ... ... 13 „

## 1602.

Tho: Garrard Izabell Henrison ... ... ... 11 Aprill
Wiłłm Kewquick Jenet Cawdrey ... ... ... 16 Maye
John Atkinson Eliz$^{th}$ Lancaster ... ... ... 23 „
Robert Holliwell Margaret Sankey ... ... 10 June
Hugh Wildinge Margaret Orton ... ... ... 13 July
Wiłłm Tomson Margerie Killshaw ... ... 29 August
Jamis Nalior Elizabeth Lathwhat ... ... ... 22 September
[*No entries*] October
Rodger Ashton Catherin Huton ... ... ... 16 November
Wiłłm Robinson Anne Sutch ... ... ... 21 „
Robert Blundell Ellin Blundell ... ... ... 3 ffebruarie
John Hey Marie Lathom ... ... ... ... 6 „
John Asshorst Margaret Huton ... ... ... 3 Martch
Edward Butchart Ellin Hoolme ... ... ... 6 „
Ric̃ Asmall Margaret Ormishaw ... ... ... „ „

## 1603.

Robert Ordes Marierie Withingeton ... ... 15 Maye
Wiłłm Crayne Marierie Spencer ... ... ... 30 „

| | | | |
|---|---|---|---|
| | John Willson Marie Giłł | 5 | June |
| | Cuthbert Goare Mowde Waringe | 13 | „ |
| | Edward Blundell Marierie Cropp | 7 | Julye |
| Fo. 240 | Ric̃ Asmall Marierie Swifte | 8 | Auguste |
| | Jamis Beconson Jenet ffeles | 4 | September |
| | Wiłłm Bankes Jaine Cropp | 12 | „ |
| | John Mercer Alis Morecroft | 25 | „ |
| | Tho: Sutch Marie Haughton | 17 | October |
| | Edw: Kewquicke Anne Jackeson | „ | „ |
| | Wiłłm Marclough Katherin Cadicke | 20 | „ |
| | Ric̃ Cowp Jaine Clarke | 24 | „ |
| | Henry Scarsbrecke Anne Preskot | 6 | November |
| | Ric̃ Whttle Agnes Gleaste | 13 | „ |
| | Wiłłm Barton Anne Whytstones | 18 | December |
| | Ric̃ Hatton Elizabeth Barton | 10 | Januarie |
| | Rodger Mawdisley Jayne Mawdisley | 19 | „ |
| | Richard Whytestones Margrett Barton | 5 | ffebruarie |
| | Peaze Neale Katheryne Hatherwood | „ | „ |
| | George Whytestones ffranses Hamlet | 12 | „ |
| | Wiłłm Gobbin Catheryn Hoolme | 14 | „ |
| | Henry Preskot Ellen Sutch | 16 | „ |
| | Wiłłm Milner Anne Molinex | 19 | „ |

## 1604.

| | | | |
|---|---|---|---|
| Fo. 241 | Henry Morecroft Anne Aiscroft | 8 | Aprill |
| | Ric̃ Macon Jaine Luskin | 16 | „ |
| | Homfrey Lythom Anne Haughton | 22 | „ |
| | George Sidgreave Jaine Moore | 29 | „ |
| | Hugh Rimmer Joanie Luskin | 6 | Maye |
| | Robert Blundell Jenet Spenser | 3 | June |
| | Gilbert Sefton Mawde Blundell | 11 | „ |
| | Wiłłm Sefton Ellin Cropp | 22 | July |
| | Gilbert Johneson Dorethie Scarsbrecke | 10 | September |
| | Tho: Lancaster Ellin Aiscroft | 23 | October |
| | Ric̃ Sankey Claris Worthingeton | 2 | „ |
| | John Tuson Marierie ffarclough | 23 | December |
| | Wiłłm Barton Marie Haille | 8 | Januarie |
| | Hugh ffrith Elizabeth* Harresdoughter | 4 | ffebruarie |

## 1605.

| | | | |
|---|---|---|---|
| | Henry Wythingeton Saray Waynewright | 7 | Aprill |
| Fo. 242 | Hector Alker Margaret Wardman | 2 | Maye |
| | John Ruter Ellin Swifte | 5 | „ |
| | Robert Holland Emlin Aspinwall | 12 | „ |
| | ffrances [*sic*] Gowlbron Catherin Davie | 21 | „ |

* Henryse doughter *in Chester Transcript.*

Robert Norres Jaine Mawdisley ... ... ... 6 June
Robert Sefton Margaret Kewquicke ... ... 4 July
Richard Killshaw Anne Barber ... ... ... 11 August
Gilbert Barton Anne Alker ... ... ... ... 12 „
Thomas Ashton Anne Beconsaw ... ... ... 25 „
Witt͞m Gill Elizabeth Tyrer ... ... ... ... 12 September
Peeter Westhead Emlin Stannanought... ... 22 „
Thomas Hoolme Margaret Killshaw ... ... 6 October
Thomas Garstange Elizabeth Morecroft ... 5 Novemeber
Richard Morecroft Alis Waynewright ... ... 26 „
Edw: Kewkeicke Jaine Kilshaw ... ... ... 8 December
Henry Gill Elizabeth Shawe ... ... ... 10 „
Jamis Lea Alis Smyth ... ... ... ... ... 22 „
John Alker Marierie Cropp ... ... ... ... 22 Januarie
Witt͞m Rydinge Anne Ellam ... ... ... ... 25 „
Hector Walles Anne Preskot ... ... ... 17 ffebruarie
Richard Hoolme Margreat Crosse ... ... 26 „
Anthoney Ambrose Jenet Jamisdaughter ... „ „

## 1606.

Thomas Stopforth Katherin Voce ... ... 11 Maye
Jamis Tyrer Jaine Chadocke ... ... ... 18 „
Richard Killshaw Ellin Killshaw ... ... ... 29 „
Rodger Barton Jaine ffletcher ... ... ... 2 June
John Runckehorne Marie Mollinex ... ... 12 „
Henrie Linicar Grace Barber ... ... ... 3 July
Hector Morecroft Anne ffarrer ... ... ... 6 „
Witt͞m Lunt Elizabeth Asmall ... ... ... 24 August
Witt͞m Harden Jaine Morecroft ... ... ... 21 September
Richard Holland Ellin Towne ... ... ... 9 October
Edw: fforster Claris Gill ... ... ... ... 23 „
Henry Kenion Margerie Longley ... ... ... 13 November
Tho: Sutch Alis ffishe ... ... ... ... ... 16 „
Jamis Aiscroft Emlin Hesketh ... ... ... 19 „
John Greaves Anne Balle ... ... ... ... 3 December
Gabriell Walker Margaret Stopforth ... ... 18 „
Witt͞m Westhead Katherin Pwye ... ... ... 22 „
Richard Sumner Claris Parker ... ... ... 26 Januarie
Witt͞m Mawdisley Anne Waringe ... ... ... „ „
Jamis Hughson Ellin Haughton ... ... ... 2 ffebruarie
Cristopher Woofall Eideth Mawdisley ... ... 3 „
Alexsander Gowlbron Marie Sefton ... ... 9 „
Robert Killshaw Katherin Butchard ... ... 17 „

## 1607.

Rodger Scarsbrecke Anne Lea ... ... ... 23 Aprill
John Williamson Ellin Preskot ... ... ... 3 Maye

| | | | |
|---|---|---|---|
| | Jamis Hey Elizabeth Tyrer ... ... ... ... | 10 | Maye |
| | Hugh Martindaile Margerie Koket ... ... | 14 | June |
| | Thomas Owdam Anne Westhead ... ... ... | 29 | „ |
| | Peeter Talior Jaine Asmall ... ... ... ... | 9 | July |
| | Edward Scarsbrecke Elizabeth Tunstall ... | 14 | „ |
| | Richard Hodgeson Katherin Aiscough ... | 10 | September |
| | Henrie Robertson Jaine Asmall ... ... ... | 17 | „ |
| | Thomas Burscough Jaine Caunce ... ... | 24 | „ |
| | Richard Smyth Margreat Holland ... ... | 15 | October |
| | Richard Bleckeledge Katherin Wainewright.. | 18 | „ |
| | Jamis Atherton Jane Huton ... ... ... ... | 4 | ffebruarie |
| | Jone Kilshaw Ellin Barton ... ... ... ... | „ | „ |
| | Richard Asmall Elizabeth Asmall ... ... | „ | „ |
| | Richard Ashton Margaret Barker ... ... | 9 | „ |

## 1608.

| | | | |
|---|---|---|---|
| Fo. 246 | Wiłłm Lea Margerie Hunter... ... ... ... ... | 10 | Maye |
| | John Mellinge Ellin Swifte ... ... ... ... | 19 | „ |
| | Edward Burscough Izabell Hodgeson ... ... | 20 | „ |
| | John Aiscroft Jaine Ashton ... ... ... ... | 26 | „ |
| | Henrie Bradshaw Margerie Gilbertson ... | 28 | „ |
| | Thomas Kilshaw Jaine Sefton ... ... ... | 19 | July |
| | Jamis Sutch Alis Shaw ... ... ... ... ... | 29 | September |
| | Thomas Kirkeham Margreat Whatton ... ... | 2 | October |
| | Ewain Lea Katherin Sutch ... ... ... ... | 9 | „ |
| | Thomas Ormishaw Sislie Lancaster ... ... | 20 | „ |
| | Richard Kekewicke Alis Burscough ... ... | 6 | November |
| | John Cowp Elizabeth Hill ... ... ... ... | 23 | „ |
| | John Hodgeson Katherin Kellet ... ... ... | 6 | December |
| | Thomas Spencer Dowse Pendlebury ... ... | 21 | „ |
| | Ellis Hurst ffrances Haughton ... ... ... | 2 | Januarie |
| Fo. 247 | Robert Tasker Katherin Jumpe ... ... ... | 2 | ffebruarie |
| | Robert Tarbocke Jaine Withingeton ... ... | 5 | „ |
| | Edward Allin Anne Milner ... ... ... ... | 12 | „ |
| | Henry Mawdisley Mawde Westhead ... ... | 13 | „ |
| | Richard Droñinge Ellin Smolte ... ... ... | 20 | „ |
| | Wiłłm Alker Margaret Birtchwood ... ... | 23 | „ |

## 1609.

| | | |
|---|---|---|
| Wiłłm Gyles Katherin Cropp ... ... ... | 18 | Aprill |
| Gilbert Jackeson Margreat Barton ... ... | 20 | „ |
| John Voce Jaine Haughton ... ... ... ... | 14 | Maye |
| John Blundell Anne Houlte ... ... ... ... | 30 | „ |
| Edward Simkin Margerie Westhead ... ... | 6 | June |
| Thomas Higson Elizabeth Swift ... ... ... | 19 | „ |
| Thomas Winstanley Margaret Blundell ... | 4 | July |

| | | |
|---|---|---|
| Gilbert Gill Margaret Sutch ... ... ... ... | 10 | July |
| Will̃m Holland Margaret Haughton ... ... | 17 | „ |
| Thomas Parker Ellis Sumner ... ... ... | 23 | „ |
| Will̃m Killshaw Alis Scarsbrecke ... ... ... | 10 | August |
| George Haughton Elizabeth Rutter ... ... | 28 | „ |
| Will̃m Cowp̄ Jaine Croskell ... ... ... ... | 25 | September |
| Hugh Egicar Elizabeth Henryson ... ... | 28 | „ |
| Will̃m Swifte Margaret Westhead ... ... | 1 | October |
| John Kirkebie Izabell Hunt ... ... ... ... | 9 | „ |
| George Stanley Anne Allexson ... ... ... | 26 | November |
| George Charles Jaine Aspinwall ... ... ... | 5 | December |
| Thomas Bower Margaret Madocke ... ... | 7 | „ |
| Thomas Rim̃er Anne Abott ... ... ... ... | 26 | „ |
| Richard Chadocke Sislie Hoolme ... ... | „ | „ |
| Thomas Stopforth Margaret Holland ... ... | 8 | Januarie |
| George Barton Emlin Barton ... ... ... | 5 | ffebruarie |

## 1610.

| | | |
|---|---|---|
| Gilbert Voce Katherin Gorton ... ... ... | 9 | Aprill |
| Will̃m Holworth Anne Hoolme ... ... ... | 11 | „ |
| Homfrey Winstanley Elizabeth Ormishaw ... | 12 | Maye |
| Matthew Abraham Elizabeth Aspinwall ... | 21 | „ |
| Will̃m Waringe Ellin Sumner ... ... ... | 5 | June |
| Thomas Lea Ellin Daille ... ... ... ... | 27 | „ |
| Hugh Aiscough Marie Barton ... ... ... | 3 | July |
| Henry Asmall Ellin Hey ... ... ... ... | 19 | August |
| Peeter Cropp Ellin Sutch ... ... ... ... | 29 | „ |
| John Sanderson Alis Crofild ... ... ... ... | 24 | September |
| George Mollinex Katherin Hunter ... ... | 1 | November |
| Hugh Sutch Eideth Woodhowse ... ... ... | 5 | „ |
| Gilbert Blundell Sislie Mollinex ... ... ... | „ | „ |
| Ric̃ Rimmer Katherin Spencer ... ... ... | 18 | „ |
| Henry Lailand Margreat fforshaw ... ... | 26 | „ |

## 1611.

| | | |
|---|---|---|
| Hugh Sephton Jenet Blundell ... ... ... | 20 | Aprill |
| Tho: Longley Elizabeth Moare ... ... ... | 25 | „ |
| Thomas Simkin Emlin Hoolme ... ... ... | 5 | Maye |
| Will̃m Gill Joanie Garthes ... ... ... ... | 28 | „ |
| Thomas Spencer Jenet Rimmer ... ... ... | 6 | June |
| Edward Hunter Margrea [*sic*] Husdaughter... | 17 | „ |
| Homfrey Aspinwall Jaine ffogge ... ... ... | 23 | „ |
| John Shawe Anne Yat ... ... ... ... ... | 24 | „ |
| Tho: Sephton Margreat Morecroft ... ... | 5 | September |
| Hughe ffrith Alis Mollinex ... ... ... ... | 3 | October |
| Richard Shires Joane Holland ... ... ... | 10 | „ |

Henry Morecrofte Jaine Rodgerson ... ... 18 October
Thomas Jumpe Elizabeth Whatton ... ... 22 „
Edmund Walker Ellin Breykell ... ... ... 11 November
John Kekewicke Jaine Hunt ... ... ... 2 December
Rodger Gregson Sislie Preskot ... ... ... 2 Januari
John Sowerbutes Elizabeth Haile ... ... 28 „
Jamis Coockeson Katherin Parr ... ... ... 3 ffebruarie

## 1612.

Tho: Mawdisley Jaine Halworth* ... ... 14 Aprill
Willm Rigbie Elloner Wainewright ... ... „ „
Willm Abot Marie Shelton ... ... ... ... 28 „
Fo. 251 Rowland Barton Margreat Hardman ... ... 3 Maye
John Anderton Elizabeth Beconsow ... ... 4 „
Jamis Doson Ellin Bury ... ... ... ... 6 „
Jamis More Elizabeth Bankes ... ... ... „ „
Robert Ormishaw Margerie Richardson ... 21 „
Raffe Gore Elizabeth Croskell ... ... ... 24 „
John Barton Ellin Haughton ... ... ... 23 August
Willm Marrow Elizabeth Aspinwall ... ... 27 „
Hugh Aspinwall Anne Robertson ... ... 24 September
John Craine Dorethie Scarsbrecke ... ... 29 „
Robert Suthwort Ellin ffarclough ... ... ... 11 October
Jamis Morecroft Marie Morecroft ... ... 12 „
Richard Smallshaw Izabell Barton ... ... 25 „
Henry Kilshaw Alis Haughton ... ... ... 29 „
Bryhan Davie Katherin Coockeson ... ... „ „
Fo. 252 Alexander Sumner Margreat Sutch ... ... 14 Januar
Richard Allerton Dorethie Balshaw ... ... 21 „
Richard Lathom Marie Halsall ... ... ... 31 „
Robert Ridinge Ellin Blundell ... ... ... 2 ffebruarie
Henry Cadicke Katherin Cawsey ... ... ... 4 „
Henry Croston Izabell Ort ... ... ... ... 11 „
George Wilkinson Jaine Gilbertson ... ... 16 „

## 1613.

Willm Swifte Anne Huginson ... ... ... 6 Aprill
Willm Kilshaw Jenet Whytestons ... ... 8 „
John Scarisbricke Marie Modisley ... ... 6 May
Willm Sumner Jennett Clapam ... ... ... 8 June
Alexander Lee Martha Ambrose ... ... ... 19 Julie
Hector Alcar Ellen Wainwright ... ... ... 24 August
Fo. 253 Thomas Howcrofte Isabell Hale ... ... ... 5 Januarie
Thomas Martinscroft Alice Cockett ... ... 14 „
William Woodes Elizabeth Astley ... ... 30 „

* Haworth *in Chester Transcript.*

Henrie Scarisbrick Anne Gill ... ... ... 3 ffebruarie
John Hesketh Eliza: James daughter ... ... 21 „
Henrie Ryding Anne Barton... ... ... ... 28 „
William Houlme Marie Johnson ... ... ... 3 March

## 1614.

Hector Morcrofte Marie Wright ... ... ... 8 June
Huan Swyfte Anne Ecclestone ... ... ... 23 „
John Sutton Ellen Werrall ... ... ... ... 26 „
Gilbert Gill Emlin Woan ... ... ... ... 18 Julie
Thomas Bankes Anne Haskinges ... ... ... 21 „
Richard Haughton Margerie Johnson ... ... 28 „
George Rainforth Emlin ffairclough ... ... 8 August
James Roistron Emlin Dawber ... ... ... 18 October
Robte Woodes Marie Sutton ... ... ... 3 November
Richard Clapum Alice Stopford ... ... ... 13 „
Robte Lathom Clarice Haughton... ... ... 28 „
Edward Hesketh Ellen Ormishawe ... ... 1 December
James Sutch Margrett Symkin ... ... ... 12 „
George Pye Jane Prescott ... ... ... ... 22 „
William Aughton Marie Lawrenceson ... ... 18 Januarie
William Butler Anne Chisnall ... ... ... 24 „
William Chadocke Agnes Prescott ... ... 13 ffebruarie
George Rigmaden Alice Houlme ... ... ... „ „
John Symcocke Ellin Chisnall ... ... ... „ „
Hugh Lassell Jane Lowe ... ... ... ... 20 „

## 1615.

James Prescott Margrett Walthew ... ... 4 May
Henry Houlme Katherine Atherton ... ... 11 June
Willm Woosie Jaine Chadick ... ... ... 25 „
Robte Withington Elizabeth Withington ... 29 „
John Wainwright Margrett Parkes ... ... 2 Julie
ffardinando Wardman Katherine Layland ... 17 „
Richard Shawe Jane Rose ... ... ... ... 22 „
John Lydeat Elizabeth Hunt ... ... ... 20 August
Willm ffairclough Ellen Balle ... ... ... 24 „
Peter Wilding Katherine Cowp ... ... ... „ „
Roger Letherbarrow Alice Butler ... ... 14 September
Thomas Westhead Head Jony Birchall ... 12 October
William Leadbetter Margret Glasburrow ... 4 November
Edward Croston Alice Waring ... ... ... 23 „
James Pemberton Grace Waring ... ... ... 27 „
Christopher Layland Alice Layland ... ... 21 December
Thomas Morcroft Marie ffarrer ... ... ... 27 „
Robte Wilson Anne Haughton ... ... ... 22 January

Lyonell Swyfte Ellen Clapum ... ... ... 29 January
George Hesketh Anne Clapum ... ... ... „ „
Huan Hampson Jane Blundill ... ... ... „ „
Fo. 256 Hector Lea Mary Prescott ... ... ... ... 1 ffebruary
Wiłłm Johnson Margrett Cowp ... ... ... 3 „
Thomas Scarisbricke Margery Streethey ... „ „
John Shawe Jonie Lawrenson ... ... ... 4 „
Henry Woan Margrett Johnson ... ... ... 5 „
Henry Oliverson Emlin Gille ... ... ... „ „
Edward Platt Margrett Rainforth ... ... „ „

## 1616.

Richard Chadocke Katheryne Nayler ... ... 18 Aprill
James Crapper Alice Mason ... ... ... ... 30 „
John Hunswoorth Alice Hooton ... ... ... 20 May
Edmunde Ormshawe Anne Janeson ... ... 21 „
Wiłłm Holland Alice Meanelie ... ... ... „ „
James Tyrer Lettice Clarke ... ... ... ... „ „
James Blundill Katheryne Yate ... ... ... 22 „
Henry Whalley Anne Hille ... ... ... ... 23 „
Edward Houlme Mary Lathom ... ... ... 9 June
Edward Ashurst Margery Crapp ... ... ... 10 „
Wiłłm Marclewe Elizabeth Croocke ... ... 19 „
Fo. 257 Homphrie Greaues Jane Sutch [?] ... ... 21 Julie
Wiłłm Cowper Elizabeth Sallett ... ... ... 19 August
Henry Marton Anne Hesketh ... ... ... 20 „
Rauffe Kilshawe Ellen Burrie ... ... ... 31 „
Thomas Rowley Ideth Houlme ... ... ... 11 September
Ellice Sumner Margret Walton ... ... ... 13 „
Hugh Whitestones Jane Mason ... ... ... 6 October
Homphry Lunt Ellen Croock ... ... ... 14 „
James Ascroft Elizabeth Spencer ... ... 18 „
Richard Caritam Anne Blundill ... ... ... 23 „
John Ascroft Anne Haton ... ... ... ... 27 „
Wiłłm Berrie Jane Sharples ... ... ... ... 11 November
Richard Kilshawe Elizabeth Sutch ... ... 20 „
Wiłłm Aspes Jane Whitestones ... ... ... 8 December
Edward Spencer Ellen Blackledge ... ... 9 „
George ffarclough Katheryne Ascroft ... ... 16 „
Fo. 258 Phillip Hey Mrgery Kenion ... ... ... ... 9 ffebruary
John Stopford Alice Prescott ... ... ... 13 „
Thomas Wright Ellen Houlme ... ... ... 25 „
Thomas Lowe Jane Martindale ... ... ... 3 March
Henry Webster Jony Houlme ... ... ... „ „
Richard Nelson Cisley Ascough ... ... ... 4 „

## 1617.

Robte Wright Alice Gille ... ... ... ... 22 Aprill
Edward Edwardson Jane Marrall ... ... ... 7 May
Edward Blundill Ellen Gorsutch ... ... ... 14 "
Gabriell Haughton Ellen Swyfte ... ... ... " "
Daniell Sephton Margrett ffidler ... ... ... 25 "
Richard Smult Anne Moodie ... ... ... 28 "
Henry Symkin Clarice Holland ... ... ... 10 June
Richard Wilson Elizab: Westhead ... ... 16 "
Edward Smyth Elizabeth Gobben ... ... 22 "
Richard Halsall Alice Johnson ... ... ... 25 "
Arthur Greenells Margery Whitestones ... 13 July
Henry Harker Jenniett Kilshawe ... ... ... 20 "
Edward Croocke Alice Blackledge ... ... 22 "
Alexander Blundill Margrett Hey ... ... 24 "
Gilbte Gobben Jane Hampson ... ... ... 7 August
John Breers Margrett Mason ... ... ... 4 September
Phillip Morcroft Anne Morcrofte ... ... ... 22 "
John Gitte Jane Williamsdaughter ... ... 21 October
Thomas Hayton Jennett Ascroft ... ... ... 15 December
John Bower Ellen Prescott ... ... ... ... 18 "
Richard Whitestones Mary Morcrofte ... ... 18 January
ffardinando Hodson Margrett Crosse ... ... 2 ffebruary
John Barton Cisley Gregson ... ... ... ... 3 "
Hugh Marclewe Elizab: Hodgkinson ... ... 5 "
John Durdon Margrett Hey ... ... ... ... " "
Thomas Lawrenson Katheryne ffletcher ... 10 "
Thomas Whitestones Jane Coockson ... ... 15 "
John Hille Jane Blackledge ... ... ... ... " "

## 1618.

Hugh* Holland Margrett Woozie ... ... ... 19 Aprill
Richard Kilshawe Anne Clearke ... ... ... 23 May
Henry Robinson Jane Crane ... ... ... 21 June
Richard Jackson Alice Smyth ... ... ... 2 July
Rich: Hawghton Esquier Mary Garrard gentlew: ... ... ... ... ... ... ... ... 12 August
Richard Chadocke Mariery Sales... ... ... 13 "
James Jarman Anne Prescott ... ... ... 29 Septemb:
Peter Rainforth Jane Hesketh ... ... ... 30 "
James Case Margrett Keakwicke ... ... ... 18 October
Robte Berry Ellen Spencer ... ... ... ... 28 "
Willm Kilshawe Alice Houlme ... ... ... 8 November
James Hasselden Katheryne Mosse ... ... 12 "

* William *in Chester Transcript.*

John Melling Ellen Hesketh... ... ... ... 7 December
Lawrence Woofall Margery Crapper ... ... 23 „
John Wetherby Katheryne Ryding ... ... 21 „
Richard Balle Mary Aughton ... ... ... 14 January
Richard ffletcher Ellen Taylor ... ... ... 26 „
Richard Monck Anne Rigbie ... ... ... 28 „
Fo. 261 Raph Houlme Debora Clough ... ... ... 8 ffebruary
George Steele Ideth Winder ... ... ... 9 „

## 1619.

Wittm Alcar Alice Spencer ... ... ... ... ... 6 Aprill
James Smalshawe Anne Sutch ... ... ... 11 „
John Houlme Jane Holland ... ... ... ... ... 13 „
Wittm Bond Clarice Sumner ... ... ... 20 „
Homphry Laithwaitt Elizabeth Swyft ... ... 6 May
Henry Jackson Anne Layland ... ... ... 10 „
John Harrison Jane Ascough ... ... ... 17 „
ffardinando Whitesyde Margrett Barton ... 23 „
John Brighouse Martha Bowker ... ... ... 8 June
James Sumner Jony Kilshawe ... ... ... 26 „
Alexander Breers Isabell Mason ... ... ... 7 July
Henry Houlme Katheryne Lunt ... ... ... „ „
Wittm Johnson Katheryne Walthewe ... ... 12 August
Richard Croston Ellen Holland ... ... ... 2 Sept
James Hey Ellen Blundill ... ... ... ... 12 „
Hugh Rainforth Margrett Hille ... ... ... 10 October
Fo. 262 John Seddon Isabell Walworth ... ... ... 30 November
Richard Hunter Alice Barker ... ... ... 14 December
Richard Smyth Jane Kilshawe ... ... ... 21 „
Adam Tompson Jane Badger ... ... ... 23 January
Thomas Stopforth Elizabeth Clapam ... ... 13 ffebruary
Peter Barton Margrett Aspinwall ... ... ... „ „
Edward Aspinwall Anne Barton ... ... ... 14 „
Cuthbte Chadocke Margrett Easthead... ... 18 „

## 1620.

Henry Coockeson Anne Chadocke ... ... 18 Aprill
Richard Layland Emlin Westheade ... ... 1 May
Christopher Nicolson Mary Mason ... ... 4 „
Robte Draper Margery Rigby ... ... ... „ „
Thomas Wardman Margery Gille ... ... 14 „
Robte Harryson Anne Wilson ... ... ... 15 „
John Bonnd Anne Balle ... ... ... ... 18 „
Peter Cowper Elizabeth Berry ... ... ... 1 June
Hughe Houlme Clarice Blundell ... ... ... „ „
Gowther Barton Margrett Wynder ... ... 20 July
William Shawe Jane Wignall ... ... ... „ „

John Walsh Anne Johnson ... ... ... ... 27 July
53 Willm Bate Clarice Harryson ... ... ... August*
Percivall Peterson Elizabeth Sutton ... ... 10 September
Willm Webster† Edith Houlme ... ... ... „ „
Henry Modesley Elizabeth Hesketh ... ... 5 October
Myles Danbie ffleetwoode Breers ... ... ... 22 „
Willm Bootle Jony Wilding ... ... ... ... 6 November
James Robinson Ellen Shawe ... ... ... 4 December
Ranald Mason Alice Ascough ... ... ... 14 „
John Shawe Alice Rigbie ... ... ... ... 21 „
John Kilshawe Anne ffletcher ... ... ... 26 „
Alexander Parre Margery Haughton ... ... 13 January
Willm Georgson Isabell Winstanley ... ... 3 ffebruary
Thomas Burscough Margrett Waynwright ... 5 „

## 1621.

Richard Rymer Margrett ffazakerly ... ... 6 May
Thomas Wignall Katheryne Alcar ... ... 22 „
Thomas Iddon Alice Thornton ... ... ... 24 „
John Crosse Dorithy Garrard ... ... ... 1 July
Henry Belle Alice Wilkinson ... ... ... 8 „
Willm Blundill Katheryne Vauce ... ... 9 „
264 Richard Ashurst Ellen Mollyneux ... ... 10 „
Willm Hynde Katheryne Hale ... ... ... 16 „
John Walton Anne Hille ... ... ... ... 23 „
Raphe Burscough Jane Anderton ... ... 25 „
Thomas Hunt Jennett ffletcher ... ... ... 5 August
Silvester Laythwaitt Anne Hille ... ... ... 20 „
Thomas Wynstanley Margery Alcar ... ... 2 September
Thomas Ashurst Margrett Ascrofte ... ... 9 „
Henry Lathom Elizabeth Parbolde ... ... 4 October
Hugh Smyth Jennett Lowe ... ... ... ... 6 „
Symon Smyth Anne Barton ... ... ... ... 18 „
Christopher Balle Margrett fformby ... ... 12 November
Gabriell Gille Elizab: ffletcher ... ... ... 5 December
Henry Waynwright Cicely fforster ... ... 11 January
James Jumppe M^r^grett Harryson ... ... 29 „
Thom̃ Cowborn Elizabeth Waring ... ... 31 „
265 Willm Ascough Amery Allerton ... ... ... 3 ffebruary
Thurstain Wilding Mariery More ... ... 19 „
Arthur Wynstanley Elizabeth Woosie ... ... 26 „
Huan Hodson M^r^grett Cowper ... ... ... 28 „
Raphe Wynder ffrancis Ashton ... ... ... 4 March

* *The date has been cut away.*

† Westhead *in Chester Transcript.*

## 1622.

Gilb̄te Gille Mrgery Sutch ... ... ... ... 7 May
Henry Worthingtō Mary Stopford ... ... 14 „
Hugh Tasker Margrett Balshawe ... ... 30 June
Phillipp Ascroft Elizabeth Rigbie ... ... „ „
Thomas Stanynought Jane Parkes ... ... 1 July
Thomas Kendale Margrett Morcroft ... ... 28 „
Rob̄te Rothwell Anne Crane ... ... ... 13 August
John Greaues Elizab: Penkethman ... ... 26 „
John Hey Jane Modesley ... ... ... ... 27 „
Wiłłm Modesley Alice Ashe ... ... ... ... 29 September
Rob̄te Holland Alice Smalshawe ... ... 30 October
Fo. 266 Henry ffoster Tomasin Hankin ... ... ... 21 November
Richard Prescott Katheryne Allerton ... ... 25 „
Wiłłm Jones Ellen Turner ... ... ... ... 26 December
John Gildoes Margrett Charles ... ... ... 19 January
Edward Hesketh Alice Keakwicke ... ... 27 „
Thomas Aspinwall Jennett Laithwaitt ... ... 2 ffebruary
Henry Smyth Elizabeth Woodes ... ... ... 14 „

## 1623.

Wiłłm Gyles Anne Mease ... ... ... ... 28 May
Roger Scarisbricke Alice Morcroft ... ... 29 „
John Blundill Elizabeth Gille ... ... ... 30 „
Huan Swyfte Mary Ascroft ... ... ... ... 19 June
Thomas Shorlokers Jennett Westbie ... ... 22 „
Neale Bay Elizab: Vrmston ... ... ... 3 July
Hugh Sumner Ellen Clapum ... ... ... 3 August
Wiłłm Swyfte Jane Holland ... ... ... ... 23 Octob:
John Johnson Grace Penkethm̄ ... ... ... 26 „
Fo. 267 Ravhe* Bradshawe Ellen Aspinwall ... ... 21 December
Wiłłm Crookhooe Elizabeth Bay ... ... ... 8 January
Nicolas Whittle Mary Haughtō ... ... ... 9 „

## 1624.

Wiłłm Molyneux Alice Wynstanley ... ... 2 Aprił
Richard Webster Mary Blundill ... ... ... 29 „
Xpofer ffynch Elizab̄: Prescott ... ... ... 13 May
Thomas Woodes Ciceley Barton ... ... ... 24 „
John Lewis Regs Conciator Anne Ambrose... 26 „
John Poole Ellen Haughton ... ... ... 6 June
Edward Symkin Alice Gore ... ... ... ... 7 „
Rob̄te Hunter Margrett Chadock ... ... ... 9 „

* Raphe *in Chester Transcript.*

Richard Lathom Ideth Crapp ... ... ... 8 July
Thomas Spencer Margrett Rosen... ... ... 10 Auguste
Wiłłim Morcroft Elizabeth Barton ... ... 3 September
George Rigmaden Jane Drap ... ... ... 6 „
Robte Woodes Katheryne Hunt ... ... ... 26 „
John Waring Jane Modsley ... ... ... ... 2 October
Richard Banester Grace Cockett ... ... ... 3 „
George fforshawe Alice Shawe ... ... ... 13 „
Thomas Webster Alice Jackson ... ... ... 1 November
Silvester Laithwaitt Jennett Jackson ... ... „ „
Henry Croston Mary Houlme ... ... ... 4 „
Willim Jolly Elizab: Hutchin ... ... ... 25 „
Henry Waynwright Jane Ascroft ... ... ... 27 „
George Marclewes Elizabeth Prescott ... ... 2 December
Wiłłim Blundill Anne Eccleston ... ... ... 5 „
James Aspinwall Isabell Gleaste ... ... ... 28 „
Thomas Gleaste Mary Morcroft ... ... ... 7 January
Henry Sutch Ellen Blundill ... ... ... ... 23 „
Gilbte Ambrose Alice Topping ... ... ... „ „
Thomas Woodes Isabell Carter ... ... ... 2 ffebruary
Thomas Ormishawe Mary Goldborne ... ... 5 „
Phillipp Hey Anne Modesley ... ... .. 6 „
Henry Coates Alice Kenyō ... ... ... ... 16 „
James Watkinson Margery Blundill ... ... 22 „
Robte Hankinson Ellen Berry ... ... ... 24 „
Richard Modesley Clarice Gille ... ... ... „ „

[*The last entry is written in the margin of the original and also the following note*]

Ift any body would search for a Wedding made in año Dñi 1625 lett them looke in the latter end oft this booke where the ꝑsons att this Church that yeare marryed are sett downe

## Weddings in Ano Dni 1625.

Edward Crapp Idith Gille ... ... ... ... 18 Aprill
Richard Barton Ellen Rannill ... ... ... 24 „
Wiłlim Hutchin Grace Croocke ... ... ... 25 „
John ffleetwoode Jane Tatlocke ... ... ... 26 May
Thomas fforshawe Ellen Leadbetter ... ... 20 July
Thomas Modesley Margrett Orton* ... ... 26 „
Hugh Scarisbricke Elizabeth Cheetam ... 30 „
Nicolas Nayler Elizab: Blackledge ... ... 4 August
Edward Rylons Katheryne Ashurst ... ... 10 „
Lawrence Lathom Alice Keakwicke ... ... 18 „

* Allerton *in Chester Transcript.*

George Collyer Margrett Keakwicke ... ... 18 August
Wiłłim Rande Grace Dod ... ... ... ... 30 "
John Tarlton Elizab: Ashton ... ... ... 8 September
Thomas Goolden Alice Astley ... ... ... " "
Gryffyth Whytestones Myldred Haughton ... 11 "
Hugh Lathom Alice Threlfall ... ... ... 13 "
John Greaues Mary Ormshawe ... ... . 6 October
Thurstan Hesketh Mary Hey ... ... ... 18 "
Fo. 435 Wiłłim Barton Margrett Hallywell ... ... 21 November
Thomas Sharrocks Jennett Blundill ... ... 24 "
Hugh Whittle Jane Molyneux ... ... .. " "
Edward Orme Elizab: Halsall ... ... ... 2 December
John fformby Alice Hale ... ... ... . 9 January
Henry Gorsutch Mary Sephtō ... ... ... 31 "
James Higginsō ałs Thomasō Mary Topping 6 ffebruary
Robte Lathō Cicely Brighouse ... ... ... 9 "
Nicolas Morcroft Elizab: Modesley ... .. 12 "
Wiłłim Sutch Idith Sutch ... ... ... ... 13 "
Alexander Wilson Alice Morcroft ... ... 14 "

# Indexes.

## I.

## Of Christian Names and Surnames.

---

| | | |
|---|---|---|
| *Christenings* . . . . . . . . . . | *pp.* *1—128* | *inclusive.* |
| *Burials* . . . . . . . . . . | ,, *129—252* | ,, |
| *Marriages* . . . . . . . . . . | ,, *253—288* | ,, |

---

Where a name has variants the Head-name has been selected which now exists or which most closely resembles the modern equivalent. All variants are separately Indexed with cross references to the Head-name.

Where a Surname has an *alias* each form of the Surname is Indexed under its initial letter.

The Christian names are, with some few exceptions, Indexed under their modern form—the first spelling of the name having generally been continued in connection with the same Surname.

Illegitimate children are Indexed under the Surnames of both Mother and putative Father.

"N.X.N." signifies "No Christian Name."

An asterisk following a page number signifies that that combination of Christian and Surname occurs more than once on the page number asterisked.

The name "Johne" proves to be written both for "Joan" and "John," and accordingly when it was impossible to determine which of these two names was intended "Johne" has been printed.

---

### A

*Christenings* . . . . . . . .
*Burials* . . . . . . . . .
*Marriages* . . . . . . . .

. . *pp.* *1—128* *inclusive.*
. . ,, *129—252* ,,
. . ,, *253—288* ,,

*Christenings* . . . . . .
*Burials* . . . . . . .
*Marriages* . . . . . . .

. . *pp.* *1—128 inclusive.*
. . ,, *129—252* ,,
. . ,, *253—288*

Ashurst—*Continued.*
,, John, 82, 86, 154, c. of 205, c. of 207, 228, 255, 275
,, Katherin, 82, 123, 136, 268, 287
,, Lewes, 121
,, Margaret, 6, 43, 172, 225
,, Richard, 56, 121, 126, 212, 255, 285
,, Thomas, 15, 28, 38, 43, 56, 86, 109, 123, 127, 181, 191, c. of 242, 260 270, 285
,, William, 28, 116, 138
Asimall, see Asmall
Askough, Askowe, see Ascough
Askroft, Askrofte, see Ascroft
Asley, see Astley
Asmall (Asimall, Asmalle, Asmole, Asmoll, Asmolle), see also Aspinwall,
,, Alice, 2, 26
,, Ann, 26,* 142, 154, 181, 204, 212, 260, 273
,, Bartholomew, 83
,, Edward, 57, 82, 210
,, Elizabeth, 5, 25, 176, 203, 277, 278
,, Ellen, 43, 75, 89, 199, 214, 269
,, Ellis, 26, 154
,, Gilbert, 19
,, Grace, 270
,, Henry, 133, 279
,, Hugh, 5, 19, 179, 213, 264
,, Isabell, 8, 151, 256
,, James, 181, 254
,, Jane, 5, 266, 272, 278*
,, Jenet, 140
,, Joan, 21
,, Katherin, 8, 58, 168, 203, 268
,, Lawrence, 177
,, Letyse, 19
,, Margaret, 6, 160, 267, 271
,, Mary, 179
,, Peter, 26, 55, 75
,, Ranold, 19
,, Richard, 21, 55, 86, 87, 275, 276. 278
,, Thomas, 43, 57, 82, 174, 210, 255
,, Thurstan, 86
,, William, 26, 58, 83, 87, 89, 203, 206, 258
Aspes, George, 56
,, Roger. 56
,, William, 263, 282
Aspinwall (Aspinal, Aspmall, Aspnal, Aspnall, Aspinwal,

*Christenings* . . . . . . . .
*Burials* . . . . . . . . . .
*Marriages* . . . . . . . . .

Aspinwall—*Continued.*
Aspinwap, Aspinwatt (*sic*), Aspinwell),
see also Asmall,
,, Adam, 137
,, Ade (*sic*), w. of 142
,, Agnes. 167
,, Alice, 12, 84, 128, 211, 255, 265, 271. 274, 275
,, Ann, 9, 17, 61, 69, 77, 81, 91, 97, 151, 206, 229
,, Annes, 23
,, Anthony, 92, 101, 114
,, Blanch, 141
,, Edmund, 67, 216
,, Edward, 16, 17, 21, 52, 54, 62, 84, 87, 93, 103, 116, 120, 125, 180, 211, 243, 284
,, Elizabeth, 9, 18, 20, 22, 34,* 47,* 108, 125, 147, 151, 158, 169, 173, 190, 268, 270, 273, 279, 280
,, Ellen, 17, 21, 28, 80, 91, 100, 116, 166, 215, 241, 286
,, Ellis, 16, 18, 21, 28, 147, 259
,, Emlin, 276
,, George, 151, 170
,, Grace, 11
,, Henry, 10, 35, 97, 161, 176, 215. 229, 261
,, Hugh, 42, 44, 47, 54, 94, 97, 180 185, 268, 280
,, Humphrey, 17, 20, 22, 35, 51, 94, 99, 108, 114, 116, 120, 279
,, Isabel, 53, 266
,, James, 21,* 54, 62, 127, 151, 183. 259, 287
,, Jane, 40, 58, 62, 93, 96, 116, 144, 169, 265, 279
,, Jenet, 141, 145
,, Joan, 239
,, John, 17, 31, 128, 146, 175
,, Johne, 167
,. Katherin, 9, 42, 96, 191
.. Laurence, 18, 147
,, Lore, 34
,, Margaret, 30, 85, 97, 120, 158, 234. 272, 284
,, Margery, 104, 230
,, Mary, 36, 92, 103, 127, 217
,, Nicolas, 31, 47, 140, 222, 267
,, N.X.N., 13, 248
,, Peter, 23. 34, 52, 69, 74, 80, 81, 85, 91, 96, 102, 104, 108, 114,* 120, 181, 273

. . . . . *pp.* *1—128 inclusive.*
. . . . . ,, *129—252* ,,
. . . . . ,, *253—288* ,,


Babott—*Continued.*
,, Gilbert, 46, 208
,, Henry, 65, 239
208, ,, Richard, 38, 54, 111, 164
,, Robert, 177
,, Thomas, 42, 46, 54, 65, 111, 164, 210
Backestonden (Backstendeyle),
,, Hugh, 268
,, Katherine, 272
Badger, Hugh, 44, 48, 216
,, Jane, 284
,, Ralph, 196
,, Richard, 166
,, Thomas, 44, 48
217 Bagilay, see also Balie,
,, Isabel, 183
Baines, Alice, 254
Baker, John, 187
Balard (Ballert), Henry, 253
,, Margare, 275
Balie (Bale), see also Bagilay,
,, Jane, 227
,, John, 212
,, Ralph, 84
,, Robert, 212
,, Roger, 84
Ball (Balle), Ann, 35, 43, 277, 284
,, Christopher, 285
,, Edward, 225
,, Elizabeth, 231
,, Ellen, 281
,, George, 260
,, Katherin, 257
,, Margery, 35
,, Richard, 43, 257, 265, 273, 284
,, Robert, 263, 268
Ball *alias* Talior, Margery, 138
Ballert, see Balard
Balshaw (Ballshaw, Balshawe, Balshewe, Bashawe), see also Bellsha,
,, Ann, 62
,, Dorothy, 280
,, Edward, 58, 110
,, Ellen, 48, 95
,, Gilbert, 27, 39, 48, 52, 228
,, Henry, 52
,, James, 41, 86, 87, 93, 95, 107, 220
,, Jane, 39, 170, 262, 267*
,, Jenet, 43, 170
,, Jo: 32, 38, 41, 48, 52, 62
,, John, 35, 45, 48, 57, 103, 107, 110, 147, c. of 195, 217, 220
,, Katherin, 38, 165, 217, 268

*Christenings* . . . . . .
*Burials* . . . . . . . .
*Marriages* . . . . . . .

Balshaw—*Continued.*
,, Margaret, 32, 57, 58, 66, 86, 198. 261, 286
,, Richard, 87, 93
,, Robert, 266
,, Thomas, 45, 52, 66, 103
,, William, 274
Banburie, Symond, 254
Bancke, Banckes, see Bankes
Baner, Gilbert, 139
,, Margaret, 270
Banerster, Banester, see Banister
Banet, Alice, 140
Banister (Banerster, Banester),
,, Alice, 248
,, Ellen, 15
,, James, 28, 65, 197
,, John, 168
,, Katherin, 201
,, Nicholas, 65
,, Richard, 126, 287
,, Robert, 263
,, Thomas, 126
,, William, 145
Bankes (Bancke, Banckes, Bank, Banke),
see also Bonke,
,, Ann, 112
,, Edward, 23, 59, 73,* 271
,, Elizabeth, 21,* 25, 280
,, Ellen, 266
,, Grace, 255
,, Henry, 21,* 23, 34, 59, 164, 257
,, Hugh, 133
,, Isabel, 164
,, Ja: 190
,, James, c. of 2, 11, 34, c. of 134, 134, 142
,, Joanie, 190
,, John, 112, 221
,, Jone (? meaning John), 190
,, Katherin, 20, 102, 133
,, Margaret, 145, 160
,, Margery, 136
,, Mary 73
,, Richard, 13, 20, 155, 259
,, Robert, 102, 112
,, Thomas, 73, 103,* 112, 134, 140, 281
,, William, 134, 276
Barber, Ann, 277
,, Grace, 277
Baricke, see Barwicke
Barker (Barkar, Barke, Barkere),
,, Alexander, 19, 64, 113, 121, 148, 150, c. of 241

*Christenings* . . . . . . . . . . pp. *1—128 inclusive.*
*Burials* . . . . . . . . . . . ,, *129—252* ,,
*Marriages* . . . . . . . . . . ,, *253—288* ,,

on, Alice—*Continued.*
154, 167, 222, 226, 231, 244, 263
Andrew, 70, 121
Ann, 8, 11,* 20, 46, 52,* 57, 60, 67, 87, 91, 97, 108, 110, 127, 150, 160,* 185, 202, 234, 238, 242, 272, 281, 284, 285
Arthur, 57, 67, 125, 233, 270
Barbarie, 196
Bryhan, 201
Christopher, 18, 35, 168, 195, 208, 238
Ciceley, 286
Claris, 96, 98, 225
Edith, 261
Edward, 24, 32, 39, 67, 83, 87, 113, 117, 120,* 126, 218, 221, 229
Elizabeth, 14, 21, 22, 32, 35, 38, 51, 56, 63, 78,* 79, 92, 97, 101, 111, 116,* 118, 121, 137, 159, 174, 205, 208, 215, 233, 234, 239, 244, 252, 261, 263, 264, 265, 274, 276, 287
Ellen, 4, 5, 18, 28, 99, 116, 126, 150, 160, 173, 175, 192, 238, 239, 240, 250, 278
Ellis, 113
Emlin, 21, 39, 61, 92, 101, 161, 183, 259, 260, 279
Gabriel, 8, 26, 35, 39, 44, 48,* 104, 178, 186, 266
Genet, 56, 118, 122, 144, 162, 245
George, 4, 20, 24, 33, 37, 97, 104, 114, 122, 126, 161, 256, 279
Gilbarton (*sic*), 13
Gilbert, 24, 28, 36, 38, 41, 58, 60, 65, 66, 82, 87, 88, 94,* 127, 143, 151, 192, 194, 196, 212, 231, 256, 270, 277
Gowther, 55, 57, 58, 61, 62, 66, 69, 109, 111, 115, 120, 125, 238, 269, 284
Grace, 10, 229, 265
Hathor (? Arthur), 86
Hector, 154, 173
Henry, 28, 42, 62, 65,* 67, 69, 71,* 73, 84, 91, 97, 108,* 192, 201, 208, 272, 274
Hugh, 10, 48, 62, 67,* 69, 71, 79, 83, 84, 87, 91, 96, 100, 108, 116, 123, 182, 197, 200, 205, 239, 273

Barton—*Continued.*
,, Humphrey, 28, 125
,, Isabel, 23, 36, 71, 112, 169, 237, 244, 267, 275, 280
,, Ja: 36, 41, 45, 51, 52, 55,* 57, 62, 63, 69, 197
,, Jac, 51
,, James, 32, 40, 48,* 52, 58, 67, 76, 78, 82, 87, 98, 116, 128, 175, 183, c. of 185, two c. of 204, 205, 247, 252, 266
,, Jane, 3, 18, 58, 69,* 94, 95, 100, 120, 131, 158, 178, 197, 206, 211, 214, 215, 270, 271, 272
,, Jdeth (*sic*), 7
,, Jo: 36, 42,* 48, 52, 65
,, John, 3, 26, 55, 57, 61, 67, 69, 71, 73,* 78, 82, 83,* 85, 92, 113, 122, 126, 148,* 150, 154,* 158, 165, 182, 186, 201, 218, 229, 246, 266' 269, 280, 283
,, Katherin, 4, 6, 48, 84, 91, 97, 112, 115, 190, 217, 230, 237, 241
,, Lewis (Levis), 24, 26, 28, 36, 47, 154, 230, 236, 261
,, Margaret, 6, 16, 17, 32, 35, 41, 48, 56, 58, 82, 83, 86, 118, 122, 126, 154, 169, c .of 182, 184,* 208, 212, 257, 262, 268, 276, 278, 284
,, Margery, 18, 62, 114, 169, 181, 230, 249, 257,* 266
,, Mary, 48, 52, 62, 78, 83, 125, 160, 209, 279
,, Mather, 17
,, Miles, 28, 35, 41, 52, 56, 60, 88, 114, 117, 230, 240, 242, 247, 262
,, Nicolas, 12, 53
,, N.X.N., 73, 91, 169, 171, 208, 233, 234
,, Ottiwell, 12
,, Peter, 16, 20, 23, 24, 26, 57, 64, 67, 71, 82, 87, 92, 98, 104, 112, 118,* 122, 123, 128, 151, 192,* 200, 226, 234, 258, 284
,, Ralph, 35, 90
,, Richard, 4, 23, 33, 36, 37, 42,* 47, 51, 56, 60, 73, 77, 83, 90, 97, 101, 109, 128, 132, 167, 172, 212, 239, 258, 272, 287
,, Ro: 82
,, Robert, 27, 53, 64, 87, 93, 99, 127, 192, 200

*Christenings* . . . . . .
*Burials* . . . . . . .
*Marriages* . . . . . .

. . . *pp. 1—128 inclusive.*
. . . ,, *129—252* ,,
. . . ,, *253—288* ,,

*Christenings* . . . . . . . . . . pp. 1—128 inclusive.
*Burials* . . . . . . . . . . . ,, 129—252 ,,
*Marriages* . . . . . . . . . . ,, 253—288 ,,

*Christenings . . . . . . . . . . pp. 1—128 inclusive.*
*Burials . . . . . . . . . . „ 129—252 „*
*Marriages . . . . . . . . . . „ 253—288 „*

*Christenings* . . . . . . .
*Burials* . . . . . . . . .
*Marriages*. . . . . . . .

Butcher—*continued.*
,, Isabel, 181
,, John 150
,, Katherin, 47, 150, 277
,, Lyonel, 19,* 147
,, Margaret, 138, 222, 254
,, Margery, 130
,, Thomas, 167
,, William, 19,* 147
Butelor, see Butler
Butle, see Bootle
Butler (Buler, Butelor, Butlere),
,, Albanie, 225
,, Alice, 62, 68, 281
,, Ann, 107
,, Edward, 2
,, Ellen, 28, 46, 48, 171, 262, 273
,, Gabriel, 61
,, Gilbert, 28, 57, 262
,, Henry, 85, 88
,, Jane, 57
,, Jo: 40, 47, 56, 62
,, Joan, 40
,, John, 69, 136, 184
,, Katherin, 122, 185, 227, 246
,, Margaret, 39, 64, 85, 125
,, Mr., 85, 88
,, Richard, 56, 88, 183
,, Robert, 35, 48, 114, 122, 125, 163, 187
,, Thomas, 35, 39, 42, 46, 47, 48,* 56, 61, 64, 68, 69, 78,* 114, 185, 190, 211, 236
,, William, 42, 107, 255, 281
Butrie (Butterie), Margerie, 164
,, Richard, 129
Butrie *alias* Goare, Elizabeth, 161
Butterfeild, Roger, 113
,, Thomas, 113
Butterie, see Butrie
Button, Robert, 228
Bycarstaffe (Bicarstaff, Bycarstaf, Bycarstafe, Bycarstaff, Bycarstaffe, Byckstaff, Bykarstaff, Bykarstaffe),
,, Alison, 135
,, Elizabeth, 10, 19, 64, 171
,, Ellen, 140
,, Emlin, 23, 203
,, Gilbert, 132
,, Godfrey, 143
,, Gowther, 212
,, Henry, 36
,, Hugh, 19, 23, 28, 40, w. of 132, 142, 183, 200, 256, 260
,, Ja: 24

*Christenings* . . . . . .
*Burials* . . . . . . .
*Marriages* . . . . . .

Bycarstaffe—*continued.*
,, James, 260
,, Jane, 28, 183
,, Jo: 64
,, John, 206
,, Katherin, 40
,, Margaret, 179
,, Richard, 265
,, Robert, 162, 261
,, Thomas, 24
Bygehouse, see Brighouse
Byggot, Jane, 159
Bykarstaff, Bykarstaffe, see Bycarstaffe
Bylame (Bylanes), Ellen, 28
,, Jo: 28
Bylinge, see Billinge
Bynson, Agnes, 192
Byram, Robert, 155
Byrch, Byrtch, see Birche
Byrchwood, Byrtchwood, see Birtchwood
Byspam, see Bispam

C

Cadicke (Kadicke), see also Chadock,
,, Anthony, 19, 202, 274
,, Cislie, 254
,, Edward, 45
,, Elizabeth, 49
,, Ellen, 78, 142
,, George, 64
,, Henry, 280
,, James, 16, 204
,, Jane, 213
,, Katherine, 34, 276
,, Ralph, 26, 165
,, Richard, 42, 139, 266
,, Robert, 49, 59, 64, 68, 73, 78, 268
,, Silvester, 73
Thomas, 68, 160, 201
,, William, 19, 34, 40,* 42, 45, 59, 168, 182, 254
Cadwell, Jenet, 248
Car, see Carr
Carbee, Carbie, Carby, see Corbay
Carr (Car, Care, Carre, Kar, Kare, Karre),
,, Alice, 35, 231, 257, 275
,, Ann, 151
,, Bartholomew, 40, 167
,, Catherine, 208, 251
,, Christopher, 27, 35
,, Cisley, 107, 222, 259

*Christenings* . . . . . . . .
*Burials* . . . . . . . . .
*Marriages* . . . . . . . .

. . pp. *1—128 inclusive.*
. . ,, *129—252* ,,
. . ,, *253—288*

Cooper—*Continued.*
,, Peter, c. of 243, 284
,, Ralph, 44
,, Randle, 31, 105, 219
,, Richard, 1, 24, 31, 73, 80, 104, 114,* 138, c. of 196, c. of 201, 220, 237, 245, 276
,, Ro: 31
,, Robert, 6, 26, 80, 82, 89, 146, 157, 170, 182, c. of 184, 250
,, Thomas, 120, 121
,, William, 29, 83,* 89, 97, 106, 111, 120, 228, 279, 282
Cooton, see also Cotton,
,, Richard, 246
Cophull (Coppall, Coppo, Coppoe, Coppowe),
,, Elizabeth, 8
,, Ellen, 232
,, Richard, 3
,, Thomas, 9
,, William, 253
Corbay (Carbee, Carbie, Carby, Corbott),
,, Alice, 7
,, Ann, 105, 227
,, Francis, 108
,, Isabell 96, 222
,, James 239
,, Jane, 250
,, Joan, 123
,, Joseph, 96, 105, 108, 116, 123, 222, 239, 250
,, Margery, 116
Corker, Elizabeth, 178
,, John, 178
,, Richard, 44
,, William, 44
Corneforth, Richard, 106
,, Thomas, 106
Cosey, see Cawsey
Cothere, see also Cawdrey,
,, William, 258
Cottam, Edward, 97
,, Mary, 97
Cotton (Cvtune), see also Ccoton,
,, Elizabeth, 227
,, Margaret, 82, 138
,, Mrs., 227
,, Ro: 82
Cottrell, John, 211
Couldock, see Cowdocke
Coupper, see Cooper
Coventrie, Alice, 181
,, Margaret, 164
Cowbann, see Cubbon

*Christenings* . . . . . . .
*Burials* . . . . . . . .
*Marriages* . . . . . . .

*Christenings* . . . . . . . . . . *pp.* *1—128 inclusive.*
*Burials* . . . . . . . . . . . ,, *129—252* ,,
*Marriages* . . . . . . . . . . ,, *253—288* ,,

*Christenings* . . . . . . . . . . *pp.* *1—128 inclusive.*
*Burials* . . . . . . . . . . . ,, *129—252* ,,
*Marriages.* . . . . . . . . . . ,, *253—288* ,,

. . . . pp. *1—128 inclusive.*
. . . . ,, *129—252* ,,
. . . . ,, *253—288* ,,

Dowber, see Dawber
Dowren, see Darwen
Dozon, see Doson
Draninge, see Droning
Draper, Henry, c. of 192, 216, 248, 257
,, Jane, 287
,, Margaret, 248
,, Robert, 284
,, Thomas, w. of 142, 152
Dreage, Elizabeth, 260
Droning (Draninge, Dronninge),
,, Alice, 219
,, Charles, 62, 194
,, John, 62
,, Richard, 219, 278
121, Duckenfeild, Anna, 125
,, Richard, 125
Duddill, Joh, 238
,, Margaret, 238
Dughtie, see Doughtie
Dukes, Jane, 230
171, Duncon (Donkon, Dunkon, Dvmcon, Dvncon),
,, Alice, 179
,, Ann, 113, 237
,, Catherin, 74
,, Elizabeth, 5, 237
,, Emlin, 70
,, George, 3, 135
,, Henry, 74, 123, 237, 246
,, Hugh, 215
,, James, 143
,, Jennett, 126, 248
,, John, 70, 74, 106,* 113, 115, 123, 126, 179
,, Margaret, 184
,, Mary, 166
,, Thomas, 115, 198, 208
Duncon, Dunkon *alias* Seale, Seall, Sheal,
,, Jo: 62
,, John, 217
,, Thomas, 257
,, William, 62
Durdon, John, 283
Durham, George, 128
,, Robert, 128
Dutton, Richard, 178
,, Susanna, 72
,, Thomas, 72
Dvmcon, Dvncon, see Duncon
Dwarrehowse (Dwarihouse, Dwarihows),
,, Emlin, 254
,, Robert, 173
Dye, Ewan, 10

*Christenings* . . . . . .
*Burials* . . . . . . . .
*Marriages* . . . . . . .

## E

Fazakerley—*Continned.*
„ Hu h, 51, 233
„ Jane, 27, 267
„ Margaret, 51, 285
„ Roger, 95
„ Thomas, 95
Feetewood, see Fleetewood
Feles, Jenet, 276
Fenes, see Finne
Fenton, Agnes, 225
„ Margaret, 101
„ Thomas, 101
Ferar, see Farrer
Ferie, Peinbiall (*sic*), 203
„ Rowland, 203
Feriman, Elizabeth, 182
Ferrer, see Farrer
Ferris (Feris), Mr. c. of 203*
„ Paul, 72
„ Rowland, 72
Fetcher, see Fletcher
Fidler (Fydler), Ann, 110
„ Elizabeth, 104
„ James, 46, 55, 98, 171
„ Jane, 38, 98, 117
„ Margaret, 98, 283
„ Richard, 65, 200
„ Robert, 50, 98, 104, 110, 117, c. of 221, c. of 251
„ Roger, 41, 169
„ Thomas, 38, 41, 46, 50, 55, 65, c. of 185, c. of 190, 200, 223
Finch (Finche, Fintch, Fynch),
„ Christopher, 286
„ Emlin, 32, 158
„ Richard, 25
„ Thomas, 25
Finne (Fenes, Fine, Fines),
„ Edward, 261
„ Roger, 213, 272
Fintch, see Finch
Firkin, Thomas, 12
Fishe, Alice, 277
„ Thomas, 186
Fisher (Fysher), Elizabeth, 214
„ John, 6, 41, 167
„ Richard, 41, 214, 229, 274
„ Thomas, 6
„ William, 138
Flecher, Fledgger, see Fletcher
Fleetwood (Feetewood, Fleetewood, Fleetwoode),
„ Edward, 57
„ Elizabeth, 256
„ John, 287
„ Peter, 57

*Christenings* . . . . . . .
*Burials* . . . . . . . .
*Marriages* . . . . . . .

Garnett—*Continued.*
,, Henry, 241, 270
,, John, 158
,, Richard, 261
,, Robert, 250
Garrard, Garrarde, Garrerd, see Gerrard
Garret (Geret), see also Gerrard and Jarrard,
,, Cuthbert, 178
,, Edward, 153
,, Hugh, 210
,, Isabel, 211
,, Margery, 135
,, Thomas, 211
,, William, 178
Garstange, Edward, 14, 144
,, John, 82, 90, 93
,, Margaret, 246
,, N.X.N., 93
,, Ranolde, 145
,, Richard, 90, 274
,, Thomas, 82, 277
Garston, Richard, 4
Garthes, Joanie, 279
Garthife, Cuthbert, 191
Gaskin (Gasken), Lawrence, 255
,, Margaret, 174, 271
Gathe, Cuthbert, 63
,, Jo: 63
Geldard (Gelder, Gilder), see also Gildoes,
,, Ann, 99, 234
,, Ellen, 233
,, Gabriel, 84
,, Grace, 91
,, Henry, 97
,, Michael, 84, 91, 97, 99, 228
Gellibrund, see Gillibrond
Georgson, see also Gorhson,
,, Ciceley, 128
,, Henry, 242
,, Katheryne, 123
,, William, 123, 128, 285
Gerard, see Gerrard
Geret, see Garret
Gernere, John, 268
Gerrard (Garard, Garerd, Garrard, Garrarde, Garrerd, Gerard, Gerrarde, Gerrerd), see also Garret and Jarrard,
,, Agnes, 173
,, Ann, 76, 222, 272
,, Catherin, 26, 50, 51, 80, 155, 175, 176
,, Cuthbert, 4, 53, 56, 59 62, 68, 121, sons of 176, 182, 198, 204, 235, 268

*Christenings* . . . . . . . .
*Burials* . . . . . . . . .
*Marriages* . . . . . . . .

| | | |
|---|---|---|
| *Christenings* | *pp.* | *1—128 inclusive.* |
| *Burials* | ,, | *129—252* ,, |
| *Marriages* | ,, | *253—288* ,, |


l Margaret—*Continued.* 108, 131, 150, 164, 170, 191, 197, 209, 232, 245, 258, 261, 264, 269, 271, 272
,, Margery, 10, 35, 84, 135, 151, 165, 193, 221, 239, 261, 274, 284
,, Martha, 99
,, Mary, 24, 54, 94, 276
,, Nicholas, 3
,, N.X.N., 2, 217
,, Par (Parre), 48, 199
,, Persevall, 23, 27, 52, 150,* 219, 256, 261
,, Ralph, 52
,, Ranould, 22, 26, 98, 224
,, Richard 10, 17, 24, 28, 29, 37, 47, 59, 64, 70,* 73, 74, 79, 81, 89, 95, 107, 146, 155, 157, 161, 192, 200, 204, c. of 205, 211, 229, 244, 260, 263, 271
,, Robert, 5, 37, 52,* 55, 59, 73, 83, 100, 107, 184, 186, 204, 229, 233, 249, 269
,, Roger, 26, 56, 93, 155, 219
,, Thomas, 14, 20, 48, 58, 64, 84, 94, 98, 106, 107, 118, 148, 165, 175, c. of 186, 186, 191, 215, c. of 230, 239, 255, 270
,, William, 21, 23, 28, 32, 34, 39, 47, 81, 93, 97, 103,* 112, 160, 167, 217, 242, 244, 261, 277, 279

Gillibrond (Gellibrund, Gillibrund, Golibrand, Golibrannd, Golibrond, Goliebrand, Gollibrand, Gollibrond, Jolibran, Jolibrand, Jolibrond, Jolibrone, Jollybrand),
,, Alexander, 123
,, Alice, 136, 245
,, Ann, 168
,, Edward, 87, 182
,, Elizabeth, 235
,, Hugh, 50, 114, 213, 233, 241
,, Isabel, 217
,, Jenet, 141
,, John, 118, 150, 242
,, Katherin, 144, 184
,, Margaret, 149, 213
,, Margery, 85
,, Richard, 50, 85, 87, 101, 114, 118, 123, 131, 144, 149, 170, 207, 213, 233, 242, 245
,, Robert, 101, 172

Gineson, Margaret, 256
Glasburrow (Glaisbarow, Glaisburrow),
,, Ann, 227
,, Ellen, 46
,, Margaret, 57, 281
,, Richard, 46, 57, 225
,, Robert, 46
,, Thomas, 46

Gleast (Gleaste), Agnes, 29, 276
,, Ann, 73, 202
,, Edith, 246, 274
,, Elizabeth, 54, 228
,, Ellen, 95, 198, 233
,, Ellis, 22, 64, 66, 68, 70, 73, 75, 80, 86, 95, 105, 197, 202, c. of 210, c. of 215, 228, 233
,, Emlin, 29
,, Hugh, 66, 197
,, Isabel, 39, 75, 275, 287
,, James, 66
,, Jenet, 144
,, Jo: 54
,, John, 193
,, Katherin, 219
,, Margaret, 68, 105, 198, 231
,, Mary, 80, 86
,, Ralph, 26
,, Richard, 19, 64, 66, 272
,, Thomas, 19, 22, 26, 39, 70, 199, 287

Goare, see Gore
Goare *alias* Butrie, Elizabeth, 161
Gobbin (Gobben, Gobin, Gobine),
,, Alice, 255
,, Ann, 19, 190, 200, 270
,, Barbarie, 207
,, Elizabeth, 3, 14, 23, 52, 248, 272, 283
,, Gilbert, 84, 119, 221, 283
,, Henry, 62, 76, 84, 95, c. of 217, 221
,, Isabel, 135
,, James, 127
,, Jane, 146, 153
,, Jo: 20, 23, 57, 68
,, John, 29, 52, 62, 76, 147, 175, 228, 237, 259, 266
,, Margaret, 10, 148, 270
,, Margery, 20, 183
,, N.X.N., w. of 135
,, Robert, 46, 57, 118, 127, 135, 138, 169, 242
,, Thomas, 19, 29, 68, 118, 119, 147, 156, 203, 242, 257
,, Thurstan, 183

*Christenings* . . . . . . . . . . pp. 1—128 inclusive.
*Burials* . . . . . . . . . . ,, 129—252 ,,
*Marriages*. . . . . . . . . . ,, 253—288 ,,


Gobbin—*Continued*.
,, William, 5, 84, 95, 276
Godbeere, William, 225
Golborne (Golbourne, Golbrane, Golbron, Golbrone, Goldborne, Goulbron, Gowborn, Gowbron, Gowlb, Gowlbron, Gowlbrond),
,, Alexander, 54, 85, 101, 277
,, Alice, 14
,, Ann, 31, 101
,, Anthony, 33, 37
,, Catherin, 24, 153, 217
,, Ellen, 142, 156, 175, 267
,, Francis, 30, 81, 86, 217, 276
,, Henry, 35, 49, 215
,, Hugh. 114
,, Humphrey, 52, 54, 63, 81, c. of 187, 199, 238
,, James. 254
,, Jo: 24 39, 49
,, John, 28, 35, 37, 44, 153, 236, 259. 263
,, Lawrence. 33
,, Margaret, 63, 199
,, Margery, 2, 44, 55
,, Martha, 86, 234
,, Mary, 10, 287
,, Richard, 5, 35, 52, 114, 175, 257
,, Roger. 35
,, Silvester, 39
,, Thomas, 28
,, William, 25, 55, 85, w. of 131, 142
Golibrand, Golibrannd, Golibrond, Goliebrand, Gollibrand, Gollibrond,
see Gillibrond
Gollie, see also Jolly,
,, Alice, 190
,, Elizabeth, 177
,, Henry, 171
,, Jenet, 270
,, Margaret, 59, 186, 192
,, Robert, 192
,, Thomas, 59, 73, 190, 274
,, William, 73
Goodes (Guddes), Elizabeth, 29
,, Jo: 25
,, John, 29, 262
,, Thomas, 161
,, William, 25
Goolden, Thomas, 288
Gore (Goare), Adam, 59
Gore—*Continued*.
,, Alice, 286
,, Ann, 78, 96, 162
,, Cuthbert, 276
,, Elizabeth, 95, 124
,, Henry, 95, 96, 103, w .of 13
,, Humphrey, 115, 124
,, Jane, 59
,, Jo: 190
,, Margaret, 223
,, Ralph, 280
,, Richard, 78, 234, 274
,, Robert, 190
,, Thomas, 103
,, William, 115, 261
Gorhson, see also Georgson,
,, William, 269
Gorsutch (Gorsatch, Gorsuch, Gorsuche, Gorsuth),
,, Ed: 27
,, Edward, 75, 218*
,, Elizabeth, 6, 80, 258
,, Ellen, 283
,, Frances, 30, 157
,, Gabriel, 18, 199
,, Henry, 12, 288
,, Ja: 27
,, James, 18, 29, 96,* 139
,, Jane, 146, 261
,, John, 171, 194
,, Margaret, 258, 273
,, Margery, 7, 169*
,, Nicolas, 75, 80
,, Richard, 141, 256
,, Robert, 131, 146
,, Thomas, 2, 142
,, William, 145, 158
Gorton, Katherine, 279
,, William, 178
Goulbron, Gowborn, Gowbron, Gowlb, Gowlbron, Gowlbrond,
see Golborne
Goye, John, 267
Graine, (?) meant for "Craine,"
,, John, 28
,, Ran: 28
Grason, Thomas, 45
,, William, 45
Graystocke Agnes, 192
Greaves (Greaues, Greave, Greves
,, Ann, 84, 181, 252
,, Christopher, 64
,, Elizabeth, 84
,, Ellen, 90, 235
,, Emlin, 12, 144

Grove—*Continued.*
„ Eme, 150
Guddes, see Goodes
Gyles, Henry, 3, 34, 119
„ Isabell. 274
„ Jane, 119
„ Katherin, 182
„ Richard, 34
„ Robert, 57, 124, 189, 270
„ Thomas, 142
„ William, 3, 35, 57, 124, 174, 278 286
Gyll, see Gill

H

Haale, see Hale
Hadley, Ann, 57
„ John, 57
Hadocke (Haidocke), Adrian, 24
„ Alice, 173, 207
„ Anne, 267
„ Charles, 24, 158
„ Edmund, 19, 148
„ Elizabeth, 9, 140, 246
„ Henry. 27
„ Huan, 220
„ Jane, 269
„ N.X.N., 220
„ Richard, 107. 221, 246
„ Robert, 17, 221, 235
„ Thomas, 17, 97, 107, w. of 207
„ William, 97
Haide (Haid), Alice, 28, 273
„ Catherine, 188, 195
„ Edmund, 198
„ Edward, 188
„ Elizabeth, 160
„ Margaret, 183
„ Richard, 28, w. of 188, 188
„ Thomas, 188
„ Walter, 189
„ William, 195, 263
Haidocke, see Hadocke
Haidon, N.X.N., 186
Haighton, see Hayton
Haile, Haill, Haille, see Hale
Hainde, see Hynde
Haiton, see Hayton
Haiworth, see Haworth
Hale (Haale, Haile, Haill, Haille),
„ Alice, 288
„ Anne, 242
„ Catherine, 21, 118, 185, 241, 285
„ Edward, 126, 128, 250

*Christenings . . . . . . . . . . pp. 1—128 inclusive.*
*Burials . . . . . . . . . . . ,, 129—252 ,,*
*Marriages . . . . . . . . . . ,, 253—288 ,,*


Halton, see also Holton,
,, Elizabeth, 224
,, Ellen, 159
,, William, 242
Halword, see also Hallworth,
,, Alis, 159
Hamerson, John, 159
Hamlett (Hamlet), Frances, 224, 276
Hampson (Hamson), Huan, 282
,, Jane, 283
,, Nicalas, 272
Hancocke (Hankick),
,, Ellen, 34, 161, 259
,, Francis, 34
,, William, 148
Hand, Margery, 274
Hankick, see Hancocke
Hankin, Alice, 178
,, Ann, 37, 82, 213, 235
,, Elizabeth, 181
,, Isabel, 184
,, James, 72, 226
,, Jane, 34 154
,, Jo: 152
,, John, 152
,, Katherine, 153
,, Margaret, 78
,, Robert, 34, 37, w. of 235, 238
,, Roger, 150
,, Thomas, 75, w. of 154, 156, 177
,, Tomasin, 286
,, William, 30, 72, 75, 78, 82, 213
Hankinson, Edward, 95
,, Elizabeth, 99
,, Jane, 126, 251
,, Margaret, 243
,, Robert, 95, 99, 126, 243, 287
Harber, Isabel, 71
,, John, 71
Harden, see also Hardman,
,, Jane, 214
,, John, 63
,, Katherine, 82
,, William, 63, 82, w. of 214, 236, 277
Hardman (Herdman),
see also Harden,
,, Alice, 54
,, Anne, 149
,, Ellen, 19, 152
,, Jo: 50
,, John, 54, 183
,, Katherin, 267
,, Margaret, 50, 280
,, Margery, 2, 136, 137
,, Robert, 7, 149
Hardman—*Continued.*
,, Thomas, 12, 19, 143, 149,* 183, 256
[Haresnape], see Harsnep
Harison, see Harrison
Harker (Harkar), see also Arker,
,, Alice, 176
,, Emlin, 24
,, Henry, 283
,, Isabel, 38
,, Richard, 142
,, Thomas, 24
Harlinge, Ann, 47
,, Thomas, 47
Harresdoughter, Elizabeth, 276
Harrison (Harieson, Harison, Harrson, Harryson, Herryson),
see also Harson and Henrieson,
,, Abigall, 81
,, Alis, 197
,, Ann, 57, 112
,, Clarice, 285
,, Cristopher, 263
,, Cuthbert, 261
,, Elizabeth, 69, 168, 170, 175, 267
,, Ellen, 122, 174,* 239
,, George, 256
,, Henry, 65, 110, 231
,, Hugh, 40, 49, 239
,, Humphrey, 65, 259, 271
,, Izabell, 220
,, James, 199, 224
,, Jane, 11, 64
,, Jenet, 139
,, John, 15, 38, 49, 112, 122, 184, 193, 253, 284
,, Katherine, 171
,, Margaret, 40, 60, 176, 220, 285
Margery, 233
,, Miles, 180, 243
,, Richard, 251
,, Robert, 38, 41, 57, 129, c. of 187, w. of 233, 284
,, Sislie, 272
,, Thomas, 16, 60, 64, 69, 81, 110, 192
,, William, 4, 41, 105, 174
Harsnep, Bartholomew, 85
,, Cislie, 92
,, James, 85
,, Robert, 92
Harson, see also Harison,
,, Jane, 158
Hartley (Hartleye), James, 80
,, Mary, 80
,, N.X.N., 234

*Christenings* . . . . . . .
*Burials* . . . . . . . .
*Marriages* . . . . . . .

. . *pp.* *1—128 inclusive.*
. . ,, *129—252* ,,
. . ,, *253—288*

Hayton—*Continued.*
,, Humphrey, 65
,, Isabel, 185
,, James, 118
,, John, 75, 86, 91, 110, 133, 223
,, Margery, 73
,, Richard, 73, 86
,, Thomas, 40, 50, 110, 118, 124, 132, 223, 283
,, Trymor, 65
,, William, 40
Heaton, Ann, 107
,, Elizabeth, 89
,, Ewan, 89, 95, 107, 115
,, Jane, 95
,, Richard, 115
,, Sislie, 257
Hebleforth, Katherin, 271
Heddringeton, Henry, 75
,, John, 75
Heicclif, Thomas, 155
Heie, Heies, see Hey
Henrieson (Henrison, Henryson, Herryson),
see also Harrison,
,, Alice, 43, 130, 215
,, Ann, 13, 48, 73, 262
,, Bryan, 264
,, Edward, 48, 78
,, Elizabeth, 279
,, Ellen, 130
,, Gilbert, 16
,, Grace, 89, 198
,, Henry, 6, 35, 86, 91, 202
,, Hugh, 2, 3, 156, 157, 253
,, Humphrey, 198
,, Isabel, 157, 220, 275
,, James, 6, 10, 33, 91, 259, 265
,, Jane, 89, 156, 166
,, John, 87,* 149, 253
,, Katherine, 207, 240, 266
,, Margaret, 183, 220
,, Myles, 149
,, N.X.N., 45
,, Richard, 43, 87, 89, 147, 251, 266
,, Robert, 32, 45, 86
,, Roger, 131
,, Thomas, 10, 44, 73, 78, 89, 114, 182, 202, 269
,, William, 10, 87, 136, 251, 262
Henrysedoughter, Elizabeth, 276
Herdman, see Hardman
Herlickers, see also Shurlicars,
,, John, 23
,, Margaret, 23

*Christenings* . . . . . . . . . pp. 1—128 inclusive.
*Burials* . . . . . . . . . . ,, 129—252 ,,
*Marriages* . . . . . . . . . ,, 253—288 ,,

. . pp. 1—128 inclusive.
. . ,, 129—252 ,,
. . ,, 253—288 ,,

Hodgson—*Continued.*
,, Ann, 26, 118, 173
,, Blanch, 213
,, Elizabeth, 219
,, Ellen, 254
,, Ellis, 92
,, Ewan, 26, 122, 180, 183, 258, 285
,, Fardinando, 110, 118, 122, 283
,, Henry, 264
,, Hugh, 15, 17, 122, 219
,, Izabell, 278
,, Jane, 265
,, Jenet, 142
,, Jo: 36
,, John, 21, 110, 183, w. of 213, 241, 278
,, Johne, 138
,, Katherine, 122, 270
,, Margaret, 111, 163, 270
,, Margery, 36
,, Richard, 92, 103,* 111, 120, 124, 134, 184, 248, 249, 269, 278
,, Robert, 21
,, Thomas, 11, 120, 142, 205
,, William, 124, 244, 249
Hodson, see Hodgson
Holande, see Holland
Holcroft (Holcrofte), see also Howcroft,
,, Alice, 111, 237
,, Ann, 123
,, Claris, 101
,, Elizabeth, 246
,, John, 101, 111, 116, 123
,, Thomas, 116, 271
Holden (Houlding, Howlden, Howldinge), see also Howden,
,, Ann, 199
,, Bright, 102
,, Elizabeth, 199
,, Ellen, 265
,, Ellinor, 235
,, Gabriel, 63
,, George, 91, 102, 108, 149, 179, 221, 227
,, Henry, 149, 156, 221, 252, 259
,, Jo: 63
,, Margaret, 91, 195, 263
,, Richard, 156
,, Robert, 163
,, Sisley, 227
,, William, 108, 268
Holey, John, 202
,, Thomas, 202

*Christenings* . . . . . . . . . .
*Burials* . . . . . . . . . . .
*Marriages.* . . . . . . . . .

Holiwell, see Halliwell
Holland (Holande, Hollande, Hollanes, Hollond, Hollonde, Holond, Holonde, Hoolond),
,, Alice, 55, 162, 263
,, Ann, 57, 218, 263, 267
,, Clarice, 283
,, Edith, 194
,, Edmund, 253
,, Edward, 110, 112, w. of 205, 228, 235, 256
,, Elizabeth, 57, 60, 86, 134, 197, 204, 218, 256,* 269*
,, Ellen, 7, 58, 178, 179, 222, 284
,, George, 51, 60, 176
,, Gilbert, 145
,, Grace, 151
,, Henry, 266
,, Hugh, 43, 49, 78, 84, 110, 116, 124, 151, 170, 174, 176, 205,* 209, w. of 218, 260, 283
,, Isabel, 269
,, Izabeth, 3
,, James, 68, 116
,, Jane, 61, 140, 175, 220, 266, 284, 286
,, Jo: 53, 57, 68
,, Joan, 79, 224, 279
,, John, 57, 65, 75, 79, 110, 154, w. of 218, 220, 224
,, Katherine, 49, 55, 107, 148, 205, c. of 235
,, Lettis, 191
,, Lewes, 72, 235
,, Margaret, 43, 53, 112, 124, 181, 203, 214, 278, 279
,, Margery, 15, 54, 95, 179, 185, 255, 266
,, Mary, 266
,, Nicholas, 275
,, N.X.N., w. of 153
,, Peter, 258
,, Ralph, 51, 54, 176, w. of 179, 269
,, Richard, 12, 17, 29, 78, 84, 89, 95, 116, 132, 140, 148, 209, 215, 224, 227, 237, 260, 270, 273, 277
,, Robert, 23, 58, 61, 72, 86, 89, 116, 144, c. of 188, w. of 203, c. of 209, c. of 213, 220, 271, 276, 286
,, Sislie, 75, 273
,, Thomas, 23, 29, 65, 178, 255, 260
,, William, 107, 110, 154, 165, 222, 275, 279, 282, 283

. . *pp.* *1—128 inclusive.*
. . ,, *129—252* ,,
. . ,, *253—288* ,,

*Christenings* . . . . . . .
*Burials* . . . . . . . .
*Marriages* . . . . . . .

Hunsworth, John, 282
Hunt (Hunte, Hvnt),
,, Abraham, 19, 64
,, Alice, 255
,, Edward, 29
,, Elizabeth, 57, 258, 281
,, Ellen, 4. 123, 235, 271, 273
,, Emlin, 11, 123
,, Henry, 126
,, Izabell, 279
,, Ja: 27, 134, 155
,, James, 2, 19, 27, 64, 126, 134, 177
,, Jane, 160, 280
,, Jenet, 197
,, Jo: 44, 66
,, John, 15, 27, 36, 54, 57, 61, 85, 155, 197, 263, 269
,, Katherine, 66, 287
,, Margaret, 44, 85, 169, 246
,, Margery, 54
,, Maud, 231
,, Nicholas, 119
,, Silvester, 36
,, Thomas, 8, 61, 119, 123, 127, 131, 172, 285
,, William, 127, 251
Hunter, Adam, 139, w .of 144
,, Ann, 21, 148, 274
,, Cecelie, 2
,, Christopher, 10, 38, 72, 76, 81
,, Edward, 5, 20, 94, 97, 103, 111, 119, 140, 224, 247, 279
,, Elizabeth, 42, 154, 275
,, Ellen, 103, 139, 216, 230
,, Elynor, 248
,, Gabriel, 22
,, Henry, 15, 26, 79, 189
,, James, 22, 81, 144
,, Jane, 42, 51, 171
,, Jenet, 76, 233
,, Jo: w. of 149
,, John, 121, 257
,, Katherine, 143, 258, 279
,, Margaret, 72, 210, 249, 256
,, Margery, 5, 149, 203, 278
,, Mary, 200
,, Mawde, 39
,, Peter, 48, 147, 148, 174
,, Richard, 8, 72, 112, 121, 149, w. of 203, 205, 284
,, Robert, 11, 20, 27, 39, 66, 94, 97, 126, 154, 179, 197, 199, 224, 257, 258, 286
,, Sislie, 27
,, Thomas, 11, 21, 26, 38, 42, 48,

. . . *pp.* *1—128 inclusive.*
. . . ,, *129—252* ,,
. . . ,, *253—288*

Jackson—*Continued.*
,, James, 17, 40, 45, 54, 57, 97, 107, 113, 124, 152, 184, c. of 185, 199, 258, 265, 266
,, Jane, 17, 37, 47, 49, 167, 172, 254, 257, 264, 270
,, Jenet, 8, 173, 175, 227, 268, 287
,, John, 2, 3, 8, 26, 42,* 45, 53, 97, 101, 104, 106, 110, 114, 115, 121, 125, 132, 135, 161, 170, 212, 232, 269
,, Jon, 26
,, Katherin, 177
,, Lyonell, 209
,, Margaret, 8, 25, 54, 155, 156, 194, 216, 260
,, Margery, 56, 187, 220*
,, Mary, 39
,, Nicholas, 131, w. of 149
,, Peter, 156, 165, 253, 263
,, Richard, 26, 45, 47, 49, 53, 57, 73,* 97, 100, 101, 108,* 155, 192, 203,* 225, 227, 238, 267, 275, 283
,, Robert, 18, 21, 25, 37, 155, 179
,, Silvester, 18
,, Thomas, 14, 18, 26, 42, 108, 204, 237
,, William, 40, 45, 49, 114, 164, 170, 172, 194,* 203, 210
Jahnsen, see Johnson
Jamesdaughter (Jamisdaughter, Jamisdoughter),
,, Elizabeth, 106, 281
,, Jenet, 277
,, Margaret, 256
Jameson (Jamson), Ann, 47
,, Edward, 127
,, Isabel, 206
,, Jo: 47
,, John, 261
,, Thomas, 127, 161, 255
Jamis, Alice, 79
,, Richard, 79
Jamisdaughter, Jamisdoughter, see Jamesdaughter
Jamson, see Jameson
Janeson, Anne, 282
Jarman, James, 113, 119, 124, 283
,, Margaret, 119
,, N.X.N., 124
,, Richard, 113
Jarrard, see also Garret and Gerrard,
,, Henry, 29
,, John, 29

*Christenings* . . . . . .
*Burials* . . . . . . .
*Marriages* . . . . . .

*Christenings* . . . . . . . . . *pp.* *1—128 inclusive.*
*Burials* . . . . . . . . . . ,, *129—252* ,,
*Marriages* . . . . . . . . . ,, *253—288* ,,

kewicke—*Continued.*
,, Agnes, 164
,, Alice, 1, 50, 92, 114, 240, 264, 286, 287
,, Ann, 67, 76, 203, 259
,, Arthur, 26
,, Bartholomew, 107
,, Catherin, 36, 54, 160, 233, 267, 274
,, Claris. 63
,, Cuthbert, 89
,, Ed: 86
,, Edward, 22, 77, 83, 87, 89, 99, 102, 109, 120, 137, c. of 223, 276, 277
,, Elizabeth, 13, 55, 109, 129, 173, 230, 265, 269, 273
,, Ellen, 67, 86, 197
,, Emlin, 8, 50, 173, 261, 266
,, George, 44, 50, w. of 131, 132
,, Godfrey, 133
,, Henry, 68
,, Hugh, 19, 35, 43, 51, 54, 60, 67, 203, 230, 248, 269
,, Isabel, 39
,, Ja: 25, 54, 155
,, James, 106, 120, 199, 268
,, Jane, 82, 87, 163
,, Jo: 22
,, John, 25, 94, 97, 107, 119, 120, 149, 151, 157, 222, 257, 269, 280
,, Margaret, 24, 54, 60, 120, 129, 161, 162, 172, 263, 277, 283, 288
,, Margery, 127, 166, 200, 264
,, Mary, 24, 44, 52, 164
,, One, 196
,, Ralph, 99
,, Richard, 22, 27, 35, 59, 65, 83, 92, 114, 119, 125, 127, 155, 157, 193, 243, 257, 278
,, Robert, 43, 55, 59, 63, 68, 79, 92, 97, 102, 106, 211, 229
,, Roger, 22, 26, 51, 151, 177
,, Silvester, 20, 149
,, Thomas, 9, 77, 94, 97, 125, 143, 185, 222, 253
,, William, 11, 19, 27, 39, 50, 52, 65, 67, 76, 79, 82, 92, 97, 99,* 193, w. of 195, 211, 275
Kellet (Kelett), Alice, 183
,, Elizabeth, 193
,, Jane, 168
,, John, 176
,, Katherin, 178, 278
Kellet—*Continued.*
,, Margaret, 59
,, Richard, 59, 168, 178, 193, 205, 274
Kendale, Elizabeth, 122
,, Mary, 126
,, Thomas, 122, 126, 286
Kenion (Kenian, Kenione, Kennion, Kenyon),
,, Alice, 85, 287
,, Edward, 151
,, Elizabeth, 243, 244
,, Ellen, 75, 204
,, George, 73
,, Henry, 62, 67, 73, 75, 77, 82, 85, 90, 204, 209, 213, 217, 272, 277
,, James, 235
,, Jane, 209
,, Margaret, 151, 186, 201
,, Margery, 62, 282
,, Mary, 82, 103, 213
,, Robert, 67, 103, 244
,, Samuel, 77
,, Sannel (*sic*) 235
,, Thomas, 90, 217
Kequicke, see Kekewicke
Kerfoote, Jane, 120
,, Margery, 122, 251
,, Robert, 128
,, Thomas, 120, 122, 128
Keuqick, Keuquick, Kewqkeicke, Kewquicke, see Kekewicke
Key, Ellen, 188
Keykwicke, see Kekewicke
Kidd (Kidde, Kydde), Ellen, 256
,, Ja: 156
,, James, 134
,, Katherin, 270
,, Margaret, 156
,, Richard, 268
Kilingworth, Margaret, 268
Killshaw (Kilsh, Killshawe, Kilshaw, Kilshawe, Kilshshawe, Kylshawe),
,, Alexander, 48
,, Alice, 22, 71, 93, 124, 125, 260, 262, 275
,, Allen, 37, 42, 47, 53, 59, 66, 69, 199, 232, 235, 265
,, Ann, 22, 60, 61, 87, 95, 105, 116, 125, 159, 188, 203, 214, 231,* 232, 262, 265, 272
,, Claris 12, 182, 260
,, Cuthbert, 100

Killshaw—*Continued.*
,, Edmund, 49, 113, 132, 174
,, Edward, 10, 24, 66, 71, 119, 142, 250, 272
,, Elizabeth, 22, 46,* 47, 73, 91, 96, 111, 120, 171, 204, 217, 223, 237
,, Ellell (*sic*), 239
,, Ellen, 27, 33, 51, 59, 68, 94, 98, 115, 121, 126, 189, 191, 201, 220, 230, 235,* 239, 252, 254, 273, 277
,, Emlin, 5, 137
,, Gabriel, 21, 150
,, Gilbert, 16, 65, 68, 72, 74, 85, 132, c. of 190, 201,* 214, 217, 272
,, Hector, 8, 38, 44, 51, 52, 56, 65, 100, 104, 182, 266, 269
,, Henry, 5, 49, 50, 96, 98, 104, 108, 115, 116, 124, 181, 223, 235, 280
,, Hom: 56
,, Isabel, 267
,, Ja: 39, 46, 49, 53, 189
,, James, 33, 38, 54, 99, 100, 108, 168, 182, 191, 203, 249, 266
,, Jane, 59, 66, 113, 165, 171, 182, 186, 277, 284
,, Jenet, 178, 283
,, Jo: 34, 38, 42, 47, 50, 54,* 180, 188
,, Joan, 218, 278, 284
,, John, 37, 39, 42, 47, 49, 59, 61, 66, 82, 91,* 93,* 97,* 99, 104, 106, 116,* 119, 125, 152, 162, 165, 186, 204, 215, 216, 217,* 238, c. of 250, 252, 285
,, Johne, 148
,, Katherin, 54, 65, 85, 99, 108, 180, 214, 266
,, Lettice, 103
,, Margaret, 28, 48, 65, 94, 116,* 120, 162, 205, 230, 263, 277
,, Margery, 275
,, N.X.N., 53
,, Ralph, 44, 56, 104, 120, 183, 282
,, Ranete, 196
,, Richard, 22, 53, 74, 85, 89, 93, 94, 95, 100, 108, 109, 111, 115, 116, 120, 123, 125,* 126, 151, 212, c. of 216, 218, 230, 261, 277,* 282, 283
,, Robert, 42, 69, 130, 199, 277
,, Thomas, 28, 33, 37, 38, 39, 42,

*Christenings* . . . . . . . . . . *pp.* *1—128 inclusive.*
*Burials* . . . . . . . . . . ,, *129—252* ,,
*Marriages* . . . . . . . . . . ,, *253—288* ,,

ithwait—*Continued.*
,, Elizabeth, 11, 69, 73, 84, 92, 99, 183, 221, 274, 275
,, Ellen, 25, 68, 73, 93, 144, 203, 241. 263
,, Emllin. 36, 163, 230
,, George, 65, 192
,, Henry, 2, 4, 9, 33, 51, 61, 65, 69,* 71, 73, 76, 86, 88, 96, 97. 99, 103, 119,* 123, 132, 148, 153, 160, 192, 203, 223, c. of 251, 262, 269, 271
,, Hugh, 70, 202
,, Humphrey, 43, 284
,, Isabel, 38
,, Ja: 48, 51, 54, 65
,, James, 9, 51, 59, 68, 73, 77, 89, 96, 100,* 102, 110, 193, 212, 223, 227,* 241
,, Jane, 65, 85, 193
,, Jenet, 76, 150, 213, 286
,, John, 4, 86
,, Katheryne, 252
,, Margaret, 54, 66, 76
,, Marie, 193
,, Miles, 71, 201
,, Peter, 34, 36, 38, 43, 52, 80, 161, 185, 210
,, Richard, 48, 57, 84, 96, 99, 132, 150, 173, 218, 223
,, Robert, 17,* 65, 66, 67, 71, 80, 84, 93, 99,* 152, 193, 210
,, Roger, 69, 77, 96, 200, 223
,, Silvester, 59, 62, 118, 242, c. of 251, 285, 287
,, Thomas, 33, 37, 54, 106, 110, 118, 121,* 183, 221, 272
,, William, 6, 25, 34, 37, 51, 54, 57, 62, 67, 70, 73,* 76, 84, 85, 88, 92, 96,* 97, 99, 102, 103, 143, 161, 202, 210,* 212. 218, 221, 223,* 241, 252
aland, see Leyland
ancaster (Lancestere), Alice, 62, 190
,, Ann, 192
,, Elizabeth, 173, 245, 255, 275
,, Gilbert, 154, 155
,, Isabel, 88, 177, 215
,, James. 77, 186
,, Jenet, 169
,, Jo: 62, 190, 192, 198
,, John, 17, 77, 83, 146, 210, 215, 217. 225, 247
,, Margery, 83, 210
,, Richard, c. of 134, 198
,, Sislie, 17, 247, 278
,, Thomas, 88, 198, 276

Langley (Langeley), see also Longley,
,, Catherine, 1
,, Huan (Ewan), 109, 194
,, Jane, 82
,, Jenet, 218
,, John, 178
,, Margery, 123
,, Ralph, 94, 109, 123
,, Thomas, 5, 82, 94
,, William, 231
Lappinge, Ja: 40
,, Margery, 40
Lassell, Hugh, 100, 281
,, Thomas, 100
Latham, see Lathom
Lathfoot, Lathfott see Laithwait
Lathom (Laithom, Latham, Lathome, Lathomm, Lathon, Lathum, Laythom),
,, Alice, 41, 91, 181, 183, 186
,, Ann, 37, 44, 170
,, Catherin, 2, 52, 63, 236, 239
,, Claris, 20, 176, 248
,, Dorothy, 65
,, Edward, 108
,, Elizabeth, 23, 147, 197, 199
,, Ellen, 31, 159, 256
,, Emlin, 35
,, Francis, 39, 261
,, Gabriell, 20, 149
,, George, 91
,, Gilbert, 33, 35, 39, 178, 264, 271
,, Goulter, 91
,, Gultheric, 74
,, Henry, 20, 27, 31, 52, 54, 56, 58, 61, 65, 75, 210, 235, 262, 268, 269, 285
,, Hugh, 12, 25, 34, 41, 44, 61, 84, 150, 170, 233, 255, 260, 288
,, Isabel. 29, 249
,, Jaine (probably John), 269
,, James, 75, 210, 230, 245
,, Jane, 162, 164, 266
,, Jenet, 27
,, Jo: 20, 23, 29, 37
,, John, 25, 135, 192
,, Lawrence, 287
,, Margaret, 12, 33, 63, 173, 174, 188, 191, 230, 235, 268, 275
,, Margery, 143
,, Mary, 30, 37, 65, 275, 282
,, Matthew, c. of 191
,, N.X.N., 141

*Christenings* . . . . . . . . . . *pp.* *1—128 inclusive.*
*Burials* . . . . . . . . . . . ,, *129—252* ,,
*Marriages.* . . . . . . . . . ,, *253—288* ,,


Lathom—*Continued.*
,, Richard, 37, 54, 63,* 65, 74, 80,* 84, 91, 146, 149, 152, 191, 210,* 250, 263, 280, 287
,, Robert, 58, 102, 111, 248, 281, 288
,, Sislie, 196
,, Thomas, 33, 34, 56, 102, 108, 149, 156, 183
,, Walter, c. of 183, 270
,, William, 25, 111, 149, 198
Lathwaitt, Lathwat, Lathwate, Lathwhat,
see Laithwait
Law (Lawe), see also Lowe,
,, Jo: 57
,, Katherin, 162
,, Richard, 57
Lawrance (Lowrance), Anthony, 55
,, Elizabeth, 270
,, John, 137
,, Thomas, 55
Lawrancedoughter, Margaret, 15
Lawransondowghter,
,, Elizabeth, fi: of 44
Lawranson alis Robertson,
,, James, 150
Lawrenson (Lawranson, Lawrence son),
,, Anthony, 38, 62, 240
,, Doughter, 44
,, Elizabeth, 44
,, Jane, 38
,, Jonie, 282
,, Margaret, 62, 72, 115, 241, 250
,, Mary, 72, 281
,, Thomas, 16, 72, 115, 126, 274, 283
,, William, 126
Lay see Ley
Layland, Laylande, Laylloyd,
see Leyland
Laythom, see Lathom
Laythwaitt, see Laithwait
Lea, see Ley
Leadbeater (Leadbeter, Leadbetter, Ledbeter, Ledbetter),
,, Alice, 111, 157, 205, 207
,, Ann, 270
,, Edith, 138
,, Elizabeth, 208, 262
,, Ellen, 122, 287
,, Grace, 260
,, Hamlet, 137
,, Henry, 107, 110, 178, 265
,, Isabel, 219
,, Jane, 122, 254
Leadbeater—*Continued.*
,, John, 106, 110, 117
,, Margaret, 66, 86, 115, 130, 192, 212
,, Margery, 14
,, Mary, 128
,, Peter, 66, 86, 107, 122, 212*
,, Richard, 86, 117, 212, 240
,, Robert, 111, 115, 137, 204, 243, 251
,, Thomas, 254
,, Trymor, 188
,, William, 106, 281
Leadbetter *alias* Cocket,
(Ledbetter *alias* Cocket)
,, Ralph, 37, 164
Leae, Leay, see Ley
Lee (Le, Leee), see also Leigh and Ley,
,, Alexander, 61, 98, 280
,, Ann, 98, 225
,, Charles, 255
,, Elizabeth, 203
,, Hector, 128
,, Huan, 128
,, Jane, 5
,, Margaret, 71
,, Margery, 138
,, Richard, 6, 61, 71, 76
,, Rowland, 264
,, Thomas, 76
Leech, Ellen, 154
,, Hugh, 133, 154
Leee, see Lee
Leegh, see Leigh
Lei, see Ley
Leigh (Leegh, Ligh, Lighe),
see also Lee and Ley,
,, Alexander, 101, 107
,, Ann, 101
,, John, 205
,, Margery, 130
,, Mary, 107
,, Richard, 66,* 209, 226
,, Von, 205
Leister, George, 84
,, Nicholas, 84
Leiusley, see Livsey
Leivers, Margaret, 211
Leland see Leyland
Lemman, Mary, 90
,, Richard, 90
Lenard (Lennard), Alice, 257
,, Elizabeth, 263
,, Robert, 154

. . *pp.* *1—128 inclusive.*
. . ,, *129—252* ,,
. . ,, *253—288*

Ley—*Continued.*
,, Jane, 39, 70, 149, 205, 214, 274
,, Jefferey, 95
,, Jo: 23, 26, 35
,, John, 13 17, 21, 29, 32, 67, 83, 90, 102, 149, 158, 164, 177, 180, 186, 254, 258
,, Johne, 75, 78, 206
,, Margaret, 44 61, 87, 109, 171, 211, 213, 237
,, Margery, 19, 225, 261, 268
,, Mary, 81
,, N.X.N., 10, 195*
,, "One." c. of 195*
,, Paul, 29
,, Peter, 16, 146, 163
,, Phelis, 168
,, Ralph, 41
,, Richard, 30, 69, 95, 119, 137, 250
,, Robert, 15, 23, 62, 87, 190
,, Roger, 8, 27, 63, 67, 70, 76, 81, 87, 89, 95, 102, 119, 157, 180, c. of 182, c. of 190, c. of 195, 213, 269
,, Thomas, 56,* 81, 90, 95, 115, 229, 279
,, William, 9, 13, 17,* 29, 53, 54, 56, 60, 61, 62, 72, 84, 89, 149, 179, 195,* 205, 211, 227, 278
Leyland (Lailand, Lailon, Lailond, Laland, Layland, Laylande, Laylloyd, Leland, Leylande),
,, Alice, 244, 281
,, Ann, 46, 117, 121, 223, 244, 284
,, Catherin, 35, 281
,, Christopher, 102, 108, 117, 222, 281
,, Ellen, 241
,, Ellis, 17
,, Grace, 81, 220
,, Henry, 279
,, Hugh, 15, 18, 104, 148, c. of 209
,, James, 132
,, Jane, 172
,, Jo: 152*
,, John, 18, 92, 108, 152,* 167, 224, 239
,, Margaret, 41, 128, 168, 273
,, Margery, 102, 224, 231
,, Mary, 75
,, N.X.N., 189
,, Richard, 46, 121, 124,* 128, 189, 254, 284

*Christenings* . . . . . . . . . . *pp.* 1—128 *inclusive.*
*Burials* . . . . . . . . . . . . ,, 129—252 ,,
*Marriages* . . . . . . . . . . . ,, 253—288 ,,

Leyland—*Conitnued.*
,, Robert, 17
,, Thomas, 35, 75, 81, 92, 104, 117, 161, 220, 222, 223
,, William, 270
Lidya, Mary, 70
,, Thomas, 70
Ligh, Lighe, see Leigh
Linicar, see Lynaker
Litham, see Lytham
Litherland, Jane, 19
,, John, 159, 263
,, Margery, 19, 219
Lithom, Lithon, see Lytham
Littler, Henry, 161
Livesey, Livesley, Livessey, see Livsey
Livinge, Stven, 266
,, Livisley, see Livsey
Livsey (Leiusley, Livesey, Livesley, Livessey, Livisley, Lyuesley, Lyvesley),
,, Emlin, 260
,, Henry, 225
,, Hugh, 3
,, Katherin, 260
,, Margaret, 36, 162
,, Margery, 175
,, Robert, 138
,, Thomas, 36, 165
Locker (Loccar, Lockere, Lockker),
,, Alice, 258
,, Ann, 14, 272
,, Catherin, 202
,, Dowse, 155
,, Ellen, 269
,, Emlin, 11, 144
,, Frances, 175
,, Francis, 5
,, Hugh, 254
,, Humphrey, 136
,, Jane, 267
,, John, 7, 138
Lockeye, Hugh, 148
Loncton, see Longton
Longe (Lunge), Douse, 132
,, Elizabeth, 258
,, Ellin (m), 254
,, Ellis, 47, 128,* 132, 158, 179
,, Isabel, 261
,, John, 156
,, Margery, 179
,, Mary, 5, 267
,, Peter, 47, 173, 266
,, Richard, 234
Longely, see Longley
Longeton, see Longton
Longeworth (Longewoorth),
,, Henry, 60, 243
,, Jane, 206
,, William, 60, 191
Longhey, Thomas, 273
Longley (Longely, Longlay, Longlaye), see also Langley,
,, Ann, 10
,, Cisley, 112
,, Elizabeth, 215, 273
,, Ewan, 60, c. of 181
,, George, 117
,, Henry, 274
,, Jo: 20
,, John, 58, 72, 154,* 221
,, Margaret, 146, 216
,, Margery, 254, 277
,, Mary, 20, 61, 128
,, Ralph, 60, 112, 117, 128
,, Thomas, 72, 146, 216, 279
,, William, 58, 61
Longton (Loncton, Longeton),
,, Ellen, 21, 151
,, Gabriel, 88
,, George, 30
,, Jenet, 88
,, Richard, 21, 151, 265
Lowe (Low), see also Law,
,, Alice, 180
,, Arthur, 184
,, Ja: 37
,, Jane, 37,* 237, 281
,, Jennett, 285
,, Jo: 63
,, John, 41, 69
,, Katherin, 114, 249
,, Margaret, 169
,, Robert, 69
,, Thomas, 37, 41, 114, 167, 18 197, c. of 235, 282
,, William, 63
Lowrance, see Lawrance
Lucas, William, 182
Ludgate, Thomas, 203
,, William, 203
Lufkin, see Luskin
Lune, Elizabeth, 255
,, Oliver, 37
Lunge, see also Longe,
,, Elizabeth, 255
Lunt (Lunte, Lvnt),
,, Alice, 100, 114, 140, 194, 245
,, Ann, 101, 114, 208
,, Catherine, 21, 284

*Christenings* . . . . . . . . . *pp.* *1—128 inclusive.*
*Burials* . . . . . . . . . . . ,, *129—252* ,,
*Marriages* . . . . . . . . . . ,, *253—288* ,,

*Christenings* . . . . . .
*Burials* . . . . . . .
*Marriages* . . . . . .

. . pp. *1—128 inclusive.*
. . ,, *129—252* ,,
. . ,, *253—288*

Mason—*Continued.*
,, Jane, 20, 43, 47, 59, 88, 98, 130, 165, 216, 270, 282
,, Joan, 104
,, John, 39, 139, 140, 180, 194, c. of 213
,, Johne, 41
,, Katherin, 57, 119, 158, 184, 246, 250, 269
,, Laurence, 116, 124, 128
,, Margaret, 11, 17, 72, 116, 139, 143, 179, 224, 228, 264, 283
,, Margery, 24, 116, 124, 153, 247, 268, 269
,, Mary, 42, 51, 68, 150, 169, 177, 284
,, N.X.N., 74, 179
,, Peter, 197
,, Ralph, 34, d. of 194
,, Ranold, 20, 35, 90, 119, 217, 227, 255, 285
,, Richard, 8, 24, 33, 34, 35, 38, 43, 64, 81, 139, 148, 159, 160, 162, 179, 194, 199, 202, 206, 214, 216, 250, 265, 276
,, Robert, 90
,, Sislie, 139, 214 222
,, Thomas, 34, 41, 45, 47, 52, 57, 58, 64, 81, 90, 94, 98, 104, 106, 123, 220, 227, 243
,, William, 9, 33, 57, 76, 90, 94, 106, 141, 220, 221
Massey (Massie), Elizabeth, 139
,, Hugh, 18
,, Richard 18
,, Thomas, 125
,, William, 125, 250
Masson, see Mason
Mather, Margaret, 270
Matthew (Mathew, Mathewe),
,, Alice, 239
,, Ann, 107, 170
,, Bryan, 243
,, Elizabeth, 14
,, George, 24, 114, 184, 250
,, Henry, 24, 107, 114, 221, 246
,, John, 174, 258
,, Lawrence, 232
,, Margaret, 242, 243
,, Margery, 138, 221
,, Sislie, 169
Maudesley, Maudisley, see Mawdisley
Maundy, see also Mundie,
,, Ann, 233
Mawdisley (Madisley, Maudesley, Maudisley, Mawdisle,

*Christenings* . . . . . . .
*Burials* . . . . . . . .
*Marriages* . . . . . . .

Mawdisley—*Continued.*
Mawdisleye, Modesley, Modisley, Modsley, Moudiseley, Moudisley, Moudsley, Movdisley, Mowdisle, Mowdisley, Mowdsley, Mudisley, Mwdisley),
,, Agnes, 31
,, Alice, 18, 34, 86, 122, 133, 161, 163, 208, 213, 268, 272
,, Ann, 7, 17, 19,* 23, 43, 46, 65, 74, 79, 88, 115, 119, 126,* 167, 188, 200, 215,* 223, 258, 263, 272, 287
,, Dorothy, 71, 149
,, Edward, 74, 109, 193
,, Eideth, 112, 277
,, Elizabeth, 16, 22, 24, 39, 74, 86, 123, 127, 131, 149, 166, 181, 182, 191, 215, 222, 251, 262, 265, 270, 273, 288
,, Ellen, 2, 13, 50, 86, 99, 124, 149, 152, 156, 171, 198, 207, c. of 207, 250, 270
,, Emlin, 183, 247
,, Ewan 4, 28, 45, 57, 136, 222, 239
,, Gabriel, 43
,, George, 35, 61, 105, 121, 160, 218, 262
,, Grace, 209
,, Hector, 2, 9, 19, 21,* 22, 28, 40, 57, 67, 72, 78, 81, 90, 139, 152, 179, 185
,, Henry, 12, 28, 29, 34, 41, 43, 45, 52, 59, 75, 79, 86, 87, 89, 95, 98,* 102, 111, 112, 115, 118, 124, 166, 172, 187, 215, 221, 224, 242, 254, 261, 274, 278, 285
,, Hugh, 3, 59, 187
,, Humphrey, 25
,, Isabel, 34, 37, 95, 164, 188
,, Ja: 91, 149,* 150
,, James, 17, 38,* 46, 52, 72, 86, 95, 97, 104, 112, 121, 145, 164, 181, 206, 265, 267
,, Jane, 3, 28, 31, 35, 60, 61, 72, 100, 102, 118, 153, 158, 171, 190, 206, 257, 258, 263, 266, 276, 277, 286, 287
,, Jenet, 139, 140, 154, 162, 199
,, Jo: 22, 35, 37, 41, 46, 49, 53
,, Joan, 218
,, John, 5, 6, 13,* 21, 33, 36, 40, 53, 59, 74,* 80, 96, 103, 110,

*Christenings* . . . . . . . . . . *pp.* *1—128* *inclusive.*
*Burials* . . . . . . . . . . ,, *129—252* ,,
*Marriages* . . . . . . . . . . ,, *253—288* ,,

adows—*Continued.*
, Katherine, 226
, Philip, 89
, Thomas, 58, 73, 81, 89, c. of 211, c. of 219, 226, 231, 243, 271
eanelie, Alice, 282
ease, Ann, 286
edow, Medowe, Medowes, see Meadows
elling (Melinge, Mellinge),
,, Ann, 53, 129, 261
,, Anthony, 39, 48, 53, 60, 140
,, Catherin, 60, 117, 159, 178, 241, 248
,, Dorothy, 27
,, Edward, 124
,, Elizabeth, 35, 101
,, Ellen, 101, 111, 234, 260
,, Grace, 228
,, Henry, 124
,, James, 132
,, Jane, 44, 120
,, Jo: 178
,, John, 1, 4, 113, 124, 133, 208, 234, 278, 284
,, Johne, 43
,, Margaret, 32, 97, 271
,, Margery, 39, 115, 166, 172, 255
,, Ralph, 44, 48, 57, 97, 101, 106, 111, 117, 120, 124, 185, 228, 241, 262
,, Richard, 1, 34, 35, 43, 76, 109, 132, 168, 171, 193
,, Roger, 34
,, Thomas, 30, 76, 106, 124, 172, 240, 251
,, William, 57, 101, 109, 113, 115, 124, c. of 208
ercer (Marcer, Marser, Marsher),
,, Ann, 95, 262
,, Elizabeth, 74
,, George, 135
,, Grace, 103
,, Henry, 111
,, Isabel, 213
,, Jane, 223
,, Janet, 82
,, John, 89, 95, 103, 111, 119, 275, 276
,, Margaret, 89
,, Margery, 272*
,, N.X.N., 15
,, Ralph, w. of 144, 188, 259, 268
,, Richard, 71, 201, 240
,, Robert, 71, 74, 82, 103, 119, 213

Mercer—*Continued.*
,, Roger, 125, 201
,, Thomas, 27, 125
,, William, 103, 262
Miller (Milere, Myller), Ann, 83
,, Dorothy, 54
,, Edith, 119
,, Ellen, 50
,, James, 97, 107, 112, 119
,, Jane, 101, 208
,, Katherine, 112, 239
,, Richard, 107, 233
,, Thomas, 50, 54, 97
,, William, 83, 101, 208, 239
Millingeton, Ellen, 31
,, Jane, 263
Milner (Millner, Milnor, Mylner),
,, Ann, 35, 278
,, Dorothy, 194
,, Elnor, 194
,, Henry, 41, 194
,, James, 45
,, Jane, 77, 194, 264
,, Jenette, 197
,, Margaret, 92
,, Thomas, 35, 41, 45, 164, 194, 200
,, William, 77, 92, 276
Minshaw, Catherine, 26
,, Richard, 26
Moare, see Moore
Modesley, Modisley, Modsley, see Mawdisley
Molines, see also Molyneux,
,, James, 5
,, Thomas, 6
Molyneux (Molinex, Molinxe, Mollinex, Mollyneux, Mollynex, Molnexe, Mulinex, Mulinexe, Mulinxe, Mullinex), see also Molines,
,, Agnes, 245
,, Alice, 74, 79, 156, 172, 194, 204, 279
,, Ann, 71, 80, 148, 163, 194, 243, 276
,, Cislie, 63, 119, 279
,, Dorothy, 110, 237
,, Edward, 96
,, Elizabeth, 99, 148, 169, 221, 268
,, Ellen, 2, 43, 89, 117, 163, 202, 245, 285
,, Eloner, 9
,, George, 20, 279

*Christenings* . . . . . .
*Burials* . . . . . . . .
*Marriages* . . . . . . .

| | | |
|---|---|---|
| *Christenings* . . . . . . . . . | *pp.* | *1—128 inclusive.* |
| *Burials* . . . . . . . . . . | ,, | *129—252* ,, |
| *Marriages* . . . . . . . . . | ,, | *253—288* ,, |

rcroft—*Continued.*
, James. 17, 42, 47, 55,* 95, 98, 106. 124. 168, 174, 175, 186, 226, 228, c. of 231, 280
, Jane, 6, 21, 24, 26, 42, 44, 47, 71. 81, 87, 138, 168, 169, 172,* 193, 196, 210, 223, 254, 261, 263, 273,* 277
, Jenet, 19, 144, 154, 160, 226, 233
, Joan, 32, 59, 100, 119
, John, 6, 14, 18, 21, 69, 123, 234
, Margaret, 34, 46, 50, 61, 71, 75,* 88, 94, 125,* 151, 152, 171. 175, 185, 204,* 205, 211, 215. 222, 233, 250, 259, 264, 265, 266, 279, 286
, Margery, 14, 255
, Martin, 8, 140
, Mary, 34, 66, 79, 87, 213, 274, 280, 283, 287
, Nicholas, 74, 123, 221, 269, 288
, N.X.N., 30, 66, 140
, Peter, 62, 119, 153, 229, 255
, Philip, 108, 113, 119, 125, 283
, Ralph, 18, 19, 22, 24, 26, 233, 244
, Rañ, 136
, Richard, 6, 22, 36,* 38, 39, 42, 44,* 45, 46, 50, 51, 54, 55,* 59. 61, 62, 64, 69, 72, 75, 76, 79, 80, 82, 83, 85,* 86, 91, 94,* 95, 99,* 100, 102, 111, 112, 125, 139, 150, 185, 186, 201, 204, c. of 206, 209, 214, 215, 221, 244, 265, 272, 277
, Ro: 26
, Robert, 33, 34, 36, 40, 44, 85,* 115, 221, 222, 239, 259
, Roger, 34, 91, 119, 147, 221
, Sara, 24, 213
, Susan, 75, 125
, Thomas, 10, 18, 26, 33, 36, 41, 45, 47,* 50, 51, 52, 55,* 57, 59,* 62, 66, 67, 69, 71, 74, 76, 81,* 87, 104, 107, 113, 151, 153, 154,* 173, 195, 197, 202, 213 215, 217, 229, 251, 258, 264, 266, 281
, William, 3, 18,* 22, 25,* 29, 34,* 37, 38, 39, 42, 47,* 49, 54. 55, 59, 64, 71, 99,* 104, 107, 115, 119, 125, 128, 150, 151, 162, 163,* 212, 238, 255, 258, 264,* 287

Moore (Moare, More, Mores), see also Morris,
,, Elizabeth, 202, 234 279
,, Ellen, 96, 222
,, George, 106
,, James, 96, 99, 105, 117, 222, 234. 280
,, Jane, 276
,, John, 207
,, Katherin, 99
,, Margaret, 245
,, Margery, 285
,, Mary, 207
,, Miles, 117
,, Robert, 202
,, Thomas, 52, 105
,, William, 52, 106, 245
Morcroft, Morcrofte, Morecroft, Morecrofte, see Moorcroft
More, Mores, see Moore
Morer, Elizabeth, 11
Morgan, George, 256
,, Thomas, 7, 147
Morris, see also More,
,, Ellen, 143
Mortimer (Mortmeer),
,, Andrew, 91, 216
,, John, 91, 216
Morton, Thomas, 257
Moscrop (Moscrofte, Moscropp, Moscroppe),
,, Elizabeth, 223, 257
,, Ellen, 250
,, Fardinando, 9, 250
,, Izabell, 220
,, James, 131, 153
,, Jane, 233, 253
,, John, 130
,, Margaret, 153, 158, 254
,, Robert, 166
,, Roger, 158
,, William, 220
Mosocke, Mosoke, see Mossocke
Mosse, Ann, 246
,, Edward, 20
,, Elizabeth, 84, 159, 160
,, Ellen, 189
,, Ewan, 164
,, Gilbert, 168
,, Hugh, 20
,, James, 12
,, Jenet, 138
,, John, 84, 143, 163, 184, 185
,, Katherin, 283
,, Margaret, 7, 138

*Christenings* . . . . . . .
*Burials* . . . . . . . . .
*Marriages* . . . . . . . .

. . *pp.* *1—128 inclusive.*
. . ,, *129—252* ,,
. . ,, *253—288* ,,

Ormishaw (Ormeshaw, Ormeshawe, Ormisha, Ormishawe, Ormshaw, Ormshawe),
,, Agnes, 150
,, Alice, 263
,, Ann, 68, 106, 197, 209, 257, 266
,, Anes, 5
,, Ciceley, 252
,, Dorothy, 134
,, Dowse, 180
,, Edmund, 106, 282
,, Eideth. 203
,, Elizabeth, 64, 140, 180, 217, 249, 260, 271, 279
,, Ellen, 31, 60, 160, 180, 199, 248, 281
,, Gabriel, 64
,, George. 157, 259
,, Gilbert, 17, 21, 38, 94, 179, 224, 241
,, Godfrey, 30, 158
,, Henry, 69, c. of 199, 213, 249
,, James, 17, 38, 250
,, Jane. 260
,, Jenet, 24, 117, 248, 264, 273
,, Jo: 69
,, John. 2, 60, 64, 100, 270
,, Katherin, 84, 260, 262, 271
,, Margaret, 127, 192, 255, 275
,, Margery, 251
,, Mary, 34, 288
,, Peter, 21, 139, 180
,, Richard. 14, 64, 68, 134, 197, 203, 230
,, Robert, 180, 251, 280
,, Roger, 31, 34, 100, 146, 150, 203, 239
,, Thomas, 1, 10, 29, 68, 70,* 84, 94, 108, 134, 179, 197, c. of 215, 237, 249, 251, 278, 287
,, William, 21, 108, 117, 127, 199
Orrell, Alexander, 14
,, Elizabeth, 35
,, Jane, 40
,, Jo: 36
,, Joanie, 40, 166
,, John, 40, 132, w. of 132, 184
,, Margaret, 210
,, Peter, 8
,, Ralph, 36
,, William, 35
Orte (Ort), Humphrey, 78
,, Izabell, 280
,, James, 212
,, Joanie. 78
,, John, 212
,, William, 182

*Christenings* . . . . . . .
*Burials* . . . . . . . .
*Marriages* . . . . . . .

*Christenings* . . . . . . . . . . *pp.* *1—128 inclusive.*
*Burials* . . . . . . . . . . . ,, *129—252* ,,
*Marriages* . . . . . . . . . . ,, *253—288* ,,


rr—*Continued.*
,, Peter, 91
,, Robert, 257
,, William, 72
rsivall, Sir John, 132
rson, Jo: 39
,, Ralph, 39
rtingeton, Thomas, 183
rye, Jeffrey, c. of 226
tricke, Robert, 270
ulsey, see Powsey
ver (Pavor), Katherin, 151
, Thomas, 133
wsey, see Powsey
yntersdoughter, N.X.N., c. of 50
arte, Henry, 30
ckvance, see Picavance
cocke (Peycocke), Emlin, 9, 141
,, James, 4
,, Margery, 138
,, William, 6, 255
edder, N.X.N., 258
eeter, see Peter
eeterson, see Peterson
emberton (Pemerton),
,, Elizabeth, 105, 242
,, Ellen, 111
,, James, 102, 105, 117, 281
,, Jane, 29
,, John, 102, 141, 229
,, Roger, 26, 29
,, Sislie, 262
,, Thomas, 160
,, William, 26, 117
'endlebury (Pendleberis, Pendleburie),
,, Dowse, 278
,, Elizabeth, 165, 182
,, John, 147
,, Margaret, 185
,, Margery, 264
,, Thomas, 182, c. of 185, 219
'endleton, Agnes, 238
'eningeton, see Pinnington
'enketh (Penket, Penkett),
,, Brichet, 272
,, Catherin, 45
,, George, 190, 267
,, Henry, 43, 45, 52, 76, c. of 78, 85, 171, 180, c. of 206, 274
,, Hugh, 43
,, Jane, 76
,, Margaret, 85, 166
,, Mary, 180
,, Richard, 52
'enkethman, Elizabeth, 286
,, Grace, 286

Percivalson, John, 118
Percy, Elizabeth, 120
,, Ferdinand, 120
Perker, see also Parker,
,, George, 131
,, Henry, 209
,, Jane, 209
Peter (Peeter, Peeters),
,, Alice, 78, 206
,, Ann, 53
,, Elizabeth, 172
,, James, 118
,, Jo: 51, 53, 56
,, Joanie, 60, 125, 250
,, John, 51, 60, 65, 74, 78, 83,* 109, 218, 260, 269
,, Katherin, 56
,, Margaret, 78, 206
,, Richard, 74
,, Thomas, 65, 109, 118, 125, c. of 251
Peterson (Peeterson),
,, Edward, 78, 244
,, Perceval, c. of 249, 285
,, Peter, 78
Peycocke, see Pecocke
Phillipps (Phillipes), Elizabeth, 94
,, Henry, 100
,, William, 94, 100
Picavance (Peckvance, Pickvance),
,, Alice, 182
,, John, 175
,, Margaret, 131
,, Thomas, 261
Pickett (Picket), Alice, 271
,, Anne, 267
Pickvance, see Picavance
Piningeton, Pinington, see Pinnington
Pinner, Peter, 189
Pinnington (Peningeton, Piningeton, Pinington, Pinniton),
,, Alice, 69
,, Ellen, 152
,, Humphrey, 56, 69, 84, c. of 190, 248*
,, Jane, 84, 248
,, John, 56, 84, 182, 206
,, Thomas, 205
Platt (Platte), Edward, 282
,, John, 275
Plumbe (Plombe, Plommbe, Ploumbe, Plowmbe, Plumbe, Plume, Plvmbe, Prombe),
,, Alice, 161, 176, 192
,, Ann, 274
,, Edw: 61, 193

*Christenings* . . . . . . . .
*Burials* . . . . . . . . .
*Marriages* . . . . . . . .



P

*Christenings* . . . . . . . . . . *pp.* *1—128 inclusive.*
*Burials* . . . . . . . . . . . ,, *129—252* ,,
*Marriages* . . . . . . . . . . ,, *253—288* ,,


scot—*Continued.*
, Nicolas, 25, 154
, Oliver, 131
,, Peter, 18, 25,* 33, 79, 129, w. of 134, 154, 160, 199
, Richard, 14, 27, 32, 37, 40, 41, 42, 46, 47, 50, 59, 122, 154, 166, c. of 184, c. of 188, 200, 202, 228, 230, 265, 286
,, Robert. 21, 40, 59, 127, 133, 141, 147, 202, 228
,, Roger, 41
,, Syslye, 20, 173, 280
,, Thomas, 12, 20, 32, 33, 36, 37, 41,* 42, 45,* 50,* 51, 54, 55, 56, 61,* 66, 68, 74, 85, 160, 171, 173, 186, c. of 202, c. of 203, 226, 241, 248, 250, 263
,, Tomazin, 258
,, William, 4, 20, 29,* 33, 38, 41,* 42, 45, 54, 61, 74, 99, 129, 147, 216, 259, 268
'eston, Elizabeth, 231
,, Thomas, 256
rice (Pryce), Margaret, 2
,, William, 254
rice *alias* Showen, John, 140
ryce, see Price
rombe, see Plumbe
rynne, Katherin, 225
uye, see Pye
wsey, see Powsey
wye, see Pye
ye (Puye, Pwye, Py),
,, Elizabeth, 27, 234
,, George, 104, 114, 117, 267, 281
,, Henry, 272
,, John, 104, c. of 198, 265
,, Katherin, 114, 257, 277
,, Margaret, 257, 267, 271
,, Robert, 117
'yke, Isabel, 166

R

ACHDAILL, Elene, 186
adley, Margaret, 253
ainforth (Rainfforth, Ranforth, Rayfornth, Raynforth, Raynforthe),
,, Alice, 133, 253
,, Ann, 110, 111
,, Catherine, 2, 133, 164
,, Dorothy, 81
,, Edith, 117
,, Elizabeth, 124
,, Ellen, 23

Rainforth—*Continued.*
,, George, 135, 281
,, Hugh, 43, 74, 113, 119, 124, 284
,, Ja: 81
,, James, 74, 84, 101, 117
,, Jo: 39
,, John, 43, 84, 119, 158
,, Margaret, 2, 23, 251, 282
,, Margery, 39
,, Mary, 78, 209, 212
,, N.X.N., 113
,, Peter, 78, 111, 283
,, Richard, 101, 110, 115
,, Robert, 115, 176, 273
,, William, 162
Ramer, John, 127
,, Margaret, 127
Ranal, Rande, see Ranold
Ranforth, see Rainforth
Ranold (Ranal, Rande, Rannill, Ranould),
,, Anthony, 106
,, Ellen, 287
,, John, 106
,, Nicholas, 216
,, Ozed, 216
,, William, 288
Raskem, Jo: 23
,, Margaret, 23
Ratcliffe (Ratclife), Dorothy, 101
,, Henry, 101
,, William, 266
Ratheram (Rathra, Rathram),
,, Edward, 97, 104, 112, 121
,, Gabriel, 104
,, Hugh, 97
,, Thomas, 121, 246
,, William, 112, 240
Rathwell, see Rothwell
Rayfornth, Raynforth, Raynforthe, see Rainforth
Read (Reade), Emlin, 208
,, Ja: 46, 195
,, James, 267
,, Robert, 46
,, William, 226
Reader, Cuthbert, 100
,, William, 100
Redfurthe, Isabel, 156
,, Ralph, 156
Rethrop, Rethrope, see Rithrop
Rethrope allis Mossocke, James, 94
Rgerson, see Rodgerson
Rhodes (Roades, Rodes), Edward, 118
,, Elizabeth, 93
,, Jane, 89

*Christenings* . . . . . . . .
*Burials* . . . . . . . . . .
*Marriages* . . . . . . . . .

Rhodes—*Continued.* R
,, John, 96, 224
,, Margaret, 122
,, N.X.N., 106
,, Thomas, 89, 93, 96, 100,* 106, 112,* 118, 122, 227
Richardsdoughter (Ric$^{d}$doughter, Richardesdoughter),
,, Ann, 264
,, Ellen, 162, 260
,, Katherin, 189
,, Margaret, 262
Richardson (Ric$^{r}$son, Ric$^{d}$son, Ryc$^{9}$son),
,, Alice, 155, 177
,, Ann, 145, 155
,, Christopher, 264
,, Edmund, 22, 258, 263
,, Edward, 136, 150, 259
,, Henry, 254
,, Jane, 150, 261
,, Jenet, 156, 164
,, John, 42, 257
,, Lawrence, 155, 258 R
,, Margery, 280
,, N.X.N., 155
,, Richard, 42
,, Robert, 129
,, Thomas, 261
,, William, 22, 37
Richardson alis Jackeson,
,, Robert, 260
Ridgbie, see Rigby R
Riding (Ridinge, Ryding, Rydinge, Rydinges, Rydynge), R
,, Alice, 90, 265
,, Ann, 27, 83, 270
,, Elizabeth, 151, 231, 247
,, Ellen, 22, 98, 158
,, Henry, 281
,, Isabel, 243
,, James, 52, 93, 98, 100, 112, 118, 219, 234
,, John, 34, 63, 83, 90, 112, 161, 177, 247
,, Katherin, 55, 284
,, Loare, 19
,, Margaret, 209, 257
,, Richard, 100, 234
,, Robert, 19, 22, 27, 37, 158, 161, 245, 260, 280
,, Roger, 52, 55, c. of 58, 63, 93, c. of 192, 205, 219, 269
,, Rowland, 37, 86, 216
,, Silvester, 118
,, William, 86, 143, 151, 200, 231, 243, 277

*Christenings* . . . . . . .
*Burials* . . . . . . . . .
*Marriages* . . . . . .

Rothwell—*Continued.*
,, James, 109, 116
,, John, 218
,, Margaret, 109, 116
,, Robert, 116, 121, 128, 286
Roughley, Thomas, 203*
Rowe (Rowes), see also Rose,
,, Elin, 146
,, Peter, c. of 188, c. of 215
Rowley, Thomas, 106, 282
,, William, 106
Rozaway (Rosheye), Abraham, 114
,, Homfray, 268
,, Sarah, 114, 239
Runckehorne, John, 277
Rutter (Ruter Ruttere, Rutters),
,, Ann, 259, 269
,, Elizabeth, 11, 57, 112, 142, 279
,, Ellen, 64
,, Henry, 102
,, James, 133
Jane, 140, 152, 257
,, Jo: 39, 57, 68
,, John, 39, 64, 102, 112, c. of 188, 248, 276
,, Margaret, 96, 263
,, Margery, 201, 271
,, Richard, 256
,, Robert, 8, 68, 223
,, Roger, 96
,, Sislie, 258
,, Thomas, 12, 146, 152, 175
Ryanson, Edmund, 17
,, Elizabeth, 17
Ryce (Ryesse, Ryse), Katherin, 268
,, Margaret, 275
,, Margery, 258
Rycroft (Rycrofte), Elizabeth, 60, 191
,, Ewan, 57
,, William, 57, 60, 191
Ryc[d]son, see Richardson
Rydde, Margaret, 253
Ryding, Rydinge, Rydinges, Rydynge,
see Riding
Ryesse, see Ryce
Rylands (Rilans, Rylance, Rylandes, Rylanes, Rylans, Rylanse, Rylons, Ryylanes),
,, Edward, 127, 287
,, Elizabeth, 34, 158, 221
,, Frances, 20, 149
,, Lawrence, 227
,, Mary, 65
,, Robert, 20, 34, 127, 149, 190, 255, 264
,, Thomas, 4, 65
,, William, 9, 141

. . pp. *1—128 inclusive.*
. . „ *129—252* „
. . „ *253—288* „

Scarisbrick—*Continued.*
„ Frances, 33, 45, 194
„ Gabriel, 39, 45, 55, 164, 181
„ George, 33, 72, 102, 180
„ Gilbert, 28, 37, 52, 89, 93, 229, 246
„ Gowther, 180
„ Grace, 92
„ Henry, 38, 80, 82,* 88, 92, 96, 99, 106, 112, 114, 122, 128, 167, 213, 221, c. of 227, 276, 281
„ Hugh, 42, 82, 89, 102, 109, 115, 164, 214, 267, 287
„ Humphrey, 55, 104, 123, 125
„ Izabell, 41, 131, 139, 167, 171, 180, 255
„ Ja: 33, 58, 131
„ James, 72, 82, 114, 134, 135, 249, 268
„ Jane, 4, 29, 31, 37,* 104, 158, 162, 174, 177, 190, 198, 238, 254, 256, 275
„ Jenet, 130, 182, 228
„ Jo: 42
„ John, 19, 106, 109, 114, 125, 127, 206, 235, 280
„ Judith, 98, 250
„ Katherin, 35, 72, 88, 170, 202, 256, 258, 269*
„ Margaret, 8, 20, 24, 58, 96, 136, 142, 165, 190, 197, 221, 249, 265
„ Margery, 7, 180, 265
„ Mary, 26, 45, 105, 115, 125, 128, 172, 249
„ Maud, 205
„ Mhill [Michael], c. of 183
„ Mr., 18, 20, 23, 82, 88, 92, 154, 178, 180, 191, 198, 199, 202,* 203, 205, 207,* 208, 209, 213, 216, 218, 225, 226, 232, 233,* 238,* 240, 243, 250, 251*
„ Mrs., 165, 198, 205, 214
„ Miles, 151
„ Nicholas, 212
„ Peregrina, 100
„ Peter, 1, 28, 31, 99, 154, 155, 156, 164
„ Richard, 165, 174
„ Robert, 105
„ Roger, 4, 45, 99, 133, 167, 176, 226, 250, 254, 256, 277, 286
„ Thomas, 5, 24, 28, 34, 41, 45, 48, 52, 79, 80, 82, 89, 92, 98, 105, 127, 153, 154, 207, 208, 259, 282

*Christenings* . . . . . . .
*Burials* . . . . . . . .
*Marriages* . . . . . . .

Scarisbrick—*Continued.*
,, William, 37, 38, 43, 45, 82, 103, 156, 158, 221, 234, 261, 264
Scath, Elizabeth, 256
,, James, 112
,, Ralph, 112, 237
Scersbreke, see Scarisbrick
Scoefeild, see Scotfeild
Scofelt, Ellen, 117, 246
,, John, 117, 126
,, Margaret, 126
Scotfeild (Scoefeild), Alexander, 111
,, John, 111
Scott, Jane, 243
,, Jenet, 178
,, Mrs., 178
Seale (Sele), Elizabeth, 9
,, Ellen, 180
,, Henry, 6
,, Jane, 258
,, Jo: 67
,, John, 180, 270
,, Thomas, 5, 67, 136
,, William, 3, 135
Seale *alias* Duncon, (Seall *alias* Duncon),
,, John, 217
,, Thomas, 257
Seddon (Sedon, Sedone),
,, Elizabeth, 259
,, Ellen, 257
,, John, 115, 122, c. of 252, 284
,, Margery, 172
,, Robert, 122
,, Thomas, 115
Sefton (Sephton), Ann, 109,* 117
,, Brichet, 202
,, Daniel, 283
,, Edmund, 73, 76, 81, 90, 222, 223
,, Edward, 207
,, Elizabeth, 17, 103, 151
,, Ellen, 37, 73, 95, 167, 173, 223
,, Emline, 144, 230
,, George, 19, 23, 25, 32, 37, 49, 117, 152, 158, 203, 259
,, Gilbert, 15, 65, 67, 276
,, Henry, 76, 77
,, Hugh, 19, 94, 106, 279
,, Jane, 38, 128, 249, 274, 278
,, John, 32, 80, 81, 158, 202, 223, 275
,, Margaret, 94, 151, 219
,, Margery, 182
,, Mary, 49, 73, 78, 90, 277, 288

*Christenings* . . . . . . . . . *pp.* *1—128 inclusive.*
*Burials* . . . . . . . . . . ,, *129—252* ,,
*Marriages* . . . . . . . . . ,, *253—288* ,,

aw—*Continued.*
,, Ellen, 9,* 54, 75, 96, 104, 116,* 141, 203, 225, 241, 285
,, Emie, 74
,, Emlin, 188
,, Gabriel, 55, 69, 79, 128, 205
,, George, 71, 75, c. of 207
,, Gilbert, 146
,, Grace, 7
,, Henry, 23, 28, 190
,, Hugh, 29, 59, 98, 137, 190, 244,* 263
,, James, 13, 21, 43, 143, 145, 184
,, Jane, 81, 82, 171, 215, 230, 247
,, Jenet, 90, 216, 243
,, Jo: 26, 39, 188
,, John, 29, 48, 93, 97,* 104,* 111, 122, 124, 135, 218, 219, 241, c. of 242, 261, 279, 282, 285
,, Johne, 4
,, Katherin, 200
,, Margaret, 16, 26, 47, 79, 81, 90, 126, 172, 174, 190, 216, 268, 271, 272, 274
,, Margery, 201
,, Mary, 69, 121
,, Nicholas, 35, 81, 85, 90, 95, 98, 161, 191, c. of 210, 216*
,, N.X.N., 229
,, Peter, 82, 111, 133, w. of 142, 148, 154, 215, 222, 234, 257, 270
,, Ralph, 176
,, Richard, 30, 39, 43, 96, 104, 107, 114, 127,* 131, 226, 230, 281
,, Robert, 4, 12, 21, 24, 96, 136, 151, 152, w. of 190, 197, 223, 257, 262, 263, 273
,, Roger, 20, 43, 93, 151, 201, 206, 216, 219, 255
,, Silvester, 20, 64
,, Thomas, 1, 4, 11, 31, 43, 45, 55, 74, 114, 116, 121, 122, 126, 135, 138, 142, 165, 205, 243, 267
,, Widow, 192
,, William, 4, 5, 27, 28, 35, 45, 47, 48, 54, 59, 64, 95, 96, 116, 121,* 129, 136, 138, 144, 164, 247, 248, 262, 284
he, see Shaw
heal als Dunkon, Jo: 62
,, William, 62

Sheill (Shell), Elizabeth, 269
,, Emlin, 228
,, John, 260
Shelton, Marie, 280
,, William, 133
Sheppard (Shepard, Sheparde, Shepert, Sheperte, Sheporđ, Sheppord),
,, Alice, 138, 257, 263
,, Elizabeth, 7, 270
,, Henry, 63, 66, 78, 99, 196
,, James, 105, 141
,, Jane, 176, 258
,, Jenet, 94
,, John, 63
,, Margery, 164
,, Mary, 66, 196
,, Roger, 99
,, William, 78, 94, 105
Sherringeton (Shervingeton, Shervington, Shirvingeton),
,, Christopher, w. of 129, 151
,, John, 140
,, Margaret, 184
,, Margery, 174
Shirdley, Margery, 261
Shires (Shyres), Henry, 102, 229
,, James, 95, 98, 221
,, Margery, 106
,, Richard, 95, 98, 102, 106, 221, 279
Shirvingeton, see Sherringeton
Shorlakers, Shorlicars, Shorlikares, Shorliker, Shorlikers, Shorlokars, Shorloker, Shorlokers,
see Shurlicars and Herlickers
Showe, see Shaw
Showen *alias* Price, John, 140
Shurlicars (Shorlakers, Shorlicars, Shorlikares, Shorliker, Shorlikers, Shorlokars, Shorloker, Shorlokers, Shurlacars, Shurlecars, Shurlokars, Shurlekers, Shurlikar, Shurlikars, Shurliker),
see also Herlickers,
,, Alexander, 53, 125, 223
,, Alice, 141
,, Ann, 176
,, Edmund, 141
,, Elizabeth, 174, 254, 264
,, Ellen, 35
,, Genet, 259

*Christenings* . . . . . . . . . . *pp.* *1—128 inclusive.*
*Burials* . . . . . . . . . . ,, *129—252* ,,
*Marriages* . . . . . . . . . . ,, *253—288* ,,

*Christenings* . . . . . . .
*Burials* . . . . . . . . .
*Marriages* . . . . . . . .

Sounse, Elizabeth, 141
Sowerbutts (Sourbutts, Sowerbutes, Sowerbuts, Sowrbutts),
,, Alice, 126, 251
,, Ann, 95
,, Emlin, 100
,, Joanie, 91, 217
,, John, 91, 94, 95, 97, 100, 115, 126, 219, c. of 225, c. of 231, c. of 233, 280
,, Katherin, 97
,, Richard, 94, 115, 219
Sowter, Richard, 251
Sowthwork, see Soothworth
Speakeman (Spackeman, Spackman, Spakem, Spakeman, Spakman),
,, Elizabeth, 203, 262
,, Ellen, 243
,, Henry, 84, 149
,, John, 72
,, Margaret, 84, 154, 173
,, Peter, 168, 262
,, Richard, 43, 72, 203, 233, 265
,, William, 43
Specer, see also Spencer,
,, Edmund, 175
,, Peter, 270
Spencer (Spenser), see also Specer,
,, Alice, 25, 33, 67, 247, 284
,, Ann, 106, 121, 242
,, Dorothy, 271
,, Edith, 108
,, Edmund, 150, 255
,, Edward, 65, 69, 97, 108, 116, 224, 272, 282
,, Elizabeth, 61, 82,* 91, 154, 170, 206, 261, 273, 282
,, Ellen, 99, 247, 256, 263, 272, 283
,, Emlin, 86
,, Frances, 62, 212
,, Hamlet, 150
,, Henry, 54, 56, 105, 247
,, Hugh, 38, 70, 84, 90, 94, 99, 108, 130
,, Isabel, 255
,, Ja: 33, 68, 91
,, James, 29, 65, 82, 87, 94, 97, 104, 111, 114, w. of 133, 135, 164, 224, 256, 268
,, Jane, 38, 87,* 89, 165
,, Jenet, 25, 68, 102, 229, 237, 276
,, Jo: 29, 33, 54
,, Joan, 165

*Christenings* . . . . . . . . . . *pp.* *1—128 inclusive.*
*Burials* . . . . . . . . . . . ,, *129—252* ,,
*Marriages* . . . . . . . . . . ,, *253—288* ,,


Stanley—*Continued.*
,, Dame, 166
,, Denize, 145
,, Dorothie, 49, 72, 130, 225
,, Edward, 31, 60, 62, 66, 69, 71,* 98, 104, 107, 111, 115, 119, 121, 180, c. of 188, 190, 201, 205, 206, 209, 216, 224, 226
,, Elizabeth, 69, 93, 137, 201, 213
,, Emaniwell, 91, 217
,, Fardinand, 101
,, Frances, 71
,, Francis, 121, 167
,, George, 91, 93, 98, 101, 149, 217, 226, 240, 243, 262, 279
,, Henry, 31, 46, 49, 71, 107, 180, 196, 204, 257
,, Isabel, 166
,, James, 77, 111, 236
,, Jane, 83, 271
,, Je: 166
,, John, 119, 266, 271
,, Katherin, 180, 209, 224, 243, 269
,, Ladie Dorothie, 130
,, Lady Elizabeth, 213
,, Margaret, 62, 77, 93,* 190, 223, 251, 257
,, Mary, 259, 268
,, Mr., 71, 84, 104, 167, 180, c. of 188, 201, 204, 205, 208, 209,* 216, 236, 244, 248
,, Mrs., 137, 147, 180, 223, 224, 257, 259
,, Peter, 57, 147, 184
,, Ralph, 208
,, Richard, 84, 171
,, Robert, 115
,, Roger, 152
,, Sir, 145, 149, 206
,, Sislie, 147
,, Thomas, 84, 104, 208, 209, 236, 268
,, William, 12, 57, 72, 77,* 83, 93, 101, 193, 209, 243
Stannanought, see Stananought
Stanton (Stonton), Catherin, 25
,, Ellen, 258
,, Isabel, 188, 262
,, Ja: 24
,, John, 173
,, N.X.N., 14
,, Roger, 24
Stanynought, see Stananought
Starkey, Anne, 265
Steele, Ann, 108, 245
,, George, 108, 113, 121, 233, 284
,, James, 95,* 220, c. of 233
,, Jane, 113
,, Margaret, 233
,, Mary, 121
,, Richard, 246
Stevenson (Steenson, Stivenson),
,, Alice, 272
,, Ann, 113
,, Edward, 257
,, Henry, 113
Stonton, see Stanton
Stopford (Spopford, Stopforth, Stopforthe, Stophford),
,, Alice, 57, 128, 133, 189, 212, 239, 281
,, Anne, 80, 103,* 115, 120, 135, 170, 257
,, Ciceley, 237
,, Claris, 75, 211
,, Edward, 28
,, Elizabeth, 150, 151, 177, 181, 195, 212, 262
,, Ellen, 18, 124
,, George, 28, 154, 166, 193, 237, 262
,, Grace, 161
,, Henry, 40, 45, 57, 65, 70, 75, 80, 126, 145, 162, 202, 205, 211, 228, 240, 267
,, Hugh, 92, 113
,, James, 17, 65, 115, 124, 187, 223
,, Jane, 78, 110, 117, 123, 206, 228
,, Jenet, 184
,, Joan, 170
,, John, 23, 120, 150, 151, 174, 178, 179, 282
,, Katherin, 70, 113, 175, 204, 257
,, Margaret, 45, 92, 112, 120, 145, 228, 263, 267, 277
,, Margery, 186, 235
,, Martha, 237
,, Mary, 286
,, N.X.N., 239
,, Peter, 109, 117
,, Ralph, 23, 151, 243
,, Richard, 122, 154, 164, 245, 254
,, Robert, 177, c. of 215
,, Roger, 123
,, Thomas, 37, 40, 44, 94,* 103, 109, 112, 120, 126, 131, 133, 151, 162, 195, 198, 205, 239, 277, 279, 284

*Christenings* . . . . . . .
*Burials* . . . . . . . .
*Marriages* . . . . . . .


Stopford—*Continued.*
,, William, 17, 37, 44, 78, 103, 110, 116,* 122, 128, 162, 193, 224
Strange, Ann, 47
,, Isabel, 51
,, Miles, 47, 51
Streete, George, 102
,, Richard, 102
Streethey, Margery, 282
Streyker, see Stryker
Strongarme, Thomas, 240
Stryker (Streyker), Dorothy, 62
,, Jane, 69
,, Mary, 232
,, Michael (Micall), 62, 203
,, Myhell [Michael], 58, 69
,, Richard, 58, 203
Sturbacre, Philip, 105
,, Robert, 105
Styam (Styham, Styhan, Styhom),
,, Arthur, 25, 196
,, Jo: 21, 25
,, Joan, 31
,, John, 14, 17, 21, 258
,, Margaret, 17
Such, Suche, see Sutch
Sulbie, Ranould, 149
,, William, 149
Sumner (Somner, Soomner, Sumpner, Symner),
,, Alexander, 28, 81, 93, 280
,, Alice, 12, 55, 75, 208, 264
,, Amery, 226
,, Ann, 25, 76, 81, 210, 259
,, Christopher, 19, 113, 139, 209
,, Claris, 284
,, Cycely, 113, 238
,, Edward, 14, 20, 66, 70, 75,* 81
,, Elizabeth, 43, 90, 205
,, Elis, 269, 279, 282
,, Ellen, 2, 11, 45, 81, 87, 112, 129, 213, 214, 257, 279
,, Emlin, 38
,, Gilbert, 20, 23, 34, 71, 75, 86, 99, 129, 174, 257
,, Henry, 16
,, Hugh, 33, 45, 55, 117, 127, 214, 286
,, Isabel, 19, 113
,, James, 33, 86, 112, 167, 284
,, Jane, 83
,, Jenet, 9, 258, 264, 270
,, Jo: 19, 28, 38, 43
,, John, 33, 40, 70, 90, 95, 99, 106, 113, 117, 161, 205, 206, c. of 227, 256

*Christenings* . . . . . . . . . . *pp.* 1—128 *inclusive.*
*Burials* . . . . . . . . . . . . ,, 129—252 ,,
*Marriages* . . . . . . . . . . . ,, 253—288 ,,

Sutch—*Continued.*
,, John, 15, 29, 51, 59,* 74, 80, 85, 145, 146, 156, 157, 158, 187, 213, 220, 252, 270
,, Jonie, 226
,, Katherin, 13, 71, 184, 193, 259, 278
,, Lucie, 34
,, Luke, 18, 22, 187, 226, 256
,, Margaret, 22, 26, 27, 30, 46, 51, 67, 95, 150, 155, 163, 173, 192, 257, 279, 280
,, Margerie, 60, 162, 165, 178, 187, 256, 272, 286
,, Martha, 232
,, Mary, 75, 80, 98, 103, 231
,, Peter, 32, 102, 105, 116, 124, 230
,, Ralph, 52
,, Richard, 74, 80, 87, 190
,, Robert, 3, 62
,, Roger, 7, 15, 43, c. of 62, 62, 64, 68, 75, 84, 87, w. of 141, 145, 153, 196
,, Sibell, 181
,, Silvester, 41, 72, 76, 80, 89, c. of 213, 215, 216, 274
,, Sislie, 254
,, Thomas, 41, 46, 64,* 72, 81, 87, 96, 105, 111, 115, 116, "theldest" 133, 185, 214, 228, 249, 265, 270, 276, 277
,, William, 10, 26, 58, 64, 75, 81, 99, 124, c. of 183, 185, two children of 188, 193, 255, 272, 288
Suthe, see Sutch
Suthwort, see Soothworth
Sutton (Svtton), Edward, 263
,, Elizabeth, 54, 285
,, Frances, 216
,, Francis, 83
,, George, 31
,, Gilbert, 78, 212
,, Hector, w. of 147, 148, 156
,, Henry, 127
,, Ja: 27
,, James, 262, 269
,, Jane, 73, 103, 186, 216, 239
,, John, 34, 99, 103, 112, 118, 127, 281
,, Margaret, 30, 118, 153, 199
,, Margery, 25, 40, 148, 163, 255, 263
,, Mary, 281
,, Richard, 58, 112
Sutton—*Continued.*
,, Robert, 28, 70, 73, 78, 83, 216,* 274
,, Thomas, 27, 28, 34, 40, 70, 99, 129, 196, 227, 262
,, William, 54, 58, c. of 199, 239, 241
Svmner, see Sumner
Svtch, see Sutch
Svtton, see Sutton
Swabricke, Elizabeth, 124
Swift (Swifte, Swyft, Swyfte),
,, Alice, 22, 41, 58, 168, 187, 255, 264
,, Ann, 54, 98, 152, 225, 267
,, Annes, 270
,, Bryham, 15, 157
,, Christopher, 6, 156
,, Cisley, 121, 124, 244
,, Claris, 219
,, Edmund, 210
,, Edward, 121, 128, 244
,, Elizabeth, 7, 40, 58, 82, 138, 163, 176, 179, 188, 209, 278, 284
,, Ellen, 45, 70, 153, 173, 276, 278, 283
,, Ellis, 32, 199
,, Ewan, 22, 45, 63, 72, 105,* 110, 116,* 119, 121, 123, 124,* 175, 241, 249, 260, 268, 281, 286
,, George, 6, 47, 118, 137, 196
,, Gilbert, 76, 227
,, Henry, 24, 53, 100, 105, 109, 118, 124, 127, 153
,, Hugh, 41, 72, 80, 111, 123
,, Humphrey, 44, 49, 265
,, Izabell, 64, 121, 139, 267
,, Ja: 19, 24, 153
,, James, 13, 33, 54, 72, 74, 76, 80, 82, 86, 87,* 92, 93, 98, 105,* 123, 153, 188, 227, 255, 273
,, Jane, 61, 106, 166, 186, 192, 197, 217, 231, 237, 239
,, Jo: 22, 35, 51, 55, 58, 63, 68
,, John, 5, 9, 15, 18, 22, 32, 72 77,* 88, 111, 124, 133, 135, 137, 163, 168,* 170, 185, 188, 236
,, Katherin, 41, 88, 92, 109, 110, 121, 209, 244, 254, 261
,, Lionell, 18, 35, 106, 110, 119, 121, 123, 128, 141, 179, 208, 282

*Christenings* . . . . . . .
*Burials* . . . . . . .
*Marriages* . . . . . . .

Swift—*Continued.*
,, Margaret, 14, 22, 49, 55, 93, 100, 105, 107, 116, 165, 178, 230, 239, 262, 274
,, Margery, 153, 209, 276
,, Mary, 178
,, Micell, 50
,, Myles, 49
,, N.X.N., 2
,, Nicolas, 58, 63
,, Oliver, 49
,, Peeter, 220
,, Philip, 70, 73, 77, 83, 126, 192, 204, 240, 261, 273
,, Richard, 15, 19, 22,* 51, 64, 68, 107, 110, 111, 116, 121, 124, 128,* 175, 221, 252, 260, 264, 269
,, Roase, 164
,, Robert, 33, 41 47, 86, 124, 179
,, Thomas, 22, 50, 73, 83, 105, 114,* 118, 134, 151, 152, 156, 165, 186, 204, 209, c. of 214, 221, 246, 263
,, Threstram, 139
,, Trayamore, 267
,, Trymer, 127
,, Trymour, 217
,, Trymower, 218
,, William, 22, 44, 47, 49, 53, 61, 63, 74, 77, 111, 118, 126, 138, 192, 267, 279, 280, 286
Sworton, see Sorton
Swyft, Swyfte, see Swift
Symcocke, John, 281
Symkin, see Simkin
Symond, Alice, 140

T

TABERNER, Ann, 241
Talier, Talior, see Taylor
Talior *alias* Ball, Margery, 138
Talylior, Talyor, see Taylor
Tandanoughte, see Stananought
Tarbocke (Torbocke), Ann, 60
,, Edward, 274
,, Elizabeth, 107
,, Jane, 218
,, Jo: 60
,, Robert, 218, 278
,, Thomas, 107
Tarbut, Elizabeth, 148
Tarior, see also Tayrare,
,, Loare, 201,

*Christenings . . . . . . . . . pp. 1—128 inclusive.*
*Burials . . . . . . . . . . „ 129—252 „*
*Marriages . . . . . . . . . „ 253—288 „*

aylor—*Continued.*
„ Richard, 8, 60, 68, 78, 88, 94,* 103, 118, 203, 274
„ Robert, 37, 42, 47, 53, 61, 189, 265
„ Sislie, 5, 170
„ Thomas, 33, 60, 107, 118, 125
„ William, 12, 23, 78,* 93, 94, 104. 113, 121, 185, c. of 220, 248
Tayrare, see also Tarior and Tyrer,
„ Gilbert, 42
„ Symonde, 42
Thackerow (Thakarowe),
„ Alexander, 255
„ Ellen, 3
Tho:daughter, Elizabeth, 130
„ Jane, 261
Thomason als Higginson, James, 288
Thompson (Thomasson, Thomson, Tompson, Tomson, Tumson),
„ Adam, 284
„ Agnes, 255
„ Alexander, 191, 267
„ Alice, 80, 202, 228, 259
„ Anne 40, 170, 171
„ Edeithe, 267
„ Ellen, 85, 105, 231, 241
„ Ferdinand, 67, 201
„ Hugh, 202, 209
„ Humphrey, 75
„ Ja: 40
„ James, 80
„ Jane, 75, 165, 202, 204, 212, 242
„ Jenet, 148, 260
„ Jo: 48, 67, 148
„ John, 44, 70, 75, 77, 105, 201, 204, 212, 215, 231
„ Katherin, 70
„ Margaret, 44, 77, 164
„ Margery, 197
„ Richard, 64, 192
„ Roger, w. of 144, 260
„ Thomas, 80
„ Thurstan, 244
„ William, 48, 64, 75, 80, 85, 192, 202, 228, 271, 273, 275
Thornall, see also Thorne,
„ Edward, 228
„ Elizabeth, 98
„ Gabriel, 86, 212
„ Robert, 98, 104
„ Susan, 104, 236
„ Thomas, 86, 212
Thorne (Thornow), see also Thornall,
„ Gabriel, 73
„ Mary, 79
„ Thomas, 73, 79, 275
Thornton (Thorneton, Thorton),
„ Alice, 285
„ Ann, 6, 112 259
„ Cuthbert, 95
„ Edward, 100
„ Elizabeth, 235
„ Ellen, 93, 107, 234
„ Gabriel, 251
„ Jane, 250
„ John, 92, 255
„ Katherin, 110
„ Margaret, 104
„ Mary, 251
„ Robert, 93, 95, 104, 110, 112, 120, 250, 251
„ Susan, 120, 236, 244
„ Thomas, 92, 100, 167
„ Thurstan, 107
Thorpe, Thomas, 264
Thorston, Hugh, 270
Thorton, see Thornton
Threlfall, Alice, 288
Thrope (Throppe), George, 125, 250
„ Hugh, 105, 108, 125, c. of 241
„ Jane, 108
„ Myles, 105, 231
„ Thomas, 264
Tireyer, see Tyrer
Tobie, Elizabeth, 202
„ Richard, 202, 212
Tockholes (Tockeholes, Toccoles),
„ Ann, 253
„ Ellen, 256
„ Margaret, 255
Todd (Todde), Henry, 51, 177
„ William, 51
Tomes, Jenet, 142
Tomlinson, Anne, 119
„ James, 127
„ Richard, 119
„ Roger, 127
„ Thomas, 246
Tompson, Tomson, see Thompson
Topping (Toppinge),
„ Alice, 79, 265, 287
„ Ann, 119, 234, 242, 274
„ Ellen, 72, 132, 179
„ Elloner, 211
„ Henry, 87, 103, 236
„ Hugh, 79
„ Humphrey, 72, 75, 79, 87, 95, 206, 238, 274

*Christenings* . . . . . . . . . . *pp.* 1—128 *inclusive.*
*Burials* . . . . . . . . . . ,, 129—252 ,,
*Marriages* . . . . . . . . . . ,, 253—288 ,,

Topping—*Continued.*
,, James, 105, 126, 231
,, Jo: 22
,, John, 14, 74, 79, 145, 151, 211
,, Margaret, 13, 121, 142
,, Mary, 75, 206, 288
,, Ralph, 103, 105, 113, 119, 121, 126, 236
,, Robert, 202
,, Thomas, 22, 74, 151, 175
,, William, 95, 113, 132, 157
Torbocke, see Tarbocke
Towne, see also Taune,
,, Alice, 79, 249
,, Ann, 145
,, Annes, 15
,, Ellen, 277
,, Humphrey, 11, 142
,, James, 72, 208
,, John, 184
,, Richard, 4, 147
,, Robert, 72, 79, 239, 274
,, Simon, 131, 192
,, William, 147, 229
Townley, James, 110
,, Maud, 188
,, William, 110
Towson, Thomas, 34
Traves (Travas, Traveise, Trves),
,, Anne, 66, 84, 192, 215, 246, 267
,, Brian, 78
,, Catherine, 23, 39, 91
,, Elizabeth, 98, 206
,, Ellen, 173, 183
,, Ewan, 178
,, George, 13
,, Henry, 23, 39, 206
,, Humphrey, 74
,, Jane, 43, 78, 267
,, John, 70, 78, 141, 164
,, Margaret, 70, 189, 199, 230, 272
,, N.X.N., 9
,, Richard, 36, 43, 96, 192, 210, 215, 222
,, Thomas, 66, 78
,, William, 8, 36, 74, 78, 84, 91, 96, 98, 139, 222, 230
Ttyem (*sic*), Jo: 152
,, John, 152
Tumson, see Thompson
Tuner, Ja: 22
,, Thomas, 22
Tunstall (Tunstual), Elizabeth, 278
,, Ellen, 196
,, Gowther, 22, 258
,, Silvester, 22
Turnebridge, Hugh, 185
Turner (Turnere), Elizabeth, 63,
,, Ellen, 73, 286
,, Hugh, 59
,, Humphrey, 56, 59, 63, 73, 241
,, Ja: 26
,, James, 260
,, John, 125,* 127
,, Robert, 127
,, Simon, 56, 183
,, William, 26
Tuson, Elizabeth, 90
,, Ellen, 80
,, Hamlet, 31
,, John 80, 86, 90, 96, 101, 276
,, Katherin, 101
,, Margaret, 86, 245
,, Richard, 80, 221
,, Thomas, 96
Tyldsley, Anne, 125
,, Gilbert, 125
Tyrer (Tireyer), see also Tarior a Tayrere,
,, Alice, 274
,, Anne, 83
,, Cisley, 107
,, Elizabeth, 75, 113, 249, 278
,, Ellen, 24, 79
,, George, 50
,, Gilbert, 55, 181
,, Henry, 98
,, James, 75, 79, 83, 88, 99, 216, 226, 277, 282
,, Jane, 103
,, John, 196
,, Mary, 99, 226
,, Mawde, 60
,, Richard, 79*
,, Robert, 98, 103, 107, 113
,, William, 50, 55, 60, 88, 216
Tysinge, John, 255

U

[Unsworth], see Hunsworth

V

Vace, see Vauce
Vackeffeeld, see Wackefeeld
Vallentyne, William, 244
Vauce (Vace, Voce), Adam, 88
,, Alice, 30, 44, 63, 100, 121, 179, 209, 226

*Christenings* . . . . . . . . . *pp.* *1—128 inclusive.*
*Burials* . . . . . . . . . . ,, *129—252* ,,
*Marriages* . . . . . . . . . . ,, *253—288* ,,

ace—*Continued.*
,, Ann, 94
,, Catherine, 32, 277, 285
,, Claris, 178
,, Elizabeth, 116, 215
,, Emlin, 35
,, Gilbert, 35, 39, 44, 48, 94, 215, 240, 279
Henry, 54, 62, 179
,, Hugh, 58, 63, 68, 70, 81, 85, 91, 98*
,, Isabel, 118
,, Jane, 54, 70
,, Jenet, 48, 177
,, John, 47, 68, 88, 94, 100, 108, 118, 127,* 278
,, Margaret, 68, 85
,, Margery, 108
,, Mary, 81
,, Peter, 54, 60, 91, 116, 121, 127, 179, 226, 269
,, Richard, 47, 54, 58, 60, 62, 68, c. of 193, c. of 203, 226, 240, 268, 271
,, Thomas, 39, 94, 127
Vaudrie (Vaudry), John, 116, 121
,, Margaret, 121
,, Richard, 116
Veale, Edward, 147
,, Frances, 147 (m)
,, Jenet, 14, 145
,, Margaret, 146
,, Mr., 147
,, Mrs., 146
Verguse, John, 163
Vlster, Denis, 206
Voce, see Vauce
Vrmston (Vrmeston, Vrmiston),
,, Alice, 23
,, Elizabeth, 176, 217, 286
,, Lyonell, 23, 164, 261
,, Margery, 144

W

Wa: (*sic*), Jane, 12
Wackefeeld (Vackeffeeld, Wackfeild),
,, George, 247
,, Gilbert, 40
,, Hugh, 40
,, Jane, 187
,, Peter, 40
,, Robert, 187
Wackenson, see Watkinson
Wadington (Wadingeton),
,, Edward, 40
,, Fardinando, 62
,, James, 43
,, Jenet, 58
,, John, 51, 176
,, Margaret, 269
,, Mary, 53
,, Thomas, 48
,, William, 40, 43, 48, 51, 53, 58, 62, 199
Wailch, see Walsh
Wainwright (Waineright, Wainewright, Wainwrighte, Waynewright, Waynwrigh, Waynwright),
,, Adam, 14
,, Alice, 19, 182, 241, 277
,, Ann, 6, 15, 27, 89, 104, 124, 171, 172,* 254
,, Bartholomew, 2
,, Claris, 164
,, Edward, 117, 240, 245
,, Elizabeth, 10, 85, 150, 166, 267
,, Ellen, 14, 23, 149, 150, 152, 244, 280
,, Ellis, 28
,, Elloner, 280
,, Ewan, 27, 28, 144, 155, 226
,, G: 23
,, George, 9, 37, 79, 140, 150, 173, 180, 182, 186, 198, 207, 263, 265
,, Gilbert, 177
,, Grace, 22, 212
,, Henry, 64, 120, 124, 128, 150, 159, 247, 285, 287
,, Hugh, 45, 64, 227
,, Humphrey, 32, 159
,, Isabel, 78
,, Ja: 47
,, James, 27, 37, 96, 214, 269
,, Jane, 21, 35, 47, 48, 122, 174
,, Jenet, 30, 58
,, Jo: 32
,, John, 5, 43, 104, 109, 115, 122, 144, 281
,, Jonie, 186
,, Joseph, 121
,, Katherin, 10, 37, 105, 109, 150, 165, 180, 268, 273,* 278
,, Margaret, 39, 56, 92, 100, 171, 218, 227, 285
,, Margery, 2, 64, 182, 254
,, Marie, 45, 129
,, Peter, 11, 47, 124

*Christenings* . . . . . . . . . . *pp.* *1—128 inclusive.*
*Burials* . . . . . . . . . . . ,, *129—252* ,,
*Marriages* . . . . . . . . . . ,, *253—288* ,,

Wainwright,—*Continued.*
,, Ranould, 111, 147, 255
,, Richard, 16, 58, 79, 81, 92,* 117, 209, 216, 251
,, Sara, 120, 276
,, Sislie, 18, 180
,, Sy: 56, 64
,, Symon, 46, 78
,, Thomas, 19, 21, 26, 37, 39, 43, 46, 48, 81, 85, 89, 92, 96, 100, 105, 111, 115, 117,* 121, 124, 128, 142, 149, 150, 198, 209, 218, 236, 252, 257, 265, 275
,, William, 18, 22, 24, 26, 46,* 47, 155, 172, 180, 189, 254, 263, 267
Waiworth, see also Walworth,
,, Edward, 20
,, Richard, 20
Wakker, see Walker
Walas, see Wallis
Walcar, see Walker
Walche, see Walsh
Walener, Waliner, see Walliner
Walison, John, 16
Walker (Wakker, Walcar, Walkar, Walkare),
,, Alice, 176
,, Ann, 9, 47, 90, 177, 216, 264
,, Edmund, 51, 95, 169, 246, 280
,, Elizabeth, 254
,, Ellen, 112, 246
,, Gabriel, 38, 84, 89, 95, 100, 112, 122, c. of 234, 277
,, George, 81, 90, 97, 209, 216, 224
,, Henry, 100
,, Jane, 231
,, Jo: 35
,, John, 35, 89
,, Katherin, 81, 209, 244
,, Margaret, 163
,, Richard, 38, 47, 51, 84, 245, 250, 265
,, William, 2, 97, 122, 224
Wallas, see Wallis
Wallen (Wallne, Walne), see also Wollen,
,, Agnes, 171
,, Elizabeth, 207
,, Henry, 67, 207, 273
,, Hugh, 44, 89
,, Jane, 89
,, Jo: 44
,, John, 141, 171, 266
,, Richard, 67
Wallener, see Walliner
Walles, see Wallis
Walley, see Whalley
Wallice, see Wallisy
Walliner (Walener, Waliner, Wallener), Alice, 82
,, Edward, 155
,, Humphrey, 82
,, Margaret, 28, 269
,, Margery, 25, 212
,, Mary, 238
,, Thomas, 28
Wallis (Walas, Wallas, Walles, Wallice, Whalese), and see Wlles,
,, Alice, 93, 144, 272
,, Ellen, 120
,, Hector, 41, 83, 86, 88, 93, 10 110, 114, 120, 125, 144, 21 277
,, Henry, 114
,, Jane, 88, 208
,, John, 101, 130, 234
,, Katherin, 86, 213
,, Margaret, 3
,, Robert, 125
,, Thomas, 41, 83, 186, 266
,, William, 110
Wallne, see Wallen
Wallworth, see Walworth
Walmsley, Richard, 245
Walne, see Wallen
Walsh (Wailch, Walche, Walshe, Welsh, Welshe, Weltch, Weltche),
,, Ann, 27, 63
,, Cuthbert, 73
,, Edward, 121
,, Elizabeth, 266
,, Gilbert, 58, 63, 68, 73, 80, 8 201, 270
,, Jenet, 27, 128
,, John, 117, 121, 266, 285
,, Margaret, 24, 228
,, Mary, 128
,, Richard, 128
,, Robert, 80, 117, 240
,, Roger, 68, 201
,, Silvester, 58, 189
,, Thomas, 86, 128
,, William, 260
Walthew (Waltheu, Walthewe),
,, James, 49
,, John, 40
,, Katherin, 284
,, Margaret, 281

. . . *pp.* *1—128* *inclusive.*
. . . ,, *129—252* ,,
. . . ,, *253—288*


Wariner—*Continued.*
,, Ellen, 23
,, Emlin, 152
,, Margaret, 141
,, Thomas, 23, 36, 152, 196
,, William, 258
Waring (Wareinge, Waringe, Wering),
,, Alice, 33, 181, 265, 281
,, Ann, 40,* 50, 67, 89, 219, 255, 272, 277
,, Christopher, 19, 67, 69, 72, 76, 80, 86, 90, c. of 190, 203, 274
,, Edmund, 176
,, Elizabeth, 44, 228, 285
,, Ellen, 50, 100, 141, 142, 157, 215, 253
,, Ewan, 201, 262
,, Frances, 69
,, Francis, 203
,, Gilbert, 14, 71, 90
,, Grace, 55, 281
,, Harie (*sic*), 40
,, Henry, 55, 60, 69, 200, 266
,, Izabell, 234
,, Ja: 33, 40, 50, 63, 142
,, James, 42, 44, 80, 96, 135, 139, w. of 151, 152, 221, 234, 264, 267
,, Jane, 32, 169,* 257
,, Jenet, 144
,, Jo: 44, 50
,, John, 13, 60, 76, 77, 107, 135, 186, 256, 287
,, Katherin, 135, 198
,, Margaret, 18, 169, 171, 194
,, Margery, 8, 139, 230
,, Mary, 44
,, Matthew, 157
,, Mawde, 13, 69, 200, 276
,, Nicholas, 141
,, N.X.N., 177
,, Paul, 32
,, Perret, 7, 138
,, Richard, 19, 44, 71, 72, 150, 200, 257
,, Robert, 71, 77, 89, 200, 219, 275
,, Sislie, 63
,, Sybell, 5
,, Thomas, 8, 44, 86, 92, 138, 159
,, William, 18, 71, 92, 96, 100, 107, 180, 221, 234, 279
Warriner, see Wariner
Waterworth, Alice, 256

*Christenings* . . . . . . . .
*Burials* . . . . . . . . .
*Marriages* . . . . . . . .

. . pp. *1—128 inclusive.*
. . . ,, *129—252* ,,
. . . ,, *253—288* ,,

Whalley—*Continued.*
,, Nicholas, 41, 47, 49, 267
,, Richard, 111
,, Robert, 75, 78, 82, 87, 92, 97, 229
,, Roger, 49
,, Thomas, 109, 111, 118,* c. of 218,* 247
,, William, 87, 233
Whatton, Anne, 261
,, Elizabeth, 280
,, James, 17, 118, 121, 125
,, John, 118, 138
,, Margaret, 278
,, Margery, 12, 157
,, Mary, 26, 274
,, Thomas, 17, 26, 121, 258
,, William, 31, 125, 211
Whetherby, see Wetherby
Whetstones, see Whitstons
Whicke, Thomas, 262
Whitacre, Thomas, 241
Whickliffe (Whiclife, Whicliffe, Whitcliffe),
,, Anthony, 223
,, Henry, 222
,, John, 223
,, Richard, 222
,, William, 227
White (Whyte), Agnes, 132
,, Cislye, 167
,, Edward, 46, 132, 254, 267
,, Gabriell, 145
,, James, 23, 261
,, Jane, 2, 135
,, John, 267
,, Katherin, 46
,, Margaret, 233
,, Margery, 175
,, Thomas, 23
Whitefeld, see Whitfeeld
Whitehead (Whytehead), Alice, 66
,, Henry, 66, 127, 252
,, John, 127
Whitestones, Whitestons, see Whitstons
Whitesyde, see Whytesyde
Whitfeeld (Whitefeld, Whitefild, Whitffelde, Whitfilde),
,, Alice, 204
,, Elizabeth, 208
,, Margaret, 187
,, Margery, 221
,, Thomas, 184
Whithington, see Withington

*Christenings* . . . . . . .
*Burials* . . . . . . . .
*Marriages* . . . . . . . . .

: : pp. 1—128 inclusive.
: : ,, 129—252 ,,
: : ,, 253—288 ,,

Watson—*Continued.*
,, Ann, 23, 76, 152, 284
,, Christopher, 23, 152
,, Elizabeth, 6, 147
,, Ellen, 89
,, Izabell, 265
,, James, 79, 264
,, Jane, 148
,, Jo: 55
,, John, 4, 76, 79, 85, 89, 93, 96,* 162, 219, 265, 268, 276
,, Katherin, 45, 175
,, Lawrence, 93, 96, 219
,, Margaret, 85
,, Margery, 4, 136, 155
,, Richard, 155, 283
,, Robert, 151, 232, 268, 281
,, Thomas, 147, 219, 267
,, William, 45, 96
Wilson *alias* Palmer, (Willson alis Pamer),
,, Henry, 140
,, Katherin, 9
Winde, Jayne, 202
,, Jenet, 165
,, Margery, 130, 135
Winder (Wynder), Cisley, 107, 233
,, Elizabeth, 99
,, Ellen, 245
,, George, 101, 221, 232
,, Henry, 18, 21, 232, 253, 260
,, Ideth, 284
,, James, 155
,, Jane, 222
,, Katherin, 101, 232
,, Margaret, 284
,, Ralph, 122, 149, 285
,, Richard, 18, 102,* 122, 222
,, Roger, 21, 226
,, Thomas, 99, 107, 155, 221, 232
Windle, see Wyndle
Windrow (Windgrow, Windraie, Windraw, Windrawe, Windrowe, Wingrow),
,, Alice, 74, 91, 185, 204
,, Ann, 21, 74, 81
,, Bartholomew, 89
,, Edw: 70, 200
,, Eline, 145
,, Elizabeth, 79, 204, 207
,, Ellen, 15
,, Emlin, 11
,, Gabriel, 82
,, George, 86, 91, 95, 204
,, Henry, 66, 86, 194
,, Isabel, 18

*Christenings* . . . . . .
*Burials* . . . . . . .
*Marriages* . . . . . .

*Christenings* . . . . . . . . . . *pp.* *1—128 inclusive.*
*Burials* . . . . . . . . . . ,, *129—252* ,,
*Marriages* . . . . . . . . . . ,, *253—288* ,,

Wood—*Continued.*
,, Elizabeth, 3, 74, 107, 126, 182, 204, 228, 286
,, Ellen, 182
,, Eme, 274
,, Emlin, 66, 211
,, Gabriel, 81
,, George, 77, 103, 153, 181, 193, 230, 254
,, Henry, 28, 30, 55, 70, 81, 89, 107, 110, 126, c. of 245
,, Hugh, 251
,, Izabel, 77, 256
,, James, 69, 110
,, Jane, 262
,, Jennet, 224
,, John, 93, 182, 206, 218
,, Lawrence, 49, 268
,, Margaret, 23, 153, 159, 237, 242
,, Margery, 271
,, Mary, 69
,, N.X.N., 67, 140
,, Richard, 27, 66, 69,* 70, 72,* 78, 93, 103, 106, w. of 132, 137, 211, 216, 218, 257
,, Robert, 23, 27, 51, 64, 78, 105, 159, 182, 185, 229, 281, 287
,, Thomas, 12, 53, 59, 83, 105, 179, 247, 286, 287
,, William, 49, 51, 53, 55, 59, 64, 67, 74, 77,* 89, 193, 204, 215, 216, 217, 228, 230, 269, 280
Woodcocke, John, 75
,, Raffe, 75
Woode, Woodes, see Wood
Woodfall, Alice, 161, 254
,, Ann, 253
,, Ellin, 254
,, Gilbert, 139
,, Humphrey, 27
,, Ja: 27
Woodhouse (Woodhovse, Woodhows, Woodhowse),
,, Alice, 102, 198
,, Ann, 99, 165, 242
,, Edith, 32, 279
,, Elizabeth, 2, 133
,, Hugh, 36, 45, 152, 225, 245
,, Jane, 267
,, John, 14
,, Margaret, 110, 129, 254
,, Margery, 266
,, N.X.N., 225
,, Richard, 45, 99, 102, 110, 119

Woodhouse—*Continued.*
,, Sibell, 201
,, Thomas, 36, 150, 163, 259
,, William, 119
Woods, see Wood
Woodworth (Woodwordthe, Woodworte),
,, Alison, 160
,, Hugh, 144
,, John, 179*
,, Robert, 218
,, Thurstan, 212
Woolfall (Wolfall, Woofall),
,, Alice, 92, 254
,, Ann, 15, 104
,, Christopher, 42, 88, 92, 98, 104, 207, 244, 270, 277
,, Ellen, 88, 135, 172, 207, 251
,, Henry, 98, 216, 256, 269
,, Hugh, 260
,, Jane, 116
,, John, 254
,, Lawrence, 116, 284
,, William, 42, 169
Woollen, Elizabeth, 274
Woolsey, see Wolsey
Woorthington, see Worthington
Woosey, Woosie, Woozie, see Wolsey
Worrall (Werall, Werrall, Worall, Worrolle),
,, Alice, 130, 256
,, Ann, 48
,, Elinor, 8
,, Elizabeth, 170
,, Ellen, 54, 281
,, Grace, 10, 166
,, Henry, 7, 138
,, James, 2, 135
,, John, 143, 158, 191, 254
,, Margery, 135
,, Nicholas, 256
,, Richard, 48, 54, 63,* 191,* 211
Worsley, Nicholas, 136
Worthington (Woorthington, Worthingeton),
,, Ann, 22, 105, 123, 273
,, Bartholomew, 161
,, Catherin, 25, 109, 198
,, Christopher, 131
,, Claris, 27, 276
,, Edw: 67, 88, 262
,, Edward, 36, 105, 109, 111, 114, 119, 123
,, Elizabeth, 29, 166, 171, 257
,, Ellen, 88, 202
,, Fleetwood, 111

*Christenings* . . . . . . . . . *pp.* *1—128 inclusive.*
*Burials* . . . . . . . . . . . ,, *129—252* ,,
*Marriages* . . . . . . . . . . ,, *253—288* ,,

Worthington—*Continued.*
,, George, 122, 246
,, Grace, 105
,, Henry, 56, 118, 170, 286
,, Hugh, 30, 40, 43, 56, 67, 77, 93, 114, 116, 138, 201, 204, 219
,, Jane, 40, 77, 123, 169, 204
,, Jenet, 269
,, John, 180, 228, 250
,, Margaret, 19, 96, 167, 242, 257, 263, 269
,, Mary, 40, 43, 167, 229
,, N.X.N., 119
,, Richard, 19, 22, 25, 27, 29, 40, 93, 96, 116, 118, 122, 123, 170, 178, 219, 229, 242
,, Sislie, 218
,, Thomas, 36
,, William, 177, 255
Wosey, Woulsey, see Wolsey
Wrennall, Jenet, 259
Wrest, Elizabeth, 7
Wright (Wrighte, Wryght),
,, Anne, 191
,, Elizabeth, 147
,, George, 77
,, Hugh, 36, 195
,, James, 140
,, Jenet, 194
,, Jo: 190
,, John, 45, 83, 228
,, Margaret, 190, 246
,, Mary, 39, 281
,, Rangle (*sic*), 77
,, Robert, 283
,, Thomas, 17, 45, 146, 147, 233, 282
,, William, 17, 36, 39, 83, 146, 266
Wrightinton, Anne, 133
,, Richard, 133
Wroe, Elizabeth, 98
,, Peter, 98, 227
,, Sisley, 227
Wryght, see Wright
Wyet, Richard, 206
Wynder, see Winder
Wyndle (Windle), Ellen, 115, 239
,, John, 115
Wynstanley, see Winstanley
Wythingeton, Wythington, see Withington

## Y

Yate (Yat, Yeate, Yeatt, Yeatte),
,, Alice, 17, 20, 24, 153, 197, 257, 265
,, Ann, 62, 279
,, Catherin, 7, 23, 168, 268, 282
,, Edward, 17,* 23, 27, 32, 60, 112, 132, 153, 228, 272
,, Elizabeth, 28, 32
,, Ellen, 73, 212
,, Ewan, 42
,, Henry, 168, 203*
,, James, 70, 119, 120, 266
,, Jenet, 217, 272
,, Jo: 20
,, John, 17, 120, 191, 217
,, Johne, 257
,, Lawrence, 28, 263, 266
,, Margaret, 27, 132, 271
,, Margery, 10, c. of 60
,, Mary, 94
,, Richard, 77
,, Thomas, 13, 42, 60, 70, 73, 77, 94, 112, 119, c. of 205, c. of 209
,, William, 24

## II.

# Index of Places.

| | | |
|---|---|---|
| *Christenings* . . . . . . . . . . | *pp.* *1—128* | *inclusive.* |
| *Burials* . . . . . . . . . . . | ,, *129—252* | ,, |
| *Marriages* . . . . . . . . . . | ,, *253—288* | ,, |

[All places left without the addition of a County may be presumed to be in Lancashire.]


A

ATHERTON, 230
Aughton (Aug, Aught, Augton), ,, 7, 8, 13,* 24, 26,* 27, 28, 32, 36,* 37, 40, 43, 44, 50, 52,* 57, 71, 78, 81, 83, 84,* 86,* 88, 90, 91, 94, 95, 96,* 97, 98,* 100. 102, 103, 105,* 106, 107,* 109, 110, 116,* 117,* 118, 119, 120, 121, 123' 124,* 125, 126, 127. 128, 131, 169,* 227,* 228, 229, 230, 232, 233, 241, 242

B

BECCURSTETH, 224
Bickerstaff (Bycar, Bycarstafe, Bycarstaffe), .. 71, 170, 184, 189, 196, 200, 223
Bispam, 80, 105
Burscough, 130

C

CHESHIRE, 120
Crosse Hall, 180
Croston, 73, 76, 91,* 116

D

DALTON, 119, 239, 250

E

EAST (? a place name), 158
Eccleston (Ecclestone), 23, 63, 104, 118, 138

H

HAITON, 163
Halsall (Hal:), 20, 24, 27, 32, 53,* 54, 56, 60,* 121, 128, 132, 153

L

LAR (? Lat), 78
Lathom (Latham), 1, 4, 160
Lathom Chapel, 92
Layland, 113

M

MAGEHUL, 113
Marton, 84
Marton in Cheshire, 120
Meales, 55
More Hall, 60, 188, 201, 209, 216

O

ORMSKIRK (Ormis[h]), 1, 129, 152, 221
Ormis[h] Churche, 253

P

PRESCOT (Prekot), 18, 45, 54
Preston, 179

R

RACLIF, 85, 88
Rainforth (Rain: Rañfford), .. 36, 54. 72, 113
Rufforth (Rufford), 53, 118, 125

S

SCARISBRICK (Scarsbrecke, Scer:), ,, 56, 88, 169, 184, 198, 213
Sephton Parish, 106
Snap, 96
Stand, 131

W

WIGAN, 232
Writhington (*i.e.*, Wrightington), ,, 241

III.

# Index of Trades, Descriptions, and Various Matters.

*Christenings* . . . . . . . . . . *pp.* *1—128* *inclusive.*
*Burials* . . . . . . . . . . . . ,, *129—252* ,,
*Marriages* . . . . . . . . . . . ,, *253—288* ,,


A

ADOLESCENS, 235,* 236,* 237, 239, 242
Armiger, 23, 31,* 33, 34, 45, 111, 119, 127, 147, 251

B

BACHELOR, 232,* 235, 236, 238, 239,* 243. 246, 249,* 250, 251*
Burial and Funeral, Interval of time between, 196
Burial without the Vicar's Consent, 223
Butler, 184

C

CHANCEL (Chancell, Channcell, Chonc: In Choro),
,, 138,* 139,* 140, 157, 158, 178,* 179, 180, 185,* 189, 199
Chancel, high, 144,* 147,* 148, 149,* 150,* 151, 152,* 153, 154, 164,* 166,* 167,* 169,* 170,* 174, 175,* 176, 177, 180, 181, 194, 195,* 198, 200, 201, 202, 204, 205,* 210, 211, 214, 216, 218,* 219,* 221, 222, 223,* 224,* 226, 227, 228, 229,* 230, 232,* 233, 236, 238, 239, 240, 241, 242,* 244, 246,* 247, 248, 249,* 250, 251*
Chancel, Mr. Scarsbreckes, 154, 191, 202,* 205, 207, 216, 225, 232, 233,* 238,* 240, 243, 250, 251*
Chancel, Mr. Stanley's, 190, 201, 224, 236, 241, 244, 248
Chancel, My Lord's, 208, 232, 235, 248. 252
Chancel, Saint Nicholas, 138, 141,* 142,* 143, 144, 153,* 154, 165
Chancel, the new, 172, 181, 182, 186, 207
Chapel, 179
Chapel, Derby, 186
Chapel, Earl of Derbies, 231
Chapel, Lathom, 92
Chapel, My Lord's, 206, 209. 213
Chapel, Mr Scarsbreck's, 198,* 199, 203, 204, 205, 208, 209, 213, 214 218, 226
Chapel, Mr. Stanley's, 209, 216, 223
Chapel, New, 177*
Choro, In (In the Choir), 158
Clerk, 97, 99, 131, 186, 221, 223*
Conciator Regis (King's Preacher), ,, 286
Conjugat, p, 47
Curat: 106

D

DAME, 166
Derby, Chapel, 186
Drowned, 178, 206
Dueeli (twins), 13

E

EARL, 1st, 186
Ecclia, in, *passim*
Ecclesia lata, 182
Esquire, 26, 43, 46,* 49,* 66, 69, 71, 88, 90, 104, 107, 115, 121, 131, 178, 180, 184, 196, 213, 224, 257, 283

F

FRENCHMAN working at Bycarstaff, 200
Funeral, 186, 187, 196
Funeral and Burial, Interval of time between, 196

G

GENTLEMAN. 50, 57. 62,* 63,* 65, 70, 105. 109, 113, 119, 121, 125, 128, 167, 186,* 187, 190, 207, 218, 230, 231, 233, 235, 252, 263. 270, 271, 274
Gentlewoman (Generosa), 233, 241, 244, 263, 271, 274, 283
Gipsie, 84
Glassemen, 200

*Christenings* . . . . . . . . . *pp.* *1—128 inclusive.*
*Burials* . . . . . . . . . . ,, *129—252* ,,
*Marriages* . . . . . . . . . ,, *253—288* ,,

H

HERALD, 249
His Majesties Preacher, 112
Honourable, Right, 130, 167, 186, 187, 235

I

INFANCE, 221, 222
Infant, *passim*
Interval of time between Burial and Funeral, 196
Irisheman, the, 43

J

Junior, *passim*
Juvenis, *passim*

K

KING'S Preacher, 229
Knight, 149, 235

L

LABOURER, 233
Ladie, 213
Lame, 119
Ludi Magister, 245

M

MAIJ, c. of 230
Master of Arts, 207
Miles, 166
Minor, 22
Mr., 18, 20, 23, 27, (m^9sr) 49, 71, 73, 82, 84, 85, 86, 88,* 92, 104, 124, 147, 154, 167, 178, 180,* 188, 190, 191, 198, 199, 201, 202,* 203, 204, 205,* 207,* 208,* 209,* 213,* 216,* 218, 224 225, 226,* 232,* 233,* 236, 238,* 240,* 243, 244, 248,* 250, 251,* 259
Mrs., 137, 145, 146, 147, 165, 173, 178, 180,* 198, 199, 205, 214, 223, 224, 227, 257, 259
Muxeman, the, 141

N

NORTHEREN woman, 140
Northren Robin, 178

P

PARSON of Eccleston, 138
Pawper, 194
Peř, 220
Peregrina, 227
Poor child, 187, 194,* 195,* 198, 201, 204, 237
Poor man, 190, 194, 196
Poor woman, 187, 188, 192, 195, 197
Pore felow, 139
Preacher, 89, 112
Preacher, His Majesties, 112
Preacher, King's, 229
Priest (Preeste, Priste),
,, 131, 132, 135, 145,* 158
Pryor of Burscough, 130
Puer, *passim*
Puere, 146

R

RECUSANT, 223
Regis Conciator, 286

S

SCHOOLMASTER, 179, 245
Senior, *passim*
Servant, 178
Shumaker, 206
Sir (Ser), 130, 131,* 132,* 135, 138, 139, 145,* 149, 158, 192, 206, 235
Slain, 168, 200
Spinster, 183, 188, 214, 221,* 222, 223, 224,* 226,* 227,* 228,* 230, 231,* 232,* 233,* 234,* 235, 236,* 237,* 238,* 240, 241, 242, 243,* 244, 245,* 246, 247,* 248,* 249,* 250,* 251
Strange boy, 246
Strange man, 248
Stranger, 37, 41, 44, 47,* 54, 59, 62, 84, 85, 90, 91, 92, 95, 97,* 110, 114, 120, 130, 133, 169, 170, 171,* 173, 182, 183, 200, 208, 211, 216, 225, 228,* 230, 231, 232, 233, 234,* 235, 240, 243,* 245, 247, 248*

T

TALIOR, 56, 81
Tanner, 189

V

VICAR, 49, 51, 54, 57, 60, 102, 152, 221, 226
Virgo, *passim*

Y

YEOMAN, 228

# IV.

# Baptisms and Burials

apparently on the same day, but entered *together* either in Christenings or Burials.

---

| PAGE. | | |
|---|---|---|
| 7 | Windrowes iij children .......... | These among Christenings |
| 8 | John Coockeson .................. | |
| ,, | Jenet and Marget Jackson...... | |
| 11 | John Craine ........................ | |
| 13 | John Lea ........................... | |
| ,, | John Waringe ..................... | |
| 32 | Jaine Wetherbie .................. | |
| ,, | Marget Blanch .................... | |
| ,, | Joanie Morcrofte ................. | |
| 34 | Willim Bradley ................... | |
| ,, | Jaine Hankin ...................... | |
| 49 | Rodger Wholey .................. | |
| 50 | John Hesketh ..................... | |
| ,, | Anne Ambrose .................... | |
| 51 | John Peeter ........................ | |
| 161 | Jaine Chadocke ................... | These among Burials |
| ,, | John Jonson ........................ | |

# Errata.

Page 15, *for* 'Bryham Swyfte' *read* 'Bryhan'
„ 54, *for* 'Hesekth' *read* 'Hesketh'
„ 77, *for* 'Sunforth' *read* 'Sanforth'
„ 88, *insert* 'Fo. 126' *opposite* 'Willm Tyrer'
„ 177, *for* 'chaꝑ' *read* 'chap'
„ 190, *for* 'Alic Lanc̃' *read* 'Alis'
„ 227, *for* 'Gliasburrow' *read* 'Glaisburrow'
„ 237, *for* 'Ascorft' *read* 'Ascroft'
„ 241, *for* 'generoso' *read* 'generosa'
„ 253, *for* 'C adocke' *read* 'Chadocke'

JAMES CLEGG, THE ALDINE PRESS ROCHDALE.

Lightning Source UK Ltd.
Milton Keynes UK
UKHW010646010219
336547UK00009B/542/P